Dr Ambedkar and the
Revival of Buddhism II

THE COMPLETE WORKS OF SANGHARAKSHITA include all his previously published work, as well as talks, seminars, and writings published here for the first time. The collection represents the definitive edition of his life's work as Buddhist writer and teacher. For further details, including the contents of each volume, please turn to the 'Guide' on pp. 757–65.

FOUNDATION

1 A Survey of Buddhism / The Buddha's Noble Eightfold Path
2 The Three Jewels I
3 The Three Jewels II
4 The Bodhisattva Ideal
5 The Purpose and Practice of Buddhist Meditation
6 The Essential Sangharakshita

INDIA

7 Crossing the Stream: India Writings I
8 Beating the Dharma Drum: India Writings II
9 Dr Ambedkar and the Revival of Buddhism I
10 Dr Ambedkar and the Revival of Buddhism II

THE WEST

11 A New Buddhist Movement I
12 A New Buddhist Movement II
13 Eastern and Western Traditions

COMMENTARY

14 The Eternal Legacy / Wisdom Beyond Words
15 Pāli Canon Teachings and Translations
16 Mahayana Myths and Stories

17 Wisdom Teachings of the Mahayana
18 Milarepa and the Art of Discipleship I
19 Milarepa and the Art of Discipleship II

MEMOIRS
20 The Rainbow Road from Tooting Broadway to Kalimpong
21 Facing Mount Kanchenjunga
22 In the Sign of the Golden Wheel
23 Moving Against the Stream
24 Through Buddhist Eyes

POETRY AND THE ARTS
25 Poems and Short Stories
26 Aphorisms and the Arts

27 Concordance and Appendices

COMPLETE WORKS 10 **INDIA**

Sangharakshita

Dr Ambedkar and the Revival of Buddhism II

EDITED BY VIDYADEVI

Windhorse Publications
38 Newmarket Road
Cambridge CB5 8DT

info@windhorsepublications.com
www.windhorsepublications.com

First published in 2021.

Cover design by Dhammarati
Cover images: Front: Dr Ambedkar delivering a speech during the
mass conversion in Nagpur, 14 October 1956.
Back flap: Dr Ambedkar and his followers become Buddhists, 1956.
Mural, Nava Jetavana Vihara, Shravasti, India.
Typesetting and layout by Tarajyoti
Printed by Bell & Bain Ltd, Glasgow

**British Library Cataloguing
in Publication Data:**
A catalogue record for this book is
available from the British Library.

ISBN 978-1-911407-06-5 (paperback)
ISBN 978-1-911407-05-8 (hardback)

CONTENTS

List of Illustrations xv
Acknowledgements xvii
Editor's Preface xix
Foreword xxii
Voices from the Dhamma Revolution xxxv

REMEMBERING AMBEDKAR: AN INTRODUCTION 1

Remembering Ambedkar 3
The spirit of Dr Ambedkar 15
B. R. Ambedkar, a great Buddhist 21

BUDDHA AND THE FUTURE OF HIS RELIGION: A COMMENTARY ON DR AMBEDKAR'S ARTICLE 29

Introduction 31
1 The many founders of religion 33
2 Comparing Buddhism with Hinduism 43
3 The parent of the caste system 51
4 The revival of Buddhism in India 57
5 Buddhism is the only religion the world can have 63
6 The opium of the people 70
7 Dr Ambedkar's vision 75

THE MASS CONVERSION AND THE YEARS AFTER: 1956–1969 91

The tide turns 93
A whirling programme at Nagpur 95
Dr Ambedkar 106
A great injustice 109
Diksha Bhumi 112

Preaching tours 1958–1961 115

First tour 116
Are Hinduism and Buddhism the same? 117
The real Buddha 118
Character building 119
Buddhism in the modern world 119
The bodhisattva ideal and the six *pāramitās* 121

Second tour 124
What the *Diksha* movement means 124
The impact of conversion on Indian life 125
Dr Ambedkar and Buddhism 126

Third tour 131
The origin of Buddhism 132
Hīnayāna and Mahāyāna 133
The fundamentals of Tibetan Buddhism 134
The middle way 135
Tantric Buddhism 136
Karma and rebirth 137
Atheism 138
Buddhism in England 139
Buddhism 140
The central philosophy of Buddhism 142
Oṃ maṇi padme hūṃ: notes for a series of three lectures 144

Fourth tour 149
Buddhism and God 150
Mindfulness 150
Oṃ maṇi padme hūṃ 151
The spiritual path in Buddhism 152
Literature and Ethics 153
Buddhism today 156
Practical Buddhism 157
Anātman and *śūnyatā* 159
Duties of *Upāsakas* and *Upāsikās* 161
The *Diamond Sūtra* 162
The great life of Dr Ambedkar 167
The universality of Buddhism 170
The four *brahma vihāras* 172
Oṃ maṇi padme hūṃ 174

Social training course in Buddhism at Poona 179
Manners and customs 180
Poona District Buddhist Women's Association and Buddhist Society of Gujarat 181
The position of women in Buddhism 182
Ambedkar Jayanti 185

A NEW BUDDHIST MOVEMENT: TALKS IN INDIA AND ENGLAND 1979–1992 189

1979 191
Mettā is the most important thing 193
The energy of the Windhorse 199
What attracts Westerners to Buddhism? 204
Whatever helps us grow 210
Why did the Buddha leave his house? 219
The Buddha – man or god? 229
The path of the Dhamma 239
Lessons from the life of the Buddha 254
The future of the Sangha 261
Questions at Ahilya Ashram, Poona 276

1982–1983 285
A miscellany of impressions 286
The ex-untouchable Indian Buddhists 305
What death reminds us of 316
Buddhism in one word 326
Dr Ambedkar's true greatness 335

1988 353
The foundation stone of the Mahavihara 354
On *Ambedkar and Buddhism* 358

1992 365
Keeping the Mahavihara beautiful 366
Return to Nagpur 372
Dhamma revolution for the world 374
A visit to the IAS training institute 381
Why start a new Buddhist movement? 383
The ten ornaments of the Buddhist 391
The opening of the boys' hostel at Dapoli 399
A visit to the girls' hostel at Vishrantwadi 401
The opening of the shrine hall at Bhaja 404
Bhaja shrine dedication, Order convention 407
Interview with Nagabodhi 410

WISDOM BEFORE WORDS: AN EXPLORATION OF THE *UDĀNA* 419

Editorial Note 421
Introduction 424
1 The Bodhi Tree 427
 1.1 Seeing the nature of causation 427
 1.2 This not being, that does not become 432
 1.3 Scattering the armies of Māra 433
 1.4 Who is the real brahmin? 436
 1.5 Those who wander, always mindful 443
 1.6 Kassapa refuses dinner from the *devas* 447
 1.7 A dark and stormy night 451
 1.8 Free from all ties 454

1.9 You don't become pure by bathing 457
1.10 In the seen, only the seen 458

2 Mucalinda 469
2.1 The serpent king shelters the Buddha 469
2.2 Talk about the Dharma or keep quiet 471
2.3 The Buddha teaches some boys not to be cruel 476
2.4 The Buddha's advice about handling criticism 477
2.5 The Buddha and the businessman 483
2.6 Happy indeed are those who have nothing 487
2.7 Don't fall into the King of Death's power 490
2.8 A difficult pregnancy 493
2.9 Being under another's power is all suffering 498
2.10 Ah, what bliss! 500

3 Nanda 502
3.1 Bearing the consequences of your actions 502
3.2 Nanda and the nymphs 504
3.3 The Buddha and the noisy *bhikkhus* 508
3.4 Sāriputta sits like a mountain 511
3.5 Mindfulness of body and Nirvāṇa 512
3.6 Five hundred lives of conditioning 514
3.7 The king of the gods makes curry for Kassapa 515
3.8 The advantages of going for alms 517
3.9 Elephant-craft and other matters 520
3.10 The difficulty of communicating Enlightenment 521

4 Meghiya 526
4.1 Meghiya and spiritual friendship 526
4.2 A home territory of perfect emotion 532
4.3 The Buddha and the cowherd 533
4.4 Sāriputta gets a slight headache 534
4.5 The Buddha and the elephant seek solitude 536
4.6 Piṇḍola the rag-robe wearer 537
4.7 Sāriputta apparently doing nothing 538
4.8 The *bhikkhus* are accused of murder 539
4.9 Rejoicing in merits 541
4.10 Sāriputta reviews his own calm 542

5 The Elder Soṇa 543
5.1 No one dearer than one's own self 543
5.2 The pattern of the Buddha's life 546
5.3 The Buddha gives a public lecture 549
5.4 Do you fear suffering and dislike pain? 556
5.5 The taste of freedom 557
5.6 Soṇa learns the Dharma by heart 572
5.7 Passing beyond doubt 577
5.8 Devadatta decides to break away 579
5.9 Why do people go on talking? 581
5.10 Setting up mindfulness before him 581

6 Born Blind 583
6.1 Why didn't Ānanda ask the Buddha to live longer? 583
6.2 The Buddha and the king's spies 588
6.3 The Buddha reviews his state of mind 593
6.4 The blind men and the elephant 594
6.5 Sinking in the middle of the flood 599
6.6 Going beyond self-agency 600
6.7 Thoughts burned up like incense 605
6.8 A fight over a courtesan 607
6.9 Like moths that fall into the lamp's flame 610
6.10 The sun and the glow-worms 611

7 The Little Chapter 613
7.1 Bhaddiya the dwarf gains insight 613
7.2 Sāriputta doesn't realize Bhaddiya is awakened 615
7.3 Stuck on pleasure's ties 616
7.4 Like fish in the mouth of a net 617
7.5 A beautiful royal chariot 618
7.6 Working on all your imperfections at once 619
7.7 The abandonment of proliferation 621
7.8 Mindfulness of the body is enough 621
7.9 The Buddha and the well 622
7.10 The women of the harem gain insight 627

8 Pāṭali Village 632
8.1 Neither earth nor water nor fire nor wind 632
8.2 One who sees holds on to nothing 633
8.3 The unborn, unbecome, unmade, unconditioned 634
8.4 There is agitation for one who is dependent 637
8.5 The Buddha's last meal 639
8.6 The Buddha gives the villagers tips on ethics 641
8.7 The Buddha and the foolish disciple 649
8.8 The death of Visākhā's grandchild 651
8.9 Dabba attains final Nirvāṇa 653
8.10 Unwavering happiness 655

Appendix 1 657
Dr Ambedkar's twenty-two conversion vows 657

Appendix 2 659
Ambedkar and Buddhism, reinstated passage 659

Sources 662
Notes and References 664
Indexes 726

A Guide to *The Complete Works of Sangharakshita* 757

LIST OF ILLUSTRATIONS

VOICES FROM THE DHAMMA REVOLUTION

Bronze statue of Dr Ambedkar at Nagaloka Campus, Nagpur xxxiv
'An unfathomable, fascinating, and somewhat scruffy friend', Cambridge, August 1973 xlv
Bakula and Dharmarakshita after their ordination, with Sangharakshita and Lokamitra xlv
Lokamitra helping build the retreat centre at Bhaja xlix
Padmasuri leads the first women's retreat at Bhaja l
First ordinations of women by women: Srimala, Vimalasuri, Ratnasuri, and Jnanasuri lii
Nagaloka campus, looking across to the Walking Buddha lv
Order convention at Bodh Gaya, 2018 lxiii
Sangharakshita and Tarahridaya at their final meeting lxiv

REMEMBERING AMBEDKAR: AN INTRODUCTION

The garlanding of Dr Ambedkar's statue, Diksha Bhumi, Nagpur 1965 2
Sangharakshita and Mrs Ambedkar, Poona, 1988 6

BUDDHA AND THE FUTURE OF HIS RELIGION: A COMMENTARY ON DR AMBEDKAR'S ARTICLE

Dr Ambedkar's letter to Sangharakshita 30

THE MASS CONVERSION AND THE YEARS AFTER: 1956–1969

The Diksha Bhumi, Nagpur 92
Sangharakshita's schedule, Bombay, December 1959 132
Giving a talk in an alleyway, Ahmedabad 1965 155
With the Poona District Buddhist Women's Association 162

A NEW BUDDHIST MOVEMENT: TALKS IN INDIA AND ENGLAND 1979–1992

The Mahavihara, Dapodi, Poona 192
Padmavajra, Yuvaraj, Sangharakshita, Lokamitra, Virabhadra 194
Padmapani's windhorse mural, London Buddhist Centre 200
The entrance to the Bhaja caves 334
The opening of the Hsuan Tsang Retreat Centre, Bordharan 393
The opening of the new shrine-room, Vishrantwadi girls' hostel, Poona 403

WISDOM BEFORE WORDS: AN EXPLORATION OF THE *UDĀNA*

On the *Udāna* seminar in the tent in Cornwall 420

ACKNOWLEDGEMENTS

This has been a very special volume to put together, and I wish Sangharakshita himself could see it – but at least we had the chance to talk about it and plan it before his death in 2018. Believe it or not, it began as a potentially slim volume, but as more and more material came to light, it became rather substantial, as you can see.

Each volume of the *Complete Works* is a collaboration, and that is particularly true of this one. I'm deeply grateful to Lokamitra for helping the volume to take shape, somehow finding time to do so when at full stretch dealing with many other matters. His lifelong dedication to the Buddhist revival in India shines through his contributions to the section 'Voices of the Dhamma Revolution'. Many thanks also to Maitriveer Nagarjuna (Dr Santosh I. Raut), who has also been a wonderful collaborator, and has given to the Foreword the insights of his scholarly perspective.

I'm delighted to be able to include Amitamati's reflective and inspiring contribution to 'Voices of the Dhamma Revolution'; many thanks to her. And thanks also to three alumni of the Nagarjuna Training Institute, Maitreyaratna, Dhivya Ethiraj, and Lakhindar Soren, for sharing their moving stories with us. I'm grateful as well to Nagabodhi for the transcript of a remarkable interview with Dharmarakshita once upon a time, and to Jnanasuri for the no less remarkable reminiscences she shared with Vassika.

Thanks also to Paramartha and Mokshapriya for their help with retrieving documents from the archives at Urgyen House, Adhisthana, and also to Mokshapriya for his assistance with archive photographs and the supply of original footage of Sangharakshita's tours in India, without which we would not have had access to some of the talks included in this volume. My gratitude also to Kalyanaprabha and Akasasuri for transcribing some of the talks, and to Padmasuri, Dhammadinna, Lokamitra, and Dhammarati for photographs.

Dhammarati has created the design of the *Complete Works* from the outset, and has given generously of his tremendous creative energy to the making of these volumes, with beautiful results. Many thanks to him for everything he has put into our work together on this volume. My gratitude also, as ever, to our copy-editor Shantavira, whose commitment to his work on Sangharakshita's writings has now lasted almost four decades. And many thanks to all the *Complete Works* team for their dedication to the project: Maitiu O'Ceileachair for checking the Pāli and Sanskrit, Michelle Bernard for coordinating the whole project, Tarajyoti for typesetting, Kalyanasri for proofreading, Satyalila for indexing, and Helen Lewis and Dhammamegha for their work to get the *Complete Works* out into the world through Windhorse Publications.

Vidyadevi

EDITOR'S PREFACE

In 1950, Sangharakshita, 24 years of age and newly ordained, wrote to Dr B. R. Ambedkar congratulating him on his article 'Buddha and the Future of His Religion', recently published in the *Maha Bodhi* journal. Somehow finding time to reply, the great Indian statesman, while applauding the young man's work for Buddhism in Kalimpong, urged him that 'You should be more active than that.' Sangharakshita treasured that letter for the rest of his life, and this volume tells the story of how he indeed became 'more active than that' in the cause to which Dr Ambedkar had devoted his life: the revival of Buddhism in India, and throughout the world.

To my mind the volume is a bit like a musical work in five movements, each with its own harmonies and textures, but all variations on the main themes. As overture, in his Foreword Maitriveer Nagarjuna introduces those themes, conjuring Dr Ambedkar's vision of an equal society based on Buddhist values. Then, as counterpoint, comes a medley of stories from some of the people who witnessed the events this volume describes, those whose history this is, ranging from the memories of someone who was present on the occasion of the great mass conversion to young people whose lives have also been transformed by Dr Ambedkar's Dhamma Revolution. And then we come to the main work, Sangharakshita's own writings and teachings.

1. REMEMBERING AMBEDKAR: AN INTRODUCTION

The introductory section gives us Sangharakshita's reflections on the long history of his involvement with the Buddhist movement in India and his personal relationship with Dr Ambedkar.

2. BUDDHA AND THE FUTURE OF HIS RELIGION: A COMMENTARY ON DR AMBEDKAR'S ARTICLE

Next we have a commentary on the very article which first made the connection between Dr Ambedkar and Sangharakshita. The text is based on a seminar held in 1986 during an ordination retreat in Tuscany, and those present evidently knew little of the subject, so this serves as an introduction to Dr Ambedkar's thinking about Buddhism, and also introduces the theme of connections and contrasts between Buddhism as practised in India and in the West.

3. THE MASS CONVERSION AND THE YEARS AFTER: 1956–1969

In the third part of the book, we move to the mass conversion ceremony in 1956, and Sangharakshita's teachings among the new Buddhists in the years that followed. This section includes recently unearthed archive material: an eye-witness account by Dr A. R. Kulkarni of Sangharakshita's 'whirling programme' in Nagpur at the time of Dr Ambedkar's death; and Sangharakshita's own notes for some of the talks he gave on his tours of India in the late 1950s and early 1960s, which cover everything from ethics and etiquette to *śūnyatā* and the *Diamond Sūtra*, the notes being interspersed with the report of the tours he published at the time. Also in this section are notes from talks Sangharakshita gave in England in the 1960s, to raise awareness of Dr Ambedkar and the Buddhist revival.

4. A NEW BUDDHIST MOVEMENT: TALKS IN INDIA AND ENGLAND 1979–1992

Volume 9 of Sangharakshita's *Complete Works* presents the talks delivered on his tour of India in 1981–2. Here, in a talk given in England on his return from that tour, Sangharakshita describes it from his own point of view. There are also talks given on his other visits to India between 1979 to 1992, charting the progress of the Buddhist movement in India from its earliest days to its development into a substantial organization. Lokamitra, who organized all the tours, gives us the inside story in 'Voices from the Dhamma Revolution' which follows the Foreword.

5. WISDOM BEFORE WORDS: AN EXPLORATION OF THE *UDĀNA*

The final section introduces a new theme – or rather a very ancient one. Now we go right back to the beginning, to the Buddha himself. According to the Pāli canon's *Udāna*, which is the text studied here, the first question the Buddha was asked after his Enlightenment was 'What is a true brahmin?', and his reply makes clear his rejection of the caste system in favour of worth, not birth, as Maitriveer Nagarjuna puts it in his Foreword, to bring this volume full circle. The text is based on two seminars given by Sangharakshita in the 1970s. (Dhammadinna, who attended the first one, gives us some of her memories in the introduction to this section.) The *Udāna* depicts a world in which the Buddha's experience was completely new, a sense of freshness and creativity which obviously moved Sangharakshita and the seminar participants in those very new days of the Western Buddhist Order (later the Triratna Buddhist Order). So newness, paradoxically, is another recurring theme. Indian and Western Buddhists alike are 'new Buddhists', and so were the Buddha's first followers. Indeed, there is really no other kind. To add to the sense of newness, the commentary includes new translations of the *Udāna* verses specially made by Dhivan (Dr Thomas Jones).

FOREWORD

The Liberation: the Revival of Buddhism in India

> The greatest thing that the Buddha has done is to tell the world that the world cannot be reformed except by the reformation of the mind of the man and the mind of the world.[1]

The world is changing at an increasing pace. Developments in technology have brought comfortable lives for many, but have also resulted in the abuse of ecology. Similarly, information technology brings many benefits, but information spread irresponsibly through social media leads to prejudice rather than freedom. This scenario, combined with the present global tendencies towards populism and authoritarianism, and the widening gap between classes, is threatening the future of human life. A close contemplation reveals a triple trap. Firstly, with the rise of globalism and increased access to unfiltered and untested information, societies are facing an unparalleled speed of change. Secondly, environmental catastrophe due to growing technologies, materialism, and consumerism is hinting at upcoming disastrous times. Thirdly, democracies are deteriorating and there are resultant moves towards totalitarian populist states. How does a society absorb such unprecedented change? Do we embrace it, opening our minds to new influences, or do we close down and attempt to preserve an idea of the past which was dominated by mental prejudices of various kinds? We are also experiencing a vertically developing society, in which the wealthier and more powerful accrue more capital, instead of a horizontal growth where wealth and power are shared equally. How do we bring about equitable change?

In Dr Ambedkar's revival of Buddhism, India witnessed a unique phenomenon, the exemplification of positive change in a modern society not only in theory but in practice. The great statesman precipitated a social, political, and spiritual revolution in India on the basis of non-violence and egalitarian human values, affecting the lives of millions of Indians who were considered lower caste by Hindus. Dr Ambedkar saw the means of the Constitution, law, and non-violence (inspired by the Buddha) as the best way to bring about a new society, defining such a society in terms of self-respect, non-violence, liberty, equality, and fraternity. For him these were not mere political slogans but deep spiritual principles. In a 1954 All-India Radio broadcast, he declared:

> Positively, my social philosophy may be said to be enshrined in three words: liberty, equality, and fraternity. Let no one, however, say that I have borrowed my philosophy from the French Revolution. I have not. My philosophy has roots in religion and not in political science. I have derived them from the teachings of my Master, the Buddha.... He gave the highest place to fraternity as the only real safeguard against the denial of liberty or equality or fraternity which was another name for brotherhood or humanity, which was again another name for religion.[2]

Dr Ambedkar came into socio-political public life during the most crucial period of modern Indian history, a period marked by the decline of British colonial power. At that time the aspiration towards the dream of a free society with the promise of humanity and liberation for every citizen in the country was at its peak. The newly independent India was passing through a unique phase, with complicated currents of various ideologies. The only vital issue of dissension over the firestorm of independence was the appropriation of centralized power as it was released by the receding colonial authority. With the rise of a nationalistic movement which was mainly led by privileged castes, the question took a dramatic turn when it came to establishing principles for the future nation based on equal freedom for everyone. The transfer of leadership and equitable power-sharing became central points of an existential struggle for a community which was divided into castes, and the promise of egalitarian society remained unfulfilled. Among the people of India, privileged classes and castes consolidated to enjoy the fruits of independence in spite of the sacrifices made by all sections of the society to achieve it. The sufferings of unprivileged sections remained unanswered and they were left behind as the dream of a shining and developing India was sketched. The evolution of a power structure empowered minuscule upper castes and classes which insisted on a monopoly of power, excluding underprivileged and oppressed social groups.

India is a Hindu caste-based society with other religious minorities, and the caste system remains one of the dominant factors in the perpetuation of an oppressive, violent, and unjust society. Caste has been a chronic disease of the mind of India for thousands of years. The *varṇāśrama* (caste system)[3] is a hierarchical and complex socio-religious model with little reform, used as an ideological weapon to claim society, culture, and nation. Nationalism can therefore be defined as a ruling class discourse. In spite of political freedom, India remained divided into several castes and communal groups. In his speech to the Constituent Assembly on 25 November 1949, Dr Ambedkar warned:

> I am of the opinion that in believing that we are a nation, we are cherishing a great delusion. How can people divided into several thousands of castes be a nation? In India there are castes. The castes are anti-national. In the first place, because they bring about separation in social life. They are anti-national also because they generate jealously and antipathy between caste and caste. But we must overcome all these difficulties if we wish to become a nation in reality. Without fraternity, equality and liberty will be no deeper than coats of paint.[4]

Dr Ambedkar saw clearly that nothing could be built on the basis of caste: no nation, no community, and no culture which would give peace to the minds of citizens. He realized that the roots of caste lay in the mind itself, and that caste left no scope for any reform to form an egalitarian society.

THE COMPLEX CASTE CLUSTER

If a nation is to breathe harmoniously, it has to be equally represented by all sections of society, and this is only possible when citizens are economically and socially free. People also need to be free to follow without fear whatever religion they choose as long as they do not harm others. Dr Ambedkar's profound vision for the liberation of the oppressed masses of the country compelled him to go against the graded unequal society based on caste hierarchy. It is well argued in his celebrated essay *Annihilation of Caste* that 'caste has its roots not in social or political practices but essentially in religion with divine sanctity'. Once the caste system is approved by 'divine' origin and authorized by 'sacred' texts (*śāstras*), can humans even question it? It is not in their power to change or challenge it but only to accept it. Thus the sufferers of this system remain eternally helpless, with no possibility of liberation, compelled to follow *jāti-dharma* (caste-duties). If caste compels the oppressed to suffer heinous inhuman practices in the name of divinity, it is nothing but 'cosmic corruption' by religion, which is thus responsible for the oppression of the scale of caste hierarchy. Belief in such a religion cannot repair the structure; the only recourse is to give it up.

CRITICAL QUEST FOR LIBERATION

Dr Ambedkar diagnosed India's disease as birth-based caste. He analysed that 'caste in India means an artificial chopping off of the population into fixed and definite units, each one prevented from fusing into another through the custom of endogamy'.[5] Caste has never permitted society to be united or allowed mutual sympathy to flower among different castes and religions. Caste does not result in economic efficiency, but demoralizes the mind, the higher castes promoting the interests of their own class and shutting out wholesome interaction with other groups. Caste teaches and produces selfish ideals based on greed, hatred, and ignorance. It results in lack of fellow feeling. It kills public spirit, so it cannot produce a selfless ideal in the service of mankind. In any society created on the basis of class division, it is impossible to build an egalitarian nation or community.

Dr Ambedkar came to the conclusion that what India needed was a *moral and mental disposition* to change the mindset of the people, not reliance on superficial socio-political reforms. In 1936, in a speech written for the Annual Conference of Jāt-Pāt-Todak Mandal at Lahore, entitled *Annihilation of Caste* (but not delivered), he said, 'You must take the stand that the Buddha took. You must take the stand that Guru Nanak took.' He further elaborated:

> Equality is the main feature of Buddhism.... The religion of the Buddha gives freedom of thought and freedom of self-development to all. It has never taught to achieve salvation by sacrificing animals or any living being to propitiate the Gods.... Prior to the advent of Buddhism, it was impossible to even think that a Shudra would get the throne. The history of India reveals that after the emergence of Buddhism, Shudras are seen getting thrones. Verily, Buddhism paved the way for the establishment of democracy and socialistic pattern of society in India.[6]

He saw that Buddhism promotes true liberty, equality, and fraternity. It does not observe the caste system in any form. It encourages taking responsibility for one's own progress. It does not teach liberation based on God or any cosmic agent between God and the human world, but teaches that freedom can only be achieved by one's own effort. Everyone, irrespective of caste birth, colour, race, or gender, can become liberated if they make sincere efforts to cultivate a mind free of prejudice. Dr Ambedkar recognized that the Buddha is a *mārgadattā* (way finder/guide), not a *mokṣadattā* (giver of salvation).[7]

The teachings of the Buddha never promoted caste-based society but radically advocated for worth and not birth as the true measure of a human being. According to the *Udāna*, the very first person the Buddha encountered after his Enlightenment at Bodh Gaya was a brahmin called Huhuṅkajātika who asked the Buddha, 'What makes a brahmin?' He replied, with a mind free of reactivity and prejudice, that no one becomes pure or noble merely by birth. A true brahmin is 'one who is an expert in wisdom, who has lived the holy life'.[8] Likewise, in the *Vasala Sutta* of the *Sutta-Nipāta*, the Buddha said:

> One does not become an outcast by birth, one does not become a brahmin by birth. It is by deed that one becomes an outcast, it is by deed that one becomes a brahmin.[9]

In other words, the Buddha was the pioneer and founder of casteless society. He challenged an old way of thinking on the basis of birth and gave a new egalitarian vision to an unequal and prejudiced Indian society for its reconstruction and liberation.

Borrowing inspiration from his master, the Buddha, on 14 October 1956, at the Diksha Bhumi in Nagpur, Dr Ambedkar inspired millions to convert to Buddhism and thus opened a new window on Indian history. The process of building a new India initiated a fresh inspiration based on liberty, equality, and fraternity, as opposed to a caste-based foundation that cast an oppressive shadow on Indian culture. Dr Ambedkar revealed that in the past Buddhist society experienced a relief from caste prejudice and paved the way for the establishment of democracy, making a deep impression on the minds of the masses who had converted to Buddhism, and enabling them to drop their thinking in terms of caste. Historically, this was an everyday experience in the sangha founded by the Buddha. Everyone, irrespective of caste, was equally a member of the sangha. Those who joined the sangha left behind their caste identity. It was from this model for an ideal society that Dr Ambedkar took inspiration. Firmly believing that the function of the Buddha's teaching is to 'reconstruct an individual and a society', he showed that it is possible to transform the self and the world by bringing changes to the attitude of the mind on the basis of the Buddha's Dhamma.

Dr Ambedkar thus precipitated a social revolution in India on the basis of the Dhamma, affecting the lives of millions of people who were formerly considered untouchable by Hindus. When these people converted to Buddhism, they gained a new confidence in themselves and began to take their rightful place in society. The effects of this revolution are evident in statistics showing improvement in the social and economic status of the converted compared with similar caste groups in which few conversions took place.[10]

LIBERATION THROUGH SPIRITUAL DEMOCRACY

Dr Ambedkar considered that religion was absolutely essential for the development of mankind, but his vision of religion was determined by social considerations. He rejected Hinduism because of its rigid hierarchies, whereas equality was inherent in Buddhism. Even in his quest for economic and socio-political reforms, he believed that it was the Buddha-Dhamma that could bring about the change he envisaged. It was implicit in his vision that democracy is not merely a system to form a government but 'primarily a mode of associated living, of conjoint communicated experience',[11] and 'more than a political machine. It is even more than a social system. It is an attitude of a mind or a philosophy of life.'[12] He equated a successful democracy with the principles of liberty, equality, and fraternity. But above all, he anchored his conception of democracy in the Buddha's *maitrī* (Pāli *mettā*):

> What sustains equality and liberty is fellow feeling. What the French Revolutionist called fraternity. The word fraternity is not an adequate expression. The proper term is what the Buddha called *maitrī*. Without fraternity, liberty would destroy equality and equality would destroy liberty. If in democracy liberty does not destroy equality and equality does not destroy liberty, it is because at the basis of both there is fraternity. Fraternity is therefore the root of democracy.[13]

Dr Ambedkar aspired to achieve not just political and social democracy, but *spiritual* democracy, sacred unity on the basis of love. One might call it *Dhammic* democracy in the light of the Buddha's teachings. For him, liberty, equality, and fraternity were not merely political slogans but spiritual principles wherein democracy gives an individual freedom to grow to their fullest potential without any form of discrimination. It might be thought that democracy and spirituality are two different things and cannot work hand in hand. We tend to assume that spiritual movements preach unalterable truths that are impossible for a person to verify, beyond the reach of reason and human experiences. But spirituality is not an abstract idea where human intervention is not possible, nor is it a set of sacred duties or commands that have to be blindly followed. Such wrong views perpetuate the caste system, according to which caste is divine and no human intervention can alter it. It does not envision a free human but one that remains eternally enslaved to divine commands. By contrast, democracy as a spiritual principle brings human relations into the realm of the spiritual and can be a natural solution for the cultivation of an individual's fullest potential. The yardstick that must ultimately measure experiences in society should be, in the Buddha's words, *bahujana sukhāya*, *bahujana hitāya*, 'for the welfare and happiness of many people',[14] since real liberation lies in realizing that humans are essentially spiritual beings capable of seeing through ignorance and attaining liberation.

The greater part of humanity in our time is dominated by largely selfish impulses, at best moderated by some sense of religion or morality. The religious sense is often corrupted and co-opted by the struggle for survival, especially when priesthoods and ecclesiastical hierarchies become involved. In the name of the unconditioned, they are thoroughly conditioned, serving the needs of the selfish will. Whatever movement towards the unconditioned there is within the conditioned is blocked by impulses of selfish attachment, usually unacknowledged and even unrecognized. It was this vertical and horizontal insight into the true nature of reform that Dr Ambedkar made the fundamental basis for his conversion to Buddhism: vertical in the sense that he realized the deep root cause of suffering on the basis of self-identity, in other words, *ātmavāda*; and horizontal in the sense that once we liberate ourselves from the tyranny of self-identity, we come into harmony with others by recognizing them on the basis of equality and *mettā* (loving-kindness). This was his essential vision throughout his long struggle to transform a culture based on inequality to a more humane one. As he said in his last important public engagement,

> The greatest thing that the Buddha has done is to tell the world that the world cannot be reformed except by the reformation of the mind of the man and the mind of the world.[15]

Dr Ambedkar recognized the Buddha's vision of human liberation in launching the Dhamma Revolution. He certainly wanted to activate the force of *maitrī* – compassion in action. He famously said that he would like to see an image of the walking Buddha, symbolizing compassion in action and breaking down barriers to bring about an equal society.[16] His vision for the future of the people combines the possibility of spiritual democracy with the promise of Buddhist philosophy which liberates. The process of building a new human society activated Dhammic inspiration for the task of rebuilding a humanitarian society based on the proud heritage of the ancient past and the great promise of a modern future. These were the basic ingredients of Dr Ambedkar's socio-spiritual imagination. Dr Ambedkar believed that when religion ends, society will perish too. He said,

> Religion must mainly be a matter of principles only. It cannot be a matter of rules. The moment it degenerates into rules it ceases to be religion, as it kills responsibility, which is the essence of a truly religious act.[17]

It is an error to understand religion as a private and individualistic affair. It is equally mistaken to think that it is the following of rigid rules such as those found in so-called sacred texts like the *Manusmṛti* (an ancient legal text among the many *Dharmaśāstras* of Hinduism). Religion cannot be a matter of rules that evoke fear in the human mind; it must be anchored in human wisdom and compassion. It is not just a matter of faith but must aspire to realize the fullest potential of the human mind, in fact truth itself, through direct and unmediated experiences. It is a matter of personal transformation in which an individual suspends every prejudice, transforming a conditioned attitude to see themselves and others in the absence of oppressive discrimination, so that there is no duality or difference between I and you, or we and they. A religion which discriminates between human beings, gives privileges to a few and inflicts insufferable pains on many, is not religion. Religion and slavery are irreconcilable.

Dr Ambedkar's contemplation of the roots of caste over many years concluded that those roots lay in the mind itself. He recognized that 'caste is a notion, it is a state of mind'.[18] That notion was intrinsically implanted in religious belief and interwoven with supernatural powers that decided social fortune. The new way he was seeking was enshrined in the principles of liberty, equality, and fraternity, utterly rejecting caste discrimination in all its forms. It was compatible with reason and science, did not enjoin blind belief in supernatural agencies that control human fate, and did not justify poverty. His Dhamma Revolution began after hundreds of years of Buddhism's decay in the land of its birth. Among the twenty-two vows he gave to his followers[19] was the vow: 'I renounce Hinduism, which is detrimental to the fulfilment of human beings, and which considers human beings as unequal and degraded, and I embrace the Buddha Dhamma.' He said, 'I am now free from the hell of the caste and I believe that I am taking a new birth.'[20]

Urgyen Sangharakshita, who met Dr Ambedkar on three occasions, acknowledged how much he owed the great man, saying, 'After my contact with Dr Ambedkar I became much more aware of the social dimension of Buddhism, in fact the social dimension of existence itself.' Elsewhere he talked of how Dr Ambedkar's conversion to Buddhism helped him to understand the crucial significance of the act of Going for Refuge to the Buddha, Dhamma, and Sangha. 'I felt very close to my ex-Untouchable brothers and sisters.... For them as for me there could be refuge only at the feet of the Buddha.... I came closer to seeing that Going for Refuge was the central and definitive act of the Buddhist life.'[21] In 2018, a few months before he died, I was able to discuss this with Sangharakshita at his home in Adhisthana, UK, and he expressed his deep appreciation of Dr Ambedkar:

> When I was roaming in India as a Buddhist monk, I saw very little of Buddhism. It was Dr Ambedkar who had the potential to embark a new era for the future of Buddhism. I saw a flood of Buddhists flowing in all corners of India. He was undoubtedly a great bodhisattva. Cherish the Dhamma Revolution he launched.[22]

Guided by a new aesthetic shaped by the Buddhist vision of Dr Ambedkar, a new culture and creativity emerged to give a new egalitarian model and message to Indian society. Dr Ambedkar's conversion to Buddism is often understood as merely an Indian story, or worse, of relevance only to his caste-oppressed followers. But he realized that the answer to the terrible oppression his followers suffered had to be part of a universal solution to *duḥkha*, as relevant to men and women of the modern world as to his so-called untouchable followers. As such, his dynamic vision and approach to Buddhism has the potential to inspire a flowering of the Dhamma not only in India but throughout Asia and the Western world. In his remarkable essay, *Buddha and the Future of His Religion*, Dr Ambedkar clearly expressed this:

> If the countries which are Buddhist can develop the will to spread Buddhism the task of spreading Buddhism will not be difficult. They must realize that the duty of a Buddhist is not merely to be a good Buddhist. His duty is to spread Buddhism. They must believe that to spread Buddhism is to serve mankind.[23]

Ambedkar's far-reaching vision invites a fundamental change leading to a special form of consciousness, a kind of social endosmosis breaking down barriers, leading towards social egalitarianism and an ideal society. He saw this as the surest basis for a truly just and harmonious society everywhere. As he saw, real reform comes about only by the disposition of mind of many people in society. The Buddha's Dhamma offers the basis for that change of mind 'that is the surest way'.[24] He embraced Buddha's non-violent, compassionate, and liberating path to make not only a *Prabuddha Bhārata*, an enlightened India, but also a *Prabuddha Viśva*, an enlightened world.

Maitriveer Nagarjuna (Dr Santosh I. Raut)
Department of Aesthetics and Philosophy
EFL University
Hyderabad, India

Bronze statue of Dr Ambedkar at Nagaloka Campus, Nagpur

VOICES FROM THE DHAMMA REVOLUTION

Compiled by Vidyadevi, with contributions from Lokamitra and others

There are thousands of stories to be told about the impact of Dr Ambedkar's decision to embrace Buddhism upon those who chose to take the same step. Here are just a few of them, taking us from the conversion ceremony itself all the way to the present, and the future.

EYE-WITNESSES TO THE DHAMMA REVOLUTION

In the crowd at the ceremony on 14 October 1956 in which Dr Ambedkar converted to Buddhism along with his followers was a thirteen-year-old girl who was to become Jnanasuri, one of the first women to be ordained within the Order founded by Sangharakshita:

> Dr Ambedkar had announced what was going to happen, and for months beforehand we were all getting ready. The day before, people came from many different places and gathered in Nagpur. They didn't have money for trains or buses, so they had to leave their houses days before and come on foot. Some people even sold the tin sheets from their roofs in order to attend. We lived in a small house in a Nagpur slum, but almost two hundred people came to our house! They had to make arrangements for cooking outside. We were all 'ex-Untouchables', we were all very poor, and life was very difficult. Since 1927 Dr Ambedkar had been telling us about our rights, including the right to education. We had a

lot of problems because of Untouchability, and people thought if they listened to Dr Ambedkar and got themselves educated, they could come out from the caste system and life would improve. We had no idea what Buddhism was or how to practise it, but because Dr Ambedkar converted himself and wanted us to convert, we followed him.

Early in the morning, we marched to the place where the conversion was going to take place. Dr Ambedkar had asked everyone to come in white clothes. My mother didn't have a white sari, but my father had a piece of cloth from which he was going to make some pyjamas, and she wore that. People were very excited and happy and they were chanting slogans. Many people had stayed overnight at the place where the conversion happened, fourteen acres of land completely full of people, women on one side, men on the other. Luckily, I was right at the front. I didn't know much about what was happening, but I did understand that we were going to leave the caste system and go with some other religion, and that was going to give us some benefit.

When Dr Ambedkar stood up to take the *diksha*, he looked very old and sick, and yet he still managed to do so much for the people. First he himself converted to Buddhism, and after that he gave us the *diksha* and the twenty-two vows, which told us exactly what we were committing ourselves to. On each person's face one could see great faith in Dr Ambedkar, and they were so happy that they were just hugging each other. It was as though we had come out of hell. People weren't worried about money or about what was going to happen when they got back home. They were full of excitement and joy. When people went back to their villages, they literally picked up the images of gods and goddesses and threw them out. But the other caste people tortured them, because they refused any longer to clean the roads and do all the dirty jobs. The next day, when I went to school, the brahmins mocked us, and the teacher asked, 'What have you converted to? What concepts have you embraced?' But I said to her, 'Why are you asking all these questions? What difference is it going to make to you what we do? It is our life.'

Drawn by a deep intuition, Sangharakshita arrived in Nagpur on the day, six weeks after the conversion, when Dr Ambedkar died. Jnanasuri remembers it very well:

> I ran home from school and my father gave me a big hug. He was crying and saying 'Now we don't have anyone. We have lost our leader. We are helpless.' In the slums, some people were getting ready to go to Bombay for the funeral, and those who could not go went to Kasturchand Park with candles in their hands. Everyone went, whole families, but we didn't know what to do when we got there. Everyone was crying. Bhante Sangharakshita was there, and he stood on a rickshaw and gave a talk. I vividly remember that, but I don't remember what he said.[25]

Dharmarakshita, who was to become another of the first Order members, was there too:

> I was just 28, a student, and not particularly interested in the Dhamma, but on 6 December 1956 I went along to Kasturchand Park in Nagpur with a friend. A huge crowd had gathered, and there were all kinds of speakers, but they were all so sad they could hardly speak. Then, suddenly, there was Sangharakshita, standing on a rickshaw and speaking to us. Here was someone who could actually say something about the Dhamma. We needed so much support at that moment and Bhante was the only person who could give it. It didn't seem strange that he was an Englishman. It wasn't a time to think about that but a time just to listen to what he was saying. I don't think it really mattered what he said; it was more important that he was there and able to speak. In my heart I can still feel him telling us that with Dr Ambedkar's death we had to keep our courage alive, and continue to follow his lead. You see, there had been the mass conversion and then immediately afterwards there had been a death, so the caste Hindus around us were spreading the idea that we were being punished by the gods. This was not a time to be reminded of Dr Ambedkar's political views. What we needed was a taste of the Dhamma. We didn't really know anything about it. In the days that followed I heard many of Bhante's lectures in

Nagpur. He would be driven around town by car and I would jump onto my bicycle to follow him around.

By chance, Dharmarakshita got involved with Sangharakshita's preaching tours in the following years:

> I had moved to Poona to study for my MA in psychology. One Sunday afternoon I went along to a meeting to hear a *bhikkhu* give a talk, and there was Sangharakshita! All he did was announce that he was giving a talk that evening, but I could tell that his translator was struggling. Well, that evening the audience was huge. There were thousands of people. Everyone who considered themselves a Buddhist was there – except Bhante's translator! Then somebody recognized me and called out, 'Here's a boy from the university. He can speak some English. Get him on stage!' Terrified, I was dragged through the audience, and then there I was, right next to Bhante – him very tall and me very short. I think he could tell how I was feeling, but when he started talking my fear simply dropped away. I started translating and it seemed to go very well. Afterwards we had tea and talked before I went back to my hostel. A little while later he came back to Poona and once again I went along to hear him give a talk and ended up translating. That's how it began.
>
> From 1959 until 1964, for several months each year, I went everywhere he went, to towns and little villages. We were always together and we became friends. I never saw him as 'the big man', nor was there any difficulty because he was a foreigner. I just enjoyed it. Our programmes were sometimes organized by Ambedkarite or Dalit organizations, and sometimes by local people, and we more or less went wherever we were invited. Even then the Ambedkarite movement had its political divisions but Bhante would be invited to speak everywhere because he was only concerned with teaching the Dhamma. People were pleased to learn anything about Buddhism, and nobody seemed to find it strange that the most active *bhikkhu* in the region was a foreigner, perhaps because Dr Ambedkar had impressed on us that the Buddha-Dhamma is for everyone in the world, not just for Indians. No village was too far away: if an invitation came, Sangharakshita

would go, and he could cope with any conditions. There would be times when we would go off to some distant village in a bullock cart and discover that, come the evening after the programme, there was nothing to eat and nowhere to sleep. There wouldn't be anyone around to blame – except me, and it wasn't my fault! But Bhante would simply search for insects in the earth and stubble, move them gently out of the way, and lie down on the ground to sleep.[26]

THE EMERGENCE OF A NEW BUDDHIST MOVEMENT

In 1964 Sangharakshita returned to Britain, and in 1967 he founded a new Buddhist movement, then called the Friends of the Western Buddhist Order (FWBO, now the Triratna Buddhist Community). But he never forgot Dr Ambedkar and the new Buddhist movement in India. He gave talks in England about the plight of the Dalits, and before long there was another opportunity to 'be more active than that'. Lokamitra takes up the story:

> In 1976, in a series of lectures in London on 'Transforming Self and World in the *Sūtra of Golden Light*',[27] Sangharakshita showed that working on oneself implies working on the world, and working on the world implies working on oneself; the two are inextricably joined. This teaching awakened me to the vision I had been seeking for many years. The next year, when I went to India for a yoga course, Surata and I were on a train from Calcutta to Poona. The journey was very long, and noticing that it passed through Nagpur, where we knew that some of Sangharakshita's old friends lived, we decided to break our journey there for a day. To our surprise the town, including the rickshaws, was decked in Buddhist flags and garlands. We soon found out that it was the twenty-first anniversary of the momentous conversion of so-called Untouchables to Buddhism in 1956. We went straight to the house of Sangharakshita's old friend and translator, A. R. Kulkarni, who later took us to the Diksha Bhumi, the conversion ground. Being at that time an *anagārika* in yellow robes, I was seated on the stage for the *bhikkhus*, which was somewhat lower than the stage for the politicians – one of my first lessons about the situation.

Late that night, after the politicians had departed, I was expected to speak to the crowd of hundreds of thousands, the largest crowd I had spoken to before then (in the UK) being not more than 150. In the thirty-six hours we spent in Nagpur I entered a new world, a world of millions of the most oppressed people, all desperate to transform their lives and their society through Buddhism. I had stumbled blindly into a movement dedicated to the twofold transformation of self and world, and on the most auspicious of days. Sangharakshita was, as I was to understand increasingly over the coming weeks and years, one of the most significant figures in this remarkable Dhamma Revolution after Dr Ambedkar himself, and had been trusted by the great man as much as anyone to help take it forward.

The day after the anniversary I wandered round the Diksha Bhumi talking to people, many of whom remembered Sangharakshita and spoke of him with gratitude, pleading for him to return. From Nagpur I went to Poona for two months, ostensibly to learn yoga, but I spent most of my time meeting and teaching local Buddhists. Almost every night we had classes or talks; I was overwhelmed by the response. Clearly the Dhamma seeds planted by Dr Ambedkar and nourished by Sangharakshita had begun to wither since the latter returned to the West in the mid-1960s. This was also my experience in Bombay and Ahmedabad. People were starving for Dhamma nourishment. Sangharakshita wrote to me asking if we should have a centre in Poona, and I could only respond with an emphatic 'yes', even though I knew his next letter would contain a suggestion that I could not refuse: to start it myself.

I returned to Poona to live and work in August 1978, with Kularatna and Padmavajra helping me. We made Poona our base largely because it was where Sangharakshita had spent most time among Dr Ambedkar's followers, and my initial visit had given me the confidence that we could organize activities there. The immediate task before us was to prepare for Sangharakshita's first return visit six months later. At one point, Padmavajra and I were managing fourteen classes and lectures every week between us, conducting them where we could, in the garage of a Christian whose car went to church on Sundays, the veranda of a large empty Parsee bungalow whose caretaker was a Buddhist, a disused railway carriage, and such like. We ran retreats, started a Marathi magazine, *Buddhayan*, and visited Ahmedabad, where Sangharakshita also had connections.

But despite Sangharakshita's encouragement, I was not at all confident about returning to India to teach the Dhamma. How could we, brought up in the UK, possibly think of working with the followers of Dr Ambedkar, who had lived the worst imaginable lives in a totally different social environment? I was abruptly confronted by this question a couple of weeks after I returned to live and work in India. I had just given a public talk on the Dhamma jewel and one person asked me, 'How can we cultivate skilful mental states when our sisters and daughters are raped, our houses burnt and family members killed?' The questioner was referring to the terrible orgy of violence to which Buddhists living in 1,200 towns and villages around Aurangabad had been subjected by caste Hindus, who were upset because the government of Maharashtra had proposed to rename the local university after Dr Ambedkar. He was, according to the caste system, an Untouchable, and his name on their degree certificates would contaminate them. Rather than take it out on the government, they attacked local Buddhists.

As it happened, Jnanasuri, who moved to Aurangabad on her marriage, saw this at first-hand. She explains:

The government promised that the university in Aurangabad would be named after Dr Ambedkar, but the Hindus did not keep their word. People started agitating, and there was a lot of violence and chaos. I was part of the group that was trying to agitate, and I was beaten and put in jail twice. By the second time, I had attended a retreat, so I knew how to do the Mindfulness of Breathing and the *mettā bhāvanā*, and taught the other women in the jail how to meditate. The Mindfulness of Breathing was OK, but I found the *mettā bhāvanā* very difficult, both doing it myself and teaching it to others, because I found it hard to wish happiness to those people who were beating us.

Awareness of this kind of suffering preyed on Lokamitra's mind:

> Coming from safe, comfortable Britain, how could I possibly teach those facing hardships so far beyond my experience? I could not. But we could join each other in a mutual exploration of the Dhamma, sharing our experience and practice. This was possible because they, like me and other disciples of Sangharakshita, were new Buddhists, not born Buddhists. We had all come freshly to Buddhism and we wanted pure Dhamma practices that related to us in our present predicament, not encumbered with the historical and cultural baggage of other traditions. This freshness to the Dhamma created a strong sense of fellowship from the very beginning of our work.
>
> The depth of gratitude people feel towards Dr Ambedkar for rescuing them from the hell of Untouchability and taking them into Buddhism is immeasurable. However, soon after he died, this huge movement was torn apart by his feuding political heirs. Ignored by the Buddhist world, and crippled by poverty, illiteracy, and extreme oppression, few of his followers had any chance to understand much of the Dhamma. Although Dr Ambedkar had written a guide to Buddhist teachings, *The Buddha and His Dhamma*, and a book of devotional practices, as well as prescribing twenty-two vows, an initiation to guide his new Buddhist followers, without exemplars and teachers progress was difficult. His followers could relate to the enormous contribution Dr Ambedkar had made to their economic, legal, social, and political existence, but the supreme importance he gave to the Dhamma was less tangible, and many of his disciples were confused over why he converted to Buddhism. But their faith in him meant that they did not give up, and they remained desperate to know what it meant to practise the Dhamma, and how it could change their individual and social lives.
>
> In the early days of our movement in India, people were especially receptive to us because of the connection Sangharakshita made when he happened to arrive in Nagpur on the day in 1956 when Dr Ambedkar passed away. Many thought he had saved Nagpur for Buddhism. After that he spent months every year helping new Buddhists all over central and western

India understand the Dhamma. Everywhere I went I found overwhelming gratitude to him. One leading Buddhist politician, Dadasaheb Rupawate, who became a close friend of mine, had taken Sangharakshita on a teaching tour around the Ahmednagar District of Maharashtra in the early 1960s. Whenever he spoke of Sangharakshita there were tears in his eyes. 'If there was a car, he would come by car, if not, a cycle, if not, a bullock cart, otherwise he would walk. He stayed in our huts and ate our food; no one from outside our community (caste) had ever done that before!' Maharashtrians are known for their loyalty, for not forgetting those who have helped them at their time of need and distress. The mention of Sangharakshita's name took us straight into people's homes and hearts.

Although we came to Buddhism from such different worlds, we all saw that Buddhism stood for nothing less than the creation of a new society, and that this was based on individual practise of the Dhamma – the transformation of self and world. This was what had inspired me on that October day in Nagpur in 1977 and moved me to stay in India. Dr Ambedkar talked about the sangha as an ideal society, and Sangharakshita talked of it as the nucleus of a new society. Going for Refuge to the Buddha, Dhamma, and Sangha was the central act that made one a Buddhist, for both lay people and monastics. To Sangharakshita morality was the immediate expression of Going for Refuge, and to Dr Ambedkar morality was not different from the Dhamma. Both Dr Ambedkar and Sangharakshita insisted that the real meaning insisted of the precepts is to be found in their positive counterparts. Both were categorical about the need to leave behind all vestiges of the old religion in order to progress in the new. The tension between the individual and the group, and the need for the individual to rise above group tendencies, was of primary concern to both, and that tension found its resolution in the Dhamma. Dr Ambedkar based much of his approach on the Theravāda teachings, with some Mahāyāna elements, such as the bodhisattva ideal, the *paramitās*, and the fourfold bodhisattva vow, and the mantra of Avalokiteśvara, *oṃ maṇi padme hūṃ*. Sangharakshita's approach in principle was very similar.

Oṃ maṇi padme hūṃ was included in a puja book in Marathi which Dr Ambedkar had published to coincide with the conversion – Jnanasuri's family bought it at the ceremony and started reciting from it the next day. Sangharakshita often made the significance of the mantra the subject of his talks to the new Buddhists, no doubt to explain its inclusion in the puja book, but why was it important to Dr Ambedkar? Fortunately we have the record of a moving conversation that took place in May 1950 between Ambedkar and Mulk Raj Anand, who wrote the novel *Untouchable*. Anand greeted Ambedkar with the traditional *namaskar*, but Ambedkar said, 'I prefer the Buddhist greeting, *oṃ maṇi padme hūṃ*. May the lotuses awake!' Anand replied, 'I agree. How thoughtless we are! We inherit words without questioning their meanings! Of course, *namaskar* means 'I bow before you….' And Ambedkar said, 'That perpetuates submission! "May the lotuses awake" is a prayer for Enlightenment!'[28]

SANGHARAKSHITA'S VISITS TO INDIA

Between the years 1979 and 1992 Sangharakshita made several visits to India to see how the new movement was progressing. Lokamitra, who organized all the tours, remembers them very well:

> Sangharakshita came to India twice in 1979, once on his way to New Zealand, and once on the way back. These visits were emotional occasions, for him and for his Indian disciples. He was returning after an absence of thirteen years during which he had laid the foundations for a new Buddhist movement in the West. During that time, the Ambedkarite conversion movement in India had reached to a hiatus, and the Indian socialist republic was beginning to grow out of its old Nehruvian and Gandhian clothes, to become part of the global village. Sangharakshita met many old friends and disciples, wealthy and spiritually-minded Parsees and caste Hindus, politicians, Buddhist followers of Dr Ambedkar, and Buddhists from the East. It was so different from my experience of him in the West, where he was an unfathomable, fascinating, and somewhat scruffy friend in the free counter-cultural atmosphere of the time. Not only was he deeply respected by all in India, but whoever he was with, his attitude was the same, one of genuine emotional engagement and

Right: *'An unfathomable, fascinating, and somewhat scruffy friend', Cambridge, August 1973*

Below: *Bakula and Dharmarakshita after their ordination, with Sangharakshita and Lokamitra*

respect. It was renewing contact with his old disciples among the Ambedkarite communities that moved him most of all. He thought they would have forgotten him. They had certainly given up on him returning and many had begun to despair about the future of Dr Ambedkar's Buddhist movement. But they still remembered him, their respect for him seemed to have grown, and there was a great sense of relief at seeing and hearing him once again.

He made up for his long absence with three gifts that he had honed in the West: a vision of a Dhamma-based society, Dhamma teachings that were as relevant to new Indian Buddhists as new Western Buddhists, and a spiritual community that transcended all differences. Sangharakshita was a master at communicating the Dhamma in an inspiring and accessible manner to people from all backgrounds. He delighted all in the nine talks he gave on that first visit, clarifying and bringing alive the teachings they had learned from Dr Ambedkar, and opening a new dimension for our movement. Through the Dhamma, Dr Ambedkar had opened the possibility of fellowship between some of the world's most abused people, whose very touch was anathema to many of their countrymen, with people throughout the world, especially the 'new world', as he called it. But as yet his disciples had had little experience of this possibility, being largely ignored by the Buddhist world. In 1979, Sangharakshita ordained twelve people, ten from Poona and two from Ahmedabad, most of the ordinations taking place at the majestic Sinhagad Fort, which dominates the skyline south of Poona. Through these ordinations the Indian members of the Order made a connection with Western people who could not understand caste, and so could not relate to them in those terms, thus opening horizons hitherto unimagined. And the benefit was far from one way. In the West we had the tendency to see ourselves as not conditioned to the extent that people from more traditional societies seemed to be, but this was far from being the case, and through this spiritual fellowship we had an opportunity to go beyond our more subtle but just as limiting social conditioning. On the day of the first ordinations several rainbows appeared, an auspicious beginning to a unique development, transcending enormous social and civilizational extremes through fellowship in the Dhamma.

Also during this visit Sangharakshita conducted a *puṇyānumodanā* (after-death) ceremony which lived long in the memory of those who attended it. As reported in the *FWBO Newsletter*, he spoke on a verse from the *Dhammapada*: 'Some people do not realize that we are all heading for death. But those who realize this bring their quarrels to an end.'[29] 'One of those present confessed that compared with what he had just heard, the last twenty-three years since he had converted to Buddhism had been a complete waste. He had learned nothing about the Dharma in that time. For the first time in his life he had thought seriously about the Dharma.'[30]

From Lokamitra's point of view:

> Those two visits were chaotic. The local Buddhist community had little money and we didn't have much either. There were no phones, we found it hard to get cars, and when we did they were old and could break down. But none of this mattered. When Sangharakshita left us, we had an Indian wing to the FWBO, named Trailokya Bauddha Mahasangha Sahayaka Gana, at the heart of which was the Order, the Trailokya Bauddha Mahasangha. We were now able to get down to developing Dhamma activities in Poona, venturing to Bombay and other towns, finding land for a vihara in Poona and a retreat centre nearby, planning social work, and developing publications.

Here's an excerpt from Sangharakshita's explanation of the name he had given to the Indian wing of the Order, which translates roughly as 'Buddhist community of the three worlds':

> *Trailokya* means 'pertaining to the three worlds' (*triloka*). According to Buddhist tradition the three worlds are the *kāmaloka*, the world of sensuous desire, the *rūpaloka*, the world of archetypal form, and the *arūpaloka*, the formless world. These three worlds between them comprise the whole of conditioned existence. The fact that our new Buddhist movement is styled '*trailokya*' therefore means that it is addressed to all sentient beings regardless of the 'world' in which they live, or the degree of mundane development which they have attained. The term *triloka* can, however, be understood in other ways. The three worlds are

> also the three levels of material life, cultural life, and spiritual life, with progress on all of which Buddhism is concerned, as well as the three economic divisions of the (industrially) developed world, the developing world, and the undeveloped world, in two of which our new Buddhist movement is already functioning.

Sangharakshita's next tour lasted about three months, starting at the end of 1981. Lokamitra:

> The tour was brought vividly alive by Nagabodhi in his book *Jai Bhim!*[31] Sangharakshita gave forty lectures, each quite different, in towns throughout central and western Maharashtra, and in Bombay, Ahmedabad, Ajmer, and Delhi. If the talk was in a village, it was usually held in the poorest part, transformed by fairy lights and flags. If it was in a town, the local people would sometimes organize it in a prominent place, if possible in the central square, blocking the main roads, proclaiming their newfound confidence as Buddhists. The tour was a remarkable feat for him, the travelling, staying in basic lodgings, the very different food and very persuasive hosts, the mob-like clamour to get near him, and preparing a different lecture every day.[32] There were many highlights. He visited Mahad, giving a talk where Dr Ambedkar had burned the *Manusmṛti*, which articulated the laws defining the practice of Untouchability. In Delhi he gave a talk to the Buddhist wing of Kanshi Ram's social organization, BAMCEF, which eventually metamorphized into the Bahujan Samaj Party, the most successful party of Ambedkarites so far. In Bombay he gave a talk to another quasi-political organization (politics being the major dimension of Dr Ambedkar's life's work). In this talk, 'Dr Ambedkar's Dhamma Revolution', he emphasized what Dr Ambedkar had said about the need for a new kind of sangha made up of dedicated Dhamma workers. This, he said, was what our sangha was about. This theme inspired and galvanized TBMSG (as the Triratna Buddhist Community was then known) for years. The visit was a major step forward in the development of activities in Maharashtra and Gujarat, and confirmed TBMSG as making a serious and significant contribution to Dr Ambedkar's Dhamma Revolution.

Lokamitra helping build the retreat centre at Bhaja

Sangharakshita next visited India at the end of 1983, the tour again organized by Lokamitra:

> During this visit he gave three lectures, the first on the anniversary of Dr Ambedkar's death, a very emotional time for all his followers. The lecture was held in Dapodi, Poona, near the site where we were to build our magnificent Mahavihara, and next to the slums where our community health and education work had already started. The second was at the opening of our new retreat centre, Saddhamma Pradip, facing the ancient Bhaja caves, an hour's train journey from Poona. Whilst at the retreat centre he ordained eight men, most of whom embodied the ideal of the Dhamma worker that he had inspired us with on his previous visit, playing leading roles in taking the Dhamma into new areas. The last lecture was in Bombay, in the appallingly overcrowded chawls of Worli, a hub of Dr Ambedkar's movement in which thousands of Buddhists lived. Entitled 'Dr Ambedkar's True Greatness', and comparing Buddhism with the major secular philosophies of the modern age, developed by Darwin, Marx, and Freud, it proved to be another seminal lecture.

Padmasuri leads the first women's retreat at Bhaja

While inspired by the power of the Dhamma to change lives, the new Buddhist movement also addressed people's needs for healthcare, education, and ethical employment. When speaking at Dapodi during this 1983 visit, on the site where a medical centre was shortly to be built, Sangharakshita reminisced about his tours in the 1950s:

> Although I gave so many lectures, I was not altogether satisfied with my work. Everywhere I went I saw people who were suffering from all kinds of diseases and injuries. I used to think that it was not enough to preach the Dhamma, not enough to look after the mind. We also have to look after the body. Sometimes I used to wish that I had studied medicine instead of devoting so much time to poetry, philosophy, and history. I used to think how wonderful it would be if I could preach the Dhamma in the morning and give medical treatment in the afternoon.

Here was an opportunity for Western Buddhists to give. Virabhadra and Padmasuri, a doctor and nurse, pioneered the training of medical staff (as chronicled in Padmasuri's book *But Little Dust*),[33] and fundraising in England began for what was first called the 'Poona Project', became Aid for India, and then the Karuna Trust, which still funds work in India and beyond. Vajrapushpa, the current chair of the charity, writes:

> From the modest beginnings of supporting a medical project in the slums of Poona and a few hostels in Maharashtra, the Karuna Trust has evolved into a medium-size charity working with a wide range of partner organizations in India and Nepal. Many things have changed since the early 1980s, but the ethos and values remain firmly underpinned by Sangharakshita's emphasis on individual and social transformation and Dr Ambedkar's critique of caste. Karuna's partners work in three areas – education, dignified livelihoods, and gender equality – which support the overall mission to end caste-based discrimination, poverty, and inequality in India and Nepal.

While the Karuna Trust supported all kinds of social projects, different funding would be needed for Dhamma work. In the early days, not much help was forthcoming from the rest of the Buddhist world, as Sangharakshita used to lament, but that changed dramatically. Lokamitra explains:

> It was clear that the charity could fund social projects, but it was more difficult to fund Dhamma projects, as most donations were made on a non-religious basis. This was potentially problematic, as it was Dhamma practice that empowered people to engage in social projects. I discussed this with Sangharakshita in 1983, and he suggested I approach Buddhists in East and South-east Asia. He put me in touch with the Young Buddhist Association of Malaysia, who organized a tour for me in 1984. Malaysian Buddhists have close connections with Buddhists in Taiwan, where I was invited as a result, and I have been visiting annually since 1989. Our friends in Taiwan, and also China and Korea, have supported many projects, including the Hsuan Tsang Retreat Centre; the Nagarjuna Training Institute (including the magnificent Walking Buddha); earthquake, flood, and tsunami relief programmes; many community centres; and the Ashok Dhammaduta programme, in which Nagarjuna Institute alumni teach the Dhamma in many villages.

First ordinations of women by women: Srimala, Vimalasuri, Ratnasuri, and Jnanasuri

In 1987 a new development took place because Sangharakshita *couldn't* visit India. His elderly mother was ill and he couldn't leave England, so for the first time he asked other people to perform ordinations on his behalf. This was when Jnanasuri was ordained, together with Vimalasuri. Their private preceptors were Srimala and Padmasuri, and Ratnasuri was their public preceptor. Thus began the tradition which over time developed into the ordination process for women and men in India and throughout the world.

Sangharakshita visited India twice more, in 1988 and 1992. Lokamitra again:

> In October 1988, Sangharakshita came out to make a BBC documentary, *In the Footsteps of Ambedkar*. He laid the foundation stone for our Mahavihara at Dapodi, Poona, and ordained a further eight men at Bhaja, including the first from Nagpur, and two from Wardha. Since 1983 we had carried out extensive tours of Vidarbha, the north-east region of Maharashtra,

> centred around Nagpur, the hub of the conversion movement, where he had made such an emotional impact at the time of Dr Ambedkar's death.

Sangharakshita was full of praise for the work that was being done. In later years he spoke warmly of two people in particular:

> Shakyananda and Sanghasena lived for the Dharma, and they died for the Dharma. They were old men when I ordained them, and they both suffered from various ailments, but year after year they went from village to village giving talks on the Dharma. Sanghasena was a small, quiet man who operated in the northern part of Maharashtra, so he was known as the lion of the north, and Shakyananda, who was a fat, jolly man – I used to call him the Buddhist Falstaff, except that he didn't have Falstaff's weaknesses – operated in the southern part of Maharashtra, so he was known as the lion of the south. Between them in a few years they must have covered a thousand villages and towns, bringing the Dharma to each and every one of them, and they both died in harness. One might say they sacrificed their lives for the sake of the Dharma, except that they worked so happily. They loved their work, they were joyful despite their ailments, and they communicated that joy in the Dharma to thousands of people. They weren't great scholars, in fact they weren't scholars at all, but they were living embodiments of compassion and energy.[34]

On his 1988 tour, Sangharakshita next went to Wardha, near Nagpur. Lokamitra remembers:

> The programme took place the day before the anniversary of Dr Ambedkar's conversion, which is always celebrated on a huge scale in Nagpur. Although Sangharakshita did not want to return to Nagpur until we had regular activities there for him to build on, we spent six hours on a train which was going there, and that gave us a taste of the atmosphere. Fortunately we were travelling first class, as second class was jam-packed, and the roof was just as crowded. We stayed just outside Wardha, next to the ashram Gandhi developed in the last years of his life, an opportunity for

Sangharakshita to comment for the documentary on the relative significance of Gandhi and Dr Ambedkar in the eradication of Untouchability. He noted that of the eleven observances developed by Gandhi for the ashram, the removal of Untouchability was the last! On another occasion he referred to Dr Ambedkar as 'the greatest non-violent revolutionary of this century'.

Sangharakshita's final visit to India took place in the winter of 1991–2, by which time we had developed many of the activities we are running today. He was delighted with the Dapodi Mahavihara, and I was particularly pleased that he spent time there. It seemed to bring the vihara to life, rather like giving 'life' to a Buddha image. Besides a popular Dhamma centre with full classes, the Mahavihara had offices for administration for our social and Dhamma activities in Maharashtra, as well as Gujarat, Hastinpur in Uttar Pradesh, and Hyderabad. The Dhamma activities included not only centres in various towns, but tours throughout the state of Maharashtra, and also the large retreat centres at Bhaja, near Poona, and Bordharan, near Nagpur. We had developed a thriving publications wing, with many books, especially Sangharakshita's, as well as the quarterly magazine, *Buddhayan*, of which we were producing 25,000 copies. Probably the most important activity was the preparation for ordination training which was centred on the community at the Mahavihara. A number of the leading Order members of today emerged out of that training.

Important though the visit to the Mahavihara was, the main aim was to visit Nagpur, where we now had four very active members of the Order, to honour the commitment Sangharakshita had made to Nagpur Buddhists many years before. We travelled some of the way by train, and there were crowds waiting to garland him at every station. Arriving at Nagpur, we found that he had been accorded the honour of being a State Guest, so we were driven in a police convoy everywhere we went. His main talk was at the historic Kasturchand Park, where he had spoken at Dr Ambedkar's condolence ceremony. We also made an excursion to Bordharan to open the first stage of the retreat centre there, along with some *bhikṣuṇīs* from Taiwan who had helped us. Being good friends of mine, they were in awe of my teacher, Sangharakshita. The retreat centre was named after Hsüan Tsang (Xuanzang), the great

Nagaloka campus, looking across to the Walking Buddha

Chinese traveller monk, to symbolize the developing link between Indian and Chinese Buddhism.

I think Sangharakshita knew that this was probably his last visit. He was clearly very pleased with all the developments in our work. In Nagpur, he said that we should get twenty acres of land outside the town to showcase all our different Dhamma and social activities. At the time I had no idea how we could fund something like that, but two or three years later we were able to purchase fourteen-and-a-half acres of land on the edge of the city, and by 1997 we had opened the first building on the Nagaloka campus. In the end, instead of showcasing a cross-section of our work, we concentrated on training young people from all over India, something Sangharakshita fully endorsed. Until the centenary of Dr Ambedkar's birth in 1991 his followers were concentrated in the state of Maharashtra, but after that there was an explosion of interest in him among Scheduled Castes, Scheduled Tribes, and others all over India. We couldn't go to every town in India

> to teach, but we could offer residential training at the Nagarjuna Training Institute at Nagaloka. At the time of writing over 1,400 young people from twenty-five Indian states have benefited from the training and form a vibrant network. With the magnificent Walking Buddha at the centre of the campus, Nagaloka is respected throughout the Ambedkarite Buddhist communities in India and the socially engaged Buddhist world beyond. I think Sangharakshita knew in 1992 that Nagpur would be the springboard from which we would bring to fulfilment the deep connection he made on that fateful day in 1956.

LOOKING TO THE FUTURE

The future of the Dhamma Revolution rests with young people like those training at Nagaloka. Here are the voices of three alumni who grew up in villages in different parts of India: Dhivya Ethiraj in a remote area 200 kilometres from Chennai in Tamil Nadu; Lakhindar Soren in a village next to a uranium mine in Jharkand state, to the south of Bihar; and Dhammachari Maitreyaratna in Odisha, a coastal state south of Kolkata. Odisha has a long Buddhist history, as Maitreyaratna explains:

> The Lord Buddha never visited Odisha, but Buddhist chronicles refer to a relic of the Buddha brought there by two of his first disciples, Tapassa and Bhallika, the wealthy merchants from Orissa (as it is named in the Pāli canon),[35] and there were many important centres of Buddhism there during the sixth to tenth centuries CE. In the modern Lalitgiri, Udayagiri, and Ratnagiri there are the remains of ancient and medieval Buddhism, treasured by Buddhists and historians.

Things are different there now. Odisha is a poor state with much caste discrimination, from which Maitreyaratna suffered as a child.

> Once I touched the water pump while an upper caste boy was drinking, and after school his mother came after me with an axe. Sweating with fear, I hid in our henhouse, and I heard my mother say to the angry woman, 'It's such a small thing. Why are you getting so upset?' But the woman said, 'It's not a small thing. Your

> boy polluted our caste. Every day you people disrespect the caste system. You must live as you are supposed to live.' Every day I felt the demoralizing impact of caste discrimination, which was deeply rooted in my mind and reflected in my every action. I felt I couldn't do anything, and I was afraid of everything.

Things were just as difficult for Dhivya.

> The higher caste people wanted nothing to do with us. We weren't allowed to participate in village festivals, or sit near them on a bus, and if we tried to take water from the public tap we would be beaten. We were not allowed to enter the village shop, and at school we had to sit at a distance for our midday meal. We worked as landless labourers; while working in the fields we were not even allowed to wear shoes. We could not question caste Hindus on any matter but had to obey their orders. If we didn't follow caste duties, they barred us from labour and the basic necessities of life. We were literally treated as slaves.

There was trouble at home too.

> I am among the first generation of girls from our community to get an education. The belief is that girls should not be educated and they should get married as soon as they come of age. My mother worships many gods, offers animal sacrifices, and fasts on religious days. My father was drunken and violent. Once when he was angry he burned our books, and he tried to kill us many times. He sold things from our home to buy drink and went to prison for his violence. He died when I was in high school, and my mother and sister run our family now. I became interested in Christianity and used to go to church to cry and confess all my suffering and pain.

Lakhindar, too, grew up in poverty, his family so poor that although he gained a scholarship to complete his schooling, his father didn't know how to advise him what to do next. But his uncle had heard of Nagaloka, and Lakhindar decided to apply. When he arrived at the campus he was moved by its beauty, but at the interview he felt conflicted:

I wanted to go home to take an exam to work on the railways, then come back, but the interviewer said I would need to decide there and then. I phoned my father and he advised me to stay, so I decided to dedicate myself to learning. At first I found learning about Buddhism very difficult, but meditation helped me develop concentration, clarity, and confidence, the course about faith was transformative, and in Dhamma study I began to see that nothing is separate, and everything is impermanent.

Dhivya found her way to Nagaloka too.

My sister started working as the warden of a hostel in Chennai, established by Nagaloka alumni after the 2004 tsunami in Tamil Nadu. She suggested that I should go to Nagaloka to study. At first I resisted, and when I got there, I phoned my sister and told her that I wanted to go home. The food was different from what we ate at home, and I couldn't talk to anyone as I knew only Tamil. I was angry with my sister for sending me there, but she asked me to stay for a week and then come home if I still didn't like it. I am grateful to say that I made friends who were very supportive and encouraged me to stay, and I'm grateful to my sister too. During the first month I focused on learning Hindi, but gradually I started enjoying morning meditation, and we went on a meditation retreat which turned out to be very inspiring.

Maitreyaratna heard about Nagaloka from a social activist.

It was my first train journey, my first experience of the world outside the village. Nagaloka was like a dream. People I didn't even know were so welcoming and friendly, with handshakes and hugs. It was like a Pure Land, and the people were my family – more than my family. At Nagaloka I learned to distinguish science from superstition and blind belief, and came to know about the Buddha as a true individual and the ideal of the human being. The teaching of the Three Jewels gave me the direction of my life, and to this day meditation, both the Mindfulness of Breathing and the *mettā bhāvanā*, gives me the strength to break my inferiority

> complex and caste conditioning. Physical birth is not in our control, but learning and practising the precepts gave me a new birth, and cultivating positive emotion gave me fearlessness and moral strength.

As Lakhindar says, 'We create a mini-India every year at Nagaloka.' From the start Dhivya was deeply moved by the way people there treated her 'like a human being, not as a lower caste girl'. Having arrived unable to communicate with anyone, she learned public speaking, translated from English for a visitor from the UK, and went to the INEB conference (International Network of Engaged Buddhists), where she connected with the wider Buddhist world. Lakhindar works for the Manuski Trust,[36] inspired by the *Kālāma Sutta* to think for himself and for his community. And Maitreyaratna, for whom 'social action is nothing but the expression of our Buddhist practice', is working with friends from Nagaloka to bring Buddhism back to Odisha, where it flourished so many years ago. As Dhivya says:

> Nagaloka has done so much for so many of us who would otherwise have been left to live a life of slavery. Instead, we live a life of freedom and are able to help our people.

These Nagaloka alumni describe the challenges of living in village India. The big city presents different challenges, as Amitamati, of Mumbai, explains. She was born with a serious medical condition which meant that she spent a lot of her childhood in hospital. Despite, or perhaps because of, that she was drawn to medical work when she grew up:

> My grandparents were converted to Buddhism in 1956. My grandmother, a staunch Ambedkarite Buddhist, used to chant the Refuges and Precepts every day before the pictures of the Buddha and Dr Ambedkar. Of course you can't be a born Buddhist – you have to take the Refuges and Precepts, and understand and practise them – but having a Buddhist family background was very helpful, because there was no Hindu influence.
>
> Like many people, I became a practising Buddhist by accident. In 1987, when I was studying at Siddharth College, which Dr Ambedkar founded, a family friend mentioned that there was

a meditation class at the college every Saturday. I didn't know then that meditation is an integral part of Buddhist practice, but I knew that it meant learning concentration and how to integrate your mind, so I went to the class out of curiosity. I was seventeen years old. It was amazing to see three or four hundred people sitting silently in a hall with closed eyes, and a pale skinned British man (his name was Padmavajra) teaching them to meditate. I didn't know anything about Triratna, then known as Trailokya Bauddha Mahasangha, but I decided to investigate. That was the turning point of my life.

At school and medical college I struggled to get food and books and clothes, but I didn't experience caste discrimination as such. My schoolmate was a brahmin and we used to share tiffin and visit each other's families. There was a sort of social endosmosis, as Dr Ambedkar called it. But life was very different when I started work. My father lost his job and I was the eldest daughter, so I had to take care of the whole family. I was quite a meritorious student, so I had no trouble getting a job, and having a fresh young mind, I had no thoughts about caste. I just wanted to learn more about medical science. But my colleagues wanted to know my surname – this is how people in India find out your caste background – and some days after I was appointed, I was given menial tasks for which I was over-qualified. I thought it was part of the job, but one of my colleagues asked me, 'Why are you doing this?', and then I realized that my supervisor was prejudiced against me. I got another job which was better, and then I moved to the hospital where I've now been working for many years, but here too caste prejudice is very strong. Modes of caste-based discrimination are more subtle in workplaces these days, especially in Metro cities like Mumbai. It's not that you're literally 'untouchable'. At one level everything's fine, but people respond to you differently from how they treat other people, and they certainly don't want to accept anyone of an ex-Untouchable or Ambedkarite Buddhist background in a superior position. They react as if their privileges are being taken away. If you are a practising Buddhist, you are supposed to be kind and compassionate, and do the *mettā bhāvanā* for everybody, but that's a challenge if somebody's very rude and harsh to you. It's not about living in a fantasy. You have to live practically. Even if you're trying to practise all four speech precepts, it's hard if the other person is unkind.

I'm not saying that it's completely the fault of the people who are prejudiced, because it's very challenging to change yourself. Giving away privileges that you are born with is challenging in itself. It's a deeply rooted mindset and it takes proper focus and a lot of effort to change it. Some of my friends say they realize that there is something wrong about the way they are behaving, but they struggle to put what they know into practice. It happens with us too. I just leave them to it and try not to keep grievances in my mind. I think that is the best thing that Buddhism has offered me. Negative emotions create restrictions in the mind, and if you let them control you, you can't experience liberation. Sometimes when I have a bad day, when I'm rudely treated by my boss or I have to keep explaining that I'm there on my merits, not only because of my caste, in the evening I go to the Mitra class where I live, and I'm teaching them to be kind to other people. I close my eyes and try to feel *mettā*, and I feel, 'Oh, I'm not getting liberated, I'm completely bound up in all these negative emotions.' But slowly, slowly my mind gets straight. These challenges make you strong. You can use them as an opportunity.

Over the last twenty years I have seen that people from the Shudra community, the other 'backward class' apart from the Mahars, are slowly realizing how they are ruled by upper caste people. They can rule if we follow them and don't liberate ourselves from caste boundaries. Of course, some people have converted to Buddhism, but it will take a long time. As Dr Ambedkar said, 'The Buddha's way is a long way, but perhaps the surest way.' He initiated the process, and people will follow it. The Buddhist community is still dominated by the ex-Mahars, but we need to open the path of liberation to other communities if we want to realize Dr Ambedkar's vision of an Enlightened India. It's a challenge, but why not? If Dr Ambedkar could do it seventy years ago, we can do it now. It's our responsibility, as a reflection of our Going for Refuge. That's how I look at it.

It's happening at Nagaloka, in Nagpur. There are students from twenty-nine states of India, all from different backgrounds, and their stories of what they have been through are quite amazing. Young people are very socially engaged, vibrant, and politically active, and through social media they stay connected with what's going on. In the past, if a woman somewhere was raped by upper caste people, it took months for us to hear about it. That sort of thing still happens, unfortunately.[37] But young people are now protesting and they have the guts to come forward and talk about what has happened. I think the younger generation are moving forward. My concern is that they should be led in the right direction. Mobs tend to get dragged along by violent ideologies like Marxism, but Dr Ambedkar and the Buddha talked about peaceful transformation, and that is what we believe in. I have full confidence in the Buddha's teaching because I have experienced it myself. It is not easy, because ultimately it is connected with the transformation of mind, and unless that happens, social transformation will not take place.

As Buddhists we need to make sure that we are not falling into the trap of consumerism. People feel tempted by the big shopping malls and they become focused on external experience – this car, that house – rather than looking within. Of course, you have to have a good lifestyle. The Buddha and Dr Ambedkar didn't encourage poverty. But materialism should not take control of your life. If you fall into that trap, instead of becoming more insightful and reflective, life becomes an accumulation of material things, and ultimately you cause yourself more suffering.

Since I am a Buddhist and aspire to be a good practitioner, I have to reflect on my actions, not just when I am on retreat or in a Dharma class, but wherever I am, even in unfavourable conditions like my workplace. In any case, it's favourable when I see my patients, because that is how I practise kindness. I decided to be a life science student because I wanted to help those in pain, whether physical or mental. When I go to work, I walk past the mortuary, and that puts life in perspective. If I keep carrying aversion, I cannot liberate myself. I remember the last part of the Sevenfold Puja: 'Just as the earth and other elements are serviceable in many ways to the infinite number of beings inhabiting limitless space, so may I become that which maintains all beings.' There's a long way to go, and I am just a beginner, but I have committed myself to helping people who are suffering in whatever way I can. That is my way of Going for Refuge. I want to say this from my heart: people need your love, people need your help. So let us open our hearts and minds, and reach out to those in need, and stop keeping ourselves within boundaries. That is what Bhante Sangharakshita and Dr Ambedkar did throughout their lives. Their message is that our life should be dedicated to the benefit of all beings. That is the first vow we take when we are ordained, and we don't know how much life we have left. So although it is challenging, keep going, leap the hurdles on the path. We will be victorious. We are the daughters of the Buddha.

Order convention at Bodh Gaya, 2018

From the beginning, Sangharakshita wanted there to be as much contact as possible between Triratna Order members throughout the world, and over the years this has gradually developed. Many Westerners have devoted themselves to Dhamma work in India, and many Indian Order members have visited the West, and provided much inspiration. (Sangharakshita always maintained that Western Buddhists have much to learn from their brothers and sisters in India.) Triratna's international council has met in India, and Order conventions have been held at Bodh Gaya, where Triratna has a centre. Although Sangharakshita's visit to India in 1992 was to be his last, many people from the Indian sangha have visited him in the UK.

Sangharakshita died in 2018, nearly seventy years after his first contact with Dr Ambedkar, 'the greatest man I ever met in all my life'. So much had been achieved in the light of their shared vision of the revival of Buddhism in India and far beyond, and yet, to echo Dr Ambedkar's words at the final meeting of the two men, there was still so much to do. Now it was time to hand on the challenge to 'be more active' to

Sangharakshita and Tarahridaya at their final meeting

future generations. Sangharakshita's last personal visitors were two Indian Dhammacharinis, Tarahridaya and Abhayanavita.[38] Tarahridaya shares something of that last meeting:

> I entered his room with a big red flower to offer him. I bowed three times and tried to offer him the flower, but he was trying to shake my hand. I asked him, 'Bhante, do you still remember Hindi?' and with a soft gesture he replied '*Bhul gaya*', which means, 'I have forgotten.' But after that he spoke a few sentences in Hindi. I talked about my difficulty in visualizing in my *sādhana* practice, and he said, 'The work you are doing is Tārā's work, and your connection with her is more important than seeing her. Keep chanting her mantra.' Then he chanted the Green Tārā mantra using his *mālā*, like a blessing for me. His memory was amazing. I travel in many states for my work with the women's ordination process, and he asked me about South India and Rajasthan, and mentioned a friend in Udaipur. He asked me how many women in India have asked for ordination. 'Nearly 850', I told him, 'and there are eighteen of us on the team.' Hearing that, he smiled, as though he knew something. Somehow knowing that this would be the last time I would see him, I tried to absorb every moment in my heart.

REMEMBERING AMBEDKAR: AN INTRODUCTION

The garlanding of Dr Ambedkar's statue, Diksha Bhumi, Nagpur 1965

REMEMBERING AMBEDKAR

A talk given by Sangharakshita at the London Buddhist Centre in October 2006 to mark the fiftieth anniversary of Dr Ambedkar's conversion to Buddhism.

On this day, when we are remembering Dr Ambedkar, my thoughts immediately go further back than 1956, the year in which the event we are celebrating took place, to 1950. At that time I was living in Kalimpong, in the eastern Himalayas. I'd been taken there by my teacher, Jagdish Kashyap, and he left me there with the injunction that I should stay there and work for the good of Buddhism. I was then twenty-four years of age, and a *śrāmaṇera*, not quite a *bhikṣu*, but anyway, my teacher had told me to stay in Kalimpong and work for the good of Buddhism, so that is what I proceeded to do. I set up an organization called the Young Men's Buddhist Association under whose auspices we conducted various activities, both religious and social.[39] And one day it so happened that a recent copy of the *Maha Bodhi*, which later on I was to edit,[40] came into my hands, and in it there was an article which I found of particular interest. This article was entitled 'Buddha and the Future of His Religion', and it was by someone called B. R. Ambedkar.

Now I'd heard of Dr Ambedkar before. In fact, in India in those days you couldn't help hearing of him, because he was a very controversial figure, and we mustn't forget that. Millions of people are now celebrating this day, but there were others who weren't at all happy at the conversion of so many Dalits to Buddhism. I first heard of Dr Ambedkar as a controversial figure in connection with some legislation which had been passing through the Indian parliament, the Hindu Code Bill. I won't go into the details of that – it's rather complex – but he was the law minister at the time and made certain proposals for changing the law governing Hindu families, and these proposals weren't at all popular. So he was a very controversial figure, a politician and a law-giver, in fact the architect of the Indian constitution. And here he was in the *Maha Bodhi* writing about Buddhism. Obviously I was interested that such a well-known person should be writing about Buddhism, because in those days there were very, very few Buddhists in India, at the most just a few thousand of them – mostly what we sometimes call born Buddhists – in the north-east and north-west of India, and perhaps a few hundred in Calcutta and Bombay, most of them from Buddhist countries. So it was very unusual in those days to meet a Buddhist. I used to consider myself lucky if I met even one Buddhist in the course of the year. (Of course, this was before the arrival in Kalimpong of the many refugees fleeing Tibet.) Finding that this prominent and controversial politician had written about the Buddha and the future of his religion in the *Maha Bodhi*, I thought I should have some contact with this man, so I wrote him a letter introducing myself and the Young Men's Buddhist Association, and telling him what we were doing and what we hoped to do. I very quickly received a very warm and friendly and encouraging reply written with his own hand, some four pages which I still have in my possession.[41]

That was my first contact – not direct, but through correspondence – with Dr Ambedkar. Two years later I found myself in Bombay, where he lived, and I thought to myself, 'We've had some contact. Maybe I should go and see him.' Dr Ambedkar lived in the district of Bombay called Dadar, halfway up the peninsula, in a house he built himself and called Rajagriha, which of course gave some suggestion of his Buddhist sympathies.[42] His followers liked to think of him as 'Bhim Raja', so they thought that Rajagriha or Rajgir, the King's House, was a very appropriate name for his residence. So I went along there. In those days I was a *bhikṣu*, and *bhikṣus* can go anywhere. The yellow robe is a passport in itself, one could say.

Being a politician, Dr Ambedkar had a sort of office or surgery, and there were quite a lot of people already there wanting to meet him, so he asked me to wait. So I sat and waited, and I observed what was going on, as I like to do. I remember very well seeing Ambedkar standing there in the middle of the room, in front of his desk. He was a tall man, maybe a little above average height, and strongly built, even a bit bulky. He was then about sixty. Evidently some delegation had come to meet him, six or seven people, and they were standing in front of him, some of them carrying one of those enormous marigold garlands. If you've been to India you've probably seen these things. People are fond of welcoming one with marigold garlands, and this delegation had a really big one with lots of marigolds and tinsel which they were attempting to put over Ambedkar's head. But he wouldn't have any of it. He just brushed it aside with some impatience. Listening to the conversation, I couldn't understand what was being said – they were speaking in Marathi – but it was clear that Dr Ambedkar was giving these people a good scolding about something or other. But they clearly didn't mind. They just stood beaming at him with evident feelings of devotion, and in the end something was agreed upon, or decided, or settled, and they left.

Dr Ambedkar seated himself behind his desk, I came forward and sat on a bench in front of him, and he looked at me with a rather grim look and said, 'Why has your Maha Bodhi Society got a Bengali Brahmin as its president?' So I said, 'Look, it's not *my* Maha Bodhi Society. I know it's got a Bengali Brahmin as its president, and I'm not very happy about it either. I hope it can soon be changed.'[43] After that we had a friendly conversation, but I learned from this that Ambedkar was a very outspoken person. He was not a man to be trifled with. In fact he gave the impression of someone who was belligerent, formidable, even a bit of a fighter. Of course he needed to be like that to do what he had done for the Dalit people.

So that was my first meeting with Dr Ambedkar. Three years later I again found myself in Bombay and I thought I should go and see him again, so off I went, this time not to his residence but to Siddharth College, which he himself had brought into existence especially for the benefit of Dalit people.[44] In his office at the college, he was sitting behind his desk and his wife – his second wife – was standing beside him. As I entered, he said, 'Oh, I'm so sorry I can't get up. I'm suffering from arthritis.' This time when we talked he was much milder, not so belligerent. Maybe he'd heard a bit about me in the meantime, because I was also a bit of a controversial figure, not on the scale he was, but sufficiently controversial, as I think I've remained. We got talking, and it was clear that he'd been thinking very seriously about changing his religion. For years, even for decades, he'd been trying to work for the uplift of the people whom we then called Untouchables, but whom we now call Dalits, the downcast

Sangharakshita and Mrs Ambedkar, Poona, 1988

or downtrodden people, trying to relieve them from all the disabilities, religious and social and economic and educational, from which they'd been suffering, but especially from caste discrimination. As the word untouchable suggests, the Dalits were at the very bottom of the social scale of the caste system, so low down that any member of a higher caste who touched them felt that they had been polluted and had to go and purify themselves. The Dalits were kept out of temples and even out of schools sometimes, and they were obliged to do the lowliest, dirtiest work, scavenging work. They were often brutally oppressed and persecuted, and sometimes even killed. Dr Ambedkar had worked for their uplift for years, trying to encourage the caste Hindus to treat them more humanely – of course he himself was born into a Dalit family – but they wouldn't, or at least the majority of them wouldn't. They just continued in the same old way. So Ambedkar had come to the conclusion that there was no future for his community, for the Dalits, in Hinduism. If they wanted to uplift themselves, if they wanted to progress socially, economically, educationally, even spiritually, they'd have to change their religion. But which religion should they adopt? He pondered this question for some years. Should it be Islam? Should it be Christianity? Should it be Sikhism? He was clear that it had to be another religion rather than any secular system of thought. He believed that human beings could not live without religion, and that spiritual values of some sort must underpin the whole of social life. So he was looking for another religion, and eventually his thoughts turned more and more towards Buddhism.

It was at that stage that I met him at Siddharth College, and after we'd talked for a while, he asked me, 'How does one become a Buddhist?' Nowadays we think that's a simple matter, but in the India of those days it wasn't known. I explained that one became a Buddhist by Going for Refuge formally and publicly to the Buddha, the Dharma, and the Sangha, and by undertaking the five precepts. Then he said, 'Who can make one a Buddhist?' I said, 'Well, any senior Buddhist, whether a *bhikkhu* or a senior lay person, can make one a Buddhist by adminstering the Three Refuges and the five precepts.' He pondered this and then asked, 'Could you do it?' I said, 'Yes, I could do it. Any Buddhist monk can. But if you want your conversion, and the conversion of your followers, to be taken seriously by the rest of the Buddhist world, it would be good if you were initiated into Buddhism by the seniormost monk in India.' This happened to be U Chandramani, who had made me a *śrāmaṇera* some years earlier.[45] Dr Ambedkar didn't say anything about this at the time, but he asked me to write it all down for him when I got back to Poona, where I was staying. So when I got to Poona I wrote to him explaining how one became a Buddhist, who was the best person to officiate at the ceremony, and so on.

Before we parted on that second occasion he also asked me to address a meeting of his followers. He said that he would organize a public meeting, and he would like me to speak on the subject of what it means to be a Buddhist. I agreed, and a few days later, on New Year's Day, I addressed a couple of thousand people in the Worli district, which was a working-class area of Bombay. The talk took place in the evening, in the open air. Many of the people who were present on that occasion worked in the mills – there were hundreds of mills in Bombay in those days – and they came home from work quite late in the evening, so it wasn't much before ten o'clock when we started. It was a very cold night and I had only my thin monk's robes on, so I was very cold indeed, but I got up and spoke. I had a translator, who was then president of the Scheduled Caste Federation[46] and afterwards became a friend of mine, and I spoke about what it meant to be a Buddhist, how one became a Buddhist, and especially about the Three Jewels, about the Buddha, the Dharma, and the Sangha. I was at pains to clear up all sorts of misunderstandings. I explained that the Buddha was not an *avatāra* of Vishnu, as the Hindus believed, but an ordinary human being, a genius if you like, who had become Enlightened by his own efforts. I also explained that the word Dharma had quite a different meaning in Buddhism from its meaning in Hinduism. In Hinduism it often meant the performance of your caste duty, whereas in Buddhism it meant something of a far more ethical and spiritual nature. I explained all of that as clearly as I could. That was the first time I had addressed a Dalit audience, and I remember them very well. They were sitting on the ground out in the open, having recently come home from work. They were very poorly dressed, but I remember how thoughtfully and seriously they listened to me, and I could sense that what I had to say made an impression on them.

The following year, on 14 October 1956, the great mass conversion took place, and as I had suggested, the Refuges and Precepts were administered to Dr Ambedkar by U Chandramani, a Burmese monk who had lived for many, many years in Kusinara, and from whom, as I mentioned, I'd received my own ordination as a *śrāmaṇera*. On the occasion of the mass conversion, which took place in Nagpur, approximately 380,000 people became Buddhists. First of all, U Chandramani administered the Refuges and Precepts to Dr Ambedkar and his wife, and then Ambedkar himself administered them to the crowd who had gathered, all dressed in white, in the open space which became known as the Diksha Bhumi. That was a very great occasion, a historic occasion, though not everybody was pleased about it. Some of the daily papers contained very scathing comments, some commentators dismissing it as a political stunt on Ambedkar's part and others quite disturbed that so many people should be leaving the Hindu fold, because that had political and even electoral implications of various kinds. But anyway, the great mass conversion took place. I wasn't there myself – the invitation reached me rather late, and I'd already made arrangements to give some lectures in Gangtok – but of course I heard all about the event, and I wrote something about it at the time.[47]

I must also mention another remarkable feature of the conversion programme. After he had administered the Refuges and Precepts to his followers, Ambedkar administered a further twenty-two vows, or *pratijñās*, as they were called in Marathi, and he explained why. These vows were to safeguard the integrity of the Buddhism of those who had converted. He didn't want any mixing with Hinduism. The vows, which may not sound very relevant to us here in the West, consisted of such things as not worshipping this or that Hindu god, not supporting the caste system, and so on.[48] I think they were quite important, because in India Hindus very easily mix things together. Even a very recent news item reported that the government of one of the states in India has passed a law that Buddhism is part of Hinduism, which of course Buddhists don't agree with. Dr Ambedkar was hoping to safeguard against that sort of thing, so that what people followed after the conversion was Buddhism, not a mixture of Buddhism and Hinduism. Later on, when I used to travel around the small towns and villages lecturing on the Dharma, I found that there were a few people who, though they considered themselves Buddhist, were still performing animal sacrifices to this or that local god. Ambedkar wanted to have a clear line of division, as it were, between Buddhism and Hinduism. He wanted his followers to be Buddhists, not a mixture of Buddhism and something else, and perhaps that's a lesson for us in the West also.

I met Dr Ambedkar for a third time in Delhi, shortly after the mass conversion, towards the end of 1956. It was the time of the celebration of the 2,500th anniversary of Buddhism, reckoning from the date of the Buddha's *parinirvāṇa*. (It was partly on account of its being the 2,500th anniversary of Buddhism that Ambedkar had chosen that particular year for the mass conversion.) Ambedkar happened to be in Delhi at the same time as I was there in connection with the celebration, so again I went to see him, this time taking with me a number of other Buddhists. We went with the intention of congratulating him on his own conversion to Buddhism and on the success of the conversion movement, because by that time, in addition to the 380,000 who had converted personally at his hands, several hundred thousand had converted elsewhere. But I was sorry to see that he was greatly changed. When I met him the second time he was suffering severely from arthritis, but by the time of our third meeting he was suffering from all sorts of complaints, and he was clearly an old, tired, and very sick man. But he insisted on talking. He was sitting at a table out in the compound in the sunshine, and my companions and I sat on chairs in a semicircle around him, and he and I talked at some length. I could see that he was very tired and that he really shouldn't be sitting out in the sun, even though he was wearing a solar topee, and talking so much, but he insisted on talking. More than once I tried to say goodbye, but he said, 'No, no. Stay. I have more to say.' I could see that he was very, very worried about the movement he'd started. He seemed to be very aware of his own frailty. He was only in his middle sixties, but he'd led a very difficult and very active life. Towards the end of our conversation he was leaning forward resting his arms on the table, and his head was almost on the table too, he was so tired, but he wanted to talk, and we talked for two hours, which was astonishing considering his state of health. I could see his wife getting more and more anxious – she was a doctor – and in the end I said, 'I really must go. You really must take rest.' So off I went.

He seems to have recovered a bit during the next few days, because he went off to Kathmandu, to a meeting of the World Federation of Buddhists, and gave a lecture on the Buddha and Karl Marx, which was a bit controversial.[49] He was, by the way, not a Marxist, and he was very critical of communism, and didn't like any of his followers to be communist. At that time I was in Bombay, staying with some friends. They were anxious that I should stay longer, but although I can't explain it, I had a strong feeling – one might call it an intuition – that I had to be in Nagpur by a certain date. I already had an invitation to visit the city from the Buddhists there and I was keen to meet them as soon as I could after the mass conversion, but I felt impelled to go by a certain date, despite the efforts of my friends in Bombay to detain me. So I caught the overnight train to Nagpur, and at the station I found about 2,000 new Buddhists waiting to greet me. They gave me a wonderful reception and conducted me to the house of a friend where I was to stay. I settled in, but shortly after lunch, when I was just about to have a rest, there was a disturbance outside, and the friend with whom I was staying said, 'There's three or four people, and they say they must see you, it's very urgent.' Just as he was speaking, these people burst in, and they said, 'What do you think? Babasaheb is dead.' It was as sudden as that. They were very, very upset, because it was totally unexpected.

The people who had come to see me were the leaders of the local Buddhist and political organization, and they said, 'Thousands of people have come to our office, having heard the news, and we want you to speak to them. They need to be consoled.' I said, 'Well, it had better be a proper meeting with loudspeakers if I'm to address so many people.' So it was agreed that there would be a condolence meeting in Kasturchand Park at seven o'clock that evening. Kasturchand Park is a well-known area of Nagpur. It's not like an English park, it's just an open space. There were no proper arrangements for the meeting. I had to stand on a rickshaw with the microphone in my hand, and there were just a couple of Petromaxes for illumination. I could see people coming from the four quarters of Nagpur and converging on the park. Each person carried a lighted candle and there was a dead silence. The park gradually filled up, and there must have been 100,000 people there in the end. At the beginning some of the local leaders tried to speak, but they were so overcome by emotion that they couldn't say anything. They burst into tears and sat down again. Ambedkar had meant so much to them. He had done so much for them. They had the sort of feeling for him that I think for us in the West it's very hard to imagine, because he had delivered them from such difficulties, from, as he said himself, the hell of caste.

So in the end it was up to me to speak. I felt quite moved by all that I saw and heard, but I thought, 'I've got to speak. This is a very critical time. It's only six weeks since the mass conversion took place. Ambedkar was the leader of these people and now he's dead, so they're disconsolate, they're in despair, they don't know which way to turn.' I felt I must give them as much encouragement as I possibly could. That was the tenor of my speech: yes, Ambedkar may be dead, and that's a tragedy, but it's not the end of the world. You have to carry on the torch that he lit; you need to practise and spread the Dharma. They felt some comfort and hope, that was clear. During the following days I gave many speeches in different parts of Nagpur to the same effect, and as a result I forged a strong link with the Buddhists of Nagpur, and indirectly with the new Buddhists of other parts of India. And thus the Buddhist conversion movement continued after Ambedkar's death, and it's very encouraging to see that on this very day, as we're sitting here, more conversion movements are going on in India, and perhaps as many as two million more Buddhists will be joining the sangha, the sangha in the widest sense of the term, on this day.

I spent quite a lot of time during the fifties and early sixties going from Kalimpong down to Calcutta, then on to Nagpur, where I gave lectures, to Poona, where I gave lectures and admitted more people into the Buddhist fold, and to Gujarat, Ajmer, Delhi, all sorts of places.[50] I got to know Dr Ambedkar's followers very well, and I think they got to know me, and I could feel the depth of their appreciation of Ambedkar. They really saw him as their deliverer, almost as their saviour, who had delivered them from the cruelty and oppression of the caste system. It wasn't of course that Hindus ceased to treat them badly, but the people who had converted, the new Buddhists, *felt* different. They were quite ordinary people and most of them were illiterate, but when I asked them, 'Now that you're Buddhists, how do you feel? What difference does it make?' they would invariably say, 'Now we are Buddhists, we feel free.' In a sense they weren't free. Being Buddhist didn't necessarily mean that they had better jobs, or that they were treated better by the caste Hindus, but they felt free, they felt that they were independent of the Hindus, and they had the Dharma to practise, and the sangha to develop among themselves and with other Buddhists. That's the great difference that Ambedkar made to their lives. In the course of the last fifty years, many of the Dalits have improved their economic position, though in the villages and small towns the caste system continues to be rife and many of them are still badly treated by the caste Hindus.

I remember all this today, when we're celebrating the fiftieth anniversary of that great mass conversion. It was certainly a very important period of my life. I sometimes contrast the position and the attitude of new Buddhists here in the West with the background and the attitude of the new Buddhists in India. Here we're much more concerned, it seems, with our subjective psychological states, with our feelings. 'How do I feel today? Do I want to do this or would I rather do that?' There's nothing like that in India. For the Dalits, the point of departure was social. They saw the teaching of the Buddha, which was critical of the caste system, as the key to their social and economic and even political uplift as well as a spiritual path. So we may say that here in the West we go from the psychological to the spiritual, or hopefully we do – sometimes I think we get bogged down in the psychological – but in India they go from the social to the spiritual, to the Dharma. You need to have both. You need to balance the two.

That's why I think it's very good that in our Buddhist movement we have our two great wings, as it were. We have our western wing, where people are more concerned with psychological problems, and our eastern wing, where people are more concerned with social problems. I won't say that I hope people in India will become more concerned with psychological problems! I hope they won't have them. But I certainly think that people in the West – certainly Order members and Mitras – should pay more attention to objective and social issues rather than just to their own subjective feelings. I have noticed over the decades that there has been rather a drift away from public activities, even on the part of some Order members, a sort of retreat into subjectivity. People are concerned about their personal practice and their own friends, but they are not so concerned to help out around the Buddhist centre, to spread the Dharma so that others may be benefited just as they have been benefited themselves. I hope we can learn from our friends in India, who are very much concerned with social and economic and other such issues. We must have a balanced spiritual life. Part of that drift towards the personal and away from the public is reflected in the fact that not so many people these days seem so interested in team-based right livelihood, or living in a community, or helping out around the centre. We have become a bit overbalanced, placing too much emphasis on the purely personal and private side of our life and activities.

I'm led to think and speak about these things because it's such a contrast with what we see in India. The Dharma means so much to people there. This was very evident to me as I moved around among the new Buddhists in the fifties and sixties. They were so intensely grateful to Dr Ambedkar for having given them the Dharma. If you visit places in India where there are Buddhists, you see his statue and his picture everywhere, and his name is mentioned by Buddhists all the time; they call him Babasaheb. They use the greeting '*Jai Bhim!*', which means 'Victory to Bhim!' 'Bhim' of course is Dr Ambedkar – his first name was Bhimrao. The Sanskrit word *bhim* means 'fearsome one', which is very suitable for Dr Ambedkar. He was rather fearsome, rather formidable, as I've said. That's a side of the Buddha's life that's not often emphasized. We like to think of a nice, sweet, gentle, kind, compassionate Buddha, and that's all true, but perhaps we don't like to think so much of the strong, fierce, even controversial Buddha. We have to be careful that our Buddhism, our Dharma, our Triratna culture, doesn't degenerate into something weak and wishy-washy, something that is a bit of an option rather than an essential, integral part of our life. If you go to India – and some of you have been there, no doubt, and some of you have met our Buddhist friends there – you'll see a very different approach to the Dharma, because the Dharma has made a total revolution in the lives of so many people on every level, and especially on the religious or spiritual level. Of course it does that for us too, here in the West. But a change should mean a change. When we go for Refuge and undertake to observe the five or the ten precepts, it should mean a turnabout in our whole way of life, a new way of looking at things, a new way of relating, in fact a new way of living.

So these are some of my thoughts on this occasion. I'm delighted to be able to share with you my recollections of Dr Ambedkar and the movement he started, and I really do hope that through the kindness of the Internet many of our Buddhist friends in India are able to listen to me and to hear my words. In conclusion I want to wish all of them, and you as well, three hearty *Jai Bhims*.

THE SPIRIT OF DR AMBEDKAR

An interview with Dhammachari Maitriveer Nagarjuna,[51] *2011*

When did you become aware of Dr Ambedkar, and do you think you had an impression of his significance at that time? Did you feel moved to meet him, and did you feel that that meeting would have any significance for you?

I must have heard about Dr Ambedkar for the first time either in 1949 or 1950. At that time I didn't read the newspapers, but I think I knew that there was a big debate going on in the Indian parliament about the Hindu Code Bill, and I knew that someone called Dr Ambedkar was involved with that. But then in 1950, I read an article that he had written called 'Buddha and the Future of His Religion', so I wrote to him. I was at that time living in Kalimpong, and I'd started the Young Men's Buddhist Association, so I wrote to him telling him that, and I think I also sent a copy of the little magazine I was publishing. I got a reply from him written in his own hand. I still have that letter. He said he was very glad I was carrying on those activities in Kalimpong and he was very encouraging. But I don't think at that time I had much idea about his position, especially his position with regard to the Dalit community.

We heard that Dr Ambedkar was very strict and always to the point, and very forceful and fearless in character. You describe him in Ambedkar and Buddhism as like a great black storm cloud that might discharge thunder and lightning at any minute.

Yes, that was my impression. He didn't smile, and when I was waiting to talk to him that first time, I noticed how he was with the people who came to see him. There must have been seven or eight people in a group who came to see him, and he received them, but he wasn't smiling. He looked very grim. They tried to put marigold garlands over his head, but he just put them aside. He didn't look particularly pleased; in fact he may have been frowning a little. So he did give an impression of being a rather stern, grim sort of person.

Tell me something more about that first meeting.
I was a *bhikkhu* then, of course, and wearing my yellow robes. So as soon as we had exchanged greetings, Dr Ambedkar said, in an almost belligerent way, 'Why has your Maha Bodhi Society got a Brahmin for its president?' So I said, 'It's not *my* Maha Bodhi Society. I don't belong to it, and one of the reasons I don't belong to it is that it's got a Brahmin for its president. But I do cooperate with it, and I hope that one day it will have a Buddhist for a president.' And actually some years later it did – the Maharaja Kumar of Sikkhim was elected as its president, with some help from me.[52] But when he was elected, some of the Hindus connected with the Maha Bodhi Society said, 'These Buddhists are very narrow-minded. They want to have a Buddhist as president of the Maha Bodhi Society!' I was quite astonished that after two Hindu presidents, we couldn't have a Buddhist president without being thought narrow-minded.

What happened after that in your meeting with Dr Ambedkar?
After that – well, I won't say he became more amicable, but he lost his belligerent look. I can't remember the conversation we had. I didn't stay long, because I could see he was busy and a lot of people were waiting to see him. But anyway, I had established contact, and a few years later, when I was in Bombay, I made arrangements to see him at Siddharth College. The meeting took place in his room at the college. His wife (his second wife) was with him, and he was sitting behind the desk. When I entered he said, 'I'm sorry I can't get up to receive you. I've got bad arthritis in my legs.' I thought, 'He may be a bit stern, but he's basically a very polite man.' So we had some talk, and he asked me if I would be ready to give a lecture to some of his followers. I said yes, I'd be very happy to do that, so he arranged for me to give a talk.

And when you met him the last time, after his conversion, you took some delegates to his home in Alipur Road, Delhi?
That was in 1956, at the time of the Buddha Jayanti, and I was on pilgrimage in north-east India with a number of other Buddhists, so I went to meet him, taking all of them with me. Most of them didn't understand English, so discussion was mainly between Dr Ambedkar and me, and he was clearly very ill. It was a very hot day and he was wearing a solar topee. Mrs Ambedkar was there, and she was very anxious that he was talking too much for the good of his health, but he went on talking, and he expressed his fears for the Buddhist movement in India. He was very aware of the obstacles which it faced.

How did you experience the change from that first meeting, when he was a very strict and forceful man, and that last meeting, when he was becoming emotional and saying 'So much is to be done', and you had a sense that he was wanting to transfer some of the responsibility on his shoulders to you? How did that feel?
Well, I could see there was a very big change in his physical condition. The first time I met him, he may have had some illness, I don't know, but he seemed strong and healthy. The second time he was clearly an ill man. And the third time I met him he was very ill indeed, so when a short time later I heard that he had died, I was not surprised.

And you were present at Kasturchand Park on 6 December 1956, on the day when Dr Ambedkar passed away.
Yes, I was.

You've described how you could feel that over the crowd hung an enormous presence. Could you say something more about the mood of that day? How did you feel when you heard that he passed away?
I'll go back a little bit. I was staying in Bombay with a Parsi friend of mine, and I got a very strong feeling that I must go to Nagpur. My Parsi friends urged me not to go. They thought that I shouldn't go at that time, and that if I did, something bad would happen. But I said, 'No, I have this strong urge to go to Nagpur.' I didn't know why I had that urge, but I acted on it and caught the train to Nagpur. I was staying in the house of an old friend of mine, A. R. Kulkarni,[53] and quite soon after I arrived, someone came to say that the news had arrived that Babasaheb was

dead. He said that people were in a state of shock and confusion. Would I come and speak to them? There was a big crowd, it seemed, outside the Bharatiya Bauddha Maha Sabha office in Sitabuldi. I said, 'Since it's such a large crowd, there had better be some proper arrangements. You'd better arrange for a loudspeaker and all that, so I can speak to people.' So arrangements were made for a meeting in Kasturchand Park that evening. It was quite dark, and I saw streams of people coming from all directions and converging on the park, all carrying lighted candles. They were completely silent. As you know, in India when you get a crowd of people all together you don't often get silence, but they were completely silent.

And then the meeting began. They'd been able to arrange for a loudspeaker, but not much else. There were several people who wanted to speak, but they were so overcome by emotion that after a few minutes they broke down crying and couldn't carry on. Many people in the audience were also shedding tears. Two or three people tried to speak, and then it came to my turn. I felt quite moved, but I thought, 'I've got to stay collected. I've got to say something. No use me just shedding tears.' There was no stage, so I had to stand up on a rickshaw. A microphone was held in front of me and I spoke. The gist of what I said was, 'Dr Ambedkar may be dead, and that is very sad, but we have to carry on with his work. The spirit of Dr Ambedkar is not dead, and his work must continue.' People told me afterwards that they were very encouraged by that, and some people even said that on that day, with that speech, I saved the Dharma for Nagpur. But while I was giving my talk, I felt as though – it's very difficult to explain, but I felt as though in a way Dr Ambedkar was there – a very big Ambedkar consciousness hovering over the meeting. That's the sort of experience I had, quite definitely.

I stayed in Nagpur for four or five days, and I gave many talks. I tried to get round to all the localities. I must have given about thirty-five talks, and in every locality I gave the same message – that Dr Ambedkar is dead, but his work must carry on. People must fulfil his legacy.

So in your view, what is the significance of conversion and its impact on Indian society and culture?

I well remember the response of many Hindus at the time. I had many Hindu friends, and there was a variety of responses. A few said, 'It's good that these people have converted to Buddhism because they couldn't have risen socially in any other way.' A few did admit that. But many other Hindus were outraged. Who were these people to reject our glorious Hindu heritage? How dare they? And others were afraid from a political point of view. They felt that if the Untouchables converted to Buddhism there would be fewer Hindus, and that would have political implications. A few others said, 'At least they haven't become Muslims.' But on the whole the Hindu community was quite disturbed by the conversion. That was very clear.

And how does it feel to emancipate the ex-Untouchables? Quite a significant phenomenon happened in the modern history of India with the embracing of Buddhism by Dr Ambedkar.
It's well-known nowadays in Maharashtra that those Dalits who converted to Buddhism through their faith in Dr Ambedkar forty, fifty, sixty years later are much better off in every way. They're better off economically, socially, and educationally, and of course they have the Dharma, and what could be a greater gain than that? I think it's generally recognized that the movement of mass conversion was a great success, not just from the religious point of view, but from the social and economic and educational points of view as well. So it was a very great achievement, and that's why we speak of the Dharma revolution.

How do you feel about having missed the great event of conversion? Do you have any regrets about having missed it? What difference would it have made to our movement if you had been there?
I don't think it would have made any difference at all. I think what is important is that I was in Nagpur on the day Dr Ambedkar died. I think that is the important thing insofar as my own relationship with the mass conversion movement is concerned. I was there at the right time, when I was really needed. So I don't have too many regrets about not being there at the time of the original conversion.

You were in India after the conversion in 1956 until 1964. Were you able to contribute to Dr Ambedkar's conversion movement after his death, and what else did you do during your stay in India?
I divided my time between Kalimpong, where I studied the Dharma, practised meditation, and wrote books, and my lecture tours in the plains.

My lecture tours were mainly among Dr Ambedkar's followers, because they had converted to Buddhism out of faith in Dr Ambedkar, and many of them didn't know anything about Buddhism at all, so I took it upon myself to give as many talks as I could, wherever I went. I think I visited every state in India except Kashmir, and in every state I gave lectures on Buddhism. But I concentrated my activities in three cities: Nagpur, Bombay, and Poona. There I built up a very strong connection with the local Dalit, now Buddhist, community. I must have given hundreds of lectures about the fundamental principles of the Dharma. Lectures were important because so many of the people were illiterate. They couldn't read books on Buddhism, so it was only from talks that they could get information about the Dharma. I found that they were very keen indeed to learn about the Dharma. I used to talk about the Three Jewels, the five precepts, meditation, the three *lakṣaṇas*, the four noble truths, the Noble Eightfold Path. In some places, where I developed a regular audience, I was also able to talk about more philosophical things. Even an illiterate person can be very intelligent, and if even quite deep aspects of the Dharma are explained to them in simple language, they can understand. So that was how I spent many, many months, touring around.[54]

But there was another side to it. I had to remove certain misunderstandings about Buddhism, certain wrong beliefs and practices carried over from the days when the new Buddhists were Hindus. For instance, I used to talk a lot about the evil of the dowry system, that is to say, the system whereby the father of the girl has to pay money to the bridegroom and his family. Many people used to get into debt and borrow money to pay the dowry, and sometimes the debt was handed on from one generation to another and the family never became free of it. So I spoke very strongly against the dowry system. I also spoke against spending a lot of money on the wedding ceremony, because the father of the bride would have to borrow money in order to feed four or five hundred people when he couldn't really afford to feed more than ten or twelve. Also, in some places, especially out-of-the-way villages, I found that people were still practising animal sacrifice. Usually when someone became sick, people thought, 'Oh, some bad goddess is responsible. We have to kill at least a chicken, or maybe a goat.' So I had to speak against that and say, 'Animal sacrifice is not part of Buddhism. It's against the Buddha's teaching.' Those evils were still present among the new Buddhists, and I felt it necessary to deal with them.

B. R. AMBEDKAR, A GREAT BUDDHIST

An excerpt from Great Buddhists of the Twentieth Century

In 1995 Sangharakshita gave a lecture at the London headquarters of the Maha Bodhi Society,[55] *which was founded by Dharmapala, the first of Sangharakshita's choice of five great Buddhists. Sangharakshita had a connection with the society going back some fifty years, and edited its publication, the* Maha Bodhi, *for twelve years from 1952. The lecture was given – by an unforeseen but auspicious coincidence – on 14 October, the anniversary of the great mass conversion initiated by Dr Ambedkar in 1956.*

So far we have looked at individuals from wealthy, middle-class families. By contrast, Bhimrao Ramji Ambedkar came from the very bottom of the social heap. He was born in 1891 at Mhow in central India into an 'untouchable' Hindu family, and this background to his life is very much what his career was about. To have any idea of what Ambedkar achieved one has to be clear about what this term 'untouchable' really means.

Hindu society is divided into castes, with the Brahmins, the priestly caste, at the top, and the Shudras, or labouring caste, at the bottom, and others, with all sorts of subdivisions, in between. Having been born into a particular caste you can't get out of it – it is regarded as very wrong even to try. As for 'Untouchables', they are even lower than Shudras, and in a sense they are outside the caste system altogether. They are called 'Untouchables' because any contact with them pollutes so-called caste Hindus. Even their shadow is believed to pollute.

Traditionally, Untouchables lived in ghettoes outside the main community. They could engage only in very menial occupations such as removing night-soil, and they would serve the caste Hindu villagers in this way in return for a few scraps of food. They weren't allowed to enter Hindu temples or attend Hindu schools. They had no economic or political rights – they could not even own property. They were not allowed to better themselves in any way. Once an Untouchable, always an Untouchable – at least, so far as this life was concerned. This system had been rigidly in force for a thousand years (and to all intents and purposes it still is in many areas). But when Ambedkar was born there were already faint signs that it was beginning to weaken. The rule of the British over India was no doubt unfortunate in many ways, but for the Untouchables it did have its advantages, because the British army accepted them into its ranks. In fact it had Untouchable regiments, and Ambedkar's father belonged to one of these. Members of these regiments were given a certain amount of education, and some, including Ambedkar's father, even became army schoolmasters.

With help and encouragement from his father, Ambedkar became a brilliant student, and at the age of seventeen was the first Untouchable to matriculate. He was given a scholarship by a liberal Indian prince, and eventually graduated in politics and economics. He studied further at Columbia University and then at the London School of Economics, and also qualified as a barrister. He returned to India in 1923, aged thirty-two, and took his place as one of the most highly gifted and qualified men in Indian public life.

However, he had not equipped himself so comprehensively for a political career out of self-interest. He never forgot that he himself was an Untouchable – nor was he allowed to. Many Indians continued to treat him as an Untouchable, and this was a source of great disappointment and bitterness to him; but it only hardened his resolve to devote his life to the uplift of his people.[56] He founded newspapers, he started schools and colleges, he entered politics, he fought legal battles; and we may say that from 1923 until his death in 1956, the story of his life is inseparable from the history of modern India.

In 1927 Dr Ambedkar focused attention on the problems faced by his people by provoking the 'Chowdar Tank case'. In the town of Mahad in what is now Maharashtra state, Untouchables were not allowed to take water from this tank until 1927, when it was opened to them by the local municipality. Whether or not the Chowdar Tank actually belonged to the municipality would be later contested. But meanwhile, Ambedkar held a conference of 3,000 Untouchables at Mahad, and at its conclusion led them to the edge of the tank to drink from it.

This may all seem a very tame business to us – a local dispute over who is allowed to use a water tank, and 3,000 people gathering together in order to dare to make use of what has been made available to them. But in India in those days it was a terrific, extraordinary, revolutionary thing to do. There was a furious reaction from the caste Hindus, and some of Ambedkar's followers were assaulted in one way or another for their impious – in the eyes of the caste Hindus – temerity. The Untouchables had, by drawing water from the tank, polluted it. The question now was how to purify it. Brahmins were called together, and they took 108 earthenware pots of water from the tank and mixed the water with curds, milk, cow-dung, and cow's urine. Then the pots, with the water and the aforementioned 'purifying' elements, were put back in the tank and Vedic mantras were recited. In this way the tank was purified.

Naturally, a response to this insulting procedure was called for on the part of the Untouchables under Ambedkar, and it had to be an appropriate response, one that would get to the heart of the issue. In the same year, 1927, they burned a copy of the *Manusmṛti*, or the 'Laws of Manu'. The significance of this book as a symbol resided in the fact that it is the source of all the laws regarding caste. It lays down who can eat with whom, who can marry whom, who can touch whom, and it also lays down how those who infringe those laws should be punished. Thus, for example, it is decreed that any Shudra who presumes to teach Brahmins their duty should have boiling oil poured into his mouth and into his ears. The burning of the *Manusmṛti* had the desired effect. It shocked orthodox Hindus all over India, and it symbolized the repudiation by the Untouchables of the authority of the Hindu scriptures.

The man generally lauded nowadays as the great hero of this period in India, during the drive towards independence, is of course Mahatma Gandhi. But the Untouchables cannot see him in quite this idealized light. Gandhi was himself a caste Hindu who claimed to represent the Untouchables as well as caste Hindus, but the Untouchables did not recognize him in this role. They believed that only an Untouchable could safeguard their interests.

Gandhi had already agreed that Muslims, Christians, and Sikhs should have separate electorates, and Ambedkar argued that in a democratic India there should be a separate electorate for Untouchables as well. This was because Untouchables did not want to be governed by caste Hindus. However, in 1932 Gandhi resisted Ambedkar's demands by going on one of his 'fasts to death', and during the period of the fast Ambedkar described himself as the most hated man in India.[57] Gandhi did indeed come close to death, and in the end Ambedkar was forced to compromise. If Gandhi had fasted to death Ambedkar would have faced the prospect of the wholesale murder of Untouchables by caste Hindus.

In 1935 Ambedkar's wife died. He had married her very young, when he was sixteen and she was just nine; only one of their five children had survived. By this time his political position was hardening. He no longer believed in the possibility of reform within Hinduism. He was convinced that the caste Hindus were not going to change their ways; they weren't going to treat the Untouchables as human beings. And in 1935 he made his famous declaration that though he had been born a Hindu, he would not die one.[58]

In 1947 Ambedkar became Minister of Law and Justice in the first government of the independent state of India, but he resigned from the Cabinet four years later because of fierce opposition from caste Hindus – even in the Cabinet – to his attempts to reform Hindu law. It was at about this time that I myself had some correspondence and then a series of meetings with him.

At the end of 1954 Ambedkar announced that he would devote the remainder of his life to the propagation of Buddhism in India. This was not a sudden decision. He had been a student of Buddhism for some time, and had known something about it ever since he was sixteen, when he had been given a copy of the Marathi translation of Edwin Arnold's *The Light of Asia*, a life of the Buddha in English verse.

Over the years Ambedkar had gradually become convinced that Buddhism was the best religion for himself and for the Untouchable community as a whole. There were various reasons for his choice, but the main ones were, firstly, that Buddhism did not conflict with the dictates of reason; secondly, that it did not condone man's inhumanity to man, and it certainly did not condone the caste system; and thirdly, that it was of Indian origin, it was not the product of a foreign culture.

So in 1956, in a ceremony at Nagpur in central India, Dr Ambedkar became a Buddhist – along with 380,000 of his followers. The conversions in Nagpur sparked off others all over India. It was the greatest event for Buddhism in India for hundreds of years. Though these were 'mass conversions' the effect on the individuals who took part, who became Buddhists at that time, was profound. I used to ask people, months or even years afterwards, 'What difference has becoming a Buddhist meant for you?' And nine times out of ten they would reply, 'Now that I'm a Buddhist I feel free.' That seems to have been the most important aspect of the experience: a sense of freedom. They felt socially, psychologically, spiritually free.

Six weeks later, Ambedkar was dead, at the age of sixty-four. I was in Nagpur at the time and I well remember the reaction of shock and grief that swept through the newly Buddhist community. There were fears that the conversion movement would simply collapse. But happily it didn't collapse, and it continues to this day.

The significance of Dr Ambedkar's life and work is exceptionally profound and far-reaching. The problem he faced was how to lift up his people, socially, economically, educationally – in every respect. And he felt that the only overall solution to this problem was a change in religion. It wasn't enough just to reject Hinduism, just to leave the religion that generally condoned the caste system. Ambedkar was a deeply religious man; he believed that religion is essential to human life, that we cannot live without it. So for him there was no question of pursuing, for instance, the communist option. He believed that a real social and economic revolution was possible only on the basis of a spiritual revolution. It was for this reason that he inaugurated what we now call the 'Dhamma Revolution'. This is not just a nominal change of religion, but a transformation of one's whole life in every aspect. It is not just individual transformation, but collective transformation as well. This is the movement that Ambedkar set in motion. He showed that a change in religion, even in the midst of the twentieth century, could bring about a change for the better in the lives of millions of people.

The conversion movement in India is of profound significance for Buddhism itself. Ambedkar was well aware that Buddhism had already disappeared once from India, and having revived it he didn't want it to disappear again. So he looked at why it had disappeared. He saw that one of the principal factors leading to its decline was the separation which had developed between the monks and the laity. The monks lived together in monasteries, and in the course of centuries these monasteries became bigger and bigger, each in the end housing thousands of monks leading self-contained lives apart from the laity. Without much contact with the monks and without any lay ordination, the lay people began to feel less and less that they themselves were Buddhists at all, and they came more and more under the influence of the Hindu Brahmins. This process was accelerated after the great monasteries were destroyed by Muslim invaders in the tenth, eleventh, and twelfth centuries, and eventually the lay Buddhists were simply absorbed into the Hindu community. Buddhism disappeared from India, and only ruins marked what it had once been.

On the basis of this analysis of the decline and fall of Indian Buddhism, Ambedkar decided that there had to be ordination for lay people corresponding to monastic ordination for monks. He called this lay ordination '*Dhammadiksha*', and it consisted of two parts: first, taking the traditional Three Refuges and five precepts; and secondly – and this was quite new – taking twenty-two vows.[59] These twenty-two vows were devised by Ambedkar himself, and their purpose was to clearly and completely separate the new Buddhists from their old Hindu religion. They constituted an explicit renunciation of every vestige of Hinduism, of every Hindu practice, like, for example, offering animal sacrifices to gods and goddesses. These vows made it clear what it was to be a Hindu and what it was to be a Buddhist, and that it was not possible to be both. They helped to root out a commonly held belief in India at this time that if you were a Buddhist you were necessarily also a Hindu, that Buddhism was an accretion on the main body of Hinduism. I myself remember a Hindu swami asking me after my ordination why I had not done the job properly and become a Hindu monk. 'Hinduism is like the great ocean,' he said, 'Buddhism is just a little stream.' In fact, any idea that Buddhism might be combined with another faith represents a serious confusion of thought. Dr Ambedkar thought that this principle was so important that it needed to be embodied in vows taken as part of the ordination ceremony.

The way it was done at Nagpur on 14 October 1956 was as follows: Dr Ambedkar took the Three Refuges and five precepts from U Chandramani, a very senior *bhikkhu*. After this, Ambedkar publicly recited his twenty-two vows. He then proceeded to administer the

Refuges and Precepts and the twenty-two vows to the 380,000 of his followers who were assembled there at Nagpur. In this way he established a very significant principle. Ambedkar was initiated into Buddhism by a monk, but his followers were initiated into Buddhism by a layman. Thus the monk and the layman were placed, in a sense, on an equal footing. Dr Ambedkar was asserting the fact that it is Going for Refuge to the Three Jewels – the Buddha, the Dharma, and the Sangha – which makes one a Buddhist, not one's lifestyle. Going for Refuge is the primary act of a Buddhist; lifestyle – whether one is monk or lay – is secondary.

BUDDHA AND THE FUTURE OF HIS RELIGION: A COMMENTARY ON DR AMBEDKAR'S ARTICLE

The following commentary is based on a question-and-answer session given on a men's ordination retreat in Tuscany, Italy, in 1986. Study groups on the retreat had been studying Dr Ambedkar's article and were 'finding their bearings in the Indian world', as one of the participants explained. In the commentary, Dr Ambedkar's article is quoted section by section, followed by Sangharakshita's comments and reflections in answer to the seminar participants' questions.

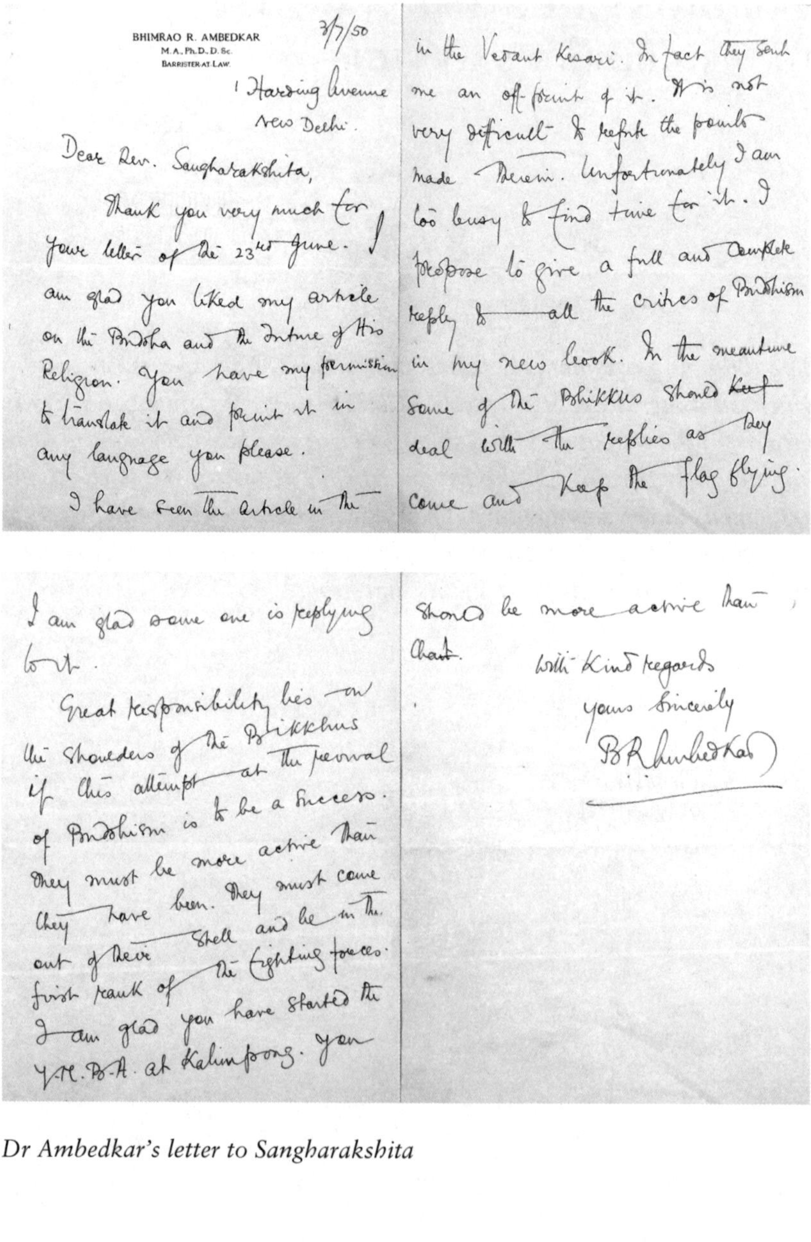

BHIMRAO R. AMBEDKAR
M.A., Ph.D., D.Sc.
BARRISTER-AT-LAW.

3/7/50

1 Harding Avenue
New Delhi.

Dear Rev. Sangharakshita,

Thank you very much for your letter of the 23rd June. I am glad you liked my article on the Buddha and the Future of His Religion. You have my permission to translate it and print it in any language you please.

I have seen the article in the Vedant Kesari. In fact they sent me an off-print of it. It is not very difficult to refute the points made therein. Unfortunately I am too busy to find time for it. I propose to give a full and complete reply to all the critics of Buddhism in my new book. In the meantime some of the Bhikkhus should deal with the replies as they come and keep the flag flying. I am glad some one is replying to it.

Great responsibility lies on the shoulders of the Bhikkhus if this attempt at the revival of Buddhism is to be a success. They must be more active than they have been. They must come out of their shell and be in the first rank of the fighting forces. I am glad you have started the Y.M.B.A. at Kalimpong. You should be more active than that.

With kind regards
Yours sincerely
B.R. Ambedkar

Dr Ambedkar's letter to Sangharakshita

INTRODUCTION

Dr Ambedkar's article 'Buddha and the Future of His Religion' was written in 1950 and published in the Wesak issue of the *Maha Bodhi* for that year.[60] (Wesak is the annual celebration of the Buddha's Enlightenment, held at the full moon of April/May.) The Wesak issue was an especially large one, and the usual practice was to write to all sorts of Buddhist scholars and prominent people asking them to contribute to it, so it's possible that Dr Ambedkar was invited to submit an article.[61]

The *Maha Bodhi* was and still is the official organ of the Maha Bodhi Society of India, read by those sympathetic to Buddhism in India as well as English-speaking Buddhists in South-east Asia and in the West, so Dr Ambedkar was mainly addressing a South-east Asian Buddhist audience who could read English. At the time he wrote the article he hadn't said in so many words that he was going to become a Buddhist, and the mass conversion was still six years away; he seems to have been feeling his way, voicing some of his ideas about Buddhism and advancing some criticisms of contemporary Buddhist practice.

To the best of my knowledge the article elicited very little response. It is perhaps significant that the Buddhist world took little notice of it. I myself noticed it; indeed, it was reading this article that prompted me to write to Ambedkar. We had a brief correspondence, and I met him a couple of years later.

Bhimrao R. Ambedkar
M.A., Ph. D., D.Sc.
Barrister-at-Law
1 Harding Avenue
New Delhi
3/7/50

Dear Rev. Sangharakshita

Thank you very much for your letter of 23 June. I am glad you liked my article on the Buddha and the Future of His Religion. You have my permission to translate it and print it in any language you please.

I have seen the article in the *Vedanta Kesari*.[62] In fact they sent me an off-print of it. It is not very difficult to refute the points made therein. Unfortunately I am too busy to find time for it. I propose to give a full and complete reply to all the critics of Buddhism in my new book. In the meantime some of the *bhikkhus* should deal with the replies as they come and keep the flag flying. I am glad someone is replying to it.

Great responsibility lies on the shoulders of the *bhikkhus* if this attempt at the revival of Buddhism is to be a success. They must be more active than they have been. They must come out of their shell and be in the first rank of the fighting forces. I am glad you have started the YMBA at Kalimpong. You should be more active than that.

With kind regards,
Yours sincerely
B. R. Ambedkar

I

THE MANY FOUNDERS OF RELIGION

> Out of the many founders of Religion, there are four whose religions have not only moved the world in the past, but are still having a sway over the vast masses of people. They are Buddha, Jesus, Mohammed, and Krishna. A comparison of the personalities of these four and the poses they assumed in propagating their religions reveals certain points of contrast between the Buddha on the one hand and the rest on the other, which are not without significance.

So let's consider the opening paragraph of Dr Ambedkar's article. In comparing the Buddha to the founders of three other religions, he seems to refer to Krishna as a historical person. Hindus, of course, do see Krishna as a historical character, but in the form in which they see him he can't be regarded as fully historical. There's a Vedic *rishi* who is called Kṛṣṇa and referred to by the Buddha in the Pāli canon as the Pāli equivalent, Kaṇha,[63] but he is clearly a historical figure who happens to have that name (which just means 'dark one'). There is the Krishna of the *Mahābhārata*, who is represented as the teacher of the *Bhagavad Gītā*. And then there is the Krishna of the *Śrīmad Bhāgavatam*, a quite late Hindu scripture, a *purāṇa*, which presents a quite different Krishna: not the warrior, not the teacher of Arjuna on the battlefield of Kurukṣetra, but the playmate of the *gopis*, the milkmaids of Brindaban. Tending to fuse these quite distinct figures, none of which may in fact be historical, certainly not fully historical, traditional Hinduism regards Krishna as one of the incarnations of the god Vishnu, who is one of the most prominent figures in the whole of Hindu mythology. Vishnu's two most prominent incarnations are Rama and Krishna, and they are worshipped all over India. The Hare Krishna people especially worship Krishna in his Brindaban form, together with Radha, his favourite among the *gopis*; that double form is often called Radhakrishna. But Hindus don't see Krishna as a founder of Hinduism. Here Dr Ambedkar is taking a semi-historical view. Orthodox Hindus do not see Hinduism as having any founder at all. They believe that Hinduism, to use a comparatively modern term, is based upon the Vedas, and that the Vedas are what they call *apauruṣeya*, that is to say they have no human author. Inasmuch as the Vedas have no human author and inasmuch as Hinduism is based on the Vedas, Hinduism has no human founder, or no founder at all, and modern apologists for Hinduism regard this as a strong point. As they see it, all other religions, like Buddhism and Christianity, Islam and Zoroastrianism, had individual founders, and stand or fall with the founder, whereas Hinduism is based on the Vedas, which are eternal and indestructible, so they say that Hinduism has a much stronger foundation. Sometimes they say that 'Veda' means knowledge, meaning that Hinduism is based upon divine knowledge, not on any particular individual, and that is one of the sources of its strength. From a Buddhist point of view, Hinduism is an ethnic religion, and, unlike universal religions, ethnic religions usually don't have individual founders.

> The first point which marks off Buddha from the rest is his self-abnegation. Throughout the Bible, Jesus insists that he is the son of God and that those who wish to enter the kingdom of God will fail if they do not recognize him as the son of God. Mohammed went a step further. Like Jesus he also claimed that he was the messenger of God on earth. But he insisted that he was the last messenger. On that footing he declared that those who wanted salvation must not only accept that he was a messenger of God, but also accept that he was the last messenger. Krishna went a step beyond both Jesus and Mohammed. He refused to be satisfied with merely being the son of God or the messenger of God, or even the last messenger of God. He was not even satisfied with calling himself a God. He claimed that he was *Parameswhar* or as his

> followers describe him *Devadhideva*, God of Gods. Buddha never arrogated to himself any such status. He was born as a son of man and was content to remain a common man and preach his gospel as a common man. He never claimed any supernatural origin or supernatural powers, nor did he perform miracles to prove his supernatural powers. The Buddha made a clear distinction between a *Margadata* and a *Mokshadata*. Jesus, Mohammed, and Krishna claimed for themselves the *Mokshadata*. The Buddha was satisfied with playing the role of a *Margadata*.

A *mokṣadattā* (i.e. *parama-īśvara*, supreme lord) is a giver of salvation or emancipation, *mokṣa* meaning salvation or freedom or emancipation or liberation (the Pāli is *mokkha*) and *dattā* coming from root *dā* (like *dāna*), thus one who gives. A *mārgadattā* is one who gives, in the sense of shows, the path or way; and that the Buddha certainly was. To the best of my knowledge the terms are not found in the Pāli canon, or for that matter in the later Sanskrit works of Buddhism. It is possible that they do occur, but they are certainly not used in that technical sense, though the distinction represents the sense of the Buddha's teaching in that the Buddha did make it clear that Enlightenment was not something that he could give you, but something you had to achieve by your own spiritual efforts.[64]

Dr Ambedkar says that Jesus, Mohammed, and Krishna all made certain claims, and then goes on to say that the Buddha was born a son of man and was content to preach his gospel as a common man, never claiming any supernatural origin or performing miracles to prove supernatural powers. I am not sure quite what he means by 'son of man'; perhaps there was some idea in his mind of the way that expression is used to describe Jesus in the Gospels. But anyway, he means an ordinary human being. I don't think any special significance is to be attached to that expression.

The Buddhist tradition tells us that the Buddha was born from his mother's side rather than in the usual manner. But is there a rational explanation? Does this legend relate to something like birth by Caesarean section? To the best of my knowledge there isn't any evidence for this in the Buddhist scriptures. It was quite common in ancient Indian mythology to represent heroes as having been born in unusual ways; there are a number of examples in the *Mahābhārata* and the *Purāṇas* of heroes being born from the thigh and the knee and so on. This would seem to be a retrospective testimony to their heroic status. In his *Buddhacarita*, Aśvaghoṣa, when describing the Buddha's birth from the side of his mother, refers to some of these parallels from Indian mythology.[65] So I don't think it can be regarded as any sort of evidence that the Buddha's birth was surgically assisted or anything of that sort. It is the usual Indian attempt to indicate a man's greatness by suggesting that his birth was not a normal birth. I think it's really no more than that. It isn't a question of whether it would be *useful* for us to regard the Buddha as being born a normal human being in the usual way, or inspiring to regard him as having been born as described in traditional legend. One is concerned here with what the facts might have been, useful or otherwise. The legend of his birth from his mother's side doesn't appear in what seem to be the oldest records of his life – in fact the oldest records contain very little about his early life and nothing about his birth at all – so it is probably safe to assume that he was born in the usual manner.

The Buddha didn't 'preach his gospel as a common man' in the sense of being a *pṛthagjana*, one who is not Enlightened. The Buddha preached as a Buddha. I think what Dr Ambedkar is getting at is that the Buddha didn't claim divine authority in the way that Krishna, Jesus, and Mohammed did. He didn't say that people should believe what he taught because he was God. He spoke from his own spiritual experience and taught people that if they followed the path that he had discovered they could become Enlightened in the same way that he had.

It is correct that the Buddha 'never claimed any supernatural origin', but what about 'supernatural powers'? I don't know whether Dr Ambedkar was aware of the distinction between supernatural and supernormal, but there *is* a distinction. Christians would speak of Christ having supernatural powers because he was a supernatural being. As the son of God, he shared God's powers. He could raise people from the dead and perform other miracles. The Buddha did not claim supernatural powers because he wasn't God, or the incarnation of God. According to the Pāli canon, he did have supernormal powers – that is to say, powers that were extensions of ordinary human faculties – but the fact that one has supernormal powers does not constitute any evidence of insight or wisdom or Enlightenment. Devadatta had some of those powers. They are merely supernormal, they do not in themselves have any spiritual, i.e. transcendental, significance.[66]

According to the Pāli canon, the Buddha did from time to time exhibit what one might call supernormal powers, though to what extent those are authentic records is another matter. But clearly his overall appeal was to reason and experience. He is represented as rebuking one of his disciples for trying to impress people with his supernormal powers.[67] Also, as I have argued in some of my lectures and writings, at least some of the 'supernormal powers' exhibited by the Buddha are to be understood symbolically. For instance, the famous *yamaka iddhi*, when the Buddha rose into the air and emitted fire and water simultaneously from his body – is one to take that literally?[68] It seems as though the compilers of the scriptures are trying to tell us something about the Buddha on the spiritual level, though the incident is represented as having actually happened.

Sometimes Ambedkar's language is a bit clumsy. He doesn't always make very fine distinctions. But one could say that in trying to dissociate the Buddha from God, he is emphasizing his humanity, which is a quite extraordinary thing in the Indian context, because the last thing the Indians want to emphasize about any great teacher is his humanity. They want to make him into a divinity, an incarnation of some sort, as quickly as possible. I have seen this happening with people I have actually known, who have ended up being regarded as incarnations of God, or even God himself. I sometimes get literature from people in India and other places claiming to be incarnations of God. The Indian, or the Hindu at least, has this very strong tendency. Dr Ambedkar himself spoke strongly against what he described as the very unhealthy Indian tendency to hero-worship. He regarded this as most unfortunate. In a way it goes back to a famous verse in the *Bhagavad Gītā* where Sri Krishna says, 'Whenever unrighteousness prevails, I will take birth to restore righteousness.'[69] Hindus are always quoting this verse. This is the tendency of the Indian, to believe that some higher power will put things right. If you read Indian newspapers and magazines, you see that politicians and chief ministers in different states are almost made into deities by their followers, in a way that just doesn't happen in the West. The chief minister of a particular state at this moment, who is governing a state of sixty million people, has become a sort of sannyasin, going around in sannyasin's gear, and his picture appears in the papers with one of the Hindu divinities behind him. Probably in the next issue one will read that he has proclaimed himself an incarnation.

He used to be a film star! So Indians have this tendency, and this is what Dr Ambedkar is protesting against. And, of course, Hindus see the Buddha as an incarnation, the ninth *avatāra* of Vishnu, removing the Buddha from the human sphere, and substituting worship of the Buddha as an incarnation for the actual practice of his teaching. This is what Dr Ambedkar is really getting at.

There's some similarity between the tendency of Hindus to regard people as incarnations of divinities and the Dalai Lama being regarded as the incarnation of Avalokiteśvara, but on the whole the Tibetans tend to be much more sober and realistic in their attitude towards religion. Hindus really do go over the top and are often totally uncritical, whereas the Tibetans scrutinize their incarnate lamas carefully, at least to begin with. Dr Ambedkar saw the fondness for hero worship as a great weakness in the Indian character. He believed very strongly in Western parliamentary democracy. He was a socialist, one might even say a state socialist, and he believed that the Indian attitude of worshipping political leaders and religious leaders as supermen and incarnations of God was dangerous for democracy. He was dead against it, not only on religious but on practical political grounds, and his fears seem to have been justified.[70]

In many ways Dr Ambedkar was a rationalist. He seems to have regarded Krishna, Jesus, and Mohammed as historical personalities and ordinary human beings, common men, to use his phrase, who made exaggerated claims on their own behalf. But I'm not sure that he fully realized the distinction that makes an Enlightened being different from a human being. He is not alone in that. Traditionally in the West we have two categories: ordinary human being or incarnation of God, as Jesus is believed by Christians to have been. We don't have a category of Enlightened humanity. Dr Ambedkar had tremendous admiration for the Buddha and strong devotional feelings towards him, and he did believe that the Buddha was an Enlightened human being, and therefore higher than any other human being, but I think his understanding of Buddhism was not such that he could fully appreciate the difference between an ordinary human being and an Enlightened human being. He went some way towards seeing it, but not the whole way. It is quite difficult to see that difference; you need a deep understanding of Buddhism, and some spiritual knowledge and experience. One might say that in his anxiety to show that the Buddha was not God, or an incarnation of God, he probably leaned too far to the other extreme.

Dr Ambedkar seems to have strongly discouraged his followers from hero-worshipping him, but they insisted on doing so, especially after his death, in ways of which I think he would have disapproved. He did so much for them, and they were quite right to appreciate that, but the form their appreciation took sometimes didn't meet with his approval even during his lifetime. He was not charismatic. He never went out of his way to please people, or humour them, or court popularity. He was rather grim, unsmiling, uncompromising. The Dalits recognized that he had worked selflessly for them over many years, and they had the very highest regard for him on that account, but he was highly regarded on account of his achievements and his work, not on account of any superficial tricks of personality. He just didn't have those.

He is still hero-worshipped today. People believe, rightly, that he did the best he could for the Dalits during his lifetime, and he succeeded in raising their status considerably. They are still in a bad condition, but not nearly as bad as before, and they are grateful to him for that. So in a way they do hero-worship him. That has a positive side inasmuch as, out of their regard for him, they have taken to Buddhism. But sometimes they follow him, or follow what they think he thought or said, quite uncritically, and they are sometimes very closed if they think that what somebody is saying is opposed to what he said. Some of them don't really understand what he said. Some are illiterate, so they can't read his writings and have only a very general idea of what he said. So their hero worship has its positive and its negative aspects, but if one is skilful one can utilize it in a positive way. There is a line to be drawn between a justifiable appreciation of someone's services and an irrational hero worship. I've met followers of Dr Ambedkar who believed quite firmly that he was the most learned man that has ever lived, and almost literally knew everything. Clearly one can't encourage that – and it is in the Hindu rather than in the Buddhist tradition.

> There is also another distinction between the four religious teachers. Both Jesus and Mohammed claimed that what they taught was the word of God and as the word of God what they taught was infallible and beyond question. Krishna was according to his own assumption a God of Gods and therefore what he taught, being the word of God, uttered by God, they were original and final and the question of infallibility did not even arise. The

> Buddha claimed no such infallibility for what he taught. In the *Mahaparinibbana Sutta* he told Ananda that his religion was based on reason and experience and that his followers should not accept his teaching as correct and binding merely because they emanated from him. Being based on reason and experience they were free to modify or even to abandon any of his teachings if it was found that at a given time and in given circumstances they do not apply. He wished his religion not to be encumbered with the dead wood of the past. He wanted that it should remain evergreen and serviceable at all times. That is why he gave liberty to his followers to chip and chop as the necessities of the case required. No other religious teacher has shown such courage. They were afraid of permitting repair. For they felt that the liberty to repair may be used to demolish the structure they had reared. Buddha had no such fear. He was sure of his foundation. He knew that even the most violent iconoclast will not be able to destroy the core of his religion.

Dr Ambedkar talks of the claimed infallibility of Jesus and Mohammed, and then goes on to say, 'The Buddha claimed no such infallibility for what he taught.' But did the Buddha not claim infallibility in, for example, the *Lion's Roar Sutta*?[71] It depends what one means by infallibility. The point is really that the Buddha didn't claim omniscience. According to the Pāli canon, Mahāvīra, the Jain leader, claimed omniscience, or at least it was claimed on his behalf, in the sense that he would know, for instance, the exact number of leaves on a tree.[72] The Buddha never claimed omniscience with regard to any mundane fact, but only with regard to Nirvāṇa and the path to Nirvāṇa.[73] One could say that he professed to be infallible in that respect because Nirvāṇa and the way to it was a matter of his own experience.

Dr Ambedkar's accounts of the Buddha's life and teachings have some surprising features. The attitude of his followers outside our own Buddhist movement in India is that Ambedkar's interpretation of Buddhism is the right one; they have blind faith in that. They would accept any version of the Buddha's life that he gave, and he has his own version. He has his reasons for his version, but it is not one that is usually accepted by Buddhists, whether rightly or wrongly. So far as our movement in India is concerned, we encourage people to look critically at Dr Ambedkar's interpretation of Buddhism, but one has to be quite careful about this. His followers have such a strong belief in him that if they feel that you are criticizing him or you are against him (and often they think in terms of either being for or against) they won't listen to anything else you have to say. So you have to be very careful how you put your point across, gently at least suggesting that there are other interpretations of the Buddha's life and that we have to take those into consideration too.

Dr Ambedkar says that 'the Buddha gave liberty to his followers to chip and chop as the necessities of the case required'. One might think that Ambedkar himself did that to the Dharma in a way that was politically advantageous to his way of seeing things. His conversion wasn't at all politically advantageous to him, because it meant that he isolated himself, but he was certainly concerned to stress the social aspect, or the social bearing, one might say, of the Buddha's teaching, especially with regard to the caste system. In India there is a rigid social structure characterized by the caste system, one of the logical consequences of which is Untouchability. One of the features of Hindu philosophy is that social life and spiritual life are kept in separate compartments, and higher spiritual teachings have never been allowed to influence social life. You get Hindu teachers who profess to have realized the Absolute, but who still strictly observe the caste system, as I saw myself in the cases of Anandamayi and Ramana Maharshi.[74] They claim to have realized non-dual reality and all the rest of it, but in their social life they observe these invidious distinctions, and in this way the so-called higher spiritual life is prevented from having any ameliorating effect on the social order. Ambedkar was absolutely opposed to that. Insisting that the Buddha had applied his spiritual principles and realizations to the amelioration of humanity generally and the reform of society, he found it necessary to break down that division which is set up in Hinduism between the social order and the spiritual life.

But in giving an account of the Buddha's life which would not be accepted by most traditional Buddhists, isn't he using the Dharma as a means to his own ends? In a sense he is, and rightly so, because Buddhism is for human beings' ends. In the West people tend to suffer more psychologically than materially, so we approach Buddhism from a psychological point of view, to give us peace of mind, for instance;

at least that may be our approach initially, and we consider it quite justified. But in India, in view of the general condition of the Dalits in the social system, they approach it more from a social than a psychological point of view. Westerners eventually balance the psychological attitude with the realization that there has to be some kind of transformation of society too, and Indians eventually balance their social approach with what could be considered the psychological one; they become interested in meditation and so on. This is what we find with those who become involved in Triratna activities in India. Their approach may look strange to Westerners, but the Western approach looks no less strange to them. They find it very difficult to conceive of the sort of psychological problems that people in the West suffer from. They think it all really rather odd.

2
COMPARING BUDDHISM WITH HINDUISM

> Such is the unique position of Buddha. What about his religion? How does it compare with those founded by his rivals? Let us first compare Buddhism with Hinduism. In the short space available the comparison must be limited to a few important points; indeed only to two. Hinduism is a religion which is not founded on morality. Whatever morality Hinduism has it is not an integral part of it. It is not embedded in religion. It is a separate force which is sustained by social necessities and not by the injunction of Hindu religion. The religion of Buddha is morality. It is embedded in religion. Buddhist religion is nothing if not morality. It is true that in Buddhism there is no God. In place of God there is morality. What God is to other religions morality is to Buddhism.

Dr Ambedkar points out that the basis of Hinduism is not morality. But if that is the case, what *is* the basis of Hinduism? The basis of Hinduism, as of all ethnic religions, is social; it's concerned to maintain and protect the group. And the group, like the ordinary individual (not the individual in the spiritual sense but in the sense of a social unit), is concerned to preserve itself. This is why ethnic religions don't usually favour celibacy: because that practice doesn't make for the perpetuation of the group. One could say that Hinduism, considered in this very broad sense, is a social system rather than a religion in the sense of a universal religion, and all its customs, beliefs, and practices are concerned, except in very marginal instances, with the preservation of that social order, especially as exemplified in the caste system. I relate in my memoir *The Rainbow Road* a discussion I had in South India with an old brahmin as who was a Hindu.[75] What it really came down to was that a Hindu is one who believes in the caste system. In other words, the caste system really is the basis of Hinduism. You can't say that a Hindu is one who believes in God, because you can be a Hindu without believing in God, but you can't be a Hindu without believing in the caste system or having a caste.

If a European took to following a Hindu guru, would he have to adopt the caste system in order to practise that guru's teaching? It depends on what level. There is a story about Akbar the Mogul emperor, a broad-minded man who wanted to become a Hindu. He sent to the pundits of Benares to inquire how he might become a Hindu, and they sent back a donkey and said that, in the same way that the donkey could not become a horse, the emperor could not become a Hindu. The word *jāti*, caste, also means species. It is the same word in both Sanskrit and Pāli, which is perhaps significant. In India I met a number of Western disciples of orthodox Hindu gurus. If you're a sannyasin, there's no problem, because they are outside the caste system, but if you wanted to live as a lay person, you wouldn't be able to marry into an orthodox Hindu family. Even if you could find a family that was sufficiently broad-minded to accept you, they couldn't do it, because they'd be shunned by their caste fellows, and no one would want to marry their daughters.

There are some Hindu gurus who don't accept the caste system, but then they tend to create a new caste. My memoir *The Rainbow Road* includes quite a few illustrations of the sort of thing that Dr Ambedkar is getting at. For example, during my stay at Anandamayi's ashram I discovered that some of the Ramakrishna Mission sannyasins were discriminated against by orthodox Hindu sannyasins because they were known to eat with Europeans. In the ashram there was a very devoted Austrian woman who was treated as an Untouchable. When Anandamayi wanted to drink a glass of water, non-Brahmins were asked to leave the room, and in Ramana Maharshi's ashram there was a screen down the middle of the dining hall with Brahmins on one side and non-Brahmins on the other, although he was a teacher of the non-dualist Advaita. As I mentioned earlier, Hindus keep their social system completely separate from their philosophy and don't allow the one to influence the other. Very few teachers have been able to break through this, and it shows us what Dr Ambedkar was up against.

> It is very seldom recognized that he propounded a most revolutionary meaning of the word *Dharma*. The Vedic meaning of the word *Dharma* did not connote morality in any sense of the word. The *Dharma* as enunciated by the Brahmins and as propounded in the *Purvamimamsa* of Jaimini meant nothing more than the performances of certain *karmas* or, to use the terminology of the Roman religion, observances. *Dharma* to Brahmins meant the keeping up of observances, i.e. *Yagnas*, *Yagas*, and sacrifices to Gods. This was the essence of the Brahmanic or Vedic Religion. It had nothing to do with morality.

The terms *yajña* and *yāga* refer to two different kinds of Vedic sacrifice. Vedic sacrifices are sacrifices usually of animals, sometimes of libations of ghee poured into the sacred fire, always to the recitation of Vedic mantras for a particular mundane purpose. They are mentioned constantly in the Pāli texts; especially in the *Dīgha Nikāya* there is a lot about the inefficacy, according to the Buddha, of Vedic sacrifices, which were very elaborate and involved vast expenditure, and from which of course the Brahmins, who alone were entitled to perform these sacrifices on behalf of other people, greatly profited.[76] These days *yajña* and *yāga* are comparatively rare, because owing to the influence of Buddhism animal sacrifice virtually disappeared from India and was not revived to any extent even after the disappearance of Buddhism. Only very occasionally do you find animal sacrifices of the Vedic type being performed in India. You get animal sacrifices of the Tantric type much more frequently, especially in connection with the worship of Kali, the mother goddess. One of the things we have had to do among the new Buddhists is to weed out the practice of animal sacrifice, because they were in the habit of sacrificing goats and chickens to a variety of minor gods and goddesses, and I frequently had to speak against this practice when explaining to them what as Buddhists they ought and ought not to be doing. It is still quite common among those in outlying villages who profess to be Buddhists. Often they are not aware that it is not in accordance with Buddhism, having received no teaching.

The technical distinction between Vedic and Tantric rituals is that Vedic rituals are generally performed with Vedic mantras and Tantric rituals are performed with verses taken from the *Purāṇas* or the Tantras. Also, Tantric rituals are of a more popular character. They are less associated with Brahmanism, so you don't necessarily have to have a Brahmin to officiate. Probably the most famous centre for animal sacrifice of the Tantric type in India is the Kalighat temple in Calcutta; when I visited it, as briefly mentioned in *The Rainbow Road*, black goats were still being sacrificed.[77] The Hindu Nepalese are great animal sacrificers, and at the time of Dussehra (called Dassain in Nepal) they sacrifice hundreds of buffaloes.

This is to use the term Tantric as distinct from the way it is used in Tibetan Buddhism. There are at least six different Tantric traditions in India. There is the Buddhist Tantra. There is the Jaina Tantra, which is very small and little-known, but does exist. There's the *Śaiva Tantra*, the Tantra associated with Shiva; those works are sometimes called *āgamas*. There's the Tantric tradition associated with the mother goddess, Kālī or Durgā, Śrīdevī, and so on – that's usually called *nigama*. There's a tantra associated with Gaṇapati, the elephant-headed god; and there's a tantric tradition associated with sun worship. The Buddhist Tantra is the most highly spiritualized, and it's that, of course, which went to Tibet. Most of the other tantric traditions involve animal sacrifice, though not the Jaina one, of course. Usually Tantric Hinduism means the *shakti* cult, the worship of the mother goddess as the supreme, all-pervading power, either under the form of Kālī, Durgā, Pārvatī or even the local smallpox goddess, who is widely worshipped. It's very difficult to say how much influence the different Tantras have on each other. There was a substratum of popular, semi-Tantric practice which was worked up by the different religious traditions in various ways in accordance with their particular principles and utilized for their particular purposes. Buddhism also made use, so to speak, of that trend in Indian culture and religious life.

> The word *Dhamma* as used by the Buddha had nothing to do with ritual or observances. In fact he repudiated the *Yagnas* and *Yagas* as being essence of religion. In place of *Karma* he substituted morality as the essence of *Dhamma*. Although the word *Dhamma* was used by Brahmanic teachers as well as by the Buddha, the

content of both is radically and fundamentally different. In fact, it might be stated that the Buddha was the first teacher in the world who made morality the essence and foundation of religion. Even Krishna as may be seen from the *Bhagavad Gita* was not able to extricate himself from the old conception of religion being equivalent of rituals and observances. Many people seem to be lured by the doctrine of *Nishkam Karma* otherwise called *Anasaktiyoga* preached by Krishna in the *Bhagavad Gita*. It is taken to mean the Boyscout sense of doing good without the expectation of reward. This interpretation of the *Nishkam Karma* is a complete misunderstanding of what it really means. The word *Karma* in the phrase *Nishkam Karma* does not mean action in the generic sense of the word, *Karma* meaning 'deed'. It is used in its original sense in which it is used by the Brahmins and Jaimini. On the point of observances there is only one point of difference between Jaimini and the *Bhagavad Gita*. The observance which used to be performed by the Brahmins fall into two classes: (i) *Nitya Karmas* and (ii) *Naimittika Karmas.*

The *Nitya Karmas* were observances which were enjoined to be performed regularly, for which reason they were called *Nitya* and as a matter of religious duty, for which there was not to be any expectation of reward. On that account they were also called *Nishkama Karmas*. The other category of *Karmas* was called *Naimittika*, that is to say they were performed whenever there was occasion, that is, whenever there was a desire to perform them, and they were called *Kamya Karmas* because from their performance some benefit was expected to come. What Krishna condemned in the *Bhagavad Gita* was *Kamya Karmas*. He did not condemn *Nishkama Karmas*. He extolled them. The point to be borne in mind is even for Krishna religion did not consist of morality. It consisted of *Yagnas* and *Yagas* though of the *Nishkama Karmas* category.

This is one point of contrast between Hinduism and Buddhism. The second point of contrast lies in the fact that the official gospel of Hinduism is inequality, for the doctrine of *Chaturvarna* is the concrete embodiment of this gospel of inequality. On the other hand Buddha stood for equality. He was the greatest opponent of *Chaturvarna*. He preached against it, fought against it, and did

> everything to uproot it. According to Hinduism neither a *Shudra* nor a woman could become a teacher of religion nor could they take *Sannyasa* and reach God. Buddha on the other hand admitted *Shudras* to the *Bhikkhu Sangha*. He also admitted women to become *Bhikkhunis*. Why did he do so? Few people seem to realize the importance of this step. The answer is that Buddha wanted to take concrete steps to destroy the gospel of inequality. Hinduism had to make many changes in its doctrines as a result of an attack made by Buddha. It gave up *Himsa*. It was prepared to give up the doctrine of the infallibility of the *Vedas*. On the point of the *Chaturvarna* neither side was prepared to yield. Buddha was not prepared to give up his opposition to the doctrine of *Chaturvarna*. That is the reason why Brahmanism has so much more hatred and antagonism against Buddhism than it has against Jainism.

Dr Ambedkar says that Hinduism had to make many changes to its doctrines as a result of the Buddha's teachings, and one of these changes was that it gave up *hiṃsā*, which literally means violence, and here means the sacrifice of animals. There is no doubt that Hinduism gave those up as a direct result of criticism from Buddhists and Jains. In the Buddha's day, as one can tell from reading the Pāli canon, especially the *Dīgha Nikāya*, sacrifice occupied a central place in Hindu religious life.[78] That isn't the case now. Those Vedic sacrifices very rarely take place, and Hinduism has become almost a religion of non-violence. That is definitely due to the criticism of Buddhism and Jainism. The Brahmins found that if you wanted to beat the Buddhists, you had to join them. To use the term Hinduism to refer to the religion in India at the time of the Buddha is a misnomer, by the way; there's a definite break between what we should more accurately call Brahmanism and modern post-Buddhistic Hinduism. Elements of Hinduism are the product of the influence of Buddhism on Brahmanism, one could say. For instance, before Buddhism there were no temples or image worship in Hinduism. Religious life revolved around elaborate sacrifices, at which sometimes hundreds of Brahmins officiated and thousands of animals were sacrificed.

As Ambedkar shows in his book *The Untouchables*, in the Buddha's day Brahmins ate meat, even beef.[79] Vegetarianism came in under the auspices of Buddhism and Jainism. If you speak to a modern Hindu about killing a cow, he's deeply shocked, but in the Buddha's day cows were regularly sacrificed and Brahmins partook of the beef. Modern Hindus don't like to be reminded of these things. Scholarly Hindus know that this is what happened, but if you were to mention to ordinary Hindus that their ancestors in the Buddha's day ate beef, they would deny it point blank. So that aspect of Hinduism, or Brahmanism, was greatly modified under the influence of Buddhism.

In the Buddha's day, Indians on the whole were non-vegetarians. *Bhikkhus* were permitted to be non-vegetarian because they were dependent upon alms, but they were only allowed to eat the flesh of animals that had not been killed especially for them.[80] The whole thrust of Buddhism was definitely in favour of vegetarianism, and eventually Buddhist India did become predominantly vegetarian. There is, for instance, the *Laṅkāvatāra Sūtra*, with its chapter against meat-eating.[81] The Sarvāstivādins and even the *bhikkhus* seem to have been strongly in favour of vegetarianism. The whole trend of Buddhism was against the slaughter of animals, especially for sacrifice, and against meat-eating, and that tendency seems to have become stronger as Buddhism itself became stronger in India.

It is unfortunate that in the Buddhist countries of South-east Asia *bhikkhus* don't want to be vegetarian, and in fact will strongly defend non-vegetarianism. I've been told by Burmese monks that if you're a vegetarian you're not a Buddhist, you're a Hindu, which seems quite amazing. In Sri Lanka there are some vegetarian *bhikkhus* and they are generally well respected by the lay people, but the majority of them eat meat, justifying it by saying that the Buddha permitted it, or that if you're a vegetarian you're picking and choosing, which monks mustn't do. Many *bhikkhus* say, 'The lay people give us meat and we can't refuse.' I've found that one can't even discuss the matter with Burmese *bhikkhus* – they just get angry – but when I used to talk with Thai *bhikkhus* I would say, 'Thailand has been a Buddhist country for hundreds of years. You've taught the lay people to bow down to you in certain ways. You've taught the women to offer everything on a cloth so that their body doesn't come into contact with the body of the *bhikkhu*. Could you not have taught them to give you vegetarian food?' Then they used to say, 'Ah, well, we have been brought up as meat-eaters, we can't change.' I would reply, 'Well, I was brought up as a meat-eater too. I became vegetarian when I was in the army. If I can change, so can you.' Then they just used to laugh weakly and say, 'Well, your mind is very strong!'

The Tibetans have their own philosophy in this respect. They believe that if you have to eat meat – and in Tibet it's difficult to grow vegetables and people subsist mainly on barley flour and meat – it's better to kill one large animal than a number of small ones. That's why the Tibetans don't eat fish or birds, but they eat the yak and the sheep, on the basis that if you just take one life that will feed a large number of people, that is less of a sin. But Tibetans will always admit that it is better to be vegetarian; it's just that conditions in Tibet don't allow them to be. I met one old Tibetan monk, a refugee, who was a vegetarian. He was very thin, but he was active and healthy, so he was proof that you could be a vegetarian even in Tibet. A great many Tibetans in India and the West keep eating meat, which is unfortunate. When the Dalai Lama came to India, he was strongly criticized in Indian newspapers for eating meat, and I think the Dalai Lama gave it up for a while, but I believe he then returned to meat-eating, saying that he just couldn't manage on a vegetarian diet. But at least Tibetans accept vegetarianism in principle, and if you are a vegetarian, they will rejoice in your merits.

Dr Ambedkar talks about Hinduism giving up *hiṃsā*, violence, under the influence of Buddhism. Are there other examples of elements of Buddhism being incorporated into Hinduism? There's image worship, which seems to have started with Buddhism, although for its first couple of hundred years the Buddha was represented by a symbol. It was the Buddhists who introduced the installation of images, and temples and pujas. Before that, Hindus had Vedic sacrifices. That was their form of ritual. You could say the *Purāṇas* are modelled on Mahāyāna *sūtras*; they are a mixture of myth and legend and ethical and spiritual teaching. There wasn't much monasticism in Hinduism before the time of Buddhism and Jainism. Broadly speaking, Hinduism isn't really in favour of monasticism. The Brahmin is usually a householder. One could say that the teaching of karma was taken over to some extent from Buddhism, though in a garbled form. There are only one or two references to karma in Vedic literature, perhaps even only one, which is in one of the Upanishads.[82] Lots of philosophical teachings were taken from Buddhism by Hinduism, especially in the form of Vedānta. The doctrine of the two truths,[83] the doctrine of *māyā*, and the doctrine of the beginninglessness of *saṃsāra* are all generally admitted to have been taken over from Buddhism.

3

THE PARENT OF THE CASTE SYSTEM

Hinduism has to recognize the force of the Buddha's arguments against *Chaturvarna*. But instead of yielding to its logic Hinduism developed a new philosophic justification for *Chaturvarna*. This new philosophic justification is to be found in the *Bhagavad Gita*. Nobody is able to say for certain what the *Bhagavad Gita* teaches. But this much is beyond question that the *Bhagavad Gita* upholds the doctrine of *Chaturvarna*. In fact it appears that this was the main purpose for which it was written. And how does the *Bhagavad Gita* justify it? Krishna says that he as God created the system of *Chaturvarna* and he constructed it on the basis of the theory of *Guna* – Karma – which means that he prescribed the status and occupation of every individual in accordance with his innate *gunas* (or qualities). Two things are clear. One is that this theory is new. The old theory was different. According to the old theory the foundation of *Chaturvarna* was the authority of the Vedas. As the Vedas were infallible so was the system of *Chaturvarna* on which it rested. The attack of the Buddha on the infallibility of the Vedas had destroyed the validity of this old foundation of *Chaturvarna*. It is quite natural that Hinduism, which was not prepared to give up *Chaturvarna*, which it regarded as its very soul, should attempt to find for it a better foundation, and this the *Bhagavad Gita* proposes to do. But how good is this new justification given by Krishna in the *Bhagavad Gita*? To most

Hindus it appears to be quite convincing, so that they believe it to be irrefutable. Even to many non-Hindus it appears to be very plausible, very enticing. If the *Chaturvarna* had depended only on the authority of the Vedas I am sure it would have long disappeared. It is the mischievous and false doctrine of the *Bhagavad Gita* which has given this *Chaturvarna* – which is the parent of the caste system – apparently a perpetual lease of life.

The basic conception of this new doctrine is taken from the *Sankhya* philosophy. There is nothing original about it. The originality of Krishna lies in applying it to justify *Chaturvarna*. It is in its application that the fallacy lies. Kapila, the author of the *Sankhya* system held that there is no God, that God is necessary because matter is believed to be dead. But matter is not dead. It is active. Matter consists of three *gunas*: *Rajas*, *Tamas* and *Satva*. *Prakriti* appears to be dead only because the three *gunas* are in an equilibrium. When the equilibrium is disturbed by one of the *gunas* becoming dominant over the other two, *Prakriti* becomes active. This is the sum and substance of the Sāṃkhya philosophy. There can be no quarrel with this theory. It is perhaps true. It may therefore be granted that each individual as a form of *Prakriti* is made up of the three *gunas*. It may even be granted that among the three *gunas* there is a competition for dominance one over the other. But how could it be granted that a particular *guna* in a particular individual which at one time – say at the time of his birth – happens to dominate his other *gunas* will continue to dominate them for all times, till his death? There is no ground for this assumption either in the *Sankhya* philosophy or in actual experience. Unfortunately neither Hitler nor Mussolini were born when Krishna propounded his theory. Krishna would have found considerable difficulty in explaining how a signboard painter and a bricklayer could become dictators capable of dominating the world. The point of the matter is that the *Prakriti* of an individual is always changing because the relative position of the *gunas* is always changing. If the *gunas* are ever changing in their relative position of dominance there can be no permanent and fixed system of classification of men into *varnas* and no permanent and fixed assignment of occupations. The whole theory of the *Bhagavad Gita* falls to the ground. But as I have said the Hindus have become infatuated by its plausibility and its 'good look' and have become slaves of it. The result is that Hinduism continues to uphold the *Varna* system with its gospel of social inequality. These are two of the evils of Hinduism from which Buddhism is free.

The doctrine of the *guṇas* is part of the Sāṃkhya philosophy, as the article says, but it has entered into general Indian thought. According to the Sāṃkhya philosophy there are two ultimate principles: *puruṣa* and *prakṛti*. *Puruṣa* literally means person or even male, but the real meaning, roughly speaking, is what we would call Spirit, with a capital S. *Prakṛti* is Nature with a capital N. *Prakṛti* is supposed to consist of three *guṇas*: *sattva*, *rajas*, and *tamas*. It is very difficult to translate these three terms, because they have a number of different meanings and connotations, but *sattva* is roughly peacefulness; *rajas* is energy and activity and fieriness; and *tamas* is darkness, sloth, torpor, ignorance. According to Sāṃkhya philosophy, to begin with these three *guṇas* are in a state of equilibrium, but under the influence of *puruṣa*, which does not itself move, the balance of the *guṇas* is disturbed and the whole process of evolution takes place.

But if Sāṃkhya philosophy sees the *guṇas* starting off evolution, where is that evolution tending? To put it very simply, the Sāṃkhya believes in cycles, holding that having reached a certain point the whole process reverses itself. The Sāṃkhya stresses, though, that *puruṣa* does not do anything; it is the mere proximity of *puruṣa* to *prakṛti* that sets it in motion. The famous analogy that the Sāṃkhya gives is that it's like the master of the house; he doesn't do anything, he just sits in the house, but the mere fact of his presence means that all the people in the house go about their respective duties. The Sāṃkhya also teaches that some of the qualities of *puruṣa* are as it were reflected onto *prakṛti*, and that the two get apparently mixed up – not in reality, but they appear to be mixed up – and they regard salvation as consisting in the dissociation of *puruṣa* from *prakṛti* and realizing that the qualities reflected in *prakṛti* do not belong to *prakṛti* but to *puruṣa*. The Sāṃkhya is therefore a dualistic system, and the state of liberation, which they usually call *kaivalya* (freedom or detachment), consists in the complete dissociation from nature.

The connection with the *Bhagavad Gītā* is that in the *Bhagavad Gītā* the different castes are described on the basis of the amount of particular *guṇas* in each. The Brahmin is supposed to be the embodiment of the *sattva guṇa*, the best of the *guṇas*, the Kshatriya is a combination of *sattva* and *rajas*. The Vaishya is *rajas*, and the Shudra is *tamas*. The *Bhagavad Gītā* seeks to justify the caste system on the grounds that it represents a natural division of people in accordance with their *guṇas*, and their karmas in accordance with those *guṇas*. There is a well-known verse in which Sri Krishna is supposed to say, 'The caste system is of my creation, in accordance with the difference of *guṇa* and karma' – that is to say, the *guṇas* and the actions that are the results of the *guṇas*.[84] Ambedkar strongly disapproves of the *Bhagavad Gītā*, regarding it as giving a pseudo-philosophical basis to the caste system and thereby justifying it. The verse I quoted is in the mouths of Hindus all the time.

The 'Untouchables' don't really enter into the picture. They don't enter into the *Bhagavad Gītā*, as though they are so low they can't even be mentioned, they're below even the Shudras. According to Dr Ambedkar in his book *The Untouchables*, Untouchability in the full sense originated between about 200 and 400 CE,[85] and the *Bhagavad Gītā* is probably somewhat prior to that. Untouchability is mentioned in the Pāli canon – the Buddha himself came up against instances of it[86] – but the systematic treatment of whole communities of people as untouchable came some hundreds of years later.

In the article, Dr Ambedkar says that to use the difference of *guṇas* as a basis for a justification of the caste system assumes that people's natures remain unchanged, which he says is not the case. But the Hindu theory assumes that you are born with one or another *guṇa* predominating, and it's because that *guṇa* predominates that you are born into that particular caste. One of Dr Ambedkar's arguments against that is that you can't regard people in this cut-and-dried way, that in this person such-and-such a *guṇa* predominates throughout his life and in another person another *guṇa* predominates. He regards that as completely unrealistic. But traditional Hindus see the proportion of *guṇas* in a person as determining their character.

The *Bhagavad Gītā* goes into this, describing the different lifestyles, as we would say, of the different castes according to the *guṇas* that predominate in them. The *guṇas* are often referred to in the everyday language of India. For instance, the *Bhagavad Gītā* refers to the kind of foods that are liked by sattvic people, rajasic people, and tamasic people. Sattvic people like sweet, oily foods, rajasic people like hot, pungent dishes, and tamasic people like rotten things. (I suppose ripe cheese would be included in that category.) So in India you may be told, 'Oh, this food won't do you any harm, it's very sattvic,' or 'He's a very sattvic sort of person', or again, 'He is very rajasic'. Even now this idea influences Hindu thinking very strongly. Hindus regard it, as Dr Ambedkar mentions, as a logical explanation of the caste system. They would probably say it was highly scientific.

Ambedkar himself was a living contradiction of the *guṇas*, but nobody bothered to try to defend that way of thinking. When custom is strongly established, you don't have to defend it when it is attacked, because you are confident that it can't be shaken. To give an example, just recently a book called *Gandhi and his Critics* was published.[87] Who was Mahatma Gandhi's strongest critic? Dr Ambedkar. But in the book there is only a brief mention of him and the Poona Pact. One of his major works, called *What Congress and Gandhi have done to the Untouchables*, a devastating attack on Gandhi and his whole attitude towards the Untouchables, is not even mentioned, although it is probably the strongest of all the criticisms, and very well researched.[88]

The standard Hindu doctrine is that your *guṇas* determine your position in the caste system, and if you want to improve your lot and be reborn in a higher caste, the only way to do that is faithfully to observe the duties of your caste in this life. If you are born as a Shudra or an Untouchable, you should accept that status and faithfully discharge your duties, and then you may be reborn in a higher caste. There is no other way. The proportions of your *guṇas* are modified by your fidelity to your caste *dharma*. In the context of the *Bhagavad Gītā*, *dharma* means your duties in society as determined by your caste. This, not the Buddhist use of the term, is the general sense of the word *dharma* in India. Your *dharma* is your social duty as prescribed by the caste into which you have been born. As Ambedkar pointed out in several places, there are castes whose *dharma* is to steal and even to murder, like the thugs whose *dharma* was to assassinate people.[89] It's estimated that they assassinated many tens of thousands before they were stamped out by the British. They were devotees of the goddess Kali. Sri Krishna even says in the *Bhagavad Gītā*, 'There is danger in the duty of another.'[90] That is in a way the whole point of the *Bhagavad Gītā*, because Arjuna, who was a Kshatriya, was unwilling to fight, and the whole thrust of the text is to convince him that he should perform his *dharma* as a

Kshatriya. In refusing to fight, he is in a way wanting to change to the *dharma* of the Brahmin, but Sri Krishna says he should act in accordance with his *dharma* as a Kshatriya and leave the results to God, as it were. One could say that in doing that, he is an agent for karma. The *Bhagavad Gītā* doesn't actually say that, but it does make the point, in one of its later chapters, that in any case Arjuna is deluded in thinking that he acts in any way; it is really Sri Krishna himself who is acting through all these various forms. Arjuna should not have the deluded idea that he is killing anybody; it's the god who is killing them. In the eleventh chapter there is what is called the vision of universal form, the Vishvarupa, showing Sri Krishna as the All-Destroyer, Time, who swallows everybody.

You can see the social implications of these teachings. I think Christmas Humphreys was a bit influenced by these sorts of ideas, he being basically a Theosophist. When he was a prosecuting lawyer he used to demand the death penalty, and on several famous occasions he was successful and the person was executed. He was sometimes asked how he reconciled his Buddhism with his activities as a barrister and a judge, and he stated many times that he believed that he was an instrument of karma. He seemed to believe that the law of karma was reflected in the British judicial system and that he was just its humble instrument. I heard him once being interviewed on the radio and he spoke very strongly indeed in these terms.[91]

As to the difference between Hindu and Buddhist ideas on the workings of the law of karma, the Hindus don't seem to have a systematic account in the way that Buddhism has, especially in the later Abhidharma-type works. Hindus often identify karma with fate or even with the will of God. In theory it's the result of your own actions, but very often it's spoken of as though God visits those results upon you, being regarded as the administrator of the results of karma in a rather Christmas Humphreys-like way. Hindus don't have the Buddhist philosophy of the *niyamas*, the different orders of cause-effect relationship, of which karma is only one.[92] They tend to think that everything that happens to you is the result of karma, whether that is reflecting the will of God or not. So one might say that the Hindu doctrine of karma tends to be fatalistic. But Buddhism never teaches that everything that happens to you is the result of some action that you have done in the past.

4
THE REVIVAL OF BUDDHISM IN INDIA

> Some of those who believe that only the acceptance of the Gospel of Buddha can save the Hindus are filled with sorrow, because they do not see much prospect of the return or revival of Buddhism in India. I do not share this pessimism. In the matter of their attitude to their religion, Hindus today fall into two classes. There are those who hold that all religions are true, including Hindus, and the leaders of other religions seem to join them in this slogan. There cannot be a thesis more false than the thesis that all religions are true. However this slogan gives the Hindus, who have raised it, the support of the followers of other religions. There are Hindus who have come to realize that there is something wrong with their religion. The only thing is that they are not ready to denounce it openly. This attitude is understandable. Religion is a part of one's social inheritance. One's life and dignity and pride are bound up with it. It is not easy to abandon it. Patriotism comes in. 'My country right or wrong', so also 'My religion right or wrong'. Instead of abandoning it the Hindus are finding escape in other ways. Some are consoling themselves with the thought that all religions are wrong, so why bother about religion at all.

Here Dr Ambedkar says that Hindus fall into two classes: those who hold that all religions are true and those who say, 'Why bother about religion at all?' I think that's still broadly true. Those who say, 'Why bother about religion?' are mostly the Marxists, a very small minority compared with the others, but the general Hindu attitude is that all religions are the same. Of course, they are concerned to keep their social structure intact; so long as you follow the caste system and that is your effective religion, it doesn't matter what you believe.

> The same feeling of patriotism prevents them from openly embracing Buddhism. Such an attitude can have only one result. Hinduism will lapse and cease to be a force governing life. There will be a void, which will have the effect of disintegrating the Hindu society. Hindus then will be forced to take a more positive attitude. When they do so, they can turn to nothing except Buddhism. This is not the only ray of hope. There is hope coming from other quarters also.
>
> There is one question which every religion must answer. What mental and moral relief does it bring to the suppressed and the downtrodden? If it does not, then it is doomed. Does Hinduism give any mental and moral relief to the millions of Backward Classes and the Scheduled Castes? It does not. Do Hindus expect these Backward Classes and the Scheduled Castes to live under Hinduism which gives them no promise of mental and moral relief? Such an expectation would be an utter futility. Hinduism is floating on a volcano. Today it appears to be extinct. But it is not. It will become active once these mighty millions have become conscious of their degradation and know that it is largely due to the social philosophy of the Hindu religion. One is reminded of the overthrow of Paganism by Christianity in the Roman Empire. When the masses realized that Paganism could give them no mental and moral relief they gave it up and adopted Christianity. What happened in Rome is sure to happen in India. The Hindu masses when they are enlightened are sure to turn to Buddhism.

Dr Ambedkar speaks of modern Hinduism sitting on a volcano which is bound to erupt once these downtrodden depressed castes come to realize their degradation. Does that have a political, even Marxist, flavour? In a way it's a statement of fact. At present there are a hundred million former Untouchables.[93] Even though they are in a minority, a hundred million is quite a lot of people, so if they did all suddenly realize how they had been treated, and also had the means to put things right, there could be an upheaval which really was volcanic. But I think if it happens at all, it will happen quite gradually. These people don't all live in one area. Many Dalits are village servants, and a village of a hundred caste Hindus might have five or six or ten Dalits to perform menial services, so everywhere they are in a minority. They don't possess weapons. They've only got strength of numbers in the big cities to which they've emigrated to get away from their position of slavery in the villages, and even in the big cities they are in a minority. And they are still on the whole uneducated and poor, so they are still dominated and bullied by the caste Hindus.

Things are gradually changing in some areas. Dalits have begun to resist the caste Hindus and refuse to be oppressed, refuse to perform menial services without proper pay, and so on. But even now, every year hundreds of Dalits are killed, usually because the caste Hindus think that they are getting above themselves. Tens of thousands are beaten, thousands have their houses burned down, every year; there are accounts in the Indian newspapers almost every week. Caste Hindus still can't accept that the Dalits are bettering themselves, the background of their attitude being that if you are born as an Untouchable, that is because of sins committed in previous lives, so if you try to better your condition you are going against the law of karma. You are not accepting your punishment, as it were. Caste Hindus seem to think of it as part of their religious duty to keep the Dalits in their place. For instance, there have been examples where a Dalit bridegroom has ridden in the marriage procession on horseback, which is the caste Hindu custom, and he's been assaulted because he is behaving in a way that is not proper for a Dalit to behave. There have been other cases where a Dalit has been thrashed for daring to wear his sandals when walking through a caste Hindu street. If he's not sufficiently polite or obsequious to the caste Hindus he can be thrashed. There have been examples of Dalits being punished for turning the ends of their moustaches upwards, because that is supposed to be the prerogative of the Rajput. Sometimes Dalits have been thrashed and half the moustache shaved off as a punishment. Sometimes as a punishment the Dalits' wells are polluted. These things, and far worse, are still happening today.

Gradually, here and there, Dalits are resisting, especially those who have converted to Buddhism, but sometimes they are punished for it.

If Dalits report incidents, often the police officers are caste Hindus, so nothing happens. If a police officer happens to be a non-caste Hindu, or a Christian or Muslim, they may get some sympathy, and occasionally a more liberal caste Hindu may give them justice. Most of them are landless labourers, and if they refuse to behave as they are supposed to, the caste Hindus sometimes refuse to give them work, or refuse to pay them for work they have done. What are they to do? They have no money to engage a lawyer to fight their case. They are in a minority, so they can't do anything by force. This is the background of some of the people in our sangha in Poona and other places, though to us in the West it's quite incredible. To them Buddhism represents a way out of this sort of treatment. They can take a stand on the fact that they are Buddhists, they are outside Hinduism, so they are not Untouchables, and they refuse to be treated as such.

Sometimes caste Hindus take action against Dalits practising Buddhism, seeing that as the Dalits trying to better themselves. There are many cases of caste Hindus smashing Buddha images, not because of direct religious antagonism but because they're annoyed that the Dalits are getting above themselves, as they see it, so they want to humiliate them. They do it by assaulting them, raping the women, burning down their huts, and smashing images of the Buddha and Dr Ambedkar. Statistics of the different types of atrocities perpetrated by caste Hindus on Dalits list about 1,200 different types, from murder downwards. There are various degrees of discrimination. A Dalit may not be admitted to the teashop in the village; instead he is given tea in a special cup kept for Dalits, and he has to drink it standing in the road. In village India you don't usually shave yourself; you get the barber to do it, and he goes round from house to house, but he won't shave Dalits.

I haven't been aware of any risk to our social projects in India. Most of them are in predominantly Buddhist localities. If there was a large-scale riot, if the caste Hindus started attacking the Dalits, it's not inconceivable that our properties could be involved, but there haven't been any signs of that. Poona, where we mainly function so far, is a relatively peaceful place, not given to riots even when there is unrest in places like Bombay and Ahmedabad. Perhaps surprisingly, in places like Bombay and Poona, Buddhists, Christians, and Muslims are on quite friendly terms. It's partly because Dalits don't have any restrictions about dining together. Caste Hindus wouldn't invite a Muslim or a

Christian into the house to eat or to drink tea, but Christians, Muslims, and Buddhists dine together quite freely, and often invite one another to weddings and other social events, despite their religious differences, which don't seem to trouble them at all. Perhaps rather oddly, they all regard themselves as oppressed minorities.

The Dalits certainly have grievances, to say the least, and those who take Dr Ambedkar seriously, see Buddhism as the solution ultimately to those grievances. They don't believe that if they become Buddhists they will at once become more prosperous, and of course that hasn't happened. The Buddhist countries of the East haven't rushed to help them. But once they say that they are Buddhists, they feel that if anyone tries to treat them as an Untouchable, with all that that implies, they can say, 'No, I am not a Hindu. I am a Buddhist, and I refuse to be treated in that way.' This gives them a great feeling of strength. When I was moving around among them shortly after the conversion, I used to ask them, 'What difference has becoming Buddhist made to you?' And I always got the same reply: 'I feel free.' That sense of liberation from the tyranny of the caste system has released a tremendous amount of energy, which shows itself in all sorts of ways.

Dalits are able to take advantage of the positive discrimination practised by the Indian government on their behalf,[94] but that presents them with a problem. Indeed, this was one of the biggest problems they had to face after the conversion, because the central government withdrew those concessions from those who declared themselves to be Buddhists. One can only say that that was a move on the part of the caste Hindus in the government to block the process of conversion. There are two kinds of concessions: those given by the central government and those given by the different state governments. After the mass conversion, both the central government and the state governments declared that those who became Buddhists were no longer eligible for concessions given to members of the Scheduled Castes, so if they wanted to become officially Buddhist, they had to sacrifice those. There was a big attempt on the part of the new Buddhists and some of their friends to get the government to reverse this decision; there was correspondence on the subject in the *Maha Bodhi* of the time. In the end, only one state government gave back those concessions to those who had become Buddhists, and that was the government of Maharashtra. Some people believe that is one of the reasons why Buddhism prospers more in

Maharashtra than anywhere else. Elsewhere, if you declare yourself a Buddhist, then you and your children cease to be eligible for those concessions.

I'm afraid that sometimes people took the *Dhammadiksha*, as they call it, they became Buddhists, but in the census they continued to declare themselves to be Hindus, so that they could benefit from those concessions. They were aware that it wasn't quite honest, but they felt they had no alternative because their economic position was so weak. People asked me hundreds of times in the course of my tours what they should do. I said that if they possibly could, they should declare themselves to be Buddhists and take the consequences, but if they didn't feel able to do that, I certainly wasn't going to criticize them. There have been riots in Ahmedabad in recent times originated by caste Hindu students who were demonstrating against Scheduled Caste students being given special places in a medical college, and many Dalits and others were killed.[95] So some caste Hindus deeply resent the fact that Scheduled Caste people are still being given these concessions.

Some of the antagonism against the Dalits is from people in the Shudra classes, who feel that the Dalits have an unfair advantage over them now. Sometimes the people who are just above you resent you coming up more than do those who are very much above you. In some areas the Shudras are quite prosperous peasants and farmers, and they are often just as resentful as the Brahmins that the Dalits are improving their position, or even more resentful. In Maharashtra some years ago there was a political alliance between the Dalits and the Brahmins, strange to say, because they were both minorities. The majority caste there is the Mahratta caste, and they are both anti-Brahmin and anti-Dalit, the Brahmins being above them, and the Dalits being below them. So the people at the very bottom and the people at the very top made certain political alliances. They say that in politics necessity makes strange bedfellows. This didn't mean that the Brahmins relented socially – they wouldn't inter-dine with the Dalits or anything like that – but they were prepared to have political alliances with them.

5
BUDDHISM IS THE ONLY RELIGION THE WORLD CAN HAVE

So much by way of comparison between Hinduism and Buddhism. How does Buddhism stand in comparison with other non-Hindu Religions? It is impossible to take each of these non-Hindu Religions and compare it with Buddhism in detail. All I can do is to put my conclusions in a summary form. I maintain that:

(i) Society must have either the sanction of law or the sanction of morality to hold it together. Without either, society is sure to go to pieces. In all societies, law plays a very small part. It is intended to keep the minority within the range of social discipline. The majority is left and has to be left to sustain its social life by the postulates and sanction of morality. Religion in the sense of morality must therefore remain the governing principle in every society.

(ii) Religion as defined in the first proposition must be in accord with science. Religion is bound to lose its respect and therefore becomes the subject of ridicule and thereby not merely loses its force as a governing principle of life, but might in course of time disintegrate and lapse, if it is not in accord with science. In other words, religion if it is to function, must be in accord with reason which is merely another name for science.

(iii) Religion as a code of social morality must also stand together another test. It is not enough for religion to consist of a moral code, but its moral code must recognize the fundamental tenets of liberty, equality, and fraternity. Unless a religion recognizes these three fundamental principles of social life, religion will be doomed.

(iv) Religion must not sanctify or ennoble poverty. Renunciation of riches by those who have it may be a blessed state, but poverty can never be. To declare poverty to be a blessed state is to pervert religion, to perpetuate vice and crime, to consent to make earth a living hell.

Which religion fulfils these requirements? In considering this question it must be remembered that the days of the Mahatmas are gone and the world cannot have a new Religion. It will have to make its choice from those that exist. The question must therefore be confined to existing religions.

It may be that one of the existing religions satisfies one of these tests, some two. The question is – Is there any religion which satisfies all these tests? So far as I know, the religion which satisfies all these tests is Buddhism. In other words Buddhism is the only religion which the world can have. If the new world – which be it realized is very different from the old – must have a religion – and the new world needs religion far more than the old world did – then it can only be the religion of the Buddha.

All this may sound very strange. This is because most of those who have written about Buddha have propagated the idea that the only thing Buddha taught was Ahimsa. This is a great mistake. It is true Buddha taught Ahimsa. I do not want to minimize its importance, for it is a great doctrine. The world will not be saved unless it follows it. What I wish to emphasize is that Buddha taught many other things besides Ahimsa. He taught as part of his religion, social freedom, intellectual freedom, economic freedom and political freedom. He taught equality, equality not between man and man only, but between man and woman. It would be difficult to find a religious teacher to compare with Buddha, whose teachings embrace so many aspects of the social life of a people, and whose doctrines are so modern and whose main concern was to give salvation to man in his life on earth and not to promise it to him in heaven after he is dead!

Dr Ambedkar says that the Buddha taught social freedom, intellectual freedom, economic freedom, and political freedom. I don't think we can say that the Buddha taught these things in so many words – this is modern terminology – but his teaching does seem to assume that the individual is a free agent in all the spheres of life. Certainly there is social freedom, and intellectually one must think for oneself and therefore one must have the freedom to do so. And the Buddha does seem to teach that you should have the freedom to better your economic condition. That's quite clear from some texts.[96] The idea of political freedom isn't so clear, because in the Buddha's day there was no politics in the modern sense. The king administered justice, punished criminals, and defended the country from outside attack, and to meet his expenses he gathered taxes, but he didn't have anything to do with health or welfare or education. In many of the cities the guilds ran their own affairs, so the king had very little to do compared with the tasks of a modern government. Ordinary people, it seems, didn't participate in the government, if one can call it that. The king did everything, with the help of his ministers, his army, and his police. Rich men seem to have exerted a certain amount of influence, and so did wise men, in the guise of advisers, but most people didn't participate in politics at all as far as we can see. The so-called republics were not republics in the modern sense, but oligarchies in which the aristocratic or well-to-do minority governed, rather than government by a single individual or monarch. There wasn't full political participation in the Buddha's day and therefore, in a sense, there wasn't political freedom. It was very different from the Athenian democracy, in which every adult male who was free-born and a citizen participated in the administration. There wasn't that sort of pattern in ancient India as far as we know. But you were almost completely free to live your own life, with far less governmental interference than there is today, so in a sense people had more political freedom in the Buddha's day. In India today, the Dalits have less freedom than other people, being poor, oppressed on religious grounds, and uneducated. If you can't read and write, the law may say that you are free to study, but you can't take advantage of it. But even in a modern society, does anyone really feel free, or have we just got used to our lack of freedom? If you live in a democracy and accept that what the majority says has to prevail, then you may not as an individual be able to enjoy certain freedoms.

> How could this ideal of spreading Buddhism be realized? Three steps appear to be quite necessary.

First: To produce a Buddhist Bible.
Second: To make changes in the organization, aims and objects of the *Bhikkhu Sangha*.
Third: To set up a world Buddhist Mission.

The production of a Bible of Buddhism is the first and foremost need. The Buddhist literature is a vast literature. It is impossible to expect a person who wants to know the essence of Buddhism to wade through the sea of literature. The greatest advantage which the other religions have over Buddhism is that each has a gospel which everyone can carry with him and read wherever he goes. It is a handy thing. Buddhism suffers for not having such a handy gospel. The Indian *Dhammapada* has failed to perform the function which a gospel is expected to. Every great religion has been built on faith. But faith cannot be assimilated if presented in the form of creeds and abstract dogmas. It needs something on which the imagination can fasten – some myth or epic or gospel – what is called in journalism a story. The *Dhammapada* is not fastened around a story. It seeks to build faith on abstract dogmas.

The proposed gospel of Buddhism should contain (i) a short life of Buddha, (ii) the Chinese *Dhammapada*, (iii) some of the important Dialogues of Buddha and (iv) Buddhist Ceremonies, birth, initiation, marriage, and death. In preparing such a gospel the linguistic side of it must not be neglected. It must make the language in which it is produced live. It must become an incantation instead of being read as narrative or as ethical exposition. Its style must be lucid, moving, and must produce a hypnotic effect.

In this 'proposed gospel' Dr Ambedkar includes the Chinese *Dharmapada* rather than the Indian *Dhammapada*. So far as we can judge from Beal's translation, the Chinese *Dharmapada* includes various illustrative stories giving the circumstances under which the Buddha gave the teachings embodied in the *Dhammapada* verses.[97] There is a similar work that does that for the Pāli *Dhammapada*, though perhaps Ambedkar wasn't aware of it – the *Dhammapada aṭṭhakathā*, a commentary which has been translated into English in three volumes.[98] But in the Pāli tradition that commentary is kept quite separate from the *Dhammapada* verses, whereas the Chinese *Dharmapada* is like the Pāli *Udāna*, in which the verse and the illustrative story go together. Ambedkar was concerned that there should not be just dry precepts but also something more interesting, something story-like.

> There is a world's difference between a Hindu *Sannyasi* and a Buddhist *Bhikkhu*. A Hindu *Sannyasi* has nothing to do with the world. He is dead to the world. A *Bhikkhu* has everything to do with the world. That being so a question arises. What was the purpose for which the Buddha thought of establishing the *Bhikkhu Sangha*? What was the necessity for creating a separate society of *Bhikkhus*? One purpose was to set up a society which would live up to the Buddhist idea embodied in the principles of Buddhism and serve as a model to the laymen. Buddha knew that it was not possible for a common man to realize the Buddhist ideal. But he also wanted that the common man should know what the ideal was and also wanted there should be placed before the common man a society of men who were bound to practise his ideals. That is why he created the *Bhikkhu Sangha* and bound it down by the rules of Vinaya. But there were other purposes which he had in his mind when he thought of founding the *Sangha*. One such purpose was to create a body of intellectuals to give the laymen true and impartial guidance. That is the reason why he prohibited the *Bhikkhus* from owning property. Ownership of property is one of the greatest obstacles in free thinking and application of free thought. The other purpose of Buddha in founding the *Bhikkhu Sangha* was to create a society the members of which would be free to do service to the people. That is why he did not want the *Bhikkhus* to marry.
>
> Is the *Bhikkhu Sangha* of today living up to these ideals? The answer is emphatically in the negative. It neither guides the people nor does it serve them. The *Bhikkhu Sangha* in its present condition can therefore be of no use for the spread of Buddhism. In the first place there are too many *Bhikkhus*. Of these a very large majority are merely *Sadhus* and *Sannyasis* spending their time in meditation or idleness. There is in them neither learning nor service. When the idea of service to suffering humanity comes to one's mind everyone thinks of the Ramakrishna Mission. No one thinks of the Buddhist Sangha. Who should regard service

> as its pious duty? The *Sangha* or the Mission? There can be no doubt about the answer. Yet the *Sangha* is a huge army of idlers. We want fewer *Bhikkhus* and we want *Bhikkhus* highly educated. The *Bhikkhu Sangha* must borrow some of the features of the Christian priesthood, particularly the Jesuits. Christianity has spread in Asia through service – educational and medical. This is possible because the Christian priest is not merely versed in religious lore but because he is also versed in Arts and Science. This was really the ideal of the *Bhikkhus* of olden times. As is well known the Universities of Nālandā and Taxila were run and manned by *Bhikkhus*. Evidently they must have been very learned men and knew that social service was essential for the propagation of their faith. The *Bhikkhus* of today must return to the old ideal. The *Sangha* as composed cannot render this service to the laity and cannot therefore attract people to itself.

This passage seems to imply that Dr Ambedkar didn't have a very high opinion of meditation. When he says of *bhikkhus*, 'Of these a very large majority are merely *Sadhus* and *Sannyasis* spending their time in meditation or idleness', it is not clear whether he regards meditation and idleness as the same thing or two different things. But he also says that they are 'merely' sadhus and sannyasins, which suggests that he does not have a very high opinion of that way of life. He speaks more highly of the Ramakrishna Mission, the founder of which, Swami Vivekananda, was strongly influenced by the example of the Christian missionaries, and also by what he had read about the ancient Buddhist monastic orders.

Here one must bear in mind Dr Ambedkar's Hindu background. Though he doesn't state it in so many words, the impression is that he regarded meditation, in the light of his Hindu experience, as consisting in a selfish self-absorption in inner blissful states, regardless of what is happening in the world and the sufferings of other beings. Perhaps one could say that he was looking at meditation much as a Mahāyānist might look at the *arhant* ideal. One must remember that sannyasins in India traditionally had no conception of concern for society at large, and until very recently didn't consider that they had any sort of responsibility towards other living beings, so their attitude could be regarded as a complete negation of the bodhisattva ideal. Ambedkar saw Buddhism very much in terms of the bodhisattva ideal, and though he doesn't speak of the ideal *bhikkhu* as being a sort of bodhisattva, that does seem to represent his way of thinking. Sometimes he admitted that he tended to see the *bhikkhu* rather too much in terms of the social worker – that can't be denied, and it is in a sense the other extreme. But at his best, he saw the ideal monk, or the spiritual life itself, in terms of the bodhisattva ideal rather than the *arhant* ideal. In view of the fact that he came from a Dalit family and that the Dalits had at that time (and still have) such a degraded position in Hindu society at that time, one can hardly be surprised at that.

To what extent was Dr Ambedkar himself leading a spiritual life? That depends what one means by a spiritual life. He didn't meditate in any formal sense, to the best of my knowledge, but despite his intellectuality he was a very emotional man, and he had very strong devotional feelings towards the Buddha, particularly at the end of his life. There is no doubt that he led a spiritual life in the sense that throughout the whole of his career he was concerned with the needs of others. In India politics can be a very dirty game and there is a lot of corruption, but so far as one knows, Ambedkar was completely free from anything of that sort. He certainly had a very strong moral sense and very strong ethical principles, and he based his life very much on those.

6

THE OPIUM OF THE PEOPLE

Without a Mission Buddhism can hardly spread. As education requires to be given, religion requires to be propagated. Propagation cannot be undertaken without men and money. Who can supply these? Obviously countries where Buddhism is a living religion. It is these countries which must find the men and money at least in its initial stages. Will they? There does not seem to be much enthusiasm in these countries for the spread of Buddhism.

On the other hand the time seems quite propitious for the spread of Buddhism. There was a time when religion was part of one's own inheritance. A boy or a girl inherited the religion of his or her parent along with the property of the parent. There was no question of examining the merits and virtues of religion. Sometimes the heir did question whether the property left by the parents was worth taking, but no heir was there to question whether the religion of his or her parents was worth having. The times seem to have changed. Many persons throughout the world have exhibited an unprecedented piece of courage with regard to inheritance of their religion. Many have, as a result of the influence of scientific inquiry, come to the conclusion that religion is an error, which ought to be given up. There are others who as a result of the Marxian teaching have come to the conclusion that religion is opium which induces the poor people to submit to the domination of the rich and should be discarded. Whatever be the

> causes, the fact remains that people have developed an inquiring mind in respect of religion. Whether religion is at all worth having and if so which religion is worth having are questions which are uppermost in the minds of those who dare to think about this subject. The time has come. What is wanted is will. If the countries which are Buddhist can develop the will to spread Buddhism the task of spreading Buddhism will not be difficult. They must realize that the duty of a Buddhist is not merely to be a good Buddhist. His duty is to spread Buddhism. They must believe that to spread Buddhism is to serve mankind.

Marxism seems to fulfil Dr Ambedkar's four criteria for a religion, so why did he decide not to adopt it? He wasn't at all happy with Marxism, or with communism, let's say, taking communism to mean Marxism in action. At one stage of his career Ambedkar was a labour leader in Bombay. Many Dalits worked in the mills, Bombay being a big industrial centre with lots of cotton mills and other factories. During that period he learned to distrust the communists, because he found that the communist leaders who were working in the factories and trying to organize the workers were not really concerned with the improvement of the workers' conditions, but wanted to use them for political purposes of their own. He was convinced that the communists didn't really have the interests of the workers at heart. Also, he didn't believe in violence as a means of achieving social and political ends. He didn't believe in non-violence in all circumstances – he believed that a state had the right to defend itself against attack – but he certainly didn't believe that social and political objectives could be achieved by means of violence, whereas Marxism believes that violence is in the end the only way. He rejected Marxism mainly on those grounds.

Also, Marxism isn't strictly speaking a religion, and Dr Ambedkar believed that religion is essential both to the individual and to the state. It is essential to society because society can't be held together by force or by law, but only by ethical principles, which in the last resort have a religious basis. Some people have claimed that Marxism has some features of a religion. It certainly has missionary zeal, and it even has a prophet and a 'bible' (in the form of *Das Kapital*), but there isn't the transcendental dimension which is the most essential element of religion, or at least of universal religion. Throughout his career, Ambedkar was strongly opposed to communism, though it must be said that nowadays some of his followers are attracted to it, especially in Bombay.

Another reason for Dr Ambedkar's decision against Marxism was that it was foreign. One of the reasons he chose Buddhism was that it was an indigenous religion, and so far as his Indian followers were concerned this was a strong point. Centuries ago India was Buddhist, so they had Buddhistic roots, as it were, which meant that they had a strong feeling for Buddhism that they wouldn't have had for a teaching or a system that had originated outside India. In a way this was an appeal to something ethnic, but he was after all dealing with very large numbers of people. But I think his real objection to Marxism was that it advocated violence as a means of social revolution, and he didn't believe that social revolution could be brought about in that way.

Dr Ambedkar says, quoting Marx, that religion is the opium of the people. Often people don't quote the whole of that passage; the well-known phrase is part of a longer one: 'Religion is the sigh of the oppressed creature, the heart of a heartless world, and the soul of soulless conditions. It is the opium of the people.'[99] So what Marx says about religion as the opium of the people isn't as negative as it might sound. He almost suggests that under certain circumstances people need the consolation of religion. In the nineteenth century opium was widely taken in Britain, in the form of laudanum. It was a universal panacea; they even used to give it to babies to keep them quiet. So opium, in the Victorian context – and Marx was one of the great Victorians in many respects – doesn't have quite the connotation that it has for us today. Religion helps to keep the people quiet, it helps to keep them satisfied with their lot. Marx didn't consider that a good thing, but he doesn't seem to have thought that it was altogether a bad thing that people should have some consolation in the midst of their trials and difficulties. Opium provides relief from physical pain, which was initially why it was taken during the Victorian period, but it is addictive. Apart from relieving pain, it seems to give intensely pleasurable sensations, including visionary experiences, in a self-indulgent, self-centred way, which no doubt did alienate people. In a well-known book on Coleridge and opium, Molly Lefebure, who had considerable knowledge of poisons and their effect on people, showed quite clearly that Coleridge's bondage to opium resulted in his becoming alienated from people, especially those who were nearest and dearest to him.[100] That seems to be one of the side effects of opium.

One might say that there is an analogy with religion in that perhaps religion wrongly understood, or an Eastern or spiritual tradition wrongly understood in the West, would alienate one from other people. One has to be mindful of that possibility. Sometimes you need to separate yourself from other people, to withdraw, to intensify your experience of yourself, which might have been rather crushed in the group, but there mustn't be an emotional alienation from other people. Of course, one must take care to use the word alienation in the strict sense. You are only alienated from people if you cease to feel for them. You may be separated from them, or your interests may diverge, but if you still feel friendly towards them, even though you no longer have any common interests, you are not alienated from them.

Dr Ambedkar took up the social dimension of religion and approached it much more from the altruistic point of view than from the individualistic point of view. Have we gone so far the other way in the West that religion, even Buddhism, has become for us an opiate, a way of retreating to the positive group?[101] Are we becoming more positive and enjoying ourselves more while ignoring the social difficulties that the majority of people are experiencing? You are justified to some extent in withdrawing into the positive group, if the group is genuinely positive, and trying to transform it into a spiritual community as a basis for operations later on, when you are bigger and stronger, in society as a whole. You need to have a basis of operations, a launching pad. But there is a tendency on the part of some people in our own Buddhist movement to take refuge within the movement not with a view to qualifying themselves to move outwards *to* the wider society, but as a self-indulgent escape *from* the wider society.

When reading one of Charles Dickens' novels recently, and also a life of Dickens, one thing that struck me was the great importance in the society of his time of the family and the group to which one belonged. In the Victorian period the family meant a large, extended family, not only mother, father, and ten or twelve children, but aunts and uncles and cousins and second cousins and all the rest of it, quite a network of relationships, and it seems that in that context there was quite a lot of warm intercommunication. Though that pertains to the group, it does seem to represent a necessary stage in the development of the individual. We don't have that very much nowadays. Some children are brought up in one-parent families with little or no contact with other relatives. As people grow up, there's a sense of alienation from social life in the wider sense, from the political and economic life of the country, especially if they are out of work. If you grow up with a very impoverished experience of the group, when you come into contact with something like the Triratna community you may see it as a group because that is what you need. You may use the right spiritual language and talk about the spiritual community, but what you really want is a group, or even a family. On its own level, that is quite legitimate. You mustn't get stuck there, you must go beyond that, but in itself it represents a legitimate stage of development. People often come to the Triratna community in a rather battered condition. Sometimes within the spiritual movement we have to complete the work that society should have done.

7
DR AMBEDKAR'S VISION

Dr Ambedkar's language in this article may seem populist or simplistic, but sometimes you have to oversimplify things to say anything at all. You can make the oversimplification the starting point, and refine it more and more until you can say what you really want to say. His style may be a bit rough, but he is always vigorous and direct. He wrote the article for an English-language magazine, and the readership wouldn't have been more than a couple of thousand. He certainly wasn't writing it for his own followers, who wouldn't have been able to read it anyway. Many of the contributions in the *Maha Bodhi* are very scholarly, and perhaps the populist style Ambedkar adopts is surprising, but perhaps he didn't have much idea about the readership of the journal and was just airing his views, trying them out and seeing what sort of response he might get. Or perhaps he was unburdening himself, or wrote the article hastily.

He didn't have much contact with other Buddhists, or any teachers to go to, and one shouldn't underestimate the difficulties this brings. There were many Indian scholars who had a good knowledge of Buddhism, but they were almost all Hindus, and often Brahmins at that, and he deeply distrusted their interpretations, often with reason. Radhakrishnan is not a reliable interpreter of Buddhism.[102] At the same time, the *bhikkhus* in India were not intellectually or spiritually up to the mark. Dr Ambedkar did visit Sri Lanka and Burma, but he wasn't impressed by many of the things he saw there. So with whom could he talk things over? I had some contact with him myself, but it was quite limited. At that time I wasn't well known, and I was quite young, not much more than half his age. Perhaps he couldn't take me as seriously as he might have done if I'd been a bit older. Also, by the very nature of his career and achievement, he was an independent person who thought for himself. Perhaps he accepted the invitation to write for the *Maha Bodhi* in the hope that he might stir these supposedly indolent Buddhist scholars.

He was a bit of a sledgehammer, in a way. He sometimes got very frustrated and desperate and even angry, because he was so much on his own, battling against this completely indifferent Hindu society. He stood virtually alone. He had some lieutenants, as they are usually called in India, very junior colleagues, but they weren't up to much. Really there was just Ambedkar and the vast illiterate masses. It's ironic that his article appeared in the *Maha Bodhi*, because in the early 1950s the president of the society was an orthodox Brahmin. Indeed, every president of the Maha Bodhi Society since it started had been an orthodox Bengali Brahmin. This was the Buddhist organization of India, and it was headed by Brahmins. What do you imagine Ambedkar's feelings were? One of the last of the Bengali Brahmin presidents, Shyama Prasad Mookerjee, had been a past president of the All-India Hindu Mahasabha, and was one of Ambedkar's principal opponents in Parliament when Ambedkar was trying to push through the Hindu Code Bill, which would have meant a reform in Hindu personal law. It's almost as though in England we had as the president of the Buddhist Society not our comparatively innocuous Christmas Humphreys but some scheming Jesuit. So this was the sort of thing Dr Ambedkar was up against, and indeed I was up against it myself, as I describe in my memoirs.[103] Partly due to me, when Shyama Prasad Mookerjee died we got a Buddhist elected as president, the Maharaja Kumar of Sikkim, who was a friend of mine. When that happened, we were all accused of narrow-mindedness for wanting a Buddhist as president. This was another famous example of Sangharakshita's intolerance! So one mustn't be surprised if Ambedkar hammers away with his arguments in a rather ferocious manner, or even if he is one-sided or exaggerates a bit.

I don't think that the political influence Dr Ambedkar wielded by virtue of his office had much connection with his influence on the masses. His political career having taken a downward turn, some people who were trying to minimize the significance of his conversion to Buddhism said that it was a compensation for his dwindling political influence. But he was trying to operate on two fronts at the same time. In Parliament he was concerned with legislation which would ameliorate the lot of the Dalits. A lot of his time was taken up with parliamentary work, and for a time he was a minister, first of labour and then of law. After he resigned as law minister when his Hindu Code Bill failed, he was freer to devote himself to purely religious activities. I think he would have preferred to have gone on in politics too, because he felt there was a lot of work still to be done there, but he was taking on too much, and in some ways it is fortunate that he did have to resign, because then he could devote himself to Buddhism. Also, there was a rapid deterioration in his health during the last year of his life. He may have hoped to have another ten or fifteen years to live, whereas in fact he only had another year, and it must have become obvious to him as the year progressed that his life was nearly over.

I never thought of going into politics myself when I lived in India. For many years I never looked at a newspaper as a matter of principle. I started reading newspapers at the time of the trouble in Tibet and the Dalai Lama's flight, and from then on I thought I'd better look at the papers sometimes, to keep myself informed as to what was going on in the world. But I had no idea of getting politically involved in India. When I was working among Dr Ambedkar's followers, some of their political leaders tried to get me on their side against other leaders, but I always avoided that and confined myself to strictly religious activities. Since my return to England, I have sometimes wondered whether it might be a good or necessary thing to get involved in politics, because it does seem that one needs to operate on that front too, but in Britain politics is party politics, and I couldn't see any party with which I could sympathize. I could occasionally agree with some of the things that some of them did, but I couldn't say more than that. Certainly I couldn't see myself joining a political party, and in Britain unless you belong to a political party you can't really get anything done. One could, I suppose, start a new party. There are one or two new parties, the Green Party, for example, and there are parties that put up a single candidate, though if he gets 150 votes and forfeits his deposit, that hardly seems very helpful. For some years I've not thought seriously about politics. I've almost given it up as a bad job. But I've encouraged members of our sangha to get involved on the local level, because there you can do something.

Attending meetings of the parish council helps neighbourly relations, and if you've got a planning application in, it helps to have the parish council on your side. That low-level participation is just common sense if you're going to conduct activities on any scale. I think it's a shame if idealistic people don't see any opening for them in politics. Why should politics be left to the power-hungry people? But nowadays it is very difficult to get on in politics, regardless of your particular political predilection, unless you've got an absolute lust for power, and that isn't very Buddhistic.

Might there be any significance in the fact that the new Buddhist movement came about at the time that India was gaining its freedom? There was a connection, because Dr Ambedkar was very worried about what would happen to the Dalits after India gained independence. He felt that they were better off under the British than under the caste Hindus. He saw quite clearly that when independence came it would be the caste Hindus who seized power, and he was afraid of what they might do to the Dalits. His long-term strategy, although he didn't live long enough to see it through, was to spread Buddhism to such an extent that Hinduism would be completely undermined. He felt that the more Buddhist India was, the better chance there was for democracy, and the better the chance for democracy, the more likely it was that the Dalits would be decently treated. But towards the end of his life he realized that Buddhism wasn't going to have the influence in India as a whole that he had hoped, at least not yet; so he decided that he had better do what he could and lead the Dalits, or at least a percentage of them, into Buddhism. Really he wanted to revive Buddhism in India for the whole population, because he believed that religion was necessary for humanity and that society had to have a moral basis. He had no faith in Hinduism, which he believed negated all human values, so his vision was to convert the whole of India to Buddhism.

People in India often ask why Ambedkar left conversion so late. I think there were several reasons. First of all, he hoped to be able to persuade a lot more people to follow Buddhism. He certainly didn't want it to be confined to his own community. Initially he seems to have hoped that the whole of India could be swayed in the direction of Buddhism. Then he seems to have felt that at least all the Scheduled Caste communities – about a hundred million now, nearly sixty million in his day – could convert to Buddhism. But his influence was not so strong with all of them as it was with the Mahar community in which he was born, which is about four or five million strong. He held off as long as possible in the hope of bringing more people in, but in the end he realized, it seems, that it was only with the Mahars that he had sufficient influence to swing them round to Buddhism. He also felt that he was getting old. He was very ill for the last few years of his life; it was now or never. But it seems that he postponed the conversion as long as possible in the hope that he could persuade more and more people to follow him.

Following the death of Dr Ambedkar, which left millions of newly converted Buddhists without spiritual guidance, the Buddhist world as a whole responded very poorly, and still, with the exception of our own movement, doesn't seem to be helping much. Why? I once tried to encourage some Thai *bhikkhus* to come to India and work among the Dalits, but one of them said, 'Why should we? We're quite comfortable in our own country.' A very few *bhikkhus*, some of whom I knew, did try, but the majority were quite indifferent. Some South-east Asian *bhikkhus* weren't too happy with the idea of all those Dalits becoming Buddhist, thinking that it would lower their prestige in some way. There was that sort of feeling especially in Sri Lanka, where they aren't completely devoid of caste feeling. These people were poor and wretched, and that's not the sort of person they were very keen on welcoming into Buddhism. They wanted highly intellectual Europeans with plenty of money. So there was that aspect too, though I don't want to overemphasize it.

The few *bhikkhus* who did get to India found it almost impossible to work among the Dalits. One reason for that was that the approach of the *bhikkhus* was very rigid. They expected just to be able to say 'Buddhism is this and Buddhism is that' and have everyone accept it. They were not used to being asked questions or challenged or asked for further explanations. Also, many of them couldn't put up with the low standard of living, because most *bhikkhus* in South-east Asia have a far higher standard of living than the ordinary Dalits. They couldn't eat the food because it was too coarse; they couldn't live under those simple conditions. They were accustomed to a comfortable, easy life. Another thing was that the Dalits didn't treat them with the sort of respect that they were accustomed to. They treated them with respect, but not in the full formal way that they were used to back home. Many *bhikkhus*, if they are not treated in that way, are completely thrown off balance. So it was just too big a job for them, and they hadn't the imagination or the adaptability to cope with it. That is the sad truth. Tibetans, of course, have flocked to the West. They've not bothered with the Dalits at all, even though many of them are living in India. They've not wanted anything to do with them, though they know perfectly well that they are there, and they have managed to get to every other part of the world. One can't help wondering why, with all that bodhisattva spirit and all those incarnate lamas, they couldn't help these very poor people who needed the Dharma more than anybody else, indeed were begging for it.

Is there not a Buddhist world organization that could respond? Since 1950 we have had the World Fellowship of Buddhists. Dr Ambedkar attended the first meeting, and he said it wasn't enough to have a World Fellowship of Buddhists, they needed a programme of action. That hasn't happened yet, though they still meet every two years in one Buddhist country or another. It is certainly a useful venue for making contacts, but it has no activities of its own. It has a constitution and in principle it's supposed to be doing all sorts of things to propagate Buddhism, but in effect it is mainly this meeting every two years, and a magazine which contains news of Buddhist activities all around the world.[104]

I'm afraid the eastern Buddhist world failed the Dalits when they first converted to Buddhism. A few individuals or organizations sent Buddha images, or invited a few young Dalits to Sri Lanka or Burma and made them into monks for a while, but that's about all they've done in thirty years. To me it was quite an eye-opener that there was such a lack of response from the rest of the Buddhist world. If the Dalits had become Christian, you would have had missionaries and money pouring in from all over the Western world. It's ironic that the Buddhist movement that has done most for them, though that is so far a drop in the ocean, is Triratna, based in England, of all places – and we got involved simply because I happened to meet Dr Ambedkar and became involved in the effort to support the teaching of Buddhism among his followers while I was living in India. Groups from eastern Buddhist countries have built quite a lot of temples and so on in India over the last twenty or thirty years, mainly in the Buddhist holy places, but these are mainly to cater for the needs of their own pilgrims.[105]

When it comes to cultural life generally, the new Buddhists are in a difficult position, because Indian culture is steeped in Hinduism, and they don't want anything to do with it. Hindu music, even, has a semi-mythological basis that they want to avoid. Some of our Indian Order members have started appreciating Western classical music, believe it or not. Over the last few years there has been a very interesting literary movement called Dalit literature (Dalit meaning 'oppressed'). Dalit literature consists mainly of poetry, short stories, and a few novels, but it is a quite distinctive form of Marathi literature and has begun to be recognized by the Marathi literary scene generally.[106] Some of these stories and poems have been translated into English. The Dalits formerly didn't participate much in Hindu cultural life; they were excluded from that. They had a bit of folk culture of their own, though again that is tied up with popular Hinduism. I tried to encourage them to keep up their dances, which were folk dances mainly. If you are welcomed on your arrival in a village, very often there's a troupe of young men with castanets and drums to dance you in, and they are very wild and vigorous. It's quite savage, but very energetic. There's no obvious link with Hinduism, so I tried to encourage them to keep up things of that sort. But the few of them who have some education have some interest in Western culture because it's not Hindu. They don't want anything to do with Hinduism, and one can understand that.

There's an issue to do with images of bodhisattvas. Someone in our sangha, seeing an image of Mañjuśrī, wondered why we should have an image of a bodhisattva with a sword,[107] but the sword wasn't the only concern. Iconographically, Indian Buddhist bodhisattvas look very like Hindu gods, and the new Buddhists don't want anything to do with Hindu gods, so they tend to be suspicious of representations of bodhisattvas, although they certainly appreciate the bodhisattva ideal. It is rather as if Buddhists in Britain were to be presented with pictures of Buddhas and bodhisattvas that were depicted exactly like Jesus and the Christian saints. We wouldn't be too happy! We love to see Indian bodhisattvas because for us they don't have associations of Hindu gods and goddesses, but iconographically it is very difficult to distinguish bodhisattvas from Hindu deities.

There's a similar issue with vegetarianism. The new Buddhists sometimes say they don't want to be vegetarian because Hindus are vegetarian. They are concerned to be as different as possible from Hindus. They want nothing to do with Hinduism, or even those areas which Buddhism and Hinduism share, because their feeling against

Hinduism is so strong, understandably, on account of the way they have been treated. There are those who are more educated and articulate, and understand what is Buddhism and what is Hinduism, but there are still millions of people who haven't got a very clear idea of what Buddhism is all about.

Did Dr Ambedkar have much of a feeling for spiritual hierarchy? One has to understand that for the Dalits the whole idea of hierarchy is absolutely out, because they have been so oppressed by an iniquitous social hierarchy, having been right at the very bottom of it, that it is going to take generations before they can think of spiritual hierarchy in a positive sense, because to them hierarchy means the hierarchy of Brahmins, Kshatriyas, Vaishyas, and Shudras, and themselves right at the bottom. In the West we can have no idea of their feelings in this respect. Are people who have suffered in the social hierarchy likely to bring their fear or hatred of any idea of hierarchy into the spiritual community? This does not seem to have happened within our own movement in India at all, I am glad to say. If anything, they are less susceptible to reactivity to authority than many people are in England.

Dr Ambedkar started off with a social vision because he saw the state that the Dalits were in and that something had to be done about it. To Ambedkar the social meant the ethical, and the ethical meant the other-regarding, and that led you straight to the bodhisattva ideal. Ambedkar seems to have been deeply convinced that the social order had to be a moral order, that society had to have a strongly positive ethical basis. A legal basis wasn't enough; a basis of power wasn't enough. Eventually he defined ethics in terms of brotherhood, fraternity, and love between human beings in the sense of *mettā*. That was his vision. It wasn't a vision of society in the Marxist sense; he repudiated Marxism. It was a conception of society which was deeply humanistic, in the most ideal sense.

So at first he seems to have thought more in social terms, then he seems to have seen that his social vision required a religious underpinning, and he found that religious underpinning in Buddhism. It's as though he began with a vision and then set about finding the principles to contain his aspiration. His passions were already engaged. One can see this in the number of people inspired to embrace Buddhism in India. There are far more Buddhists in India now than there are in Britain, so why is this? It's the same teaching. If anything, it's presented more clearly and effectively here than it is there, because it has been presented consistently for a longer time. Why the great appeal in India? The reason is that there it links up with matters which are of deeply personal interest to a very large number of people. A lot of people feel the injustice with which they are treated very strongly because they experience it every day, and they see Buddhism as the remedy. It is as though you need to latch on to a cause, or even a grievance, to have a large-scale movement. Otherwise you've got to add one person to another until you've got ten, fifteen, twenty, thirty.... That's a sound process, but it's a very slow one. Sometimes you need to have a large movement to make any sort of impression on society as a whole.

And you also need vision. Dr Ambedkar's vision certainly fires our movement in India. There's no doubt that our Order members in India are much more fired up than those in Britain. One rarely gets the impression in Britain that Order members are fired up – perhaps they are from time to time, after a particularly good lecture or retreat or meditation, but it's usually not sustained. In the 1960s there was some enthusiasm and idealism around, though sometimes it took rather strange forms. It's still around now, in the Greenpeace movement, for example, but it's not so widespread or so noticeable as it was then. When the FWBO started, it took advantage of that wave; most of our original members were drawn from it, and some of those who are still very prominently with us were hippies. I've got photographs of them to prove it! Maybe if there hadn't been that wave, it wouldn't have been possible to make a start with the FWBO. But there isn't all that much of that enthusiasm around now. In those days people did believe that you could change society radically, even if they thought that the way to do it was by dropping acid in everybody's coffee. Oh yes, those were exciting days! Some people wanted to change society overnight.

But, as I have observed before, the besetting sin of Buddhism is laziness and indifference. It's difficult to understand why, particularly in the light of the Buddha's exhortation to his disciples to go forth and spread the Dharma.[108] Buddhists aren't usually fanatical or intolerant, and they don't persecute people – those are the characteristic weaknesses of other faiths – but time and time again they have been guilty of laziness and indifference and neglect. I can't even begin to think why. Perhaps it's a question of the near enemy. Indifference is the near enemy of tolerance, one might say, and laziness is the near enemy of peacefulness. I suppose one can only conclude that the gravitational pull is very strong. In some ways it's not surprising that people often don't practise the spiritual teachings that they profess to believe in. Even in our own Order, there are teachings clearly known to everybody, but does everybody live up to them? Why isn't one full of enthusiasm for the Dharma? Why does one want to watch television or go and see some third-rate film? Why does one waste one's time reading detective stories, or in pursuit of members of the opposite sex? Why does one quarrel with other members of the sangha? Why doesn't everybody succeed in attaining *dhyāna* states when they meditate? Everybody knows exactly how to do it. Why are people unmindful? They've all heard *appamādena sampādetha* hundreds of times and they know exactly what it means.[109] They could probably give an excellent lecture on the four stages of mindfulness, but you still find them forgetting to keep appointments, or to turn up for chapter meetings or council meetings, or to post letters. If you want to know why the Buddhist world hasn't succeeded in practising the Dharma to the extent that it might have done, ask yourself why *you* haven't practised it to the extent that you might have done. I suspect that the answer is exactly the same. You might even say there's less excuse in the case of members of our own Order, because it has all been spelled out for them so clearly. Some people can't even get up in the morning to meditate, extraordinary as that may seem.

Also, there's the question of going out into the world to spread the Dharma. One of the models we have is the zeal of the Christian missionary, but that is quite different. It's very difficult for us to realize now the extent to which the nations of the West in earlier centuries believed that they represented a superior civilization and that they had a God-given duty to civilize the rest of the world, whether through their trade or their culture or their religion. They really believed that they were superior, and the missionary movement was closely associated with this. Many people genuinely believed that the West had attained its position of supremacy because it was Christian, and because God had blessed it. I have heard Christian missionaries in Kalimpong speaking to local people in exactly this way. They used to say, 'Well, look at England, look at America, look at Germany: consider how wealthy they are, compared with you. And why is that? Because God is pleased with them, God has blessed them, God has given them all that wealth. Why? Because they are following the right path, because they are Christian.

You are so poor and miserable because God is angry with you, because you are worshipping idols. If you want to be rich, you should become Christian. God will be pleased with you and bless you, and you'll have everything you want.' I have heard these things with my own ears. But that was the last sunset glow of Western imperialism. There may be missionaries in remote Indian villages still singing the same tune for all I know, but I don't think it will be happening in the same way as before. The missionary movement in the main was one aspect of the dominance of the West, and in Christianity there was an inherent proselytizing zeal which lent itself to that sort of movement. But in a sense there is an inherent proselytizing zeal in Buddhism. It is there in the scriptures, and there were Buddhists who travelled thousands of miles under difficult conditions to propagate the Buddha's teachings. It was usually individual monks, just going because they were individually inspired to go forth and spread the Dharma. There was nothing very organized. But they must have gone forth in considerable numbers for Buddhism to have spread so widely.

There have been some successful mass religious movements in the UK. Not long before I left India in 1964, I happened to read a book on Methodism, and I must say I was quite impressed by the personality and methods of John Wesley, who went around on horseback preaching three or four sermons a day all over Britain until he was in his eighties. He was particularly effective in Cornwall. The Cornish tin miners at that time were living in dreadful conditions and were totally neglected by the religious authorities of the day. From Wesley's point of view they had relapsed into paganism and they had apparently hardly heard of Christianity. Many of them were illiterate. But through the sincerity of his preaching Wesley managed to have a tremendous effect on them and produced what was called the Cornish religious revival. He had a strong ethical influence on people, and he was something of an organizational genius. He would organize his followers into cells; they would have weekly meetings, and each member had to pay a penny a week into a fund. These weekly meetings were organized into groups: there was a sort of local chapter, as we would call it, and then a district and then something else; he built up a very systematic organization. He used to ride around inspecting people, and if anyone was backsliding, he struck their name off the register without hesitation. And of course he was always preaching at them, or to them. He seems to have been a very kindly old gentleman with great sincerity and enthusiasm, and he achieved quite a lot. The Methodists eventually became one of the biggest and most successful of the nonconformist denominations. Methodism did rather harden at the arteries later on, I would say, but it is still one of the larger churches in the United Kingdom, and in the United States and elsewhere in the world.

One thing to be learned from Wesley's life and example is that he directed his attention to people whom everybody else neglected; he went to the industrial slums as well as the Cornish mining areas. At that time there had been great shifts of population and there were vicars and bishops in places where there weren't many people, while in places where there were thousands of people there weren't any vicars or bishops. Wesley went where there were people, and they responded, appreciating his sincerity and the fact that he had gone out of his way to approach them when nobody else would. Perhaps we don't have people like that in the United Kingdom any longer, people living in degradation and thoroughly neglected by all the powers that be – not on that scale, anyway. He directed his attention to those people whom the ecclesiastical authorities wanted to avoid, people who were not respectable, people of whom others were even perhaps afraid. Wesley himself had to face hostility to the point of violence many a time, but he seems to have been able to overawe people by sheer force of personality. Not that he was a strong or overbearing person – he was a very kindly, gentle old man – but it seems that he was able to communicate something of his sincerity, so that he had a positive effect even on wild and violent people. He was never actually injured, as far as I remember. There is a multi-volume edition of his journal of his tours which is quite interesting.

Very concerned about the ethical aspect of life, he was very much against drunkenness and favoured virtues like thrift – rather unimaginative virtues in a way, but useful. He was in favour of literacy, and wrote and published a lot of simple books for newly-literate people. So he was concerned with social and educational work as well as religion. In modern Britain we don't have mass illiteracy any more, although there is the problem of alcoholism, of course, and drugs. It would seem that the problems that people suffer from in modern Britain, and perhaps in the modern West as a whole, are not so much problems of poverty or material deprivation as psychological problems, so perhaps if one were to have a mission of this type, it would need to be more to people who suffer psychologically. But you can't get people like that together in great masses; you have to approach them individually because of the nature of the problem. I must say I am a bit surprised sometimes that some of our Buddhist centres don't take more interest in the local community. I think we should try to do more in this way, not necessarily as a method of spreading Buddhism and making converts, as it were, but just out of human concern. If you were a doctor, rather than trying to treat all the patients yourself, it might be better to train up other doctors so that in the long run more sick people would get attention. Likewise, if you were a solitary Buddhist, you might do better to concentrate on training up others to teach, and this has been the policy of our movement so far. But we are beginning to reach a point where we have got quite a few doctors, so to speak, and perhaps we should start spreading ourselves more widely in the community. It's a sensible thing to do too, because it's prudent to be on friendly terms with the non-Buddhist people in whose midst you are living and functioning.

This concern for society is certainly one of the things we can learn from the Indian wing of our movement. I think every Western Order member who has gone there and has seen something of what is happening has been deeply impressed. Nagabodhi has recently written a book about it, and I think it's going to be quite an eye-opener.[110] After I come back from India, I sometimes find the movement in Britain quite dull in comparison. It seems strange that one has to work hard to stir up people's enthusiasm, especially when they are already Order members. Maybe one has to blame the British, or at least English, character.

The Campaign for Nuclear Disarmament is one thing about which people are enthusiastic in Britain, at least at the moment, but I got a tiny response to my lecture 'Buddhism, World Peace, and Nuclear War'.[111] It's not surprising – there's so much literature on the topic of nuclear war, and in some ways I haven't said anything new; the newness is the way I've linked the subject with Buddhism. But people's energies aren't engaged even in an issue like that in the same way that the energies of the Dalits are engaged with the issue of leaving Hinduism and becoming Buddhist, because in their case their disadvantages are felt every hour of the day, every day of the week. The only comparison would be if we were turfed out of our homes so that nuclear weapons could be installed there, and if we were reminded of that inconvenience every day.

Then we'd have a cause, then we'd have a grievance. So long as nuclear weapons are installed somewhere else, so that we don't see them and they don't affect our day-to-day life, we can easily forget all about them. The Dalits can't forget their grievances in this easy manner, because they are constantly being reminded of them by the way they're treated.

So what can Western Buddhists do to help? It would certainly help if suitable people did go to India from time to time, even to spend three or six months, but you would have to be prepared for a lot of culture shock and be ready to adapt and do whatever was needed, not go with too many ideas of your own. You'd have to be young and healthy, and pretty resilient. You'd have to know your Dharma fairly well, and also know the background, because if you went there not really knowing what the caste system is, you wouldn't be able to function. Order members in India love to have contact with Order members from the West, but to visit India you need to have a bit of understanding of the situation, a bit of sensitivity. Sometimes people have gone out there and been rather a nuisance, because they haven't realized that people are tremendously busy. Visitors may hope to be looked after, but they can't expect this.

On the other hand, the mere fact that people go is encouraging to our Indian Buddhist friends, because they feel very isolated. As Buddhists among the majority Hindu population, they feel that Hindus are very much against them, so they feel isolated in their own country. They feel that the Buddhist world doesn't care much about them either, so they are very happy to see Buddhists from overseas; indeed, they are desperate for contact with other Buddhists. It's a great encouragement to them to feel that there are other Buddhists who know about them and sympathize with them, and have a fellow feeling for them. They are encouraged and even inspired just to see a Western Buddhist among them, and if he or she can go around giving talks, that's even better.

But if you really want to help, probably the best thing you can do is to join a door-knocking appeal or send some money.[112] They still need a lot more money, especially for Dharma work. Not that lack of money is the only thing that is holding the development of Buddhism in India back. A lack of Indian Order members is holding it back even more. We've got work for probably a thousand Indian Order members, but we've only got about forty.[113] So the need is for personnel even more than for money, but money comes a good second, and money is easier to find, in a way.

I would like to see more contact between Indian Order members and Order members in the West, and eventually I'd like to see some of the Indian Order members coming over here.[114] At present, they just can't be spared; also, it's very expensive. Then there is the question of culture shock. We experience a bit of culture shock when we go to India, and they would certainly experience culture shock if they came to Britain, if only to see that people aren't so enthusiastic, perhaps, as they are. They would probably find it difficult to understand why people take things so easy here and why they are doing so little for the Dharma when they've got such good resources and have such an easy time. In many ways Order members in the West have more to learn from Order members in India than vice versa. That's not the way people usually think, but it is my settled conviction.

It's good that people in the West learn something about Dr Ambedkar and what he did, because if it wasn't for him and his work we probably wouldn't have any movement in India at all. I wrote my book *Ambedkar and Buddhism*[115] with no clear idea of who I was writing it for – to some extent, I wrote it for my own satisfaction – but if pressed, I would say that I wrote it for the Buddhist movement in the West, to give people a better understanding of the background of many of the people involved in our movement in India. I hope that people outside our community who have some interest in social conditions in India and therefore in the Dalits, or some interest in the revival of Buddhism in India, may also find this book helpful. It's quite shameful that so few people in the world know anything about the position of the Dalits in India. Everybody knows about apartheid in South Africa, but you hear hardly a word about the plight of the Dalits, which is in many ways worse, even though Untouchability is now illegal. Dr Ambedkar made it illegal when he framed the constitution.

One of the things Dr Ambedkar wasn't able to do was to leave a team of people behind him to carry on his work. He did have some very junior colleagues, but they soon started quarrelling among themselves after his death, and his movement split. For years and years there was no real Dharma teaching. The *bhikkhus* weren't equal to it, and neither was anybody else. Well, we've taken on that job, as it were, and those people we've been able to contact have responded very warmly. People from all over western and central India are asking us to send people to establish viharas and hostels, and offering us land, but we need more

Indian Order members to do the work. A lot of people just want to know more about the religion that they are supposed to have accepted.

I think it's important that those in our community in the West know something about the background of people who come into our movement in India, and no doubt it's important that people in India know something about the background of people here too. We need to have a movement that transcends national and cultural barriers. If we are limited to our own cultural context, we can't fully appreciate what it means to be an individual and to lead the spiritual life. It's not easy to transcend these barriers. Even in Britain we are conscious of the differences that exist north and south of the border, and if you go from Britain to India you will be struck by even greater differences of approach, but we have to transcend those differences and recognize that we are all following the same Dharma.

THE MASS CONVERSION AND THE YEARS AFTER: 1956–1969

The Diksha Bhumi, Nagpur

THE TIDE TURNS

Maha Bodhi, *October 1956*

Ever since the inception of the Maha Bodhi Society more than sixty years ago we have been accustomed to regard our work for the revival of Buddhism in India as constituting a hopelessly minority movement. Though as the decades went by more and more people acquired knowledge of and developed sympathy for the Dharma of the All-Enlightened and All-Compassionate One, it was but rarely that some courageous soul came forward and declared himself to be not merely a sympathizer with Buddhism but a Buddhist.

Mighty unseen forces were, however, all the time at work behind the visible framework of events, and when, shortly after the glorious day on which our country achieved independence, the Sacred Relics of the *arhants* Sāriputta and Mahāmoggallāna were brought back from London to be re-enshrined at the site whence they had been removed a century earlier, all India rose as one man to welcome them.[116]

Now comes the news that on the 14th of this month, which by a strange coincidence is the Vijayadashami day, the day which, according to Hindu mythology, commemorates the victory of the forces of light over the powers of darkness, one of our great national leaders will be converted to Buddhism together with hundreds of thousands of his followers.[117]

Let none think that Dr B. R. Ambedkar has taken this momentous step hastily or without due consideration, or that he has embarked upon this truly revolutionary course without full consciousness of its socio-religious implications and its far-reaching historical significance. It is perhaps five-and-twenty years since Dr Ambedkar first declared that though he had been born a Hindu he did not intend to die a Hindu.[118] Twenty-five years back is a big enough slice of anybody's life, and a period of time sufficiently long for the pondering even so momentous a step as the changing of one's religion. Brahminical clamours to the contrary notwithstanding, Dr Ambedkar knows what he is doing, and his followers know what they are doing, too.

Not theoretical considerations merely but their own bitter experience of all the unspeakable cruelty, the soul-searing injustice and systematic relentless inhumanity through the ages has eventually convinced them that Hinduism is incapable of reformation and that the only course now open to them is to break away from it and embrace Buddhism.

Within the Buddhist fold they will find not only social emancipation but, what is even more important, a way of life conducive to the attainment both of happiness here and hereafter and that unshakeable deliverance of mind which is the gist of the Buddha's teaching. They will also find the hand of brotherhood stretched out to them from every side, not only welcoming but assisting and supporting them as they make their first step along the Noble Eightfold Path.

When, on the coming Vijayadashami day, the lion-hearted leader and his followers make that momentous step forward, a threefold shout of 'Sadhu!!!' will surely rise from every part of the Buddhist world and be taken up by the *devas* and other celestial beings and echoed from heaven to heaven until finally it reaches the foot of the Throne of Enlightenment; and those who labour in the heat of the day in the field of Buddhist revival in India, hearing that shout, will pause a moment in their work, and know, with joy in their hearts, that at last the tide has turned.[119]

A WHIRLING PROGRAMME AT NAGPUR

Written by A. R. Kulkarni, Nagpur[120] *on 27 December 1956*

THURSDAY 6 DECEMBER 1956

It was a strange coincidence that Venerable Bhikshu Sangharakshita of Kalimpong happened to be at Nagpur on 6 December 1956, the date of death of Dr B. R. Ambedkar. Although his visit was prearranged it was never thought that he would be at Nagpur to mourn the death of Baba Saheb Ambedkar along with the people of Nagpur which he had already visited about two years back and where he had delivered several lectures on Buddhism. His visit at this moment was quite opportune and could be said to be God-sent. It should here be remembered that the memorable event, viz. the conversion of about half a million of people into Buddhism, took place at Nagpur on 14 October 1956 on the Dasera or Vijayadashami day as it is called. The people of Nagpur naturally cherished that event, which was quite fresh in their minds.

On his arrival at Nagpur by the Bombay–Calcutta mail on 6 December at about 11.30 a.m. the Venerable Bhikshu was received at the station by Shri Waman Rao Godbole, the secretary of the Nagpur Branch of the Buddhist Society of India, and was taken to the residence of Shri A. R. Kulkarni in Dharampeth. At about 1.15 p.m. a written message was received which read as follows:

Rev. Sangharakshita,
We have lost our revered Baba. I am today proceeding to Bombay for his funeral.
(Sd) W. M. Godbole

It was a great shock to us all. In no time the gloom spread over the whole of Nagpur. Myself and Venerable Bhikshu Sangharakshita sent telegrams to Mrs Ambedkar condoling the death. The previously arranged meeting in the Kothari Mansion which was to be addressed by the Venerable Bhikshu Sangharakshita was of course cancelled.

In the evening at 6 p.m. a huge mass meeting was held in the Kasturchand Park under the Presidentship of Shri Sakharam Meshram, an eminent Buddhist advocate, to pay homage to the memory of Dr B. R. Ambedkar, or Baba as he was popularly known. The meeting was attended by over 50,000 people, mostly Buddhists. The meeting was originally scheduled to take place in the Chitnavis Park, which is in the heart of Nagpur city. Apprehending that the Chitnavis Park would be insufficient to accommodate the huge crowd that would be participating in the meeting the organizers shifted it to the Kasturchand Park. Though there was no time to announce the time and place of the meeting the people poured into the Kasturchand Park like a regular stream. The torch procession which came from the side of the city was a sight for the gods to see. The people of Nagpur had last seen Baba on 14 October on the occasion of the mass conversion ceremony. That function was still ringing in their ears and in grateful remembrance of it they flocked in large numbers to pay homage to Baba's memory. The processionists were regularly reciting *tisaraṇa*, namely *Buddhaṃ saraṇaṃ gacchāmi, Dhammaṃ saraṇaṃ gacchāmi, Saṅghaṃ saraṇaṃ gacchāmi*, the immortal mantra which Baba had given to them at Nagpur on 14 October 1956.

The huge crowd that had gathered in the Kasturchand Park was in a mourning mood. The people had lost their shepherd and were therefore helpless. The death of Baba had created a void in their minds. But this void was to a certain extent made good when they noticed Venerable Sangharakshita, the English *bhikṣu* from Kalimpong, in the customary yellow robe, in their midst. Though no dais was prepared for the meeting, Venerable Bhikshu Sangharakshita was seated on the cushion seat of a rickshaw so that he might be visible to the huge crowd that had gathered to pay homage to Dr B. R. Ambedkar. The condolence meeting commenced with the Venerable Bhikshu administering *tisaraṇa* and *pañcasīla* to those assembled.[121] A half-masked portrait of Dr B. R. Ambedkar which was hung on a small tree was then garlanded. Several institutions and persons paid their homage to the Baba. Shri A. R. Kulkarni on behalf of the Buddha Society of Nagpur also spoke a few words. In fact the people had not come to make speeches. The typical homage was paid by Shri Kawade, President of the Buddhist Society of Nagpur. As he rose to speak he was tottering along and he could not even stand. His voice was choked up and with tears flowing from his eyes he said, 'A brilliant star appeared on the horizon and has vanished, vanished, vanished.'

But Venerable Bhikshu Sangharakshita, who was the last to speak, in his speech said, 'Dr B. R. Ambedkar is not dead. He still lives in your hearts – and the work that he did. Dr Ambedkar commenced the work of reviving Buddhism in the land of its birth and that work has devolved on us all and to walk in the path shown by him is true homage paid to him.' The Venerable Bhikshu further said that the climax of Dr Ambedkar's work was the conversion of lakhs of people into Buddhism at Nagpur and that 'he will shine more gloriously after his death'. The *bhikṣu* spoke in English and his speech was rendered into Marathi by Shri A. R. Kulkarni, who acted as his interpreter in all the subsequent programmes at Nagpur. Shri Meshram, the President, offered his homage to Baba Saheb, after which the meeting came to a close at about 10 p.m. It was clear that new spirit had been infused into the people, who dispersed with a grim determination to carry ahead the work of Dr Ambedkar. The meeting had adopted a resolution condoling the death of Dr B. R. Ambedkar, all standing for five minutes.

FRIDAY 7 DECEMBER 1956

This was observed as a day of dedication to the memory of B. R. Ambedkar by the labourers of Nagpur. These people went in a procession through the principal streets of Nagpur. The processionists carried the portrait of Lord Buddha and Dr Ambedkar with them and were regularly reciting Trisharan and Panchshil. The procession terminated at the conversion ground near the Vaccination Depot or Mata Kacheri as it is called. Precisely on the spot where Dr B. R. Ambedkar took the *diksha* (Sanskrit *dīkṣā*) on 14 October at the hands of the Venerable Bhikshu Chandramani, a wooden pole on which a Buddhist flag was hung was fixed in the ground. This had become a sacred place to the Buddhists, who therefore made it their rallying point. The people were seen wearing black bands in token of their mourning mood. At 3 p.m. a meeting was held on the conversion ground. To begin with the Venerable Bhikshu Sangharakshita administered *tisaraṇa* and *pañcasīla* to the people and then in a short speech explained the meaning of *diksha* or initiation. He also explained the meaning of Buddha, Dharma, and Sangha and laid particular emphasis on implementing the work begun by Dr Ambedkar. The gathering consisted of about 50,000 to 60,000 people, both male and female combined.

In the evening there was another public meeting in the Kasturchand Park. This gathering was bigger than the gathering of 6 December. About a lakh of people attended this meeting. The people were gradually realizing that Dr B. R. Ambedkar had left a definite programme for them and they were therefore anxious to know about it from Bhikshu Sangharakshita. The meeting commenced with the Bhikshu administering *tisaraṇa* and *pañcasīla* to the gathering. He then delivered a short speech in which he urged the importance of unity. Several persons garlanded the portrait of Bhagwan Buddha and Dr Ambedkar. Bhajan parties recited bhajans in praise of the Buddha. We left this meeting at about 10 p.m.

SATURDAY 8 DECEMBER 1956

Venerable Bhikshu Sangharakshita paid a visit at 8 a.m. to the Nagpur Branch of the Buddhist Society of India, Kothari Mansion, Sitabuldi, Nagpur. Shri Panchbai explained to the Bhikshu the steps the Society had taken to acquire the conversion ground as they proposed to erect a suitable memorial on it.

At about 9 a.m. the Venerable Bhikshu attended a public meeting at Indora held to pay homage to the memory of Dr B. R. Ambedkar. In his speech the Bhikshu explained the necessity of propagating Buddhism.

The Venerable Bhikshu and Shri A. R. Kulkarni were then entertained to a sumptuous dinner by Shri Gondana. After this the Bhikshu paid a visit to the library in Indora. There was a great demand for Pāli classes among the younger generation and this was a matter of satisfaction. The Bhikshu then spent some time in the office of the local branch of the Buddhist Society answering questions put to him. Here the Bhikshu explained the meaning of *oṃ maṇi padme hūṃ*.[122]

At 6 p.m. the Venerable Bhikshu Sangharakshita delivered a lecture on 'Buddhism and Culture' in the meeting room of the Nagpur University Building under the Presidentship of Shri K. T. Mangalmurti, ICS, Vice-Chancellor, Nagpur University. This was lecture no. 4 in the University Extension Lecture Series. To begin with the Vice-Chancellor garlanded a portrait of Dr B. R. Ambedkar and moved a resolution condoling the death of Dr B. R. Ambedkar which was adopted, all standing for five minutes. The Vice-Chancellor then introduced the speaker and requested him to deliver his speech. The learned Bhikshu in his speech said that it was wrong to suppose that Buddha was against art and culture. He quoted chapter and verse to support this statement. In fact that which ennobles the mind is the best art and from that point of view the Buddhist art stood supreme in the world, said the Bhikshu. The President in his concluding speech paid a glowing tribute to the learned Bhikshu. Shri A. R. Kulkarni then thanked the Venerable Bhikshu for his learned and illuminating lecture and also the Vice-Chancellor and the Nagpur University for having arranged the lecture under its auspices and thus afforded the public an opportunity to hear the Bhikshu. This meeting terminated at about 7.30 p.m.

At about 8 p.m. a public meeting was held in Gaddigodam to pay homage to the memory of Dr B. R. Ambedkar. The Venerable Bhikshu Sangharakshita administered *tisaraṇa* and *pañcasīla* to the gathering. Shri Kawada and Shri A. R. Kulkarni spoke explaining the significance of Dr Ambedkar's work. The Bhikshu in his speech urged upon the gathering to be united and carry on the work of Dr Ambedkar unitedly. The meeting terminated at about 10.30 p.m.

SUNDAY 9 DECEMBER 1956

At about 8 a.m. the Venerable Bhikshu was entertained to tea and light refreshments by Shri G. G. Kulkarni, nephew of Shri A. R. Kulkarni.

By now the fame of the English Bhikshu had spread far and wide and the people were anxious to fix his programme in their own locality. Many were also anxious to receive *diksha* at his hands. Consequently at the instance of the people of Lashkari Bagh a mass conversion function was arranged at 9 a.m. The people had created a beautiful rostrum for the occasion. The Bhikshu took his seat on it. It was also a function to pay homage to Dr Ambedkar. Two portraits, one of Bhagwan Buddha and the other of Dr Ambedkar, were placed in front of the rostrum and several persons garlanded them. The Bhikshu then administered *tisaraṇa* and *pañcasīla* to the people and in addition the twenty-two vows formulated by Dr B. R. Ambedkar were also administered. These additional vows consisted in abstaining from worshipping Ram and Krishna and other traditional Hindu deities like Gauri and Ganesh and doing any act which would be contrary to the Buddhist faith. These were in fact meant as a safeguard against the new entrants lapsing into the traditional mode of worship. In his speech the Bhikshu explained the significance of *diksha* and urged upon them the necessity of implementing the vows in their lives. While the speech was going on it was brought to the notice of the Bhikshu that about a thousand more persons from the neighbouring village had arrived at the place of the meeting and were keen to receive *diksha* at his hands. As the meal was ready and as it was nearly 11 a.m. it was thought advisable to finish the meal. The people were therefore asked to wait. The newly arrived people were given *diksha* at about 12.30 p.m. in the formal manner.

At 3 p.m. a public meeting was held at Vakil Peth to pay homage to Dr B. R. Ambedkar. The people had erected a special rostrum for the Bhikshu to sit. Though the gathering was small the function was neat and clean. As usual the meeting commenced with the Bhikshu administering *tisaraṇa* and *pañcasīla* to those assembled. In the course of his speech the Venerable Bhikshu explained the meaning of Sangha. He said that Sangha meant the Bhikshu Sangha wearing the yellow robe. And since the Sangha was preaching the Dharma of the Buddha it was the duty of the laity to honour them, to hear the Dharma from them, and to be guided by them.[123] The function came to a close at about 4.30 p.m.

The Bhikshu then attended the function at Siraspeth. It was both a homage and a *diksha* function. This function commenced at 5 p.m. and lasted up to 6 p.m. To begin with the Bhikshu administered *tisaraṇa*, *pañcasīla*, and the twenty-two special vows formulated by Dr Ambedkar. The Bhikshu then made a short speech in which he explained the meaning of *diksha* and the best way to pay homage to Dr Ambedkar. The best way to pay homage to their leader was to carry on his work with unabated vigour, declared the English Bhikshu.

The venerable Bhikshu then attended a public meeting held in the Shivanand Hall of the Ramakrishna Mission at Nagpur. The hall was packed to the full and the people had occupied every available space in the veranda outside. The meeting was scheduled to begin at 6.15 p.m. and the Bhikshu arrived precisely at 6.14 p.m., maintaining punctuality typical of an Englishman. The subject of the lecture was 'Buddha's conception of Nirvāṇa and the way to attain it'. Swami Vyomanand of the Rama Krishna Ashram presided over the meeting. After the Bhikshu was introduced by the President the Bhikshu made his speech. It was in fact a regular religious discourse. In his fluent and forceful speech the learned Bhikshu pointed out that Nirvāṇa could not be described in words as it was beyond words and description. The learned Bhikshu pointed out that the bodhisattva ideal was the right ideal in life. The bodhisattva in fact lived for humanity, sacrificing his comforts and even his life for humanity. The audience, which was English-knowing, listened with rapt attention to the speech of the learned Bhikshu. The speech was both an intellectual and a spiritual feast to the people of Nagpur. The meeting was over at 8 p.m.

At 8.30 p.m. the Bhikshu attended a public meeting held in the Indora Primary School, under the auspices of the Indora Education Society. In his speech the Bhikshu laid stress on education as a step towards fullness of life. The meeting was over at 9.30 p.m.

The Bhikshu then attended a huge mass meeting at Bhankheda at about 10.30 p.m. It was attended by over 5,000 people who were sitting on open ground unmindful of the bitter winter cold, only to have a *darshan* of the Bhikshu and listen to his words. To begin with the Bhikshu administered *tisaraṇa* and *pañcasīla* to the people assembled. In the speech that followed he inculcated upon the people the necessity of carrying further the work of revival of Buddhism commenced by Dr B. R. Ambedkar, and that was true homage to him, said the Bhikshu. We were then treated to tea. We returned home at about midnight.

MONDAY 10 DECEMBER 1956

The day commenced with a public meeting at Dharampeth at about 8.30 a.m. The Bhikshu administered *tisaraṇa* and *pañcasīla* to the people assembled and delivered a short speech pointing out the advantages that were implicit in taking refuge in the Buddha, whose message had a universal significance.

At 2.30 p.m. the Bhikshu addressed the students of the Swastik High School, Lashkari Bagh. In his speech the Bhikshu pointed out that the student's life was the period when the foundations of a citizen's life were laid. It was difficult, the Bhikshu said, to correct an old man as he was very firm in his views. But that was not the case with boys who had an open mind, and therefore, if right views are inculcated on them they would get a right direction in their lives. From that point of view the *tisaraṇa* and *pañcasīla* had a great significance to them. The Bhikshu was then entertained to light tea by the school authorities.

The Bhikshu then addressed the students of the Kurve High School, Sitabuldi, Nagpur at about 4.30 p.m. He told the students to understand the implications of Buddhism. Buddha was the only personality of which they could be legitimately proud, declared the Bhikshu. Buddhism was undoubtedly reviving in India after a lapse of about a thousand years. He told the students that if Buddhism revives in India then it revives in the whole world and that was the reason why he himself, though an Englishman, was striving to revive Buddhism in India.

At 6 p.m. the Bhikshu proceeded to Shanti Nagar, a suburb of Nagpur mostly inhabited by Buddhists. Here the entire locality was in festive mood. Their joy knew no bounds when they learnt that a *bhikṣu* was coming to their locality with a message of the Buddha. The people were now conscious that Dr Ambedkar lived in them in the message that he had given to them. Though the meeting was originally organized with the idea of paying homage to Dr Ambedkar the people thought that the best way to do it was to take refuge in the Buddha, Dharma, and Sangha. So those who had not taken the *diksha* on 14 October 1956 decided to do so now. The people were therefore in a festive mood. They had cleaned their houses and courtyards and had decorated them with beautiful designs made out of powdered sandstone. They had constructed a beautiful rostrum for the Bhikshu to sit. The gathering, which consisted of about 3,000 persons, both male and female, was highly disciplined. The Bhikshu was naturally impressed by the enthusiasm of the people and the systematic way in which they were conducting the proceedings of the meeting. He administered *tisaraṇa* and *pañcasīla* and the twenty-two special precepts formulated by Dr Ambedkar and thus initiated them into Buddhism.

He then delivered a short speech in which he explained the meaning of Buddha, Dharma, and Sangha. Buddha was not a god or an incarnation of God, declared the Bhikshu. He was a human being like any other human being. But by his own efforts he had eliminated lust, greed, and hatred from himself and had become a fully Enlightened person and was therefore a teacher of men and gods. We therefore look upon him as a guide and no more. Dharma is the path shown by the Buddha, and Sangha meant the *bhikṣus* wearing the yellow robes who preach the Dharma taught by the Buddha. The Bhikshu then visited the Library in Shanti Nagar and expressed satisfaction at the work done by the people in reviving interest in Buddhism.

At 7.30 p.m. the Bhikshu attended a small function in the Timki locality of Nagpur city. The function was organized by the people of the locality to pay homage to Dr B. R. Ambedkar's memory. To begin with the Bhikshu administered *tisaraṇa* and *pañcasīla* to those assembled. This was followed by a short speech in which the Bhikshu explained the meaning of true homage. True homage was paid not merely by offering flowers but by following in the footsteps of Dr Ambedkar, declared the Bhikshu. It was therefore incumbent on them to understand, study, and spread Buddhism. He therefore urged the intellectual youths to create *bhikṣus* from amidst them, who could do the work of propagating Buddhism.

At 8.30 p.m. the Bhikshu attended a well-attended function in New Shukarwari, organized to pay homage to Dr B. R. Ambedkar. It was now getting late and we had yet five more programmes before us. We doubted if it could be possible for us to finish them all. But the enthusiasm we noticed amongst the people inspired us to carry them out without dropping a single one. This meeting as usual commenced with the Bhikshu administering *tisaraṇa* and *pañcasīla* to the people assembled. In a short speech that followed the Bhikshu pointed out vividly the greatness of the work of Dr Ambedkar which consisted in making them self-reliant in their lives. Self-reliance was the keynote of Dr Ambedkar's work.

Then there was a small function at Utkhana at about 9 p.m. attended by about 500 persons. The fact was that every locality of Nagpur wanted to avail of the presence of the Bhikshu and was keen on having him in its midst. The people thought that the Bhikshu was a link between them and their departed Baba. The function in Utkhana, as most functions, commenced with the Bhikshu administering *tisaraṇa* and *pañcasīla* to the gathering. It was followed by a short speech in which the Bhikshu explained the meaning of true homage.

9.30 p.m. The Bhikshu then attended a well-attended function in Kumbharpina near the orange market. Here the gathering was pretty big. It might be about 2,000 persons. The people here were keen on receiving *diksha* at the hands of the Bhikshu. The Bhikshu initiated them into Buddhism by administering *tisaraṇa*, *pañcasīla*, and the twenty-two special vows formulated by B. R. Ambedkar. In a brief speech the Bhikshu explained the meaning of Buddha, Dharma, and Sangha.

10 p.m. The Bhikshu then attended a small function in Khalasi Lines. Here, about one hundred persons received *diksha* at the hands of the Bhikshu, who formally initiated them into Buddhism. In a brief speech the Bhikshu explained the significance of taking *diksha*.

10.30 p.m. The Bhikshu then attended a function at Siddhartha Nagar. This function was organized to pay homage to Dr Ambedkar. The Bhikshu administered *tisaraṇa* and *pañcasīla* to the people and explained to them the true way of paying homage.

11.30 p.m. All the above functions were at Nagpur. The last but the most important function was arranged by the people of Kamptee, a place about ten miles from Nagpur. We went in a taxi to Kamptee and reached that place at about 11.30 p.m. We noticed that about 20,000 people were anxious to receive *diksha* at the hands of Venerable Bhikshu Sangharakshita. In fact we already knew that people from the neighbouring villages had come to Kamptee for the *diksha* ceremony. We were, therefore, equally anxious to avail of the function and since it was the last function of the day we were no longer troubled by the thoughts of having to attend another function. We were in a way glad that we had kept up every engagement and that circumstance made us buoyant. The determination with which the people were sitting for hours together exposing themselves to the shivering cold of the winter created a deep impression on our minds and we were glad that we could witness such a spectacle rarely to be seen in life. The people had erected a beautiful rostrum for the occasion. To begin with the Bhikshu administered *tisaraṇa*, *pañcasīla*, and the twenty-two additional vows formulated by Dr Ambedkar. The Bhikshu then delivered a short speech in which he explained the meaning of Buddha, Dharma, and Sangha. He further pointed out to the huge gathering that the best way of paying homage to Dr Ambedkar was by following in his footsteps and not by merely offering flowers. The meeting terminated at about 12.30 a.m. We had now stepped into the morning of the next day i.e. 11 December. After this function the Bhikshu was shown the Old Shio Temple in which the image of the Buddha was installed at my hands about a year back. The Bhikshu then conferred his blessings on the gathering and we came to Nagpur at about 2.30 a.m.

TUESDAY 11 DECEMBER 1956

8.30 a.m. The Bhikshu addressed the students of the Yugantar High School Sadar. The Bhikshu asked the boys to cherish and be proud of the Buddha. Buddha and Buddhism was the richest and noblest heritage of Bharat and that was the reason why the people of India had adopted Ashok-chakra as the emblem of their nation.[124]

10 a.m. The Bhikshu then paid a visit to the Medical College Hospital, Nagpur, and blessed Shrimati Tara Joshi, daughter of Dr D. R. Kulkarni, and her newborn baby.

Bhikshu Sangharakshita left Nagpur by Calcutta Mail at about 11.40 a.m. Mr M. Y. Koli had come to the station.

DR AMBEDKAR

Maha Bodhi, *January 1957*

The death of Dr Ambedkar, at the comparatively early age of sixty-five, has come as a shock not only to his followers but to Buddhists all over the world. Only six weeks earlier, on 14 October, he had launched a major social and religious revolution by taking the Three Refuges and Five Precepts at Nagpur together with half a million of his supporters. On that historic occasion he spoke with all his accustomed fire and brilliance. Again, when he addressed the inaugural assembly of the World Fellowship of Buddhists at Kathmandu on 15 November, despite his obvious bodily weakness few who heard him could have thought that the end of one of the most colourful careers of modern times was so close at hand. After going on pilgrimage to the holy places Dr Ambedkar returned to his home at Delhi. On 5 December he finished writing the Preface to his book on Buddhism, working far into the night. Next day, the servant who took him his early tea found him dead. His last waking thoughts must have been of the Buddha.

Born into an Untouchable family of Maharashtra, Bhimrao Ambedkar experienced very early in life the soul-sickening cruelty and injustice of the socio-religious system under which he had had the misfortune to be born. Forced to drink foul water, refused food and drink for days together, thrown out of a public vehicle in which he had dared to seat his polluting carcase, stoned and beaten when he ventured to protest, humiliated at school, where he was relegated to a corner and where caste Hindu teachers refused to touch his copybooks, grim and terrible were the memories of Hinduism with which he grew up. Unlike his millions of oppressed brethren, however, he was not destined to suffer in silence. As he grew in years and experience, and as, despite heart-breaking difficulties, he gradually carved out for himself a place in the political life of the nation, he became more and more outspoken in his condemnation of the evils of caste. The harsh unpalatable truths he uttered naturally awakened the fierce resentment and implacable hatred of the champions of orthodoxy, who till the end of his days treated him as their sworn enemy. Tens of millions of Scheduled Caste people, however, hailed him as their leader and saviour. But not even at the height of his power, not even when as Minister of Law and Justice of the central government he drafted the Constitution and the Hindu Code Bill, did either his friends or his enemies realize how wide and how deep his influence extended. That became apparent only on 14 October and afterwards. A lifelong student of religions, Dr Ambedkar had step by step come to the conclusion that orthodoxy was incapable of reformation, and that the victims of age-old socio-religious oppression and exploitation in India could be freed from their disabilities only by embracing Buddhism. Towards this consummation he gradually bent more and more of his energies. Some, even among his own people, opposed him, feeling perhaps that no mere 'religion' could solve a problem of such tremendous complexity. But Dr Ambedkar's faith in Buddhism stood firm as a rock. With characteristic boldness, he declared that he was going to become a Buddhist even if nobody else became one. But when the time for taking the momentous step actually came, far from taking it alone he carried hundreds of thousands with him. All over India, wherever the name of Dr Ambedkar was honoured, people gathered in their thousands and in their tens of thousands to take refuge in the Buddha, the Dharma, and the Sangha.

Before the movement of mass conversion could reach its height Dr Ambedkar, worn out by the labours of a lifetime, died. Some there were who thought that with his death the movement would come to an end, or at least receive a serious setback. Never were prophets more false. The ashes of his funeral pyre were hardly cold before the movement gathered a momentum beyond the expectations even of the most wildly optimistic. Nay, even as all that was mortal of him was consigned to the flames the sacred chant *Buddhaṃ saraṇaṃ gacchāmi* rose spontaneously from the lips of the tens of thousands of mourners assembled there. Since then reports have come in of mass conversion ceremonies at Nagpur, Poona, Ahmedabad, Agra, and a score of other important centres. Great as Dr Ambedkar's influence was during life evidently it is greater still in death.

The disciplined courage and enthusiasm which Dr Ambedkar's followers have displayed since their great leader's demise should not cause us to think that the movement can be safely left to look after itself. Repetition of the Three Refuges and Five Precepts is not by itself sufficient to make one a Buddhist. One must put the Three Refuges and Five Precepts into practice in one's life. But practice proceeds from understanding, and understanding depends upon proper instruction. Unless the Buddhist countries come forward with at least a few hundred full-time *dharmadūta* workers, preferably *bhikkhus*, there is every danger that the movement so gloriously inaugurated by Dr Ambedkar will not be properly consolidated. Organizations which have no trained personnel to spare should at least contribute funds for the publication of books and pamphlets in Hindi, Marathi, and other languages. But under no circumstances should the Buddhist world fail to do its duty by those who are struggling towards the light of Buddhism after dwelling for centuries in darkness. There is no better way for any of us to honour the memory of Dr Ambedkar than by devoting ourselves to the continuation of his work.[125]

A GREAT INJUSTICE

Maha Bodhi, *July 1957*

One of the greatest events of the 2500th Buddha Jayanti year was, undoubtedly, the conversion to Buddhism of the late Dr B. R. Ambedkar together with hundreds of thousands of his followers. Certain interested parties have questioned the genuineness of a change of faith affecting such a vast number of people. But those who, under Dr Ambedkar's guidance, took the *tisaraṇa* and *pañcasīla* at Nagpur on 14 October last year did not change their convictions overnight. For years Dr Ambedkar and a handful of devoted henchmen had been endeavouring to impress upon the minds and hearts of the 'Untouchables' the fact that only in Buddhism was there to be found a spiritual force strong enough to effect their all-round amelioration, and slowly but surely their efforts bore fruit. Even after the tragically sudden demise of the lion-hearted leader the great movement of mass conversion did not slacken off. Indeed it increased in momentum. This fact alone should be sufficient to convince even the most sceptical that we have to deal, not with a 'political stunt', as some of them tried to make out at the beginning, but with the greatest spiritual upheaval that India has known in modern times.

But even spiritual upheavals take place within a specific socio-economic framework. The Neo-Buddhists, as they are now generally styled (the term meaning not those who follow a new form of Buddhism, but simply those who have newly become Buddhists) are drawn almost entirely from what are officially known as the Scheduled Castes, Scheduled Tribes, and Other Backward Classes, or in other words, from those people, numbering between seventy and eighty millions, whom the orthodox Hindus have for centuries despised and ill-treated as outcastes and untouchables. Recognizing that on account of generations of systematic degradation and social persecution these Depressed Classes, as they were also called, stood in need of special consideration, the Indian Government granted them, though on a small scale, certain special political and educational facilities. Among these facilities were scholarships for deserving Untouchable students. The Constitution envisaged their continuation for a period of ten years from the date of its promulgation.

Now, however, comes the news that the Government of India and the State Government of Bombay (the State in which the majority of Neo-Buddhists are to be found) have decreed that on becoming Buddhists the Neo-Buddhists shall automatically forfeit the facilities to which as members of the Scheduled Caste communities they were formerly entitled. When an Untouchable renounces Hinduism he does, of course, cease to be an Untouchable at the same time that he ceases to be a Hindu, for from its very inception Buddhism has resolutely refused to countenance the inhumanity that, in the name of religion, degrades a fellow human being to a level lower than that of a beast. But change of religion is not necessarily synonymous with an immediate improvement of socio-economic conditions. By getting themselves converted to Buddhism the Scheduled Caste people have not automatically become rich, well educated, and respected. The vast majority of them continue to live as they have lived for centuries – in poverty, ignorance, and ignominy. The only difference is that while as Hindus they lived without hope, as Buddhists they live full of hope, for Buddhism tells them, not that they have been born Untouchables as a result of sins committed in past lives and that unquestioning submission to the insults of the caste Hindus is the only means of expiation, but that they are the masters of their own fate, the architects of their own destiny, and that by right effort every man can become the peer of the Buddha.

Since the socio-economic conditions of the Neo-Buddhists are the same as they were before their conversion it is difficult to understand why the Central Government and the State Government of Bombay should have discontinued even the meagre facilities that they were formerly enjoying. One would have thought that the government of a secular state would have welcomed the opportunity of continuing to help a socially and economically backward section of the community without having to place itself in the anomalous position of recognizing *de facto* those very caste distinctions which it does not recognize *de jure*. By discontinuing the scholarships and other educational concessions of such Scheduled Castes students as become Buddhists the Government of India and the State of Bombay have in fact discriminated against Buddhism in favour of Hinduism. They have indirectly encouraged Untouchability. They have set a premium on social injustice and inequality.

We sincerely hope that the damage so far done is not irreparable and that saner counsels may in the end prevail. In celebrating the 2500th anniversary of the *parinirvāṇa* of the Lord Buddha the Government of India set an example to the whole world. It would be a thousand pities if the Buddha Jayanti celebrations should be followed up by an action which seems strangely like a deliberate attempt to discourage people from trying to put into practice the very principles which those celebrations were intended to recall. Unless the educational concessions to which, as members of a still backward community, the Neo-Buddhists continue to be entitled are promptly restored to them, certain national leaders will find it hard to escape the charge of paying lip sympathy to Buddhism for purposes other than strictly religious.

Whether the Neo-Buddhists continue to enjoy the same social and economic concessions after conversion as they enjoyed before, or whether they do not, of one thing all those concerned would do well to be assured: that the movement of mass conversion started by Dr Ambedkar cannot be halted or even checked. Surely it is not too much to expect that after treating the Untouchables with cruelty for centuries the majority community will now at least refrain from attempting, however vainly, to frustrate their efforts to achieve not merely a higher standard of living but a better standard of life. By helping the Neo-Buddhists at the present juncture the caste Hindus will be sowing the seeds of future friendship. By renewing their efforts to harm they will only enlarge the gulf of hatred and misunderstanding which is already alarmingly wide.

DIKSHA BHUMI

Maha Bodhi, *July 1959*

On 14 October 1956, the greatest religious revolution which India has seen in modern times took place when the late Dr B. R. Ambedkar of revered memory, was publicly initiated into Buddhism by the Ven. Chandramani Maha Sthavira[126] along with half a million of his followers. It is now a matter of history that the great movement of Buddhist revival thus inaugurated has since swept over the whole of central and western India, besides penetrating into many other parts of the great subcontinent and despite the tragically sudden demise of the lion-hearted leader shortly after his conversion it continues to make tremendous progress.

It is only natural that, to those who received the light from Dr Ambedkar, as well as to fellow Buddhists all over the world, the Diksha Bhumi, or Initiation Ground, as the spot where the historic event took place is now universally known, should be regarded as a place of pilgrimage, 'with odours visited and annual flowers'.[127] Natural, too, is their desire that on that spot, hallowed by so many memories, should be erected not only a worthy memorial to Dr Ambedkar but also Viharas and other institutions which would further the cause of Buddhism in India.

Since the land in question belongs to the Bombay State Government no difficulty was anticipated in connection with its acquisition. However, it is reported that despite vigorous pressing of their claim by the newly initiated Buddhists and other interested persons, the Bombay State

Government refuses to grant more than the tiny plot on which stands an obelisk, erected shortly after the conversion ceremony, to mark the exact spot on which Dr Ambedkar stood when he accepted the Three Refuges and Five Precepts. The excuse given is that the land in question is required for an agricultural college.

That an agricultural college in Nagpur is a desideratum, even a necessity, may be freely admitted; but alternative plots no less suitable for the purpose are easily available. The religious sentiment which attaches to the Diksha Bhumi, on the other hand, cannot be transferred to any other piece of land, however convenient. We therefore earnestly hope that the Bombay State Government will graciously accede to the legitimate request of the Indian Buddhists by handing over to them the fifty or sixty acres of land which to them constitute the hub of the great wheel of revival of the Dharma set revolving by their intrepid leader.[128]

PREACHING TOURS 1958–1961

Extract from Triyana Vardhana Vihara, Kalimpong Report 1957–1962 (published in Kalimpong in 1963).[129] *The report is written by Sangharakshita, although it refers to him ('the Bhikshu') in the third person. Interspersed with the text of the report are transcripts of Sangharakshita's handwritten notes for a number of the talks given on the tours. Please bear in mind that we don't know how closely he followed his notes when giving the talks, but they are included here to give an idea of the sort of thing he said. We have added endnotes to enlarge on points where that seemed justified, but some points will have to remain mysterious matters of conjecture. We have been able to link many of the sets of notes to the occasions on which the talks were given, but guesswork has been involved in a few cases, and some of the notes do not include a place or date.*

FIRST TOUR

On 6 December, which was the second anniversary of the death of Dr B. R. Ambedkar, the Bhikshu addressed several meetings in Nagpur and paid tribute to the memory of the great leader who had been responsible for the conversion of the Depressed Classes to Buddhism. The most important of these meetings was the one held at the Diksha Ground where on the memorable Dasera Day of 1956, namely on 14 October, Dr B. R. Ambedkar had taken his *diksha* at the hands of the Ven. Chandramani Maha Sthavira of Kusinara along with several lakhs of his followers. Thousands of people had gathered at this historic site to pay their homage to the late 'Baba Saheb'. In his speech the Bhikshu eulogized the work of the late Baba Saheb and paid homage to his memory, pointing out that true homage consisted in carrying out the work of propagation of the Dharma in a resolute and united manner. He also addressed meetings at Dharampeth, Humpyard, Kurve's Model High School, Sitabuldi, and Kamptee.

The Bhikshu's first preaching tour in the plains occupied the greater part of February and March, 1959, and took him to Nagpur, Bombay, and Poona. On his arrival at Nagpur on 3 February from Sarnath he was received at the station by Shri A. R. Kulkarni and Shri W. R. Godbole of the Bharatiya Bauddha Maha Sabha and others. During his short stay of about six days Bhikshu Sangharakshita addressed several meetings.

Leaving Nagpur on the morning of 7 February Bhikshu Sangharakshita went to Manegaon, a village about sixty miles from

Nagpur, accompanied by Shri W. R. Godbole, Shri A. R. Kulkarni and others. At Manegaon he was accorded a reception by the Buddhists of the place and blessed the handing over of a piece of land to the Bharatiya Bauddha Mahasabha for the construction of a Vihara. From Manegaon he proceeded to Singori, walking a distance of about five miles, and addressed a huge meeting of the Buddhists who had gathered at Singori. The Bhikshu expounded the Dharma and stressed the necessity of unity among the Buddhists.

ARE HINDUISM AND BUDDHISM THE SAME?: LECTURE NOTES

People are perplexed about this question, but we should understand clearly. It's strange that those who say they are the same object to the conversion to Buddhism. If they are the same, why object? There must be some ulterior motive, an attempt to stifle Buddhism.

Various arguments are made: 'Same words, different meanings'; 'The Buddha did not start a new religion'. 'In Magadha'. Brahmajāla Sutta. *His words to Subhadra.*[130]

Hinduism and Buddhism are different. There is more difference between them than there is between Hinduism, Christianity, and Islam. Buddhism stands alone.

God	*No God*
Incarnation/prophet	*Teacher*
Revealed Book	*Tripiṭaka*
Faith	*Understanding*
Conflict with science	*No conflict*
bhakti	maitrī
grace	*self-help*
inequality	*equality*
priests	bhikkhus

When we take diksha, *we must appreciate the change. Those who say Buddhism and Hinduism are the same are enemies of Buddhism. They want to spoil the success of the movement. If they're the same, why change? We must change because they are different, but we must understand the points of difference. This is not spreading hatred; but we must stick to the truth.*

Duties – Viharas. Need to expand diksha. *Ambedkar's dream was that all India will become Buddhist. This needs unity among people, and integrity among leaders.*

The party returned to Nagpur on the morning of 8 February and the same day the Bhikshu left Nagpur for Bombay accompanied by Shri A. R. Kulkarni.

In Bombay Bhikshu Sangharakshita spent six weeks and delivered no fewer than forty lectures to large and appreciative audiences in various parts of the city. Under the auspices of the Society of Servants of God he spoke on 'The Real Buddha', 'Bodhisattvas in the Mahāyāna' and 'Preliminaries of Meditation', and delivered a series of twelve discourses on the *Dhammapada*, dealing in each discourse with one chapter of this celebrated work.

THE REAL BUDDHA: LECTURE NOTES

February 1959, Bombay, The Society of Servants of God

*'Real' implies 'unreal'. Reality is one, but there are grades according to our perception. Illustration of gold. Illustration of light and curtains. Three principal planes: Absolute (*śūnyatā*); relative; illusory. They correspond to: Enlightenment;* samādhi*; sense-perception. Anything perceivable comes under one of these three aspects, and hence is more or less real. We can apply this to the Buddha and his spiritual experience. He was one with the Absolute –* dharmakāya. *As he appears in the heavenly (meditative) realms to bodhisattvas –* sambhogakāya. *As he appears on earth plane –* nirmāṇakāya.

This doctrine was not fully unfolded during the Buddha's lifetime. Early disciples stressed the rūpakāya/nirmāṇakāya *and interpreted the* dharmakāya *as 'teachings'. This was part of a general narrowing. The reaction of the Mahāyāna: The appearance of SP [Six Perfections] and PP [*prajñāpāramitā, *perfection of wisdom]. The revelation of the Eternal Buddha; like a young man with old sons.*[131] *'Those who see me by eye are wrong.'*[132] *Later Buddhism rather neglects the* nirmāṇakāya.

Aspects of saṃbhoga*: Five Buddhas.*[133] *Bodhisattva. Spiritual practice. All are to be meditated on as* śūnyatā. *Thus the Real Buddha is realized.*

He also gave three talks on 'Character Building' to trainees undergoing a course in Statistical Quality Control organized by the N. C. Corporation Private Ltd, the filial organization of the Society of Servants of God.

CHARACTER BUILDING: LECTURE NOTES

What is character? How is it built? Why is it built? 'Character is an habitual attitude of mind connected with a net of actions.' Two factors are involved: external behaviour and mental attitude, body and mind. These are different aspects of the same reality; they interact, and we may start at either end. Bodhisattvas.

Action or thought tends to repeat itself, and this forms character. There is influence from without – family, society, religion; and influence from within – desires, ideas. The process is largely unconscious – our character is formed before we know it – but it can be made conscious if we develop awareness. This is the beginning of character-building.

But where is the norm of character? How do we know what to think and do? In Buddhism the criterion is psychological: wholesome and unwholesome thought and action. Practising the pañcasīla *(five precepts) etc., we act from without. Meditation is the constant repetition of wholesome thoughts. Character is not an end in itself. Lower and higher types. Appearance of instability.*

At the Ānanda Vihara the Bhikshu gave lectures on 'The Noble Eightfold Path', 'Right Livelihood' and the *Sahassavagga* of the *Dhammapada*; at the Bahujana Vihara on 'Buddhism in the Modern World' and 'The Six *Pāramitās*'.

BUDDHISM IN THE MODERN WORLD: LECTURE NOTES

February 1959, at the Bahujana Vihara, Bombay

First, Buddhism. It's a very old religion. It spread to many countries and took different forms. In all religions there is spirit and form. Buddhism is a path, a way of life. Śīla, samādhi, prajñā. *Bodhidharma.*[134] *I will say no more at present; it will emerge from the lecture. I will only add that the path is to be followed for self* and *others. Four types of persons.*[135]

Now a look at the modern world. How does it differ from the ancient world?

1. *Quicker communications. One world. No longer possible to isolate national problems – health, food, etc.*
2. *Political awakening of masses. Started with French Revolution. Previously only despotism.*
3. *Conception of the welfare state. Anticipated by Aśoka.*
4. *Increased control over nature. Scientific inventions.*
5. *Decay of religious faith. As we will see later, some more than others.*

All these factors have given birth to problems. For instance:

1. *One nation can interfere in another's internal affairs. Congo.*
2. *Conflict not between kings but nations.*
3. *Material satisfaction leads to frustration. Sweden.*
4. *Atomic weapons. Danger of destructive war.*
5. *Decay of religious faith means restraints removed. No fear of God.*

These are some of the present-day world's problems. There are many more, but they are all reducible to one: how to find a spiritual basis for life? Jung's testimony.[136] *True on world scale. It has always been a problem, but it is more urgent in the modern world because:*

1. *Nations are closer; a higher principle to govern relations is needed.*
2. *The masses now involved, not only rulers.*
3. *The means of material well-being are more abundant.*
4. *There is the danger of destructive war unless restrained.*

This spiritual basis was formerly found in religion, but it is not now so in the West. The modern world needs a religion that combines intellectual clarity with a moral force strong enough to guide one on the spiritual path. This is not found in theistic religions. Belief in God. Revelation. Authority. Conflict with science. Militant record. Justification of social etc. injustice.

What of Buddhism? It stands a little apart from other religions. It is questionable whether one can call it a religion at all, but no matter.

(1) Its intellectual clarity and precision. Reason and experience. Scientific outlook. Psychology. (2) Strong moral emphasis, pañcasīla, *Eightfold Path. (3) Practical.* Mettā bhāvanā. *Goodwill to* all. *(4) Non-theistic. (5) Human responsibility. (6) No glorification of poverty. (7) Equality. (8) Pacific record.*

Hence Buddhism provides a spiritual basis for the modern world. It is spreading in the West, though there are no missionaries, and there is a demand for books. There is a revival in many Buddhist countries, and now it has returned to India. Hope for the modern world lies in Buddhism – not its forms, but its spirit. Essentially it is a path to be followed for the benefit of self and others. Then problems will be solved.

The Bhikshu spoke at the Japanese temple on 'Parables of the *Saddharma Puṇḍarīka Sūtra*' and 'The Four Noble Truths and Noble Eightfold Path'; and at the Khar Vihara on '*Anuttara* Pūjā' and 'Characteristics of the Buddha, Dharma, and Sangha'. At the Blavatsky Lodge he spoke on the four *brahma vihāras*. The audience at many of these lectures consisted chiefly of newly initiated Indian Buddhists (all followers of the late Dr B. R. Ambedkar), who gave Bhikshu Sangharakshita a particularly warm and enthusiastic reception. So great, in fact, was their interest, that they organized more than a dozen special meetings in the predominantly Buddhist localities of the city such as Agripada, Byculla, Kamathipura, Worli, Bellasis Road, Nagpada, and Sayami Road. Most of these meetings were held late at night, not finishing until after midnight, as most of the Buddhists are factory hands working long hours in local mills. The Bhikshu, who addressed them on such topics as 'The Three Refuges', 'The Five Precepts', 'Transformation of Life Through Buddhism', 'The Bodhisattva Ideal and the Six *Pāramitās*' and 'Duties of the Upāsaka', found them solidly united in their determination to tread the Path of the Buddha as indicated by their great leader Dr Ambedkar.

THE BODHISATTVA IDEAL AND THE SIX *PĀRAMITĀS*: LECTURE NOTES

February 1959, Bombay

Humanity requires a living ideal, and this ideal must be human. The Buddha personifies the Goal and the Bodhisattva personifies the Path.

The Origins of the Bodhisattva Ideal

The Buddha mentioned his previous births but not in detail. After his death interest in the Buddha's previous lives increased and the Jātakas *were written. As the Buddha was no longer alive, the lack of a concrete ideal was felt and the bodhisattva ideal was developed.*

Since Buddhahood is the goal of the bodhisattva, it is first necessary to describe the Buddha. He is not an incarnation, or mere ethical teacher. He is not even merely a liberated being like Sāriputta etc. The Buddha is one who rediscovers the way to Nirvāṇa.[137] *An understanding of the cosmological background is necessary* – kalpas. *Buddhas arise and teach the Dharma known in previous* kalpas. *Gautama's career as Sumedha. He sees Dīpaṅkara, then practises the ten or six* pāramitās – dāna, śīla, kṣānti, vīrya, samādhi, prajñā. *As the* Jātakas *illustrate, he renounces individual salvation for the good of the world.*[138] *This is the essence of the bodhisattva ideal. Dogmatic details are not important – the attitude is essential.* Vessantara Jātaka.[139]

The essence of the bodhisattva life is in prajñā *and* karuṇā. Prajñā *means the knowledge that things have no self – not intellectual.* Karuṇā *means universal compassion, the desire to help – not emotion. They are inseparable. It will be noticed that the idea of individual salvation is given up. This does not mean that Buddhahood should not be aimed at, but that it should not be regarded as a personal possession. 'May I attain Nirvāṇa for the good of all sentient beings.' The bodhisattva ideal has no parallel. In Christianity there is only one Christ, but in Buddhism all must become Christs and save the world. The bodhisattva ideal is not a dogma but an attitude to life. We should develop our highest potentialities for the sake of helping others. The bodhisattva ideal is of great use to society. The betterment of society is impossible on a materialistic basis. Modern antagonism is not applicable to Buddhism or the Buddhist. Appeal to adopt the bodhisattva ideal.*

Two meetings were of special significance. One, held at Worli, when about 7,000 people sat in the piercingly cold night wind for two hours hearing the Bhikshu speak on the Three Refuges and Five Precepts. Another, when accompanied by 500 newly initiated Buddhists he marched from Borivli Station, thirty miles out of Bombay, to the ancient and famous Kanheri Caves, five miles away.[140] After administering the Three Refuges and Five Precepts to the assembled devotees in the great Chaitya Hall, he led them thrice round the chaitya in single file to the chanting of Pāli *gāthas*. Later, he delivered a sermon in the Cave of Assembly. Both these functions were organized by Shri R. D. Bhandare, a noted leader of the Indian Buddhists, who on each occasion rendered the Bhikshu's speeches into simple yet elegant Marathi.

Bhikshu Sangharakshita also contacted Shri Yeshwantrao Ambedkar, President of the Bharatiya Bauddha Mahasabha, with whom he had several important discussions concerning the material difficulties and spiritual needs of the newly initiated Buddhists. Shri Yeshwantrao Ambedkar, Shri R. D. Bhandare, and other Buddhist leaders of Bombay, including Ven. H. Dhammananda, Ven. Dhammaloka, and Ven. Watanabe, gave the Bhikshu every cooperation during his stay in the city. Many of the meetings referred to above were held under the auspices of local branches of the Bharatiya Bauddha Maha Sabha. In addition to Shri R. D. Bhandare, Shri A. R. Kulkarni, Shri H. M. Pagare, and Prof. N. M. Shewalay were tireless in interpreting Bhikshu Sangharakshita's speeches into Marathi whenever necessary, besides rendering him assistance in many other ways. Prof. Shewalay took advantage of the Bhikshu's presence in Bombay to organize under his guidance a Buddhist Literary Circle in the name of the great poet-preacher Aśvaghoṣa.

While in Bombay Bhikshu Sangharakshita paid a brief visit to Poona, where he spoke on 'The Three Refuges and Five Precepts' to a large and enthusiastic audience at a meeting organized at Kirkhee by the local branch of the Bharatiya Bauddha Maha Sabha.

SECOND TOUR

The second preaching tour took place during the following summer (1959). On 25 May, two days after the Vaiśākha Pūrṇimā, Bhadanta Sangharakshita left Kalimpong for central India where, in the course of a month, he visited nearly a dozen towns in the United Provinces, Madhya Pradesh, and Bombay State; presided over or spoke at nine Buddha Jayanti meetings; performed the opening ceremonies of two temples and a library; initiated nearly 25,000 people into Buddhism; and delivered upwards of fifty lectures and sermons. Among the places visited by the Bhikshu were Benares, Sarnath, Jahalpur, Khamaria, Nagpur, Dhamangaon, Shirpur, Raipur, Wardha, and Kamptee, in all of which he contacted local Buddhist leaders and workers, delivered discourses, and performed *paritrāṇa*[141] and other ceremonies for the benefit of the people. *Diksha* ceremonies were held at Dhamangaon on 4 June, when the Bhikshu initiated 3–4,000 people into Buddhism, at Shirpur on 6 June, when at two o'clock in the morning he initiated 15–20,000, and at Raipur on 10 June, when the number of new converts was about 500.

WHAT THE *DIKSHA* MOVEMENT MEANS: LECTURE NOTES

I'm happy to be here; this is my first visit. Many here are Buddhists; formerly there were no Buddhists here. I want to investigate what the diksha *movement means, first very simply and then through a more advanced explanation.*

1. One who takes and practises tisaraṇa *and* pañcasīla, *plus various other duties.* Tisaraṇa: *(a) Buddha, (b) Dharma: study (no blind faith, must understand), practice, propagation, (c) Sangha.*

Pañcasīla: *duties: (a) meetings regularly, need of vihara, (b) social ceremonies, (c) position of women, (d) pilgrimage.*

2. One who strives to become like the Buddha

'Buddha' is a title; it comes from the word bodhi. *So to become like the Buddha means to develop* bodhi. *But what is* bodhi? *A state of mind characterized as* mahāviśuddhi, mahāprajñā, *and* mahākaruṇā. Bodhi *is to be attained for the good of* all. *This aspiration is called* bodhicitta. *One who develops* bodhicitta *is a bodhisattva. No selfish aim. How does a bodhisattva actually become a Buddha? By practice of the six* pāramitās: dāna; śīla; kṣānti; vīrya: *four kinds of people – work for the good of all;* samādhi: *mindfulness, contentment, getting rid of hindrances (simile), concentration (*kammaṭṭhānas*),* jñānas; prajñā: *three kinds – the third sees reality. All can practise and attain. The story of the tiger.*[142] *I hope everyone will practise this. It is not enough to take* tisaraṇa *and* pañcasīla. *We must all be bodhisattvas and practise the* pāramitās. *Reminder about vihara. I hope to come again for a longer stay.*

THE IMPACT OF CONVERSION ON INDIAN LIFE [NO PLACE OR DATE GIVEN]: LECTURE NOTES

This is a big subject. I assume that conversion to Buddhism is meant. Indian life is composed of individuals. How does Buddhism affect the individual? Conversion means change. True miracle.[143] *A change in the ethical standard of individual life must affect society. Application of* pañcasīla – *vegetarianism and abstention from drink. Eightfold Path – Right Livelihood.*

Other examples: The Buddha taught social equality. This goes against the caste system. In Hinduism belief is unimportant and caste duties are all in all. We must not limit the conversion movement to one group. We cannot be Buddhist until all are Buddhist. No 'reform' of Hinduism is possible. The social implications of the Buddha's teachings were not fully realized in ancient times – hence Buddhism's disappearance.

Economic impact: Application of adinnādāna – *no exploitation. Poverty is not a virtue – socialism.*

Political impact: Hinduism is connected with monarchy, which favours submission. Buddhism is republican and democratic, and by making a person intelligent and self-reliant fosters democracy. There is no place for 'God's will'.

The conversion should have an impact on language and literature. Indian languages and literature are saturated with Hindu conceptions. There is need for a literary revolution.

Presentation of Buddhist ideal. Importance of study of Pāli. Revival of Aśvaghoṣa etc. Buddhist philosophy also to be studied – Nāgārjuna.

The conversion to Buddhism means a thoroughgoing revolution in every aspect of Indian life. Through Buddhism we can make a new India. The impact will be rejuvenating and creative. Not by hate, but by love. Sympathy for Buddhism is not enough. Conversion is the need of the day.

Next to these, the most important meeting function was the exceptionally well-organized meeting at which Bhikshu Sangharakshita and Shri Yeshwantrao Ambedkar jointly installed a Buddha image in the newly constructed vihara at Gautam Nagar, Nagpur, after which both addressed the huge gathering.

DR AMBEDKAR AND BUDDHISM

June 1959, People's Education Society at Siddharth College, Bombay

We have gathered to pay homage to the memory of Dr Ambedkar. On such occasions it is usual to recount the life and achievements of the person being remembered, but here I am faced by certain difficulties. First, Dr Ambedkar was a man of extraordinarily varied interests and attainments. He was an economist, a sociologist, a lawyer, a politician, an educationalist, a legislator, a reformer, a writer, and an editor, and in all these fields he was not a mere dabbler, but an expert. He touched nothing that he did not adorn. Consequently, it is impossible to do him justice in one lecture. A symposium would be needed.

Moreover, I have a personal difficulty. Many of those present knew Dr Ambedkar personally, whereas my own acquaintance with him was limited to three meetings, one of them here in Siddharth College. Hence, I cannot say much that you do not know already. I have therefore decided to confine myself to one aspect of his career – the most important aspect in my view. I will deal with Dr Ambedkar and Buddhism.

At this stage I can imagine an objection. Some will say that Buddhism occupied only a small place in Dr Ambedkar's life. He embraced Buddhism only two months before his death. How can it be the most important aspect of his life? I cannot agree. In the lives of all great men, there is a certain pattern. They were born as it were to achieve a certain great end, but this is often discernible after their death. Only then is it realized that they were all the time working towards a goal which was immanent in their activities from the beginning. Dr Ambedkar was a very great man, but even after two and a half years it is possible to get a glimpse of the main pattern of his life. My contention is that the chief purpose of his life was the revival of Buddhism in India.

Some of course say that the Nagpur conversion was a political stunt, but a glance at his career will dispel this illusion. His first recorded contact with Buddhism was in 1907, at the age of sixteen, when on passing Matric he was presented with a copy of the *Life of Gautama Buddha*. Then twenty years later, in March 1927, we get the first reference to the possibility of conversion, thirty years before the actual event. This was after the Chowdar Tank incident at Mahad, when the tank was 'purified' and there was much orthodox opposition. At a conference in Mahad that December, Dr Ambedkar burned the *Manusmṛti*. And after the conference he visited Buddhist excavations in the neighbourhood, praised the *bhikkhu* life, and asked those present not to sit on the stone seats there.[144] Thereafter he made frequent references to a possible change of religion. Hence it is not surprising that in about the middle of 1933 there were rumours of his impending conversion to Islam, though he wrote in a letter that this was not true. He was determined to leave Hinduism and embrace some other religion, but he would never embrace Islam and was for the present inclined towards Buddhism. In 1934 he built a new home at Dadar and called it Rajagriha.[145]

In October 1935, at the Yeola Conference, he declared that his ten-year struggle for equal rights with caste Hindus had been useless. He declared that he was born a Hindu but would not die one, and he advised his followers to change their religion. It is interesting that he did not advise them to abandon religion completely. He was a deeply religious man. In 1935 he said, 'Some people think that religion is not essential to society. I do not hold this view. I consider the foundations of religion to be essential to life and practices of society.'[146] The same year he vehemently attacked Hinduism in his book *Annihilation of Caste*. He also declared at the Mahar Conference at Dadar, 'There is no other feeling than that of spiritual feeling underlying my religious conversion. Hinduism does not appeal to my conscience.'[147] He closed with a quotation from the Buddha and advised his followers not to worship Hindu deities, observe Hindu festivals, or visit Hindu places of worship.

During the next few years he had many offers from Muslims, Christians, and Sikhs, and if his object had been political he could easily have embraced one of them. But in 1946 he founded the People's Education Society and called this college Siddharth. In 1948 he published *The Untouchables* and opined that they were depressed Buddhists who resisted reabsorption into the Brahminical fold. In 1950 at the Buddha Vihara in New Delhi he said that the Buddha is superior to the founders of other religions because he claimed to be *margadata* only. In the same year he contributed an article, 'Buddha and the Future of His Religion', to the *Maha Bodhi*.[148] My own contact with him dates from this time. He attended the World Fellowship of Buddhists in Ceylon and asked Sinhalese Untouchables to embrace Buddhism, and in 1951 he founded and named Milinda College in Aurangabad. In 1953, addressing the Indo-Japanese Cultural Association, Bombay, he said that mankind would have to choose between Marx and the Buddha. They could not be combined. And he declared his determination to devote his life to the propagation of Buddhism.

All these events culminated in his conversion to Buddhism on 14 October 1956 at Nagpur along with four lakhs of his followers. Some said no one would follow him. Even Gandhi had predicted that the Untouchables would never forsake their ancestral religion. Such people underestimated the strength of Dr Ambedkar's influence and the extent to which he had prepared the ground. It was the greatest event in Buddhist history since the destruction of Nālandā. Other organizations had worked for Buddhism, but they had not touched the masses. Unfortunately, Ambedkar died after two months. But the movement goes on.

It is interesting to observe Dr Ambedkar's reasons for choosing Buddhism. First of all, it is Indian, whereas Christianity and Islam are foreign religions. You will recall that Ambedkar considered religion to be the foundation of society. But the foundation must be good. No doubt Hinduism contains certain lofty ideals, but these were never made the basis of society. The basis of society was the *Manusmṛti*, with all its injustices. Buddhism believes in the application of the highest ideals directly to social, economic, and political life. It believes in equality. On the religious plane, it believes that all are capable of gaining Enlightenment. Hence Dr Ambedkar found in Buddhism a basis for all his activities. There was no question of political opportunism. Archimedes was asked if he could lift the earth with a lever, and he said, 'Yes, if you give me a place to stand outside the earth.'[149] Dr Ambedkar was an Archimedes of sociology. He needed a place to stand outside Hinduism to uplift the Untouchables, and ultimately all in India. This was provided by Buddhism. Moreover, Buddhism is in accord with reason and experience. There is no clash with science. But having a powerful brain, Dr Ambedkar did not accept Buddhism without criticism. He put his finger on the weak spot. He saw that there should be no separate laity. It was the separation of monastic and lay that led to Buddhism's downfall in India. Hence he insisted on *diksha*. One cannot be both Hindu and Buddhist.

His further views on Buddhism find expression in his book *The Buddha and His Dharma*, to a limited extent. Since its posthumous publication, this work has had a mixed reception, and some criticism is justified.[150] For the second edition, I would suggest these changes: (1) all references to be supplied, (2) passages of Dr Ambedkar's own composition to be in italics, (3) regularize terminology.

This will obviate criticism. I also suggest removing the preface. As other general suggestions to this Society, as appropriate, I would suggest (1) a volume of studies about Dr Ambedkar, (2) a biography, (3) a bibliography, (4) a collected edition of Dr Ambedkar's works.

I suggest the setting up of a committee. All these will provide a fountain of inspiration for the movement he founded. We must not only honour his memory but follow his example. Dr Ambedkar was one of the greatest men in modern India. We are too close to him to measure his real height. Like a mountain, he is best seen from a distance. He will seem greater with the passing centuries. And the most important elements in that greatness are his care for his people and his love for Buddhism. In that he was a real bodhisattva. We may apply to him Goldsmith's lines speaking of a pastor and his flock:

Their welfare pleased him, and their cares distressed;
To them his heart, his love, his griefs were given,
But all his serious thoughts had rest in heaven,
As some tall cliff that lifts its awful form
Swells from the vale, and midway leaves the storm,
Though round its breast the rolling clouds are spread,
Eternal sunshine settles on its head.[151]

The outstanding success of the Bhikshu's tour was due largely to the cooperation of the various branches of the Bharatiya Bauddha Maha Sabha. Shri R. Kawade and Shri H. L. Kosare deserve special mention in this connection. Meetings and other functions were also arranged by Shri T. Bhagat, Jabalpur, Shri A. R. Kulkarni, Prof. N. M. Shewalay, Shri H. D. Awode, Shri R. Janorkar, and Shri R. Moon, Nagpur, and Shri R. P. Ramteke, Wardha, as well as by a number of other devoted workers. Shri A. R. Kulkarni, Prof. N. M. Shewalay and Shri R. Moon also rendered great service by interpreting the Bhikshu's speeches into Marathi. The Bhikshu returned to Kalimpong on 27 June.

THIRD TOUR

On his third preaching tour, which occupied the whole of the winter of 1959–60, and which took him to Bombay, Poona, and Ahmednagar, Bhikshu Sangharakshita was accompanied by three Thai *bhikkhus*, Ven. Sukitt, Ven. Maha Phrom and Ven. Accadhara, who not only gave him the moral support of their presence but also assisted him in various ways. Leaving Kalimpong on 19 November, he reached Bombay on 27 November after paying brief visits first to Sarnath and then to Bodh Gaya, where the Thai *bhikkhus* joined him. During the month of December he delivered twenty-four lectures in Bombay to highly interested and receptive audiences drawn from all sections of the community. Under the auspices of the Society of Servants of God,[152] the Bhikshu delivered a series of four Sunday morning lectures and conducted six study groups. The study groups were devoted to Tsongkhapa's 'Three Chief Paths', which Bhadanta Sangharakshita had recently had translated from Tibetan into English at the special request of His Holiness the Dalai Lama.[153] At the Ananda Vihara three Sunday morning lectures were delivered. Lectures were also given at Siddharth College under the auspices of the Dr Ambedkar Institute of Pāli, Buddhism and Social Sciences. The Bhikshu gave two lectures under the joint auspices of the Bombay branches of the All-India P.E.N.[154] and the Indian Institute of World Culture, the Forum for Cultural Freedom, the Maha Bodhi Society of India, etc.

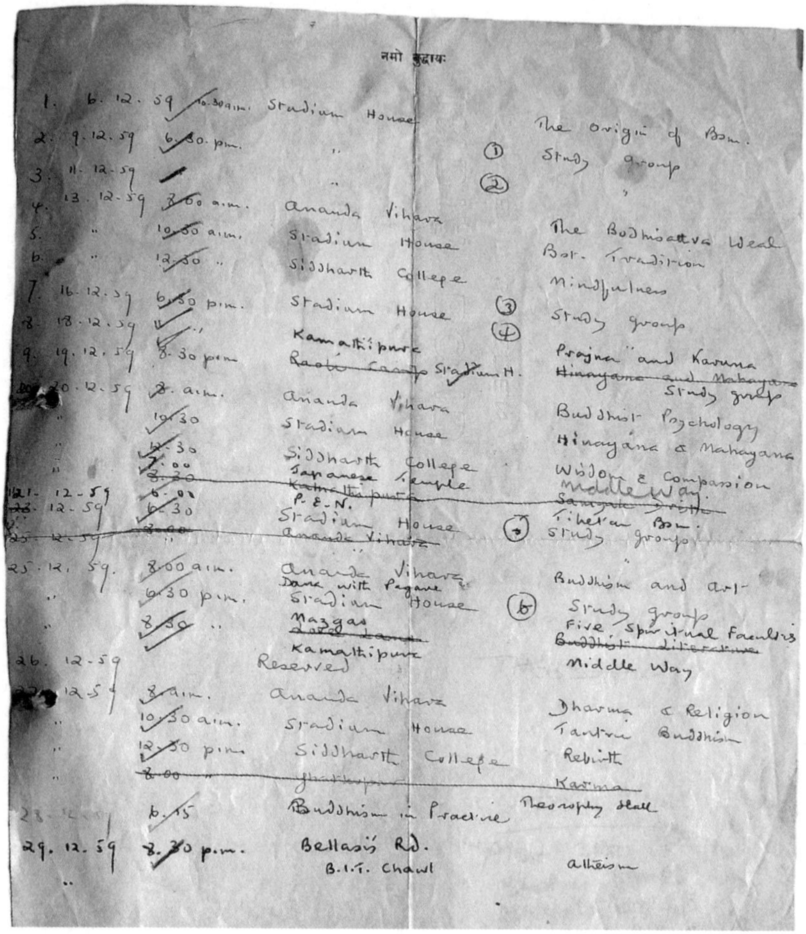
नमो बुद्धाय

1. 6.12.59 10.30 a.m. Stadium House — The Origin of Bsm.
2. 9.12.59 6.30 p.m. " — ① Study group
3. 11.12.59 " — ②
4. 13.12.59 8.00 a.m. Ananda Vihara
5. " 10.30 a.m. Stadium House — The Bodhisattva Ideal
6. " 12.30 " Siddharth College — Bst. Tradition
7. 16.12.59 6.30 p.m. Stadium House — ③ Mindfulness
8. 18.12.59 " — ④ Study group
9. 19.12.59 8.30 p.m. Kamathipura Stadium H. — Prajna and Karuna
20.12.59 8. a.m. Ananda Vihara — Study group
10.30 Stadium House — Buddhist Psychology
12.30 Siddharth College — Hinayana & Mahayana
7.00 Japanese Temple — Wisdom & Compassion
21.12.59 6.00 P.E.N. — Middle Way
23.12.59 6.30 Stadium House — ⑤ Tibetan Bsm. Study group
25.12.59 8.00 a.m. Ananda Vihara — Buddhism and Art
" 6.30 p.m. Dana with Pagane; Stadium House — ⑥ Study group
" 8.30 " Mazgaon — Five Spiritual Faculties
26.12.59 Kamathipura Reserved — Middle Way
27.12.59 8 a.m. Ananda Vihara — Dharma & Religion
" 10.30 a.m. Stadium House — Tantric Buddhism
" 12.30 p.m. Siddharth College — Rebirth
" 8.00 Ghatkopar — Karma
28.12.59 6.15 Buddhism in Practice — Theosophy Hall
29.12.59 8.30 p.m. Bellasis Rd. B.I.T. Chawl — atheism

Sangharakshita's schedule, Bombay, December 1959

THE ORIGIN OF BUDDHISM– LECTURE NOTES

6 December 1959, Stadium House, Bombay

I'm glad to be back in Bombay. This lecture is the first of a series. It will be elementary, but necessary for understanding the subsequent lectures. The subject 'The Origin of Buddhism' implies that Buddhism has *an origin. Buddhism is twofold: unformulated principle and formulated expression. The question of origin arises only in the latter case. We must guard against misunderstanding. The ordinary workings of the human mind. Attempts to explain lower in terms of higher – mind a product of matter, for instance. Historical events due to economic factors – human element ignored. Illustrated in Buddhism. Buddhism as social protest.*

Some people see Buddhism as a product of the Upanishads. There is an element of truth in that but it is not basically the case. The origin of Buddhism is in the Buddha's spiritual experience. This experience was not fortuitous. He lived many lives as a Bodhisattva. His spiritual experience has two aspects: wisdom and compassion. These two are really inseparable. By the first, he realized the truth. By the second, he wished to impart it, to share his experience. This determines the nature of Buddhism: it is a Path to Enlightenment. This Path is threefold etc.

The Buddha taught in the language of his time and used contemporary concepts, but there is no question of borrowing. Did he intend to found a new religion? His attitude to contemporary teachings.

The origin and end of Buddhism are the same. Buddhism is a tradition originating in Enlightenment and ending therein. If we understand that, then we can follow the subsequent lectures.

HĪNAYĀNA AND MAHĀYĀNA– LECTURE NOTES

20 December 1959, Stadium House, Bombay

I'm often asked about the difference between Hīnayāna and Mahāyāna. Wrong ideas of scholars. The literal meaning of the terms. Neither is found in the oldest Buddhist literature. The original meaning of 'Mahāyāna'. Its historical origins; the Vaiśālī split.[155] *Mahāyāna literature is in Sanskrit, Hīnayāna in Pāli. Geographical distribution. I will not treat the subject historically. We must first of all understand what Buddhism is.*

The Buddha's Enlightenment. The Dharma is a means. The danger of understanding conceptual expressions literally. The example of the Abhidharma. The arhant *ideal.*

Because it was aware of the limitations of formulations the Mahāyāna was able to achieve new formulations, so the Mahāyāna is a development, not a degeneration. The Hīnayāna is conservative. The importance of the oral tradition. The Mahāyāna interpretation of Reality and the Buddha has its seeds in the Pāli canon. The Mahāyāna is a universalization. Example of monastic dress. But the Mahāyāna includes the Hīnayāna. Buddhism is to be studied as a whole – as in

Tibet. There is one Vinaya. There's a need for mutual study. Reform movement in the Mahāyāna. Position in Sikkim.

Recapitulation: Hīnayāna and Mahāyāna correspond to the two tendencies of the human mind: centripetal and centrifugal forces. Nāgārjuna on the Two Truths.[156] *I hope you will study* both *Hīnayāna and Mahāyāna.*

THE FUNDAMENTALS OF TIBETAN BUDDHISM: LECTURE NOTES

21 December 1959, PEN, Bombay (originally titled Poets, Essayists, Novelists)

The title raises the question of the classification of different types of Buddhism. In what sense can we speak of Tibetan *Buddhism? The answer to this question will help to determine the nature of the fundamentals of Tibetan Buddhism. Lamaism is a misnomer, unknown to Tibetans. Meaning of lama.*

The development of Buddhism in India. The three yānas. *Hīnayāna (Conze's work), Mahāyāna, and Vajrayāna. Buddhism spread outside India while still developing in India. Each Buddhist country follows the type of Buddhism prevalent in India when it was first introduced into that country. Thus, Sri Lanka became Hīnayānist and China Mahāyānist. Buddhism was introduced into Tibet from the seventh century* CE *onwards, during the height of the Vajrayāna period.*

But was only the Vajrayāna introduced to Tibet? No, *the whole Buddhist tradition was introduced there. It's very important to understand that the development of Indian Buddhism represents a process of accretion. There was no rejection of previous schools, as in Christianity. Sometimes later schools regarded earlier ones as belonging to a lower level, though the Indian Buddhism of the Pala period was, as it were, removed bodily to Tibet. This was Hīnayāna + Mahāyāna + Vajrayāna = Triyāna Buddhism. Tibetan Buddhist historians are very conscious of the continuum of their tradition with Indian Buddhism. The fundamentals of Tibetan Buddhism are identical with those of the mostly highly developed phase of Indian Buddhism. So is 'Tibetan Buddhism' merely a geographical expression?* No, *original contributions were also made. There are four main schools of Tibetan Buddhism, and each made a distinctive contribution.*

The Nyingma, founded by Padmasambhava, is the most purely tantric school, and continues the Indian conception of continuous revelation – termas *– even down to the present. Occult sciences. The Kagyu concentrated on meditation. Milarepa is well known, famous for his psychic powers. The Sakya are known for their scholarship and the codification of the canon and history. And the Gelug specialized in organization and reform. Tsongkhapa developed Atiśa's idea of the three* yānas *as successive stages of the spiritual path,*[157] *and this idea is now common to the whole of Tibetan Buddhism. The Buddhist recapitulates Buddhism.*

Tibetan Buddhism's original contributions transcend the limitations of schools. I will consider them by way of the three yānas*. Tibet takes the Vinaya as characteristic of the Hīnayāna and developed enormous monasteries. In India these were the exception, but in Tibet they were the rule. The Mahāyāna bodhisattva ideal was developed in* tulkus*. Heads of monasteries were* tulkus *and so were the heads of government – the Dalai Lama. There are about a thousand* tulkus *in Tibet – reincarnations of Indian teachers. Plurality – overlapping. More than in Indian Buddhism there was a consciousness of compassion descending, and hence a corresponding upsurge of faith. The Tibetan people are intensely religious and* abhiṣeka *is a standard proceeding, though only considered valuable when given by a* tulku.[158] *There are grades among Rimpoches, a hierarchy. Reflections in society. In fact, if Indian Buddhism developed the three* yānas *and various levels of spiritual status, Tibet embodied them in society. One is a dynamic aspect, the other static. The need for conserving Tibetan Buddhism so that the ideals of spirituality are not lost.*

THE MIDDLE WAY: LECTURE NOTES

25 December 1959, Kamathipura, Bombay

The Middle Way can be thought of as the middle way between indulgence and asceticism, and in terms of philosophy the middle way is between satkāryavāda *and* asatkāryavāda.[159] *In Buddhism we have the principle of conditionality: A existing, B arises. Neither identity nor difference.*

Now let's apply this to human beings. Five skandhas*. Neither the same nor different. In dependence on a previous state, the succeeding one arises. Applying the middle way to rebirth, ordinary views are* śāśvata *and* uccheda, *but the Buddhist view is* punarbhava. *This is explained in detail in* pratītya-samutpāda. *If there is* tṛṣṇā, *there must be rebirth, either on earth or in other worlds. Some think that we automatically gain Nirvāṇa when we die, but this is a great mistake. Nirvāṇa and* parinirvāṇa. *Some confuse Buddhist* puṇya anumodanā *with* śraddhā.[160] *This is also wrong. 'No man can purify another.'*[161] *Can only advise.*

Dead people are out of sight, but we should honour their memory. How? Do something for the Dharma. Lectures, publications etc. Need for propagating the Dharma. More should study. Classes. Also this celebration. I am very glad to be here.

TANTRIC BUDDHISM: LECTURE NOTES

27 December 1959, Stadium House, Bombay

The last lecture [20 December] was on Hīnayāna and Mahāyāna. The difference between them is twofold: doctrinal and psychological. The Mahāyāna eventually became 'Hīnayānistic', and this led to what is loosely called 'Tantric Buddhism'.

The Mahāyāna was subdivided into pāramitāyāna *and* mantrayāna. *Mahāyāna thought became highly conceptualized, and the* mantrayāna *was perhaps a reaction to that.* 'Dhāraṇī' *chapters of* sūtras.[162] *Over-literalization of the bodhisattva ideal. The Tantra aims at Buddhahood in this life. Buddhahood is threefold* – trikāya – *transmutation of body, speech, and mind.* Mudrā – mantra – samādhi.

The Tantrayāna is called the short path. It is concerned solely with technique. It accepts existing Buddhist philosophies. Broadly speaking, its method is through esoteric meditation. Was this an innovation? Refer back to 'mind to mind' transmission. The more exoteric doctrines were written down first. The Tantrayāna was an oral tradition eventually made public. It has many types of meditation. Classification of Buddhas. Identification with the Void through one's yidam. *All Tantric practices require* abhiṣeka.[163]

Moreover, all activities are to be utilized on the Path. Everything has a 'vajra' *aspect: hence Vajrayāna. To follow the Vajrayāna one needs a guru. The Tantra is a very complex system – this is only an outline. It's a living tradition, and now great Vajrayāna gurus have come to India. I hope Buddhism will spread.*

27 December 1959, Siddharth College, Bombay

Four questions:

(1) The meaning of karma and rebirth. (2) Proofs. (3) Nature of and how takes place. (4) Practical results of believing in.

1. *Explanation of meaning*

2. *Proofs*

Philosophical – every action must have a reaction (karma = action; rebirth = reaction). Moral – if there is only one birth, there is no explanation of inequality at birth and the universe would be unjust. So if we believe in a moral order of the universe we must believe in rebirth. Scientific – ordinary people sometimes remember. Religious – the Buddha's ability to remember his past lives – this can be developed.

3. *Nature of rebirth*

It is the mind that is reborn, not the body. There are six different worlds, and rebirth is possible in any of them. On one hand there is mind, on the other, world. What determines the connection between them? We go to the world for which we are suited. We do not really 'go'; each world corresponds to a state of consciousness. When we die, our mind is in a certain condition, and according to that condition we have a body, and hence 'go' to a particular world. If our mind is good we go to heaven; if evil, to hell. If it is mixed, we are reborn on earth. And if our mind is beyond good and evil, we enter Nirvāṇa.

4. *Practical results*

We must be careful of our actions. Śīla *leads to a good rebirth on earth.* Samādhi *leads to a good rebirth in heaven. And* prajñā *leads to Nirvāṇa in this life, and afterwards no rebirth.*

29 December 1959, Bellasis Road, B.I.T. Chawl, Bombay

Before talking about atheism, we need to consider theism. The development of theism was really a crude scientific hypothesis.

Is Buddhism theistic? Some people say that the Buddha was silent when asked about God, but this is a misinterpretation. Issara-nimmāna-vāda *is a 'wrong view' in the* Brahmajāla Sutta. Avyākatas *is a different question.*[164]

Why Buddhism does not believe in God:

(1) An ethical reason: belief in God stultifies self-effort. (2) A philosophical reason: a first cause is inconceivable.

The origin of the universe is a matter for science, not religion. Religion aims at spiritual *Enlightenment. Buddhists are free to accept the scientific view of the universe. Buddhism is definitely atheistic, and Buddhist atheism has important consequences:*

No avatāravāda *– the Buddha is a human teacher. No one is recognized as the son or messenger of God. There is no priest, no mediator between God and man. There is no revealed sacred book – Tipiṭaka may be criticized. There is no* īśvara-bhakti *– only* guru-bhakti *and* maitrī. *No prayer – only meditation.*

Its atheism affects the whole character of Buddhism, so it is strange that there should be any doubt. Some people say that Buddhism is not a religion. This is because they think in terms only of either theism or materialism. But Buddhism follows a middle path. It doesn't matter whether you call Buddhism a religion or not, but you must remember that it is definitely atheistic.

Ven. Maha Phrom and Ven. Accadhara addressed several gatherings on 'Buddhism in Thailand'. During January and February 1960, the Bhikshu was hardly less busy. Under the auspices of the Dr Ambedkar Institute of Pāli, Buddhism and Social Sciences he delivered a lecture on 'Buddhism in England' and conducted five study classes on the *Dhammapada*.

January 1960, Dr Ambedkar Institute of Pāli, Buddhism and Social Sciences, Bombay

Spencer Hardy's Manual of Buddhism *1850. Theosophical Society.* Sacred Books of the East. *Edwin Arnold's* Light of Asia, *1879. At this period there was no separate Buddhist movement, but several Englishmen became* bhikkhus *in the East. The first English* bhikkhu *to return to England was Allan Bennett – Ananda Metteyya. He was born in 1872 – left the Catholic Church – 'analytical chemist' –* Light of Asia *– in Burma for ten years. Meanwhile, English Buddhists were springing up. R. J. Jackson, who preached Buddhism from a soapbox in Hyde Park together with another Englishman, Colonel J. R. Pain, founded in 1906 the Buddhist Society of England, which, in 1907, became the Buddhist Society of Great Britain and Ireland. This paved the way for Ananda Metteyya, who arrived back in England in 1908 to promote a Buddhist Mission, on which he worked for nearly a year.* The Buddhist Review *was founded in 1909. During the Great War there were only lectures.*

In 1924 Christmas Humphreys founded the Buddhist Lodge of the Theosophical Society, 'to form a nucleus of such persons as wished to study, disseminate, and attempt to live the fundamental principles of Buddhism'. In 1925 the periodical Buddhism in England *was founded; later renamed* The Middle Way. *Anagarika Dharmapala came to England and founded the London Buddhist Vihara in 1926.*[165] *In 1926 the Buddhist Lodge separated from the Theosophical Society to become the Buddhist Society. Since then there has been steady growth. During the Second World War there were naturally setbacks, but after the war there was revival and expansion, the Society's main activities being lectures, study groups and meditation, publications, and summer schools. But people as a whole are only just beginning to understand.*

India was in the same position until recently. Only Dr Ambedkar's act made Buddhism a mass movement. Now something more than lectures is needed. The reorientation of the whole of life – a new type of person. Viharas and Buddhist schools. Young men becoming sāmaṇeras *for three months. Reorganization of the economic basis of life. Right Livelihood. Creation of new literature and art. Other countries will help, but India must stand on its own feet. This is the lesson of Buddhism in England and it will be even more so in India. There is the possibility of Indian Buddhists leading the whole Buddhist world, but they must be energetic. It is good to see students enrolling today, but they must not fall away. I hope to see them – and more – next year.*

On 21 January the Bhikshu delivered an address inaugurating the Pāli Union of Siddharth College. In the evening of the same day he conducted a question-and-answer meeting at the Theosophy Hall under the auspices of the Indian Institute of World Culture, Mme Sophia Wadia occupying the chair.

Proceeding to Poona on 25 January, the Bhikshu gave lectures on 'Duties of an *Upāsaka*', on '*Maitrī Bhāvanā*' and on the 'Five Spiritual Faculties'. Together with Ven. Bhikkhus Sukki, Accadhara, and Maha Phrom he performed a *paritrāṇa* ceremony on the occasion of the unveiling of a statue of the late Dr B. R. Ambedkar on the morning of the 26th.

Returning to Bombay, Bhikshu Sangharakshita addressed an exceptionally well attended meeting on 'Buddhism' at Theosophy Hall on 1 February.

BUDDHISM: LECTURE NOTES

1 February 1960, Theosophy Hall, Bombay

The time at my disposal is very short – 45 minutes for twenty-five centuries – and I am not a Zen master. Two methods would be possible – a complete theoretical survey or a practical cross-section, a cake recipe or a slice of cake.

Buddhism is concerned with human beings. Religions are often concerned with God, but not Buddhism, in which belief in īśvara *is a 'wrong view'. Two kinds of human being are found: the* pṛthagjana *and the* āryan, *bound and free. They are not two races or creations. The freed man was once bound. This is what Buddhism is concerned with: how can the bound man or woman become free? It is not concerned with theoretical questions but only with what can be experienced. It is not even concerned with this question theoretically. Free men and women actually exist, no less than those who are bound. The first in historical times was the Buddha, and what we call Buddhism is the interplay between a free man and the unfree.*

It's a challenge, like that of a swimmer to a sleeper, because we can *become free – otherwise it would have no meaning. But* how *to become free? The Dharma supplies the answer. In fact, it supplies nothing but this answer. Its function is purely practical. It's a means to an end. Mahāpajāpatī's question. Like a raft, it can be thrown away.*[166] *The Dharma says, understand your unfreedom. Understand how you have become unfree. We bind ourselves –* pratītya-samutpāda. *We must accept responsibility. We limit ourselves from minute to minute by our own thoughts, words, and actions. This is known as karma. Because we bind ourselves, we can unbind ourselves. There is no need for grace. We are our own saviour. Buddhas only show the way. The state of freedom is to be achieved by ourselves in* this *life. Reality is this state of freedom. No one can experience it for us.* Ehipassiko dhammo. *The nature of freedom cannot be determined theoretically. The Tathāgata is 'unfathomable'. But freedom is recognizable, and it manifests as compassion.*

Some of you may be surprised that I have not mentioned the Eightfold Path etc. These represent the graduated approach to the understanding of our unfreedom. In this understanding lies freedom. The mind must be prepared – hence śīla, samādhi, *etc. But these do not, by themselves, give freedom, though there is no freedom without them. We must never lose sight of the fundamental aim of Buddhism. 'One taste'.*[167] *Freedom is to be achieved by wisdom and understanding, and manifest as love. The world needs all three of these today. Perhaps only Buddhism can survive, because it is clear and uncompromising, and because it deals with human beings and their problems in a practical and convincing way.*

On 6 February the Bhikshu visited Mulund, where he delivered a sermon on the *Maṅgala Sutta*. On the 10th and 13th respectively he gave lectures on 'The Central Philosophy of Buddhism' and on '*Śīla, Samādhi, Prajñā,* and *Karuṇā*' in Bombay.

10 February 1960, Bombay

First, I'll examine the meaning of 'philosophy'. There are many definitions: 'science of values', 'thinking consideration of things' etc. These do not help very much. Tracing the origin of the word, it comes from Greek – Socrates, Oracle, Sophists. It means 'a lover of wisdom', not 'wise'. This meaning persists throughout Western philosophy. Philosophy is a quest for truth, reality, etc. And the instrument of the quest is reason. We can see now that it is not very correct to speak of 'Buddhist philosophy', though many do.

Buddhism springs from the Buddha's Enlightenment. This includes Buddhist philosophy. Hence 'philosophy' in the West and in Buddhism are quite opposite. So the question arises: What, then, is Buddhist philosophy? To understand this, we must refer to the Path. It has three main stages – śīla, samādhi, *and* prajñā *– which I will describe briefly.*

There are two aspects of śīla *– social and individual. The principle of social ethics is 'Do as you would be done by'. The principle of individual ethics is psychological. Thought and deed are interrelated. Thought can influence deed, but deed also influences thought.* Samādhi *comprises mindfulness, concentration. Fourfold practice of mindfulness. Then one-pointedness of mind gives rise to various experiences and* samādhi. *Many people get stuck here. Formulate* dṛṣṭis *or* mithyādṛṣṭis.[168] *The parable of the blind men and the elephant.*[169]

So the question arises, how to develop prajñā? *By meditation on the conceptual formulations of the Buddha's Enlightenment. These formulations constitute what we call Buddhist philosophy. The most important formulation is that of the conditionality of existence. It is expressed in the formula 'This arising, that arises; this not arising, that does not arise.' It is not a theory of causation.* Satkāryavāda *and* asatkāryavāda.[170] *Buddhism follows a middle path. Its most important application is to psychical life. This gives rise to the doctrine of* anātman, *which is much misunderstood. One thought-moment arises in dependence on the previous one. These form a stream. Rebirth – but there is none who is reborn. Neither the same nor different. Middle way between materialism and* ātmavāda.[171] *The same principle can also be applied to existence as a whole or Reality. In this way arises* śūnyavāda. *This too is misunderstood. It means that reality is logically indescribable. It is not existent nor non-existent, nor both, nor neither.*

The principle of conditionality is handled differently by different Buddhist schools: (1) Abhidharma: occupied chiefly with analysis, classification, and interrelation of states of mind – sometimes called 'psychological ethics'. (2) Madhyamaka: concerned to show dialectically that reason is self-contradictory, hence all formulations are of relative value only. (3) Yogācāra: shows that the so-called objective universe arises in dependence on consciousness sullied by subject–object relation.

These are important Indian schools. There are many others, but the principle is the same. They all deal with conceptual formulations which in samādhi *act as support for the development of* prajñā. *We should guard against a mistake: this is not speculation, only pure awareness. In this way* vipassanā *arises, then* vimukti, *then* bodhi. *So, to sum up, the function of Buddhist philosophy is practical. It's the expression of the Buddha's realization in conceptual terms. One of the most important formulations is conditionality. This is applied in* anātman *and* śūnyatā, *and explained from different points of view by various schools. It's a vast subject, of which this is only a glimpse.*

At the invitation of the Bahujan Sikshan Sangh, Ahmadnagar, the last week of February was spent touring the Ahmadnagar District of Bombay State. Accompanied by Shri R. D. Pawar MLA, Bhadanta Sangharakshita first visited Bhandardar, in the extreme west of the District, and inspected a plot of land which had been acquired by the Sangha for the construction of a vihara and training centre. On the morning of 25 February he left for Ahmadnagar, passing through the villages of Rajur and Akola, in each of which he contacted local Buddhists. At Sanghamner, a small town, the Bhikshu gave a short talk to the inmates of the Siddharth Hostel. Reaching Ahmadnagar town the same evening the Bhikshu delivered a lecture on 'The Noble Eightfold Path' at the District Board Hall. On the morning of 27 February he delivered a lecture at Nalegaon, where a vihara and library were under construction. After visiting the Buddha Vihara, Bhingar, he gave another lecture at the Bhima Gautami Vidyarthini Ashram. At 8 p.m., after travelling for several hours by bus and bullock-cart, he spoke on 'The Ten Duties of the *Upāsaka*' at the village of Karare. More than a thousand Buddhists from twenty adjacent villages attended this meeting. On the following morning the Bhikshu visited the vihara at the village of Kanur, where he installed an image of the Buddha after it had been taken out in procession by the local Buddhists, and delivered a sermon. In the afternoon he addressed the inmates of the Siddharth Hostel, Parner.

From 8 March to 21 May Bhikshu Sangharakshita stayed in Poona. Besides participating in the Buddha Jayanti celebrations, he delivered during this period, in Poona and the adjoining districts, a total of fifty-eight lectures on the Dharma, from simple talks on the meaning of the Three Refuges and the Five Precepts to a series of three philosophical lectures on the meaning of the mantra *oṃ maṇi padme hūṃ*.

OṂ MAṆI PADME HŪṂ: NOTES FOR A SERIES OF THREE LECTURES

Spring 1960, Poona

1

Buddhism teaches the Threefold Path: śīla, samādhi, prajñā. *We are now concerned with the transition from* śīla *to* samādhi. *Forty* kammaṭṭhānas. *Temperaments.* Śraddhā-carita. Buddhānusmṛti, Dharmānusmṛti, Saṅghānusmṛti. 'Iti'pi so', *etc.*[172]

Two stages of repetition: (a) rosary and words; (b) only words. Many mantras developed after the time of the Buddha. One such is oṃ maṇi padme hūṃ. *This was recommended by Dr Ambedkar, but many people do not understand either the practice or the meaning.*[173] *You can concentrate the mind by simple repetition, without understanding the meaning. There is no magic power in the mantra – it's all from the mind. But if the meaning is understood also, you can go from* samādhi *to* prajñā.

The mantra consists of four words, but contains the whole Buddhist teaching. Its origin is in the Kāraṇḍa-vyūha Sūtra.[174] *It is Avalokiteśvara's gift to the world. The mantra is very famous in Tibet, constantly repeated and carved on rocks, walls, etc.*

Today we will see the meaning of oṃ *and* maṇi. Oṃ *signifies the goal of the path, generally called Nirvāṇa. But language is inadequate. Language was created for practical purposes, not for philosophical discussion. The fish and the turtle.*[175] *We must guard against understanding words in a non-Buddhist sense. Nirvāṇa equals no greed, anger, or ignorance. It's a state of mental freedom. There's no concept of 'I' or* ātman. *It's not a state of nothingness. It's a state of absolute wisdom and compassion.* Oṃ *comes first since at the beginning of the practice we visualize the goal.*

Maṇi *stands for mind. The* cintāmaṇi *of Indian mythology.*[176] *Everything depends on mind.* Manopubbaṅgamā dhammā *etc.*[177] *The mind, controlled, can give Nirvāṇa. No one else can give it – not grace of God. Each one is a potential Buddha. But how? The mind has two aspects: one turned towards the world and the other turned away from the world. We must give up the former and cultivate the latter. But this is not enough. We must cultivate love for all. The desire for Nirvāṇa must be joined with* maitrī. *This produces the* bodhicitta. *One aspires to Nirvāṇa, or Buddhahood, for the sake of all.* Maṇi *in a special sense means the* bodhicitta. *The* bodhicitta *is difficult to develop. It's like a blind man finding a jewel on a rubbish heap.*[178] *Its development makes one a bodhisattva. There is much to be said on this subject, but it must wait for tomorrow.*

2

Yesterday we saw the meaning of oṃ *and* maṇi. Oṃ *represents Nirvāṇa, the goal.* Maṇi *represents (a) the mind, and (b)* bodhicitta. *Today, the meaning of* padme. Padme *is the vocative of* padma, *lotus. The lotus has an important place in Buddhism. It is one of the four symbols of important events in the Buddha's life:*

(1) Lotus – birth. (2) Bodhi tree – Enlightenment. (3) Dharmacakra *– First Sermon. (4) Stupa –* parinirvāṇa.

Early Buddhist art and iconography used these symbols to represent the Buddha rather than making images of the Buddha himself. We now have Buddha images, but the symbols are still used for decoration. The lotus also appears in the story of the Buddha's decision to teach. He saw humanity as a bed of lotuses, some in the mud, some half-emerging from the mud, etc. Here the lotus stands for different stages of spiritual development.[179] *The* Dhammapada *says that the true disciple is like a lotus,*[180] *and the Buddha is represented seated on a lotus. The lotus therefore symbolizes spiritual birth, stages of development, and attainment. It specially represents stages of growth.* Udāna: *the Dharma proceeds gradually, not all at once.*[181]

Let us see what these stages are. They can be viewed as: (1) stages of attainment. (2) vices to be abandoned. (3) virtues to be cultivated. Too much detail would be confusing, but an understanding of the general outline is more important.

1. stages of attainment

This is of more theoretical interest. The Mahāyāna texts speak of ten bhūmis, *and the Hīnayāna texts of four* maggas *and four* phalas. *We will deal with the latter, as this list comes in the* Tiratana Vandanā: *(1) Path and Fruit of* srotāpanna. *(2) Path and Fruit of* sakṛdāgāmin. *(3) Path and Fruit of* anāgāmin. *(4) Path and Fruit of* arhant.

Difference between Path and Fruit. These stages are reached by breaking fetters or saṃyojanas. *They are ten in number. The* srotāpanna *breaks: (1)* satkāyadṛṣṭi, *(2)* śīlavrata-parāmarśa, *and (3)* vicikitsā. *The* sakṛdāgāmin *loosens: (1)* kāma-rāga, *and (2)* vyāpāda. *The* anāgāmin *breaks these. These are the five lower fetters. The* arhant *breaks the five higher fetters: (1)* rūpa-rāga, *(2)* arūpa-rāga, *(3)* māna, *(4)* auddhatya, *and (5)* avidyā. *These four kinds of people, with two subdivisions known as* āryapudgalas, *form the Āryasaṅgha. The Sangha is threefold: (1) Āryasaṅgha, (2) the sangha of four directions and three times, (3) Local sangha of five or ten* bhikṣus.

Now we come to the virtues to be practised. There are many formulations, but we will take the pāramitās. *These are ten in number, but four belong to tomorrow's lecture. The remaining six are:* dāna, śīla, kṣānti, vīrya, samādhi, prajñā. *Practising them makes one a* bodhisattvacaryā; *you attain six* bhūmis.

You may not be able to remember the details of all this, but remember the symbolism of the lotus, the beautiful symbol of natural growth.

3

We have now reached Buddhahood, but is that the end? We can refer to the Dhammapada *verse:* puttā m'atthi, dhanam m'atthi, iti bālo vihaññati.[182] *Selfishness can also take a spiritual form, if one thinks in terms of salvation for oneself alone. St Augustine.*[183]

According to the Buddha, there are four kinds of people: (1) people who care neither for their own nor for others' salvation, (2) people who care for their own salvation, but not for that of others – Christian, Vedāntin, etc., (3) people who care for others' salvation, but not their own – useless – social reformers, (4) people who care for their own salvation, then that of others. The fourth type is praised as the best.[184]

The meaning of Tathāgata.[185] Prajñā *and compassion are one. The bodhisattva must descend into the world. The story of Avalokiteśvara.* Oṃ *represents ascent and* hūṃ *represents descent. The two are opposites but complementary, one at the beginning and the other at the end of the mantra.* Hūṃ *includes* oṃ, *and is therefore greater.* Oṃ *may be found in other religions, but* hūṃ *is found only in Buddhism.*

Padme *equals the first six* pāramitās. Hūṃ *equals the last four.*[186] *These are: (1)* Upāya-kauśalya *(skilful means), consisting of (a) four* saṃgraha-vastus *(means of conversion): (i)* dāna *(generosity), (ii)* priyavāditā *(loving speech), (iii)* artha-caryā *(beneficial activity), (iv)* samānārthatā *(exemplification). (b) four* pratisaṃvids*: (i)* dharma-pratisaṃvid *(analytical knowledge of phenomena), (ii)* artha-pratisaṃvid *(analytical knowledge of meaning), (iii)* nirukti-pratisaṃvid *(analytical knowledge of etymology), (iv)* pratibhāna-pratisaṃvid *(analytical knowledge of courage). (2)* Praṇidhāna pāramitā – *not to rest until all are delivered; (3)* Bala pāramitā – *list of ten; (4)* Jñāna pāramitā – *Nirvāṇa in* saṃsāra, *the jewel* in *the lotus.*

Some may say that all of this is beyond us, but we must understand the principle. We must not only go up, but come down. We must first realize the principle, then apply it. Our Buddhism is not only for Sundays (example of ceremonies) but must also be applied to politics, economics, social life, etc.

Recapitulation of the whole mantra: Oṃ *equals goal, or philosophy;* maṇi *equals mind, or psychology;* padme *equals path, or ethics;* hūṃ *equals world, or sociology. Thus the mantra includes not only the whole of Buddhism, but in a sense the whole of knowledge. Dr Ambedkar's selection was not arbitrary. Here I have given some hints on how to practise it, and I advise all to do so.*

Among the places visited by the Bhikshu were Range Hills, Bhimapura, Aundh Village, Ganjpeth, Paud Village (where 3,000 people were converted to Buddhism at his hands), Vishwantwada, Camp, Village Rahu, Erode, Chikkalwadi, Village Koregaon (where 1,000 people embraced Buddhism), Guruwarpeth Bhawanipeth, Dapoli (Kirkhee), Ahmadnagar, Sanwarwade, Village Wade, Village Alandi, and Village Akuda. Most of these talks were translated into Marathi by Shri D. R. Maheshkar. The Bhikshu also opened viharas and ceremonially installed images of the Buddha and performed *paritrāṇa* ceremonies. Returning to Bombay he was given a rousing send-off by the Bharatiya Bauddha Maha Sabha on 24 May and left Bombay on 25 May. On 29 May he arrived in Kalimpong, having delivered, in the course of his whole tour, 120 lectures on Buddhism and held important discussions with Buddhist leaders on the future of the movement.

FOURTH TOUR

The fourth and longest of the Bhikshu's preaching tours covered the winter months of 1960–1 as well as the following spring and early summer. Starting as usual from Kalimpong, the tour gained strength at the Thai Vihara, Bodh Gaya, where Ven. Bhikkhu Vivekananda (of Chiang Mai, Thailand) and Śrāmaṇera Sujiva (of England) were staying and joined to make a party of three. The first stop after leaving Gaya was Jabalpur, where on the evening of 12 October there was both a private function, a name-giving ceremony, and a public one, a lecture in the Jaina library. Here, as in many other places, all three spoke upon different topics, thus providing the audience with varied fare.

Nagpur presented the party with an ample number of lectures and other engagements. Time was in great demand on 14 October, being the anniversary of Dr Ambedkar's *diksha*, and on that day there were four meetings. In the course of the following week the Bharatiya Bauddha Maha Sabha arranged a series of six meetings in different districts of the town, all of which were well attended. Besides this series there were meetings in various other places: Model Mills, Bhankeda, Sitabuldi, Barse Nagar, Shraddhanand Peth, and Lakargunj.

Arriving in Bombay at the end of October, the three *bhikṣus* spent more than a month in that city. Bhikshu Sangharakshita spoke on 'Buddhism and God' at the Bahujana Vihara, Parel, on 3 November.

3 November 1960, Bahujana Vihara, Parel

There are many religions in the world, divisible into two groups, theistic and non-theistic. Definitions of God: (1) Person – eternal; (2) Creator; (3) Saviour and answerer of prayer. Buddhism is definitely non-theistic. There are many misinterpretations – the Buddha was not silent. Some ask why Buddhism doesn't believe in God, what is the proof of no-God. But the onus is on them *to prove that God exists. Some people believe in God because they say that the universe must be made by someone, others desire help etc. Some say that their mystical experiences prove that God exists, but the Buddhist would reply that this is a misinterpretation of experience, which is the product of our own mind.*

Not believing in God has important consequences. Since there is no God, there is no incarnation. Hinduism believes in avatāras, *but they are not found in Buddhism. Who then is the Buddha? He is the teacher – he shows the way.* Bhagavan. *His teaching is not handed down through authority or revelation. In Buddhism there are only two* pramāṇas.[187] *These points all have important practical consequences: (1)* No God *– man is responsible. (2) The Buddha is a shower of the way but we must follow it – the Eightfold Path. (3) There is no authority – we must use our own judgement.*

The Bhikshu spoke on 'Mindfulness' at Stadium House.

MINDFULNESS: LECTURE NOTES

Mindfulness embodies the practical aspect of Buddhism. Its importance: sati, appamāda. *It is the seventh step of the* Noble *Eightfold Path – two* suttas – Dhammapada *– the last words of the Buddha.*[188]

1. *How mindfulness makes us more efficient in daily life.* Kāyagatā-sati*: Memory improved.*
2. *Freedom from emotional disturbances.* Vedanā-sati – *anger.*
3. *Peace of mind.* Citta-sati

These are the first three satipaṭṭhānas. *The fourth will be dealt with later.*

4. *Balanced personality. Five* indriyas – *Hindu yogas.*

5. Removal of obstacles to concentration, conscious and unconscious. Unmindful suppression builds up subconsciously, and becomes active in sleep and meditation. Hence we need sammā-sati *first, then* samādhi. *Japanese story.*[189] *A completely mindful person has no subconscious.*

6. How mindfulness helps us meditate. We have already noticed that mindfulness, applied to vedanā-citta, *makes us subtler. This is now applied to breathing.* Ānāpānasati, *not* prāṇāyāma. *This carries us up into the* dhyānas.

7. Cultivation of wisdom. The fourth satipaṭṭhāna *is the mindfulness of* dharmas, *i.e. the nature of reality as expressed in Buddhist 'philosophy'.*

But there's another way, whereby one can go directly from mindfulness to wisdom. Story of Bāhiya.[190] *To explain this, we must glance at* pratītya-samutpāda. *(1)* avidyā *(2)* vijñāna *(3)* jāti *(4)* saṃskāras *(5)* nāma-rūpa *(6)* jarā-maraṇa *(7)* ṣaḍāyatana *(8)* sparśa *(9)* vedanā *(10)* tṛṣṇā *(11)* upādāna *(12)* bhāva.

One can become aware of vedanā *in such a way that no* tṛṣṇā *arises. This is very difficult, but it's the shortest and quickest way. It's most effective when backed up by other forms of mindfulness.*

So, to sum up, we have seen the practical aspect of Buddhism summed up in mindfulness. 'Mindfulness is always useful.'[191] *Universal principle.*

And the Bhikshu spoke on '*oṃ maṇi padme hūṃ*' at Worli Chawls on 6 November.

OṂ MAṆI PADME HŪṂ: LECTURE NOTES

6 November 1960, Worli Chawls

The Buddhist path has three stages. How to pass from śīla *to* samādhi? *There are many methods. One is the repetition of a mantra. Nothing magical.* Oṃ maṇi padme hūṃ *is one such mantra. External repetition. Internal repetition. Transition from* samādhi *to* prajñā.

The meaning of the mantra:

Oṃ – *the goal – forget Hindu meaning*

Maṇi – *potentiality in all* – bodhicitta

Padme – *steps – six* pāramitās

Hūṃ – *descent:* upāya kauśalya, praṇidhāna, bala, jñāna

Prajñā *and* karuṇā. *This is not easy to understand, but in ordinary terms it's the implementation of Buddhism in daily life: viharas; training centres;* sāmaṇera *period; pilgrimage; regular meetings; unity.*

The Bhikshu spoke on 'The Spiritual Path in Buddhism' at Theosophy Hall on 7 November.

THE SPIRITUAL PATH IN BUDDHISM: LECTURE NOTES

7 November 1960, Theosophy Hall, Bombay

The concept of the path or way is very prominent in Buddhism. This has the advantage of helping us to realize that Buddhism is something practical, not a mere system of philosophy. At the same time, we cannot fully understand it without recourse to Buddhist philosophy.

There are two trends in existence, one a process of reaction between opposites, the other progressive between factors which progressively augment one another. The first is saṃsāric, the second Nirvāṇic, or we could say 'worldly' and 'spiritual'. The first is represented by pratītya-samutpāda, *and more elaborately by the wheel of life.*

A more detailed examination of the twelve nidānas.

(1) avidyā *(2)* vijñāna *(3)* jāti *(4)* saṃskāras *(5)* nāma-rūpa *(6)* jarā-maraṇa *(7)* ṣaḍāyatana *(8)* sparśa *(9)* vedanā *(10)* tṛṣṇā *(11)* upādāna *(12)* bhāva.

These are subdivided into cause/action-process and effect/result-process. The crucial point is where the effect/result-process of the past ends and the cause/action-process of the present begins. This is vedanā-tṛṣṇā.

At this point you either begin to swing round into saṃsāra *or keep progressing in accordance with the second trend. This constitutes the path. The Buddha and Bāhiya: 'In the seen only the seen.'*[192] *The path is in the mind. If we can make the necessary effort, we can realize Nirvāṇa instantaneously. But* avidyā *is very strong, hence progress is gradual.*

The subdivision into stages is characteristic of the Buddhist spiritual path. There are many ways of reckoning it, but the basic one is the threefold path: śīla, samādhi, prajñā. Śīla *is represented by rules,* samādhi *by meditation exercises, and* prajñā *by doctrines. Some say that this is wrong, that there is no particular method to attain freedom, but Buddhism disagrees. Freedom is not attained by any particular method, but it is not attained without any method. The method must be left behind. For this mindfulness is necessary as a constant factor.*

Other consequences of the Path being in the mind: No real distinction between spiritual and worldly. Path from instant to instant. No distinction between Path and pilgrim. Some ask, 'Who treads? Who realizes?', but this is wrong. 'Thou canst not tread the Path.'[193] *We should all try to* become *the path.*

The Bhikshu spoke again on 'Mindfulness' at Stadium House on 13 November, on 'Literature and Ethics' at Theosophy Hall on 14 November, and on 'The Bodhisattva Ideal' at the Japanese Temple, Worli, on 16 November.

LITERATURE AND ETHICS: LECTURE NOTES

14 November 1960, Theosophy Hall, Bombay

The title may give rise to different ideas in different people's minds. The relation between literature and ethics is part of the general problem of the relation of art and ethics. Are they independent, or should one be subordinated to the other? Recent case of Lady Chatterley.[194]

We must first investigate the meaning of the terms:

Literature

De Quincey's classification: literature of (1) information, (2) power.[195] *The first appeals to the mind, the intellect, and comprises science, philosophy, etc. The second appeals to the imagination and comprises poetry, drama, novels, etc. There are of course some intermediate forms which are difficult to classify, but the main distinction is clear. We are concerned with the literature of power, or imaginative literature.*

Ethics

We can take ethics in two senses: (1) certain patterns of behaviour, or rules; (2) certain principles. What type of principle? We may call it value-principle in its positive/negative application to human life.

We are now in a better position to discuss the relation between literature and ethics. The first point is that we cannot discuss them without reference to human personality, by which they are produced. They are both products of human life and activity.

There are two ways in which literature can be related to human personality: (1) expression of merely aesthetic or literary personality; (2) expression of the total personality. To understand the basis of the distinction as applied to modern literature, we must go back into European history. From the time of the Reformation, there was a breakdown of the traditional synthesis of knowledge, and more and more specialization. This was reflected in human nature in the form of the compartmentalism of activities. Thus we speak of 'religious man', 'economic man', 'political man' etc. There's no unifying principle, hence no interaction or mutual influence. In this way emerges aesthetic or literary man, movements like 'pure poetry' or art for art's sake expressing the literary aspect of personality. This gives rise to what may be called minor literature. It may be beautiful, but something is lacking. The question of the relation between literature and ethics, and whether one is to be judged by another, arises only in the case of such literature. In the case of literature which is an expression of the total personality, this question does not arise. Such literature may be called great literature, and great literature is ethical, which does not mean didactic.

Great literature

(1) Expresses total personality. (2) Therefore expresses preoccupation with value principle. (3) This principle is apprehended and expressed not conceptually but imaginatively.

For this reason such literature has permanent appeal, while minor literature is comparatively ephemeral.

We should be careful not to separate ethical and imaginative too sharply. In reality they all work together. Also, we should not think that a fundamentally ethical work may not offend our moral sense in particular passages. The work should be judged as a whole.

Modern literature is aware of its limitations and in search of wholeness. Modern man, in fact, is searching. This is sometimes expressed as a search for tradition, but it's more than that. Traditions can be good or bad. The search is really for spiritual principles, and

Giving a talk in an alleyway, Ahmedabad 1965

when we find them, life will be unified. Then there will be the possibility of literature expressing the whole personality, and the chance of great literature again.

Śrāmaṇera Sujiva spoke on 'The Centre Point of Mind-Control' at Stadium House on 30 October. The *bhikṣus* also performed a number of name-giving ceremonies.

On 17 November the party travelled on to Ahmedabad, the capital of the new state of Gujarat, where Bhikshu Sangharakshita spoke on 'Buddhism Today' under the auspices of the International Academy of Philosophy on 18 November and on 'Why Dr Ambedkar Embraced Buddhism' under the auspices of the Maha Bodhi Ambedkar Mission, on '*Tisaraṇa* and *Pañcasīla*' at Kolol, forty-five miles away, under the auspices of the Bauddha Upasak Mandal, and on 'The Five Spiritual Faculties', again at Ahmedabad, all on 19 November.

18 November 1960, International Academy of Philosophy, Ahmedabad

Here are two topics: 'Buddhism' and 'today'. In a sense they're contradictory. Buddhism is akāliko, *based on spiritual and psychological principles which are eternal. Buddhism is the same yesterday, today, and tomorrow. But certain aspects are particularly relevant at particular times. We can take 'Buddhism Today' in two senses:*

(1) Those aspects particularly applicable today. (2) External conditions.

Of course, the two are connected. We will see both, but first we need to see the nature of Buddhism generally. (It is not 'Buddhism' but the Dharma.)

The Tiratana Vandanā[196] *contains a useful generalization:* Svākkhāto bhagavatā dhammo*: 'well-preached'. The outcome of the Buddha's spiritual experience.* Prajñā *and* karuṇā. *The way to Enlightenment:* śīla, samādhi, prajñā. *The parable of the raft.*[197]

Sandiṭṭhiko*: gives results in this life. Nirvāṇa can be attained here and now.* Parinirvāṇa. *Not for self alone.*

Akāliko*: never out of date. Something internal, not external.*

Ehipassiko*: no blind belief. Test and see for yourself. In this sense Buddhism is scientific. Three meanings of 'scientific':*

(1) pertaining to material inventions and discoveries, (2) attitude of openness, (3) method of enquiry – hypothesis, experiment.

Buddhism is scientific in senses 2 and 3.

Opanayiko*: progressive, leading forward. Both spiritual and material. Buddhism is not indifferent to cultural values, but they are not an end in themselves.*

Paccataṃ veditabbo viññūhi*: to be known by the wise, each for himself. No one can purify another of ignorance.*

I have given a general characterization. We will now see the aspects that are particularly relevant today. First, Buddhism does not demand belief. Modern man is sceptical. Second, it is practical – the Path. Thirdly, there's an emphasis on meditation, peace of mind. Fourthly, there are definite methods. Example of mettā bhāvanā. *All religions say 'Love your neighbour', but how? Description of practice.*

Now external conditions. Buddhism has been dormant for centuries, but it is now reviving. Sujiva could have told more about Buddhism in the West. Our knowledge is very limited, but we know it is spreading. There is a great deal of literature. We know more about India: the Maha Bodhi Society, Ambedkar's conversion, vigorous Buddhist movement in India today. I am sure it will be greater in the future. Buddhism is akāliko, *but we need Buddhism more desperately than ever today. There is the threat of atomic war, and the need for peace in the mind of man. We can find it through the Dharma. Buddhism today is in a better position than it has been for centuries.*

In the course of a three days' stay at Ajmer, the beautiful second city of Rajasthan, the Bhikshu delivered four lectures under the joint auspices of the Maha Bodhi Asok Mission and the Maha Bodhi Society, Ajmer.

The Delhi programme began with a lecture on 'What is Buddhism?' at the Buddha Vihara, Reading Road, under the auspices of the Maha Bodhi Society, on 27 November, followed by two at the Ceylon Pilgrims' Rest House. The first of these, which was presided over by H. E. Sir Richard Aluwihare, the Ceylon High Commissioner, was held on 29 November and dealt with 'Practical Buddhism', and the second, held two days later, with '*Anātman* and *Śūnyatā*'.

PRACTICAL BUDDHISM: LECTURE NOTES

The same thing can be looked at from different points of view, and there are different ways of looking at Buddhism – archaeological, historical, artistic, philosophical, etc. But all of these are intellectual, theoretical – they do not touch our life – and Buddhism is above all else practical, in the way that, say, making a pot is practical. In making a pot, you would consider the material the pot was to be made from, the values in accordance with which it is made, by whom it is made, and for what purpose. Practical Buddhism works in the same way. What is it made from? The mind – momentariness – good and bad thoughts. The method is the way to purify the mind, which is naturally radiant. By whom is it made? By oneself. And what is its purpose? Nirvāṇa for the sake of all sentient beings – bodhisattva and arhant.

We may understand all this theoretically, but what starts us upon the path? We make a pot because we need *one. And we start on the path because of feelings of dissatisfaction with worldly things. This is the Buddhist teaching of* duḥkha. *It is not pessimistic, but opens the door to progress. Buddhist doctrines are not speculative, but state the conditions of spiritual progress. It's similar with the doctrines of* anicca *and* anattā. *If things were not in the process of constant transformation no progress would be possible. Nāgārjuna says that those aspirants who deny* śūnya *are like a man who rides but denies a horse.*[198]

Now, to give a more detailed treatment of the method, Buddhist spiritual practice is divided into three stages: śīla *(ethics),* samādhi *(meditation), and* prajñā *(wisdom). Buddhist ethics are the same as ethical teachings all over the world, except for one important difference. Buddhist ethics have only relative, not absolute, value. They are not divine commands but conditions of spiritual progress; the criterion is not teleological but scientific. As a result of ethical training, gross desires will gradually be controlled and the mind will be turned inwards.*

Five hindrances remain: kāmachanda, pratigha, styāna-middha, auddhatya, vicikitsā. *There are methods for eliminating hindrances, for example thinking of, or developing, the opposite* – karuṇā *or* maitrī *to drive out hate, faith to drive out doubt.*

Before entering upon samādhi, *work on the equilibrium of the five spiritual faculties – faith, wisdom, contemplation, energy, and mindfulness. The Buddha said, 'Mindfulness is always useful.'*[199] *Let us take it as a transitional term to meditation. Every action should be done with full mindfulness: bodily mindfulness, mindfulness of feelings, mindfulness of thoughts, mindfulness of things. If we are mindful, and watch the arising and falling of thoughts etc. in our mind, they gradually lose hold over us. Control is difficult, but at least we should be mindful – this requires honesty with oneself.*

Next, one should take up an object of concentration. These are of various kinds. Images are also a means to concentration; by fixing the mind on a luminous image concentration is attained. There are four dhyānas *(levels of concentration) described by the tradition; Buddhism is rich in supernormal psychology. The assimilation of spiritual truths in meditation will permanently change our nature.*

*This path underlies all schools of Buddhism. Many people are interested in Buddhism from various points of view, but we are not Buddhist unless we practise. Buddhism is practical in all spheres, including the social. It refused to occupy itself with [*text unclear*]* *to maintain the social status quo, so it was driven out. It must be brought back.*

ANĀTMAN AND *ŚŪNYATĀ*: LECTURE NOTES

1 December 1960, Ceylon Pilgrims Rest, Delhi

There are two ways of developing prajñā*: (1) mindfulness,* samādhi, prajñā*; (2) mindfulness,* prajñā. *Today we're going to consider* anātman *and* śūnyatā, *a subject of much misunderstanding. But first, an account of the* jhānas/dhyānas. *There are two sides, negative and positive. The negative side is the suppression of the* nivaraṇas, *the hindrances. If mindfulness/concentration is good, this takes place automatically. The hindrances are traditionally likened to five states of water:*

kāmachanda	*colours*
vyāpāda	*boiling*
auddhatya-kaukṛtya	*waves*
styāna-middha	*weeds*
vicikitsā	*mud*

The positive side is the attainment of the four dhyānas. *In the first* dhyāna, *five mental factors are present:* ekāgratā, sukha, prīti, vitarka-vicāra. *In the second, just* ekāgratā, sukha, *and* prīti *are present. In the third,* ekāgratā *and* prīti *are present. And in the fourth, just* ekāgratā *and* upekṣā. *The four* dhyānas *are likened to four similes: soap-powder, a subterranean spring, a lotus in water, and a person wrapped in a pure white sheet after a bath.*[200] *The mind has become purer and purer.*

Conceptual symbols are like the moon's reflection. From reflection to object. There are many different reflections, and anātman-śūnyatā *are two of the most important. Their interconnection. True understanding of the conditioned is the way to the Unconditioned, freedom. Difference of aspects –* lakṣaṇas *and* vimokṣas*:* duḥkha – apraṇihita*;* anitya – animitta*;* anātman – śūnyatā.

Let's first take up anātman. *It's usually translated as 'no soul', and much misunderstood. It's difficult to explain; the structure of language is against us. But take the example of a chair. It does not exist apart from its arms, legs, etc. It's the same with a human being. There is a multiplicity of psychological states, but no* ātman *to which they belong.* Ātman *is an abstraction, a mere name. We may use the term, but we should not be deceived. But people say, 'If there is no* ātman, *how can there be rebirth? What is reborn? Buddhism contradicts itself.' We must understand conditionality. 'B' arises in dependence on 'A'. In philosophy, 'A' is the cause and 'B' the effect.* Satkāryavāda *and* asatkāryavāda.[201] *Buddhism follows a middle course. Neither the same nor different. Change, but nothing which changes. Modern physics. Apply to psychical life, then rebirth. Neither the same nor different. The Middle Way. Death is not the end, yet there is no transmigration. Rebirth, but no one reborn. Not* punarjanman *but* punarbhava. *Distinctive to Buddhism, difficult to understand.*

Śūnyatā *is also misunderstood – Śaṅkara, Aurobindo.* Śūnyatā *is to existence as a whole what* anātman *is to the individual. There is no substance, pure flux, energy, neither material nor spiritual. Four meditations:* samskṛta *and* asamskṛta*:*

(1) samskṛta *empty of* a samskṛta, *(2)* asamskṛta *empty of* samskṛta, *(3) distinction itself empty, (4)* śūnyatā-śūnyatā.

Beyond thought – catuṣkoṭi.[202] *Paradox – known by not knowing.*

We have seen how samādhi *leads to* prajñā, prajñā *to* anātman, *then to* śūnyatā, *and this to* vimukti. *What is Buddhism? The means to freedom. The taste of salt. I hope these lectures have helped.*

3 December was devoted to a visit to a village near Mehrauli, where Bhadanta Sangharakshita spoke in Hindi on 'The Three Refuges and Five Precepts'. On 6 December he addressed a large gathering at Agra on the occasion of the Death Anniversary of Dr B. R. Ambedkar, and on 7 December spoke at a similar function at the Ambedkar Bhavan, New Delhi.

After a brief visit to the Rev. Lama Anagarika Govinda at Almora,[203] the Bhikshu returned to Ahmedabad, where, between 17 and 19 December, he delivered a second series of nine public lectures under the auspices of the Maha Bodhi Ambedkar Mission. These lectures created great interest not only among the Buddhists but also among several persons sympathetic towards Buddhism and it was decided that steps should be taken to construct a vihara in Ahmedabad as soon as possible.

On 5 January Bhikshu Sangharakshita, accompanied by Bhikkhu Vivekananda, arrived at Poona and was given a grand reception at the station by the local Buddhists. His programme during the months of January and February was a very busy one. To begin with he conducted thirteen mass conversion ceremonies inside and outside the Poona

District: on 16 January at Baramati, on 17 January at Shirshupal; from 26–29 January at Kumbharagaon, Palasdeo, Lasurne, Anthurne, Kati, and Indapur; from 3–5 February at four places including Bhigawan, Indapur (again), and Kalas; on 11 February at Wagholi. In all about 25,000 persons were converted. At each meeting the Bhikshu delivered a comprehensive discourse to the new initiatives explaining their duties and responsibilities as Buddhists.

DUTIES OF *UPĀSAKAS* AND *UPĀSIKĀS*: LECTURE NOTES

1. Understand significance of Triratna
2. Observe pañcasīla *regularly*
3. Aṣṭaśīla, *occasionally*
4. Regular meetings: (a) at least Vandanā, *(b) if possible, book-reading, (c) even lectures.*
5. Observe Buddhist manners and customs: (a) Name-giving, marriage, after-death, (b) In the home – shrine, (c) Public meetings, (d) General dignity and decency.
6. Train children: (a) Teach cleanliness, good behaviour, (b) Kindness to animals, (c) Consideration for others, (d) Give education, (e) Religious teaching.
7. Position of women: (a) Social equality, (b) Participation in religious activities – PDBWA *(Poona District Buddhist Women's Association).*
8. Pilgrimage
9. Contact with outside groups
10. Propagation of the Dharma
11. Support of the Sangha
12. Raise cultural level
13. Preserve unity

Under the auspices of the Poona District Buddhist Women's Association, founded under his guidance the previous year, the Bhikshu delivered a series of eight weekly lectures on 'The Position of Women in Buddhism'. On 8 February the Bhikshu went to Panchgani, a small hill station sixty-five miles from Poona, where he delivered a public lecture on 'Who is a Buddhist?' On 10 February he paid a visit to Ahmadnagar, where he delivered a lecture on 'The Principles and Practice of Buddhism' at the Municipal Board Hall to an audience of 300 Buddhist social workers,

With the Poona District Buddhist Women's Association

and performed a house-warming ceremony. On 27 February the Bhikshu lectured on the *Diamond Sūtra* at Theosophy Hall, Bombay, under the auspices of the Indian Institute of World Culture. Mme Sophie Wadia was in the chair.

THE *DIAMOND SŪTRA*

27 February 1961, Theosophy Hall, Bombay

This is the fourth lecture in the series, and we have already heard from speakers on the Vedas *and the Upanishads, the* Bhagavad Gītā, *and the*

Gāthas. *Now we come to a Buddhist text. It was difficult to make a choice. The* Dhammapada *sprang first to mind, but it's too well-known. What then? Before giving the reasons for my selection, I'll say a few words about Buddhist scriptures in general.*

Few people realize how vast the collection of Buddhist scriptures is. The Pāli Tipiṭaka has forty-five volumes and the Tibetan Kanjur has 108. There are 100 volumes in the Taishō edition of Chinese Tripiṭaka (about 1,600 separate works). And there are also uncollected Sanskrit and Prakrit works. All this is canonical (commentary and exposition are separate) – that is, discourses attributed to the Buddha or, in some cases, to an Enlightened disciple. This is a vast store from which to choose, and I hesitated for some time, but I eventually chose the Vajracchedikā-Prajñāpāramitā, *or* Diamond Sūtra *(literally 'Diamond-Cutter')*

The reasons for the choice: (1) Because it is a Prajñāpāramitā sūtra, *(2) Because of its historical importance, (3) Because it is analogous to the* Dhammapada, *(4) Because of its intrinsic value, (5) Because of its connection with meditation, (6) Because of its literary importance, (7) Because it is unknown in India.*

1. It is a Prajñāpāramitā sūtra

To understand this, we must understand something of the history of Buddhism. There is no time for details, but broadly, within 500 years of the parinirvāṇa, *Buddhism had become stereotyped, and a reaction set in. This new movement was called the Mahāyāna, in contradistinction to what it called the Hīnayāna. Hīnayāna scholasticism finds expression in the Abhidharma literature, which is highly scholastic and technical. Its basic assumption was that* prajñā *or wisdom consisted in analysing things into their ultimate psychophysical constituents, or* dharmas, *in order to dispel the delusion of selfhood. 'Self' was unreal, but* dharmas *were real. Against this, the Mahāyāna contended that the* dharmas *are not ultimate, being in reality just as much products of thought as the 'self'. The only ultimate is* śūnyatā *– not 'void', but the ineffable reality of things, both conditioned and unconditioned.* Prajñā *consists in the realization of* śūnyatā. *The Mahāyāna called it* prajñāpāramitā, *the perfection of wisdom, to distinguish it from the Hīnayānic* prajñā.

This aspect of the Mahāyāna finds expression in the Prajñāpāramitā sūtras. *They are thirty-eight in number, written in Hybrid or Buddhist*

Sanskrit. Their composition ranged in date from 100 BCE *to 600* CE. *We must remember that no Buddhist* text *is earlier than 100* BCE. *They all embody earlier traditions, worked up in various ways. There were four periods of composition of the Prajñāpāramitā* sūtras*:*

(a) The composition of the Aṣṭasāhasrikā Prajñāpāramitā, *in thirty-two chapters, in about 100* BCE, *probably among the Mahāsaṅghikas of Andhra. (b) The composition of the* Mahā-Prajñāpāramitā *in three versions: in 18,000, 25,000 and 100,000 lines. (c) The composition of shorter* sutras. *The* Diamond *and the* Heart Sūtras *are the most famous of these. They were written down in about 400* CE. *(d) Tantric versions.*

So we have now 'placed' the Diamond Sūtra. *It is a Mahāyāna* sūtra *of the Prajñāpāramitā class, composed in about 400* CE *as a summary of the teachings. It deals with* prajñāpāramitā, *the faculty by which* śūnyatā *in the Mahāyāna sense is realized. I should also add that it is in the form of a dialogue between the Buddha and Subhūti, in prose, with two verses.*

2. *Its historical importance*

I can deal with this only briefly. There are twenty Pala commentaries extant in Tibetan translations. In Tibet, Mongolia, China, and Japan, the Diamond Sūtra *enjoys fame like that of the* Bhagavad Gītā *in India. It's particularly important for the Chan or Zen school. You will all have heard of Zen; there are many books in English, and Suzuki was in Bombay recently.*[204] *Zen is an attempt to realize the import of the* Diamond Sūtra. *Huineng, the sixth Patriarch, became enlightened after hearing this* sūtra.[205] *It is recited in all Zen monasteries, and there are hundreds of editions, translations, and commentaries. It is now becoming known in the West; there are nine English translations, two French, and two German.*

3. *Analogous to the* Dhammapada

The length of the two texts is about the same. The Dhammapada *is an anthology of verses from the Pāli Tipiṭaka, and those who cannot study the whole Tipiṭaka may read the* Dhammapada. *The* Diamond Sūtra *stands in the same relation to the Prajñāpāramitā. As the* Dhammapada *is in the Theravāda countries of South-east Asia, so the* Diamond Sūtra *is in Tibet and the Far East.*

4. The intrinsic value of its teaching

First of all, it's the highest teaching of Buddhism so far as that can be formulated in words, in highly concentrated form. It's meant for bodhisattvas. At the beginning, Subhūti asks, 'How should a bodhisattva stand, how progress, how control his thoughts?' The answer in essence is that he should see everything as void of self, *i.e.* as śūnyatā. This is the basic Buddhist doctrine. But like the rest of the Prajñāpāramitā literature, the Diamond Sūtra works it out in various ways:

a. Ontologically. The Abhidharma has analysed everything into dharmas. But these are also śūnyatā. All so-called objects of perception and thought are discriminated by mind, so they have no real, ultimate existence. They do not constitute so many separate entities. Even the various categories of Buddhist doctrine do not correspond to any really existing object. They represent only relative truth, and hence are ultimately to be abandoned. Even ideas like 'Buddha' and 'bodhisattva' are to be given up if śūnyatā is to be realized.

b. Logically. If there is no entity, there is no identity. Logic says that a thing identical with itself is hence not its not-self. 'A cannot be both A and not-A.' This is the Law of Contradiction. But it is upset by the Diamond Sūtra, which says that 'A is A because it is not-A, and because it is not-A it is A.' Consequently, the Diamond Sūtra is full of paradoxes, such as 'The bodhisattva should vow to save all sentient beings and at the same time realize that in reality there are no sentient beings.' If this sounds absurd, it's because we are logic-bound.

c. Psychologically. The bodhisattva should not think of śūnyatā in terms derived from sense- and mind-experience. They should 'produce an unproduced thought' – that is, a thought which is a no-thought. This can be done only on the basis of meditation.

5. Connection with meditation

We can understand the sūtra intellectually to some extent, but we can benefit from it spiritually only when we meditate on it. As I mentioned, the text is connected with Zen, a meditation school. It's the same with the Mahāmudrā in Tibet. Hence, I have not gone much into the teaching. I suggest you buy Conze's translation[206] and read and reflect thereon.

6. Literary importance

The Diamond Sūtra *is the first known printed book,*[207] *given a date of 11 May 868* CE. *By contrast, the first Bible was printed in Europe in the fifteenth century.*

7. Unknown in India

This is very strange. In fact, it is very strange that Buddhism itself is so little known in India. Vague ideas about ahiṃsā *are no good. Buddhism has been almost completely forgotten for about 800 years. The Sanskrit text of the* Diamond Sūtra *has been carefully preserved in Japan, but not a single* sūtra *has been preserved in India. This is really very shameful, and we should try to understand the reason. Meanwhile, I am grateful for the opportunity to make the* Diamond Sūtra *better known.*[208] *I hope some will realize its importance, and the importance of the Buddhist scriptures to which it belongs.*

Bhikshu Sangharakashita also delivered lectures at Range Hills High School, St Helena's High School, Poona University, and other places in Poona, besides performing numerous name-giving and other ceremonies for the benefit of the local Buddhists.

The last lap of the Bhikshu's preaching tour covered the months of April and May and took him to Bangalore, Poona, Ahmadabad, Bhusawal, Nagpur, Calcutta, and Ranchi. At Bangalore in the course of a three-day visit devoted mainly to re-establishing old contacts, he spoke on 'The Progressive Path of Spiritual Perfection' at the Maha Bodhi Sangharama on 5 April.

Returning to Poona, he spoke on 'Buddhism and Education' at Range Hills on 8 April and participated in the First Anniversary celebrations of the Poona District Women's Association. On 14 April, the seventieth birth anniversary of the late Dr B. R. Ambedkar was celebrated with great enthusiasm and in the course of the day the Bhikshu addressed large public meetings at Poona City, Modikkhana (where he also dedicated the site of a vihara), Bhawanipeth, and Kirkee.

14 April 1961, Kirkee, Poona

I'm very happy to be here giving my first lecture in Kirkee, especially because today is the seventieth anniversary of Dr Ambedkar's birth. This is the first time the day has been declared a public holiday in Maharashtra State, but I hope next year the day will be celebrated throughout India.

First, a few words about history. Thinking about the story of mankind, not individually but as groups, there are two theories, both about a hundred years old: (1) History is the product of material factors, mainly economics. This is the theory of Karl Marx. (2) History is made by great men. This is the theory of Thomas Carlyle.[209] *The first theory contains elements of truth, but not the whole truth; the second theory is more correct. Great men and women are very important – they are the pathfinders whom others follow. For this reason we celebrate their birth anniversaries. We celebrate the lives of many kinds of individuals: religious, scientific, literary. Even Marxists celebrate.*

But how are we to celebrate these great lives? There are two kinds: those who were merely great – conquerors etc. – and those who were great and good*. I am concerned only with the latter kind, and their anniversaries are best celebrated by following their example.* Dīgha Nikāya *episode – true worship.*[210] *Dr Ambedkar was a great man of the second type, and we must follow his example, which is twofold: personal characteristics and work. We cannot follow him unless we know these.*

Dr Ambedkar had many great characteristics. Here I will select only four:

1. Fearlessness

Dr Ambedkar was a man of tremendous courage. At one time almost the whole country was against him. He said, 'I am the most hated man in India.'[211] *But he did not flinch. He taught his followers fearlessness. The story of the tiger and the sheep. He taught you not to bleat like sheep, but to roar like tigers – or lions. I was very sorry to hear that in Delhi a* namkaran[212] *was performed behind closed doors. It's the same in Gujarat – people are afraid to become Buddhists. But we should be fearless.*

2. Adherence to principle

Dr Ambedkar studied widely and thought deeply before he made up his mind. But when he made up his mind, he was unshakeable. He could not be influenced or bribed. We should have the same firmness. Some people take diksha, *then deny it, which is very shameful. Do not give up your principles, even at the cost of sacrificing life.*

3. Hard work

Dr Ambedkar lived not one life but many. As a young man he studied incessantly. He practised as a lawyer, taught, wrote books, engaged in political and educational activities, then religious work. He was never idle, never wasted time. He was an exemplar of vīrya pāramitā. *We too should practise* vīrya.

4. Self-sacrifice

Dr Ambedkar did not work for himself. He devoted his life to the uplift of the downtrodden masses. His exterior was rough, but his heart was full of compassion. He wore himself out working for all-round uplift.

This brings us to the second aspect of his greatness, his work. This was many-sided, but tonight I will take only two aspects of it, perhaps the most important.

1. Education

He realized the importance of education. He gained the best education himself, and tried to educate his followers. His speeches were educative. People's Education Society.[213] *Why? Because knowledge is power. The Brahmins realized this, so they kept education from the masses. Dr Ambedkar followed Buddhism in this respect, and we should follow him. I'm very happy that evening classes have been started by young men at Range Hill. All should help with that.*

2. *Religious activities*

Dr Ambedkar brought Buddhism back to India, a tremendous achievement. There was the great conversion ceremony in Nagpur. He decided to change religion only after long study. But why Buddhism? He had many reasons, but tonight I will give just one. This is the age of science. Science is making great progress, and a man has even been put into space. Many religions are losing their hold because they are unscientific and ask us to believe impossibilities just because they are found in the scriptures. Buddhism is the sole exception, being based on reason and experience, and thus having nothing to fear from science. So Dr Ambedkar chose Buddhism.

Unfortunately he died, but the diksha *movement is spreading. In Madras there are 40,000 Buddhists. But our work is not finished. I have already mentioned schools. Viharas are also needed, and arrangements for training* śrāmaṇeras. *Young men must come forward. And we need publications.*

For all this, unity is essential. But how are we to safeguard unity? By regular religious meetings. By not mixing religion with politics. We may perhaps have political differences, but we are united as Buddhists. Too much importance is given to politics. People are ambitious. More emphasis should be placed on constructive work, and we should guard against outside attempts to undermine unity. People ask the divisive question, 'Are you Hīnayāna or Mahāyāna?' but we are simply Buddhists.

If we can work in the way I have suggested, all India can become Buddhist, because Buddhism is for all. And this would truly honour Dr Ambedkar.

On 18 April, accompanied by Bhikkhu Vivekananda, Sangharakshita left Poona for Ahmedabad via Bombay. At Ahmedabad a busy programme awaited him organized jointly by the Buddhist Society of Gujarat and the Friends of Buddhism. From 21–23 April the Bhikshu delivered a series of three lectures at the Prarthana Samaj Hall, his subjects being the universality of Buddhism, the four *brahma vihāras*, and the significance of Buddha Jayanti. On 23 April he also delivered a discourse on the *Sigālovāda Sutta* at the Lakshman Bhavan and addressed a public meeting organized in connection with Dr Ambedkar's Birth Anniversary celebrations.

21 April 1961, Prarthana Samaj Hall, Ahmedabad

I'm happy to be back in Ahmedabad.

Buddhism is like a many-faceted gem, and these three lectures will show a few aspects. Today we will consider Buddhism as a universal religion. Universal means 'for all', which suggests that there are religions that are not 'for all'. To make the distinction clearer, there are national religions, part of the cultural heritage of a particular country, for example Daoism, Confucianism, Hinduism, Shintoism. Then there are ethnic religions, for example Zoroastrianism, Judaism. You have to be born into a particular country or race to follow these religions. This is not so with universal religions, which are open to all. This implies the possibility of conversion.

Principally three religions claim to be universal: Christianity, Islam, and Buddhism. Today we are concerned with Buddhism, which I believe to be more universal than the others. To bring this out, I will discuss the universality of Buddhism under seven headings, or from seven points of view. Buddhism is universal: (1) in origin, (2) in appeal, (3) in principle, (4) in practice, (5) in attitude, (6) in ideal, (7) in application.

1. Universal in origin

What is the origin of Buddhism? This is a very important question, and there are many misunderstandings. Some say that it was borrowed from previous teachings, the Upanishads. We should remember the first Vaiśākha Pūrṇimā, when Siddhārtha attained sambodhi, *became* sambuddha. *We should notice the prefix* 'sam', *which implies completeness, universality, no limitation or one-sidedness. If we consider the parable of the blind men and the elephant,*[214] *the Buddha was like the seeing man. Many small sects and even religions have been started by people who experienced one side of the truth, but the Buddha's experience was universal. Therefore Buddhism is universal in origin.*

2. Universal in appeal

This means Buddhism appeals to what is universal in human beings. What is this? Intelligence. Some religions appeal to prejudices and emotions. Since these vary, they will appeal to some and not to others, so they cannot be universal. Some may object that intelligence also varies, but it only does so when under the influence of the emotions. If one is free from these, one can always come to agreement. This is because intelligence is the same in all; only the degree may differ. Buddhism appeals to this innate reasonableness. In the Kālāma Sutta *the Buddha says, 'My teaching is to be tested.'*[215] *Hence Buddhism is universal in its appeal.*

3. Universal in principle

This brings us to Buddhist philosophy. We've already had one lecture on that subject. The difference between science and philosophy. Spencer's three kinds of knowledge.[216] *Two kinds of conditionality. Applies to both body* and *mind. Buddhist psychology.* Anattā. *Buddhism is universal because it is based on principles which admit of no exception.*

4. Universal in practice

Buddhism can be practised by all. But how, when people have varying degrees of ability? The objection is answered by the Buddhist conception of the path, which has successive stages: śīla, samādhi, prajñā, vimukti. *The path is the same for all, only the stages differ. There is no question of 'higher' and 'lower' teachings, which only leads to exploitation. Hence Buddhism is universal in practice.*

5. Universal in attitude

Buddhism should inculcate the same attitude to all. This is taught in the brahma vihāras. *'May* all *beings be happy' is the motto of Buddhism. Other religions are often lacking in this respect. Some teach hatred of other religions and sects, so their records are full of bloodshed. Buddhism has a tolerant and peaceful record. Some religions teach love to human beings only, leaving out animals. Buddhism includes* all. *This is not a mere pious aspiration, but actual practice. Karle caves.*[217]

6. Universal in ideal

What does this mean? Every religion sets a goal before its followers. Being universal in ideal means that the highest spiritual status is open to all who make the effort. This is not so in all religions. The Christian cannot become Christ, but can merely worship Christ. In Buddhism all can become Buddhas. This is the bodhisattva ideal.

7. Universal in application
In the social aspect of Buddhism, there is no discrimination between high and low. All rivers lead to the ocean. This applies not only to the sangha, but to the whole of society. To Buddhism, all human beings are brothers and sisters.

I have now shown in what sense Buddhism is universal. Only Buddhism is truly universal. For this reason it appeals to many people. Thousands have embraced it in the West, and there is a revival in India. I hope it will flourish in Ahmedabad also, through the cooperation of the two societies.

THE FOUR *BRAHMA VIHĀRAS*: LECTURE NOTES

22 April 1961, Prarthana Samaj Hall, Ahmedabad

Yesterday I spoke on the universality of Buddhism. Buddhism's universality of attitude is summed up in the four brahma vihāras. *Today I will deal with these in detail.*

First, we must recollect the path. It consists of three great stages: sīla, samādhi, paññā.

There are four kinds of sīla:[218] *(1)* Pāṭimokkha-samvara-sīla: *for the laity, there are five or eight* sīlas. *(2)* Indriya-samvara-sīla: *this implies mindfulness. In a way it's intermediate between* sīla *and* samādhi. *(3)* Ājīva-pārisuddhi-sīla: *for the monk, this means dependence on the laity. For the layman, it means right livelihood. (4)* Paccaya-sannissita-sīla: *traditionally for the monk this concerns the wise use of four necessities: food, clothing, shelter, medicine. For the layman, it means the simple life.*

It is on the basis of sīla *that one becomes ready to take up meditation. It's impossible to plunge straight in. Many people make this mistake, then wonder why they cannot succeed. There are forty* kammaṭṭhānas, *but it's not necessary to practise all of them. They are to be practised according to temperament. There are six* caritas *(temperaments). How are the temperaments to be recognized? – walking, eating, sweeping, dressing etc.*[219] *A meditation master must study these. Today, we'll take up the four* brahma vihāras: mettā, karuṇā, muditā, upekkhā. *These are very popular in all Buddhist countries. They are an integral part of other practices.*

First some general remarks: We are composite beings, made up of thought, emotion, and volition. All must be developed. Especially, intelligence and devotion are to be balanced. The brahma vihāras *develop and refine the emotions. Other religions do this through devotion to God. Buddhism develops the emotions with regard to human beings and even animals. The object of the* brahma vihāras *is 'all beings'.*

1. Mettā bhāvanā *(the development of love)*

The word mettā *comes from* mitra, *'friend'. All religions say 'love others', but how? Only Buddhism teaches an actual method. You sit as for meditation, at the same time each day. Then you develop* mettā *towards yourself. This is very important. We hate others because we hate the self. But why do we hate ourselves? Modern psychology would say that it's because of feelings of guilt, which are suppressed, and then hatred is projected. Hence the importance of* sīla. *So first, love yourself, wish yourself well.*

Then direct mettā *towards a dear friend, someone of the same sex and age as yourself, someone who is alive. Then bring to mind a neutral person and direct* mettā *towards them. Then think of an enemy – though don't do this stage at first, because it's fatiguing. In the last stage, develop the same feeling towards all. It must be a* feeling, *not a thought of a feeling. Now make the* mettā *universal. It shouldn't have any limit, as a mother's love for her only child.*

Each vihāra *has a near and a far enemy. Here the near enemy is attachment and the far enemy is anger. The* mettā bhāvanā *is suitable for the* dveṣa-carita.[220] *It is the foundation of the other* brahma vihāras, *which are usually practised in succession.*

2. Karuṇā bhāvanā *(the development of compassion)*

Follow the same procedure. Imagine your nearest and dearest experiencing dukkha, *suffering. Then bring to mind a neutral person. Then an enemy. (If you put the enemy in the first stage, you will feel pleasure.) Finally, universalize.* Karuṇā *becomes the bodhisattva's aspiration to gain Enlightenment for the good of all. The near enemy is contempt; the far enemy, cruelty.*[221] *The practice is good for cruel people.*

3. Muditā bhāvanā *(the development of sympathetic joy)*

Imagine someone very happy in an innocent manner. Share that happiness. Then the neutral person. Then the enemy. (If you think of them first, you will feel sorrow.) Then universalize. Near enemy, vicarious satisfaction. Far enemy, jealousy.

4. Upekkhā bhāvanā *(the development of equanimity)*

This is the highest and most difficult of the four practices. It's a feeling of sameness towards all beings. It's implicit in the other brahma vihāras, *but here isolated from feelings of* mettā, karuṇā, muditā. *It's neither love nor hate, but complete equanimity. It's not indifference, which is its near enemy. Its far enemy of course is restlessness. It's the basis for the higher practice of meditation.*

Through the brahma vihāras *lower emotions are transmuted into higher ones. This gives the motive power for the spiritual life.* Emotions *are very important. I hope this lecture makes clear the universal attitude of Buddhism. And I hope some of you will practise the* brahma vihāras. *They can transform our life and world.*

OṂ MAṆI PADME HŪṂ: LECTURE NOTES

23 April 1961, Prarthana Samaj Hall, Ahmedabad

This is the third lecture in the series. The first was philosophical, the second was practical, and this lecture will be a synthesis of both. Many of you will have read the words oṃ maṇi padme hūṃ *in connection with Tibet. They also appear in Dr Ambedkar's puja book.*[222] *Many questions are asked about the phrase, so it is the topic of this talk.* Oṃ maṇi padme hūṃ *is a mantra. There are two kinds of mantra: without meaning, a sound syllable; and with meaning. The first kind develops* samādhi, *and the second kind also develops* prajñā. Oṃ maṇi padme hūṃ *is of the second type, so we must understand its meaning. The literal meaning does not help very much, so I will explain it word by word. Rightly understood, it contains the whole of Buddhism. Today I will give only an outline.*

Oṃ *stands for the ultimate goal of the spiritual life, i.e. Nirvāṇa.*

In reality it is ineffable. There are some symbolic descriptions, not to be taken literally:

1. destruction of the five nivarāṇas*:*

(a) kāmachanda	*coloured water,*
(b) vyāpāda	*boiling water,*
(c) auddhatya-kaukṛtya	*water with waves,*
(d) styāna-middha	*water full of weeds,*
(e) vicikitsā	*muddy water.*

Nirvāṇic consciousness is like clear water.

2. cessation of rebirth

3. seeing things as they are – yathābhūtam[223]

4. irreversible, yet not static – spiral order

5. attainable in this life. Nirvāṇa and Parinirvāṇa.

Maṇi *stands for the human potential to realize Nirvāṇa. Technically,* bodhicitta. *Very interesting.* Bodhicitta-utpāda *in Buddhism, especially the Mahāyāna, corresponds to conversion, the beginning of spiritual life. It's the coming together of two trends: (1)* vairāgya, *desire for salvation; (2)* karuṇā. *The conjunction produces* bodhicitta, *definable as 'the aspiration to Enlightenment for the sake of benefiting all'. When the* bodhicitta *arises, we become a bodhisattva. Four kinds of person; can choose. All have this potentiality.*

Padma, *literally lotus. It unfolds gradually, passes through stages, and so too does the bodhisattva. We can speak of three stages, six* pāramitās, *seven* visuddhis, *the Noble Eightfold Path – but in this connection, I generally speak of the six* pāramitās*:*

1. Dāna *(giving). (a) To whom? (i) friends and relatives, (ii) poor, sick, afflicted, helpless, (iii) Sangha. (b) What? (i) material things, (ii) fearlessness (*abhaya*), (iii) education (*śikṣā*), (iv) life and limbs, (v) merits, (vi) the Dharma. (c) How? (i) courteously, (ii) happily, (iii) quickly, (iv) habitually. (d) Why? Not for worldly benefit, not for our own salvation, heaven, but only for Enlightenment for* all. *Otherwise it is not a* pāramitā.

2. Śīla. *Abstention from* daśa-akuśala-dharma*: that is, abstention from taking life, stealing, sexual misconduct, false, malicious, harsh, senseless speech, intoxicants,* lobha, dveṣa, moha *(wrong views).* Śīla-pāramitā, *however, means observance without ego-sense.*

3. Kṣānti. Kṣānti *is a composite term which means forbearance, endurance, humility, acceptance, patience, love.* Kṣānti *is mainly of three*

kinds: (a) patience with harsh words, (b) patience with physical suffering – not mere stoicism, positive, (c) acceptance of anātman, śūnyatā *etc.*

4. Vīrya. Vīrya *is 'energy in pursuit of the good of self and others'. It is both physical and mental. It is not restlessness. 'If you want something done, ask a busy man.'*

5. Samādhi. *There are forty* kammaṭṭhānas *as well as many other kinds of meditation. Take, for example, the meditation on the red* kasiṇa.[224] *As you do it, you go through different stages: (a)* parikamma *(preliminary)* nimitta, parikamma samādhi, *(b)* uggaha-nimitta, upacāra samādhi, *(c)* paribhaga-nimmita, appanā samādhi. *No body-consciousness. First* dhyāna. Ekāgratā, sukha, prīti, vitarka/vicāra.

6. Prajñā. *Fundamentally* prajñā *is the faculty which realizes* anattā *and* śūnyatā. *It has three levels –* śruta-mayī, cintā-mayī, bhāvanā-mayī. *And fully developed, it has five aspects: (a) All-discriminating Wisdom, (b) Wisdom of Equality, (c) Mirror-Like Wisdom, (d) All-Performing Wisdom, (e) Wisdom of the* dharmadhātu. *These wisdoms are personified in different Buddhas.*

Having traversed these six steps, the bodhisattva reaches Nirvāṇa, becomes a Buddha. But there's still one word of the mantra to explain. But how can there be anything further? Avalokiteśvara in the Kāraṇḍa-vyūha Sūtra.[225] Hūṃ *stands for the process of descent, embodied in four additional* pāramitās.

7. Upāya-kauśalya pāramitā. *This is the same as compassion. It consists of the four* saṃgraha-vastus *(means of conversion): (a)* dāna, *generosity, (b)* priyavāditā, *loving speech, (c)* artha-caryā, *good advice, (d)* samānārthatā, *exemplification. Also the four* pratisaṃvids *(analytical knowledges): (a) Comparative science, philosophy, religion, (b) Categories and schools of Buddhism, (c) Words, speaking, writing, (d) Self-confidence, ready address. Japanese story – only a legend, but illustrates.*

8. Praṇidhāna. *To go on working for all sentient beings.*

9. Bala. *Strength, especially spiritual.*

10. Jñāna. *Understanding of the non-difference of* saṃsāra *and Nirvāṇa. Four* śūnyatās.

So we can now understand why this mantra is popular in Tibet, and recommended by Dr Ambedkar. It contains both the philosophy and the practice of Buddhism. A fitting end to this series.

At Bhusawal, where he stayed from 25 to 27 April, Bhikshu Sangharakshita performed a name-giving ceremony and spoke on the significance of Buddhist ceremonies, delivered a lecture on 'Buddhism and other Religions' and addressed a very large public meeting in connection with Dr Ambedkar's birth anniversary.

On 28 April the Bhikshu arrived in Nagpur for the Buddha Jayanti celebrations, and during the next few days full advantage was taken of his presence there on the thrice-sacred occasion. At 5 p.m. on 29 April he gave a lecture on 'The Significance of Buddha Jayanti' at the Accountant-General's office, Post and Telegraph Dept., and at 8 p.m. he installed a Buddha-image and delivered a religious discourse at Juni Mangalwadi. On 30 April, the Buddha Jayanti day, proceedings began with the administration of *tisaraṇa* and *pañcasīla* at the Ambedkar Bhavan. At 8.30 a.m. Bhikshu Sangharakshita addressed a large gathering at the Mor Hindi Bhavan on 'The Universality of Buddhism' under the presidency of Shri N. V. Gadgil, Governor of the Punjab, the meeting being organized by the Buddhists and Scheduled Castes Welfare Association. At 10 a.m. the Bhikshu addressed a meeting at Lashkaribagh and at 11 a.m. he announced the examination results and gave a short speech at the Milinda Vachanalaya, a girls' school established by the Buddhists of the same locality. At 6 p.m., a grand torchlight process, organized by the Bharatiya Bauddha Maha Sabha, Nagpur Branch, wound its way through the streets of Nagpur bearing a life-size standing image of Lord Buddha. At 9 p.m. it reached the Diksha Ground, where Bhikshu Sangharakshita and local Buddhist leaders addressed the vast gathering on the significance of the great occasion. At 10 a.m. on 1 May the Bhikshu addressed a Buddha Jayanti meeting under the auspices of the Model Mills Chawls Vihara Committee. In the evening, he motored about forty miles out of Nagpur to the village of Deoli. En route he was given receptions at Hingna and Munda by the local Buddhists and delivered a short speech at each place. At Deoli he installed the image of Lord Buddha in the newly constructed temple and addressed a public meeting. On 2 and 3 May Buddha Jayanti meetings were held at Indora and other parts of Nagpur at which the Bhikshu spoke on the significance of the occasion.

In Calcutta Bhadanta Sangharakshita spoke on 'The Universality of Buddhism' in the Maha Bodhi Hall on 11 May under the presidency of Dr N. Dutt. On 11 and 12 May he participated in the Buddhist

Convention held at Gautamdhara, 25 miles from Ranchi, due to the initiative of Shri Mehta, Secretary of the Chota Nagpur Pancha Sila Parishad. The Convention was held at a vihara situated in the midst of dense jungle and the three meetings which the Bhikshu addressed were attended mainly by tribespeople, many of whom are now turning towards Buddhism. As this was Bhikshu Sangharakshita's first contact with these simple people he made a thorough study of their social, economic, and religious condition.

On 19 May Bhikshu Sangharakshita returned to his Kalimpong headquarters after completing a preaching tour lasting seven and a half months in the course of which he had visited towns and villages in more than half the states of India, delivered upwards of 200 lectures, and received 25,000 people into the fold of Buddhism.

SOCIAL TRAINING COURSE IN BUDDHISM AT POONA

As part of the vihara's work among the followers of Dr B. R. Ambedkar a special Training Course in Buddhism for *upāsakas* and *upāsikās*, believed to be the first of its kind in modern India, was held at 6 Todiwala Road, Poona, from 1 to 31 March 1961. The classes, which were held daily (except on Sundays) from 7.30 to 10.30 p.m., were conducted by Bhikshu Sangharakshita assisted by Śrāmaṇera Sujiva. Besides the *Dhammapada*, which was expounded in its entirety, verse by verse, the subjects taught included all the more important doctrines of Buddhism, such as the four truths, the eightfold path, the three characteristics, the *pratītya-samutpāda*, *anātmavāda*, and Nirvāṇa, as well as Buddhist history, canonical literature, manners and customs, monastic law, etc. Each day the class began with the taking of *tisaraṇa* and *pañcasīla* and offering of Buddha-puja and consisted of two main periods separated by a short break for tea. After the second period time was allotted for the asking of questions and for discussion, after which the evening's work ended with meditation and concluding *vandanā*. Shri D. R. Maheshkar acted as interpreter. For the trainees – most of them workers who came to the classes straight from their duties in office and factory – the course was a means of great spiritual enrichment, while for the monks conducting it, it was a valuable experience which deepened their own knowledge of the Dharma and brought them into fruitful contact with their Buddhist friends in Poona. It is hoped that in future similar courses may be held in other parts of India where there is a demand for them.

Social Training Course in Buddhism, 6 Todiwala Road, Poona, March 1961

Manners and customs are part of śīla. *It teaches us to avoid what is inconvenient or displeasing to others, and makes us more disciplined, because it influences the mind. There are three kinds of manners and customs: (1) domestic; (2) public; (3) religious.*

1. Domestic. The home should be kept neat and tidy – but don't throw rubbish in the street. Dress in white if possible. When eating and drinking, don't make any noise. Don't point with your finger. Have respect for elders, and consideration for women and when bringing up children.

2. Public. Some people think there is no harm in doing outside what they would not do inside – spitting (including spitting pan juice) and urinating; but do not do any of these.

Public meetings should be properly organized: punctuality; regular programme; selection of speakers – point by point; audience should listen quietly and attentively; especially religious lecture – pañcaśīla.

No disputes or quarrelling. Arbitration.

3. Religious. Daily vandanā. *Care of Buddha-image: treat respectfully, clean etc., no garlanding, correct* mudrā *etc. This also applies to vihara. Treatment of* bhikkhus – *not* sadhus. *Offer everything with both hands. Pilgrimage.*

POONA DISTRICT BUDDHIST WOMEN'S ASSOCIATION AND BUDDHIST SOCIETY OF GUJARAT

As a means of consolidating Bhikshu Sangharakshita's work among the newly converted Buddhists of Western India, two organizations were established under his guidance during the period under review. The Poona District Women's Association, Poona, came into existence in April 1960, with the object of conducting religious, cultural, social, and educational activities among the women of the area, most of whom are illiterate. The Association celebrates Buddha Jayanti, Dharmachakra Day, and the anniversaries of Dr Ambedkar's birth, death, and conversion to Buddhism, besides holding weekly religious meetings in various parts of the town. Many of Bhikshu Sangharakshita's Poona lectures were given under its auspices. The Association also publishes booklets on Buddhism in Marathi. In 1961 it brought out *Buddha Dharmanta Striyanche Sthan* ('The Position of Women in Buddhism'), based upon a series of eight lectures delivered by the Bhikshu under its auspices, which speedily went into a second edition; in 1962, *Arya Ashtangik Marg* ('The Noble Eightfold Path') by Miss K. V. Kedari, the energetic young General Secretary of the Association, and in 1963 *Dharma ke ahe?* ('What is Dharma?'), being a translation by Shri D. R. Maheshkar of a talk by Bhikshu Sangharakshita. All these publications were well received by the Marathi-reading public. During the second half of 1961, after the terrible Poona floods, the Association conducted extensive relief work among the thousands who had been rendered homeless and destitute, distributing among them food, clothing, blankets, and other necessaries.

The Buddhist Society of Gujarat was founded in 1961, the initial nucleus of membership being provided by five young men whom Bhadanta Sangharakshita had initiated into Buddhism during one of his visits to Ahmedabad. The organization is working steadily and systematically. Buddha Jayanti and other Buddhist festivals are regularly celebrated, and weekly study classes conducted. The Society also holds meetings in different parts of Ahmedabad wherever there are Buddhists and members of the Scheduled Castes.

THE POSITION OF WOMEN IN BUDDHISM

Pamphlet No. 1, Poona Women's Buddhist Association

1. *The Buddha's Dharma teaches equality amongst all humanity.*
2. *So amongst Buddhists, women and men are equal and opportunities must be the same for both sexes. Woman is* not *the slave of man.*
3. *Women have rights to participate actively in the Buddha's Dharma as either* upāsikās *living the household life or as* śikṣāmāṇā, *having left the household life and devoting all their time to the Buddha-Dharma.*
4. *Women are encouraged to form their own societies for understanding and propagating the Dharma and for all social and cultural works.*
5. *Buddhist women should read or have read to them the Buddhist scriptures.*
6. *Socially, women are in no way inferior and must not be treated as such. Women in ancient texts are always mentioned, out of courtesy,* before *the men. Such good manners and their practical application in society should be extended to them in all circumstances in the present time.*
7. *In education, women must make great efforts to raise their standard of knowledge and understanding – either by their own efforts or with the help and guidance of any woman or man from their family or neighbourhood.*
8. *Sufficient time must be allowed for girls to complete their formal education.*
9. *In Buddhism, it is* not *considered that the only course or career for women is marriage. Women need not marry and are* not *to be despised if they do not wish to do so.*
10. *It is a crime amongst Buddhists to bring pressure to bear on women to marry against their will, or force them to marry an unwelcome suitor.*

11. Marriage need not be within any particular community, as the Dharma does not recognize the caste system.

12. It is a crime to offer or demand a dowry at the time of marriage.

13. A married woman has the following five obligations towards her husband: (a) To do all her work in an orderly and methodical fashion. (b) To be hospitable to all his friends and relations and friendly with neighbours. (c) Not to commit adultery. (d) To look after and protect all the stores, possessions, etc. of the house. (e) To be industrious and clever in all her duties.

14. A married man has the following five obligations towards his wife: (a) To honour and respect her. (b) Not to despise her, i.e. to treat her as an equal. (c) Not to commit adultery. (d) To leave her in charge (of her part of the work). (e) To give her dresses and ornaments.

15. Women have the duty of educating their children according to Buddha-Dharma. That is, teaching them the pañcaśīla *and what these mean, teaching them how to practise these in their lives and in general bringing them up to be responsible citizens of the world having those good manners and high standards of politeness so much prized among Buddhists.*

16. Girl-children are as welcome in Buddhist families as boys.

17. Women are not to be despised in any way because they fail to bring forth children.

18. Divorce is not prohibited in the dispensation of the Buddha, provided there are adequate grounds for this.

19. Widows may remarry and are encouraged to do so if they are unable to lead a life of brahmacarya.

20. In the Buddha's teaching it is recognized that women (as well as men) may take up any post in public life for which they are qualified – as educationists, doctors, and posts in the administration.

21. A woman has rights of property according to Buddha-Dharma. She may own land and buildings etc., as well as the contents of a house, all of which may be quite separate from the control of any man. She has the sole right of disposal of any property of which she is the owner.

22. In Buddhist communities, women are an integral part of society. They work on many levels: as students, married women, mothers, managers of the household; engaged in commerce, having their own business, etc.; as doctors, nurses, teachers, government officials, etc.;

or fourthly, as those who have left the house and who feel their whole time should be devoted to their understanding and practice of the Buddha-Dharma, helping others to do likewise.

AMBEDKAR JAYANTI

The following is a combination of notes for three very similar talks, all given in England in the 1960s. One of them was given at Linacre House, Oxford, on 19 January 1965 and another at Burgh House on 14 April 1965; so in those contexts Sangharakshita was presumably speaking to a non-Buddhist audience. But the third took place on 14 April 1969, so was presumably given in the context of the newly begun Friends of the Western Buddhist Order, at a celebration of Dr Ambedkar's 78th birthday, 'Ambedkar Jayanti', as Sangharakshita called it.

Religion is apparently on the decline. More and more areas of human life and thought are breaking away from control, and fewer and fewer people are concerned with religion, at least in traditional Western form. Any distinct contrary movement should therefore be of interest. It should be of interest when four million people abandon the religion their ancestors followed from time immemorial and take to a religion which has been dead in their country for a thousand years; when they come from socially and economically the most backward classes of the community; when they embrace that new religion voluntarily. And this is what has happened in India. Four million Untouchables in Western India have recently become Buddhists. For various reasons this is not known outside India, hence I am glad to speak on what Buddhism has done in India for the Untouchables. I have a certain amount of personal experience, and naturally I am more concerned with the religious aspects, having no sociological training. However, the movement is of great human as well as religious and sociological interest, and tonight I am mainly concerned with that.

To begin at the beginning, some thousands of years ago, long before the time of the Buddha, the 'Puruṣa Sūkta' of the *Rig Veda* describes how Brahmins were created from the head of the *puruṣa*, the Kshatriyas from his shoulders, Vaishyas from his thighs, and Shudras from his feet.[226] These four separations formed the basis of the caste system. It had hardened considerably by the Buddha's time. Brahmins claimed superiority on grounds of birth and colour, a claim rejected by the Buddha, who emphasized worth, not birth.

During the Buddhist period, caste could not flourish, but Buddhism never really succeeded in converting the Brahmins. It is very difficult to give up one's own superiority. As Buddhism declined in India, Hinduism revived, and the caste system hardened. Śaṅkara's punishment for Shudras listening to the Vedas. Eventually there were 2,000 castes, some occupational, others tribal. For the most part people of different castes did not intermarry, or even interdine. More than this, 'untouchability' developed. The 'Untouchables' were considered even lower than Shudras. We can have no idea of what this means psychologically. Even 'unseeability' emerged. I experienced this myself once in Travancore.[227]

The people of one of the untouchable castes were called the Mahars. They were about ten per cent of the population of the state of Maharashtra. They lived outside the villages in terrible conditions. They were not allowed to own new clothes or to take water from the village well. They migrated to cities, especially Bombay, where they became factory workers and lived in slum conditions. It was among these people that Bhimrao Ambedkar was born in 1891. I have no time to recount the story of his life, but despite tremendous hardships he gained an education: first the Mahar matriculation, and then he completed his education in England and the USA. He became a barrister and set up practice in Bombay, and he was soon the unchallengeable leader of the Mahars. Their devotion to him was extraordinary. He became a member of the Indian government, and was Labour and Minister of Law and Justice, then the maker of the constitution of independent India. It's a really epic story.

His main work was the removal of Untouchability, but he came up against orthodox Hinduism and its religious sanction of caste. In their view caste was a God-given institution, and it was a sin to change it. At first he hoped to change the hearts of caste Hindus, but after many bitter experiences he realized it was impossible. In 1924 came the Chowdar Tank case, in which the tank was purified with a hundred pots of water with *pañcagavya*. In 1927 Dr Ambedkar publicly burned the *Manusmṛti*, and at the Yeola Conference in 1935 he declared a change of religion necessary: 'Though I was born a Hindu I will not die one.' Thereafter many Mahars ceased to practise Hinduism.

Dr Ambedkar gradually settled for Buddhism. It was at this period that I had some personal contact with him. We corresponded in 1950 and met three times during the 1950s. We discussed conversion, and he asked me about the form a ceremony should take. But why did he choose Buddhism? One reason was that in Buddhism there is no caste. Another reason is that Buddhism originated in India. And thirdly, it teaches freedom of thought, self-reliance. There was a mass conversion on 14 October 1956 in Nagpur, when half a million people became Buddhist, and Buddhism spread rapidly. But Dr Ambedkar died just six weeks later, on 6 December. I happened to be in Nagpur at that time and remember those days very vividly. I had had some previous contact with Ambedkar, and I was now able to offer support to his followers. After Dr Ambedkar's death there were group rivalries, but the Buddhist movement spread.

What has Buddhism done for the Untouchables? Organizationally, almost nothing. Buddhism is the least organized of religions. Materially, the Untouchables have gained nothing. In many cases, they have undergone great hardships through embracing Buddhism. The charge that the conversion was political must be refuted. Due to the attitude of orthodox Hindus, the Buddhists faced many hardships. They were driven off their lands. Caste Hindus would not sell to them. They were harassed by hooligans and the police. There were beatings, even murders. Newspaper publicity was prejudiced against what they called the 'Neo-Buddhists'. Yet they stuck to Buddhism. Some *bhikkhus* starting going round, and changes took place. Temples were rededicated despite Hindu opposition. There was a lot of change to domestic ceremonies; this is very important in the Indian context. The tradition of getting into debt through marriage settlement was ended, and the position of women changed. There were further conversions (*dikshas*). Lectures were given, books were published, songs were composed. Viharas (Buddhist shrines) were built and statues were installed.

Buddhism has liberated tremendous energies, which partly explains the current *satyagraha* or non-violent civil disobedience movement of the R.P.I.[228] Most important: implementation of an anti-untouchability Act; land; educational grants. This brings us to contemporary Indian politics. I would like to note that these demands are supported in the Indian Parliament by Scheduled Caste members of other parties.

But we have not yet reached the heart of the matter. I asked many people, 'What difference do you experience after becoming a Buddhist?' And they would all say the same thing, 'I feel free.' This is the important point. It is the greatest thing Buddhism has done for their community. It is the greatest thing that it can do for anybody. If you don't feel free – psychologically and spiritually free – you're not really a Buddhist. So let us honour the Buddha, honour Dr Ambedkar, honour them because they showed us how to be free.

A NEW BUDDHIST MOVEMENT: TALKS IN INDIA AND ENGLAND

1979–1992

1979

Sangharakshita visited India twice in 1979, once on his way to New Zealand, and once on the way back. Returning to India after an absence of twelve years, during which he had laid the foundations for a new Buddhist movement in the West, as Lokamitra recalls (pp. xlivff), it was renewing contact with his old disciples among the Ambedkarite communities that moved him most of all. He thought they would have forgotten him, but their respect for him seemed to have grown, and there was a great sense of relief at seeing and hearing him once again. The nine talks he gave on that visit delighted everyone, clarifying and bringing alive the teachings they had learned from Dr Ambedkar, and opening a new dimension for the Buddhist movement.

The Mahavihara, Dapodi, Poona

METTĀ IS THE MOST IMPORTANT THING

Camp Education Society, Camp, Poona, 19 February 1979

Sisters and brothers in the Dhamma, I'm very glad to be back in Poona. As most of you know, it's a full twelve years since I was here last. Since then a few of the friends I knew have passed on, and quite a few young people have come into existence, but most people are as they were before, just a little older and wiser, as we say. I'm very, very glad to see all my old friends again. Yesterday I was sitting in the vihara in the Ambedkar Housing Estate and every few minutes someone whose face I knew very well would come in. Letters came too – for instance, letters from Nagpur saying, 'Don't spend all of your time in Poona; come to Nagpur too.' It seems that even though I've been away for twelve years people haven't forgotten me. I'm a bit surprised. When I was in England I certainly didn't forget you, but you're very busy – you've got your work to do, and your families to look after, young people have to go to school and college – so I thought you might have forgotten me, but I'm very pleased you haven't. Years ago I used to stay with a Parsi friend in Bombay, and I remember him saying, 'You know, these Maharashtrian people, once they become friends with you, they will never let you go.' And that's how it seems to be.

I see many differences between England and Poona. The weather's different, of course – I left England in the snow – but there are other differences too. I have given many lectures in England, and I think I can say I've given some quite good ones, but I never got even one garland. It's very nice to be given these garlands, because it's an expression of people's love, the garlands are beautiful, and while people are giving them to me I've got time to think about my lecture! So I quite like this custom.

You might be wondering what I've been doing in England all this time. Well, in one way I've been doing many things, but in another way I've only been doing one thing. I've been trying to do something for the Dhamma in England. When I returned there, I could see the need for a new Buddhist movement. There were some Buddhist organizations already in existence, but they were very small and they weren't doing much, so they weren't making much impact on society. I thought that something bigger and better and stronger was needed, especially for young people, and I think I can say I've succeeded. You can see for yourself from the people who are here with me. Lokamitra's quite young; Priyananda's even younger; Virabhadra's very young; and Padmavajra's the youngest of all. He became a full-time Order member when he was only nineteen.[229]

Padmavajra, Yuvaraj, Sangharakshita, Lokamitra, Virabhadra

I wanted to start something new and vigorous, but this was not easy. To begin with I was on my own, with very few people to help me. But twelve years ago I started renting a room in the middle of London and I held meetings there once a week, and we did some meditation and chanted the Refuges and Precepts. At first just a few people came along, but gradually things developed, and now there are about twenty centres and communities, with hundreds, even thousands, of people coming along to them. Three months ago we opened our new centre in London. It's a six-storey building with two large shrines, each with a larger than life-size Buddha image made by one of our Order members.[230] One of the images is seated in meditation and the other is standing with his hand in the *abhaya mudrā*, the gesture of fearlessness, and both are very beautiful. There are forty people living in this centre, all of them working full-time for the Dhamma. Some are running classes, some are running the printing press, some are making Buddhist images and pictures, and they're all working together. This is what we have been able to do in London, and in a number of other places in England we have created centres in the same way – not so big, but still quite big.

To do all this in the course of twelve years was difficult, but it was clearly not impossible, because we've done it. So what made it possible? I could answer this question in all sorts of ways. One answer is that money is necessary; you can't do much without money. People are necessary too; you can't do anything without people. There's a Buddhist saying, 'No human beings, no Buddhas.' But there's something else that made all this possible. In just one word, it's *mettā* (*maitrī*, loving-kindness). To do something big you need a lot of people, but to do it successfully, those people have to cooperate. There are so many different kinds of people in the world: old and young, slow and quick, educated and uneducated. It's as though you've got lots of bricks, but you need cement to hold them together. *Mettā* is the cement. It's *mettā* that holds the whole thing together. It's like that in England and it's the same here. The weather may be different, and maybe in England I don't get any garlands, but *mettā* is the same everywhere. Without *mettā*, you can't carry on Buddhist work successfully. So if you want to do something for the Dhamma together, you must develop good relationships among yourselves. If you're quarrelling you can't work for the Dhamma, because you'll have to work on your own, and on your own you can't do much. In order to work effectively you have to cooperate, and in order to cooperate you must have that feeling of *mettā*.

So how do you get it? Well, luckily the Buddha taught us a practice called the *mettā bhāvanā*, and this is something that we all need to learn. In the first stage of the practice, you work on feeling *mettā* towards yourself. If you don't love yourself it is very difficult to love others, so this is not a selfish love, but a quite objective love, wishing for yourself the things that are necessary for your life as a human being. Then, once you've developed *mettā* towards yourself, you develop it towards a very near, dear friend, someone of about the same age as yourself, the same sex as you, and someone who is still alive. If you think of a friend who is dead you may feel sad and that will get in the way of the practice. Then, having developed *mettā* towards your friend, you develop it towards a neutral person, someone you neither like nor dislike. And after that you try to do something even more difficult. You try to develop *mettā* towards someone whom you regard as an enemy, or who regards you as an enemy. You have to wish well even to him or her. As you know, enmities can arise very easily for all sorts of stupid reasons. Sometimes two people quarrel over a pencil, or someone wants to speak in a meeting and another person won't let him, and they become enemies. If you feel that kind of enmity towards somebody, or somebody feels it towards you, you have to overcome that. Next, you try to feel the same love towards yourself, your friend, the neutral person, and the enemy. And then you start expanding *mettā* in ever wider circles. First of all you expand it to all the people in your own house. Sometimes two brothers are not good friends, sometimes husband and wife don't get on well together, but inside the house there must be *mettā*. And then you expand it to the locality, the whole city, the whole country, the whole world, and in this way your heart becomes bigger.

If there is no *mettā* in the Buddhist community you can never do any effective work for the Dhamma. On the basis of my twelve years' experience of Buddhist work in England, I would say that *mettā* is the most important thing. It doesn't matter whether you're fourteen or eighty years old. It doesn't matter whether or not you can read and write. Even if you've never read a single book on Buddhism, that doesn't matter. If you feel *mettā* towards other Buddhists, then you can work for the Dhamma. *Mettā* is the first of what we call the *brahma vihāras*. Next comes *muditā*, joy. When you see other people happy, you become happy. And thirdly there's *karuṇā*, compassion. When you see other people suffering, you feel sorry for them, you want to help them. So from *mettā* comes *muditā* and also *karuṇā*. And if your mind is always full of *mettā*, *muditā*, and *karuṇā* towards everybody, then you will experience the fourth *brahma vihāra*, *upekkhā* – peace of mind. In the old days, yogis used to go off to the Himalayas to experience peace of mind, but that's not necessary. Just practise the *brahma vihāras* and you'll be in the Himalayas all the time, metaphorically speaking.

Can you have more than that? Yes. You can also have wisdom, *prajñā*. I'll say just a few words about that and then I must close. The Buddha says there are three kinds of *prajñā*.[231] First, there's the *prajñā* that comes by hearing. A disciple of the Buddha is called a *śrāvaka*, and *śrāvaka* means 'one who listens' – that is, one who listens to the Dhamma, not just with their ears but with their heart, their head, their hands, their whole being. Imagine it's a very hot day. You have been walking for miles and miles, maybe all day, and you are very thirsty. And then, right at the end of the day, you're given a drink of water. Think how much you would enjoy that water, how happily you would pour it down your throat. That's how you must listen to the Dhamma. You must be thirsty for the Dhamma and take it right in. Then you will develop the wisdom, the *prajñā*, that comes from hearing.

But listening is not enough. After listening to the Dhamma and taking it in, you've got to think about it. You've got to turn it over in your mind. You've got to really understand it. This is the second level of *prajñā*, and it is one of the things that Dr Ambedkar emphasized very strongly. It's not enough to be a blind follower of Buddhism. You must understand the teaching of the Buddha, and you will understand it only after thinking about it. There are some teachings that you can be turning over in your mind for years and years. Only then will you understand them. All the time you must have some points of the Dhamma in your mind that you're thinking about. In this way you develop the *prajñā* that comes from reflection and thinking.

There's one more kind of *prajñā*: *bhāvanā-mayī-prajñā*. *Bhāvanā* means to bring into existence something new. It means to bring into existence within yourself a new mind. It's not just a question of meditating on something, but changing your whole mind from a lower into a higher mind. So how does this happen? When you think about the Dhamma more and more, your mind becomes one with the Dhamma.

You are transformed into the Dhamma, into the Truth, and then you become like a new human being. You become at least a little like the Buddha. Somebody once said, 'It's not enough to be a Buddhist, you've got to be a Buddha.' It's not enough to say, 'I'm a Buddhist.' You've got to become a new person and try to become a Buddha. This is the essence of the Buddha's teaching.

Maybe what I've said this evening has been a bit too much, at least for some of you, but never mind. Just remember to practise *mettā* and develop *prajñā*. Have a good heart and a good head, an enlightened heart and an enlightened head. Then you can all work together for the Dhamma happily and successfully. If you can do this, you'll be very happy, and everybody who comes into contact with you will feel happy too. In the *Dhammapada* the Buddha says, 'My disciples live happily in the midst of a miserable world.'[232] This is one of the characteristics of a Buddhist, that you're happy. The Buddha himself is called Sugata, 'the happy one'. If you have *mettā*, if you have *prajñā*, you'll have happiness too.

I think I had better stop talking now because my throat is beginning to go and I've got to give another lecture this evening. I'd just like to say in conclusion that I'm very happy to be back in Poona once again and very happy to meet everybody on this occasion, my first talk in Poona on my return.

THE ENERGY OF THE WINDHORSE

Range Hills, 19 February 1979

Sisters and brothers in the Dhamma, I'm happy to be back in India, happy to be in Poona, and even more happy to be in Range Hills. I've been here many times before. There have been a lot of Dhamma activities here; I can remember one occasion when some young men read and explained Dr Ambedkar's book *The Buddha and His Dhamma*. So I know Range Hills well and I'm glad to be back. I hope it won't be another twelve years before I'm here again.

A few days ago I was still in London, where in the last three years we've been making a big new vihara. In the courtyard of the vihara is a wall on which there is a large painting, twenty feet long and fifteen feet high. It is bright and brilliant, and can be seen from the street. At night it is floodlit. It was painted by one of the members of our sangha[233] – it took him three months, working on scaffolding – and it represents a big white horse galloping on clouds. In the background is a bright blue sky with a rainbow around it. The horse is carrying three jewels: a yellow one at the top, a blue one on the left, and a red one on the right. Golden light and flames are coming out of the jewels, and fire is coming out of the horse's nostrils and hooves.

So what is the meaning of the picture? The yellow jewel is the Buddha. Yellow is the colour of the Buddha's robe, and in some Buddhist scriptures the Buddha's complexion is described as golden. The blue jewel is the Dhamma. Why blue? Blue is the colour of the sky. The sky has no limit, and the Dhamma, the Truth, is like that. And the red jewel

Padmapani's windhorse mural, London Buddhist Centre

is the Sangha. You may have thought that the colour of the Sangha should be yellow, but no – the Sangha is red. Red is the colour of love, *maitrī*. Within the Sangha there must be love. The jewels rest on a pure white lotus, which is resting on the horse's back.

The white horse represents energy, *vīrya*. *Vīrya* is needed to carry the Buddha, Dhamma, and Sangha. It's no use keeping them in the cupboard – they must go through the whole world, and this can only happen if Buddhists have energy. The white horse is the energy of all the Buddhists in the world. When the artist asked me which way the horse in the painting should face, I said that obviously it must gallop from the vihara (which is on the left) to the street, to the world (on the right). Energy is very important. It is one of the first teachings of the Buddha. If you don't have energy you're not a Buddhist, because you're not really alive, and a Buddhist is full of life. We have to be white horses. We have to join together and make one big white horse. We have to take the Buddha, Dhamma, and Sangha everywhere.

Several animals are important in Buddhism. The Buddha left home at night riding on a horse, and the horse represents the Buddha's energy, carrying him from home into the wilderness. So the horse stands for leaving home, and the lion, the king of all the animals, stands for the Buddha teaching the Dhamma. When the lion roars, all the other animals are silent, and when the Buddha teaches the Dhamma, everyone keeps quiet. And then there's the elephant. When the elephant walks through the village, a dog barks, but the elephant takes no notice, he just walks on. In the same way the Buddhist walks on. We could say that critics of Buddhism are like dogs barking, and since Dr Ambedkar's conversion a lot of dogs have been barking, but you must keep going. In Christianity we are told to be like sheep, to follow the shepherd Jesus, but the Buddha compares us to much more noble animals: 'Be like a horse – gallop. Be like a lion – roar. Be like an elephant – take no notice.'[234]

Tonight I want to talk about the horse of *vīrya*. The Buddha taught that there are five spiritual faculties.[235] There are two balancing pairs, the first pair being faith and wisdom, and the second pair being energy and meditation. *Śraddhā*, faith, towards the Buddha, the Dhamma, and the Sangha is necessary, but so that it is not blind faith, it must be balanced by wisdom, *prajñā*. But too much *prajñā* results in dry, dusty scholars, so it needs to be balanced by faith. Likewise with the second pair of faculties, we need plenty of *vīrya* – no *vīrya*, no Buddhism – but if there's too much *vīrya* and not enough *samadhi*, we just get restless. On the other hand, if there's too much *samādhi* and not enough *vīrya*, no work is done for the Dhamma. And there's a fifth faculty which balances the others: *smṛti* – that is, mindfulness. It doesn't need a balancing factor, because you can't have too much mindfulness. So, look at your own mind. See which faculties you've got too much of, and which too little. See where you've got to develop. Most people need to develop all five faculties more.

Some teachers say that *vīrya* is the most important of all, because you need it in order to make an effort to develop the other faculties. Just as you can't be successful in worldly life without energy, you can't be successful in spiritual life without *vīrya*. That's why we painted the picture of the horse. Spiritual energy is needed to propagate the Buddha, the Dhamma, and the Sangha. The horse galloping through the sky is an ancient Buddhist symbol found in India and Tibet called the Windhorse. It carries the Three Jewels as quickly as the wind. The world is in a very bad state. The Buddha, Dhamma, and Sangha are needed urgently. We must take them as quickly as we can to as many people as we can.

We also find *vīrya* in the Noble Eightfold Path, on which it is the sixth step. In that context we talk about the energy that is needed to get rid of unskilful mental states and develop skilful ones. First of all, we get rid of any unskilful thoughts or feelings that are present in the mind. Secondly, we prevent any unskilful thoughts or feelings from arising. Thirdly, we make an effort to develop any skilful thoughts and feelings already there, such as *śraddhā*, intelligence, kindness, joy. And fourthly, we bring in skilful thoughts that are not there already. This is the fourfold right effort.[236] It is important to have energy and inspiration all the time. What is the difference between these? Well, you may be making an effort with *vīrya*, but finding it difficult and painful. But with inspiration, it is not difficult or painful. You enjoy even the most difficult work. It is like a game. Work becomes easier than play. This is why the Windhorse is galloping on clouds, not on the earth. It's like flying. There are no wings, but in a way there are. Inspiration (*prīti* in Sanskrit) is needed as well as energy. As a result of our Dhamma practice great joy arises, like a spring of water, and this joy gives a lot of energy. Even the most difficult work becomes easy, especially Dhamma work.

I'm sure there is already some of this spirit in Range Hills. People are waiting with lights and garlands, and this is very pleasant to see, because it shows that people are happy. People who are in our Buddhist movement tend to be much happier than those who are not. They work hard, they give time, energy, and money. They live simply – much more simply than most people in England – but still they are happier. In the *Dhammapada* the Buddha says, 'Happily we live in the midst of those who are miserable'.[237] If we are always sad, there is something wrong with our Buddhism. Buddhism should give us energy, and we should give our energy to Buddhism.

Here in Poona there are more than eighty Buddhist localities, and three lakhs of Buddhists. A third of the population of Poona recite the Refuges. If a third of the population really become Buddhist, we will be able to change the whole city. I wish one third of the population of London were Buddhists. There are only a few hundred there, but there are millions of Buddhists in India. If they were all real Buddhists, India would be full of energy, happiness, and inspiration, and Dr Ambedkar's dream of a new India would come true. This was one of the reasons why he went for Refuge: not just for himself, or just for his own people, but for all India, for all people. We must take this very seriously.

I've told you about Buddhists in England, and Buddhists in England have read about you and Dr Ambedkar in our newsletter. They know Dr Ambedkar very well, and some like to read about his life and read his book *The Buddha and His Dhamma*. It is very good that we know one another. I hope that between us we can really do something for the Buddha, Dhamma, and Sangha. Between us we can make up a big white Windhorse to carry the Three Jewels everywhere – at least in Poona. If we can do this we will be true followers of Buddhism, true followers of Dr Ambedkar. We will be doing the best for ourselves and for the society in which we live.

WHAT ATTRACTS WESTERNERS TO BUDDHISM?

Parnakuti Housing Society, 20 February 1979

Sisters and brothers in the Dhamma, as Mr Vanashiv has just reminded you, it's twelve years since I was last in India. Most of that time I was in England, working for the Dhamma, and in a few minutes I'll say a bit about that, but first of all I'd like to say how happy I am to be back here again. I have memories of so many good meetings here, with so many people attending, sometimes very late at night. I'm glad not only to be back in Poona, but to be here in Yerawada. They say that when you speak about Yerawada, people think about just two things, the jail and the madhouse, but all the same I'm happy to be back here. After all, the Buddha said that the whole world, the world of *saṃsāra*, is a jail, and also that the whole world is like a madhouse, because all worldly people are mad.[238]

So what have I been doing all this time? Twelve years ago I started a new Buddhist movement in England. At that time there were some small Buddhist societies in England, but they weren't doing much. I thought something new was needed, so with a few friends I started classes right in the middle of London. We started with just one small room and we met there once a week to meditate for an hour and do our *vandanā*. As we carried on month by month, more and more people started coming, so we started hiring halls in London and having public lectures on the Dhamma. Then we started organizing retreats in the country for meditation and Dhamma study for one or two weeks at a time, and many people came on those. In the course of the last twelve years we have established about twenty new centres and communities in England, and in all these places there is a full programme of Buddhist activities. Not only in England; these activities are going on in New Zealand, Finland, and other places too. And just a few months ago in London we moved into an even bigger centre than we had before. In the course of the twelve years that the activities have been carried on in all these centres, many thousands of people have come to know about the Dhamma, and out of these people, many hundreds have taken a strong interest in it and some have committed themselves wholeheartedly to the Buddha and his Dhamma.

So what is it in Buddhism that attracts Western people so much? After all, to them Buddhism is quite foreign. Here in India, it is natural for people to be interested in Buddhism because the Buddha was born here and preached his Dhamma here. In fact, if people in India don't follow the Buddha, that is the surprising thing. But in the West, people have been Christians for nearly 2,000 years. Why should they now be so interested in Buddhism and want to commit themselves to it? Nowadays of course many people don't believe in Christianity any more, and some of these people turn to Buddhism. Dr Ambedkar once said that we cannot live without religion. Even if you give up Christianity, or Hinduism, you still need some religion. So what is it about Buddhism that attracts people in the West?

The first reason is very important. In Buddhism there is no supreme being, no God. There is God in Christianity, of course, and in Islam and Judaism, and so far as most Hindus are concerned there is God. In the West nowadays people find it difficult to believe in God, but usually the only religion they know about is God-based. If you look up 'religion' in the English dictionary, you'll find that it is defined as 'belief in God', and most people think that if you give up God you give up religion, so those who can no longer believe in God but want to follow a religion find themselves in a difficult position. If these people come in contact with Buddhism, they are pleased to find that Buddhism is a religion without God.

But why are people in the West so much against the idea of God? Christianity teaches that God has made and rules the whole universe, and tells you what to do through Jesus Christ, through the Christian religion. God is thought of as a sort of king ruling the whole universe, and if you don't do as he tells you, he will punish you, if not in this life, then after death. So in Christianity very often belief in God is associated with fear. Christian people believe in God, but they are very afraid of him, because they think that if they don't obey his commands, they will be punished, and that whatever they do or think, God knows it. So a lot of people don't like the idea of God, but they don't want to give up religion, and Buddhism offers them a way to develop spiritually without belief in God. This is perhaps the main reason why people in the West are drawn to Buddhism.

Another reason is that Buddhism offers us the possibility of developing as human beings. If you believe in God, your religion involves obeying God, praying to God, but if you don't believe in God, what is your religion then? It is developing yourself as a human being, physically, mentally, educationally, culturally, emotionally, spiritually – developing all your good, noble qualities – and Buddhism shows us how to do this, for instance by following the Noble Eightfold Path. After the Buddha gained Enlightenment at Bodh Gaya, at first he thought that the truth that he had discovered was too difficult to teach to people, but he looked out over the world and saw the whole human race in his mind's eye as being just like a bed of lotus flowers. He saw that some of these lotus flowers were right down in the mud, some were just emerging above the water, and some were standing clear of the water with their petals open in the sunlight.[239] In other words, he saw that each and every human being is capable of growth and development. Compassion arose in his heart, and he thought, 'At least there are a few people who will understand. For their benefit I will teach the Dhamma.' This is why the Buddha gave his teaching – to help people grow and develop. On one occasion he said, 'Whatever helps you to evolve, whatever helps you to be a better human being, that is my Dhamma, that is my teaching.'[240] So this is another aspect of Buddhism that attracts people in the West. It shows them a way to grow and develop as a human being.

They are also attracted by meditation, which is a way of developing the mind. So how is this done? In our Buddhist movement in England we teach several different kinds of meditation. First of all, we teach the mindfulness of breathing. We teach people to calm the mind, to make it quiet and concentrated by watching their in-and-out breathing. Then we teach them to practise mindfulness by watching their bodily movements, watching their thoughts, watching their feelings, and constantly allowing their minds to rest on the Buddha's teaching and reflect upon that. We also teach the *mettā bhāvanā*, which involves developing love towards your own self, then a near and dear friend, then a neutral person, then even towards your enemies, then all the people in your locality, in the city, in the country, in the whole world. Many people like this meditation very much, finding that it gives them great peace of mind. We also have the meditation on the six elements – I won't say anything about that because it's a bit more difficult – and the meditation on the Buddha. To meditate on the Buddha we close our eyes and see a picture of the Buddha in our mind. We see him seated under the bodhi tree on a heap of grass, eyes half closed, wearing yellow robes. He has a gold-coloured complexion and a compassionate smile on his lips and he is surrounded by golden light. In this way we practise until we can see the Buddha in our own mind, and then we say to ourselves, *Buddhaṃ saraṇaṃ gacchāmi, Dhammaṃ saraṇaṃ gacchāmi, Saṅghaṃ saraṇaṃ gacchāmi.* So this is another of the reasons why Buddhism attracts people in the West: because it teaches a practical method of meditation which can help them gain peace of mind.

Another thing that attracts people to Buddhism is that it teaches social improvement. Some religions say that it doesn't matter what sort of society you live in, because the important thing is just to think of God, but Buddhism is concerned with the development of the individual human being, and to some extent the individual is dependent upon the society in which they live. Living in a good society makes it easier for you to develop as a human being, and living in a bad, unjust society makes it more difficult. So it is not just the individual who has to be changed; society also has to be changed. Here there are two extreme views. Some people say that the important thing is to change society. If you change society, everything will be all right. Others say changing society doesn't matter; just change yourself and everything will be all right. Buddhism follows the middle path, saying that the individual and the society to which the individual belongs are interdependent. You have to improve the individual, but you also have to improve society, so that the individual can improve more easily. Some religions say that poverty does not matter. They say that even if you don't have proper clothes, even if you don't have enough food, you can still think of God. But Buddhism says that for the individual to develop, good conditions in society are necessary.

Something very different that also attracts people in the West to Buddhism is Buddhist art. Many people in the West love art, and ancient

Buddhist art is very beautiful indeed. People see an ancient image of the Buddha or a Tibetan Buddhist painting, and they think, 'This is not just an ordinary image.' It has some special quality, something they don't find in Western art. So they start asking, 'What is this?' and in this way they get interested in Buddhism. At our London centre in each of our shrine-rooms there is a beautiful Buddha image, larger than life, to make it easier to think of the Buddha and meditate on him, and do puja. We mustn't think that Buddhism is just a question of intellectual understanding, or ethics, or meditation, or improving society. Art also has a place.

I want to mention just one more quality of Buddhism that attracts people in the West. In some ways this is the most important quality of all. It is *kalyāṇa mitratā*. *Mitratā* means friendship and *kalyāṇa* means good, spiritual, noble, so *kalyāṇa mitratā* is good, noble spiritual friendship. If you're all interested in Buddhism, you all go for Refuge to the Buddha, you study the Dhamma together, you listen to lectures together, you meditate together, perhaps even live together in Buddhist communities, you will have very good, happy friendships with one another. Outside in the world people sometimes behave quite badly, but in the Buddhist community you find that people are friendly and kind. Many people in England are drawn to our Buddhist movement because of the spiritual friendship based upon the Buddha's Dhamma that they find there.

What is the difference between Buddhist friendship and ordinary friendship? Maybe you become friends with someone who works in the same office as you, or with whom you go to the cinema, or who lives next door. The friendship may not go very deep, and sometimes you may quarrel. But the basis of Buddhist friendship is that you all go for Refuge to the Buddha, Dhamma, and Sangha, and you're helping one another to grow and to lead a good Buddhist life. This is what we call the *Mahāsaṅgha*, the community of all the followers of the Buddha who are happily relating to one another. There is a passage in the Pāli scriptures where Ānanda says to the Buddha, 'Bhagavan, I think that *kalyāṇa mitratā* is half of the whole spiritual life.' But the Buddha said, 'No, don't say that, Ānanda. *Kalyāṇa mitratā* is the *whole* of the spiritual life.'[241] If everybody around you is against the Buddhist teaching and not encouraging you to practise it, it's very difficult, but if all the time you are associating with Buddhist friends with whom you're always talking about the Dhamma, practising the Dhamma, practising meditation, it's easier to be a Buddhist. This is why the Buddha told his disciples that if they met together regularly – not just to gossip, but to talk about the Dhamma, to do puja, to meditate – their progress in the spiritual life would be assured.[242]

In a way this is what we are doing this evening. Most of us come from India, and some of us have come all the way from England, but the Dhamma has brought us together. The Buddha, we can say, has brought us together. And because we are all together because of the Buddha and the Dhamma, we make up a Sangha and we can experience *kalyāṇa mitratā*. If you practise *kalyāṇa mitratā*, you will regard all other Buddhists as brothers and sisters, and if more and more people could do this, the world would be a much happier place.

These are just six of the reasons why people in the West are attracted to Buddhism nowadays, and I'm sure they also attract people here in India too. They are certainly among the things that attracted Dr Ambedkar to Buddhism. When he decided that he and his followers should give up Hinduism he looked around for the best possible path that they could follow, and he found it in the Buddha's teaching, partly for the reasons which also attract people in the West.

If we pick up the daily newspaper we see so many troubles in different parts of the world, and sometimes we really do feel that the world is a big madhouse. People are behaving in a completely mad way, doing the very things that will harm their own selves. What we need in the world is a little sanity. We need people to see things more clearly. The Buddha's teaching helps us to do this and this is why we need it more and more today.

WHATEVER HELPS US GROW

Pimpri, 23 February 1979

Sisters and brothers in the Dhamma, as you've heard, it's quite a long time since I was last in Pimpri. For the last twelve years I have been in England and other western countries. Before that, of course, I lived in India for nearly twenty years, mostly staying in Kalimpong near the Tibetan border, where my vihara was situated in a very beautiful spot from which I could see the snows of the Himalayas and especially the peak of Mount Kanchenjunga. I spent most of the year there, meditating, writing books, and teaching, and every winter I'd come down to the plains, sometimes to Calcutta, sometimes to Nagpur and Jabalpur, sometimes to Bombay and Delhi. But most of all I used to come to Poona, and when I came to Poona I visited Pimpri, and here we had many fine Dhamma meetings. I returned to England after being away for exactly twenty years. I meant it to be just a visit for four months, but in the end I stayed for two years. I saw that there was a lot of scope for Dhamma work in England, so I decided to spend some time there. Returning to India to say goodbye, I saw as many of my old friends as I could and told them what I was going to do, and then I went back to England and started up a completely new Buddhist movement which has kept me busy for the last twelve years.

So all these years I have been in England, busy trying to spread the Dhamma. But what do we mean by the Dhamma? People have all sorts of strange ideas about that. Sometimes people think that it is a system of abstract ideas, a system of philosophy. When I lived in India, many of my young friends were going to college and studying Indian philosophy, and sometimes I used to look at their textbooks. If you look at a textbook of Indian philosophy, what do you find? Chapter one, philosophy of the Vedas; chapter two, philosophy of Upanishads. Then there are chapters on all the other systems of Indian philosophy, including a small chapter on Buddhist philosophy. So a lot of people in India think this is Buddhism: just one of the twelve or fourteen different systems of Indian philosophy. And if you read that chapter on Buddhist philosophy, you'll find that it is very dull and dry. First of all there will be a bit about the Piṭakas and the four *Nikāyas*, and then there will be bits about Abhidharma, Madhyamaka, and Yogācāra. But there will be not one word about how to live as a Buddhist. If you got your knowledge about Buddhism from the textbooks of Indian philosophy, you would think that Buddhism is just some dry bones, not anything living. This is a very wrong idea, but it is the sort of idea about Buddhism that many people have got in India.

In England they've got even stranger ideas. When I went back there in 1964 several newspaper reporters came to see me in the small vihara in north London where I was staying. They were first of all surprised to find that there was not a high wall all the way round the vihara. They seemed to think that it would be like a sort of prison. The first question that they would often ask was, 'Why do Buddhists torture themselves?' And sometimes they would ask, 'Are you allowed to speak to other people?' as though I had to get someone's permission. I used to say, 'Well, of course, I can speak to anyone I please.' A favourite question was, 'Who has sent you to England?' They seemed to think that there must be some head of Buddhism sitting somewhere in India who had sent me, or maybe the Dalai Lama had sent me. But I used to say that nobody had sent me. It was my own idea, my own wish. In Buddhism we have this sort of freedom. For a while, maybe five or ten years, we study with our teacher, but after that we are free to go anywhere we please, and teach in any way we please. This they found very difficult to understand.

So what is the Dhamma? To put it simply, the Buddha's Dhamma is concerned with the growth and development of the individual human being. There is a Sanskrit Buddhist text called the *Saddharma Puṇḍarīka Sūtra* in which, among many beautiful stories told by the Buddha, is the story of the raincloud.[243] The Buddha said that at the beginning of the rainy season a big dark cloud appears in the sky. You hear the thunder and you see the lightning flash, and then the rain comes down, very steadily and heavily. And what happens then? All the different plants start drawing in the water. Big trees, small trees, grass, flowers – they all are very happy to get the rain, and they all start growing. Before, they were dry and thin and withered, but when the rain falls they grow big and strong and put forth flowers.

What is the meaning of this? The Buddha said, 'The cloud that sends down the rain is the Dhamma.' And just like the rain, the Dhamma falls on everybody. It doesn't fall on the Brahmin but not on the Shudra; it doesn't fall on the educated but not on the illiterate; it doesn't fall on the rich but not on the poor. The rain of the Buddha's Dhamma falls on everybody, is meant for everybody. When the Buddha sent forth his first sixty disciples, he said that his teaching was *bahujana sukhāya, bahujana hitāya*, for the welfare and happiness, of many people, which means everybody, all human beings.[244] The rain of the Dhamma falls on all alike, and as they take in the rain of the Dhamma everybody grows. They don't grow in exactly the same way. They grow according to their own temperament, their own qualities, their own understanding. But they all grow. Just as the trees and bushes, the flowers and grasses grow, every human being who receives the Buddha's Dhamma grows, becomes a better human being, becomes more and more like the Buddha.

So the Dhamma is whatever helps us to grow, whatever makes our minds more pure, whatever makes us more full of *mettā* and *karuṇā*, whatever increases our *prajñā*. This is the Buddha's teaching, and this is what he said to his own aunt and foster-mother. Her name was Mahāpajāpatī Gotami. She had become a *bhikkhunī*, and as she wandered about she met many of the Buddha's disciples. She asked them, 'What is the Buddha's teaching?' but one said one thing, another said something else, and she got a bit confused. This is what we sometimes find in England. A lama comes from Tibet and tells us that Buddhism is one thing, and then a *bhikkhu* comes from Thailand and says that Buddhism is something different, a Zen monk comes from Japan and says that Buddhism is something different again, and another *bhikkhu* comes from Sri Lanka and gives another version. Before we started our own movement, English Buddhists were getting confused. It's a bit like that in India too. There are a lot of Tibetan lamas here now, carrying on their Tantric ceremonies, and you also get Japanese *bhikkhus* building stupas and walking about going *tak tak tak* with their little drums. This is the Buddha's Dhamma, they say. In this way everybody gives a different version.

So what is the Buddha's Dhamma? This was Mahāpajāpatī Gotami's difficulty. Sāriputta said one thing; Moggallāna said something else; Ānanda said something else; Mahākassapa said something else. How was she to know which was the Dhamma? So she went to the Buddha and said, 'Lord, your disciples are giving so many interpretations of your teaching. How are we to know what is really your Dhamma?' And the Buddha said, 'It is very simple. Whatever helps you to grow, whatever helps you to develop as a human being, whatever helps you to purify your mind, whatever helps you to get rid of greed, whatever helps you to get rid of anger, whatever helps you to develop *mettā* and *karuṇā*, whatever makes you helpful to other people, clear in your thinking, independent, free, that is my Dhamma.'[245]

It is very simple. If you hear something about the Dhamma from some lama from Tibet, just ask yourself, 'Is it likely to help me to develop?' If you hear something from a *bhikkhu* from Thailand, ask yourself the same thing. You might need to try it for a while, to see its effect. Then, if it helps you to develop, accept it and keep practising it. If it doesn't help you to develop, quietly put it aside. It doesn't mean that that statement is wrong. It simply means that at this moment it is not useful to you. This is the great criterion. The Buddha's Dhamma is whatever helps the human individual to develop into more and more of a true individual, an Enlightened individual. So when I say that I've been trying to spread the Dhamma in England, I don't mean that I've been trying to spread a particular system of philosophy. I've been trying to spread those aspects of the Buddha's teaching that will actually help people to grow and develop.

There are some things that we've found very useful and other things that, although they are written in Buddhist books, are not particularly useful to us. I want to conclude this evening by giving you some idea of some of the things that we've found useful. The first thing is meditation. When I started up our new movement in England the first thing I did was to start meditation classes. The whole of our movement, which is now quite big, came out of that. All our centres teach meditation, and all our members find meditation very helpful. We teach different methods of Buddhist meditation: the mindfulness of breathing, the *mettā bhāvanā*, the meditation on death, the recollection of the Buddha. Everyone in our sangha meditates every day. Some people meditate for one hour, some for two or even more. People find meditation so useful that they wonder how any Buddhist can live without it, and they are sometimes surprised to meet *bhikkhus* from eastern countries who don't know how to do it.

Not only do we have meditation classes; some people want to do more meditation than that, so we have meditation retreats. A group of people go away from the city into the countryside. Some years ago we used to have to hire a big house, but now we have our own places. We stay there for two or three days, or a week or two, sometimes a whole month, and every day we do six or eight hours of meditation, with some puja and some study, and of course we eat once or twice every day. In this way people can get very deeply into their meditation practice and when they come back to their home or their work, even though they have got many things to do, they can still keep up their meditation quite well. Both men and women go on retreat, and sometimes the women have their own separate retreats which they run by themselves. We are creating a special retreat centre in a beautiful area of Wales which will be devoted to meditation, and all the people who go there will observe silence for half of every day. I think in India this is something that people find a bit difficult. Western people think that Indians are very quiet and always meditating like yogis, but we know it is not quite like that. Indian people are very lively, they like to talk, and they don't find it easy to sit quietly. But anyway, we are making this special retreat centre in Wales. I hope that by the time I get back in about four months' time, it will be finished.

Another aspect of the Dhamma that we find very useful is study. I don't just mean reading books; I mean studying Buddhist texts with a teacher. In the West, people are in the habit of reading a lot, and very often when people become interested in Buddhism they think it means simply reading books about it. They read book after book, but it doesn't help much. They get intellectual indigestion and their life doesn't change. In our movement we recommend reading just one or two books about the Buddha's teachings and reading them very carefully with a teacher. We have Dhamma study groups in which six or eight people take a text, sometimes only two or three pages, and go through every word and try to understand it deeply and thoroughly. Then they ask themselves, 'How can I put this into practice in my own life?' As I said at the beginning, Buddhism is not a system of abstract philosophy, it is something we must practise, something that must help us to grow. We also have Dhamma study retreats, during which we spend a week or ten days going through a text, every day studying for four or six hours. We study texts like the *Udāna* or the *Bodhicaryāvatāra* and we go through them word by word and sentence by sentence, trying to understand the text and apply it to our own lives. Most of these Dhamma study groups are led by me, and then those who have studied with me take other study groups for others. Not only that; the discussion is recorded, then someone transcribes it, somebody else types it, I correct it, and it is published in book form, so in this way it circulates through the movement. We haven't published all of them yet, but in the end I think there will be about thirty volumes.[246] We find this sort of Dhamma study very helpful to our development.

Another thing that we find useful may surprise you. Maybe you are not surprised to hear that meditation helps us, and that Dhamma study helps us. But the third thing that helps us in our Dhamma life is work. Of course most people work – it's nothing special. But in the UK young people sometimes like to have a year or two to have free time before they start working. Some young people, after leaving school or college, were coming along to our classes, and doing a bit of meditation and study, but strangely, they weren't getting on very well with their spiritual life. We discovered that if they did some work, especially physical work, they felt better and they could meditate and study better. When you work, your energy is aroused, so that when you meditate, you meditate better, and when you study, you study better. A lazy person doesn't develop very easily as a human being, and people discovered this for themselves.

I spoke about our centre in London. Forty people worked on it for three whole years. The building was already there – we got it from the local government – but we had to change it into a vihara. We had to make the shrine, the study rooms, and the office. We had to put in the central heating and the ventilation system, make the Buddha images and the library, plaster and paint the walls, put in the wiring and plumbing. All of this was done by people in our own sangha. We didn't get any help from outside. Everybody enjoyed working together. And because people enjoyed working together, because they realized it was helpful to their spiritual development, they set up Buddhist cooperatives, and whatever profit they make from those cooperatives goes into the Buddhist centre, so they don't have to ask the public for money. So work is one of the things that helps us develop spiritually. Of course, it has to be the right sort of work: work that is in accordance with right livelihood.

When I say work, I don't mean just white-collar work, but manual work too. In India some people have very strange ideas about work, and one of them is the idea that there is a big difference between the coolie and the babu. Maybe someone comes from a very poor family, maybe his father is only a coolie, but then his son gets some education, gets a job in an office, and gets promoted. Maybe he becomes quite a big man, even a gentleman. And when he becomes a gentleman, he doesn't even like to carry his own small briefcase. He is quite strong enough to carry it himself, but he gives a coolie five annas to carry it for him, because he thinks that now he is a babu, he mustn't do any work with his hands. This is not good because it means that the middle-class people look down on the people who work with their hands, 'in the sweat of their brow', as the saying is, and think that sitting in an office writing something is superior. But there is nothing low in manual work. Even if we become educated we shouldn't be ashamed of working with our hands. Most people in the West understand this. Even educated people like working on their own houses, painting walls, making furniture, digging in their garden. That's a more balanced life, because we have not only a brain but a body, and they both need exercise. If you don't get any exercise you become just like a shopkeeper who is sitting on his *gadi* all day; you get a big belly, maybe you get diabetes, and maybe you die an early death. So we should respect the physical worker, the peasant working in the fields, and the factory hand. Without their work society cannot exist. There's no need to be afraid of work. The more you do, especially the more you do for others, the better a Buddhist you are, the better a human being you are.

Another thing we find useful is puja, especially chanting. Some years ago people coming along to our classes in England didn't like the puja at all. They thought that Buddhism meant studying books or meditating and that puja was only for ignorant and uneducated people. So they just used to sit at the back and watch. But after a while there was a big change. They felt like joining in, and when they did, they found that they liked the puja very much. Even very educated people to their surprise find that the puja does them more good than all their reading. So why is this? Because the puja opens up their heart. Before that perhaps they didn't even know they had a heart; they were all brain. But when they start reciting the puja – the *tisaraṇa*, the *pañcasīla*, the *vandana*, and other verses that we have – they feel very deeply moved. They feel a lot of faith, a lot of devotion, and because of this they feel very happy and inspired; they feel like new people. They say afterwards, 'I would never have believed it. Just joining in the puja makes such a big difference.' So puja is one of the things that Buddhists in England have found really useful in their spiritual development, and it occupies a very important place in our activities in our centres. It is not the kind of puja where one person leads and everybody else just sits and listens. Everybody joins in because in Buddhism no one can do puja for you. There is no *purohit* or priest. You do the puja yourself because it is good for your Dhamma life, it helps you to grow.

I'll mention just one more thing that Buddhists in England find very helpful to their development and growth: communication. What do I mean by that? I'll give you an example. When you meet someone, what do you do? First of all you look at them. Some people don't even look at you. They talk to you, but they are looking up in the air so they don't see you. If they don't even see you, how can they talk to you properly? So this is the first thing to do when you meet someone: look at them. Just see them properly, see that there is another human being in front of you. And when you speak to that human being, try to say just what you are thinking and feeling. Be very open, very honest. Don't keep anything in your heart which you don't let out. This is what we call good communication. If Buddhists are living together, working together, practising the Dhamma together, it is very important that we should be open with one another and speak our minds to one another. This gives us a lot of energy, and we feel very happy that we are getting on well together, working together for the Dhamma.

These are just some of the things that Buddhists in England have found very useful in their spiritual life, and I'm sure that some of you in Pimpri will find them useful too. First of all, there's meditation. Secondly, there's Dhamma study. Thirdly, there's work: not just work for yourself and your family, but work for the Dhamma, for the Buddhist movement, work in accordance with right livelihood. Fourthly, there's puja, reciting the *tisaraṇa* and *pañcasīla* together. And lastly, there's communication, being very open and friendly with one another, being full of *mettā* and *karuṇā*.

The big thing we need to remember about the Dhamma is that it is whatever helps us to grow and develop as human beings. The Dhamma is not a system of abstract ideas. It is not just one small chapter in the history of Indian philosophy. The Dhamma is alive. Just like the rain that falls from that great raincloud on the whole earth, the Dhamma falls on all people so that they can grow. For many years the raincloud of the Dhamma was not seen in the Indian sky. All you could see for hundreds of years was just the sky and the sun, and everything got burnt up and dry. And then suddenly the cloud of the Dhamma appeared again in the sky of India, and the rain of the Dhamma started falling. When was that? That was twenty-three years ago in Nagpur, at the time of Dr Ambedkar's great conversion to the Dhamma. And now that rain is falling once again. It's falling in the towns and cities of Maharashtra, in Poona and Pimpri, in Nagpur and Jabalpur. It's falling in other places in India too: in the Central Province, Madhya Pradesh, the Punjab, Calcutta. It's even falling in England. In England we have plenty of ordinary rain, we have enough of that, but we can't have enough of the rain of the Dhamma. And soon I hope that the rain of the Dhamma will be falling in America, because in two years' time we are going to have a centre there too.

As the rain of the Dhamma falls, you should all be like the plants, the trees, the shrubs, or at least the grass. The ladies can be like the flowers. Just open yourself to the Dhamma, just take it in and grow. Whether you are young or old, literate or illiterate, rich or poor, you can grow. You can become a better and better human being, and in the end you can become like Lord Buddha himself, and then this rising of the raincloud of the Dhamma over twenty-three years ago will have achieved a great success.

WHY DID THE BUDDHA LEAVE HIS HOUSE?

Questions and answers, Sinhagad, 26 February 1979

Q: *Why did the Buddha leave his house? Please give your own reasons and the reasons given by Dr Babasaheb Ambedkar in* The Buddha and His Dhamma. *And if the reasons are different, which one is to be accepted?*
Sangharakshita: I am assuming that the questioner has in mind the story about the Buddha leaving home because of the four sights. This is the account that is accepted by most Buddhists, but Dr Ambedkar has suggested that perhaps the Buddha left home on account of some political disturbance within the Śākya republic. So did the Buddha leave home because of those four sights, or because of a political disturbance, or maybe for some other reason?

Before trying to answer that question, I want to make a few general remarks about the critical study of Pāli literature. This isn't easy to explain in a few words, but I shall try. I studied this question quite intensively some years ago, just before I left India, when I wrote a history of Buddhist canonical literature.[247] We know that the Buddha didn't write anything, and neither did his direct disciples, or their disciples. It was some generations later that the disciples started writing down the Buddha's teachings. What we call the Buddhist scriptures, the Tipiṭaka – that is to say, the Sutta Piṭaka, the Vinaya Piṭaka, and the Abidhamma Piṭaka – represent the writing down of teachings that had been transmitted orally for several hundred years. Leaving aside other versions (for example Sanskrit versions), the Pāli version is in forty-five large volumes.

So are all the texts in these volumes the teaching of the Buddha himself, or are some of them the work of disciples? Scholars of Pāli language and literature have gone into this question quite deeply, and there are some things they are more or less agreed about. They say that there are certain parts of the Pāli canon that probably go back to the Buddha himself and other parts that are clearly later elaborations. Modern scholars are generally of the opinion that the whole of the Abhidhamma Piṭaka is the work of disciples. In the Vinaya Piṭaka quite a lot is later, because it shows a very high degree of organization in the *bhikkhu* sangha which must have taken at least 200 years to develop; but some parts of the Vinaya Piṭaka are quite old. That leaves us with the Sutta Piṭaka. In the Sutta Piṭaka there are five *nikāyas*: the *Dīgha Nikāya, Majjhima Nikāya, Aṅguttara Nikāya, Saṃyutta Nikāya*, and *Khuddaka Nikāya*. Most scholars believe that the oldest parts of the Pāli canon and also some of the latest are found in the *Khuddaka Nikāya*, which contains fourteen different works. How do scholars know that some parts are older and some are later? There are three ways. The first is purely linguistic and philological. It's possible to trace the development of the Pāli language itself. You mustn't think that the whole of the Tipiṭaka is written in one kind of Pāli. It's written in at least three kinds, and scholars can trace the development of one kind of Pāli into another. There is a very ancient kind of Pāli which is quite close to Vedic Sanskrit, and some very old parts of the Pāli canon are written in this. Then there is a later kind of Pāli which is more developed and literary, and there is a third kind which is quite difficult and scholastic. If we find in the Tipiṭaka a text that is written in archaic Pāli we know that it is much older than a text written in a more developed form of the language. This is the first way in which scholars know that one part of the Pāli canon is older than another. Secondly, they can tell according to the degree of doctrinal development. Generally speaking, those explanations that are very simple and don't give much detail are earlier, and those that are elaborate and detailed tend to be later. And thirdly, we can know which parts of the Pāli canon are earlier and which are later according to the historical events they refer to and the degree of cultural development. To take an extreme example, if a text refers to the Emperor Aśoka, we know that that text cannot belong to the period of the Buddha. We find by applying these three criteria that the oldest texts on the whole are found in the *Khuddaka Nikāya*. These include the *Udāna* and some sections of the *Sutta-Nipāta*, especially the *Aṭṭhaka-vagga* and the *Pārāyana-vagga*.

So when you ask a question like 'Why did the Buddha leave home?' it's not only a question of looking into the Tipiṭaka, but trying to locate the oldest parts of it to find the most reliable account. Do we find this story of the Buddha leaving home because of the four sights in the oldest parts of the Pāli Tipiṭaka? Well no, we don't. In the oldest parts of the Pāli canon, as far as we can tell, the Buddha doesn't go out and see anything. He just reflects in his own mind, 'I am a human being, and therefore I am subject to disease.'[248] Some Western scholars say that the account of the Buddha going out and seeing these four sights, which comes in later parts of the scriptures, was an elaboration to make the Buddha's reflections more clear and vivid for the sake of ordinary people. But whether the Buddha reflected in his own mind or whether he went out and saw the sights, the meaning is the same.

But what about this story of political disturbance? In the whole of the Pāli Tipiṭaka there is only one slight reference to any such thing. This is in the *Sutta-Nipāta*, which as I said is one of the oldest parts of the canon, so we have to examine anything that comes in it very carefully. There is one passage in the *Sutta-Nipāta* where the Buddha says something like 'because of trouble and disturbances I left my house'.[249] So it is referred to just in one line, and how much importance we can attach to that is difficult to say. But anyway, Dr Ambedkar attached a lot of importance to it, and it is true that that single verse is there. There are two points to be considered here. One is that human beings are quite complicated, and our motives for doing things are usually quite complicated. We don't very often do something for one clear-cut reason. That was probably true in the case of the Buddha's leaving home. Very probably he did consider the nature of human life: that human beings fall sick and die. Very probably there was some trouble in the Śākya republic. In every state, in every government, there is trouble, and it is quite likely that the Buddha thought about that too. So it isn't so much a question of whether this is the right explanation; there is no doubt some importance to be attached to all these explanations. This is the first point.

The second point is that we know that the Buddha left home. No one has ever disputed that. No one has ever suggested that he remained happily at home with Yaśodharā for the rest of his life. We can be as certain that the Buddha did leave home as we can be about any historical fact. In the same way that we are certain that Julius Caesar was murdered in the capitol in Rome,[250] and Napoleon was defeated at the battle of Waterloo, we can be certain that the Buddha left home. But we're not quite so certain about the reasons, or rather we are not so sure how much weight to attach to all the different factors. It isn't always easy to answer these sorts of questions. We have to see the whole background before we can do so.

Q: *What is the role of women in the Dhamma in England?*
S: The brief answer is that there is no role at all, no special role. Men and women in the Order do exactly the same. They get ordained in the same way; they study the Dhamma in the same way; they take classes; they give lectures; they write articles. They have their own separate communities. The only difference is that there are not quite so many women in the Order as men. Why that is we are not quite sure. But once you join the Order, whether you are a man or a woman your role is exactly the same.

Maybe I should just mention one little thing. Here in India we usually find the ladies doing all the cooking, but in England the men also cook very well, and on a retreat with both men and women they share the cooking. Men don't leave all the cooking to the women. In fact, in England women do all the things men do – driving, for example. The women's communities have their own cars and vans, and they know how to look after them just like men do.

The next question is a bit complicated. In fact, some of it is not exactly a question, but more like someone's reflections. But anyway, I will read them out.

Q: *There is no material gain without proper planning, but is virtue the outcome of planning?*
S: So what have I got to say about this? You can have a five-year plan for the development of the country, but can you have a five-year plan for the development of your ethics or your meditation? The question is about virtue or *sīla*. I would like to say here that there are two kinds of people. The first kind are naturally good, even when they are children. They are good-tempered, kind, easy to get on with, and they never feel any inclination to commit any crime, so they don't need any planning to develop their virtue. But there are other people who find it very difficult

not to get angry and difficult to restrain themselves from being physically violent. Some people find it difficult to meditate regularly or to refrain from drinking. For those people who find *sīla* difficult, a plan is very helpful. Suppose you're a heavy smoker. Maybe you smoke thirty or forty cigarettes a day. Well you can have a plan. You say, 'All right, for one month I will go down from forty to thirty a day, the next month from thirty to twenty, the next month from twenty to ten.' If you make a plan like this, sometimes it is easier for you to practise what is good. So for those who find it difficult to be good, a plan is very helpful, but those who are naturally good don't need to bother about that. They're the lucky people.

Q: *First we understand ourselves, then we understand others. Then we understand the Buddha through his Dhamma. And in the end we forget everything, i.e. there is no Buddha, no self. What is the use of meditation and practising* Dhammamagga*?*
S: So you're asking, 'If you are meditating and you don't think of the Buddha any more, and there is no you any more, what is the use of meditation?' Well, if you reach that sort of state, meditation is not necessary. The only thing is that you may fall down from that state and you may need meditation to go back there again.

Q: *We read books on Buddhism. Monks also read and practise the Buddha's Dhamma. But even the greatest monk can only say what Buddha said about certain points. At the same time the Buddha's* Dhammamagga *comes through one's own experience. How can a monk or* anagārika *preach the Buddha's Dhamma principles without his own experience? If the answers of monks and* sāmaṇeras *are one and the same as the Buddha's, there is no difference between you and Buddha. But there is no Buddha other than Gautama Buddha.*
S: Let us go into this a bit. The Buddha taught certain principles out of his own experience. So what does a follower of the Buddha try to do, whether he is a *bhikkhu*, an *anagārika*, a *sāmaṇera*, or an *upāsaka*? First he tries to understand the principles taught by the Buddha, then he tries to practise them, and then he tries to experience them. He is able to explain those principles to other people only to the extent of his experience. If he has only a little experience, he is not able to explain very much, but if he has a very deep experience he is able to explain

more, and if his experience is just the same as the Buddha's, then he is the Buddha. There is one Gautama Buddha, but there is not just one Buddha, because whoever experiences *sambodhi* becomes Buddha. He can become Waghmare Buddha or Banerjee Buddha because he has gained the Buddha's Enlightenment. So it is not correct to say that there is only one Buddha. Any individual who becomes Enlightened can be called Buddha, and what he says is just like hearing the Buddha speak. But of course it is very difficult to become a Buddha. The important thing is to speak from your own experience. It is no use just reading books about Buddhism, even the Tipiṭaka. You have got to have some experience – otherwise you can't possibly explain it to other people. I would say that even experience is not enough. There are some people with experience of the Buddha's teachings but they find it quite difficult to explain them. To do this you need to develop your communication skills. If you are talking about Buddhism, you must ask yourself whether you are speaking from your own experience or just repeating something you have read in a book.

Q: *Knowledge must follow love as there is no smoke without fire. Please explain.*
S: Well, true knowledge does follow love, but love also follows knowledge. We find this in the case of relations between people. Sometimes you get to know somebody and then gradually you start loving them because you know them, but sometimes it happens the other way around. You meet someone for the first time and as soon as you meet them you like them, you love them, and you get to know them afterwards. So sometimes love comes first, then knowledge, sometimes knowledge comes first and then love. Which comes first is usually according to your temperament. There are some people who study the Buddha's Dhamma very thoroughly. They really like it, they go very deeply into it, but they don't care much for the Buddha. There is no *śraddhā*. So there is knowledge but not love, but the love develops naturally after the knowledge. But other people fall in love as soon as they see the image of the Buddha. They are full of *śraddhā*. They don't know anything about the Dhamma, but because they love the Buddha, because they have devotion, they start listening to the Dhamma. Whichever way we start, the ideal is eventually to have love and knowledge equally balanced.

Q: *Is it necessary to be a* sāmaṇera *or a* bhikkhu *to attain Nirvāṇa, or can any layman attain it by practising the Eightfold Path of the Buddha?*
S: Well, if we go by the Pāli canon, we find that there are records of lay people who live at home with their families attaining very high levels of spiritual development, becoming Stream Entrants, and some even becoming *arhants*. It wasn't so easy for them as it was for those who had left home and gone out into the forest, but it could be and can be done. The Buddha's teaching makes it quite clear that what is important is your own state of mind, your own sincerity, your own practice.

But which is the *upāsaka* and which is the *bhikkhu*? This is not so easy to answer as it might sound. For instance, there may be an *upāsaka* from Sri Lanka or Burma. He doesn't live at home with his family or have an ordinary job. He spends his time going around from place to place teaching meditation. He leads a very simple life, just working for the Dhamma, but we say he is an *upāsaka*. But in Sri Lanka, you might find a *bhikkhu* who is wearing yellow robes and has a shaven head, but he has a job in a college as a professor. Every month he draws his salary, and he's got a nice bungalow, and maybe even a car. So which is the *upāsaka*, which is the *bhikkhu*? We mustn't be misled by external things. When we ask, 'Can the *upāsaka* gain Enlightenment?' which kind of *upāsaka* do we mean? You could say that the *upāsaka* who is teaching meditation has a better chance than the *bhikkhu* who is teaching Pāli in a college and drawing a salary. In Sri Lanka, Burma, and Thailand it is very easy to become a *bhikkhu*. Sometimes the *bhikkhus* are like social workers or college professors, not like *bhikkhus* were in the Buddha's time. But whether someone is technically an *upāsaka* or a *bhikkhu* is not so important as whether he is practising *śīla*, *samādhi*, and *prajñā*. That is the important thing.

Q: *Psychologists say that mind and body is one. Can mind exist without body? Can body exist without mind?*
S. Well, not all psychologists say that. Some do, some don't. But can mind exist without body? Can body exist without mind? This is one of the questions that the Buddha called *avyākata*, undetermined: whether *rūpa* and *jīva* are the same, or not the same, or both, or neither.[251] The Buddha said that it is not necessary to decide this question one way or

the other in order to lead the spiritual life. There may be an answer, but from the Buddhist point of view it doesn't matter what that answer is. You can still practise the Dhamma.

Q: *Analysis and synthesis leads to duality. Does duality exist? Most sciences analyse and synthesize things. But does Buddhism agree with the results of the sciences?*
S: The answer is very simple. Buddhism neither agrees nor disagrees. It doesn't need to. Suppose astronomy tells you that the Earth is ninety-two million miles away from the sun. If you tell this to a Buddhist, what will he say? 'OK.' Whatever the distance, it doesn't matter to him as a Buddhist. He is quite happy to accept whatever science shows. The work of Buddhism is different.

Q: *If while one is practising mindfulness of breathing unskilful mental states arise, how does that affect the practice?*
S: We know it is very easy for unskilful mental states to arise, and sometimes it seems that they arise more strongly when we are trying to meditate, because then we are trying to bring the mind under control, and the mind doesn't like that. The Buddha says in the *Dhammapada*, '*Phandanaṃ capalaṃ cittaṃ, dūrakkhaṃ dunnivārayaṃ*'.[252] *Phandanaṃ* means vibrating and trembling. *Capalaṃ* means always moving. *Dūrakkhaṃ* means difficult to protect. *Dunnivārayaṃ* means difficult to exercise any sort of control. Naturally the mind revolts when we try to meditate, sometimes more than others. So what to do? Usually if you are doing the mindfulness of breathing very carefully and with a lot of intensity and energy, the unskilful mind, the *akusala citta*, is not so likely to arise. But if you relax the practice, if you become a bit unmindful or your thoughts start to wander, the *akusala citta* gets the chance to come in. When the *akusala citta* starts coming in, we know that we have relaxed the practice a bit, we are not doing it with complete energy and intentness. The first way of dealing with the *akusala citta* is to carry on with the practice, whether it's mindfulness of breathing or any other, with renewed energy. But if this doesn't work, you have to stop the practice and look at that *akusala citta*.

Say, for example, anger has arisen. There are different ways of looking at it. First you can try to see where it came from. You think about it, and then you think, 'Ah, yes, yesterday someone made me angry.' That has been in your mind ever since, and now at the time of meditation it is coming up. So you think to yourself, 'What a silly thing! All this time that was in my mind.' In this way you get rid of it, and then you can go back to your meditation. Or you can think of the consequences of that *akusala citta*. You can reflect that anger is a very terrible thing. Because of anger people beat one another, say all sorts of foolish things that they are sorry for afterwards, even kill one another. You don't want any of those things to happen. Reflecting like this will very often check the anger, and you can go back to your practice. Alternatively, you can cultivate the opposite. You can make a definite effort to cultivate *maitrī* and get rid of the anger in that way, then go back to your meditation. These are just a few simple things you can try.

Q: *Did* oṃ maṇi padme hūṃ *come straight from the mouth of the Buddha, and if not, how did this mantra come into practice and how far is it relevant to practice today?*
S: This mantra is not found in the Pāli Tipiṭaka but in some Sanskrit Mahāyāna *sūtras*. We don't have the original Sanskrit texts, but we have the Tibetan translation, which is called the *Maṇi Kabum*, the 100,000 verses on the *maṇi*. So far as we can tell from the history of Buddhist literature, this is much later than the Buddha. So what is the relevance of the mantra today? The Buddha says that any good thing that helps us can be considered as part of the Dhamma, so the question is: does this help us? This particular mantra is associated with the bodhisattva Avalokiteśvara, who represents the compassion, the *mahākaruṇā*, of the Buddha. In fact, Avalokiteśvara is often called Mahākāruṇika. When you repeat *oṃ maṇi padme hūṃ* you think of the Buddha's compassion and in this way you try to develop compassion within yourself; this is the usefulness of the practice. If you can develop compassion without it, that's fine, but a lot of people find that chanting *oṃ maṇi padme hūṃ* does help them. I believe there is going to be some chanting of that mantra this evening, so those who haven't had this experience before will be able to try it.

Q: *One feels pain in different parts of the body. Why? Are unskilful mental states cleared up through it, and is the pain physical or mental?*
S: I am assuming that the question refers to the experience of pain during meditation. Very often when they meditate, people experience pain in the physical body, sometimes in the knees or the back. This sort of pain

is just physical, maybe due to bad posture, stiffness, or old age. If you experience pain in the body for these physical reasons, perhaps some yoga *asanas* would help you. But sometimes pain in the body during meditation is due to mental causes, and these can be divided into two kinds. Sometimes the pain is simply due to the fact that you are trying too hard. If you get pain across your forehead or the back of your neck when you meditate, you are trying too hard. You just need to relax, sit more gently, more easily, and not worry about your meditation. It's no good sitting there thinking, 'Am I doing it wrong? Why isn't anything happening? Am I in first *dhyāna* or second *dhyāna*?' Just sit very quietly and gently and do the practice. But sometimes pains due to experiences you have had previously in your life come up in the course of the meditation. Don't take any notice of this sort of pain. Just say, 'Yes, this is coming up from the past.' There's no need to let it bother you; just carry on with your practice very gently and steadily.

The important point is that you don't have to suffer. Some people say that unless you suffer there is no progress, but that is not the Buddha's teaching. Again it is according to temperament. The Buddha said there are four kinds of people. With the first kind, at the beginning of their Buddhist life their meditation is very difficult and they experience a lot of suffering, but later, as they get more and more into it, it becomes happier and happier, more and more blissful. The second kind of person starts off very easily and happily. The first time they meditate, they have a beautiful meditation, and the next meditation is also beautiful, but after that it becomes very difficult. And the third kind of person starts off finding it very difficult, with a lot of pain and suffering, and after that there is still more pain and suffering, and eventually they attain Nirvāṇa, but it is difficult all the way. The fourth kind of person is the luckiest. Their Buddhist life, their meditation, starts off very happily, it carries on happily, and it is happy all the way until they reach Nirvāṇa.[253] So pain is not necessary. It may be there, it may not. If it is there, you are unlucky. If it is not there, you are lucky, but either way you get to Nirvāṇa in the end, so in a way it doesn't matter whether or not you have pain.

THE BUDDHA – MAN OR GOD?

Poona, February 1979

Sisters and brothers in the Dhamma, if we look at the course of human history, we see that about 2,500 years ago, all over the civilized world, a tremendous cultural and spiritual change took place in human affairs. In Europe this change took place in ancient Greece, with the arising of great writers, thinkers, and teachers, and in Palestine also great religious teachers arose. In Persia (now Iran) there was Zarathustra, and in China there were Confucius and Laozi. Here in India too many great men arose. And the greatest of all the great men who arose in that very important period of human history was Gautama the Buddha. As you know, the Buddha was born in India, he gained supreme Enlightenment in India, and after gaining Enlightenment, going forth from the bodhi tree, he went out into the streets and the bazaars to meet people and teach them and help them.

How did the Buddha travel? When I came to India just recently I came by aeroplane, and it took me nine and a half hours to cover 5,000 miles, but in the Buddha's day there were only bullock carts and they went at the rate of five miles per hour, if they were quick. But the Buddha didn't even go by bullock cart. He went on foot, walking from town to town and village to village, and he did that all his life, even when he was an old man of eighty. And how did the Buddha teach? In those days there were no books, and writing was very little known, just used by business people for keeping accounts and writing letters, certainly not used for religious purposes. The Buddha taught the disciples orally, and whatever he taught them, they remembered and passed on to their own disciples. This is why the Buddha's disciples were called *śrāvakas*, because *śrāvaka* means one who listens, and the Buddha's disciples listened with their ears and their hearts and tried faithfully to remember and practise what they had heard. For forty-five years the Buddha taught in this way. He taught many people, and he taught many different things. He explained thoroughly the path of the Dhamma leading to Enlightenment, and by the time he died, by the time of his *parinirvāṇa*, there were many people who knew quite a lot of his teachings by heart. But after the Buddha's *parinirvāṇa*, and even before it, people sometimes found it difficult to remember his teachings. The Buddha tried to make it easier for them, which is why we sometimes find his teaching taking the form of numbered lists: the four noble truths, the seven *bodhyaṅgas*, the Noble Eightfold Path, the twelve *nidānas*, and so on. These lists made it easier for people to commit the Buddha's teaching to memory, and good disciples of the Buddha usually knew a lot of them. In fact, there were not only lists, but lists of lists, because everything depended upon the human memory. There were no books. The Buddha's teaching was not written down until several hundred years after the *parinirvāṇa*. Some of the disciples were very good at remembering these lists and they used to play games with one another. One *bhikkhu* would say to another, 'What are the five?' or 'What are the ten?' and in this way they would help one another to remember.

There is a story that one *śrāmaṇera* had a very good memory, and someone once asked him questions of this sort. This *śrāmaṇera* was apparently only seven years old. Some people think that the Dhamma is not for the young. They say that you should finish your education, get married, get a job and work for twenty or even fifty years, and after that you can retire, and then you can start to practise the Dhamma. But the Buddha said the earlier you start to practise the Dhamma, the better. Educationalists say that at sixteen years of age one's intelligence is fully developed. Maybe you're not physically fully developed, maybe you need some more experience of the world, but at sixteen your intelligence is as good as it will ever be, and certainly at that age, or even younger, you can start practising the Dhamma.

Anyway, in this story we're concerned with a seven-year-old *śrāmaṇera*. He was asked '*Ekanāma kiṃ*? What is the one thing?' The young *śrāmaṇera*, who was very smart, said, 'All sentient beings depend upon food.'[254] It's true: whether you're an animal or a human being, male or female, young or old, good or wicked, you depend upon food. Even the hatha yogis of India depend upon food. But there is not only food for the body; there is food for the mind as well, and people depend upon that too. And where do you get food for the mind? You get it from books, from literature, poetry, history, mathematics, science. And the best food for the mind is meditation. If you meditate, you live upon joy, as the Buddha said.[255] The best food of all is simply the Dhamma itself. The Dhamma is the true nectar, the true *amṛta*, and sometimes we see in the scriptures that the giving of the Dhamma is compared to the giving of *amṛta*.

So then the young *śrāmaṇera* was asked, 'What is the two?', and he answered, '*Nāma-rūpa*'. *Rūpa* means body, and *nāma* is mind, and *nāma* can be subdivided into four: *vedanā*, *saṃskāra*, *samjñā*, and *vijñāna*. *Rūpa* means the matter that makes up the physical body. It is not a thing, not a hard, solid, unchanging object. It is all the processes going on in the physical body. And *vedanā* is the feeling of pleasure or pain, or a neutral feeling that is neither painful nor pleasant. Under *vedanā* are included all the emotions – love and hate, joy, faith, *mettā*, *karuṇā*, *muditā*. And then what is *samjñā*? This is a bit more difficult to understand. Suppose you see something in the distance, rather tall, and green in colour. You look at it carefully. First, you're not quite sure what it is, then suddenly you recognize it and think, 'That's a tree.' This kind of process is what we call *samjñā*, perception or recognition. And then there's *saṃskāra*, which is something like will or effort or determination or drive. It's also energy, mental power, desire – it's all these things. This is what keeps you going. And lastly there is *vijñāna*, which means your awareness of things, your sensing of things. So how are you aware? How do you sense? First of all, you are aware through your eyes, you see visual forms. Then you hear through the ear, you are aware of sounds. Through the nostrils you are aware of smells. Through the tongue you are aware of taste, and through the body you are aware of touch. Through these five organs of sense you are aware of the external material world. And then of course there is the inner organ which we call the mind, through which you know or you see ideas. When someone you know is not present, and you close your eyes and in your mind you can see that person, it is your mind organ which is operating.

I want to go a bit more into this question of *vijñāna*, especially *mano-vijñāna*, and this will mean going a little bit into the Abhidharma. This is the sixth talk that I have given so far here in Poona on this visit, and in the previous five talks I spoke about popular, easy topics, but I don't want to make it easy for you all the time. You've got to learn some new things, so listen carefully and I shall try to explain as simply as I can. So far we have covered six *vijñāna*s: the *vijñāna* of the eye, the *vijñāna* of the ear, the *vijñāna* of the nose, the *vijñāna* of the tongue, the *vijñāna* of the skin, and the *vijñāna* of the mind. That is, five *vijñāna*s of the body, and one of the mind. Going a little more deeply into this *mano-vijñāna*, we can say that it can be divided again, or that there is a particular aspect of this *mano-vijñāna*, a particular way of functioning, called *kliṣṭa-mano-vijñāna*.

The *kliṣṭa-mano-vijñāna*, the seventh *vijñāna*, is the one that divides things and makes distinctions. (By the way, the *kliṣṭa-mano-vijñāna* is not the last one. There is an eighth *vijñāna*, called the *ālaya-vijñāna*, but we won't go into that this evening, as it is very much more difficult.) We could say that the *kliṣṭa-mano-vijñāna* sees everything in terms of pairs of opposites which are mutually exclusive, or more simply that it sees the differences between things. Now there are two kinds of differences. The first kind are those differences that are natural, that exist in the world. For instance, the sun and the moon are quite different. Darkness and light are natural differences. Man and woman are natural differences, and so are the animal and the human being. But there are other differences that are not natural, but made by the human mind, by the *kliṣṭa-mano-vijñāna*. Let's take the example of land. If you look at a piece of land, you may think, 'That's Mr So-and-so's land', but that is a man-made difference; it does not exist in the land itself. There was a famous movement in England about 300 years ago which came to be called the Diggers because they said that land is nobody's private property. Everybody should be free to till the soil, because the earth belongs to everybody. The Diggers tried to dig the common land, because they had no land themselves, and they said everybody had the right to do so. It's very true that the earth belongs to everybody. In the earth itself there is no distinction between this man's land and that man's land; that distinction is made by the human mind, the *kliṣṭa-mano-vijñāna*.

Here in India somebody might look at people and say, 'This one is high caste, that one is low caste. That one is in the middle.' In this way he might come up with 2,000 castes. But is that division in the people themselves? You might be surprised to hear that someone who comes from England to India can't tell which caste is which. They can't tell a Brahmin from a Dalit. They just see a human being. In the same way, when the dhobi comes to take away the laundry, they don't think, 'Here's a man of the dhobi caste.' They think, 'Here's a man doing the work of a dhobi.' Likewise, as far as they can see the *dudh wallah* is just a man doing the work of bringing the milk, and the *pūjari* is just a man ringing the bell in the temple. All these distinctions of high caste and low caste are made by the mind, by the *kliṣṭa-mano-vijñāna*. They don't exist in nature. If you look at people, you might observe that the Brahmin is wearing a thread or ties his dhoti in a particular way or wears a particular kind of turban, but that's all man-made. Take all those things away and what do you see? Just a human body, just like everybody else. All these distinctions are made by the mind.

And, to come to my main topic, there is another distinction made by the mind: between man and God. We know what is meant by man: this strange creature, sometimes called the rational animal, or the tool-making animal, or the laughing animal, because animals don't laugh. But what about God? In so many religions there is a lot of talk of God; no one says they have actually seen him, but people talk about him a lot. So what do they mean? First of all, they mean someone who is all-powerful, who can do everything that he wishes. And they also mean someone who has created this universe – the sun, the moon, the earth, the planets, the stars, the galaxies, and so on. They may have in mind that God is like a great big person. Not all the people who believe in God say exactly the same thing. Christians say that God created the world. Many Hindus say that too, but they put it in a rather different way. The Christians believe that God created the universe out of nothing. Hindus have various theories, as expressed in the Upanishads and the *Darśan Śāstras*. Some Hindus say that first there was only God, and then he created everything out of himself, spinning the whole universe out of himself like a spider spinning a web, and others say that God spins the whole of the universe out of himself and after a while he draws it back, drawing the web out and pulling it back again forever; this is called *pralaya* and *sṛṣṭi*, sometimes called God's *līlā*, his play. So we find that there is this distinction between God and man. Of course, in this way of seeing things, God has created man. The two are quite different.

Man is very weak, but God is very powerful. Man must submit to God, obey the commands of God. There are many teachings about this sort of thing on the part of those religions that believe in God. But in Buddhism there is no teaching about God, because according to Buddhism there is no God, so this distinction between man and God is false. It does not exist in reality, but is created by the mind, by the *kliṣṭa-mano-vijñāna*.

At this point some of you may be asking yourselves a question. Christians say that God created the universe, and Muslims and Hindus say the same thing. But in Buddhism there is no God, so who created the universe? What has Buddhism got to say about this? Well, Buddhism says nothing about it; it doesn't need to. Buddhism says that the question of where the universe came from is not a question that concerns the Dhamma. How the universe originated is something to be investigated by science, and Buddhism is happy to accept whatever conclusion science arrives at. Buddhism is not concerned with God, or the origin of the universe. Buddhism is concerned with human beings, with the improvement and development of the individual and society. Buddhism regards the whole distinction between man and God as a false and unreal one created by the *kliṣṭa-mano-vijñāna*.

There is another question that arises, both in the West and in the East. If we start to hear about the Buddha, if we read about his life and learn about his teachings, sooner or later a question will arise: who is the Buddha? Usually people want to know whether he is a man or a god, but this question arises in different ways in different places. Western people, with their Christian background, tend to believe that man and God are quite separate. God is good and powerful, and he made everything. Man is weak, wicked, and miserable, and he certainly didn't make the universe. He is completely dependent upon God, he is the slave of God. When people who are brought up in this way come into contact with the Buddha, they can't help thinking, 'Is the Buddha a man or is he a god?' Some Western people think the Buddha was just a man – a good man, but of course not nearly as good as God. But other people in the West, seeing people offering flowers to the Buddha image on the shrine and lighting candles in front of him, think that the Buddha must be their god. So they put the Buddha either into the category of man or into the category of god – which, of course, is the activity of the *kliṣṭa-mano-vijñāna*. Usually Christian people say that the Buddha is just a man. But what about India? What do people say here? Well, for hundreds of years people in India forgot all about the Buddha and his teaching. It's only during the last hundred years that the Buddha has become known again, first to Hindus and then to newly converted Buddhists. The Hindus said he is not a man, he's an *avatāra* of god. In fact, they made him the ninth *avatāra* of Vishnu. Here again you see the activity of the *kliṣṭa-mano-vijñāna*. You've got these two categories, man and god, so when people come into contact with the Buddha, either they have got to make him a man or they have got to make him a god. In the West people say that the Buddha is just a man and in India they say the Buddha is a god.

But both are wrong. In Buddhism there is no God, so the Buddha can't be a God, which only leaves man. So is the Buddha man? Well, yes, but also no, because according to Buddhism there are two sorts of man: the *pṛthagjana* and the *ārya*, the lower man and the higher man, the ordinary man and the extraordinary man. In India caste is always creeping in, so we have to be very careful when we talk about lower and higher. It's got nothing to do with caste. It's a question of the lower and higher qualities of the human being – qualities of character, nothing to do with birth in a particular community. In Buddhism we've got two kinds of human being, the ordinary and the extraordinary, the one who is not enlightened and the one who is Enlightened. Both are human beings in a sense, but the second, the Enlightened human being, is the true human, the real human. So yes, the Buddha was a man, but he was not an ordinary man. He was an extraordinary man, a man who gained Enlightenment, a man endowed with the fullness of wisdom, *mahāprajñā*, the fullness of compassion, *mahākaruṇā*, and the fullness of purity, *mahāviśuddhi*. Whatever good qualities there are in the ordinary human being, the Buddha has developed them to the highest possible extent. Ordinary people have got just a little bit of *maitrī*. Sometimes it comes, sometimes it goes. But the Buddha feels full and complete *maitrī* all the time, and towards all people, not just a few. Whatever is a seed in us is fully developed in the Buddha – not only *maitrī*, but all other good, noble qualities. This contains for us a great message of hope. The Buddha was an extraordinary man, an Enlightened man, a Buddha, but in one sense he was just like us. His mind was the Enlightened mind of a Buddha, but his body was just like ours.

One of my teachers, Jagdish Kashyap, was born in Bihar nearly seventy years ago into a Hindu family and went to a Hindu school.

He learned Sanskrit, and eventually he went to a Sanskrit college, and then he became an *ārya samaji pandit*. He knew the four Vedas by heart, forwards and backwards. But he wasn't satisfied. In fact, he told me that he found reading the Vedas very disappointing. His Brahmin teachers used to tell him that when you read the Vedas the whole of knowledge is there, but when he came to read them, he found that there was not much there at all, so he was disappointed, and started looking for something else. Then he heard about Buddhism, so he started reading about the life of the Buddha, and he told me that there was something in the Buddha's life story that impressed him very much. There is a passage in the Pāli scriptures that describes the Buddha teaching the *bhikkhus*. He sat on the ground with his back against a tree and talked for hour after hour. Sāriputta, Moggallāna, Ānanda, and all the great disciples were there, together with hundreds of other *bhikkhus*. At that time the Buddha was quite an old man, and after he had been teaching the Dhamma for so many hours he said to Sāriputta, 'Sāriputta, my back is aching. You carry on teaching the *bhikkhus*. I shall lie down and have a rest.'[256] Kashyapji told me that when he read this story it was a revelation, a great shock, because he saw that the Buddha was a human being. He wasn't a superman. His body wasn't made of iron, but of flesh and blood, and he was old, so his back was aching. Kashyapji said that this started making him a Buddhist, because he saw that the Buddha was a human being with an ordinary human body, but by his own efforts he had developed the mind of a Buddha, an Enlightened mind.

This is why in the Buddha's teaching there is hope for everybody. In Christianity God is great, all-powerful, perfect, but you cannot become like God. You are low, you are weak, you are miserable. You must just pray to God to save you. But in Buddhism it isn't like that. There is the Buddha, yes. We keep an image of the Buddha on our shrine, wearing the yellow robe, sitting in meditation, or teaching. But who or what is this Buddha? The Buddha started as an ordinary human being, but by his own efforts he became an Enlightened human being. So Buddhism gives a message of hope. What one human being can do, any human being can do. The Buddha didn't start off with any particular advantages. In fact, you could say that he started off with a disadvantage. He was born in a rich family, and that can be a disadvantage, because life is so pleasant and comfortable that you don't think about spiritual things. If you were born in a poorer family and had more difficulties, you might start thinking about life more seriously.

This reminds me of a story. Once upon a time there was a flock of sheep, and one day they found a tiger cub whose parents had been killed by huntsmen. The sheep took him with them and brought him up to eat grass and bleat just like a sheep. He got bigger and bigger, but he still thought he was a sheep. One day an adult tiger came along, and thought, 'This is very strange. Here is a young tiger eating grass. But tigers eat meat – in fact they eat sheep.' The adult tiger came running towards the flock of sheep and all the sheep ran away, but the young tiger didn't have a chance to run away, because the adult tiger caught hold of him and said, 'Why are you behaving like this? Why are you eating grass? Why are you bleating like a sheep?' The young tiger said 'I'm a sheep! Baa! Baa!' But the other tiger said, 'That's rubbish! You're not a sheep, you're a tiger.' The young tiger wouldn't believe him, so the adult tiger took him by the scruff of his neck and pulled him to a pool of water. He said, 'Look in the pool. Look, you are just like me.' The young tiger thought, 'Oh yes! Look! I'm not a sheep. I'm a tiger.' And he started to roar.

This is a good story, but what does it mean? Well, we could say that the Buddha is like the adult tiger. Human beings think that they are weak and wicked, that they can't do anything, that everything depends upon God. They just follow God, even though they have never seen him, or they follow God's representatives. But the Buddha catches hold of them and says, 'You are not weak or wicked, and you are not dependent upon God. You are just like me. If you make the effort you can become Enlightened.' And when you look at yourself in the water – the water being the Dhamma – you see that you can become just like the Buddha. This is what happened in India 2,500 years ago. The Buddha spoke to all human beings. He said, 'Everything is in you – all power, all energy, all wisdom, all knowledge. You can develop from an ordinary human being into an extraordinary human being, into a Buddha.' But then, after many years, unfortunately it was all forgotten in India, even though it was remembered in other parts of the world. In India people started thinking that they were sheep. But then another tiger came along, and that tiger was Dr Ambedkar. He said to his people, 'You think that you are low. You think that you can't do anything. You think you are sheep, but you're really tigers.' It was the conversion to the Dhamma, the *diksha* ceremony, that made his people look at their reflection, think about what they were really like, what they could really do. And now they are beginning to roar like tigers. But when I say that Buddhists are like tigers, I mean that we have the energy and strength of the tiger, not that we are aggressive. Tigers eat meat, and they're very fierce, but Buddhists don't eat meat, and while we are strong, not weak like sheep, we are also gentle.

In the course of the last thirty years I've given quite a number of lectures, in India and in the West, and here I am again tonight giving another one here in Poona. One thing I've noticed about my lectures is that sometimes people remember them and sometimes they don't, but there is one thing people always remember even after years and years. They remember stories. Even very educated people with MAs and PhDs sometimes forget the Abhidharma, but they remember stories. So I don't know how much you will remember of what I've said this evening. I don't know if you'll remember the *ekanāma kin* or the *nāma rūpa*, or the *pañca skandhas* or the eight *vijñānas*. I don't know if you'll remember the *kliṣṭa-mano-vijñāna*, all those false distinctions – maybe you'll remember a bit of that because you experience it to some extent in your lives. But even if you forget all that, at least remember this one story. Remember that you are not sheep, but tigers – good Buddhist tigers, with the energy, strength, and swiftness of a tiger, but without the fierceness or the cruelty. Like the lion, the tiger roars in the jungle, and we must roar too. What is our roar? It's the preaching of the Dhamma. Don't keep quiet about the Dhamma. You may not yet be like the Buddha, but at least do something to spread the Dhamma. Maybe you can't do very much yourself, but at least help other people who are working to spread the Dhamma. If you can do this, then you will be real Buddhist tigers, real disciples of the Buddha, and true followers of Dr Ambedkar.

THE PATH OF THE DHAMMA[257]

I think everybody knows that for the last twelve years I have been in England. Before that I was here in India for nearly twenty years. And during the whole of that time I have been concerned in one way or another with the Dhamma, first studying it, then trying to practise it, and finally trying to propagate it. As I look back over my experience over the last thirty years or so, I find that I have had a very interesting time. Some people think that worldly life is interesting, but actually the Dharmic life is much more interesting and exciting, and one of the most interesting things is to see the different ways in which the Dhamma is practised in different countries. For example, even things like Dhamma meetings are conducted very differently in England and India. In England, if your meeting is scheduled to be at seven o'clock, you arrive at one minute to seven and everybody is there waiting and ready. At exactly seven o'clock the meeting begins and you are introduced by the chairman of the meeting, whose introductory speech lasts for one or two minutes. Sometimes he just announces your name and the title of your lecture, and then sits down. You stand up to give your lecture, and you speak for an hour, maybe more. I usually speak for one and a half to two hours, but my English friends say that is because I spent so long in India; in England people don't usually speak as long as that. At the end of the lecture the chairman thanks you briefly, and you all go home.

In India, as you know, it is completely different. In the first place there are all the offerings of garlands. Sometimes there may be twenty or thirty. I must say I rather like this practice; it makes me feel welcome. When I give a lecture in England, sometimes it's difficult to know whether people have liked it or not, but in India everybody makes me feel really welcome, and I like to speak, because everybody seems to be enjoying it. Dhamma meetings are usually much more colourful and much happier than they are in England.

In our own Buddhist movement in England the meetings are becoming a bit more like Indian meetings, but non-Buddhist religious meetings in England are sometimes very sad affairs indeed. When some Christians go to church on Sunday, they think that they must look very sad and serious, and that it's a great sin to laugh in church. In some parts of Scotland, I'm told, even today, if the minister were to catch you laughing on a Sunday, he would say 'Don't you know it's Sunday today?' because laughing on Sunday is not allowed. Everyone's customs are different. We started a centre in Finland two or three years ago, and the people who started coming along and practising meditation behaved in a way that was quite different to what we were used to in England. They'd come along to the centre and meditate together, but they would never speak to each other. This is the Finnish custom. But you'll be glad to hear that even the Finns, after coming along to the Buddhist centre and meditating for two or three years, in the end talk freely and become friends.

Another thing you learn as you go about is that the Dhamma has enemies. Some enemies of the Dhamma are outside and some are inside. One of the enemies of the Dhamma in England is the media – that is, the newspapers, the radio, and television. It's not that the media people want to be enemies; in fact, they want to be friends. But there is an English saying: 'May heaven protect me from my friends; I can protect myself from my enemies', and it's a bit like that with the media. They come along to meet us and ask about Buddhism, but they get it all wrong. Then they publish their incorrect report in the newspaper, or they report it wrongly on the radio, or they show something in a misleading way on television, and people get the wrong idea about Buddhism. In this way, sometimes the media is an enemy of the Dhamma.

But in addition to the enemies outside, there are enemies inside, and this evening I want to say something about one of the biggest enemies of the Dhamma. The name of this enemy is routine. Now what exactly do I mean by routine? We know what is usually meant by it: you get up at six in the morning, you wash, you have your breakfast, you go to work, you come back from work, you eat, you talk with your wife or your husband, you ask the children what they did at school, you read the newspaper, you go to bed. And you do this every day. Most people are involved in routines, at home or at the office or the factory. It's unavoidable to some extent. But if you're not careful, your whole life becomes one big routine, and then life becomes very dull.

I don't know how it is in India, but in England many young people feel this. It is as though as soon as they leave school, the whole of the rest of their life is set out in front of them like a straight narrow path, and they can't get off it. You leave school or university and get a job, and after settling down in your job you get married. When you get married you've got to buy a house, but you haven't got any money, so you get a mortgage. You need furniture too, and you haven't the money for that either, so you borrow money and pay a bit back every month. Maybe that takes you twenty years. You want colour television and a car, and you get them on the hire purchase system. Then, after two or three years, you start producing children. This is your life for twenty, thirty, forty or more years. Every year you go away on holiday for two or three weeks. Some people go to the same place every year, play the same games, do the same things. In this way the whole of life becomes a mechanical routine, and it is very difficult to get out of it. This process goes on until you retire. You're free then, but it's too late. You're too old, or too tired. You just want to sit in the garden, read your newspaper, and wait for death. This is of course not the Buddhist way – that's another story – but this is what it's like for ordinary people.

Why am I going into this in so much detail? Well, there is a very important point to be made. We say that we are Buddhists, we say that we are following the Dhamma, but if we are not careful, our following the Dhamma also becomes a matter of mechanical routine. We recite the *tisaraṇa* and *pañcasīla* every day, but it's just a routine. Maybe we light a candle in front of the Buddha image, but we don't think about what we're doing – we are thinking of something else. In this way the whole of our Dhamma life becomes a routine.

I noticed this many years ago when I was a very new *bhikkhu* and walked up through the jungle from India into Nepal, and stayed at a Buddhist vihara in a small town called Palpa Tansen. The town had many Buddhist residents, so there were many small temples with Buddha images. One morning I was sitting inside one of these, just next to the shrine, when suddenly a handful of rice came flying through the open door and hit the Buddha image right in the face. I looked out of the window and saw a woman running away. I asked people 'Why did she do that?', and I was told that in Palpa Tansen every morning the Buddhist ladies would go out with some rice and run from vihara to vihara. They would not enter any viharạ; they would stand at the door and throw a handful of rice inside, then run on to the next vihara, because they were very busy. They had to cook, and get the children to school, so they only had about five minutes to run round all the viharas.[258]

It's very easy for our Dhamma life to fall into this sort of routine. It's very easy to do the same so-called religious actions over and over again, forgetting their significance. It's very easy to recite so-called religious words, whether in Pāli or Sanskrit or any other language, over and over again. If we are not careful we do this with the *tisaraṇa* and *pañcasīla*. After all, we recite them so many times, and sometimes we may be doing it mechanically – our mind may be on something else. So every now and then we have to stop and ask ourselves, 'What am I really doing? Why, really, am I doing it? What is the meaning of it? Why am I here? Why am I in this meeting? Why am I reciting *tisaraṇa* and *pañcasīla*? Why am I listening? What does it mean to me?' We have to become more aware and know what we are doing, understand the meaning of the words that we are reciting.

Very often we recite the *Buddha Vandanā*, the *Dhamma Vandanā*, and the *Saṅgha Vandanā*.[259] This evening I want to say a few words about the *Dhamma Vandanā*. In my last lecture here, I spoke about the Buddha and tried to answer the question whether the Buddha is man or god. Now I want to go into the meaning of the *Dhamma Vandanā* which some of us recite every day. All of you know these words by heart, I'm sure, but maybe some of you have never asked yourself what they mean.

I am going to go through the words of the main section of the *Dhamma Vandanā* one by one so that we thoroughly understand what they are all about. First of all, we say *svākkhāto bhagavatā dhammo*. *Bhagavatā* here means the Buddha, Gautama the Buddha, Siddhārtha, and Dhamma is his teaching, so *bhagavatā dhammo* means the Dhamma taught by the Buddha. But what do we mean by the Buddha? The Buddha is an Enlightened human being, an extraordinary human being. He is not an ordinary human being, but neither is he a god, or an *avatāra* of any god. His Enlightenment includes so many sublime qualities: supreme purity, all-embracing wisdom, and absolute compassion. It is out of that compassion that the Enlightened One, the Buddha, speaks to other human beings, and what he communicates to them is called the Dhamma. The function of the Buddha's Dhamma is to help people to grow, to help them to develop. Therefore we say *bhagavatā dhammo* – the teaching of the Enlightened individual to the non-Enlightened individual, the teaching of the spiritually free individual to the individual who is not yet spiritually free. The Buddha's Dhamma is one human being talking to another, encouraging another, trying to help another. It is not a god coming down from heaven to help humanity. But before *bhagavatā dhammo*, there is another word: *svākkhāto*, which literally means 'well-taught', or even 'well-communicated'. The Dhamma of the Buddha is well communicated, which indicates that the Buddha is in touch with other human beings. He knows their needs, he knows their mental states, he knows how they are to be helped, he knows how to put things to them. He knows how to put his Dhamma in a way that everybody can understand.

The record of the Buddha's teaching to his disciples is found in what we call the Tipiṭaka. This comprises about forty-five printed volumes and it is full of all sorts of teachings given to people in all sorts of ways. Sometimes we find the Buddha giving a short and simple explanation, maybe only a few words. Sometimes he doesn't say anything at all, he just sits in silence, but nevertheless meaning is communicated. On the other hand, sometimes we find the Buddha giving a discourse for one hour, two hours, sometimes the whole night, explaining things in detail from every point of view. Again, sometimes we find the Buddha giving ethical teachings, sometimes psychological teachings, sometimes teachings about spiritual life, sometimes even teachings about political life – that is, the principles of political life, not anything to do with party politics. Sometimes we find the Buddha explaining things in general abstract terms. Sometimes we find him using beautiful illustrations – speaking of the trees and the flowers, the sun and the moon, animals and ordinary human life. Sometimes we find him telling stories, because some people can understand what you are trying to say only if you put it to them in the form of a story. This is one of the things I notice as I talk about the Dhamma in different parts of the world. There are many differences between the cultures of different countries, but everywhere people like to hear a story, and for many people this is the most interesting part of the lecture. So the Buddha taught in all these different ways, to all sorts of people. He wanted his message to be understood by everybody, so he spoke in a way that many people could understand. This is why we say the Buddha's Dhamma is *svākkhāto* – well-taught.

The Buddha didn't say that his Dhamma should be taught in just one special language. One day two *bhikkhu* disciples who had previously been Brahmins came to the Buddha and said, 'Please allow us to put your teachings into beautiful, cultured, polished Sanskrit, so that everybody can learn them in Sanskrit.' But the Buddha said, 'No. Let everybody learn my Dhamma in their own language.'[260] If Sanskrit is your language, all right, learn the Dhamma in Sanskrit. If your language is Pāli, learn it in Pāli. If your language is Prakrit, learn it in Prakrit. If your language is Marathi, learn it in Marathi. If your language is Hindi, learn it in Hindi. If your language is English, learn the Dhamma in English. This is the principle of Buddhism. There is no one sacred language. When the Buddha's teaching went to Tibet, everything was translated into Tibetan, and in China it was translated into Chinese. Everywhere that Buddhism went, it gave a stimulus to the local language and literature, because the Buddha's Dhamma is to be shared with everybody in a way that they can understand. In some religions they've got a priestly class with a sacred language and in this way the knowledge of the scriptures is confined to a small circle of people, but this is not in accordance with the Buddha's teaching. The Buddha's teaching, to spread as widely as possible, must be spread in as many ways as possible, in as many languages as possible. Therefore we say that the Buddha's Dhamma is 'well-taught' – well propagated. When we recite these words *svākkhāto bhagavatā dhammo*, this is what we should bear in mind.

Next, the Buddha's Dhamma is *sandiṭṭhiko*. This means that if you practise the Dhamma you will see the results yourself. Some religions say that the results of practising will come after your death, when you go to heaven, but in Buddhism you practise in this life and you see the results in this life. Never mind this life; sometimes you can see the results in five minutes, certainly in two or three days. Only recently I heard of someone who went on a retreat in the countryside. This person had a drink problem, a common problem in many countries, but after that short retreat, with its meditation and study and discussion of the

Dhamma, he didn't want to drink any more. That was about a year ago, and he hasn't drunk since. So these words of the *Dhamma Vandanā* are very true. If you practise the Dhamma intensively even for a few days, meditate just for a few days, practise the *mettā bhāvanā* for a few days, you will see the result. You don't have to wait for the next life. If you're not experiencing any results from practising Buddhism, it means you're not really practising it. You won't get any result just from saying *Buddhaṃ saraṇaṃ gacchāmi*, even if you say it every day. You have to practise the Buddha's Dhamma and the *sīlas*, the moral precepts, practise meditation and puja. You have to discuss the Dhamma with your friends, work hard for the Dhamma, teach the Dhamma. Then in your own life you will experience a definite result almost at once. Therefore we say that the Dhamma is *sandiṭṭhiko*.

Next, the Dhamma is *akāliko*, meaning 'not connected with time.' Time is made up of past, present, and future. The Buddha's Dhamma was practised for the first time 2,500 years ago and people experienced the results. It is the same today, and it will be the same in 10,000 years' time. If people practise the same *sīla*s and the same *samādhi*, they will see the same results. The Dhamma is not limited by time. It is *akāliko*. And it is universal, not limited by place. You don't have to live in a particular country to practise the Dhamma. In the course of the last few years I've seen many different Buddhist centres, especially of our own movement, and everywhere I've been, whether it's England or India or Finland or New Zealand, I've found the same kind of atmosphere. The culture may be different, manners and customs may be different, but the Dhamma is the same, because the minds and hearts of human beings are the same everywhere. We may come from the east or the west, the north or the south, but because we are all human beings, we can all understand one another. The same Dhamma can be practised and followed by all.

There are some religions that can be practised only in a particular country. If, to fulfil a particular religious purpose, you want water from the River Ganges, you have to get it from the Ganges. If you want to fulfil that purpose in England, you have to come to India, or get a bottle of Ganges water sent to you. There are Hindus living in England who do this, but it makes life very difficult. If you need *kuśa* grass, you can't get that in England, not even in the Indian shops. If your religious life depends upon some particular place, it's not universal.

But the Buddha's Dhamma is universal; you can practise it anywhere. I don't know whether there are any Buddhists living at the North Pole, but I'm quite sure that it would be possible to practise Buddhism there. The Tibetans practise the Buddha Dhamma in the snowy conditions of Tibet and the Sri Lankans practise it in the tropical heat of Sri Lanka. In England, a few thousand people practise the Dhamma, and in India hundreds of thousands of people practise the Dhamma. It doesn't matter where they are, because the Dhamma is not limited by space, just as it is not limited by time.

Then we find that the Dhamma is *ehipassiko*. (By the way, all these words are in Pāli, which is very similar to many of the modern Indian languages.) *Ehi* means 'come' and *passiko* comes from a word meaning 'see', so *ehipassiko* means 'come and see'. The Buddha's Dhamma is something you can come and see for yourself, come and know for yourself. Don't take anything on blind faith. Don't believe something simply because it is written in some holy book, or because some great guru tells you to believe it. Nowadays there are so many great gurus that I think they should start their own trade union. We have them not only in India, but in England, America, Australia – all over the place. Some of them fly round the world so many times it is a wonder they don't get dizzy. And most of them say the same kind of thing. They say that they are God, or those that are more modest say they are sent by God. They say they know everything. 'Ask me any question, and I will know the answer, because I'm God. All you have to do is believe in me, follow my teaching, do whatever I say and then you will be all right. Don't think for yourself, just come to me, I'll save you.' This is what so many of these great gurus all over the world are saying, and some of them have got a lot of followers, because people are very confused, frightened, and weak, and they want some great guru to come along and save them. But there is nothing like this in Buddhism. Even the Buddha didn't speak in this sort of way. He said, 'I'm a human being. I've had a certain experience, so listen to what I have to say, but listen to it rationally, critically.' The Buddha even went so far as to say, 'Just as the goldsmith tests the gold in the fire, so you should test my words.'[261] No other religious teacher has dared to say this. They all say 'Believe me, follow me. I will do your thinking for you, no need for you to think.' So people follow them blindly, which is very sad. People are sincere, they really are looking for a path, they want to do something with their lives, but unfortunately they hear this sort of wrong teaching and instead of becoming self-reliant and developing themselves, they develop blind faith in some great guru. But the Buddha's Dhamma is quite different. It's an *ehipassiko* Dhamma. It says, 'Come and see for yourself.'

Next, the Dhamma is *opanayiko*, which means 'leading forward'. In other words, the Dhamma is progressive, not in the modern, scientific sense, but in the cultural and spiritual sense, in the sense that it leads the individual human being to higher and higher levels of development. This is what the Buddha's teaching is for. It's to lead you forward, to lead you up, to make you happier, kinder, more intelligent, more full of energy, more full of joy, more able to help others. Therefore we say that the Buddha's teaching is *opanayiko*.

Finally, the Dhamma is *paccataṃ veditabbo viññūhi*, which means that it is to be experienced by each wise person by himself or herself. It is not a second-hand affair. Nobody else can do it for you. You have to do it for yourself, because it's your life, your experience. You can't ask any priest or *purohit* to do it for you. You can't pay anybody to do it for you. Even a great guru cannot do it for you. The Buddha himself cannot do it for you. The Buddha shows the way, but you must tread that way. As Dr Ambedkar said in his book *The Buddha and His Dhamma*, the Buddha is not the giver of *mokṣa* (liberation); he is the shower of the path of *mokṣa*.[262] So we need to try to see for ourselves what the Dhamma really is, try to understand the meaning of these words we recite every day. As I said at the beginning, it is not enough to recite these words mechanically; we must understand their meaning and then put them into practice, and then we shall be true Buddhists. The Dhamma above everything else is something to be practised, and this is why we speak of it as a path. The path of the Dhamma is not for sitting and looking at; is something that you must actually walk on. The Buddha very often talks of the Dhamma as the *mārga*, the path. One could say that 'Dhamma' is the more theoretical side and '*mārga*' the more practical side. Sometimes we say Dhamma and Vinaya; here again, Dhamma means the more theoretical or philosophical side and the Vinaya is the more practical, everyday side. It is not enough just to understand the Dhamma; you must follow the *mārga*.

You can see this *mārga* in many different ways. Sometimes it is called the *madhyama mārga*, the middle way between extremes, especially the extremes of self-torture and self-indulgence. We also speak of the *mārga* of the Buddha as a *visuddhi magga*, a path of purity. *Visuddhi* here doesn't mean purity in the ordinary sense, it means something very much more than that. It means a beautiful path, a glorious path, a path that we should enjoy following. It's just like going along a path in one of those beautiful hill areas in the Himalayas. The higher you go, the more beautiful the view, the more you enjoy it, the more open everything becomes, the more free you feel. The *visuddhi magga* of the Buddha is a bit like this.

The *visuddhi magga* is divided into seven stages called the seven stages of purification. All of them, one after another, lead one to Enlightenment, which is the highest possible development of a human being. These seven *visuddhis* are mentioned in the *Majjhima Nikāya*, in the *Rathavinīta Sutta*, the 'relay of chariots'. In the Buddha's day of course there were no trains or cars, so most people had to walk everywhere, but if you were very rich you might have a chariot drawn by two or maybe four horses. The illustration that was given is this: there is a king who wants to get to a far distant city. He gets into his chariot, drives his horses for so many miles, and when the horses are tired, he jumps out of his chariot and there is another chariot waiting with some fresh horses. He gets into that and drives on again. After some more miles, these horses too get tired, so he jumps out and there is another chariot with some more horses waiting. In this way he changes his horses seven times. So does the first chariot take the king to his destination? No, it does not. Does the second chariot take him to it, or the third? Again, the answer is no. But does the king get to his destination without the help of the first chariot, the second chariot and so on? No, he does not. What happens is that the first chariot takes him to the second chariot, the second chariot to the third, and so on, until the seventh chariot carries him to his destination. The chariots take him to the city he wants to get to in relays.

In just the same way, each of the seven stages of purification takes you to the next one. The first stage is *sīla visuddhi*, purification of conduct, and the second stage is *citta visuddhi*, purification of mind. *Sīla visuddhi* takes you as far as *citta visuddhi*, and then *citta visuddhi*, the second stage, takes you as far as the third stage, *diṭṭhi visuddhi*, (purification of views), and so on. The seventh *visuddhi*, which is *ñāṇa-dassana visuddhi*, takes you as far as Nirvāṇa.[263] In the *sutta* somebody asks, 'Do we get to Nirvāṇa by means of *sīla visuddhi*?' and the answer is no. Then they ask: 'Do we get to Nirvāṇa without *sīla visuddhi*?' Again the answer is no. Then, 'Do we get to Nirvāṇa by means of *citta visuddhi*?' No. 'Do we get to Nirvāṇa without *citta visuddhi*?' No. The same question is asked about all the other *visuddhi*s, and each time the answer is no. You don't get to Nirvāṇa with them, and you don't get to Nirvāṇa without them.

Let us look at each of the *visuddhis* in turn. What is *sīla visuddhi*? So far as the ordinary lay person is concerned, there are five *sīla*s: not to harm living beings, not to take what is not given, not to commit sexual misconduct, not to speak falsehood, and not to take intoxicants. I won't say anything in detail about the *sīla*s, as they are well known to you, but I want to make just one point. Some people think that if you keep the first four it doesn't matter if you break the fifth. Some people, in fact, find it not so easy to practise this *sīla* number five. So I will give you a little advice. This number five is a very dangerous fellow, because if you are not careful, if you don't keep number five, you won't be able to keep number one, and you may not be able to keep numbers two, three, or four. So watch number five and be very careful about it. But if you can observe all these five *sīla*s, your *sīla* is purified and you are leading a pure moral life. This is the basis of your individual development. It is also the basis of a harmonious social life.

If you observe the five *sīla*s, you will find that it begins to have an effect on the mind. Your mind starts becoming pure and in this way you start practising *citta visuddhi*. This is much more difficult. It means getting rid of what we call the *akusala citta*s – anger, jealousy, fear, and ignorance – and filling the mind gradually with pure and friendly and noble thoughts. Here the practice of meditation is very useful. As you purify your mind, it becomes very clear. You can think clearly and straightforwardly. You are no longer mentally confused.

Then you can go on to *diṭṭhi visuddhi*. This is the stage of purifying one's views. Buddhism identifies many kinds of wrong views – the Buddha lists sixty-two altogether[264] – but here I shall mention just three: 'everything is made by God', 'everything is the result of Fate or Destiny', and 'everything happens just by chance'. When you practise *diṭṭhi visuddhi* you purify your mind of these three wrong views. You see that when things happen, they happen because of certain definite causes and conditions, and this holds good not only of the external world, but also of your own mind. If you control the cause you control the effect, and in this way you see that you can gain control over your own life and that you can develop.

The next stage is called 'crossing over by the overcoming of doubt – *kankhā-vitaraṇa visuddhi*. Here doubt doesn't mean just enquiring into things. In this sense you *should* doubt – you shouldn't take things on trust – but this is not the sort of doubt that is meant here. Here, by doubt is meant an unwillingness really to find out about things. You don't take the trouble to find out the truth. You don't *want* to, because then you may have to put it into practice, and you're afraid of that, so you raise all sorts of unnecessary difficulties and objections. You try to stop things from becoming clear because if they become clear, you will have to act upon them. This sort of doubt must be overcome because otherwise your will is paralysed. Usually we find that very educated people suffer a lot from this sort of doubt because their minds are very active, so they can raise all sorts of problems and difficulties. They can go on talking the whole night, and they enjoy that sort of talking because it doesn't come to any conclusion, and if it doesn't come to any conclusion they don't have to take any action. It's very important to overcome doubt in this sense. It's not so difficult to see through the view itself, but if you're not careful, even after you have apparently got rid of the view, you bring it all back with your doubt.

The fifth *visuddhi* is *magga-amagga-ñāṇadassana*, 'knowledge and insight into what is *mārga* and what is not *mārga*'. This stage is very important. Even if you want to follow the right path it's not easy to find it, because the word Dhamma has so many meanings. Some people say it is this, others say it is something else. Some say this is the right *mārga*, some say that is the right *mārga*. Some people say that to regard some people as high and others as low is the Dhamma, and practising that is the right *mārga*. So it's very important at this stage to distinguish the right path from the wrong path.

The sixth *visuddhi* is *paṭipadā-ñāṇadassana*, 'knowledge and vision of the path'. Once you have established what is the right path and what is the wrong path, the next step is to actually tread the path yourself. Then from your own experience you come to know that it is the path. It's no good sorting out what is the right path and what is the wrong path if you don't then follow the right path and experience it for yourself.

Now we come to the seventh stage, which is called simply *ñāṇadassana*, 'knowledge and Insight'. It is not ordinary knowledge, however; it is a very elevated, very pure, supremely clear knowledge – the knowledge that sees things exactly as they are. It is a sort of *prajñā*, a sort of wisdom, and of course it is joined with *karuṇā*, with compassion. It is a knowledge that fills you with energy and enables you to work for the benefit of other people, to work even for the benefit of the whole world. And in this way we get to Nirvāṇa. These seven stages of purification will carry us to Enlightenment, carry us along the whole course of human development.

This evening we have covered quite a lot of ground. We tried to understand the meaning of the *Dhamma Vandanā* so that we don't just recite it mechanically. Then we tried to understand just briefly the seven *visuddhi*s, so that we can see the path that we have to follow. It is very good, in fact it is wonderful, that so many people can sit quietly listening to these things. Nowadays there are so many distractions in the world. I think there are more distractions in Western countries than there are here. In Western countries nearly every house has a television set, and some families spend the whole evening sitting around watching it. They don't talk to one another, they just look at the television. They don't even spend time cooking; in the couple of minutes between programmes they dash into the kitchen and come back quickly with some food and eat it in front of the television. This is the way many people live today in the West. Watching television is a sort of addiction. In India there are not so many possibilities of addiction, just a few basic ones, and they are not so difficult to see, so you find it easier to sit quietly and listen to the Dhamma, and this is very good.

In the collection of ancient verses called the *Dhammapada* we hear the Buddha speaking, and in one of these verses he says, 'The meeting of friends to hear about the Dhamma is a very pleasant thing.'[265] I have come from England after twelve years' absence to meet with you here in Poona. Why have we come together? Not to watch television, not to watch films, not to hear songs. We've come together for the Dhamma, and for the Buddha. As we sit here we make a sort of sangha. When people come together like this in the name of the Buddha to hear the Dhamma, then the sangha is present, and when we have a sangha like this we can be very happy together. This is not ordinary worldly happiness; this is real happiness, true happiness, and the more we have of the happiness of the Dhamma, the more truly happy we shall be. We shall feel that we are being real human beings. Eating and drinking doesn't make us human beings; animals do that too. Wearing clothes doesn't make us human; in England the old ladies put little coats on their dogs in winter. Talking doesn't make us human; mynah birds can learn to talk, and when dogs bark they communicate with one another. Having children doesn't make us human; animals also have babies. Even thinking doesn't make us human; some animals – the chimpanzee, for example – can think.

So what does make us human? It's the Dhamma. The English word 'religion' is very troublesome. People often translate the Buddhist word Dhamma as 'religion', but I try to get away from that, because the word 'religion' is often connected with Christianity. Sometimes I say to people, 'Don't think about being religious; if you can just be a human being, that is enough.' Most people think that they are human beings, but you are not automatically a human being. You are not a human being because you eat and drink and talk and wear clothes. So what makes you a human being? The Dhamma – not in the sense of the English word 'religion', but in the sense of these simple practical things that I've been talking about this evening. So just think of becoming a human being. Just try to develop really human qualities. Try to be clear in your thinking, try to be intelligent. Try to be kind to other people; try to be sincere. There's no need to bring in religion.

According to the Buddha's teaching the Enlightened human being is the highest form of life in the universe. So there's no need to think about God or the gods and all the rest of it; just think about being truly human. A good human being is better than all the gods. If you read the scriptures of religions that believe in a god or gods, you usually find that the gods do all sorts of unethical things; they don't set a very good example to human beings. The ancient Greek gods, for example, are always fighting, and running off with women, and getting drunk. This is nothing to do with the right path. The good human being is better than all the gods. We don't need the gods, we only need other human beings. We need to be good human beings, and if we can do that, we shall be fulfilling the teaching of the Buddha. The Buddha is like a kind elder brother who gives us good advice which we can understand and follow. And because he's our elder brother, we know that when we grow up we can be like him. He has not come down from heaven, he has come from the earth, from the same mother earth as us, from the same womb, as it were. We know that what he did, we can do. We just have to make the effort. That is really all I have been saying this evening. If you understand the Dhamma and follow the *mārga*, you will be true to the teaching of the Buddha, you will be true to the leadership of Dr Ambedkar, you will benefit your own life as a human being, and you will make a happier society in which to live.

LESSONS FROM THE LIFE OF THE BUDDHA

Dapodi, February 1979

Sisters and brothers in the Dhamma, most of you know that it's twelve years since I was here last, and in the course of those twelve years I've been busy with Dhamma work in England and other countries in the West. But now I'm very happy to be back in India, in Maharashtra, in Poona. I'm happy to be back in India because it's the land of the Buddha. This is where the Buddha was born and grew up, this is where he gained Enlightenment, this is where he taught his Dhamma, this is where he converted so many people to his teaching. It's from India that the Buddha's teaching spread all over the East, to Sri Lanka, to Burma, Thailand, China, Tibet, Korea, Japan, and Indonesia. So we can say that India is the *buddha-kṣetra*, the Buddha-field or Buddha-land, (*kṣetra* means 'field'), and I'm very happy to be back in the *buddha-kṣetra*. I'm also happy to be back in Maharashtra, because Maharashtra is the *dharma-kṣetra*. Buddhism has a glorious history in India. It lasted here for 1,500 years, but after that it disappeared. There were the ruins of Buddhism in ancient monuments but there were no teachings and no Buddhists – except just a very few in Assam in the far east of India, a few hundred in Orissa, and a few Tibetan Buddhists up in Himachal Pradesh. About a hundred years ago one or two Sinhalese Buddhists came and tried to start up something, but they couldn't do very much. The Dhamma really came back to India some twenty-three years ago on the occasion of Dr Ambedkar's conversion to Buddhism, when so many thousands of people became Buddhists with him. This first conversion happened in Nagpur, which is in Maharashtra, so the Dhamma in strength and force came back to India in Maharashtra, and now there are more Buddhists in this state than in the rest of India put together. Maharashtra is the *dharma-kṣetra*, and this is why I'm happy to be back here. When I'm in England I sometimes hear people speaking Hindi but I never hear anybody speaking Marathi, so I'm very glad to hear its distinctive sound again. And I'm happy to be back in Poona, the *saṅgha-kṣetra*. For the last few months Anagarika Lokamitra has been here, and under his guidance some of the most enthusiastic Buddhists have become Dhammamitras. This is the beginning, the nucleus, of a sort of *Mahāsaṅgha*. This is why I say that Poona is the *saṅgha-kṣetra*. So after twelve years I'm happy to be back in India, the *buddha-kṣetra*, in Maharashtra, the *dharma-kṣetra*, and in Poona, the *saṅgha-kṣetra*.

A few days before I left England I was sitting in the shrine-room of our new Buddhist centre, looking at the large image of the Buddha there and thinking about the lessons we can learn from the life of the Buddha. Sometimes we don't take the life of the Buddha very seriously. Maybe we know the incidents in his life, but we don't think that they have much to do with us. So this evening I want to look at some of the most important events in the Buddha's life before he gained Enlightenment and try to see what lessons they have for us here and now. After all, the Buddha was not a god, nor the *avatāra* of a god. He was a human being just like ourselves, who by his own efforts gained Enlightenment and became an Enlightened human being. The life of a god or the *avatāra* of a god cannot be any lesson to us. In the life of Jesus we read that he raised the dead back to life, but we can't do any such thing, so that incident has no meaning for us. Maybe he could do it – we can't say – but we know that we can't. It's the same with the life of Sri Krishna. In one incident he is said to lift up a mountain with one finger. I don't know about you, but I know I could never do that, so although that incident may be very interesting, it has no lesson for our own life. But the life of the Buddha is the life of a human being like us, so we can learn from the incidents in his life, and certainly we can learn from the things that happened before he gained Enlightenment. This evening I want to look briefly at four or five of these incidents.

First of all, as I'm sure everybody knows, the Buddha was born into a rich family. Some people say it was a royal family, which may or may not be so, but his family was certainly very rich. He was the only son of his father, and his mother died just after he was born. When a man has only one son, he wants the boy to be very happy, and tries to protect him from all suffering. I had a Marwadi friend who was so fond of his son that he would never allow him out of his sight and carried him everywhere, even though he was ten or eleven years old. This is the sort of thing that happens when you've only got one son. In fact, after the Buddha's Enlightenment, his father said to him that the love of a father for his son is very strong, piercing the heart.[266] So in his son's younger days, the Buddha's father, wanting to protect him from any unpleasant or painful experience, kept him indoors all the time. Some accounts say that his father built three palaces for his son (who was called Siddhārtha): one for the hot weather, one for the rainy weather, and one for the cold weather.[267] In each of these palaces there was every enjoyment, every comfort, so that Siddhārtha need never look outside. But as he grew up, he started feeling curious about the world and asked his father if he could go out of the palace. His father said, 'What do you want to go out for? You've got everything here that you could possibly want.' But after some time Siddhārtha asked again, 'Please let me go out and see what is outside.' He asked three times and in the end his father had to agree. But his father said to the charioteer, 'Let my son see only good things.' He didn't want Siddhārtha to see anything unpleasant that might upset him. But as you know, Siddhārtha did see some very unpleasant things. He saw an old man, a sick man, and a dead man. He also saw a wandering monk, a sadhu, and that set him thinking.[268]

What is the lesson of this incident for us? The lesson is that you may be very peaceful and happy in your own life, but that is not enough. It's not enough just to be interested in what is going on in your own locality, or in Poona, or even just in India. Take an interest in what is happening all over the world, especially in the Buddhist world, in Buddhist countries everywhere. Don't be the frog in the well of the Indian saying, don't just think about your own locality. Have curiosity, a spirit of adventure, a wider horizon. This is the lesson that we can learn from this incident in the life of the Buddha. He wasn't satisfied with his situation at home, even though he was happy and comfortable there. He wanted to go out and see the world. It's very easy to get into a narrow rut in your own life, but that is not enough for the Buddhist. We must have a broader view than that.

After Siddhārtha had seen the four sights, he thought about these things very seriously, and then he decided to leave his comfortable home, his loving father, his beautiful wife, and his small son. He knew that if he told them what he was going to do, they would try to stop him, so he left secretly, at night. He got onto his horse and rode away. So this is another important incident in the life of the Buddha, but what lesson does it have for us? Some people might be thinking that the lesson is that we've got to give up our house, leave our wife or husband, leave our children, and find a horse. But is this the real meaning? No. What this going forth, this *parivrajā*, really means is going forth from the old situation to the new situation, from the old society to the new society, from the old life to the new life.

Dr Ambedkar gave up Hinduism and took up Buddhism. Maybe you have done the same. But what does that really mean? It's not just a superficial change, like one day eating rice and the next day eating roti. It's a much bigger thing than that. When Dr Ambedkar became a Buddhist, it meant a change in the whole way of life, from the old, bad society to a good, new society, and this is what it should mean for you too. It's not enough that one day you're chanting '*Hare Rām, Hare Rām*' and the next day you're chanting '*Buddhaṃ saraṇaṃ gacchāmi*'. You've got to change your life, become a better person, give up all your old, wrong practices and customs and beliefs. This is what is represented by Siddhārtha's leaving home and going off on horseback into his new life. He left everything he had. After he had gone a few miles he got off his horse and sent it back to the palace, and he took off his princely robes, his golden chain, and his sword, and put on the clothes of a beggar.[269] So what does this mean? It means you must give up the old things. What's the good of saying that now you're a Buddhist if you don't give up the old Hindu things – going to the temple, drinking liquor every day, fighting and quarrelling. When you become a Buddhist you give up all the old things, just like Siddhārtha gave up his rich robes when he left his palace.

After becoming a beggar, Siddhārtha went to visit some famous teachers, some rishis and munis living in the jungle, thinking that perhaps they could teach him something. He learned everything they had to teach, and in the end they said, 'Everything that we know, you also know. Please stay with us and help us teach the other disciples.' But Siddhārtha said, 'I don't want to lead any disciples. I want to find the highest truth and this you've not been able to show me. You've given me something and I'm very grateful for that, but I know there is something more, and I've got to go on my way and try to find it.' So he left them.[270]

What does this mean for us? We are learning all the time, and maybe we're achieving some success. But most people go a little way and are satisfied with that, so they don't make much progress. It's like a child who goes to school, gets as far as class six, and then decides that there's no need to go any further, and gives up education. People are doing this sort of thing all the time. They recite the *pañcasīla* and observe the first precept a little bit, and the second one just a little bit, and then they think that's enough. They get hold of a copy of Dr Ambedkar's *The Buddha and His Dhamma*, which is quite a thick book, read a page or two, then get tired and think that's enough and put the book back on the shelf, where it gathers dust week after week. Maybe someone takes up meditation. They think, 'Oh, this is very nice.' But they sit for five minutes and then think 'That's enough meditation.' And after a while they don't do any at all.

So this is what we find. People do a little good. They learn and practise a little bit of the Dhamma, and then they stop, and they don't do any more. But we should never stop. We should go forward all the time. However much we learn, we can learn more. However much work we do for the Dhamma, we can do more. In London some months ago some of my students asked me, 'When will you think that we've done enough? When will our work be finished?' I said, 'Our work will never be finished. There is always something more to do.' This should be the spirit of a Buddhist. Whatever good you do, you can always do more. This is what this incident in the life of the Buddha teaches us. The Buddha learned so much from these two teachers and he could have stayed with them and had a comfortable life, helping them with their teaching and leading the other disciples, but he wanted to learn more, so he went on his way. We should be like that. We should always want to learn more, not be satisfied with the learning that we have now and with what we are doing now.

After Siddhārtha left his teachers, he went deep into the jungle all by himself, and tried to meditate. And as he was meditating he had a strange experience. He started feeling great fear. Sometimes when people meditate they do have that kind of experience, and even if we don't meditate we sometimes experience fear. But when the Buddha experienced fear, what did he do? Some years later he told his disciples about it. He said, 'If the fear came while I was sitting down, I stayed sitting down until it went away. If the fear came while I was standing up, I remained standing up until it went away.'[271] In this way he overcame fear. So here's an important lesson for us. Many people are afraid. Sometimes they are afraid to say that they are Buddhists. This happens in England as well as India. People think other people might laugh at them, so they keep quiet. Many people's lives are ruled by fear, so that they are unable to do the good things they should be doing. This is one of the most important teachings of the Buddha: that we should be free from fear. One of the Buddhas at our new centre in London is a standing Buddha making the *abhaya mudrā*, the gesture of fearlessness. The Buddha is saying to his disciples, 'Fear not.' If our hearts are full of fear we can't really do anything. Throw the fear away – then you'll be a true follower of the Buddha and you can face the whole world. So this also we can learn from the life of the Buddha.

Now let's come to our last incident. After overcoming fear in the jungle, what did Siddhārtha do? Where did he go? He went to Gaya, sat down on a heap of grass under a tree on the bank of the river, and said to himself, 'My blood may dry up, my flesh may wither away, but until I have gained Enlightenment I shall not move from this spot.'[272] He sat there all day and all night, and he didn't move until he gained Enlightenment. So what does this incident mean? In one word, perseverance. Siddhārtha made up his mind that he was going to gain Enlightenment. He didn't care what happened to his body, he didn't care if he died, but he was going to sit there and meditate until he gained Enlightenment. Whatever difficulties arose, he was going to persevere. Here there is a very important lesson for us. People take up work of different kinds so easily, especially religious work, Dhamma work, but if there's a little difficulty, they stop. If someone opposes them, they stop and maybe have a cigarette. Or they think, 'Never mind, I can do the work tomorrow or next week.' But in this way the Dhamma work doesn't get done. If you want to do good work for society you must have this quality of perseverance.

So these are a few of the lessons we can learn from the life of the Buddha. As I said, it's not just a beautiful story. It's not the life story of a god, or an *avatāra* of god. It's the life of a human being like ourselves, a human being who gained Enlightenment. Every single incident in the life of the Buddha has a meaning. This evening I have mentioned only five, but there are hundreds of incidents, all with some meaning for us, like the occasion when the Buddha looked after the sick monk, or the time when he took water from an Untouchable woman.[273] If you can't read, you can at least look at pictures of the life of the Buddha. If you go to Sarnath, where the Buddha gave his first discourse, you will see the Mulagandhakuti Vihara, all around whose walls are beautiful Japanese paintings of the life of the Buddha. You can see the Buddha teaching, subduing Māra, taming the mad elephant, stopping the fighting between the Śākyans and the Koliyās.[274] All of these incidents have meaning for us. Whether we read the life of the Buddha or see it in pictures, we should try to learn about it and apply it as much as we can.

As I said at the beginning, I'm happy to be back in India, I'm happy to be back in Maharashtra, I'm happy to be back in Poona, and happy to see all of you, old friends and new. I'm very happy to see that the Buddhist movement is continuing here. Somebody told me that there are three lakhs of Buddhists here in Poona. That's an enormous number. If all of those people are real Buddhists, you will be able to transform the whole of Maharashtra, and if Maharashtra is transformed it won't be long before India is transformed. It could all start from Poona; it could start from you. So don't just recite *Buddhaṃ saraṇaṃ gacchāmi*. That's good, but it's not enough. Study the life of the Buddha, learn the lessons of the life of the Buddha, and then your own life, the life of your society, and the life of the country can be completely transformed. And then Dr Ambedkar's purpose in becoming a Buddhist in the conversion ceremony twenty-three years ago will be fulfilled.

THE FUTURE OF THE SANGHA

Poona, 3 March 1979

The most important things in Buddhism are the Three Jewels: Buddha, Dhamma, and Sangha. The most important things in our life, in fact, are the Three Jewels. And in the course of these three weeks, it's about the Buddha, the Dhamma, and the Sangha that we are hearing. We've already had lectures on 'The Buddha – Man or God?' and 'The Path of the Dhamma', so this evening we come to the Sangha, especially the future of the Sangha. But before we start on tonight's subject I want to go back a little – back to the Dhamma, back to the Buddha – and ask a question. That question is: Where was the Buddha born? You may be thinking that everybody knows that the Buddha was born in a place called Lumbinī, in what is now Nepal, halfway between the territory of the Śākyas and that of the Koliyās. But if you were to say that, you wouldn't be quite correct. The Buddha was not born in Lumbinī. Where, then, was he born? If you think about it a little, the answer is quite simple. Siddhārtha (also called Gautama) was born in Lumbinī, but the Buddha was born in Bodh Gaya. After all, the Buddha was not born as the Buddha. He started off as an ordinary human baby, and it was that baby who was born at Lumbinī, grew up in the palace, became a young man, married, had a son, and left it all and went off into the jungle to find the truth – not just for his own benefit but for the benefit of all. After six years of effort he found the truth at Bodh Gaya, where he realized supreme wisdom, infinite compassion, absolute purity of mind. There he was born as the Buddha. This was his second birth: his spiritual birth, his Dharmic birth.

So the Buddha was born at Bodh Gaya. But where was the Dhamma born? To find this out, we must follow the Buddha's history after his Enlightenment. The Pāli scriptures tell us that after his Enlightenment the Buddha spent several weeks in the neighbourhood of Bodh Gaya. Some accounts say that he stayed in the area for four or five weeks, others that he stayed for seven weeks. What was he doing? In a sense he wasn't doing anything. He sat for a day at the foot of one tree, then he moved to the foot of another tree and sat there for a day, and then he moved to the foot of a third tree and sat there. All this time, in one sense he was doing nothing, but in another sense he was doing everything. The text says that he was enjoying the bliss of Enlightenment.[275] During his years in the forest he had experienced so much pain, so much suffering; he had struggled so hard to find the truth. Now he had found it, and he was free from all mental bondage, so he was very, very happy. Later on, he tried to explain by means of comparisons the happiness of one who has gained Enlightenment. He said it is like how you might feel on being released from prison, or if you pay off a heavy debt and at last, after years and years of indebtedness, you are free from debt. It is how you might feel when, having lost your way in a dense forest on a dark night, you suddenly find the right path and are able to go straight home, or if you were sitting in a completely dark room, unable to see anything, and then someone comes along and lights a lamp, so you can see. According to the Buddha, this is something like what you feel when you gain Enlightenment. You feel absolutely free. You are free from the prison of the world, free from the debt of karma. You have found the right way, the path of the Dhamma. The darkness of ignorance has gone, and you can enjoy the light and radiance of the truth.[276]

So the Buddha sat for four, or five, or seven weeks just enjoying the bliss of Enlightenment. But then he realized that he now had a great responsibility – that of carrying the truth he had discovered to other people. So he left Bodh Gaya and started walking to Sarnath, a distance of more than a hundred miles. On the way he met a naked ascetic. The ascetic was very impressed by the Buddha's appearance, because the Buddha had just gained Enlightenment, and his face was bright and shining. The ascetic therefore asked him, 'Are you an Enlightened One?' The Buddha replied, firmly and emphatically, that he was. But unfortunately, the ascetic was not able to believe him. He just shook his head sceptically, remarked 'Maybe so', and went on his way.[277] He could have been the first person to hear the Dhamma, but he missed the chance. This shows how very careful we have to be. Buddhas are not around every day, of course, but there are other people teaching the Dhamma, and you may have the good luck to meet one of them. But if you are not careful, you will do just what the naked ascetic did. You will shake your head sceptically, say 'Maybe so', and go on your way. Maybe you see a notice saying that there is going to be a lecture on the Dhamma, or a friend tells you about it, but then you remember that there is a very good film on that night, so you decide to go and see the film instead. In this way you miss your chance. Or else somebody insists that you attend his brother's wife's sister's son's wedding. You think that you are obliged to go, and again you miss your chance of hearing the Dhamma. But if you get an opportunity of hearing the Dhamma, don't miss it. The Buddha said that the Dhamma does not last for ever, and that a time would come when it would be impossible to hear it. The time would come, he said, when a great king would send a man round the city on an elephant proclaiming a reward of half the kingdom for anyone who knew even a single verse of the Dhamma, but there would be no one to come forward and claim the reward, because not even a single verse of the Dhamma would be remembered any more, even for such a price.[278] In our time, luckily, the Dhamma is still available. The Buddha made the Dhamma available and in Maharashtra Dr Ambedkar has again made the Dhamma available. So don't waste the opportunity. Don't waste the Buddha's work, don't waste Dr Ambedkar's work. Hear the Dhamma whenever you get the opportunity, even if it means giving up other amusements and interests.

The naked ascetic having missed his chance, the Buddha went on his way to Sarnath. There he met the five ascetics who had been his disciples previously, when he was practising self-mortification. They were staying together in the Deer Park at Sarnath, and when they saw the Buddha coming they agreed among themselves not to show him any respect, because according to their way of thinking, he had given up the practice of self-mortification and was now living a life of ease. But as the Buddha approached they couldn't help rising to their feet and showing him every respect. The Buddha said, 'I have found the Truth. I am the Enlightened One, the Buddha. Listen to what I have to say.' But they refused to listen. They said, 'Before, when you were practising self-mortification, you couldn't find the Truth, so how can you have found it now that you are living a life of ease?' The Buddha replied, 'It's true that I have given up the path of self-mortification, but that does not mean that I am following the path of self-indulgence. I am following the Middle Path, the path of *śīla*, *samādhi*, and *prajñā*, the path of *karuṇā*. I am following the Noble Eightfold Path.' In the end they listened to him, and the Buddha taught them, explaining to them the truth that he had discovered. In this way the Dhamma was born – out of the Buddha's communication of the truth to these first five disciples at Sarnath, just a few weeks after his Enlightenment.[279]

What happened next? When he had taught the Dhamma to the five ascetics, and they had experienced for themselves the truth that he had discovered, the Buddha went to Varanasi, where he met a young man belonging to a rich family. This young man – his name was Yasa – had many friends, also belonging to rich families, and they too listened to the Buddha's teaching and became his followers.[280] They too realized the truth of his teaching. So now, including the Buddha himself, there were sixty-one people who had realized the truth, who had accepted the Dhamma, and in this way the Sangha was born. Thus we see that the Buddha was born at Bodh Gaya, the Dhamma was born at Sarnath, and the Sangha was born at Varanasi.

As soon as the Sangha was born – as soon as there were sixty disciples who had realized the Truth – the Buddha sent them forth, saying,

> Go forth, monks, on your journey, for the benefit of the many, for the bliss of the many, out of compassion for the world, for the welfare, the profit, the bliss of devas and mankind.... Proclaim the Dhamma, goodly in its beginning, goodly in its middle, goodly in its ending. Both in the spirit and in the letter make known the all-perfected, utterly pure righteous life.[281]

In accordance with the Buddha's instructions these sixty disciples journeyed all over India, and this practice continued even after the Buddha's *parinirvāṇa*. The Buddha's disciples went to Sri Lanka, to Burma, to Thailand. They went to China, Japan, Tibet, and central Asia. They went all over the eastern quarter of the world. Some of them even penetrated further west, to Palestine, Egypt, and Greece, but at that time they were not so successful there as in the East. In this way we find the Sangha, over a period of hundreds of years, carrying the Buddha's teaching in all directions. Unfortunately, after some 1,500 years the Buddha's Dhamma died out here in India. Why it died out is a long, sad story, and we haven't got time to go into it this evening. But though the Buddha's Dhamma died out in India, in modern times it has spread to other parts of the world. Probably in all countries of the world something is now known of the Buddha's teaching.

Among the western countries, Buddhism is especially strong in the United States, in Germany, and in the United Kingdom. This evening I want to say something about my experience of the sangha in England. As I think everybody knows, I went back to England in 1964, after twenty years in India, and I spent two years there working with the existing Buddhist organizations. But I saw that there was something missing. At first I couldn't quite understand what that was, but in the end I realized that what was missing was the sangha. When I say sangha, I don't mean people wearing yellow robes. I mean people really committed to the Three Jewels. In England at that time there were several Buddhist groups and their members read a lot of books about Buddhism, but there was no actual practice of Buddhism. Some of these people continued to go to church on Sunday. So as far as Buddhism was concerned, all they did was read Buddhist books. You find things like that in India too, of course. People sometimes say that they appreciate the Buddha's teaching very much, but they don't follow it. They still go along to the Hindu temple. It was rather like that in England at that time.

I therefore started thinking that a new kind of Buddhist movement was needed in England, especially as I saw that there was a lot of potential there for such a movement. Many people were interested in Buddhism, but there was no one to give them any proper guidance. Of course, there were people who thought they could give guidance – we find that sort of person everywhere – but they couldn't really, so the Buddhist movement in England was not progressing very well. I therefore decided to devote some years to working for the Dhamma in England. I came back to India for a short visit, and among other places visited Poona. (That was my last visit, twelve years ago.) Altogether I spent four or five months travelling around India saying goodbye to my friends. Then I went back to England and started this new Buddhist movement.

Before doing this I thought very deeply. It was clear that a new movement was needed in England, but what should be its basis? In the end I came to the conclusion that there could be only one real basis for it, and that was the Three Jewels: Buddha, Dhamma, and Sangha. These are the necessary things. Now it may seem to you, as it did to me, that of course the Three Jewels should be the basis of a Buddhist movement. But at that time people in England did not realize that. They thought that reading books about Buddhism, or talking about it, was the main thing. Very few people ever thought of actually practising Buddhism. I decided that since the Three Jewels were the main thing, they should be made the basis of our new Buddhist movement, and in order to do this it was necessary to make perfectly clear what was meant by the terms Buddha, Dhamma, and Sangha. By 'Buddha' was meant a human being who had attained Enlightenment, who had become a perfect human being, who was full of energy, *mettā*, and wisdom, completely pure, full of compassion, one who had developed by his own efforts all these good qualities. And 'Dhamma' meant simply the path shown by the Buddha, by following which all other people could become Enlightened as he was Enlightened. As for 'Sangha', that meant the community of all those people who were trying to practise the path of the Dhamma, trying to become like the Buddha. This was what was meant by the Three Jewels.

This was the first thing that had to be made clear, that it was the Buddha, the Dhamma, and the Sangha that had to be the basis of our new Buddhist movement in England, but there was something else that had to be emphasized too. The Buddha, Dhamma, and Sangha are called the *tiratna* or Three Jewels, but they are also called the *tisaraṇa*. *Saraṇa* means 'refuge', and there is a difference between the Buddha as *ratna* (jewel) and the Buddha as *saraṇa*. When you speak of the Buddha *ratna*, you recognize the nature of the Buddha, but you may not be making any movement in the direction of trying to become like the Buddha. It's the same with the Dhamma. When you see the Dhamma as the Dhamma *ratna*, you really see and appreciate its truth, but you do not necessarily make any movement in that direction. It's the same with the Sangha too. So the *saraṇa* is even more important than the *ratna*. What makes you a Buddhist is not just recognizing the three *ratnas*, but actually Going for Refuge, 'taking' the *tisaraṇa*. So the most important thing for all Buddhists, and the basis of our whole movement, is not just the three *ratnas* but the three *saraṇas*. It is the *saraṇa*, Going for Refuge, that constitutes your whole spiritual life as a Buddhist.

In England I found myself emphasizing the importance of the Going for Refuge more and more. Before this no one had realized its importance, and even during my long stay in India I found that many people did not understand the importance of Going for Refuge – that is to say, before Dr Ambedkar's great conversion. People would talk about Buddhist philosophy or Buddhist meditation, which are good things, but not even *bhikkhus* spoke about the *saraṇa*. I started wondering why its importance was not understood, and the conclusion I came to was that in India – and in many Buddhist countries too – people had started thinking of the Buddhist life as simply the *bhikkhu* life. They thought that the important thing was to become a *bhikkhu*. In Sri Lanka and Thailand many of the *upāsakas* (lay followers) think that an *upāsaka* does not have to take the Dhamma seriously. They don't meditate. They just give food to the *bhikkhus*, and it's the *bhikkhus* who meditate. In this way there develops a *purohit*-like system. The ordinary lay follower does not practise the Dhamma himself; he gets somebody else to practise it for him. But this is not in accordance with the Buddha's teaching. Some years ago, when I was in Calcutta, staying at the Maha Bodhi Society, I made friends with a Sinhalese *bhikkhu* who was studying biology at the Calcutta University. One day he said to me, 'You know, I don't like being a *bhikkhu*.' Naturally surprised, I asked, 'Why did you become one, then?' 'Well,' he said, 'my mother wanted me to.' 'But why did your mother want you to become a *bhikkhu*?' He replied, 'In Sri Lanka we believe that if parents give a son to become a *bhikkhu* they acquire a lot of *puṇya* (merit) and go to heaven after death. I have been sacrificed so that my wretched mother and father can go to heaven!' This is what happens in some Buddhist countries. The Buddhist community is divided into two halves: the *bhikkhus* and the others. The *bhikkhus* are supposed to practise the Dhamma and the *upāsakas* don't practise it, but support the *bhikkhus* to do so, which means that they are virtually paying the *bhikkhus* to practise the Dhamma for them. In these countries what is stressed is that one should become a *bhikkhu*.

I came to the conclusion that this was all wrong, and indeed that it was not in accordance with the Buddha's teaching. The Buddha's teaching is to be practised by everyone individually. No one can practise it for you. You have to practise it yourself, and this is what you undertake to do when you say, *Buddhaṃ saraṇaṃ gacchāmi, Dhammaṃ saraṇaṃ gacchāmi, Saṅghaṃ saraṇaṃ gacchāmi*. Reciting that means that you want to become like the Buddha, you want to follow the path of the Dhamma, and you want to be a member of the Sangha. Everybody recites the *tisaraṇa*, whether they happen to be a *bhikkhu*, a *bhikkhunī*, an *anagārika* or an *upāsaka*. Everybody goes for Refuge. This is the uniting factor. Whether you are a *bhikkhu* or an *upāsaka* does not matter so much. What is important is that you should practise the Dhamma. What is important is that you should really go for Refuge. This is what I stressed in England when I started the new Buddhist movement. You must really try to become an Enlightened human being, must follow the path of the Dhamma in your everyday life, and must have a friendly relationship with all those people who are doing the same. Whether you are living as a *bhikkhu* or as an *upāsaka* is a secondary matter. Whether you are a family person or don't have any family is a secondary matter. The important thing is that you go for Refuge. You can't escape from practising Buddhism by saying, 'Oh, I am just an *upāsaka*.' An *upāsaka* also goes for Refuge. This is what I emphasized in England: that Going for Refuge is what unites all Buddhists, and that this is the basis on which we must build our new movement.

Let me try to give you some idea of how this actually works in England. There we have a number of centres, or what would be called viharas here, some of them quite big. In all these centres various activities go on: meditation classes, Dhamma study classes, discussion groups, lectures on the Dhamma, and so on. In most centres these activities go on every evening of the week, and people start coming along to them. At first they just come along every now and then, taking only a little interest, and sometimes they may not come at all for months together, or just for the big festivals. Such people are called 'friends' ('*sahayaks*', as you would say), and there are many of them, perhaps thousands. But some of them start coming along to the centre regularly. They start practising meditation at home. If they are earning their living in a way that is not in accordance with the Dhamma, they change their job. They give up eating meat. Some of them give up drinking alcohol. In this way their life starts changing. Not only that. They start helping with the running of the centre, and develop a feeling of belonging to it. When they reach this stage, which may take one or two years, they become what we call a Mitra and there is a ceremony to mark the occasion.[282] After this they carry on as a Mitra maybe for a year, maybe for two or three, and then some of them start thinking, 'I really want to be a Buddhist. I really want to go for Refuge. I want to be an Order member.' If we think that they are really able to commit themselves in this way then they become an Order member and there is another ceremony.

From this you can see that in our new movement, it is not easy to become an Order member. An Order member must take Buddhism very seriously, and in England most of our Order members take it very seriously indeed. They devote themselves full-time to running the centres and Dhamma activities. They don't have any other job, and they just get their living expenses, no salary or wages. They live only for the Dhamma. In this way we have developed a new kind of Buddhist movement. There is a lot more I could say about this, but there isn't time this evening. But the basic thing – the uniting thing –is that all these Order members really do go for Refuge. They are not wearing yellow robes, but many of them do far more for the Dhamma than *bhikkhus* usually do in the East nowadays. The Going for Refuge is the basis of the Order, and the Order is the basis of the whole movement. It is these truly committed Order members who conduct the Dhamma activities. This is, indeed, the only way in which Dhamma activities can be carried on.

When I lived in India, I studied the workings of all the different Buddhist organizations very carefully, and I found that many of them had got the wrong idea about how to spread the Dhamma. Most of them seemed to think that all you had to do was call a big meeting and invite some famous people, mostly politicians. It wasn't necessary for them to be Buddhists. It wasn't even necessary for them to like Buddhism. They just had to be big names. Some of these organizations thought that if you got a lot of people with big names on the platform for your Buddhist meeting, the Dhamma would be propagated automatically. But the Dhamma is not propagated like that. Other people thought that all you had to do was put up lots of buildings – lots of viharas, lots of Buddhist temples – and in this way the Dhamma would be propagated. But this is not the way either. Let me give you an example. Suppose there are lots of sick people suffering from all sorts of illnesses, and the government builds lots of fine hospitals, but suppose there are no doctors, and no medicines. What use are the hospital buildings? Empty viharas are like that. If you don't have teachers, what's the use of the viharas? If you want to start a Buddhist movement there is only one thing that is necessary, and that is ordinary human beings who have gone for Refuge sincerely. Famous people who have not gone for Refuge can do nothing for the Buddhist movement. Buildings, however big and beautiful, by themselves can do nothing for the Buddhist movement. What you want are sincere people who are prepared to give up everything and work happily and harmoniously together for the Dhamma. This is the only way in which the Dhamma can be spread. This is the only way in which we can make widespread not just Buddhism but a new kind of society. It is not enough just to spread Buddhism as a religion. It is necessary to change the whole of society in accordance with the Dhamma, so that within that society it is easier for people to follow the Dhamma and live real human lives. This is also something which we are trying to do in England now, to change society in accordance with the Dhamma. I hope it's something which will be possible in India too.

Only a little while ago I was reading something written by Dr Ambedkar in 1950 and published in a Buddhist magazine, an article called 'Buddha and the Future of his Religion'. In this Dr Ambedkar has something to say about the Sangha. To begin with, he raises the question, 'Why did the Buddha start a Sangha?' And he gives two reasons for this. To put it briefly, he said that the Buddha founded the Sangha in the first place to give people an example of how to live. Sangha in this sense doesn't just mean the *bhikkhu* sangha, but all who truly go for Refuge. They give an example to the whole of society of how to live, because they are living happily together as friends working for the good of others. These few hundred or few thousand people who are living in this way – who make up the sangha – give an example of human life, of social life, to the rest of the population. Secondly, Dr Ambedkar says that the Buddha founded a sangha to teach people. It isn't enough to set an example: you have to teach people how to follow that example. It's just like parents in the home. It is not enough for them to lead good lives themselves. That will have some influence on their children, of course, but they also need to explain to the children what they should do and not do. It's the same in the case of the sangha. The sangha also needs to explain, to teach. So Dr Ambedkar says that the Buddha started his sangha for these two reasons: to give an example of an ideal human society and to teach people.

But then Dr Ambedkar goes on to say something else. Some of you may be surprised to hear what he says, but you mustn't be surprised. Dr Ambedkar was a very unusual man, and one of the ways in which he was unusual was that he said what he really thought. He always spoke the truth, whatever other people might think, and, as you know very well, he got into a lot of trouble for speaking the truth. He said on one occasion, 'I think I am the most hated man in India.'[283] What made him so unpopular? He spoke the truth. He said things that other people didn't dare to say, and he didn't care about the consequences. This is a very great quality, though we don't always appreciate that. Sometimes we don't realize how difficult it is to speak the truth. First of all you have to know the truth yourself, and then you have to have the freedom to speak that truth. In some countries it is very difficult to speak the truth. Even in democratic countries it's very difficult. Even in England there are some things you can't say in public, and if you say them the newspapers won't print them and they won't be reported on the radio. Everybody will try to stop you speaking the truth. So it's very difficult to speak the truth, but Dr Ambedkar always insisted on doing so. I'm going to tell you just one of the things he said. It's about the sangha, especially about the *bhikṣu* sangha. So brace yourself: this may give you a shock. He said, 'The *bhikṣu* sangha of today is useless.' He went to Sri Lanka, he went to Burma, he went to Nepal, and he saw the *bhikṣus* for himself, with clear eyes. He said, 'The *bhikṣus* of today are not setting a good example, and they are not teaching people. They are not doing anything. They are not useful any more. We need a new kind of sangha.'[284]

Dr Ambedkar wrote this important article in 1950. Some years later, when I was still in India, I wrote two articles, 'Wanted: A New Kind of *Upāsaka*' and 'Wanted: A New Kind of *Bhikkhu*'.[285] I wrote them because, like Dr Ambedkar, I saw that the old kind of *bhikkhu* was useless in the modern world. But though I saw this, in India I couldn't do very much about it. In India it's very difficult to change old customs. So I made a start in England. I decided to try to form a new kind of sangha, a *Mahāsaṅgha*, a sangha consisting of people who really go for Refuge, who take Buddhism seriously, who really want to practise it, who live for it and, if necessary, are ready to die for it. It doesn't matter whether we wear yellow robes or ordinary clothes. It doesn't matter whether we're young or old, educated or uneducated. What is important is that we go for Refuge. The Buddha, the Dhamma, and the Sangha should be the most important things in our lives. In England, I think we can say we've succeeded in creating the new kind of sangha that Dr Ambedkar had in mind, and this is what enables us to carry on our Dhamma activities. We don't require the help of famous non-Buddhists. We don't even need to ask the public for money. We can do everything ourselves, pay for everything ourselves, and work for the Dhamma ourselves.

I'm very happy to be able to spend some time in Poona telling you about these things. As you know, I'm not staying long. I'm going on to other places, first to Penang in Malaysia, where I'm going to meet some Chinese Buddhist friends, and then to Sydney, where I will be meeting some Australian Buddhist friends, and after that to New Zealand, where our new movement has spread, and where we have three centres. I'm just passing through Poona spending a couple of weeks here with you all, and I'm very happy to do that. I'm very happy to meet so many of my old friends. I'm very happy to be able to speak to you about the Buddha, the Dhamma, and the Sangha, and especially to tell you about the things that are happening in England. Whether we are in England or India or New Zealand, as Buddhists we all go for Refuge, so it's very important that we should all work together. We don't want divisions of nationality or language or political party. If we are Buddhists we are all together, and we should work together. How? The Buddha has given us some advice and I'll conclude with part of it. The Buddha was very well aware of the importance of the unity of the Sangha, and before his *parinirvāṇa* he gave quite a lot of advice about how that unity should be maintained.[286] He mentioned forty or fifty different points, but I'm going to mention only four or five of these, otherwise we'd be here all night – not that that would be a bad thing, but probably you've got to go out to work in the morning.

First of all the Buddha said, 'Assemble together regularly. Meet one another. Get to know one another. Be friends with one another.' I'm glad to see people coming together from so many different parts of Poona, and not only from Poona. We have got people who've come all the way from Gujarat, from Ahmedabad, to be here with us on this occasion. It's very good that Buddhists from so many different places should meet together, as the Buddha said. We can come together regularly for lectures, for festivals, for retreats. Retreats are comparatively new here.

A retreat is an occasion when a number of people who want to practise the Dhamma seriously go away to a quiet place for two or three days, or a week, just to do that, and I very much encourage you to attend one.

The next point I'm going to mention from what the Buddha said is, 'Whatever you do, do it harmoniously.' When you meet together, meet harmoniously and when you part from one another, part harmoniously. If you have any discussion, or organize any meeting, or conduct any kind of Dhamma activity, do it harmoniously. This is very important. So often one finds that Dhamma activities are organized in the wrong sort of way. People quarrel about all sorts of things. Who is to speak at the meeting? Who is not to speak? Should things be done in this way, or in that way? Where should the programme be held? In my locality or your locality? Who is getting a garland? Who is not getting a garland? Who is paying? Who is not paying? This is very unsuitable for a Dhamma function. Whatever we do for the Dhamma should be done in complete harmony, very quietly and beautifully. If we have a stage it should be very neat, with a beautiful image or picture of the Buddha and a fine picture of Dr Ambedkar. Let everything be beautifully decorated. People should sit quietly. Whatever we do together as Buddhists, let it be done in harmony. This will be good for us, and it will create a good impression on other people.

Thirdly, 'Respect those who are more experienced in the Dhamma than yourself.' It doesn't matter if they are younger than you are, or not so educated. If they are better Buddhists than you, you must respect them; otherwise you won't be able to learn from them. I'm not saying respect *bhikkhus*. I'm saying respect those who know the Dhamma. If an *upāsaka* knows the Dhamma, respect him. If a *bhikkhu* doesn't know the Dhamma, don't respect him. This is the Buddha's teaching. You must respect knowledge, and the person who has knowledge, not just someone who dresses in a particular way.

Fourthly – this is much more difficult – the Buddha said, 'Share everything.' If another Buddhist needs something you've got, share it with him. How can you be a Buddhist if you are rich and a poor Buddhist is starving? In so many countries we see this great inequality: some very rich, others very poor. On one side of the street someone has got so much food he can't manage it all; on the other side of the street someone has got nothing to eat. Buddhists should not tolerate these differences. If you are all Buddhists together, you should share with one another, and help one another, especially in times of difficulty. If someone is ill, or if someone dies, help the family if you possibly can. If there is a boy or a girl who has lost their parents, help to look after them, help to educate them. Don't just turn them away to beg. This is the spirit that there should be in the Buddhist community, the spirit of sharing everything: sharing material things, sharing knowledge and, above all, sharing the Dhamma. If you know anything of the Dhamma, pass it on to others.

Fifthly and lastly – and this is very important – there is meditating together. People don't usually think of this. They listen to lectures together or talk together, but they don't think of being quiet together, don't think of meditating together. Of course we can do this when we go on retreat. It's very easy then because it's quiet, not noisy like here in the city. But even when we are in the city – even when we gather together like this – we can meditate together, at least for a few minutes.

This is what used to happen in the Buddha's time. There is a very interesting story in this connection. You might have heard the name of King Bimbisāra. He was a disciple of the Buddha, and he had a son called Ajātaśatru. Ajātaśatru was quite a bad son. In fact, he killed his father and made himself king. Because he had done such a wicked thing, he was very uneasy in his mind. He went to all the great gurus of that time, one after the other, just as people do today, but he couldn't get peace of mind. One fine night Jīvaka, his doctor, who was a disciple of the Buddha, suggested that they should go and see the Buddha, who was staying outside the city in the forest, and the king agreed to go. Five hundred elephants were prepared for the journey, and mounted on these the king and the ladies of the court, with Jīvaka leading, went off to the forest where the Buddha was staying. On reaching the edge of the forest they all got down from the elephants and went forward on foot. It was very dark. The king started getting very afraid, because he had a very guilty mind. He said to Jīvaka, 'Where are you leading me? You are not leading me into a trap, I hope?' Jīvaka said, 'No, I'm not leading you into a trap. Please go on.' They went deeper and deeper into the forest, it got darker and darker, and the king became even more afraid. Again he said to Jīvaka, 'You are not leading me into a trap, I hope? You are not betraying me to my enemies?' Again Jīvaka said, 'No, not at all.' A third time the king asked the same thing, and a third time Jīvaka reassured him. The king had such a guilty mind!

If you do any evil action, this is how you feel. Anyway, at last they saw a light in the distance. Jīvaka said, 'Look, there is the light in front of the Buddha's vihara.' They came into a big open space, and there was the Buddha sitting under a tree. Around him were 2,500 disciples, and they were all meditating. There wasn't a single sound. The king was deeply impressed by the sight and exclaimed, 'Never in my life have I experienced such peacefulness! May my son be able to enjoy this kind of peace.'[287]

Here we see an example from the Buddha's own time of the disciples all coming together, not saying anything, just meditating. This we can do – but not only this. We not only need to meditate together; we also need to work together. If we can meditate together and work together for the Dhamma, then we shall be fulfilling the conditions of the ideal sangha which the Buddha laid down, and if those conditions are fulfilled, the new kind of sangha that Dr Ambedkar had in mind will surely come into existence here in India and we shall be able to spread the Dhamma for our own benefit and for the benefit of all.

This is all that I am really saying this evening. Let us sincerely go for Refuge to the Buddha, to the Dhamma, to the Sangha. Let us be really good Buddhists and form a real new sangha – a sangha that will be worthy of the Buddha, a sangha that will fulfil the ambitions and dreams of Dr Ambedkar, and a sangha that can bring back the Dhamma to India.

QUESTIONS AT AHILYA ASHRAM, POONA

Ahilya Ashram, Poona, 1979

Sisters and brothers in the Dhamma, as you know, it is three months since I was last in Poona, and you may have been wondering where I have been in the meantime, so I'm going to begin by saying a few words about that. When I left India three months ago, first of all I went to Malaysia, to meet some of the Chinese Buddhists. First I went to Penang, an island just off the coast, because some of the Buddhists there had been in correspondence with me and had been listening to tapes of my lectures. Then I went to a city called Alor Setar, and another city called Ipoh. Altogether I stayed in Malaysia for some four or five days, during which time I met many Buddhists, gave three public lectures, and visited some of the Buddhist monasteries and temples.

From Malaysia I went to Australia and spent three or four days in Sydney, staying with some very old friends of mine. I met them first in Singapore more than thirty-two years ago, and this was our first meeting in all that time.[288] It was very interesting to see that even though we hadn't met for thirty-two years we were able to discuss things just as though we'd only been separated for a few weeks. In Sydney I also met some Buddhist friends who had been writing to me and listening to tapes of my lectures. And then I travelled to the last country on my tour: New Zealand. I was in there for just over two months and visited our three centres there. We had lectures, retreats, and also some ordinations.

I came all the way back from New Zealand to Bombay, via Australia, in twenty-four hours – a long journey in such a short time – so when

I reached Bombay at one o'clock in the morning I was feeling a little tired, but Lokamitra and Dharmarakshita were at the airport to meet me, and from there we went to Mr Solanki's flat, got some sleep, and this morning came here to Poona, to the Ambedkar colony in Yerawada. You may be wondering why I'm telling you all this, but I'm coming to the point now. When I came to the Ambedkar colony and entered the vihara, the first thing I noticed was a loudspeaker playing very loud film music. Naturally I thought, 'Ah! It is the month of May! It is not that they are still celebrating Buddha Jayanti. I have come back to Poona in the middle of the marriage season.' I thought, 'Never mind, they'll play a few records and then it will be quiet.' But after several hours it was still going on. I wondered, 'Where has this custom come from? Since the sound is coming from the colony, I suppose it is Buddhists getting married, but this way of getting married is not quite Buddhist. It must be some relic of the Hindu way of doing things.' This set me thinking. I was thinking that it is very difficult to give up an old habit and take up something new. Here in India, even if one becomes a Buddhist, if one goes for Refuge, it is very difficult to give up the old Hindu customs.

This kind of difficulty doesn't only arise in India; it crops up everywhere. My recent experience is of England, where of course the difficulty isn't anything to do with Hinduism but has to do with Christianity. Most of the members of our sangha were brought up as Christians. When they were very small they were taken to church and taught to say their prayers, and some of them were educated in Christian schools. Sometimes the teachers would tell them that if they didn't follow the Christian religion strictly, God would be angry and send them to hell after they died. When you are told something like this when you are very young, it makes a strong impression. You may not remember what actually happened, but its influence is still with you as an adult. In England some of our friends have been thinking about this sort of thing quite a lot. Some of them have been saying that although they thought that they were Buddhists, actually there is still a trace of Christianity which they have not yet got rid of. They're trying to get rid of that Christian influence so that they can be pure one-hundred-percent Buddhists.

Likewise, in India we have to shake off the influence of Hinduism. To do this, there are two things we have to do: get rid of all the old Hindu influences from our minds, and resist the influence of our Hindu surroundings. It's very difficult to make a new start. It's very difficult to put the old things aside. It's very difficult to change. As Lokamitra was saying a few minutes ago, there needs to be a change, a transformation, in the individual and also in the society. This twofold transformation is the basic teaching of Buddhism, but it is very difficult to achieve, so we have to make a strong effort all the time not to be influenced by the past, and to make a new beginning as Buddhists. These were the thoughts that came into my mind when I heard that music playing for the marriage ceremony today. But what is your experience? Do you experience this sort of difficulty or do you find it quite easy to make this new start?

Q: *If people invite us to the functions of other religions, should we go along?*

Sangharakshita: This raises a number of questions. The first thing we have to understand is that we belong to a society within which people are following different religions. According to the Indian constitution, in law India is a secular state; at least, that's the theory. No religion is given any particular favour. Within society, there are people following different religions, and in the course of your life you will come into contact with them. Maybe you work with them; maybe you live next door to them; maybe you come into contact with them in some other way. You can't avoid being friendly with people of other religions, and this is actually quite good. Just because you follow one religion and the other person follows another, that doesn't mean that you have to be enemies, or that you can't have any contact.

If a friend or acquaintance who is following some other religion invites you to a function, what should be your attitude? In view of what I've said already, the answer begins to become clear. Basically, there is no harm in your accepting that invitation provided that it does not involve doing anything against Buddhism. If you go along to that function it doesn't mean that you are agreeing with the religion of the person who has invited you. You are just acting in a friendly way as a member of the community. These are the three things you must bear in mind. First of all, just because you go along to that function doesn't mean that you accept that person's religion. Secondly, if you do go along, don't do anything that is against your own religion. And thirdly, you go along to keep up the friendly social relationship. So I don't think that there is any real difficulty here.

When I lived in Kalimpong, there were certain Hindu functions going on which were against Buddhism, so I didn't go. For example, the Nepalese Hindus in that area are very fond of sacrificing buffalo, and when I first arrived in Kalimpong they used to invite me to these occasions, just out of friendliness. I used to say, 'Thank you for the invitation, but I'm sorry to say that I can't come because the sacrifice of animals is against Buddhism.' But if there was some function that didn't involve anything against Buddhism I was quite happy to go. This is the main thing to consider, along with the need to maintain friendly social relations with people of different religions. When people invite you, they have to do that with some respect for your principles, and likewise, if you invite someone of another religion to your function you must respect their principles. If you invite a Muslim friend to your wedding, you mustn't expect him to bow down to the image of Lord Buddha, because that is against the principles of the Muslim religion. You may not agree with his religion but you must respect the fact that he follows it. And the attitude of other people towards you must be the same. They may not accept Buddhism themselves, but they should respect the fact that you follow Buddhism.

In the UK people are faced with this sort of thing at Christmas time. Many of our Buddhist friends have relations who are Christian, and it's the custom to invite one's relations to gather for Christmas, even if those relations are Buddhist. Some members of our sangha are a bit concerned about whether to celebrate Christmas with their relations or not, so they follow a middle way. They don't join in with the religious side of the celebration, they don't go to church, but they join in with the social side, the special meals, and so on. There is no objection to that, provided that there is vegetarian food for them to eat.

So this is the principle. You can join in events with your friends of other religions, but there is no need to join in with the religious side of the occasion; just join in with the social side. We need to follow our own religion, Buddhism, very strictly, but at the same time we need to keep up friendly relationships with other people on the purely social level.

Q: *'Buddhism is a child (i.e. a sect) of Hinduism, but perhaps it may be called a revolutionary child.' Please comment.*
S: The statement that Buddhism is the rebel child of Hinduism was made by Swami Vivekananda, who was a disciple of Ramakrishna

Paramahamsa, the founder of the Ramakrishna Mission. In 1893 Vivekananda went to America, to a big meeting in Chicago of all the different religions of the world called the Parliament of Religions. Vivekananda went there to represent Hinduism, and in his speech he said that he represented the oldest and best religion in the world. He said that Buddhism is the rebel child of that religion and that Christianity is only the distant echo of Hinduism.[289] His statement that Buddhism is the child of Hinduism is of course not acceptable to the Buddhist. The Buddha's teaching represents a completely new start because the Buddha represents a completely new start. The Buddha was a real individual. He wasn't satisfied with following the old traditions. He knew about them and followed them in his early life, but he realized in the end that they are not enough. They don't lead to Enlightenment. He had to find a new path. So we can't say that Buddhism is the child of Hinduism.

Moreover, Vivekananda said that Buddhism was the *rebel* child of Hinduism. This is quite clever. Vivekananda was no fool. He knew quite well that Buddhism is not the same as Hinduism, and that the Buddha was against many things in Hinduism – for example, against the caste system and against the *ātmavāda*. At the same time he said that Buddhism is the child of Hinduism. So his explanation was that the child is a naughty child, a rebel child.

When Dr Ambedkar converted to Buddhism about twenty years ago, some Hindus tried to say the same sort of thing. They maintained that Dr Ambedkar and his followers were just being a bit naughty, as it were, like children who don't understand properly and rebel against their parents out of naughtiness. Why do people take this sort of attitude? It's because they don't want to allow you to be free to live your own life and follow your own path. They want you to follow their path, even though that path is no longer good for you. The representatives of the old religion will always try to keep you inside that religion. This is what the Christians try to do too, and so do the Muslims.

As I said, I recently visited Malaysia, where the majority of the people are followers of Islam. They've got political power, so Malaysia is a Muslim state, not a secular state like India, and the government in Malaysia officially supports the Muslim religion. They have a law that a Muslim is not allowed to change to any other religion. Islam does not give you that freedom. It was the same with Christianity in the old days, and even now the Roman Catholic church does not recognize that anybody ever leaves it. They think that if you were once a member you cannot leave, and even if you no longer consider yourself a member of the church, they will still consider that you are.

The Buddha's teaching is not like that, because it recognizes the freedom of the individual. You are not really a Buddhist unless you accept Buddhism freely because you want to accept it. In order to be free to accept Buddhism, you must be free to reject it, and Buddhism allows you that freedom. Buddhism says 'Think for yourself.' If you're convinced of the truth of it, accept it; otherwise, don't. There is no other religion that gives you this sort of freedom, and this is why many people in western countries are attracted to Buddhism. But if you take up Buddhism after having belonged to some other religion, there will always be a pull from that religion to try to get you back. Sometimes the pull may come from inside, because we aren't yet completely individuals. Sometimes it may come from outside as an influence of the society or environment you are living in. We have to be on the watch for this and we have to resist it, which means that we have to maintain our independence of thought, and think for ourselves.

Q: *What kind of Buddhism shall we follow?*
S: This question arose quite a few years ago just after Dr Ambedkar's *diksha*, when some Hindus were asking the newly converted Buddhists, 'You have converted to Buddhism, but have you converted to Hīnayāna, or to Mahāyāna?' Some of our friends felt quite confused and didn't know what to say. By that time unfortunately Dr Ambedkar had passed away and wasn't able to clarify this question, so people were coming and asking me about it. As soon as I heard that some Hindus had been asking this question, I thought, 'Aha! This is quite dangerous.' It was quite a clever question because it was meant to divide the Buddhist community. If some people said, 'We have become Hīnayāna Buddhists' and others said, 'We have become Mahāyāna Buddhists', the result would be that the Buddhist community would be divided. So I said, 'If you are asked this question, you should say, 'I have not been converted to Hīnayāna or to Mahāyāna. I have simply been converted to Buddhism.'

But our Hindu friends are very clever, and they don't give up trying. Like Māra in the Buddhist scriptures, if they can't win the argument in one way, they will try to win it in another. So the Hindu newspapers started referring to the Indian Buddhists as neo-Buddhists, with the intention of dividing the new Buddhists from the old Buddhists, and this is still going on. So again, we should say, 'I am not a new Buddhist, I am not an old Buddhist, I am a Buddhist.'

How did the Hīnayāna and Mahāyāna and the rest arise? This is a very big historical question and I haven't time to say much about it. What I will say is that there are many schools of thought in Buddhism, but there is no quarrel between them. When the Chinese pilgrim Xuanzang came from China to India during the Buddhist period he found the followers of different schools, followers of the Hīnayāna and followers of the Mahāyāna, living together peacefully in the same viharas.[290] The Buddha's teaching is vast and has many aspects. The basic principles are very simple, but those principles are developed in many ways. The different schools of Buddhism arose because some followers of the Buddha were more interested in one aspect and others were more interested in another, and they developed the aspect they were interested in. But they did not quarrel about that. They just followed the particular aspect of the Buddha's teaching they were interested in and allowed other people to do the same. It was not like that with Christianity in the West. In the history of Europe there have been wars between the Catholics and the Protestants, and they sometimes killed one another, because each side claimed that theirs was the true Christianity. In Buddhism you never find this sort of enmity. What is important is that we are simply Buddhists and we take from the Buddha's teaching whatever is helpful to us here and now, in Maharashtra in the twentieth century. For instance, what the Buddha said about caste is especially useful because of the situation here in India. In other countries people are not very interested in what the Buddha said about caste, because they don't have a caste system, but that doesn't mean that they are following a different kind of Buddhism. They concentrate on the aspects of the Buddha's teachings that concern them, just as you concentrate on those aspects that concern you. All these different aspects of the Buddha's teaching come to the same thing in the end, which is that the individual human being should be free to grow and develop. In India we try to do that under the conditions which exist here. In other countries people try to do it under the conditions that exist there.

It is very important that all Buddhists should realize that wherever we are from, if we truly go for Refuge to the Buddha, Dhamma, and Sangha, we are all following the same path. We shouldn't allow anybody from outside Buddhism to divide us in any way whatsoever. There is no need for us to be divided, and if we think in terms of division we're still thinking in the old way. Among Hindus you can find many differences: between followers of Vishnu and followers of Shiva, between followers of Advaita Vedānta and followers of Dvaita Vedānta. Sometimes swamis and sadhus will fight with those long iron things they carry around with them. In Buddhism we don't have anything like that. All Buddhists are brothers and sisters, and we have to get away from all the old ways of thinking that divide people. We don't hate someone because he belongs to another religion. The Buddhist feels love towards everybody. The strange thing is that anyone should think that if you don't belong to their religion they've got to hate you. You know very well that if you meet a Hindu and he finds out you are a Buddhist he won't be pleased. This same Hindu might say to a visitor from another country that India produced the Buddha, the greatest man who ever lived, but if you follow the Buddha the Hindu doesn't like it. We have much the same sort of thing in England, where people may like you and think you're a good person until they find out you're a Buddhist, when they get quite upset or even angry. Buddhism takes a much broader view. The Buddhist ideal is to be the friend of all. This is why we say, '*sabbe sattā sukhī hontu*' (may all beings be happy).

So let's keep up friendly social relations with the followers of other religions. Writing about the difference between Catholics and Protestants, the famous eighteenth-century writer Jonathan Swift wrote, 'We have just enough religion to make us hate, but not enough to make us love one another.'[291] This is very sad, but it is what we usually find. People have a little bit of religion, just enough to make them hate people of other religions, but not enough to make them love everybody. People's religion sometimes makes them very small in their heart, but Buddhism's idea is that your religion, your Dhamma, should make you much broader in your heart. Yes, we stick very firmly to the Buddha's teachings, but we are still very friendly towards everybody, whatever their religion.

I hope it won't be long before I'm back in India to see you all again. I must say that I've been very much encouraged by my whole trip, to Malaysia, Australia, and New Zealand as well as India. It's wonderful to see the way the Buddha's teaching is spreading and how people in countries where Buddhism wasn't known before are following it. But even though I was pleased and encouraged by what I saw in all these places, I must say quite honestly that I feel most encouraged by what I've seen in India and especially here in Poona. Why is this? The reason is very simple. In places like New Zealand and Australia, there are some very good Buddhists, but there are very few, at most a few hundred. But here in India, even here in Poona, there are thousands. So much can be done – so much more that has been done so far. It's now more than twenty years since Dr Ambedkar's *diksha*, and after his passing away not very much happened, but now things are gaining momentum. Many people in India thought that this movement was going to die away, but Buddhism is getting stronger and stronger, especially here in Poona. So, people in Poona have got a very good opportunity, and I hope that next time I come a lot of progress will have been made. I shall be back quite soon, so if you want to show me something when I come you'll have to work quite hard. If you all cooperate, a great deal can be done.

1982–1983

This section begins with a talk given in England after Sangharakshita's extensive tour of India in 1981–2 (talks in Complete Works, *vol. 9), a behind-the-scenes account of the tour and impressions of the Buddhist revival in India. The following talk, introducing Dr Ambedkar to a Western audience, was a call to action: 'We've got to do as much to transform life and society in the West as Dr Ambedkar had to do to transform life for the Mahars in India.' The rest of this section consists of the talks given on a visit to India in late 1983, during which, as Lokamitra recalls (p. xlix), Sangharakshita gave three lectures, the first in Dapodi, Poona, near the site where the Mahavihara was to be built, the second at the opening of the new retreat centre facing the ancient Bhaja caves, and the last in the chawls of Worli, Bombay. This last talk contains one of Sangharakshita's most quoted and loved statements: 'I believe that it is possible for any human being to communicate with any other human being, to feel for any other human being, to be friends with any other human being. I cannot live without this belief, and I would rather die than give it up.'*

A MISCELLANY OF IMPRESSIONS

This talk was given in England (location unknown) not long after Sangharakshita's extensive lecture tour of India in 1981–2. The talks from that tour are to be found in Complete Works, vol. 9, so this talk, and the one delivered to the Wrekin Trust that follows it, offer a coda to that volume, giving a behind-the-scenes account of the tour and Sangharakshita's impressions of the Buddhist revival in India at that time.

This isn't going to be a lecture, or even a talk really, more a miscellany of impressions. I've been in India for three whole months – not just in India, but immersed in India, in the Indian Buddhist movement. I think that if I was to put my mind to it, I could write a book about the experiences of those three months, because they were so rich and diverse. Perhaps one book wouldn't be enough. So I'm not going to be able to do justice to those three months in the course of forty or fifty minutes. At best I can offer you a slice of the cake, a slice which I hope will whet your appetite for more, because you will be getting more in different forms. Accompanying me for much of the time was Nagabodhi with his cine-camera and he has, I hope, a cinematographic record from which, when it's all been put together, edited, provided with commentary, background music and so on, you'll be able to get a fuller and richer impression.

For the benefit of those of you who don't know much about me or our Buddhist movement, or about India and our work there, I'll start by filling you in with a bit of background. During my recent visit to India, most of the time I was among ex-Untouchable Buddhists, who are in a way a very special category of Buddhist. To explain, I'll need to tell you a bit about the Indian background, and specifically the orthodox Hindu background. According to orthodox Hinduism, as embodied in various *śrutis* and *śāstras*, as they call their texts, society is made up of four main castes. There are the Brahmins, who are the teachers; the Kshatriyas, who are the landowners, the warriors, the fighters, the administrators, the rulers; the Vaishyas, who are the traders and sometimes the agriculturalists; and the Shudras, who are the servants, the serfs, who wait upon the other three castes. And then there are the Untouchables, who are outside the caste system altogether. You belong to a caste because your father and his father and his father belonged to that caste. It's an entirely hereditary system. These four main castes are subdivided into roughly 2,000 sub-castes, partly occupational, partly tribal, and these castes exist in orthodox Hindu society even today. In fact they are still very much present, and their presence is powerfully felt even in Indian politics, though I won't go into that at the moment.

Outside the caste system, outside the four main castes with their 2,000 subdivisions, there were the Untouchables. The Untouchables are, or certainly were, quite literally untouchable. They usually lived near a Hindu village, and were dependent upon the caste Hindu occupants of the village for their subsistence. They weren't permitted to own land or wear proper clothes, or even to eat proper food. They did the menial work of the village – scavenging, removing night soil, removing dead bodies and the carcasses of dead animals, and in return they were given cast-off clothing, the right to occupy a piece of land near the village, and scraps of food, and nothing else. This system has obtained in almost all parts of India for hundreds of years right down to the present day. They were not permitted to have any sort of orthodox Hindu religious teaching. They had gods and goddesses of their own, spirits whom they worshipped. They weren't properly assimilated into the Hindu fold, though they were usually regarded as Hindus for statistical purposes.

Among these communities, the one with which I've been most concerned during my time in India is that of the Mahars, one of the communities of the state of Maharashtra, which is situated in the Deccan, stretching from Bombay in the west – Bombay being the capital of Maharashtra state now – to Nagpur in the east, Nagpur being practically in the middle of India. The population of the state is a bit smaller than that of the United Kingdom, though the area is greater.[292] Like the rest of India, Maharashtra consists mainly of village communities with just a few big cities. Along with other much smaller ex-Untouchable communities, the Mahars lived near the caste Hindu villages and carried out the sort of duties that I described. Within living memory their conditions have been very bad indeed. For instance, they weren't allowed to go through the Hindu village at times of day when their shadow might fall on other people. They had to carry a spittoon hung round their neck to spit into, because they weren't supposed to spit on the wayside in case a caste Hindu foot stepped on the saliva, and they were supposed to carry a small broom with which they swept their footprints behind them, so that no trace of their passage should be left. All these customs were enforced within the memory of the people of this community. They subsisted on cast-off clothing and leftovers, and they had no rights at all. Some of our older Indian Order members remember as small children being sent by their parents to the caste Hindu houses for the scraps of food and cast-off clothing which were all that they were entitled to in the way of wages, apart from the carcasses of the dead animals that they removed, whose skin and bones they were allowed to keep. This was their plight. They had no education. They weren't even allowed access to the village well. I travelled among these people years and years ago, and when I stayed with them they sometimes couldn't offer me clean drinking water, only muddy water from the river, because that's all they were permitted to draw.

If one takes Maharashtra as a whole, the Mahars are about one tenth of the population, but they tend not to be congregated together. They usually exist in small communities near the caste Hindu communities for which they work, so they're in a minority practically everywhere, and their isolation is another cause of their state of oppression and servitude. In recent times there has been a flow of population to the big cities, so there are quite big Mahar communities in parts of Bombay, Poona, Nagpur, and so on. But the majority of these people still live in (or rather outside) the villages in the way that I've described, and their condition was very miserable indeed. There were some alleviating factors. Some of them got into the British Army, or the East India Company Army, and that way they got a bit of education. And in modern times the community produced a remarkable man whom they regard nowadays as their emancipator. His name was Bhimrao Ambedkar, and he was born towards the end of the nineteenth century. He was a quite remarkable man. His father had been with the British Army and had got a little education, and his son managed to get an education in India, although it was very difficult, and eventually pursued higher studies in England (at the London School of Economics), Germany, and America. He returned to Bombay in the early thirties determined to do something for his community, and to cut a very long story short, he did quite a lot. He started all sorts of institutions and initiated a lot of propaganda, all calculated to raise the standard of living of his people in every way, and to induce or persuade caste Hindus to treat them as human beings. He wrote, he fought law cases, he became an expert on law, education, and sociology. He eventually entered politics, standing for Parliament, and by the end of his political career he was a minister in the central government of independent India and eventually became Minister of Law and Justice. He tried as hard as he could to alleviate the condition of the Mahar people, but again and again he came up against the obstacle of orthodox Hinduism. Orthodox Hindus would simply not admit that these people, who of course were still untouchable in their eyes, despite the passing of a law (which was not enforced), were in any way equal to them.

At first Ambedkar had the idea of trying to persuade the Hindus to change their ways, but after two decades of effort he declared himself quite frustrated in his attempts. He came to the conclusion that orthodox Hinduism could not be reformed, and decided that a change of religion was needed, famously declaring, 'I may have been born a Hindu but I do not intend to die one.' After that, he searched around for another religion to follow. He looked at Christianity, Islam, Sikhism, and Marxism, but in the end he decided to become a Buddhist and to advise his people to become Buddhists. He felt that if they got out of the Hindu fold altogether, if they adopted another religion, that would give them self-respect, for they would be able to say that they were not Hindus, but just human beings following the path of the Buddha. In 1956 there was a great ceremony in Nagpur and he and about half a million of his followers became Buddhists, and after that the movement spread. But unfortunately Dr Ambedkar died six weeks after this great mass conversion.

I myself had some contact with Dr Ambedkar, starting in 1950 and continuing up to 1956, when he died, and at the time of his death I happened to find myself in Nagpur, where the great mass conversion ceremony had taken place only six weeks earlier. At that time his followers came to me, terribly distressed and disheartened, wondering what was going to happen now that he was no longer there to guide them. I spent some days in Nagpur, in the course of four days giving some thirty-five lectures in different parts of the area, rallying people and telling them that all was not lost. Thereafter I used to go down to the plains from Kalimpong and tour from place to place, trying to spread Buddhism amongst these people. Or rather, I wasn't trying to spread Buddhism – in a sense it had already been spread, because they considered themselves to be Buddhists – but I tried to clarify for them what being Buddhist meant. For instance, I explained things like the Three Refuges, the Five Precepts, the Eightfold Path, the Four Noble Truths – things that they hadn't as yet heard about in most cases. The situation was as bad as that.

Over the years, having travelled all around Maharashtra among these people, I became quite well known to them and they developed quite a lot of confidence in me. However, in 1964 I came back to England, stayed for two years, then decided to stay on and start a new Buddhist movement, perforce having to neglect my work in India. This was a conscious decision. I felt I'd done as much in India as I could for the time being, so I took up the work in England. But India was never out of my mind. I kept up my contact with my friends there, and I used to insist on our newsletter being sent there, which turned out to be a good investment. Nearly five years ago an Order member called Lokamitra visited India for a yoga course and met some of my friends there, and I put it to him that he should start up FWBO activities in India. He's been there for four years and feels very much at home, and has pledged to stay as long as is necessary, and as long as he's happy there.[293] The FWBO having been started in India, especially in Poona, I paid them a couple of visits some three years ago on my way to and from New Zealand. On each occasion I stayed only for a few weeks, though long enough to ordain a few people. At that time about a dozen people were ordained on the recommendation of Lokamitra and Padmavajra. Two of them were people whom I'd known very well years and years earlier – that is to say, Dharmarakshita and Dharmalochana.[294] So I had that brief contact then, and just recently I've had this three-month visit to see how they've all been getting on.

Since I've been back of course everyone has asked me, 'Did you enjoy your trip to India? I've had to really think about that question. I can't say just, 'Oh yes' – it isn't as simple as that, if I'm honest. I think people expect me to say that I enjoyed every minute of my visit, but I have to confess that I didn't. There were many delightful moments, but there were other moments, and even hours, which were quite painful in one way or another. So it wasn't an unmitigatedly blissful experience.

The painful experiences were largely associated with travel. I was very glad to be in India, to meet people and to give lectures, but getting from one place to another was sometimes a very painful experience. For one thing, there's such a lot of noise. If you haven't been to India and think of it as a quiet, peaceful, yogic, retreat-like place, with sages in meditation all over the place, you've got a rude awakening coming to you if ever you go there. Life in India is noisy, especially in the big cities. When I got back to London it was as though all the people of Bethnal Green were on retreat, in comparison with Bombay. There seemed to be hardly a sound, and people were walking so quietly and peacefully in the streets. No one was shouting or quarrelling or fighting, and there were no dogs barking.

Another thing that I found quite unpleasant was the dust. The villages were full of dust, the roads were full of dust, and especially the cities were full of dust and pollution, which has got much worse in India. In Bombay it's quite terrible. In the evening there's a sort of pea soup of pollution hanging over the city. Going from one part of Bombay to another by car for an evening lecture, the trip only lasted half an hour, but I was exposed to so much pollution that I at once got a sore throat, and I kept getting sore throats much of the time that I was in India. In Bombay it's largely due to the increase in the number of taxis and scooters, of which more later. In the course of one of my lectures there I spoke about pollution, because I thought perhaps people weren't noticing that things were getting worse. I mentioned it particularly because there was an old friend of mine up on the platform who was a former mayor of Bombay, so I thought he might have a bit of influence still, and be able to do something about it. Bombay was even worse than Athens, and that's saying quite a lot.

So I certainly didn't enjoy that aspect of my trip, and I've got especially horrific memories of some of the railway towns that I visited. Railway towns in India are horrible settlements that have sprung up around big railway junctions. There's a vast railway system in India; trains by the dozen puff through the junctions all the time, and a pall of smoke and pollution hangs over the whole town. Around the railway station, which is the satanic centre of the whole complex, there's huddle upon huddle of hovels, with more modern buildings in between. Everything is so dirty, so confused, so horrible. Sometimes we had public meetings right in the middle of such places, in the open space in the crossroads next to the station. They'd stop the traffic, and with clouds of dust still in the air they'd put up the stage there and people would gather – three, four, or five thousand people. And there I would have to give my talk, with the trains puff-puffing and toot-tooting in the background, and all kinds of other noises and disturbances. Sometimes I had to raise my voice to be heard, even though there was a microphone and loudspeaker system. I must confess I didn't enjoy this aspect of my trip at all. But still, these were only minutes, or half hours, or the odd day, and there were compensations. Once Nagabodhi happened to be with me, and we had a little discussion about the contribution of pollution to the visual arts. We were staying in some hotel – well, they called it a hotel, but we'd call it a doss-house – right next to the railway station, so there was a layer of grime over everything. But one evening we went outside through the pall of pollution and discovered some really beautiful atmospheric effects. The sunset was absolutely magical: a brilliant pink sky, and inky-blue mountains seen through the iridescent haze of pollution.

So it was a mixed experience: painful and pleasant, disastrous and delightful, diabolical and heavenly, all at the same time, which was a bit confusing and disorientating. But there were experiences that were unmitigatedly pleasant, especially when we were driving through central Maharashtra from one village to another. There's been a lot of irrigation done in that area, and it's much greener than it used to be. People are growing more in the way of crops, and wherever we went there were fields upon fields of sugar cane. In Norfolk, where I live, lots of sugar beet is grown, and in Maharashtra they had exactly the same sort of sugar factories as we have in Norfolk, and that made me feel at home, though usually I don't like factories. Much of Maharashtra is flat, dry, and barren, but here and there you get green fields and orchards with all sorts of what we would regard as exotic fruits, like bananas and chikus and pomegranates and oranges, though not at that time of the year. Some of the little villages of northern Maharashtra are quite squalid but picturesque nonetheless. There are cows, horses, and goats, lots and lots of little children, people working in the fields, and little temples. Sometimes there were low mountains with interesting shapes in the distance. I found it all very delightful.

In one or two places I did a bit of sightseeing. For some reason – it might have been to do with where I happened to find myself on those sightseeing days – I decided to see something of Muslim architectural remains. There are quite a few Muslim, mainly Moghul, remains in Maharashtra, especially around Aurangabad, where I spent a week, and around Ahmedabad (in Gujarat), where I spent another week. I was especially interested in some tombs of famous Sufi teachers. Usually in India Hindus and Buddhists don't mix very much with Muslims, but anyway I did go along to some of these tombs, and in some cases there were quite a lot of pilgrims visiting them, because worshipping at the tombs of Sufi saints is quite a feature of Islam in India. Some of these tombs are very beautiful from an architectural point of view, and one in particular had a strong atmosphere which seems to be coming from the tomb itself – that was quite strange and interesting.

In India I wore my yellow robes all the time, because if you don't wear your yellow robes in India, people start wondering what exactly you are. It's much simpler and easier if you just wear them. Then people think, 'Oh yes, he's a *bhikkhu*', and they know exactly where they stand. So I was wearing my yellow robes when I went to these Sufi tombs. The tombs are often associated with mosques. Muslims at first sight can't tell the difference between a Buddhist *bhikkhu* and a Hindu sannyasin or swami, and they don't usually like Hindus going into their mosques, so I received some odd looks when they saw me in my yellow robes in the precinct of the mosque or tomb. Usually there were several of our Indian Buddhist friends with me, and on several occasions Muslims came up to them and asked, 'Who is that?' My friends used to say, 'He's from England', and as soon as they heard that, it was all right, which was distinctly odd, I thought. The fact that an Englishman was visiting their mosque or tomb didn't bother them at all. They only seemed bothered by the fact that it might be some kind of Hindu monk. So yes, I enjoyed my little bit of sightseeing. I also took the opportunity of visiting the caves at Ellora, which I hadn't seen before.[295] I must also admit that I enjoyed giving and even preparing my lectures, perhaps as much as anything I did. I gave about thirty-five substantial lectures while I was there, plus some little talks.[296] And I very much enjoyed meeting old friends. There were people I hadn't seen for twenty-odd years.

So I felt very much at home in India. In some ways I was surprised by the extent to which I did feel at home. Everything was very familiar. I knew the ropes, as it were – the customs, the manners, the people, the language. I knew what people would think on certain issues and how they would react. I'd know what they were thinking without having to ask. I feel very much at home in England, but I feel no less at home in India, especially in Maharashtra. If I was pressed, I might even say that I feel more at home in India, I think partly because the Dhamma, certainly among our Buddhist friends, is more all-pervasive, and partly because there is very often a positivity among Indian people that you don't quite get here in England. One might almost say, if it wasn't for fear of being misunderstood, that there's a friendliness there that one doesn't very often experience here. I have a lot of friends there – probably far more, numerically speaking, than I've got here. I've got hundreds of friends here but I've probably got thousands of friends in India.

It seems strange to me that I can feel so much at home in two such different places. It's like being equally at home in two different worlds, or as though one might go to the moon and feel as much at home there as on the earth. It's as though there are two very different sides to oneself, one might even say. You're two people, but at the same time you are just one person. One could say that one part of you feels at home here and another part feels at home there, but it isn't quite like that either, because the whole of you feels at home in each of the two places, even though they are so different. So maybe that should give one something to think about.

Anyway, it's probably time I gave you a sketch of my itinerary. I've mentioned various places but you may not have a clear idea of exactly where I went, so I'll say without more ado that I visited three states: Maharashtra, Gujarat, and Rajasthan. I gave lectures in all of these states, and I also visited Delhi, but I did most of my work among the Mahar Buddhists in Maharashtra, that being the centre of the Buddhist movement in India. I started off by giving some lectures in Poona, and then I went up into the hills, into the Western Ghats, and gave a lecture at Panchgani and another at Mahad. Mahad is associated with the life of Dr Ambedkar because it's there that he did something that really upset the Hindus: he burned the *Manusmṛti*. The *Manusmṛti* is one of the orthodox Hindu law books which say that even Shudras, if they happen to hear the words of the Vedas, the sacred words which only caste Hindus can hear, should have molten metal poured into their ears. So as a gesture Dr Ambedkar burned the *Manusmṛti* on a famous occasion in Mahad. On this trip I was there celebrating with other Buddhists the anniversary of that great occasion, and I was shown a sort of cenotaph that they'd erected, and I gave a lecture and so on. Then I gave quite a number of lectures in Bombay, the most spectacular of which was one at a place called Worli. Worli is a working-class area in Bombay and there are tens of thousands of Buddhists living there in row upon row of slum blocks.

Travelling wasn't easy. Sometimes transport broke down. Sometimes cars didn't turn up. Trains were late. There was a party of ten or twelve of us travelling around, so we needed three cars. Sometimes some of us took the bus while others went by car and others by train. The logistics were sometimes extraordinarily complicated, but Lokamitra managed it all somehow. We took with us our tape-recording equipment, which had to be set up under very difficult conditions. As soon as we arrived somewhere, Purna and one or two of our young friends had to go straight to the place where the meeting was going to be held, without even a cup of tea after a long journey, and set up everything, and test it and check it. There were all sorts of complications and difficulties and things going wrong, as you can imagine, but they wanted to tape every lecture that I gave. We also carried around an enormous quantity of literature to sell. We've got a lot of literature available in Marathi, much of it translated from lectures I've given or things I've written, and we had a sale of booklets and magazines at every one of our meetings. At some very big meetings we had four bookstalls, one at each corner of the meeting, all selling publications like hot cakes. So we had to carry this enormous stack of material around with us, plus bedding, because sometimes we didn't get that where we were staying. We stayed in all sorts of places. There were doss-houses, as I call them, plus one or two that could be classed as hotels, and private houses belonging to very poor people, with virtually no privacy and very inadequate sanitation. Sometimes we were able to make use of palatial rest houses, which are usually only made available to high-ranking government servants and ministers, and then we revelled in luxury for a few hours.

But despite the difficulties, the programmes as a whole were very successful. During the tour I had to follow a strict routine. Every minute, almost, was regulated, because I had to prepare a talk whatever the conditions, and it had to be a good talk because people were coming in their thousands to hear it, and it was going to be tape-recorded, translated, and published in a magazine or booklet. I used to seclude myself for up to three hours every day regardless of where I was and prepare my talk. I prepared them quite carefully, and I must say I did quite enjoy doing that. The three weeks we spent in the Marathwada area of central Maharashtra were the most strenuous and demanding weeks of the whole tour, and once or twice my physique didn't quite stand up to it, but nonetheless I was able to carry on. After that tour, and then a few days in Poona and less than a day in Bombay, we went up to Ahmedabad, the biggest city in the state of Gujarat, and a place where I have a lot of connections. We had a week there, during which I gave a number of lectures and fell ill again, and then we went up into the state of Rajasthan, still going north, and spent a couple of days in Ajmer, where I also had lots of connections, and then on to Delhi. In all these places I gave talks. Then we came back to Poona, back to Bombay, and then I came back to England.

During my three months of giving public lectures and having maximum contact with people, I was mainly concerned with putting forward the Dhamma as much as I possibly could. I found the experience of giving all these lectures very satisfying, because everywhere I went I felt that people really did want to hear the Dhamma. Don't forget, until recently they haven't had much in the way of literature in their own language, and a lot of them are still illiterate anyway, especially the women, so it's only through the spoken word that many of them have an opportunity of learning about the Dhamma. It's quite an experience to have thousands of people sitting in front of you all really wanting to hear what you have to say. It's almost a vital need. It's not out of dilettante interest. After all, these people have left Hinduism for the sake of a better life in every respect, not just spiritually but socially, politically, and economically, and they feel that through Buddhism they can create a new society as well as improve themselves. So a lecture on Buddhism means a very great deal to them. I think I can say that a lecture from me meant a very great deal to them because most of them had had contact with me before, or heard about me, and they really did want to hear what I had to say. I also met people individually, and met old friends in a more social way. I attended a couple of short ordination retreats, in the course of which there were eight ordinations, so we now have eight more *upāsakas* in India, all of them of Indian origin.

So that's a sketch of the tour. Let me give you a few more general impressions about India before I come onto specifically Buddhist impressions. My main impression was that people are becoming more prosperous. I've been familiar with India since 1943, and people are noticeably much more prosperous than they were fifteen or twenty years ago. To give a simple illustration, twenty years ago the status symbols were a wristwatch, a fountain pen, and spectacles. If you were a young blood of the village who had had a bit of education and had got a clerkship in some local office and you wanted to show that you were a cut above the rest of the villagers, you sported a European-style jacket and a fountain pen – which very often didn't work. You might also have a watch, which also might not work; you'd see people shaking their watch just to show off that they had one. And they'd go to the bazaar and buy spectacles. There was no question of having an eye test – they just bought a pair of spectacles because it was a status symbol. Towards the end of my long stay in India, before I came back in 1964, the status symbol was the transistor set, usually Japanese-made. The young men would carry these around holding them to their ears, and older villagers would gape in open-mouthed wonder at these magical boxes. But it would seem that the status symbol now is the wretched scooter. You see them all over the place: in the towns and cities, in the villages, chugging along the country roads, and of course they're adding to the pollution problem, especially in cities like Bombay.

So economically things are definitely improving. The economy seems to be expanding, and that gives the whole of life in India a sense of expansion, because there's a general expectation that things are going to get better, that your children are going to have a better life than you've had, that things in five years' time are going to be better than they are now. This is very strong among the Buddhists in particular, and it's true of their feeling about Buddhism too. They feel that with the help of Buddhism things are getting better. They feel that they're becoming better Buddhists than they were, and that the Buddhist movement is expanding and becoming more influential, so there's a feeling of hopefulness and buoyancy such as you don't get here in England. Here it's almost as though the economy is dying, and that seems to affect the whole atmosphere. In India, by contrast, the keynote seems to be growth and expansion – on a modest scale from the point of view of the industrialized societies of the West, but it imparts a tonic to everything, a sense of optimism.

After Dr Ambedkar's death there was a jostling for power among his leading followers, and things were in quite a bad way for quite a number of years. That's one of the reasons why I felt that I couldn't get very much further with my own work among these people. One had to be so careful not to tread on the toes of the political leaders among the Buddhists, who were very jealous of anybody else having any sort of influence. But while I was busy in England, these people sort of – well, they blotted their copy book, let's say. The Buddhists have lost faith in their political leaders, and they're thinking much more in terms of just Buddhism. They've also lost faith in the Buddhist organizations in India. They never had much faith in the Maha Bodhi Society, but they lost faith in their own organizations, including even those which Ambedkar started, because the people running them didn't know much about Buddhism, so they couldn't do much. What we find now is that more and more people are turning to our Buddhist movement. I was very glad, but astonished, to see how much TBMSG had grown since my last visit only three years ago. I was fully prepared to see the movement three or four times bigger than it was, but I think I can say it's twenty or thirty times bigger. The fact that we don't as yet have any permanent buildings of our own means very little, because we have lectures and classes, retreats and publications. We're expanding our sphere of activities and influence, coming into contact with tens of thousands of people, all of whom are looking towards us more and more, especially the more educated and influential among them. In fact we're beginning to attract quite a bit of support; people are offering us money and land, and support is forthcoming from among the Buddhists themselves.

To give an example, there is an organization called the People's Education Society, which was started by Dr Ambedkar and has been functioning very well.[297] It runs a number of colleges and high schools in the state of Maharashtra. Several people on the governing body are old friends of mine, which helps, and they're collectively so impressed by the work of TBMSG that they've placed all their schools and colleges at our disposal free of charge for retreat purposes during vacation time.

They say they haven't seen any Buddhist organization functioning like this before, or anyone like our Order members. They're very impressed by what is going on, not having had the opportunity to come in contact with the Dhamma in that way before. Not only among the People's Education Society, but in all parts of Maharashtra and beyond there's a great demand for lectures and study classes and retreats, and of course for publications. We've got quite a few publications, in Marathi mostly, that being the language of Maharashtra. During my visit some four new publications were launched, and Lokamitra launched them in style. At a strategic point in a public meeting, with thousands of people present, the new publication is held up for everybody to see. Usually Lokamitra gets some prominent local person to launch it. He wraps a copy in coloured paper and ties it up with ribbon, and then the local dignitary has to come up onto the stage and open it and look at it in wonderment and hold it up for everybody to see. Lokamitra then gives – I was going to say a short lecture, but it sometimes goes on for forty minutes, extolling this publication. He gives a detailed account of what it contains and why it is so useful and why people should buy it, and how cheap it is. I must admit, having attended so many meetings and heard it all so often, I got a little bit bored with it, but it was new for the people attending that particular meeting. Sometimes six or eight different publications were described in detail, and the result was that the publications sold like the proverbial hot cakes.

As well as these books and pamphlets, there's a quarterly magazine called *Buddhayan*.[298] There's nothing else like it in Maharashtra. They now print and sell 5,000 copies. In a place like India, you don't get one person buying and reading his own copy. You get fifteen or twenty people reading the same copy, because a lot of people can't afford to buy it, so things are shared around. If we sell 5,000 copies, they might reach 50,000 people. There's growing literacy, and people want literature more and more. The material in *Buddhayan* consists mainly of translations of lectures that I've given. They've just come to the end of the translations of the lectures I gave on my visit three years ago. This time I've managed to supply them with material for the next eight years. They're going to bring out some of the lectures in book form, because if I go again next year, they'll have another lot of lectures to translate and publish.

Some of you might be a bit surprised that people should be turning to our movement. After all, the FWBO was started in England, and India is the land of the Buddha. Aren't we taking coals to Newcastle? It doesn't seem so. In fact, thinking things over, it does seem very much as though there's a similarity between the position of Buddhists in the West and Buddhists in India, certainly the Buddhists of Maharashtra. The main similarity is that we are all new Buddhists. Buddhism isn't something that we've inherited from our forebears. It's something that we've decided to follow. It isn't easy if you're born as a Buddhist – if indeed you can be born as a Buddhist. You tend to follow it very mechanically. You think you know it already. Buddhism isn't very fresh or alive for you. But if you choose it for yourself after a lot of thought, and perhaps a lot of suffering, you've got a very different attitude towards it.

Because Indian and Western Buddhists are all new Buddhists, we have a much better basis for understanding each other than we have with those who are Buddhist by tradition, by birth and inheritance. But apart from that, people in India just like our movement's approach. It makes sense to them. They like our methods, they like our system: our meditations, our retreats, our study groups, our Mitra system. It's as though the whole thing was designed specifically for the Indian situation. It's extraordinary. We started our movement in England for the benefit of Westerners, but transporting the whole system to India, it seems to fit their needs like a glove, as though it was tailored for them. They are quite at home with it, and the fact that it isn't of Indian origin is an additional recommendation, because they tend to think that anything of Indian origin is tainted with Brahmanism, with the caste system, and there is some truth in that. There's also the point that Buddhists from Buddhist countries, even monks and lamas, have done practically nothing for the new Buddhists of India. It's mainly Buddhists from the West who have helped them, and they appreciate this very much. They're not at all put off by the fact that we are Western. They rather like that, because they feel we're likely to be free from any Hindu influence, and they're afraid of Hindu influence because it has caused them so much suffering.

A couple of things I mentioned in lectures seemed especially to appeal to them. They very much like the idea of a Buddhist movement being self-supporting financially. They don't like the idea of religious mendicancy, depending for the support of activities on charitable donors

– it smacks too much of beggary, and of course they were formerly forced to live as beggars. They appreciate in a way that I can't describe the idea that you don't ask the public for anything, that you have right livelihood and the profits go towards running Buddhist activities. Something else I made a point of mentioning this time was that in the FWBO we don't have leaders but rely on teamwork. In India they've got a great weakness for leaders. They're always clamouring for someone to lead them. Look at the way Mrs Gandhi's surviving son is being groomed, apparently, to succeed his mother. Why? Because he's his mother's son. There's no other reason, apparently. He's a nice young man but he was interested in flying aeroplanes, not in politics, but his elder brother died, and India has to be provided with a leader from above, from heaven as it were, so this young man is being groomed, rather late in life, for political power.[299] Indians are always looking for help from outside, for some big influential person, whether political or religious, to solve all their problems, whom they can just blindly follow.

I really hammered this in my lectures. I must say, incidentally, that the way I speak in my lectures in India is rather different from the way I speak in England. The language may be the same, but I'm much more blunt. One or two of our English friends were a bit shocked at the bluntness and crudity of some of my expressions, but I was speaking much of the time to illiterate people, people with very – what shall I say? – rough and ready minds. They see things in black and white. They're not concerned with refinements of thought and language. They want it strong and straight from the shoulder. So in this way I hammered the idea of leadership, saying 'In the FWBO we don't have leaders. We have teams of people working together. This is the spirit of sangha, that people work together and do things together as teams.' This idea appealed to them, because they've been fed up with their so-called leaders, people who tried to lead them and failed dismally.

Western Buddhists and Indian Buddhists have other things in common too. We are all trying to get away from previous religious conditioning. In the West, in many cases, we are trying to get away from our Christian conditioning, our conditioning of guilt. For their part, the Indian Buddhists suffer from their Hindu conditioning, and of course from the Hindu caste system, which is still a problem. By becoming Buddhists they've gained self-respect, they've improved themselves in all sorts of ways, but a lot of Hindus still regard them as Untouchables and try to treat them as such, and become very resentful when the Buddhists get above themselves, as the Hindus see it. If the Buddhists dress well, the Hindus think that Hinduism is being insulted, because their holy books say that these people shouldn't dress well. They think that if a woman wears a nice sari or a man wears a good suit, or if they wear ornaments, they are insulting the Hindu religion and they have to be punished. All the time I was in India cases were reported in the newspapers of ex-Untouchables being attacked, not so much in Maharashtra but especially in the United Provinces: women being raped, people being murdered, houses being burned. This is in the background all the time as a constant reminder. Suppose that here in London we were to read in the newspapers that last night five Buddhists in Birmingham, were stabbed to death, or ten Buddhists in Glasgow were burned to death when their house was set on fire, what would we feel? This is the experience that these people in India have. They feel very strongly under constant threat of attack by the caste Hindus. In the course of my tour I was staying at a railway town called Daund and we were put up in a very poor house. I had a little room to myself, and there was a wooden bed with a mattress. For some reason – I don't know why – I looked underneath the mattress, and there was a big knife there. The reason was clear: self-defence. I'm afraid they don't believe to any great extent in non-violence. If they can, they retaliate, but usually they're vastly outnumbered and they're just killed. This was a bit of an eye-opener, a reminder that these are the conditions under which these people have to live.

Nonetheless, on this visit I did detect a change of heart among some Hindus. In fact, a Hindu organization called Vishvahindu Parisa pursued me, asking me to give lectures, and I gave one lecture for them in which I really spoke my mind about Hinduism. I called it 'Religion and the Secular State'.[300] This lecture was given in Aurangabad, and I had a very interesting experience in this connection. The day before the lecture, the office-bearers of the organization invited me to their office for a cup of tea. Lokamitra and I were to go along, and from there we were to go directly to a Buddhist locality for the evening meeting. There was a lot of confusion. The car didn't turn up – I won't give you the whole story – but anyway, with great difficulty we found this office. We were an hour late and I gave a little talk, and they gave us tea. About thirty people had gathered to brief me about their organization. From there we went to the meeting in the Buddhist locality, where we found one of our Indian Order members beside himself with anxiety. As soon as he saw Lokamitra he started to scold him. He said, 'Where have you been? Where have you been taking Bhante?' Lokamitra said, 'Well, we've just had tea with these people.' So he said, 'You took Bhante to have tea with those people? Do you realize you might have been poisoned?' Lokamitra was a bit taken aback, but this Order member didn't trust any Hindu organization one little bit, and when we didn't turn up, he seriously thought that the Hindus might have lured us to their office to give us some poisoned coffee or something – this is not uncommon in India – to get us out of the way. He was as worried as that, and that showed me the depth of the suspicion and almost hatred that is felt, because the Buddhists have really suffered, and continue to suffer, at the hands of orthodox Hindus.

One can see from this that although there are many similarities between Buddhists in the West and Buddhists in India, there are differences too. Their original point of departure was social. They wanted to emancipate themselves from the caste system and get back their self-respect as human beings through Buddhism. They've done that to a great extent. For most people who become Buddhists in the West, our point of departure is not social but psychological. We think in terms of solving our psychological problems, getting rid of our existential traumas, and all the rest of it. We're not so bothered about society. Well, our society is pretty well organized compared with society in India from the material point of view. For the men and women in our movement in India, the fact that their point of departure is social, the fact that they have had to emancipate themselves from the tyranny of the Hindu caste system, the fact that they're still oppressed by Hindus, the fact that they can be attacked and murdered at almost any time, gives an edge to their being Buddhist, a sort of urgency, because they see Buddhism as the means to raise them above all this, to solve all these problems. It might be difficult for us in the West to understand that, but it boils down to the question of self-respect. Buddhism, one might say, has given them back their self-respect. They feel that Buddhism sees them just as human beings, and taking their stand on that, they can work for the amelioration of their life in all its aspects. Certainly, as I indicated earlier on, there has been a great improvement in their standard of living over the years that I've been in contact with them.

I really noticed this at some of the meetings. When I used to address meetings twenty years ago, the majority of the people in the audience would be very poorly dressed, almost in rags. One doesn't see that now. Most of the people are reasonably well-dressed and many of the women have got new saris with fancy borders. So things are improving, educationally, economically, and socially, with Buddhism as a sort of lever of this upward movement. In a way Buddhism is more important to them than it is to us in the West. It's more vital, so they take it much more seriously. Buddhism has got all sorts of implications for them that it doesn't have for us, so they approach it in a much more wholehearted way.

THE EX-UNTOUCHABLE INDIAN BUDDHISTS

A talk delivered to the Wrekin Trust, March 1983[301]

Sir George and friends, a year ago I was in India on a lecture tour among the Buddhists of Maharashtra. In the course of that tour, which lasted nearly three months, I visited about two dozen towns and villages, mostly in the state of Maharashtra, in an area called Marathwada, and delivered some forty-five lectures, under conditions which were very different from those in which we're meeting this weekend. To begin with, the weather was very different: no drizzle, no chill, but blazing hot sunshine, blue skies, and very dry air. There was lots of dust, and I very quickly got a sore throat. And of course the people were very different. For a start, there were a lot more of them. India's a very big country, a subcontinent, but it seems absolutely full of people. Wherever you go, especially in a city like Bombay, where I spent a few days, you're almost literally tripping over people all the time. Every night 200,000 people sleep on the sidewalks under scraps of sacking stretched out over the pavement: a whole family – mother, father, grandmother, grandfather, seven or eight children, babies, dogs – and all their worldly goods. How they live one can only speculate, but there they are.

At all the meetings I addressed there were lots of people too: tens of thousands, sometimes crammed together in very small areas indeed, all sitting on the ground. Indians are fond of doing things in a very colourful fashion, so there were coloured fairy lights all over the place, and lights made out of revolving wheels, *dharmacakras*, to symbolize the Buddha's turning of the Wheel of the Dhamma. When you arrive to give a lecture, you are greeted in a very special fashion. Up on the stage there's a sort of throne where you have to sit, and before your lecture they insist on garlanding you. In most of these places, since I hadn't been there for quite a few years and they were very glad to see me, I sometimes got at least thirty garlands. There were people coming up every few seconds to give me a garland. They'd put it over my head, I'd take it off and hand it to an attendant, and then the next garland would come. This sometimes took half an hour or forty-five minutes, and I'd sit there, smiling through it all. And after that, when you've been properly introduced and maybe served with light refreshments on the platform, you stand up and give your lecture. In India they are great lovers of lectures. Many people are illiterate, so they appreciate the spoken word. Sometimes they say to you before you begin that you should on no account speak for less than two hours, and if you fall short they're a bit disappointed. So circumstances in India are very different from our gathering here this weekend. And of course my audiences were made up not of well-to-do, highly educated people who have been to university, but of these Dalit Buddhists, most of whom are very, very poor and occupy the very bottom rung of the social ladder in India. It's about them that I want to say something this morning.

As you know, I'm speaking this morning at quite short notice, taking the place of Miss Monica Furlong. Of course I don't presume literally to take the place of Miss Furlong, and I'm sure that she would have told you something which I'm not able to tell you. She would have made her own distinctive contribution to this conference. Nonetheless, even if I'm not taking her place, I'm at least taking up her time. When it was first suggested to me that I should fill in for Miss Furlong, I wondered what on earth to talk about. She was going to talk about angels, but I didn't feel quite equal to that, not on a Sunday morning. I recollected that if one ever has to speak at short notice, there are only two sorts of things about which one can speak: a topic on which one has a lot of information, or one with regard to which one has strong feelings. And my next thought was that among my strongest feelings are those I have for the Dalits. So that made me realize something about myself. Having been associated with them now for upwards of thirty years, I do have very strong feelings for the Dalit Buddhists in India, and in fact for the Dalits generally, whether they are Buddhists or followers of any other faith. So I'm going to speak about them, which I think will have the advantage of helping to bring us down to earth, back to something very practical, even earthy, and I understand that this was what Miss Furlong was going to do in her own way. She was going to say something about the redemption of the body. I'm not quite sure how she would have approached the topic because as a Buddhist I tend to think that the body is not in need of redemption. The body is quite innocent. It's in the mind that everything tends to go wrong. We tend to blame the body, but it's the mind, the consciousness, that is at fault. But I won't linger on that topic, but come on to the subject of these Buddhists, sometimes called 'ex-Untouchable', although that's an objectionable term. First of all, who are they, what is meant by 'untouchable', and how did they become Buddhists? And how did I come to be involved with them? I'm afraid it's quite a long story, and I'm going to be hard put to it to get it all into the sixty minutes that remain to me, so I'd better start at once.

I'm going to go right back to the beginning, back to the Buddha's own teaching, because that's where it all begins. The Buddha gained Enlightenment, became the Buddha, under the bodhi tree at Bodh Gaya 2,500 years ago. After initial hesitation he decided to try to communicate the content of his Enlightenment experience to the rest of humanity, so he started teaching. He wandered from place to place meeting people and talking with them, trying to impart to them his vision of human Enlightenment, of the potentiality of each and every individual human being, and trying to get them to plant their feet on the path that led to Enlightenment. In this way he spent forty-five years. He didn't write any books. Like Socrates, he just talked with the people that he met. The books were written later. After several hundred years of oral transmission, his teachings were written down and became what were eventually regarded as the Buddhist scriptures.

I'm not going to try to give you a résumé of the Buddha's teachings – that would be too much, and in any case I imagine that the majority of you are familiar with the general outlines. But after the Buddha's death, after what Buddhists call his *parinirvāṇa*, these teachings spread more and more widely in India, and a number of spiritual and doctrinal and organizational developments took place. If we look at the period of the development of Buddhism in India, we see that after the first hundred years, the lifetime of the Buddha and his immediate disciples, which we can call the period of archaic Buddhism, there was a period of about 1,500 years during which Buddhism developed in various ways, and spread to many other Asian countries, including Sri Lanka and Tibet, China and Japan. But while Buddhism was expanding in the rest of Asia, it was losing ground in India itself, and by about 1200 CE that decline had become quite serious. In the course of my recent tour in India I devoted a whole lecture to the subject of why Buddhism disappeared from India.[302] There were various factors at work. There was a revival of Brahmanism, and an over-centralization of Buddhism in the monasteries. There were the Islamic invasions as a result of which many Buddhist monasteries were destroyed, including Nālandā, Vikramaśīla, and Odantapuri. Some people say that another factor was that a creative spark had gone out of Buddhism itself. Be that as it may, for one reason and another, Buddhism gradually disappeared from India and was replaced largely by a renascent orthodox Hinduism and to some extent by Islam. On the whole we may say that orthodox Hinduism triumphed.

Orthodox Hindus, by which I mean mainly the Brahmins, had never really been happy with Buddhism. Some Brahmins of course had become Buddhists. Many of the Buddha's most prominent followers, including Śāriputra and Mahāmaudgalyāyana, his two leading disciples, and Mahākaśyapa, had originally been of the Brahmin caste. But later on the Brahmins became more and more dissatisfied with Buddhism, mainly because it threatened their privileged social position. As you probably know, in India society is divided into hereditary castes. At the very top you have the Brahmins, who are (officially at least) the teachers, the administrators. Then you have the Kshatriyas, who are the warriors and fighters, then the Vaishyas, who are the traders, the business people, and then the Shudras, who are the serfs. And lower even than the serfs you've got the outcastes, the Untouchables, who have no place in society at all, who shouldn't be even seen, according to some orthodox Hindus.

The four main castes are subdivided, so that in India today there are altogether about 2,000 castes, all mutually exclusive, all hereditary. There are all sorts of caste rules. You are not supposed to marry someone of another caste. If you are quite strict you are not supposed even to dine with someone of another caste. And the lowest castes of all, who are so low that in a sense they don't have a caste, are what is called by caste Hindus untouchable – that is to say, caste Hindus consider that their touch pollutes. If you happen to touch them, or if their shadow happens to fall upon you or upon your food, you become polluted and you cannot go near other members of your own caste until you've purified yourself. This whole system of caste is systematized in various Hindu works called *dharmaśāstras*, the most important of which is the *Manusmṛti*, a very thick volume, about 600 pages in the English translation, in which Manu, the primeval law-giver of the Hindus, lays down the rules to be observed by the different castes and the penalties for breaking caste. The rules are very rigid. For instance, Shudras and Untouchables are not allowed to own property. They're not allowed to wear new clothing but have to wear the cast-off clothing of the higher castes. They're not allowed even to cook food for themselves; they have to subsist on the leavings of the other castes, and if they do cook, they can only cook in an earthen pot, not a brass one. They have to live on the outskirts of the village, or a little separate from the village, and their only wealth, it is said, is dogs and donkeys. Their attitude towards the higher caste people must be one of complete subservience. This is all laid down by this great Hindu law-giver. To go forward very rapidly, in India today there are about eighty million people who are Shudras or Untouchables.[303] According to the constitution of India, according to modern Indian law, Untouchability is a penal offence, but there have not yet been any prosecutions under the law, and Untouchability is still widespread in India, especially in the villages, as I have personally witnessed.

In the state of western central India called Maharashtra, whose capital is Bombay, there's an ex-Untouchable community called the Mahars. About four million Mahars live in Maharashtra. There are small groups of them attached to every village; they live outside the village in terrible conditions. In one place I visited, the Mahars were compelled to live just outside the wall of the village, at the very spot where the drainpipes of the village terminated and all the effluent poured down. I visited them in their houses there and had a meal, keeping my fingers crossed, but there they had to live, that's how they were treated. The older people say that in their younger days they were treated even worse by the caste Hindus, especially the Brahmins. Until quite recently, if you were a Mahar you couldn't walk along a public road in the village during the day because your shadow might fall upon a caste Hindu, and you had to wear an earthen pot around your neck to spit into, because if you spat on the roadside some caste Hindu might step on your saliva.

In some villages the Untouchables had to carry little brushes to brush away the marks of their footsteps behind them.

These days it's not as strict as that, but it's still pretty strict, and your life can be pretty miserable. There are still occasions when the Mahars are attacked and murdered. Women are raped and houses are set on fire by the caste Hindus if they feel the Mahars are getting a bit above themselves – that is to say, if they're wearing decent clothes or golden ornaments, or if they acquire a bit of property, because that is not how they should be living, according to Manu's edict. When I travelled around Maharashtra four years ago, I found that just a few weeks before my arrival 2,000 huts had been burned down, and Mahar women had been paraded naked through the village streets. Some of them were raped and quite a few of them were murdered. Something of this got into the Indian papers but it was hardly reported at all in the western press. The government of India doesn't like people in foreign countries learning about these things, which are indeed disgraceful. To give the government of India its due, it is rather ashamed of these happenings, but it finds it very difficult to prevent them. So this is still the situation.

Now among these Mahars there arose a leader, one might even say a liberator, called Dr Bhimrao Ambedkar. He was born as a Mahar, and he was the first 'Untouchable' to matriculate, and to do all sorts of other things. With the help of Ashrudkar Raja, the ruler of the state at that time, who was sympathetic towards him, he studied at the London School of Economics and also in America, and he came back to Bombay and started a great movement for the uplift of the 'Untouchables', especially of his own Mahar community. It's too long a story to tell now, but he worked very, very hard for their uplift. A man of outstanding energy and ability, he eventually became the law minister in the government of India after India's independence, and was largely responsible, by a strange paradox, for framing the Indian constitution. He is sometimes known as the modern Manu, the modern Indian law-giver, though of course he compiled a quite different constitution from Manu's. His work was frustrated to a great extent by the efforts of the caste Hindus and he eventually resigned from the government, but he'd meanwhile been thinking about what to do for the uplift of his own people. They were Hindus, but they weren't allowed to enter the Indian temples, so he appealed to the caste Hindus to change their ways and allow the Dalits into the temples, and to treat them as human beings, because they were treated almost worse than animals. But after making his case to the caste Hindus for thirty years, he came to the conclusion that they were incorrigible.

Some of you may have seen the film *Gandhi* recently. It's a beautiful film and gives a very noble picture of Gandhi, but it gives only one side of the picture.[304] The Dalits do not like Gandhi, because they feel that he didn't do anything for them. In fact you may be surprised to hear that they tend to consider him as an enemy. Some years ago Dr Ambedkar wrote a book called *What Congress and Gandhi Have Done to the Untouchables*, so if you want to know the other side of the story, read that little book.

Dr Ambedkar was eventually convinced that there was no future with dignity and self-respect for the Dalits within the Hindu fold, and that they would have to change their religion. He was himself a deeply religious man. He was tempted to go over to Marxism, but he felt that human beings need a religion, a spiritual ideal, so he started looking around. He took a look at Christianity – well, he took a look at the missionary side of it, and didn't quite like that. He took a look at Islam, but he thought that if the Dalits became Muslims, that would add to the problems of India. (This was in pre-independence days, before Pakistan appeared on the horizon.) He took a look at Sikhism. He took a look at Buddhism. And over a period of a number of years he made up his mind that the best thing for him and his whole community, the Mahars, would be to become Buddhists, because in Buddhism there is no caste system. Also, Buddhism is a spiritual teaching of Indian origin, a point which weighed with him quite strongly. So he decided that they should all become Buddhists, and, to cut a very long story short, on 14 October 1956 in Nagpur he and about 400,000 of his followers became Buddhists by reciting *Buddhaṃ saraṇaṃ gacchāmi*, 'To the Buddha for Refuge I go.' One minute they were Hindus, the next minute, at a stroke, they were Buddhists. After that, he moved around Maharashtra converting people by the hundreds and thousands. But unfortunately he lived only for six weeks after the initial conversion ceremony.

This is where I come into the picture, because I happened to arrive in Nagpur on the day that Ambedkar died. To go back a bit, I was born in London, and when I was about sixteen I came upon two remarkable Buddhist texts: the *Diamond Sūtra*, which is one of the Perfection of Wisdom or Prajñāpāramitā *sūtras*, and the *Sūtra of Huineng*, which is a

Zen work. When I read these two works, I knew that I was a Buddhist. A little while later I joined the Buddhist Society, met Christmas Humphreys, continued with my Buddhist studies, and started writing articles about Buddhism. But then something unfortunate happened – or at least it seemed unfortunate at the time. I was conscripted into the army. It turned out to be very fortunate, because the army took me to India, Sri Lanka, and Singapore, all the places I wanted to visit. My duties were light, so I spent most of my time in Hindu ashrams and Buddhist viharas, and I started my career as a lecturer on Buddhism in Singapore. Then the war came to an end and I left the army, stayed on in India, and started living as a wandering ascetic. I wandered on foot over many parts of South India and I was eventually ordained as a Buddhist monk at Kusinara in north-east India. The story of my wanderings is contained in a book I wrote some years later, *The Thousand-Petalled Lotus*.[305]

After being ordained as a *śrāmaṇera* or novice monk, I went up into Nepal and spent some time there. That was before the modernization of Nepal. At that time there were only two cars in the country – how wonderful! One belonged to the king and the other belonged to the Prime Minister, and everybody else had to walk. I spent a year in Benares studying Pāli, Abhidharma, and so on, and then I went up to Kalimpong, near Darjeeling. I was left in Kalimpong by my teacher, and I started up Buddhist activities there. At that time I made contact with Dr Ambedkar, with whom I had several meetings, and this takes us to 1956, the year of the celebration of the 2,500th anniversary of Buddhism. I'd been to Delhi at the invitation of the government of India. I'd given some lectures there and visited Dr Ambedkar, then I went to Bombay, and then I moved on to Nagpur. When I arrived there, to my astonishment, at the station there were 2,000 people to meet me. They took me in procession to the place where I was to stay, and I had a little rest and something to eat, and then there was a knock on the door, and someone burst in and said, 'Dr Ambedkar is dead. We've just had the news from Delhi.' This threw his followers into consternation, as you can imagine, because only six weeks before, under his guidance, they'd all become Buddhists, and now he'd died. There was a danger that the whole movement would collapse. People came to where I was staying – there were about 5,000 people outside – and they wanted me to speak to them and console them. But there were no loudspeaker arrangements, so I said I'd speak to them in the evening if they could make arrangements for loudspeakers. We met in a place called Kasturchand Park at seven o'clock that night. They hadn't had time to erect a proper platform, so I gave my talk standing up on a rickshaw. As I stood there, I could see people coming through the darkness from all directions of Nagpur, in total silence – almost unheard of in India, but on that occasion it happened quite spontaneously. They converged on the park, each carrying a lighted candle, and gathered there until there were 100,000 people. Dr Ambedkar's leading followers were so overcome by emotion they couldn't say a word. They'd come up to the microphone but as soon as they tried to say anything they'd burst into tears and have to sit down. The only one who didn't burst into tears – being English – was me. So I had to speak, and I spoke, saying that Dr Ambedkar had started this movement, he'd advised them to convert to Buddhism, and that was the way it had to be. The movement had to continue even though Ambedkar was dead. I went around Nagpur, and in the course of four days I gave thirty-five lectures in thirty-five different places, just trying to keep things going. Because of that, my connections with the new Buddhists became very intimate indeed, and for a few winters after that I went down to the plains, especially to the cities of Maharashtra – to Nagpur, Poona, and Bombay – and gave lectures and held classes and courses, trying to instil something of Buddhist teaching and practice into them.

From what I've said, you can understand the Dalits' very, very strong feeling for Dr Ambedkar. People in India have a strong feeling for Mahatma Gandhi, but the feeling that the Dalits have for Ambedkar goes far beyond that. They know all too well what it's like to be an Untouchable so they're correspondingly grateful to him for having liberated them from the slavery of Untouchability.

In 1964 I returned to England, and in 1967 I started the FWBO. Although I was so busy with work in England and other parts of Europe, and in America and New Zealand, I didn't forget the Dalits – in fact, I couldn't forget them – but for the time being I felt I couldn't do much for them. The situation in India had become very confused, especially politically, so I thought it wouldn't be a bad idea to give my work there a rest for a while and concentrate on doing something in the West, especially in England. After a few years some of my English students went to India and started up activities among the Dalits, so that now we have a quite thriving movement there. We have Indian members, strange to say, of the Western Buddhist Order, which in India is known as the Trailokya Bauddha Mahasangha Sahayak Gana, which means very roughly 'World Buddhist Order'. Not only do we have lectures on Buddhism and lots of publications, mainly in the Marathi language, but we've also started up social activities, because the people are still very depressed economically and socially. We're setting up a medical centre, and to that end we've created an organization known as Aid For India, which is a charitable trust concerned with raising money in the West to support our social work, especially our medical work, in India.[306] I visit India and my friends there from time to time, and that's how I came to be there last year on the three-month lecture tour.

But what is the significance of this movement of conversion to Buddhism in India, and why am I talking about it this morning? The reason is that it shows – it certainly showed me – that great social change really can be brought about by religious, even spiritual means, and non-violently. Although there is a great deal of discrimination against the Dalits in India, although they still suffer quite badly at the hands of the caste Hindus, a great change has taken place, and that change has taken place mainly in the minds of the Dalits themselves. They don't feel any longer that they are untouchable. They don't feel that they're animals, or lower than animals. They feel that they're human beings, and this they were not allowed to feel before. In the very early days, twenty-five years ago, when I was going around among these people, I used to ask them, 'What difference has conversion to Buddhism made to you?' And they all gave me the same answer, wherever I went. They said, 'Now I am Buddhist, I feel free.' Before, they felt weighed down by the caste system, enslaved by this concept of Untouchability, but now they felt free.

I don't want to emphasize this idea of conversion to Buddhism too much. It doesn't have a pleasant ring, especially when you think of missionaries trying to convert people to Christianity. The fact that it is Buddhism that has helped the Dalits to feel that they are human beings is perhaps in a sense accidental. But they feel that they are human beings, they feel free, and so a tremendous amount of energy has been liberated. If you're a free human being, with self-respect and dignity and a proper position in society, you feel you can do anything. So there's been a tremendous movement of uplift on all fronts among these people, especially among the Mahars, who are at the forefront of things. There's been great economic improvement, educational improvement, cultural improvement. They look different, they speak differently, they bear themselves differently. They can look even the Brahmin in the eye. Before they could hardly look at the Brahmin even from a distance, couldn't even allow themselves to be seen.

One can see from this that change is possible, not only individual change but change of a whole society, by as it were religious means, through spiritual ideals, a spiritual vision. This is the lesson that we can learn. It's not enough to talk, it's not enough to think; we must see actual changes in society taking place around us.

In the course of this weekend we've done a lot of talking. Well, I've done quite a lot of the talking myself. That's necessary, it's good to exchange ideas, it's good to think. But sooner or later thought and talk must turn into action, not only in the sense of the transformation of the individual, but the transformation of society. I feel that we will not have achieved our objective here if we simply go away and do more thinking and more talking but on a smaller scale. We have also to do something. We have to work to change society, and I hardly need tell you how badly society needs changing.

We can of course pity the Dalits, and in many ways their condition is and was a very pitiful one, but in some ways our own position is much worse. I can't help noticing how emotionally positive they are, despite their poverty and the discrimination against them. They're very warm, friendly, positive, happy people. I can't speak about Europeans generally, but the English at least aren't always like that, aren't always overflowing with *joie de vivre*. So something is wrong. There are other larger things that are wrong, which I don't want to go into now, but which must be at the back of all our minds in one way or another all the time. All that has to be changed. Planet Earth has a wonderful opportunity, but at the same time it's in a terrible position. We can either have one world, spiritually at least, or no world. The choice is before us. I hope that the deliberations that have taken place at this conference, the thoughts that we've had and heard expressed, will help us to realize that we've got to do as much to transform life and society in the West as Dr Ambedkar had to do to transform life for the Mahars in India. We should go forth determined that we're not only going to think and talk; we're also going to act to transform ourselves and at least our bit of the world.

WHAT DEATH REMINDS US OF

Dapodi, Poona, 6 December 1983, the twenty-seventh anniversary of the death of Dr Ambedkar

Brothers and Sisters in the Dhamma, in the nearly two years since I was last in India, I've been busy with Dhamma activities in Europe. Among other things, I've been preparing material for translation into Marathi and publication in *Buddhayan*, and I'm very pleased to think that the material I prepared in England and Italy is being read by people here in Maharashtra. On my arrival in Bombay a few days ago I came straight to Poona, so this is the first public meeting I have addressed in India since my last visit. I want to begin by saying how glad I am to be here with you all today. There are three reasons for this. First of all, as many of you will know, I have been to Poona before. I came here first in 1955 and I have been here many times since. I have many friends here, some of whom used to organize my programmes, and I am very glad to meet them again and to see the way in which they are still working for the Dhamma. In the Buddha's Dhamma, spiritual friendship, *kalyāṇa mitratā* as we call it, is very important. It doesn't matter whether we are young or old, educated or uneducated. It doesn't matter whether we come from the East or the West, or from the North or the South, or from somewhere in between. What matters is that we all go for Refuge to the Buddha, all follow the same moral and spiritual path. For this reason we are all friends, all brothers and sisters, all members of the same great Dhamma family. For this reason I am very glad to be back in Poona and to see you all again. I am very glad to see in the audience the faces of people who have been coming to my lectures time and time again over a period of many years.

The second reason I am glad to be here today is that this meeting is being held in Dapodi, on a plot of land recently acquired by our Buddhist movement. This meeting is therefore being held on our own land, and I warmly congratulate all those whose efforts have made it possible for us to acquire this land and hold our meeting here today. This land has been acquired for a twofold purpose: for a vihara or Dhamma centre and also for a medical centre. The reason for this is that the Buddha Dhamma is concerned with the development of the whole human being. Buddhist thought analyses us into *nāma*, which covers the mental and emotional aspect of our being, and *rūpa*, which covers the physical aspect. According to the Buddha's teaching, attention must be given to both of these. In ancient times some people used to say that you shouldn't bother about material things. It didn't matter if you were poor and hungry. What mattered was that you should be a good man. In modern times, on the other hand, especially in the West, people tend to emphasize *rūpa* at the expense of *nāma*. They say it doesn't matter if your mind is full of greed, hatred, and delusion; what matters is that you should have a television set and a refrigerator, a fine new suit and a gold ring on your finger. But Buddhism emphasizes both *nāma* and *rūpa*, saying we should be concerned with both our mental state and our physical condition. This is why we are going to have, on this land, both a Dhamma centre and a medical centre – one to look after the mind and the other to look after the body. There will, of course, be a certain amount of overlap, because some people are qualified in both fields.

I became very aware of this need to look after both the mind and the body when, after Dr Ambedkar's great mass conversion ceremony at Nagpur in 1956, I spent time travelling around Maharashtra and giving Dhamma lectures. I gave hundreds – one of our friends here in Poona has got full notes of 340 lectures from that period.[307] Sometimes I wonder how I could have given so many, but in those days I was younger and more energetic than I am now. But although I gave so many lectures, I was not altogether satisfied with my work. Everywhere I went I saw people who were suffering from all kind of diseases and injuries. Some had big boils on their bodies, some had eye complaints, some had fever. Others had cuts and wounds that had not healed properly and had gone septic. I used to think that it is not enough to preach the Dhamma, not enough to look after the mind. We also have to look after the body. I myself was unable to give any medical treatment – all I could do was preach the Dhamma. Sometimes I used to wish that I had studied medicine instead of devoting so much time to poetry, philosophy, and history. I used to think how wonderful it would be if I could preach the Dhamma in the morning and give medical treatment in the afternoon. I am very glad to see that after so many years my wish is going to be fulfilled here in Dapodi on this plot of land, because here we are going to have both a vihara and a medical centre. The medical centre will be available to all who need help, regardless of religion or caste. The motto of Buddhism is *sabbe sattā sukhī hontu*, 'May all beings be happy'. We want to help all beings, or as many of them as we possibly can. This is the second reason I am glad to be here today in Dapodi, on a plot of land dedicated to both physical and mental development.

The third (and perhaps the most important) reason I am glad to be with you here today is that we are observing the twenty-seventh anniversary of the death of Dr Ambedkar. On my arrival I was invited to garland the statue of Dr Ambedkar, and afterwards to offer flowers to the Buddha and garland the portrait of Dr Ambedkar, and I was very glad to be able to do this. Some people, including some *bhikkhus*, are not willing to garland images of Dr Ambedkar, but I don't know the reason for their unwillingness. In the *Maṅgala Sutta* the Buddha says *pūjā ca pūjanīyānaṃ*, which means that we should honour those who are worthy of honour,[308] and Dr Ambedkar is surely worthy of all possible honour. If Dr Ambedkar is not worthy of honour, then I don't know who is. He is worthy of honour on account of what he did for himself by raising himself in the way that he did, on account of what he did for Buddhism, on account of what he did for India, and on account of what he did for the world. He is worthy of honour on account of the noble and inspiring example he set.

He is also worthy of honour on account of his practice of the six perfections. He is worthy of honour for his spirit of *dāna* or generosity. He gave his followers the gift of material things. Before him they had nothing. He gave them decent food, clothing, and shelter. He gave them the gift of education. He gave them the gift of fearlessness by giving them self-respect. Above all, he gave them the supreme gift, the gift of the Dhamma. He is worthy of honour on account of his *śīla*. He led a completely moral life. He was honest and truthful. He was absolutely free from the taint of bribery, and he took no alcohol. He is worthy of honour on account of his *kṣānti* or patience. Throughout his life he had to put up with hardships and bear tremendous responsibilities. He had to bear abuse and slander. Once he said, 'I think I am the most hated man in India.'[309] But he patiently bore it all and carried on with his work. Dr Ambedkar is also worthy of honour on account of his *vīrya* or vigour. In Bombay many years ago I was told that Maharashtrians were famous for their fighting spirit, but Dr Ambedkar's vigour was exceptional even by Maharashtrian standards. He never stopped working, and he worked not for himself but for other people. He is worthy of honour on account of his *samādhi* or one-pointedness of mind. His mind was absolutely one-pointed. Throughout his life his sole thought was how to uplift his people, and he never allowed himself to be diverted or turned aside but kept his mind firmly fixed on that goal. Finally, Dr Ambedkar is worthy of honour on account of his *prajñā* or wisdom. He was not only a highly educated man but a very intelligent one, and he displayed his intelligence in many different ways and in many areas of life. He displayed it most of all on 14 October 1956, when he himself publicly embraced Buddhism and advised his followers to do the same.

In other words, we honour Dr Ambedkar as a modern bodhisattva. We honour him as one whose life was dedicated to the uplift of the poor, the oppressed, and the ignorant. In the Bible there is a verse that says, 'The people that walked in darkness have seen a great light'.[310] (As Buddhists we are free to make use of good things whatever their source.) Before the coming of Dr Ambedkar millions of people walked in the darkness of ignorance and superstition, but now those people have seen a great light. They have seen Dr Ambedkar, and through Dr Ambedkar they have seen the Buddha. This is why we honour Dr Ambedkar. This is why we are observing the anniversary of his death, and why I am glad to be with you all today. I am glad to have the opportunity of adding my tribute to the thousands that are being paid to Dr Ambedkar today all over India and in many parts of the world.

Today is not the only day that we remember Dr Ambedkar. We remember him on 14 April, the day of his birth, and on 14 October, the day of the mass conversion ceremony at Nagpur. Indeed, we remember him and honour him every day of the year, but the three days I have mentioned have a special significance. Moreover, each has its own special flavour. Today, when we are commemorating Dr Ambedkar's death, it is only right that I should speak to you on a serious and important topic. So what shall I speak about? *Nirvāṇa*, *anattā*, *śūnyatā*? These are the kind of subjects people like to hear about. But I am not going to speak about any of them. Instead, I am going to speak to you about the most serious and important subject of all. I am going to speak to you about death – especially about Dr Ambedkar's death.

A wise man has said that life is nothing but a preparation for death.[311] The minute we are born, we begin to die, and that we will die is the only thing in life that we can be sure of. We may or may not get promotion, we may or may not become rich, we may or may not experience happiness, but there is no doubt that we shall die. Some of us like to think that because we have read a lot of books and gone to college, we know a lot, but really there is only one thing that we know for certain: that we are going to die. That is the one thing on which we can take our stand, and on which we can rely.

I am going to speak about death under four main headings, reminding us of four things that we usually forget. (1) That we too must die, (2) that we should make the best use of our life, (3) that we should end our quarrels, and (4) that we have to rely on our own efforts.

1. WE TOO MUST DIE

People are dying around us every day. I am sure that here in Dapodi at least one person has died today, perhaps several. But although this is happening all the time, we don't tend to take much notice. Every day the newspapers carry reports of the deaths of hundreds of people. Some have died in a plane crash, some when floods swept away a whole village, some when a hotel caught fire, and of course thousands have been killed fighting in the wars that are going on in different parts of the world. But we read about these dreadful things, and then we turn to the sports page. We think seriously about death only when someone near and dear to us dies, and even then, although we may feel very sad for a while, soon we may forget and go on living just as before.

A few months ago a young man came to see me at Padmaloka, the country vihara where I usually stay when I am in England. He was in a state of such great distress that he could hardly speak. His wife had died the day before in tragic circumstances. In fact, she had committed suicide. Since he had not been looking after her properly, the young man thought her death was partly his fault, and this made him even more upset. He said 'There is only one thing for me to do now. I must devote myself absolutely to the Dhamma. I want to become a monk. Please shave my head now. I won't leave your room until you have done it.' Though I didn't say no to the young man's request, at the same time I didn't say yes. I said, 'If you attend Dhamma classes at the local Buddhist centre regularly, then I will think about making you a monk.' So he promised to do this. He said, 'Yes, I'll go every day. I'll spend the whole of my time meditating. I just want to be a monk.' A few weeks later I met some of the Order members who work at that centre and asked them if the young man was attending classes regularly. They said he had not been to the centre even once. Later on, I heard that he was living in the same way as before and thinking of getting married again. This is the sort of thing that happens. Our father dies, or our mother or our brother or our sister or our friend, and for a while we are very sad, but then we get over it and life goes on as before.

But suppose a very powerful man dies. We may not feel his death personally, but it may make us think. During his lifetime he may have influenced or even controlled millions of people. Millions of people may have been afraid of him. But now that he is dead he is completely harmless. Even if someone gives him a kick he can do nothing. This makes us think. Similarly, a man may have been a multimillionaire. He may have been able to buy people by bribing them. But even the richest man cannot bribe death. The Yamarāja doesn't take bribes and even the multimillionaire's great wealth cannot keep death away for a minute. It is the same with the great thinker, the great writer. A great thought, even a sublime thought, cannot keep death away. Though someone may have written a whole pile of books, it is no use him trying to hide behind that pile. Wherever he hides, death will find him. In this way the death of any kind of great man makes us think.

Dr Ambedkar was not only a great man but also very near and dear to us, so his death affects us very deeply indeed. It makes us think very seriously. As I have already mentioned, Dr Ambedkar's whole life was dedicated to the uplift of his people. He was indeed a modern bodhisattva. But even he had to die, so how can we hope to escape death? Even if the deaths of our friends and relations don't affect us for very long, and even if the death of other great men doesn't affect us for very long, at least the death of Dr Ambedkar should affect us strongly and remind us, in a way that it is impossible for us to forget, that we too must die.

2. DEATH REMINDS US THAT WE SHOULD MAKE THE BEST USE OF OUR LIFE.

When we have a lot of anything we tend to waste it. You would be shocked to see how much food is thrown away in Western countries. Some families throw away as much food as they eat. The same sort of thing sometimes happens even in India. A wealthy businessman may invite 10,000 people to his daughter's wedding, and an enormous quantity of food can be thrown away afterwards. We tend to waste money in the same way. If we have a lot of money, we often spend it on useless things. The money burns a hole in our pocket, as we say; that is, we are restless and uncomfortable until we have spent it.

Similarly, if we think we have a lot of time we will waste that too. Young people often waste time because they think that they have got many years ahead of them. But we don't know how long or how short our life is going to be. We may die any day. Any one of us here could collapse with a heart attack at any time. So we shouldn't waste our time, but make the best possible use of it. In England people nowadays waste a lot of time watching television. They don't usually learn anything useful in this way. They don't even enjoy watching 'the box', as it is called. It's just a habit they have got into. Many of them watch television for many hours a day. If a friend comes to see them they don't talk to him. They just carry on watching the box. When it's time to eat they don't go to the kitchen. They call out to their wife to bring some biscuits or something, and sit and eat them in front of the box.

It seems a great pity to waste a human life in this way. Human life is such a wonderful opportunity. There are all sorts of wonderful things we can do. We can study the Dhamma. We can meditate. We can help other people. We can go on retreat. We can sell copies of *Buddhayan*. We can attend programmes. We can enjoy spiritual fellowship with one another. What a pity it is, then, if we waste our time in idle gossip, or fighting and quarrelling and drinking alcohol! Is that the purpose of human life? Is that why we became Buddhists? Dr Ambedkar set us a fine example of how to use time well. He never wasted a minute; he was always busy, always occupied with meaningful activities that were truly worthy of a human being. Following his example, we should make the best possible use of our time, the best possible use of our life. We should use it to develop as a human being, and help others. If we waste time, we are not true followers of Dr Ambedkar.

3. THE DEATH OF SOMEONE REMINDS US THAT WE SHOULD END OUR QUARRELS.

Unfortunately quarrels and misunderstandings are very common, and they often last a long time. Sometimes they spread from the two people immediately concerned to whole families. They may end in violence or even murder. Quarrels are dangerous things, and if they occur, we should bring them to an end as quickly as possible. Sometimes it happens that we quarrel with those who are near and dear to us, and because of the quarrel we don't speak to them. Even a husband and wife, living in the same house or even the same room, may not speak to each other for weeks. Everybody knows that this sort of thing happens. Sometimes after quarrelling with someone, we may not see him for many years. We may have been great friends, but now we don't even like to see each other. But one day we hear that the person with whom we quarrelled is dead and that it is now impossible for us to bring the quarrel to an end, impossible for us ever to be friends again. The breach between us is going to last for ever, and that thought makes us feel very sad.

Life is short, and we don't know when we are going to die, so we should end our quarrels, if they do arise, as quickly as we possibly can. In the *Dhammapada* the Buddha tells us this very thing: 'Others do not realize that we are all heading for death. Those who do realize it will compose their quarrels.'[312] According to the commentary on the *Dhammapada* the Buddha gave this teaching with reference to the *bhikkhus* of Kosambi, who had been quarrelling among themselves. It was a big quarrel and took a long time to settle, and as usual it started with something very trivial – a dispute about a water-pot, I think. The Buddha tried very hard to bring the quarrel to an end, but the *bhikkhus* wouldn't listen to him. You know how it is. Once people start quarrelling they won't listen to anybody, not even the Buddha. Eventually the Buddha became so disgusted with their behaviour that he went and lived by himself in the jungle for three months. The company of animals and birds, he thought, would be better than the company of those quarrelsome, disobedient *bhikkhus*. In the end the *bhikkhus* realized how wrong they had been and asked the Buddha's forgiveness, and the Buddha spoke the *Dhammapada* verse I have quoted.[313]

There is a very interesting and important point here. Because the *bhikkhus* refused to stop quarrelling, it was impossible for the Buddha to stay with them. In effect, the *bhikkhus*, by their quarrelling, drove him away – not just literally but metaphorically. They could not be with the Buddha physically because they could not be with him mentally, and they could not be with him mentally because they were quarrelling with one another. They were all followers of the Buddha, they were supposed to be like brothers, but nevertheless they were quarrelling, so it was impossible for the Buddha to remain with them. Even if he had remained with them physically he would not really have been with them, because they would not really have been with him. It is much the same today. People say that they are followers of the Buddha, and followers of Dr Ambedkar, but if they quarrel with one another, they drive the Buddha away, they drive Dr Ambedkar away.

Thus, the death of someone reminds us that life is short, that we should end our quarrels quickly, that we should practise *mettā* towards one another, and that we should work together for the Dhamma.

4. SOMEONE'S DEATH REMINDS US THAT WE HAVE TO RELY ON OUR OWN EFFORTS.

When we are young, we are of course totally dependent on our parents, but as we grow older we gradually become more independent, although sometimes people remain psychologically dependent on their parents even when they are grown up. Sometimes a fifty-year-old son cannot do anything without the permission of his seventy-year-old father, and in such cases dependence ends only with the parents' death. It is much the same with the spiritual life. At first the disciples are completely dependent on the spiritual teacher, but eventually they have to grow up and start relying on their own knowledge and experience. The spiritual teacher wants his disciples to become independent. If a spiritual teacher encourages his disciples to stay dependent on him, you can be sure he is not a true spiritual teacher. Sometimes, of course, as with some children, disciples don't want to grow up and become independent. When that happens, the spiritual teacher has to 'die', i.e. he has to go away. In one of the Mahāyāna *sūtras* the Buddha says that he could have gone on living longer, but if he had done this his disciples would not have become independent. It is because they have to learn to rely on themselves, the Buddha says in this *sūtra*, that he pretends to die, and this is what is known as his *parinirvāṇa*.[314] We can take this literally or metaphorically, or in both ways, but the meaning is clear. All those who are at present helping and supporting us must die. Parents must die. Teachers must die. Dr Ambedkar must die. Sangharakshita must die. Lokamitra must die. Learn from them all while you can, but be prepared to carry on one day without them.

Twenty-seven years ago, when Dr Ambedkar died, his death came as a very great shock to his followers. He was not very old, and he died only six weeks after the mass conversion ceremony. As you have already heard, I was in Nagpur at the time, and even after all these years I well remember people's grief and distress. They didn't know what they were going to do without Dr Ambedkar. They didn't know whether the movement of mass conversion was going to survive without him or not. Well, as we know, it did survive, and people continued to become Buddhists. Now, more and more people are beginning to appreciate the significance of the step taken by Dr Ambedkar. We therefore continue to remember him, honour him, and celebrate him on those three special days every year. Indeed, we celebrate on those days on a grander scale every year.

Twenty-seven years is a long time. Many of you were not born then, and those of you who are now old were young. But we still remember Dr Ambedkar, we still celebrate his birthday, and we still observe his death anniversary, as we are doing this evening. I am very glad that I could be with you here in Dapodi on our own plot of land, I am glad we will be working here together for the development of both *nāma* and *rūpa*. I thank you all very much for giving me such a warm welcome, and I hope we shall meet again.

BUDDHISM IN ONE WORD

The opening of Bhaja retreat centre, 11 December 1983

Brothers and sisters in the Dhamma, Gautama the Buddha lived 2,500 years ago, but although he lived so long ago we know quite a lot about him and about the conditions under which he lived and worked. In other words, the Buddha is a historical character, not a product of myth and legend. He actually did live here in India. We know that he was born the son of a raja, that at the age of twenty-nine he left home in search of truth, that at the age of thirty-five he attained supreme Enlightenment, and that at the age of eighty he passed away into *parinirvāṇa*. From his attainment of Enlightenment to *parinirvāṇa* there was a period of forty-five years, and for the whole of that period the Buddha was simply teaching the Dhamma. He had no other interest. Apart from half an hour for eating and two or three hours for sleeping, his whole day was spent teaching the Dhamma to all sorts of people, whether high caste or low caste. Not that the Buddha himself saw people as either high or low. The Buddha saw everybody simply as a human being: a human being who was subject to suffering, who was in search of happiness, who wanted to grow and develop, and who ultimately wanted to attain supreme Enlightenment just as the Buddha himself had done.

After the Buddha's *parinirvāṇa*, the teaching that he had given was continued by his disciples and by the disciples of those disciples. Eventually, some of the eminent Buddhists of those days started explaining the Dhamma in greater and greater detail, so as to make it clear to more and more people. Since the time of the Buddha many developments in language and culture had taken place, and these eminent teachers had to explain the Buddha's teaching in terms of the new language, the new culture, and so on. In this connection we can mention the names of people who gave profound and important explanation of the Buddha's teaching: Nāgārjuna, one of the greatest philosophers the world has ever known, Āryadeva, Asaṅga, and Vasubandhu.

Thus, as the centuries went by, more and more great scholars and thinkers explained the Buddha's teaching, so that there came to be very many teachings. First of all you had the teaching of the Buddha himself, which was extensive enough, and then you also had all the explanations of that teaching given by the great thinkers and philosophers. In the end it became difficult to study the whole of Buddhism in a single lifetime. Some great scholars started studying Buddhism when they were seven years old and were still studying it when they were eighty. You may therefore ask, 'What are we to do? We don't have time to study all these teachings. We don't have time to study the Tipiṭaka, not even a single *Nikāya* of the Sutta Piṭaka. We don't have time to study the *Dhammapada*, or Dr Ambedkar's *The Buddha and His Dhamma*.' But you need not worry. Buddhism is very extensive indeed, but its basic principles are very few and very simple. In fact I sometimes think that the whole of Buddhism can be reduced to one principle, even to one word.

So what is that one principle, that one word? It is nothing very abstruse or profound. At least, it doesn't look profound at first sight. The principle is the principle of change. Everything changes. Everything material changes; everything mental changes. There is nothing permanent, nothing eternal. In technical language, everything that is *saṃskṛta*, or compounded, is *anitya* or impermanent. We can reduce the whole of Buddhism to this principle, and we can see it at work every day. We can see it at work in nature. During the day it is light, and during the night it is dark; the one changes into the other. Even within half an hour we can see a difference if we look closely enough. Since we started this meeting, the sun has sunk a little lower, the shadows have become a little longer. Maybe you have become a little more tired. Thus we can see changes taking place all around us. We see it in the vegetation. Now everything is dry and brown, but just after the rainy season all these fields were green. Day by day there has been a change.

People too are changing. Nowadays I don't come to India very often, and when I come, I see changes in my old friends. Babies whose name-giving ceremonies I performed are now big children. Handsome young men and beautiful women have started going grey, their faces are now covered with wrinkles, and some of them have lost their teeth. Some of my old friends are not here at all. Where are they? Have they emigrated, or are they dead? If they are dead, a very big change indeed has taken place, both for them and for their friends and relations. Thus human life is constantly changing.

We see the same thing if we look at the history of the world. If you study Indian history, you find this dynasty succeeding that dynasty, this king conquering that king, this kingdom swallowing up that kingdom. You read about the Vedic period, the Buddhist period, the Muslim invasion, the East India Company, Shivaji, Indian independence. Thus in history many changes have taken place. It seems to me that in the course of the last hundred years more changes have taken place than ever before. A few days ago I was talking to my mother. She is now eighty-seven and she was telling me what things were like when she was a small girl. There were no cars, only horses and carts. There was no radio, no film, no aeroplanes, no television. All these things have come into existence in the last hundred years, and it is very difficult for us to imagine what life would be without them. I came from England by aeroplane. If I had to walk, or even come by boat, I wouldn't come very often, certainly not every two or three years. Thus our lives have been greatly changed.

There is one change in particular that I want to mention: population shift. In the course of the last hundred years there has been a big movement of people from the countryside into the towns and cities. In England this started more than 200 years ago, and nowadays in England 85 per cent of the people live in cities, which means that only 15 per cent of them live in the countryside. (I happen to be one of the 15 per cent.) In India it's the other way round – nearly 85 per cent of the people still live in the villages, and only 15 per cent, or maybe a little more now, in the towns and cities. But every year more and more people are moving like moths attracted to the light from the villages to the cities, which are bursting with people.

Why? There are several reasons. Some people move to the city because there is no work for them in the countryside, or perhaps they've acquired a little education and they don't want to labour in the fields any more. They want to get a job that will give them more money, so that they can buy nice clothes and fine jewellery and go to the cinema every week. Another reason why people move to the city is to escape from the caste system. Villages are very small, so everybody knows everybody else, which means that everybody knows your caste. But in the big city there are millions of people. They don't know your name or your caste. You can go to any teashop and no one will ask any questions. They certainly won't ask your caste. If they ask anything, it will only be, 'Have you got money?' If you have got enough money, you can go anywhere. You can even go to the best hotel. They will be glad to have you, because they are just there to make money. They don't care about your caste. Many people therefore move to the city simply in order to escape from the caste system. Dr Ambedkar used to say that the village is not such a beautiful place as some politicians try to make out, because in the village the caste system is very strong, and where the caste system is strong, injustice and oppression will be rife.

There is another reason for the population shift, though it perhaps applies more to the young men: restlessness. Nowadays it is very easy to move about. You can get onto your bicycle or your scooter, or you can catch a train. If you have the money you can go anywhere. Some years ago I was in New Zealand, which is a beautiful country with comparatively few inhabitants, and one of our Dhammacharis took me to see the village where he grew up. It was a beautiful village, situated in beautiful countryside, so beautiful that I thought I would like to live there myself. I asked the Dhammachari how old he was when he left, and he replied, 'Sixteen.' I asked, 'But how could you leave such a beautiful place?' and he said, 'When I was a boy, I didn't think it was beautiful. I hated it. My one thought was how to get away to the big city.' When he was sixteen he therefore went to Auckland, the biggest city in New Zealand, and two or three years later he came to England. Many young men are like this in India too. Feeling restless, they leave the village and go to the big city.

Nonetheless, we mustn't think that the countryside is unimportant. It is still very important indeed, and there are two reasons for this. The first reason – a very basic one – is that the countryside produces our food. You can do many things in the city, but you can't grow food there, so the city remains dependent on the village, and if everybody left the village and go and live in the city, we would all starve. The second reason is that in comparison with the city, the countryside is very quiet.

I know how noisy the city is from personal experience, since I was born in London and spent the first eighteen years of my life there. As a baby the last thing I used to hear at night before going to sleep was the sound of the traffic. The city is a very noisy place indeed. Quite a few of the people who live in the city therefore like to visit the countryside from time to time, to enjoy a little peace and quiet. Perhaps they go just for an afternoon, for a picnic. Perhaps they go for the weekend, or even for one or two weeks. And perhaps, of course, they go to meditate. Perhaps they go on a retreat, a *shibir*, as you call them here. As Lokamitra has explained, *shibirs* are very popular and very important. We try to have them in the countryside because there it is very quiet and peaceful.

It was much the same in the Buddha's time. Even in his day there were big cities like Kapilavastu, Kāśī, Rājagṛha, and Śrāvastī, and the cities were rather noisy, as the Buddha himself tells us in the Pāli Tipiṭaka.[315] So even then some people wanted to leave the city, to get away from the noise. In fact, in the Buddha's time some people found even the village noisy. Standards were different then, and there would be dogs barking, cows lowing, men shouting, women screaming, children crying. The Buddha himself didn't spend much time in cities and towns. He entered them for only two purposes: to collect almsfood and to teach the Dhamma. Otherwise he spent his time in the countryside, and he quite often stayed in the midst of dense jungle. It has been pointed out that the Buddha was born not in a house or a hospital, but in a garden, under a tree; that he attained supreme Enlightenment not in a vihara or temple but sitting under a peepul tree; that he started teaching the Dhamma not in a classroom or lecture hall but in a deer park; and that, although he was ill shortly before his *parinirvāṇa*, he didn't die in hospital, surrounded by doctors and nurses and saline drips, but in a *sāl* grove, lying between two *sāl* trees. Thus the most important events of the Buddha's life took place in the open air.

Of course the Buddha had to walk everywhere, and even when he was eighty years old, on the very day before he died, he was still walking. On the way from place to place he met many different kinds of people. One spring morning in Magadha, he came to a village where a rich farmer called Bhāradvāja was ploughing, since it was the sowing season. When the ploughing was finished, Bhāradvāja distributed food to his labourers, and it was at this point that the Buddha arrived. As his custom was, he did not ask for anything, but simply stood there with his begging-bowl. On seeing the Buddha, Bhāradvāja called out, 'I plough and sow, and having ploughed and sown, I eat. You should do the same.' To this the Buddha replied, 'I too plough and sow, and when I have ploughed and sown, I too eat.' Puzzled, Bhāradvāja respectfully pointed out that he couldn't see the Buddha's plough, or his oxen, and asked him to explain in what sense he was a ploughman. The Buddha then explained that his ploughing and sowing was of a better kind, and proceeded to give Bhāradvāja an important teaching.[316] I am not going to talk about the whole of that teaching on this occasion, otherwise we would be here until nightfall. I will just comment on a few salient points. The Buddha told Bhāradvāja, 'The seed I sow is the seed of faith (*śraddhā*), the rain that makes my seed grow is the rain of *tapas*, and my plough is wisdom.' By faith he didn't mean blind faith, but faith in the Buddha, the Dhamma, and the Sangha. But what does that really mean?

I said at the beginning that the Buddha was a historical personality. He started off as a human being just like ourselves, and through his own efforts he attained supreme Enlightenment. The Buddha therefore said to us, and still says, 'I am a human being; you also are human beings. I have attained supreme Enlightenment by my own human effort; you too can attain supreme Enlightenment by your own effort. You can grow, you can become better and better, you can develop wisdom and compassion, just as I have done.' This is our faith in the Buddha. We believe that since the Buddha was a human being, whatever the Buddha attained we too can attain, because we too are human beings.

Similarly, faith in the Dhamma means that we hear or study the Dhamma, we then practise it, and having practised it, we see that we obtain a certain result. In this way we develop faith in the Dhamma – faith based on our own experience. A little while ago Lokamitra was talking about retreats, and he mentioned that in the course of a retreat people can change: they can become different, they can become better, they can experience a new birth. But you don't have to have blind faith in Lokamitra's words. It's not a question of giving him garlands and saying, 'Yes, yes, Lokamitra, we have faith in everything you say' and then never going on a retreat. What you have to do is to listen carefully to what he says and then think, 'Yes, perhaps this really is what happens on a retreat. I'll go and see for myself.' And if you go, no doubt you'll find that it really does happen. You experience a definite change within yourself. You can come and see for yourself. The Dhamma is an *ehipassiko* Dhamma. It says, 'Come (*ehi*) and see (*passiko*) for yourself.' I don't know how many people are present: not more than a thousand. In one year you could all go on a retreat quite easily; you could all be changed. And with a thousand people who have been changed, who have been spiritually reborn, you can change the whole of Maharashtra. You can change your home and your office. You can even change your superior officer and have good feelings towards him. You can change your school. Through the Dhamma everything can be changed, but especially through the Dhamma *shibir*, the retreat.

Faith in the Sangha, too, is not blind faith. Sangha simply means other Buddhists, especially those who are more experienced than you, who have studied more, know more, and have been on more retreats. You can trust these people. You can have confidence in them. Whether they wear a yellow robe or a blue shirt doesn't matter. What matters is that you can learn from their knowledge and experience. Some people think that to be able to write MA or PhD after your name means everything, but its only value really is that it may help you to get a better job. Learning the Dhamma is quite another matter. And faith is the seed. Everything comes from your faith in the Buddha, Dhamma, and Sangha.

Having told the farmer that his seed is the seed of faith, the Buddha went on to say that the rain that makes the seed grow is *tapas*. There are many words that have different meanings in Buddhism and Hinduism, and *tapas* is one of them. In Buddhism *tapas* doesn't mean self-mortification or self-torture, as it does in Hinduism. It means intense practice of the Buddha's teaching, intense practice of *śīla*, *samādhi*, and *prajñā*, and especially *samādhi*, or *bhāvanā*. Briefly, *samādhi* consists in skilful one-pointedness of mind. There are a number of ways of making our minds one-pointed. There is *ānāpānasati*, mindfulness of breathing, and there is *mettā bhāvanā*, the development of universal loving-kindness. If you want to learn these practices, come on a *shibir*, where experienced people will teach them to you and where you will be able to experience their benefits for yourself. If we practise in this way, the way described by the Buddha, the fruit we eventually eat will be the fruit of Nirvāṇa or supreme Enlightenment. We will become perfectly happy.

Even after the Buddha's *parinirvāṇa* people used to spend a lot of time in the countryside, and this was especially the case with the *bhikkhus*. Some of them lived permanently in cave viharas, which are still to be seen all over Maharashtra. People come from all over the world to see the cave temples of Ajanta, Kanheri, Karla, and Nasik. Here at Bhaja too we have a beautiful cave vihara, and it is very appropriate that we should have a retreat centre here, near the caves and away from the noise of the big city. You can come here from Bombay, from Poona, from Nagpur, from Aurangabad. Today people have come from all these places. But don't just come for the opening ceremony. Come and use the place. Come on a retreat. Come and meditate. After all, the best kind of food is available here. I am not talking about our rice, good though that is; I am talking about the food of the Dhamma, the food of meditation. Here we grow food in the literal sense and we also cultivate our minds. We do both kinds of sowing, both kinds of ploughing.

I began by talking about change. Twenty-seven years ago, Dr Ambedkar brought about a very great change in the lives of his followers and in the life of the whole of India. He did this by taking refuge in the Buddha, Dhamma, and Sangha and encouraging his followers to do likewise. At that time, and after his passing away, lakhs upon lakhs of people in Maharashtra and elsewhere took refuge in the Buddha, Dhamma, and Sangha. All over Maharashtra one could hear the sound of *Buddhaṃ saraṇaṃ gacchāmi*. Before that time, if you said *Buddhaṃ saraṇaṃ gacchāmi* to someone, he would ask, 'What does that mean?' But now everybody knows what it means. Everybody has heard it, even those who don't like Buddhism very much.

But though it is good that one can hear the sound of *Buddhaṃ saraṇaṃ gacchāmi* all over Maharashtra, it is not enough just to recite these words. One must also practise the Buddha's teaching, seriously, and throughout one's whole life, all the time. One must be one-hundred-percent Buddhist. I feel quite disappointed when I find that some people are only ten or fifteen-percent Buddhist. That is not good enough. Even being ninety-nine-percent Buddhist is not good enough. If you tell lies, or drink alcohol, or worship Hindu gods and goddesses, you are not really a Buddhist. I hope you will all be one-hundred-percent Buddhist. And one of the best ways of making sure that you are one-hundred-percent Buddhist is to come here on a *shibir*. This is the main reason why this place has been established, and I am very glad to see it today. I have seen photographs of it, but only when I came here yesterday was I able to appreciate how beautiful it is. I hope it will grow. I hope

The entrance of the Bhaja caves

that one day there will be another centre on that hill over there, even bigger and more beautiful.

I heartily congratulate all those who have been responsible for this great achievement. I congratulate the person who had the idea. I congratulate all the people – in so many different places, so many different countries – who have contributed money. I congratulate the workers: those who have cut the stone, carried the tiles, made the doors and windows. I congratulate everybody. We can say that this *shibir* centre represents a cooperative effort, a cooperation of head, heart, and hand, and that is the sort of cooperation we need. If we have that sort of cooperation we can do anything. I therefore hope that you will continue to come here for *shibirs*, to meditate, and even to help grow food. I hope that the new Bhaja will be even bigger and more glorious than the old one.

DR AMBEDKAR'S TRUE GREATNESS[317]

Worli, Bombay, 22 December 1983

Brothers and Sisters in the Dhamma, the saying, 'History repeats itself' certainly seems to be true in my case. Having been in Bombay many times before, here I am once again, and I am very glad to see you all on this occasion. Not only have I been to Bombay many times, but I have very happy memories of my various visits. These memories go back nearly forty years, and most of them are Buddhist memories. I didn't come here on account of the big hotels or the film studios. Whenever I came here, I came for the sake of the Dhamma. For instance, I remember the old Ananda Vihara, which used to be situated in the compound of the Nair Hospital in Leamington Road. I remember the Bahujana Vihara, Parel, where my old friend Bhikkhu H. Dhammananda used to live. Now he is retired and lives in Sri Lanka, but he still writes to me from time to time. I also remember the Japanese Buddhist temple here in Worli. I remember the Japanese monks beating their big drum every evening and, as they beat it, reciting *namu myōhō renge kyō*. Another of my pleasant memories of Bombay is of going to see the Kanheri Caves with a party of 500 newly converted Buddhists. In one of the biggest of the caves we circumambulated the big stupa chanting *Namo tassa bhagavato arahato sammāsambuddhassa*; we had a very happy time. Other visitors to the caves were very surprised to see us, because they went there just as sightseers, whereas we went as Buddhists. I can also remember giving lectures in many different parts of Bombay. These too constitute very pleasant memories of Bombay.

But my happiest memories of Bombay are of the two meetings I had with Dr Babasaheb Ambedkar. Indeed, these are among the happiest and most precious memories of my whole life. The first meeting took place at Rajagriha, Dr Ambedkar's residence at Dadar, and the other in the Ananda Bhavan of Siddharth College, in the Fort area. The second of these meetings was probably the more important, since it took place about ten months before the great mass conversion ceremony in Nagpur. At that meeting Dr Ambedkar and I discussed the whole question of the conversion ceremony, and he asked me to give a lecture explaining to his people the meaning of the *tisaraṇa* and *pañcasīla* and the significance of conversion to Buddhism. Naturally I was very glad indeed to accede to his request. A meeting was therefore held here in Worli, under the auspices of the Janata Vachanalaya. I don't know why Dr Ambedkar selected Worli. Maybe he had a particularly good opinion of the people of Worli and thought that they would be particularly receptive to the Dhamma. Anyway, on 1 January 1956 a meeting was held, and like this meeting it was held in the open air. Unlike this meeting, however, it was held very late at night, at about eleven o'clock, when there was an icy wind blowing, and I remember that I was shivering in my thin *bhikkhu*'s robes. About 3,000 people attended the meeting and heard my lecture on 'What it Means to Become a Buddhist', which was ably translated into Marathi by Mr Bhandari, President of the Scheduled Castes Federation of Bombay. Afterwards I heard that Dr Ambedkar was very pleased with the lecture. So this was the first lecture I ever gave in Worli. It took place at the beginning of 1956, almost exactly twenty-eight years ago, and it was my first real contact with the people of Worli.

Since then I have given a number of lectures here, both in the open air and inside the chawls; but I like to think that the first one had a very special significance. I like to think that I met the people of Worli through Dr Ambedkar, and that by arranging that meeting Dr Ambedkar introduced me, as it were, to the people of Worli. My connection with the people of Worli is therefore a very close one, and I am very happy to see you all once again. Last time I came to Bombay, two years ago, you gave me a magnificent reception in this very place. Tonight you have, I think, given me an even more magnificent reception. Two years ago, I spoke about the Buddha's story of the man who had a jewel hidden in the corner of his dhoti but didn't know that it was there.[318] I hope you haven't forgotten what I said. If you have forgotten, though, I expect you will be able to read the transcript of that lecture quite soon, when it appears in *Buddhayan*.

Besides being very glad to see the people of Worli again, I am also very glad to see those who have come to tonight's meeting from other places. Many have, I know, come from other parts of Maharashtra – from Poona, from Aurangabad, from Nasik, and even from as far away as Nagpur. I am very glad to see all of you. In fact, I am very glad to see all Indian Buddhists. I am very glad to see all followers of Dr Ambedkar. Not only that. I am very glad to have the opportunity of bringing you a message from the Buddhists of the West, a message of *maitrī*, a message of brotherhood and solidarity, a message of unity. All Buddhists are brothers and sisters, members of the same great spiritual family, and therefore we should all work together for the sake of the Dhamma. We should work together for the uplift of the poor and the oppressed, regardless of whether we belong to England or India or anywhere else.

You may be surprised to hear that the Buddhists of the West know about you very well, especially those in England. They know about the Buddhists of Maharashtra, of Bombay, of Worli. Above all, they know about Dr Ambedkar. This was not always the case. Until a few years ago they didn't know anything about you at all. But now they know quite a lot. They know about the great movement of mass conversion to Buddhism, and they know why Dr Ambedkar asked you to take this step. The fact that they know all this is due to the work of the Trailokya Bauddha Mahasangha Sahayaka Gana (TBMSG), thanks to which the name and the work of Dr Ambedkar are now very well known indeed to Western Buddhists. Western Buddhists are now reading the life of Dr Ambedkar, as well as his own writings, and they find both his life and his writings very inspiring indeed.

Earlier this year, Dhammachari Lokamitra went to the UK for a couple of months. While he was there he met many people and visited all the British centres of our movement. Everywhere he went he was given a big reception, and everywhere he went, he spoke about the Indian Buddhists – especially the Buddhists of Maharashtra – and about Dr Ambedkar. At that time people in the UK were especially interested in India because the film *Gandhi* had just been released and was being shown in cinemas all over the country. Many British Buddhists went to see it and expressed their surprise that they had not seen any trace of Dr Ambedkar in the film. Besides Gandhiji himself, Pandit Nehru, Vallabhai Patel, Rajendra Prasad, and many other national leaders appear, but Dr Ambedkar doesn't appear even once.[319] I don't know the reason for the omission. It may be that there is a plan to produce a film devoted entirely to Dr Ambedkar. If there is no such plan, then in my opinion there should be. Gandhiji is undoubtedly a very important figure in the history of modern India, and a very great man, and I don't want to underestimate him, but Dr Ambedkar's place in the history of modern India is no less important, and some people think that it is even more important.

To change the subject, I have some good news for you – news that will show you how much Dr Ambedkar is appreciated by Buddhists in the West. Some of you may have seen our newsletter, which is published in London and goes all over the Buddhist world. It is edited by Dhammachari Nagabodhi, whom I know some of you have met, because he was in India two years ago, when I myself was here. My good news is that Nagabodhi is coming to India again in a year's time for a very definite purpose. He is going to write a book on Dr Ambedkar and the movement of mass conversion, and he wants to write it here in India. The book will be published in England and distributed all over the world. In this way, we hope, Dr Ambedkar and his work will be appreciated more widely than ever before.[320]

But some of you may be wondering why Western Buddhists appreciate Dr Ambedkar so much. What do they see in him? Obviously, they don't see him in quite the same way that you do. They don't attach the same importance as you do to certain aspects of his life. To give a couple of examples, in India Dr Ambedkar's followers are fond of emphasizing that he was a very educated man. They will tell you that he was MA, PhD, DSc, as well as Barrister-at-Law, and of course it is quite true. But Western Buddhists do not attach much importance to his academic qualifications, because in the West education is widespread. Indeed, many Western Buddhists think that in terms of human development and human happiness modern education has very little real value. Nor is that all. Western Buddhists do not attach much importance to the fact that Dr Ambedkar was once a minister in the central government. They do not even attach much importance to the fact that he was the framer of the Indian Constitution. All such things they regard as being of secondary significance.

What is it, then, that Western Buddhists appreciate about Dr Ambedkar? First of all, they appreciate him for his tremendous strength of character. They appreciate him for his absolute integrity – for the fact that he was a man who could not be bought. They appreciate him for his honesty and outspokenness, for his fearlessness, and for his great determination. And there's another side of Dr Ambedkar's character that Western Buddhists appreciate very much. They appreciate him for his compassion. As you know very well, Dr Ambedkar's tongue was sometimes quite rough and quite bitter, but his heart was very tender. His heart bled for the sufferings of his people, and his dearest wish was to deliver them from the suffering, the slavery, of centuries. That was the only thing he wanted. He didn't want fame or money. He just wanted to serve his people, and to uplift them. Some people think that Dr Ambedkar was a highly intellectual man, and indeed he was, but he was also a man of deep and powerful emotions. In fact, he was the embodiment of compassion, which is why we think of him as a modern bodhisattva.

Thus Western Buddhists appreciate all these different aspects of Dr Ambedkar's character, and they also appreciate him for the work he has done. Dr Ambedkar's achievements are, of course, very numerous. Tonight I am going to mention only one of them, but it is the most important one, and the one that Western Buddhists appreciate most. Indeed, it is an achievement for which he will be remembered for hundreds and even thousands of years. Dr Ambedkar's greatest achievement was the great mass conversion to Buddhism that took place in Nagpur on 14 October 1956. On that historic occasion, Dr Ambedkar himself went for Refuge to the Buddha, the Dhamma, and the Sangha, and lakhs of his followers went for Refuge with him. Now there are forty lakhs of Buddhists in Maharashtra and other parts of India – that is to say, forty lakhs of people who have declared themselves Buddhists. That is what I call Dr Ambedkar's Dhamma Revolution, the most important of all the revolutions that have taken place in the twentieth century. Already it has brought about great changes in the lives of Dr Ambedkar's followers. In future, it will bring about still greater changes, not just here in Maharashtra, not just in India, but throughout the world. Unfortunately, some people do not appreciate the importance of Dr Ambedkar. They do not appreciate the true nature of his greatest achievement. They do not appreciate the significance of the great mass conversion ceremony in Nagpur. They do not appreciate the Dhamma Revolution. I therefore want to say a few words on the subject.

As some of you know, at the time of the mass conversion ceremony at Nagpur I was in India, and I remember the reports that appeared in the newspapers and the comments that were made, especially by Hindus. Some people said that Dr Ambedkar's conversion was a political stunt. Others said that simply changing from one religion to another was useless. According to them, it was just a change of label, and would not make any real difference to anybody. The people who made such comments failed to recognize the true nature of religion. They thought that religion was something merely external and superficial. They did not realize how deep religion goes.

I want to go into this a little. It is important to realize that religion is not just a matter of customs and ceremonies, not just a matter of abstract ideas, or of holding to a certain philosophy. Religion is what you yourself, in your heart of hearts, most truly and deeply believe in. Religion is what you are prepared to die for. You are prepared to die for it because you cannot live without it. Your religion is in fact your life. It is what makes you what you are, what makes you act in the way that you do. This is not, of course, the usual conception of religion, so let me give you a simple example of the sort of thing I mean. It is an example from my own personal experience, and has some connection with how I became a Buddhist.

As you all know, I was born and brought up in England, and even when I was quite young I was very fond of reading. No one ever had to tell me to read. In fact, sometimes they had to tell me to stop reading. At that time I was especially fond of reading poetry, and even now I like to read it occasionally, when I can spare the time. When I was young, I read all the great English poets, such as Shakespeare and Milton, Wordsworth and Shelley, and the great French, German, and Italian poets too. In fact, I read practically all the great poets of Europe and America. I was absolutely immersed in my reading. Sometimes I would be reading in my room, and my mother would call me to come and have lunch, but I wouldn't take any notice. I would just carry on reading. My mother would call me again, saying the food was getting cold, but still I would take no notice. In the end she would bring the food to my room and put it down in front of me, and I would eat the food with one hand and hold my book with the other, and carry on reading. That is what I was like as a boy. Looking back, I find it difficult to say whether it was a good thing or a bad thing.

One day a thought suddenly struck me. I thought, 'All this time I have been reading the poetry of the West, but the East also has great poetry.' So I started reading Arabic and Persian poetry, Chinese and Japanese poetry, and Sanskrit poetry – all in English translation, of course. I found I could understand and enjoy Eastern poetry as much as I enjoyed Western poetry. I found that the great poets of the East had the same emotions as the great poets of the West. I made this discovery when I was about fourteen years old. I started realizing that whatever has been thought and felt by someone in one part of the world can be understood and appreciated by someone in any other part of the world.

This was not all. By reading translations of Sanskrit and Pāli literature, I eventually came into contact with Indian philosophy and religion, the scriptures of which are often written in poetic form. Eventually I came in contact with Buddhism and became a Buddhist – or rather, I realized that in the depths of my heart I was a Buddhist already. But that is another story, as we say, and I won't go into it now.

There are some people who believe that there are two quite different kinds of mind in the world: the Eastern mind and the Western mind. These two minds, such people say, cannot understand each other. But I simply do not believe this. In the course of my life I have had many friends of many different nationalities, both in the East and in the West. I have had hundreds of Indian friends, as well as Chinese, Tibetan, and Burmese friends. I have understood them and they have understood me. We have been able to communicate. So why is this? Why have we been able to understand one another? Why have we been able to communicate? It is because we are all human beings, and human beings are all fundamentally the same. We have the same senses, the same feelings and emotions, the same mental processes. Of course there are social and cultural differences. There are educational differences, and even intellectual differences. But all these differences are comparatively superficial. Deep down, we are all the same: we are all just human beings. That is why we can understand one another, and why we can be friends.

Some people say that Buddhism is just an Eastern religion. This is what some Christians in the West say. They say that because Buddhism is an Eastern religion it cannot be understood and practised by people in the West. Such Christians forget that Christianity itself is of Eastern origin. But Buddhism is, in fact, not an Eastern religion. It is a universal religion. Even though Buddhism originated in India, it spread over the whole earth. Buddhism can be understood and practised anywhere in the world, because Buddhism addresses itself to the individual human being, regardless of race, nationality, caste, sex, or age. Buddhism is, therefore, the religion of humanity.

This is one of the reasons why I am a Buddhist. I believe that humanity is basically one. I believe that it is possible for any human being to communicate with any other human being, to feel for any other human being, to be friends with any other human being. This is what I truly and deeply believe. This belief is part of my own experience. It is part of my own life. It is part of me. I cannot live without this belief, and I would rather die than give it up. For me, to live means to practise this belief. Therefore, this belief is part of my religion. It has nothing to do with the way in which I dress, nothing to do with what I call myself. It is a matter of the way I am, the way I exist. It is the way I naturally function in the world. This is what religion really is. It is what you most truly and deeply believe. It is what you are, what you are prepared to die for. It is your life. It is what you are, what makes you behave in the way that you do. Religion is therefore a very important thing. In fact, it is the *most* important thing.

If you want to change someone, you must change their religion. If you want to change a community, you must change its religion. If religion is not changed, then nothing is changed. If religion is changed, then everything is changed. Change of religion means a new life. That is what Dr Ambedkar saw. This is why he himself changed his religion, and why he called upon his followers to change their religion too. This is why the mass conversion ceremony at Nagpur was Dr Ambedkar's greatest achievement – because it represented a change in the lives of lakhs upon lakhs of people. It is not easy to bring about a change of this sort. Only a very great man can do it. But Dr Ambedkar brought about that change, thus doing what very few people in history have ever done. This is why Dr Ambedkar is so greatly appreciated by Western Buddhists, and by Indian Buddhists, and why he is beginning to be appreciated by thinking people throughout the world.

Some people did not agree with Dr Ambedkar's change of religion. They thought that the mass conversion ceremony at Nagpur was a big mistake. Some people still think that religion is of no importance, and that change of religion is therefore of no importance. In my opinion, such people are quite wrong. Not only are they wrong, they are in direct disagreement with Dr Ambedkar on a matter of fundamental importance. They fail to appreciate the greatness of Dr Ambedkar, or the significance of his greatest achievement. They are therefore not followers of Dr Ambedkar.

I would go further than that. I would say that anyone who has not taken the *Dhammadiksha* is not a follower of Dr Ambedkar. Now please don't misunderstand me. I am not saying you must take the *Dhammadiksha* even if you don't want to; you are free to take it or not take it as you wish. Taking the *Dhammadiksha* is an individual matter, a matter for your own conscience. What I am saying is that you cannot refuse to take the *Dhammadiksha* and call yourself a follower of Dr Ambedkar. You cannot remain a Hindu, or a Muslim, or a communist, and call yourself a follower of Dr Ambedkar. Dr Ambedkar did not change his religion and become a Buddhist overnight. Being a very responsible man, he thought about the matter for many, many years. He studied many books on Buddhism, and he spent many years compiling his own great book *The Buddha and His Dhamma*. The mass conversion ceremony at Nagpur was therefore the culmination of Dr Ambedkar's whole life's work. He took the *Dhammadiksha* himself, and he advised his followers to take it too. Well, you are free to take it or not, but if you do not take it you should not call yourself a follower of Dr Ambedkar, because you are in direct disagreement with Dr Ambedkar on the most important point of all.

I have spoken strongly about this matter because it is important, and because I want people to appreciate Dr Ambedkar's greatest achievement. I also want them to realize the greatness of Dr Ambedkar himself. The Buddha said, 'If people praise me for my morality (*śīla*) or for my concentration (*samādhi*) they do not really praise me. People truly praise me only when they praise me for my attainment of supreme Enlightenment.'[321] In the same way, we do not really praise Dr Ambedkar when we praise him for his learning, or for being a distinguished lawyer, or a minister in the government, or a great educationalist. We really praise Dr Ambedkar when we praise him for bringing about the great mass conversion to Buddhism.

A few minutes ago I said that some people do not believe in the importance of religion, and that in my opinion such people are quite wrong. At the same time, I sympathize with them. They are not bad people, but simply mistaken in their ideas, and in a way this is not surprising. Nowadays there is a lot of confusion on the subject of religion, both here in India and in the West. Nor is that all. In former times, all the important philosophies were religious philosophies. People thought in religious terms, and their beliefs and practices were of religious origin. But during the last 200 years a very important change has taken place. We now have in the world a number of non-religious or secular philosophies, as they are called, and some of them are very important and influential indeed. Between them they influence the thinking, and even the lives, of an immense number of people all over the world. They even influence the way people think about religion. I am therefore going to say a few words about the three great secular philosophies, especially about their influence on the way in which people think about religion. We will then see what Dr Ambedkar has to say on the subject of *saddhamma*, i.e. what Dhamma has to do in order to become *saddhamma*, and after that we will conclude.

The three great secular philosophies are associated with the names of three great men, from whose thought they originated: Charles Darwin, Karl Marx, and Sigmund Freud. Darwin and Marx both lived in the nineteenth century, while Freud lived in the latter half of the nineteenth century and the first half of the twentieth century. Darwin was born in England, Marx in Germany (though he spent the greater part of his adult life in England), and Freud in Austria. Both Marx and Freud came from families that were of Jewish origin. Darwin formulated the theory of evolution by natural selection, Marx was the founder of Marxism, or what we generally call communism, and Freud was the originator of psychoanalysis. All three men have had a tremendous influence on modern thought. They have influenced even those who disagreed with their ideas. Obviously it is impossible for me to deal with their philosophies in detail (otherwise we would be here all night, and all day tomorrow, and I would have to miss my plane back to England), or even to give a proper outline of their thought. I am therefore going to concentrate on the main point of each philosophy, especially insofar as this concerns religion. In particular, I am going to see how the main point of each philosophy affects Buddhism, and how Buddhism stands in relation to it.

Darwin was born and brought up in a Christian country, England. According to Christian belief, God has created everything that exists – the entire universe, and all the things in it. According to the Bible, God created the universe in six days and on the seventh day he rested. Christians therefore believe that God created human beings, and also every species of animal: the lion, the tiger, the dog, the cat, the mouse, the spider, and so on. Christians further believe that God created each species separately, one after the other, within a few days. Moreover, until a hundred or so years ago, Christians believed that all this happened in the year 4004 BC.

Darwin showed that these ideas were quite wrong. He showed that animals had not been suddenly created by God, but had come into existence gradually, over a period of millions of years. Nor was that all. Darwin showed that the higher species of animals had developed from the lower species. This process is what we call evolution, i.e. biological evolution. Furthermore, Darwin showed that man too had come into existence gradually, over a period of millions of years, and had developed from lower species, i.e. from the animals, at least as regards his physical form. In particular, Darwin showed that man had developed from certain higher apes.

Darwin also tried to explain exactly how evolution occurred. According to him, it came about by means of a process which he called natural selection; but I have no time to go into that. I am concerned simply with the fact of evolution itself, with the fact that higher forms of life develop from lower forms. Nowadays this is accepted by nearly all educated people. Even Christians usually accept it, even though they have quite a lot of difficulty reconciling the Bible and the theory of evolution.

In the West, the widespread acceptance of the theory of evolution has profoundly affected people's whole attitude to life. I will mention just two points. Firstly, it has affected their attitude towards animals. Previously, due to the influence of Christianity, people in the West used to think that there was no connection between animals and human beings, because they believed that God had created them quite separately. In fact, Christians believed that God had created animals simply for the sake of human beings – to work for us and provide food for us. As a result of Christian teaching, animals were often treated cruelly.

Christians believed that animals did not have souls like human beings, and that it was therefore not wrong to torture and maim them. Due to Darwin's theory of evolution, this attitude has changed to some extent. People now realize that we are related to the animals by blood, so to speak. We have descended from them, so we should not harm them in any way. They feel pleasure and pain, just as we do, and we should not kill them and eat them. I am happy to tell you that thousands of people in the West are now vegetarians. In this way the theory of evolution has affected the attitude of people in the West towards animals. Indeed, it has affected their attitude towards all forms of life. At least some people in the West now realize that, from the highest to the lowest, all forms of life are interconnected.

Secondly, Darwin's theory of evolution has led to a widespread belief in progress. Darwin showed how higher forms of life developed from lower forms of life, and how we human beings ourselves have developed from the higher apes. Civilized human beings developed from uncivilized human beings. In this way, according to Darwin, over a period of millions of years, things had got better and better, and would presumably go on getting better. Unfortunately, some people started thinking that things would get better indefinitely regardless of individual human effort, that progress was automatic. Moreover, they started thinking of progress in exclusively material terms, in terms of technological advances and the increased production of material goods. This misunderstanding was not Darwin's fault. He didn't teach that progress was automatic, or that it was an exclusively material thing. Nonetheless, this is what people thought for a while. But now, for various reasons, they have started to think differently. They have started to see that although nature carries human beings up to a certain point of development, after that our progress depends upon our own individual efforts – which is, of course, the teaching of Buddhism. The Buddha constantly stressed that your development as a human being depends upon your own efforts. No one else can do the work for you. No guru can do it for you; no god can do it for you. Purity and impurity, the Buddha said, depend upon one's own individual efforts.[322] Development of higher states of consciousness depends on one's own efforts. Enlightenment depends on one's own efforts.

Though we should not think of progress in exclusively material terms, material progress is not a bad thing. On the contrary, it is a good thing; but it is not the only thing. Spiritual progress is of even greater importance. In this respect Buddhism follows a middle way between two extremes. One extreme is to believe that no distinctively human progress is possible and that humans cannot develop any further. The other extreme is to believe that progress is automatic, and that one does not have to make any personal effort. The middle way consists in believing that human progress is possible, but that it depends upon human effort, and that human progress is spiritual rather than material.

KARL MARX AND COMMUNISM

Karl Marx is important on account of his work in the field of economics, for his political theories are a direct application of his economic theories. Nowadays many authorities in the field of economics disagree with some of Marx's theories and have in fact shown that they are definitely wrong. Indeed, history itself has disproved some of those theories. But I have no time to go into all that now. Despite his mistakes, Marx remains a very important and influential thinker, and he is important and influential mainly on account of one thing – because he showed the importance of economics to human life, and showed it in a detailed and scientific manner. Before Marx, people tended to think that only ideas were important. They tended to think that their subjective mental state was more important than objective material conditions. But Marx showed that objective material conditions were important too, and had to be taken into consideration, especially in connection with economic conditions. Marx showed that economic conditions and factors such as the ownership of the means of production influenced the whole of human life – political life, social life, and even the way people thought.

This sort of teaching brought Marx into direct conflict with Christianity. According to Christianity, our chief duty is simply to think of God, or to pray to God. Christianity asserts that we should not think about material things, or about subjects like economics. It doesn't matter whether you are rich or poor. In fact, it is better if you are poor, since in that case there will be nothing to get in the way of your thinking about God. But here, too, Christianity has been forced to change its attitude, mainly as a result of Marx's teaching. It has been forced to develop a social conscience, at least to a limited extent.

Unfortunately, some of Marx's followers have taken his teaching to extremes, saying that objective material conditions are the only important thing, and that life is wholly determined by economics. They even say that consciousness itself is determined by economics. Buddhism does not agree with this, maintaining that one's subjective mental state is also of importance, and that it is not entirely determined by material, economic factors. According to Buddhism, the material conditions under which we live do indeed affect our mental state. Buddhism did not need Marxism to teach it this. At the same time, our mental state affects the material conditions under which we live. In this way Buddhism follows a middle path. It says that we must change our mental state, but it also says that we must change our material conditions. In this respect it is unlike Christianity. Buddhism says that we must create an ideal individual, but it also says that we must create an ideal society. This is why the Buddha established a sangha, to provide a model for the ideal society. So if you want to create an ideal society, there is no need to turn to communism. You can do it more effectively and in a more balanced manner, without having recourse to violence, through Buddhism.

FREUD AND PSYCHOANALYSIS

Sigmund Freud was a pioneer in the field of psychology. Freud 'discovered' the unconscious mind – that is, he discovered it so far as the West is concerned. Buddhism had of course discovered the unconscious mind – what some Buddhist texts call the *bhavaṅga-sota*, and others the *ālaya-vijñāna* – many hundreds of years earlier, but it was Freud who first demonstrated the existence of the unconscious mind in a detailed and scientific manner.

Freud also showed how an understanding of the unconscious mind could be used to cure various forms of illness. His work is therefore very important. He showed that human beings exist on two different levels, a conscious level and an unconscious level, and that the unconscious mind influences the conscious mind a very great deal. We may think that we are doing something for a particular reason – that is to say, the conscious mind thinks that we are doing it for that reason – when actually we may be doing it for a very different reason, of which we are quite unconscious. For instance, a rich man gives a large sum of money to a temple. He may think he is giving the money out of pure religious devotion – that is to say, his conscious mind may think this – but this may not be the case. He may in fact be giving the money out of a desire for fame, or in order to hear people singing his praises and saying how generous and what a great devotee he is. But he may not be conscious of this. The desire for fame and so on is what we call the unconscious motive for his action.

There is a difference between our conscious mind and our unconscious mind, between our conscious reasons for doing something and our unconscious ones, as well as a difference between what we do and what we really want to do. Sometimes this difference is very great. It may be so great that an actual conflict develops between the conscious mind and the unconscious mind. This conflict may become quite extreme, and when that happens, the person concerned may fall ill. According to Freud, the illness can be cured by discovering our repressed, unconscious reasons for doing – or not doing – something, or, in other words, by discovering our repressed, unconscious desires. Generally speaking, Freud believed that the unconscious mind influences the conscious mind much more than we realize. He believed that our higher ideals are very often only our lower instincts and desires in disguise. In this connection the sexual instinct in particular, so Freud believed, played a very important part.

Some of Freud's followers went to extremes, just as some of the followers of Darwin and of Marx had done. They believed that our conscious reasons for our behaviour were nothing but rationalizations of our unconscious desires, and that it was possible to explain all our higher ideals in this way. Religion itself could be explained in this way, in their view. Buddhism does not, of course, agree with this. To begin with, Buddhism recognizes the existence of three different levels of the mind, not two. There is (1) the level of the unconscious mind, (2) the level of the conscious mind, and (3) the level of the superconscious mind, as we may call it. Buddhism recognizes that the conscious mind can be influenced by the unconscious mind, but it does not agree that the conscious mind can be explained entirely in terms of the contents of the unconscious mind. Here, too, Buddhism follows a middle way, also recognizing that the conscious mind has the power to free itself from the influence of the unconscious mind. This is why the practice of mindfulness or awareness occupies such an important place in the Buddhist scheme of spiritual self-development. Moreover,

Buddhism teaches that we are capable of passing from the level of the conscious mind to the level of the superconscious mind, i.e. that we are capable of experiencing the four *rūpa-dhyānas* and ultimately attaining Enlightenment. Thus Buddhism goes much further than psychoanalysis. Nonetheless, a knowledge of psychoanalysis is sometimes helpful in understanding and practising the earlier stages of the Buddhist path.

These, then, are the three great secular philosophies of the modern age: evolutionism, which is associated with the name of Charles Darwin; communism, which is associated with the name of Karl Marx; and psychoanalysis, which is associated with the name of Sigmund Freud. Of course, I have been able to present only the main point of these three great secular philosophies, especially insofar as this point affects religion, but one thing, at least, is very clear. Religion in the West – i.e. Christianity – has been very much influenced by these modern secular philosophies, especially by evolutionism and communism. Christianity has, in fact, been forced to change its attitude in many respects. But Buddhism has not been influenced in the same way, and has not been forced to change its attitude. In fact, the influence of these secular philosophies has only served to strengthen Buddhism.

The reason for this is that Buddhism is a very different sort of religion from Christianity, and from Islam, and from Hinduism. Indeed, it is very different from all other religions. We can even go so far as to say that the word 'religion' itself means one thing for Buddhists and quite another for the followers of all other religions. It is unfortunate that we use the same word for Buddhism and for the other religions, i.e. the word religion in English and the word *dharma* in the Indian languages. Saying that Buddhism is a religion and Christianity is a religion, that Buddhism is a *dharma* and Hinduism is a *dharma*, is the source of a great deal of confusion. It is also, perhaps, the reason – or part of the reason – why some people who call themselves followers of Dr Ambedkar are unwilling to take *Dhammadiksha*.

Such people have to understand the matter correctly. They have to understand that criticisms that apply to Christianity, Hinduism, and so on, do not apply to Buddhism. Buddhism is a completely different kind of religion, so that however much we may be influenced by these modern secular philosophies, there is no reason why we should not take the *Dhammadiksha*. But it is not enough to understand the difference between the Buddhist concept of religion and the concept of religion in other faiths. We also have to understand the difference between Dhamma and *saddhamma*, and in order to understand this we have to turn to Dr Ambedkar's book *The Buddha and His Dhamma*, in which he says that Dhamma has two functions: to cleanse the mind of its impurities, and to make the world a kingdom of righteousness.[323] Once again we see how Buddhism follows a middle way, and how it avoids extremes. It is not enough simply to cleanse the mind of its impurities. Neither is it enough merely to make the world a kingdom of righteousness. We must do both. We must develop the individual human being, and we must improve society. In fact, we cannot do one without doing the other.

Further, Dr Ambedkar says that to be *saddhamma*, Dhamma must promote *prajñā*. Dhamma is incompatible with ignorance and superstition. Learning, Dr Ambedkar says, must be open to all, but mere learning is not enough, since it may lead to pedantry. *Prajñā* is therefore necessary. Hence Dr Ambedkar says that Dhamma is *saddhamma* when it teaches that what is needed is *prajñā*, i.e. *prajñā* accompanied by *śīla* and *karuṇā*. Above all there must be *maitrī*.

Finally, Dhamma, to be *saddhamma*, must break down all social barriers. It must break down the barriers between caste and caste, as well as the barriers between one race or one nationality and another. It must break down the barriers between rich and poor. In fact, there must not be any rich or any poor. Dhamma, to be *saddhamma*, must teach that worth and not birth is the measure of man. It must promote equality between human beings. This is what Buddhism does. This is what *saddhamma* does. This is the teaching of the Buddha, and the teaching of Dr Ambedkar. There is nothing here that a reasonable person cannot accept. In fact, if you cannot accept this you are not a reasonable person. This is what religion really is.

There should be no difficulty in accepting a religion in this sense, no difficulty in taking the *Dhammadiksha*. If you take the *Dhammadiksha* you will be able to change your own life, and the society in which you live. In other words, you will be able to take part in Dr Ambedkar's Dhamma Revolution. Most of you, I know, have already taken the *Dhammadiksha*, and the fact that you have taken it is the basis of our coming together here tonight. It is Buddhism that has brought us together; it is Dr Ambedkar who has brought us together. We are all brothers and sisters in the Dhamma.

Unfortunately, this time I cannot stay in India very long. I shall be returning to England very soon, because I have a lot of work to do there. The main reason I came on this three-week visit was to receive eight people into the Trailokya Bauddha Mahasangha as Dhammacharis. Three of these new Dhammacharis, you will be glad to know, come from Bombay – in fact, one of them comes from Worli – and they will be working for the Dhamma in Bombay together with Dhammachari Vajraketu and under the guidance of Dhammachari Lokamitra. Please give them your full support and cooperation. Bombay is the capital of Maharashtra and one of the most important cities in the whole of India. It has a large Buddhist population, and it was the scene of so many of Dr Ambedkar's activities. Consequently, it is important that we should have here a flourishing Buddhist movement that is worthy of Dr Ambedkar. This is all that I have to say. It has given me great pleasure to be with you here tonight and I look forward to meeting you all again.

1988

In October 1988, Sangharakshita went to India to make a BBC *documentary. It was a brief visit, but he found time to lay the foundation stone of the Mahavihara and give a talk in Wardha in which he introduced his new book* Ambedkar and Buddhism *(for which, see* Complete Works, *vol. 9).*

THE FOUNDATION STONE OF THE MAHAVIHARA

Dapodi, Poona, 9 October 1988

Brothers and sisters in the Dhamma, I am glad to be here again, after an absence of five years. In the course of those five years quite a lot has happened in TBMSG, and I am very glad indeed to see such a great expansion. I also feel very honoured to be invited to lay the foundation stone and plant the bodhi tree sapling. I believe this is the first time in my life that I have been invited to lay a foundation stone. I have given thousands of lectures. I have installed images. I have named hundreds of babies, I have blessed weddings, and I have performed after-death ceremonies, but this is the first time I have laid a foundation stone. It is of course the foundation stone of our Mahavihara, and the whole Dapodi complex, which will comprise an administrative centre for our social work throughout India; a library which will specialize in studies on Buddhism, Dr Ambedkar, and related subjects; a residential community; and a training centre for our Dhamma workers and social workers, so that they can start similar projects elsewhere. The conception of the whole Dapodi project is really a magnificent one, in accordance with Dr Ambedkar's vision for his people. Dr Ambedkar wanted to uplift people in every respect – socially, culturally, educationally, and religiously, in body and mind alike. This is what the Dapodi complex will be doing. It will be seeking to uplift people in every possible way.

So I am very happy to lay the foundation stone of this magnificent complex. Because it is the first foundation stone that I have laid, I have given it special thought, and I have come to a definite conclusion: that one foundation stone is not enough. Now I hope I haven't upset anyone's arrangements. I hope Lokamitra is not wondering what I am going to say next. But I think we really need six foundation stones, without which our work here will not succeed. Of course, I am not talking about foundation stones in a literal sense. I am not expecting TBMSG to lay foundation stones all over the place. I am talking metaphorically. So what are these six metaphorical foundation stones? It is very simple.

The first foundation stone we need is *dāna*. *Dāna* means giving or generosity, and it can take many forms. First of all comes the *dāna* of material things, including money. As Lokamitra has informed us, this Dapodi project started with a magnificent act of generosity by the whole Bharate family, when they gave us their land here at only a fraction of the market value. So we are very grateful to the Bharate family. They have set a very great and noble example. The second kind of *dāna* is that of education and culture, which we hope to give through our library. The third kind of *dāna*, and this is also very important, is the *dāna* of fearlessness and self-confidence. We hope to give this kind of *dāna* to the resident community and to those in our training centre, because without self-confidence one can do nothing. Dr Ambedkar was a man of tremendous self-confidence, which is why he could inaugurate the Dhamma Revolution, revive Buddhism in the land of his birth after hundreds of years, and win the respect of people all over the world. We hope that here in Dapodi we are able to develop the sort of self-confidence which Dr Ambedkar had. So that is the first foundation stone of our work: *dāna*.

Second, comes the foundation stone of *śīla*, which means ethics or morality. According to Dr Ambedkar religion is essentially ethics or morality. Ethics means abandoning unskilful actions and cultivating skilful actions. It means purifying the mind. The fundamental principles of Buddhist ethics are the five precepts: not to commit acts of violence; not to take what is not given; not to commit adultery; not to use wrong speech; and not to take drinks and drugs. Ethics is one of the foundation stones of our work here in Dapodi because we want to carry out our work here in accordance with the law of the land, and in a completely ethical manner, not by giving bribes or telling lies in order to get things done. We want to carry on our work here on a thoroughly ethical basis.

The third foundation stone is *kṣānti* or patience, a very necessary quality. We can't live in this world without patience. We have to be patient sometimes with our friends and relatives. Husband has to be patient with wife, wife has to be patient with husband, parents have to be patient with children, teachers have to be patient with students. We have to be patient with our employers. We have to be patient with our employees. And we particularly have to be patient when we are doing social and religious work, because in the course of the work so many obstacles and difficulties arise. So *kṣānti* or patience must be one of the six foundation stones of our work.

The fourth foundation stone is *vīrya* or energy. In Buddhist texts this is described as energy in the pursuit of the good. Energy is necessary to do social and religious work. To illustrate this, I will tell you a little story. There's a bit of Hindu mythology in it, but don't take any notice of that. This story goes that Indra, the king of the gods, came to earth to see what people were up to. One day he came to the shore of a great ocean and there he saw a squirrel that was behaving in a very peculiar fashion. It was dipping its bushy tail into the ocean and then turning around and shaking it out on the dry land. Indra approached the squirrel and said, 'What are you doing?' The squirrel said, 'I'm emptying the water of the ocean onto the land.' Very surprised, Indra said, 'You are so small. How can you possibly do such a thing?' But the squirrel said, 'I can if I live long enough!'[324] The scriptures do not tell us the name of the squirrel, but tonight I am going to tell you its name: Lokamitra. Not only that, Lokamitra is in fact the king of the squirrels, because he has a whole regiment of squirrels working with him. And I will tell you something more. The name of the great ocean which the squirrel was emptying on the dry land was bureaucracy.

The fifth foundation stone is *samādhi*, skilful one-pointedness of mind. Usually we think of one-pointedness in connection with meditation, but *samādhi* is like *smṛti* or mindfulness. The Buddha says that mindfulness is always useful,[325] and in the same way *samādhi* or one-pointedness of mind is always useful. We cannot succeed in any great work without concentrating all our energies on it, without dedicating ourselves to that work wholeheartedly.

The sixth and last foundation stone is *prajñā* or wisdom. It is not enough to practise *dāna*, *śīla*, *vīrya*, *kṣānti*, and *samādhi*. We also have to think and to reason. We have to look ahead, we have to plan, we have to have a clear idea of what we want to do, otherwise we cannot possibly succeed. I am very glad indeed that TBMSG has a clear idea of what to do here in Dapodi, and because it has all these six great foundation stones it will succeed. I am glad to have laid the foundation stone here in Dapodi, but the metaphorical foundation stones will have to be laid by you. Some of you are already laying or helping to lay them. I have already mentioned the Bharate family. They have helped tremendously. But I would also like to mention Mr A. Gaikwad from the Indian Administrative Service, and Mr N. M. Kamble, a Member of the Legislative Assembly. Both of these gentlemen have helped us to lay the foundation stone, both literally and metaphorically. Without their help we probably would not have had this ceremony. Many people from many organizations have helped us, both here in India and abroad. I have no time to mention them all tonight. But I am very glad to be here in Dapodi and to have laid the foundation stone. I am very glad to have planted the bodhi tree, and I hope it will grow literally and metaphorically. I am very glad I have seen you all again. I hope you will practise *dāna*, *śīla*, *kṣānti*, *vīrya*, *samādhi*, and *prajñā*. I hope that this whole Dapodi complex will flourish. I hope it will be a great centre of our activities, both Dhamma and social. I hope you all will be true disciples of the Buddha and true followers of Dr Ambedkar. And I hope we will all meet again.

ON *AMBEDKAR AND BUDDHISM*

Wardha, 22 October 1988

Brothers and sisters in the Dhamma and all friends, at present I am on a three week visit to India. I have come to meet my old friends and some new friends, and to see what progress TBMSG has made since my last visit five years ago. I have been to Bombay, Poona, and Aurangabad, and I was very pleased with what I saw there. So now at the end of my tour I am here at Wardha, and I must say I am very happy to see so many people gathered together on this occasion and to see the activities of TBMSG at last extended in the Vidharbha area.

As you already know, since 1982 Dhammachari Sanghsena has been giving lectures all over the Vidarbha area and has organized many retreats, some of which have been attended by hundreds of people. Then in 1987 a hostel was started for the boys in this area. I am very pleased indeed with this development, and I heartily congratulate all those who have helped in any way. I am particularly pleased that our hostel has a building to accommodate seventy to eighty boys and I am glad to have been asked to open this hostel today and plant a bodhi tree sapling. Dr Ambedkar attached a lot of importance to education, and for education one needs not only schools and colleges, but also a place to live where one can experience peace and develop oneself. Hostels are absolutely vital, and this is why TBMSG has set up a hostel in Wardha. TBMSG has altogether five hostels in Maharashtra, four for boys and one for girls, and one in Gujarat.[326]

Since my last visit to India five years ago TBMSG has been very active, and a lot of progress has been made in Vidarbha and other parts of India. In the course of the last five years the number of Dhammacharis has more than doubled. Five years ago we had only twenty-eight Dhammacharis, and we now have seventy-two, four of them from Vidarbha itself. I take this as a very good sign. Social work and Dhamma work cannot be done just by means of money (though money is also necessary). This work can be done only by those who are fully committed to the Buddha, Dhamma, and Sangha, observe the precepts, have the willingness to help their fellow human beings, and are filled with *kalyāṇa mitratā*. In other words, social work and Dhamma work can be done only by those who are Dhammacharis in the real sense of the term.

I don't know when I will be coming to Vidarbha again, but if and when I do come, I hope that by that time the number of Dhammacharis will have doubled, or more than doubled, and the number of Dhamma activities will have increased at least tenfold. TBMSG carries on its work and Dhamma activities in many parts of the world, especially in the United Kingdom. During the last five years many Dhamma centres have been opened not only in England but in America, Germany, Spain, and other countries. I don't have time to give you the details of these developments. Instead I want to say a few words about myself. I want to tell you what I have been doing in the course of the last five years, because people often wonder what I do with my time. When I am in India I give lectures, meet people, give names to children, receive garlands, and so on. But what do I do when I am in England?

In the course of the last five years, among a number of things I have been writing books and articles, in particular a book of special importance to all the Buddhists in the world, and to the followers of Dr Ambedkar. The title of the book is *Ambedkar and Buddhism*,[327] and it was published on 6 December 1986, on the thirtieth death anniversary of Dr Ambedkar. I wrote this book for three main reasons. Firstly, there was no book on Dr Ambedkar in any western language. Secondly, I wanted to give expression to my appreciation of Dr Ambedkar's life and work. And thirdly, I wanted people from both East and West to realize the greatness and significance of Dr Ambedkar. Thousands of people in India and other countries have heard the name of Mahatma Gandhi, but hardly anybody outside India has heard the name of Dr Ambedkar, and even in India he is not as much appreciated as he should be. Respecting Dr Ambedkar does not only mean garlanding his pictures; it means understanding his thought and putting it into practice. I wrote my book in English because that is my mother tongue, but I very much hope it will be translated into Marathi and Hindi.

The book is 200 pages long and divided into nine chapters. The first chapter is about the significance of Dr Ambedkar, mainly written for those who have not heard anything about him. I give a short biography of Dr Ambedkar: his birth, his family, his education, his difficulties, and his work for his people. I emphasize the significance of Dr Ambedkar's life not only politically but from a religious point of view: how his life and work was dominated by the Dhamma Revolution, the non-violent revolution that began on 14 October 1956, when lakhs of his followers renounced Hinduism and embraced Buddhism.

The second chapter is entitled 'Three Meetings', and in it I deal with my personal contact with Dr Ambedkar. In particular, I give details of the three important meetings I had with him. I first met Dr Ambedkar in November 1952, at Rajagriha, his house in Bombay. My second meeting with him also took place in Bombay, in December 1955, at Siddharth College. On that occasion Dr Ambedkar explained his plan to revive Buddhism in India, and told me that he intended to devote the rest of his life to Buddhism. He also asked me to give a lecture to his followers, so on New Year's Day 1956, I spoke in front of 3,000 people in Worli, and told them what it means to be a real Buddhist. This was the first time that I spoke to the followers of Dr Ambedkar, thirty-two years ago, when most of you had not even been born. During the following years I gave hundreds more lectures to them and I was always glad to do so. My third and last meeting with Dr Ambedkar was in November 1956, only a few weeks after the mass conversion We met in Delhi, at Dr Ambedkar's house in Alipur Road. He was very ill, but even so we talked for two hours, and even at the end of that time, he was unwilling to let me go. I could see he was ill and kept suggesting that I should leave, but he kept saying, 'Stay a little longer.' In the course of those two hours he told me about the hopes he had for the mass conversion. Two weeks later, he was dead. I was tremendously impressed by my meetings with Dr Ambedkar, and I am very glad indeed that I had some personal contact with him. He was the greatest man I have ever met in all my life.

The third chapter has a fearful title, 'The Hell of Caste', and deals with all those things with which you are familiar: the caste system and Untouchability. Western people don't know anything about this. They do not know how lakhs and lakhs of people are treated worse than animals. So in this chapter I have given full details, and I also narrate details about Dr Ambedkar's early life and the difficulties he had to face, having been born in an Untouchable family. There is no need for me to give the details; you are already familiar with them and most of you have experienced them yourselves.

The fourth chapter is entitled 'Milestones on the Road to Conversion'. Dr Ambedkar was a very great man and he had many great characteristics, one of which was that he did nothing without thought. The more important and serious the issue, the longer he thought about it. Changing one's religion is one of the most important and serious things anyone could possibly do, and Dr Ambedkar thought about it for a very long time, for more than twenty years. In 1935 he made a solemn declaration that although born a Hindu, he did not intend to die a Hindu,[328] but it was not until 1956 that he embraced Buddhism, so no one could accuse him of taking this decision on the spur of the moment. He went through many stages, and in this chapter of my book I describe some of them. For instance, I describe how Dr Ambedkar came to realize that the caste Hindus were not going to change their ways and that the Untouchables had to adopt another religion. I also mention how in 1935 Mahatma Gandhi described Untouchability as 'being on its last legs'. Well, Untouchability is not on its last legs even now, fifty years later.

The fifth chapter, called 'The Search for Roots', is about two important books by Dr Ambedkar himself: *Who were the Shudras?* (published in 1946) and *The Untouchables* (published in 1948). In the first book Dr Ambedkar tells us who the Shudras were. According to him, they were Aryans, not Dravidians. They were originally from the Kshatriya *varṇa*, but they were degraded by the Brahmins, who ousted them. In the same way, in *The Untouchables*, he traces Untouchability back to the fourth century CE. According to Dr Ambedkar, the Untouchables were originally Buddhist and Untouchability was the punishment imposed on them by the Brahmins for sticking to Buddhism. These two books are very important, shedding light on ancient Indian history as they do. Unfortunately they are not known to Western scholars, so I have summarized them in this chapter.

The sixth chapter is about an important article on Buddhism by Dr Ambedkar, 'Buddha and the Future of His Religion', published in the *Maha Bodhi* in Calcutta in 1950, six years before the mass conversion. In this article Dr Ambedkar makes several important points. I have very little time to talk about them tonight, but I have dealt with them in my book.[329] The first point he makes is that the Buddha was an Enlightened human being. He makes it clear that the Buddha did not claim to be the son of God or the messenger of God, and certainly he did not say he was God himself. In fact, in Buddhism there is no God at all, as Dr Ambedkar points out, before going on to say that in Buddhism the place of God is taken by morality.

Religion he said should fulfil three requirements: (1) it must be in accordance with karma; (2) it must recognize freedom, equality, and fraternity; and (3) it should not glorify poverty. Among all religions, only Buddhism fulfils these requirements. In 'Buddha and the Future of His Religion' Dr Ambedkar says that change should be made in the *bhikṣu* sangha, which is not living up to its ideal. Unfortunately, he did not live long enough to form a new type of sangha himself, but fortunately we have taken some steps in TBMSG. Our Dhammacharis and Dhammacharinis are not *upāsakas* or *bhikṣus* in the old sense. They are people who are wholeheartedly committed to Buddhism, who carry out social and cultural work, and try to spread the Dhamma as much as possible by giving lectures, teaching meditation classes, and conducting retreats. In this way they are trying to fulfil Dr Ambedkar's vision of creating a new Buddhist movement – not only a new Buddhist mission but a new world.

In the seventh chapter of my book, 'The Great Mass Conversion', I give all the details of the events of 14 October 1956, the day when Dr Ambedkar with lakhs of his followers converted from Hinduism to Buddhism, when he set in motion the wheel of the Dhamma in India, when he started the Dhamma Revolution. I hope you are already familiar with all those events, so there is no need for me to tell you about them, but I will mention a few things. Before the mass conversion Dr Ambedkar held a press conference during which he was asked a number of questions, one of which was: what form of Buddhism would he and his followers be embracing? Would they embrace Hīnayāna or Mahāyāna? Dr Ambedkar was very straightforward. He said that they were not going to involve themselves in either of the two. They were just going to be Buddhist. This is the attitude of TBMSG too. Whether in India or England or anywhere in the world, we are just Buddhist, and all Buddhists are our brothers and sisters.

Another point: at the point of conversion Dr Ambedkar did not give his followers just the Refuges and Precepts. He also gave them twenty-two vows.[330] Dr Ambedkar was a far-sighted person, and he gave these twenty-two vows for a definite reason: to safeguard the purity and integrity of the Refuges and Precepts. These vows cannot be separated; we should observe them all just as Dr Ambedkar has given them to us. At the time of the mass conversion Dr Ambedkar and his followers gave up Hinduism and thereby the caste system. Because they gave up the caste system, they gave up caste and sub-caste. But I have heard that even now there are Buddhists who continue to marry only people from their sub-caste. I hope you will give up this practice. If you keep the practice of only marrying within your sub-caste, then you are not really one-hundred-percent Buddhist.

In the eighth chapter of my book, 'The Buddha and his Dhamma', I describe in detail Dr Ambedkar's book of that name. I don't need to tell you more about it now; Dr Ambedkar wrote it in English, but it has been translated into Hindi and Marathi, so you can read it for yourself. In fact, you *should* read it. Every Buddhist should have a copy.

And in the ninth and last chapter of my book, 'After Ambedkar', I have written about the mass conversion movement after Dr Ambedkar's death and the followers of Dr Ambedkar in all the parts of Western India, Maharashtra, especially Nagpur, Bombay, Poona, Jabalpur, Ahmedabad etc. I have described how TBMSG was formed, in England in 1967 and then in India in 1977. I then give an account of my visit to India in 1981–1982 and my tour of Marathwada, during which I visited fifty or sixty villages.

On my visit in 1982 I got as far as Nanded, but this time I have reached Wardha. I am very glad to see you all, to open this new hostel, and to be able to tell you about my book *Ambedkar and Buddhism*. Dr Ambedkar was a very great man indeed. He belonged not only to India but to the whole world. I am very happy that I have been able to tell the people in the West something about him. Some of you may want to know why I have not gone to Nagpur this time. I was there on 6 December 1956, the day Dr Ambedkar died, to share the grief of the people on that dreadful day, and in the course of the next four days I delivered thirty-five lectures in different parts of the city, telling people not to be scared, not to give up hope, and urging them to carry on Dr Ambedkar's work, the Dhamma Revolution. So there is a very strong bond between the Buddhists of Nagpur and myself, and I would like to visit them, but I will not go there so long as there is disharmony between the followers of Dr Ambedkar in the city. The Diksha Bhumi is a sacred place, the place where the Dhamma Revolution started, and I am very sorry to hear that there are quarrels over it. I hope that there will be peace and an amicable conclusion, and that unity and harmony will be restored. I hope that the Diksha Bhumi will be a great centre of Dhamma activity, education, and knowledge. No doubt when I visit India again I will visit Nagpur. Meanwhile I hope you will all be well and happy. I hope the work of TBMSG will flourish in Wardha and in the whole Vidarbha area. And I hope that one day we all will meet again.

1992

On this, his last visit to India, Sangharakshita visited the completed Mahavihara in Poona, and went to Nagpur for the first time in twenty-five years. Lokamitra recalls (p. liv): 'Arriving at Nagpur, we found that he had been accorded the honour of being a State Guest, so we were driven in a police convoy everywhere we went. His main talk was at the historic Kasturchand Park, where he had spoken at Dr Ambedkar's condolence ceremony. We also made an excursion to Bordharan to open the first stage of the retreat centre there.' This section includes the talks given in Nagpur; and also talks given at the opening of a hostel in Dapoli, where Dr Ambedkar spent part of his childhood; at the new women's community in Poona; and at the dedication of the shrine at Bhaja.

KEEPING THE MAHAVIHARA BEAUTIFUL

Dapodi, Poona, 1992

Brothers and sisters in the Dhamma, three years have passed since my last visit to Poona, and that's too long to be away from my old friends here, but I'm glad to be here at last. Since my last visit quite a lot of things have happened, in the world, in India, and in TBMSG. In the course of the last three years, TBMSG and Bahujan Hitay[331] have gone from strength to strength. We've opened six more hostels, three hostel buildings have been completed, and Dhamma activities have been started in ten new places, both inside and outside Maharashtra. I don't know the number of places in which we now conduct Dhamma activities, but judging by all the garlands I was receiving earlier on, it's well over a hundred. I'm very happy to see the expansion that has taken place. In the course of the last three years there have also been twenty-eight Dhammachari ordinations and several new publications have been brought out. The new shrine at Bhaja has been completed, and so has the first stage of our Bordharan retreat centre. The ordination process for men who have asked for ordination has been developed, and our first women's community has been started. Previously all the residential communities were for men, but now we have one for women too, and we hope to have more.

All this represents a very great achievement. But that's by no means all. In some ways I've kept the best thing till last, like the sweet at the end of a meal. The sweet is of course the opening one year ago of our Mahavihara. In England I saw pictures of the opening ceremony, and now I'm very glad to be able to see the Mahavihara with my own eyes. As I was looking round a couple of days ago, I couldn't help remembering a conversation I had with Lokamitra in 1979, not long after his arrival here in Poona, and at the time of my own return to India after twelve years. Lokamitra had started Dhamma activities here and we were discussing how to develop them. I said I thought we should try to rent a building somewhere in the middle of the city, but Lokamitra did not quite agree with this. Lokamitra, by the way, is a very good disciple – he doesn't hesitate to disagree with me! He didn't think we should rent a property; he thought we should buy a place, or even build one of our own. And now, twelve years later, that dream of Lokamitra's has been fulfilled. Twelve years later we have our magnificent Mahavihara.

When I heard that it was going to be called *Maha*vihara I was a bit surprised, and thought that maybe that name was a bit ambitious, but when I saw the photographs, and then saw it with my own eyes I thought, yes, it is indeed the *Maha*vihara. I would like to congratulate all of you on this magnificent achievement. I would like to congratulate the Bharate family, every single one of them, for their great generosity in making the land available to us. And of course I'd like to congratulate Lokamitra for spearheading the whole project. Lokamitra has had to overcome innumerable difficulties. I won't describe them – to do justice to them, I'd have to give a whole series of talks – but Lokamitra overcame them all. And I'd also like to congratulate Bodhidharma and Vimalakirti on their crucial role in the planning and execution of the project, and Virabhadra and Maitreyanatha for the part they played in setting up the social and medical activities. Virabhadra is not here this evening, he's in England, but he asked me to give you this message: 'Carry on with the good work, especially in preventive medicine.'

There are many more people who have contributed to the success of the project, not least all our donors. But there are two people whose names deserve special mention: the architects, Christopher Benninger and Gautam Balsekar. It's thanks to their vision and skill that we have a building of which we can be very proud. The Mahavihara has been open for not much more than a year but already it is widely known. People come to see it not just from Poona but from all over India, and even from abroad. It is becoming a place of pilgrimage for all Buddhists, and this is not surprising. The Mahavihara is the headquarters for TBMSG and Bahujan Hitay in India, the centre for Dhamma activities and social activities, and here we have our men's community, which I believe is the biggest men's community in our whole movement. It's called the Buddhaland community, and yesterday they gave me a fine reception and programme, and I was very pleased to see how bright and happy they all were, and that there was such a spirit of *maitrī*, of brotherhood, in the community.

But this is not all that one can say about the Mahavihara. It's not just very big and very useful. It's also very beautiful. It's a work of art itself and a worthy successor to the ancient Buddhist cave temples of Maharashtra. I want to emphasize this because beauty is very important in human life. Beauty nourishes and inspires us, whether it's the beauty of nature or the beauty of art. We may even go so far as to say that without beauty we cannot lead a truly human life. Unfortunately, in modern times we are surrounded by a great deal of ugliness, especially in cities, where we are surrounded by ugly streets, ugly houses, ugly buildings, and in some cases horrible slums and heaps of rubbish. As a result of living in ugly surroundings, people often lose their sense of beauty, which means that they've lost an important human quality. So I'm very glad to see that our Mahavihara is a very beautiful building as well as being very useful. I hope that it will serve as an example. I hope we shall see more beautiful buildings springing up in Poona. Even ordinary houses should be beautiful. We should try in fact to make the world in which we live more beautiful. If we can do this, then the world will be much more like a Buddhaland.

But I need to sound a note of warning. The Mahavihara is very beautiful, but we must be careful to keep it that way. We must repair and repaint it when necessary, and keep it perfectly clean and tidy. We must care for the trees and the flowers, and keep the grass neatly cut. We must be aware of the condition the Mahavihara is in, and if we see even a speck of dust, we should at once remove it. And in order to do all this we will need a very important Buddhist quality: mindfulness.

Mindfulness is one of the most important of all Buddhist qualities. As the Buddha said, mindfulness is always useful.[332] It's useful in our worldly life and it's also useful in our spiritual life. Mindfulness is the seventh step of the Buddha's Noble Eightfold Path. It's one of the five spiritual faculties, and also the first of the seven *bodhyaṅgas* or factors of *bodhi*. As you know, *bodhi* or Enlightenment is the goal of the Buddhist life. The Buddha is called 'Buddha' because he attained *bodhi*. Anyone, in fact, who attains *bodhi* is called a Buddha. Buddhahood is within the reach of every human being provided he or she makes the necessary effort. And the seven *bodhyaṅgas* are the seven factors or constituents of *bodhi*, the seven things that we have to cultivate if we want to become Enlightened. I'll say just a few words about them before I conclude.

First of all, mindfulness. In Pāli, it's *sati,* Sanskrit *smṛti.* There are four classical forms of mindfulness: mindfulness of our physical body and its movements; mindfulness of our feelings and emotions; mindfulness of our thoughts, our mental states; and mindfulness of the Buddha's teaching. But we can add two more: mindfulness of other people and mindfulness of our surroundings. If we are not aware of other people, we won't be able to treat them properly, and we may harm them or at least hurt their feelings. And if we're not aware of our surroundings, of course we won't be able to keep them clean and tidy. So this is the first *bodhyaṅga*, mindfulness or *smṛti.*

Then secondly, there comes *dharma-vicaya*. Here *dharma* doesn't mean the teachings of the Buddha, but something like 'mental states' or even just 'things', and *vicaya* means 'distinguishing', so *dharma-vicaya* means distinguishing mental states or distinguishing things. It means distinguishing between *kuśala* and *akuśala*, right and wrong, justice and injustice, truth and falsehood, the real and the unreal. Nowadays a lot of people don't want to make clear distinctions. They want to mix everything up. But unless we can distinguish in this way, then there'll be no ethical life and no spiritual life, so *dharma-vicaya* is very important.

Thirdly, comes *vīrya* or energy. *Vīrya,* like *sati,* is one of the five spiritual faculties. It's also one of the six *pāramitās* practised by the bodhisattva. In the *Bodhicaryāvatāra*, Śāntideva defines *vīrya* as 'energy in the pursuit of the good'.[333] And the good is whatever is good for us, whatever is right, whatever is just, whatever is true, whatever is real. As one of the *bodhyaṅgas*, *vīrya* is the elimination of the bad and the cultivation of the good as identified by *dharma-vicaya*. It's no use having lots of energy if you use it for the wrong purpose, or direct it towards the wrong goal.

Fourthly, there is *prīti*, which is joy or rapture. If you are constantly using your energy for the right purpose, then you'll feel very happy, joyful, rapturous, even ecstatic. You'll feel intense bliss constantly bubbling up inside you, like a spring of water bubbling up from the rocks. *Prīti* can arise in a number of different ways. Of course it can arise in connection with meditation. *Prīti* is in fact one of the five *dhyāna* factors. *Prīti* can also arise when you do puja, when you're studying the Buddha's teaching, and in the context of spiritual friendship. It can arise when you see and appreciate a beautiful work of art like our Mahavihara. *Prīti* is very similar to enthusiasm. Some of you may remember that in a speech he gave on 15 October 1956, the day after the great mass conversion, Dr Ambedkar said that without enthusiasm, life becomes mere drudgery, a mere burden to be borne. Without enthusiasm, nothing can be achieved.[334] This is a great saying, and it is also true of *prīti*. The experience of *prīti* in fact marks a turning point of spiritual life. Perhaps it is significant that *prīti* is the middle *bodhyaṅga*.

I'll deal with the remaining *bodhyaṅgas* rather more briefly. Fifthly, comes *praśrabdhi*, which means peace. *Praśrabdhi* is what we experience when a certain element of the excitement that is in *prīti* dies down. It is not a lower state than *prīti*, but a higher state, a state of peace that transcends even *prīti*. Then sixthly, comes *samādhi*, which in this context doesn't mean one-pointedness of mind, but something more like the absorption of one's whole being in positive mental states. Seventhly and lastly, comes *upekṣā*. This is usually translated as equanimity or tranquillity, but it's much more than what is usually meant by that. *Upekṣā* represents a state of complete imperturbability of mind, like the mental state of the Buddha when he sat under the bodhi tree and attained Enlightenment, completely undisturbed by all the armies of Māra, by the forces of greed, hatred, and delusion.

So these are the seven *bodhyaṅgas*: *smṛti*, mindfulness or awareness; *dharma-vicaya*, distinguishing mental states or distinguishing things; *vīrya* or energy in pursuit of the good; *prīti*, rapture; *praśrabdhi* or peace; *samādhi* or absorption; and finally *upekṣā* or complete unshakeability of mind. If we develop these seven *bodhyaṅgas* we shall progress in the direction of Enlightenment. So, let us appreciate and enjoy the beauty of our Mahavihara, and let us keep it beautiful through *smṛti* or mindfulness. Let us make it a place where we can practise all seven *bodhyaṅgas*. If we can do that, then the influence of the Mahavihara will be felt throughout Poona and throughout Maharashtra, indeed, throughout India, and even perhaps throughout the world.

I'm very glad to have been able to be here with you all this evening. I thank you very heartily for the reception which you have so kindly given me, and once again I congratulate you all on your great work in establishing the Mahavihara, which I trust will lead to an ever more vigorous turning of the Wheel of the Dhamma.

RETURN TO NAGPUR

Nagpur, 11 January 1992

Brothers and sisters in the Dhamma, I'm very glad to be back in Nagpur once again, and I must thank you very heartily for the magnificent reception you have given me. This is, of course, not my first visit to Nagpur. I've been here many times before. When I first visited in 1954 there were very few Buddhists here, but now I'm glad to say that there are tens of thousands, even lakhs of Buddhists in Nagpur. It was here, in October 1956, that Dr Ambedkar's great mass conversion took place. On that historic occasion, Dr Ambedkar set rolling once more, here in India, in Bharat, the wheel of the Dhamma, and it has been rolling ever since.

Yesterday I visited Ajanta and saw the magnificent rock-carved cave temples and monasteries and wonderful wall-paintings[335] created by your ancestors 1,500 or 1,600 years ago. At that time, Buddhism was very great in India, and underwent one of the most significant developments in its entire history.[336] Ajanta represents the past of Buddhism in India, but all of you here in Nagpur represent its future. The future of Buddhism in India depends upon all of you. You have to follow the great example set by Dr Ambedkar. After the mass conversion in 1956 some people said that it was just a political stunt and the papers said that it wasn't going to last. But they were wrong. The movement of conversion to Buddhism did not die. Dr Ambedkar unfortunately died, and that was a tremendous loss, from which it took his followers a long time to recover, but they did recover. They realized that, although Dr Ambedkar was dead, his message and his work had to continue. This is why we're all gathered together and you're giving me this reception. It's not because of anything very great that I personally have done. It's because you're trying to continue the work started by Dr Ambedkar. We still have very much more to do. We have to spread the knowledge of the Buddha's teaching and Dr Ambedkar's teaching much more widely. We need more and more Dhamma activities, viharas, hostels, social and educational work, Dhamma publications, big meetings and celebrations, and opportunities of meeting together.

At present, I'm on just a short visit to India. I shall be here for one month, and I'll be spending most of that time in Nagpur. As I said, I've paid many visits to Nagpur before, but I was last here in 1966, twenty-five years ago. Some of you weren't even alive then, and those of us who were young then are a bit older now. But whether young or old, I'm sure we're all happy to meet again. I'm very happy to see your happy faces here this evening. I believe our local Buddhist friends have arranged for me to give lectures to you on at least three occasions, the first of them in the Kasturchand Park on Sunday. I hope to see you all there.

DHAMMA REVOLUTION FOR THE WORLD

Kasturchand Park, Nagpur, 12 January 1992

I first came to Nagpur in the middle of 1954, at the invitation of a small organization called Buddha Society, and on that occasion I gave several lectures, including one at the university, in the Law College. At that time there were very few Buddhists here, perhaps a few dozen. My second visit to the city took place on 6 December 1956, and by that time, only a couple of years later, there were lakhs of Buddhists in Nagpur. So what was the reason for this great difference? The reason was of course the great mass conversion conducted by Dr Ambedkar on 14 October 1956. The *dharmacakra*, the wheel of the Dhamma, was once more set rolling here in India, in this very place.

It wasn't possible for me to attend the *Dhammadiksha*. The organizers invited me but the invitation arrived late, and I had already agreed to give some lectures in Gangtok, the capital of Sikkim. I didn't want to break my word. But I did want to visit Nagpur as soon as I possibly could after the conversion and meet with the followers of Dr Ambedkar. So on 6 December 1956, in the middle of the day, I arrived from Bombay. I didn't have any members of the sangha with me, as I have today, or even a single companion. I thought perhaps there would be a few people to meet me, but when I arrived at the railway station I found that there were thousands of people waiting to receive me, in the same way that I was received here just a few days ago. After the reception at the railway station I was taken to the place where I was to stay. I had something to eat and a little rest, and while I was resting, there came the worst possible news: that Dr Ambedkar had died in Delhi the previous night. It's not possible to describe the effect that this news had on people at the time. Even the greatest poet could not describe it. People were absolutely stunned. It was as though they'd lost their own father and mother, their best friend, the guide in whom they had complete confidence, and at whose behest they had become Buddhists. Now they were like orphans. They were without a guide. It was as though they were alone in the midst of a dark forest surrounded by dangers. No wonder they were stunned and bewildered. No wonder they didn't know which way to turn.

After I received the news of Dr Ambedkar's death, I was told that thousands of people were surrounding the office of the Bharatiya Bauddha Maha Sabha in Sitabuldi, asking that I should speak to them. So I said I would speak to them at seven o'clock that evening here in Kasturchand Park, and that night there was a condolence meeting. There must have been more than a lakh of people present; I'm sure some of the older people amongst you must have been here on that occasion. I was the only speaker. Several Buddhist leaders were present and they tried to speak, but after a few words they would burst into tears and have to sit down. In fact, all the people at that meeting were weeping for the loss of their beloved Babasaheb. I too was very much affected, but it was necessary that someone should speak, so I spoke to the people for about an hour. I sympathized with them in their sorrow and did what I could to console them, encourage them, give them heart. I told them that they should not think that Dr Ambedkar was dead. It was only his physical body that was dead. He could never die, because he still lived on in the message that he'd given them, and now it was their responsibility to carry on the work of conversion he started, and to be faithful to the Dhamma he gave them, to take it seriously, practise it, and try to understand it in its very depth.

After that condolence meeting I stayed on in Nagpur for four more days, in the course of which I visited nearly all the Buddhist localities of Nagpur and gave thirty-five lectures, in which I repeated the same message: 'Dr Ambedkar is not really dead. He is immortal. Your duty is to carry on his work, the work of the Dhamma.' These meetings went on all through the day and half of the night too. My very last lecture started at one o'clock in the morning. And before I left, people told me that I'd saved Nagpur for Buddhism. Whether I did or not I can't say, but certainly it was fortunate that I happened to be in the city at that time, so that I could be with the Buddhists of Nagpur and share their grief, and as a result of that experience I developed a very special feeling for the people of Nagpur, and I believe that they developed a special feeling for me.

In the course of the next few years I visited Nagpur a number of times, and gave many Dhamma lectures. My last visit was in December 1966, exactly twenty-five years ago. At that time I'd just spent two years in England, and for various reasons I had decided to transfer my personal headquarters to England and work for Buddhism in the West, so I came to say goodbye to all my Buddhist friends in India, at least for the time being. I visited Bombay, Poona, Delhi, Ahmedabad, and of course Nagpur, and Calcutta, and I went up into the hills to visit Kalimpong and Darjeeling, because in all these places I had very good friends. After that, for twelve whole years I did not visit India at all. I stayed in the West and started a new Buddhist movement. In the West this is known as the Friends of the Western Buddhist Order and in India it's known as Trailokya Bauddha Mahasangha Sahayak Gana, but they are one and the same organization.

In 1979 I visited Bombay and Poona after an absence of twelve years, to see the work that Lokamitra had started there and to meet some of my old Buddhist friends. And since then I've visited India several times. On one occasion, with Lokamitra and other Dhammacharis, I toured Marathwada and gave lectures in some fifty towns and villages in that area. All this time I was getting messages from my friends in Nagpur asking 'When are you going to visit us?' For various reasons I didn't think it was the right time for me to visit, even though I very much wanted to meet my old friends here, but I promised that I would definitely visit Nagpur one day. Three years ago I got as far as Wardha, but I still did not think that the time was right to come to Nagpur. But now I feel the time is right, and I'm very glad to be here and to see you all. I'm very glad that I could keep my promise. In fact, if I was to die tomorrow I would die happy because I've kept my promise today.

In the last twenty-five years many changes have taken place in the world and in India, and I'm sure that many changes have taken place in Nagpur too. But there's one thing that has not changed, and that is the significance of Nagpur. So why is Nagpur important? It's not important because of its big railway junction, or because it is a centre of the orange-growing industry, even though the oranges are very nice. Nagpur is important because it was here on 14 October 1956 that Dr Ambedkar took the Three Refuges and Five Precepts and gave them to his followers. Here Dr Ambedkar started his great Dhamma Revolution, a revolution that has now spread to almost every corner of India.

Although I was not able to be present at the *Dhammadiksha* ceremony itself, I read about it in the newspapers. As you know, newspapers are not owned or edited or written by Buddhists, and they printed some strange statements about the mass conversion. They said that it was just a political stunt, and would die away very quickly. We know that newspapers tell lies and make mistakes, but this was surely the biggest lie they ever told, the biggest mistake they ever made. The mass conversion was not a political stunt. It was nothing less than a Dhamma Revolution. It was the most significant event in the history of Buddhism for hundreds of years. Not only that; it lasted. It has lasted for thirty-five years, and it's growing stronger every year.

The newspapers also tried to confuse the minds of the new Buddhists in various ways. For one thing, they wanted to know if Dr Ambedkar and his followers had become Hīnayāna Buddhists or Mahāyāna Buddhists. This was not an innocent, honest question. It was an attempt to spread confusion. But Dr Ambedkar had already answered this question before the conversion. He said that he and his followers would be becoming not Hīnayānists or Mahāyānists, but just Buddhists. They would adhere to the tenets of the religion as taught by the Buddha himself. They would be becoming just Buddhists. Thirty-five years ago the Buddhist world was very much divided into Hīnayāna and Mahāyāna, but now Buddhists tend to think of themselves as being just Buddhists, just men and women who go for Refuge to the Buddha, Dhamma, and Sangha and undertake to observe the five precepts, and this positive development is due, at least partly, to the example set by Dr Ambedkar. I hope that the time will come when all Buddhists will consider themselves to be just Buddhists – not Hīnayāna or Mahāyāna, not Indian or English, not Eastern or Western, just Buddhists. We are all brothers and sisters, all friends. We go for Refuge to the same Buddha, Dhamma, and Sangha. We try to practise the same *sīlas* and the same meditations. We go on the same *shibirs*. We have spiritual friendship with one another. All the Buddhists of the world, regardless of differences, belong to one great universal sangha.

At the *Dhammadiksha*, Dr Ambedkar took the Three Refuges and Five Precepts from U Chandramani, and having taken them, he gave them to four lakhs of his followers, but the conversion ceremony was not finished. Dr Ambedkar then repeated the twenty-two vows, and having done so, he gave them to his followers. Only then was the conversion ceremony complete. These twenty-two vows were drawn up especially for the occasion by Dr Ambedkar himself, but why did he draw them up? Dr Ambedkar was not just a student of Buddhism. He was also a student of history, and as a student of history he was well aware that Buddhism had flourished in India for a thousand years, but then it had declined and eventually disappeared. Dr Ambedkar wanted to know why this had happened, and eventually he found that there wasn't just one reason but a number of reasons which together led to the disappearance of Buddhism in India. He didn't want Buddhism to disappear from India a second time. He set the wheel of the Dhamma revolving after centuries and he wanted it to go on revolving. So he gave his people not only the Three Refuges and the Five Precepts, but the twenty-two vows, in order to protect the Refuges and Precepts, and so that his followers could become one-hundred-percent Buddhists.

It's easy to be a ten-percent Buddhist. There are lots of ten-percent Buddhists in India. It's not very difficult to be a thirty-percent or a fifty-percent Buddhist. But it's difficult to be a one-hundred-percent Buddhist. Dr Ambedkar wanted that his followers should be one-hundred-percent Buddhists and that's why he gave them the twenty-two vows. After all, Buddhists do not exist in a vacuum. They exist in the midst of social and cultural conditions, some of which are favourable to Buddhism, but some of which are very unfavourable. It was in order to protect Buddhism from unfavourable conditions that Dr Ambedkar drew up the twenty-two vows. They are therefore of the utmost importance. We should learn them, study them seriously, and put them into practice. Otherwise the Dhamma Revolution will not be complete and we ourselves will not be one-hundred-percent Buddhists. The fact that Dr Ambedkar drew up the twenty-two vows shows how wise and far-sighted he was, and how concerned he was that the movement of mass conversion should be a complete success.

Dr Ambedkar was a very great man, probably the greatest man that India has produced for the last thousand years. Perhaps it is only now, thirty-five years after his death, that we can begin to appreciate his true greatness, and the full significance of his Dhamma Revolution. Dhamma Revolution doesn't mean just a change of religion in the narrow sense. It means a change in our whole way of life, not just our personal life but our social life and our economic life. It means the development of a new culture, a new civilization, we could even say the creation of a new world. Dr Ambedkar had a very deep understanding of human life, and in particular a very deep understanding of his own people. He had tremendous love and sympathy for them. He saw that they were living in misery, and he wanted to deliver them from that terror. And in the end, after many years of thinking and many years of effort, he saw that there was only one way to deliver his people from the hell of caste. He saw that he and his people would have to leave the old religion, which sanctified caste, and adopt a new religion. They would have to embrace Buddhism.

Dr Ambedkar did not reject religion altogether, like the Marxists, because he believed that religion was essential to human life, but he said it had to be the right kind of religion. It had to fulfil three requirements. Firstly, it must accord with science in the sense of not maintaining doctrines that could be disproved on scientific grounds. Secondly, it must recognize the fundamental tenets of liberty, equality, and fraternity. And thirdly, it must not sanctify or ennoble poverty. According to Dr Ambedkar, only Buddhism fulfilled all three requirements, and he therefore decided to adopt Buddhism and asked his followers to do likewise. And in this way he inaugurated the Dhamma Revolution.

So far this Dhamma Revolution has been more or less confined to India, but in principle it applies to the whole world. All over the world people are suffering, whether materially or psychologically. All over the world there is injustice, poverty, and conflict. There is only one solution, and that is the solution found by Dr Ambedkar: Dhamma Revolution. Dhamma Revolution means changing our whole lives in accordance with the Dhamma, basing our ethical life, our social life, our economic life, our political life, and our cultural life on the Dhamma in the sense that it was understood by Dr Ambedkar, and by the Buddha. So this Dhamma Revolution is not just for Dr Ambedkar's own followers, not just for the people of India. The message of Dr Ambedkar, and his life and achievement, are of significance for the whole world.

I don't think that Dr Ambedkar is sufficiently appreciated here in India. He's appreciated by all Buddhists, of course, but I'm sorry to say he's not so much appreciated by other people. However, things are beginning to change. Dr Ambedkar is beginning to be appreciated in the West. Books and articles are being written about him by Western scholars, and his importance is being widely recognized. He is important because it was he who started the Dhamma Revolution, and that Dhamma Revolution started here in Nagpur on 14 October 1956. Nagpur therefore occupies an important place in Buddhist history, and that means that all of you occupy an important place in Buddhist history.

I'm happy that I have been able to keep my promise to come here again after an interval of twenty-five years. I hope you will all be happy and free from suffering. I hope you will continue to work for the Dhamma Revolution. I hope you will continue to be faithful to the memory of your great leader, Dr Ambedkar. *Jai Bhim!*

A VISIT TO THE IAS TRAINING INSTITUTE

At Mr (later Dr) Munshilal Gautam's IAS *(Indian Administrative Service, later* ICS*) training institute for people from Dalit backgrounds, Gorewada, Nagpur, January 1992*

As everybody knows, India is the place where the Buddha lived and taught and therefore, for Buddhists all over the world, both in the East and the West, India is a place of pilgrimage. India, in fact, for Buddhists, is the *puṇya bhūmi*, the sacred land, and some Buddhists would go as far as to say that even the dust of India is sacred. Whether it is sacred or not, I'm afraid the dust of India, or at least the dust of Maharashtra, is not very good for the throat, so I won't be able to say more than a very few words, almost literally the two words I was invited to give.

I am, of course, very happy to be here among you this afternoon and to see this place in process of construction. As I entered, I was pleased to see not just pictures of Bhagwan Buddha and Dr Ambedkar, but also photographs of two old friends, Mr P. M. Rajbhoj, whom I met in Poona a number of times, and Bhadant Anand Kausalyayan, whom I got to know in Kalimpong in 1953 and whom I knew thereafter.[337] My last meeting with Anandji was in Glasgow, two years ago, when he visited the UK. And perhaps I shouldn't say I was pleased to see a photograph of myself also there, but I was pleasantly surprised. If that suggests that I have some special connection with this institution, then I'm very happy to acknowledge that.

To underline what Lokamitra said, I'm very pleased to see that the membership of this institution is drawn from a number of different communities – if I heard Mr Gautam aright, not excluding the Brahmins. We must remember that Dr Ambedkar said that he had no quarrel with individual good Brahmins. He had a quarrel only with the Brahmins that adhered to caste. We have to see the individual and judge by individual behaviour and conduct. Also, like Lokamitra, I was very happy to know that this venture is not confined to Uttar Pradesh, where it started, but has spread to Maharashtra, and we hope it will spread elsewhere. And last but not least, I was very happy, as I stepped out of the car, to be greeted by Mr Gautam, whom I last met in Manchester, and to see the work that is in progress. I congratulate not only Mr Gautam but all the other gentlemen from all the communities in all the states who were involved and hope that they will be quickly able to bring this promising institution to a successful conclusion, at least as far as the building is concerned. And like Lokamitra, I hope there will be plenty of cooperation between you here and our own hostel, in fact between our two organizations.

WHY START A NEW BUDDHIST MOVEMENT?

Mahendra Nagar, Nagpur 1992

Brothers and sisters in the Dhamma, it gives me very great pleasure to be with you all here this evening and see you in such large numbers, and I'm particularly pleased to have had the opportunity of unveiling the donation stone on the land which has been donated by the Bharat Housing Co-op, whose chairman is Shri Panch Bhai. We're very grateful to Mr Panch Bhai for his good offices in this matter, and I was particularly pleased to hear him say that the donation was for ever. Sometimes people give donations but after a few months or a few years they want to take the donation back. But Mr Panch Bhai has given the land not just for one or two *kalpas*, but for ever and ever. I hope we shall be able to make good use of this land donated by him on behalf of the co-op, and it makes me very happy to be present on this occasion and accept this generous gift.

These days I'm not quite so active as I used to be. I'm leaving the more active work to the younger people. I just appear from time to time, laying foundation stones, unveiling donation stones, and sometimes saying a few words, and I'm very happy to make an appearance here this evening. As everyone knows, it's not my first visit to Nagpur. It's not even my first visit to Kamptee Road. My last visit to Nagpur was in 1966 and that's more than twenty-five years ago. For most of the time I've been in the UK, though I've also visited other countries, and there I've started a new Buddhist movement. But why did I take the trouble to start a *new* Buddhist movement. After all, it's not easy to do that, whether in England or anywhere else. In fact, it's very difficult indeed, and I will say that you are all very lucky that you don't have to do it. That part of the work has been done for you. So why did I take the trouble? Well, I started it for a definite reason, and I want to tell you what that reason was because it is relevant not only to the West, but also to India.

When I returned to England in 1964, the Buddhist movement there had been going for forty years, but it was still very small. There were just two main Buddhist organizations, one tending more towards the Mahāyāna and the other tending more towards the Hīnayāna or Theravāda. Both of these organizations were based mainly in London, and between them they had a few hundred members. Not only was the Buddhist movement at that time in England very small; it was also not very effective. Not many people knew about it and it didn't do very much, so its influence didn't extend very far. So I started thinking about this. Here we had these two Buddhist organizations, and we had this wonderful teaching, the Dhamma, but nonetheless the Buddhist movement in England was very small and not very effective. But my own weekly lectures and Dhamma classes and meditation classes were very successful. Many, many people were coming along, especially young people. Previously in England only old people tended to go to Buddhist events. I went to a small retreat once run by one of these Buddhist organizations and one day one of the women came running up to me, very excited, and said, 'Oh Bhante, what do you think? A young person has come to this retreat!' And sure enough, at the door a young man was standing – a young man of forty! But young people (as well as older people) were coming to my lectures and classes. I seemed to be doing quite well.

So I started wondering why the Buddhist movement in England was so small, and eventually I came to a definite conclusion. I noticed that many members of the two Buddhist organizations were *not* Buddhists. Some of them were Christians, belonging to various sects. Others had no particular religious belief. They were just students of comparative religion, or interested in Buddhist art or Buddhist history. I also noticed that some of the most important office-bearers of those two Buddhist organizations were not Buddhists. So it was not surprising that the Buddhist movement in England was so small and ineffective. A religious movement will only grow if you put all your energy into it, and you will put all your energy into it only if you really believe in it, only if you're inspired by it. How can a Buddhist organization be successful if it is run by people who do not really believe in or practise Buddhism? So I concluded that a new Buddhist movement was needed in England – a movement that would be run by Buddhists, and indeed consist entirely of Buddhists. So I decided to start the FWBO and WBO – what we call in India the TBMSG and TBM.

But there was still a very important question to answer. I decided to start a movement that consisted entirely of Buddhists, but who was a Buddhist? I thought about this quite a lot and consulted the Buddhist scriptures, and in the end the answer became more and more clear. A Buddhist was one who went for Refuge to the Buddha, Dhamma, and Sangha, and who observed five or ten precepts. A Buddhist was one who took *Dhammadiksha*. We call it *Dhammadiksha* but really we should call it Buddha, Dhamma, and Sangha *diksha*, or Triratna *diksha*. When I started the Western Buddhist Order, I started it by giving people the Three Refuges and the ten precepts. The *pañcasīla*, five precepts, essentially cover only action and speech, although the fifth precept is about mindfulness, but the ten precepts cover action of body, speech, and also mind. Giving the Three Refuges and the ten precepts was how I started our Order. Nobody could join it by filling in a membership form or paying a subscription, even if they paid a lakh of rupees. They could join it only by going for Refuge to the Buddha, the Dhamma, and the Sangha, only by being, or becoming, a Buddhist. In other words, I did not start another Buddhist organization or *sabha*, but a Buddhist spiritual community or sangha.

Some people think that the sangha means just the *bhikkhu* sangha. They think that only *bhikkhus* are real Buddhists and that if you want to be a Buddhist you have to become a *bhikkhu*. But this is a very big mistake. The sangha, the *mahāsaṅgha*, consists of all those who go for Refuge to the Buddha, the Dhamma, and the Sangha, all those who observe the five precepts or the ten precepts. It doesn't matter whether you live at home with your family and have a regular job or live in a vihara and spend all your time meditating. The important thing is that you go for Refuge, that you are a Buddhist. Everything else is secondary. The great difference is not between the *bhikkhu* and the layman, but between one who has gone for Refuge and one who has *not* gone for Refuge. Now it's not easy to go for Refuge, it's not easy to be a Buddhist. It's not easy to be a member of the sangha – in fact it's very difficult. It's not just a question of saying *Buddhaṃ saraṇaṃ gacchāmi* or declaring, 'I am a Buddhist.' It's very much more than that. As Dr Ambedkar himself said on the occasion of the great mass conversion in 1956, Buddhism is very difficult to practise. We should not forget those words. Dr Ambedkar knew very well what he was saying. He'd studied Buddhism very deeply. He had compared it with other religions and come to the conclusion that it was the best religion for his people. But he also realized that because it was the best, it was very difficult to practise, so he gave his people on the occasion of the mass conversion this solemn warning: Buddhism is a religion that is very difficult to practise. But fortunately we don't have to practise Buddhism all at once. There are many different levels of practice, many different levels of Going for Refuge. On this occasion, I'm going to mention just three different levels of Going for Refuge, because these are the ones that concern all of us.

The first level of Going for Refuge that I want to mention is what I call provisional or cultural Going for Refuge. In this case you happen to be born in a Buddhist country, maybe in Sri Lanka, Thailand, or Japan, or at least into a Buddhist environment. Perhaps your family, or someone in your family, is Buddhist. Two or three years ago in London, I had to go to the dentist and the dentist was a young lady from Malaysia. In between the work she was doing on my teeth, she asked me if I was Buddhist. I said I was, and she was very pleased to hear that. So I asked her, 'Well, what about you? Are you a Buddhist?' So she said, 'Well, no – but my grandmother is!' In Buddhist countries there are many people like that. They are not Buddhist, but at least their grandmother (or whoever) is Buddhist, so sometimes they think they are Buddhist too. Many people are born into Buddhism in this sort of way. They take part in Buddhist ceremonies and festivals. Sometimes they even shave their heads or wear yellow robes. But they don't take it very seriously. They don't try to *understand* Buddhism. This is what I call provisional Going for Refuge. This is the first level.[338]

The second level is what I call effective Going for Refuge. This means you think very seriously about the significance of Going for Refuge. You think very seriously about the significance of Going for Refuge to the Buddha. You ask yourself, 'Who was the Buddha? What does the word Buddha mean?' And in the same way, you think very seriously about the significance of Going for Refuge to the Dhamma. You ask yourself what the word Dhamma means. Does it mean the same thing as it means in your old religion? And you think very seriously about the significance of Going for Refuge to the Sangha. You understand that sangha is not *sabha*, not just an organization. And you make a serious effort to practise the five or ten precepts. In other words, on the level of effective Going for Refuge, you put all your energy into being a Buddhist. You take it very seriously. You decide that Buddhism is the most important thing in your life, and you act on that decision. You put it into operation. You actually practise it.

Then, thirdly and lastly, I want to mention what I call Real Going for Refuge. This is the Going for Refuge of the great disciples of the Buddha like Śāriputra and Maudgalyāyana. In the case of these great disciples, a higher, transcendental wisdom has arisen. In the case of those on the second level, the level of effective Going for Refuge, this transcendental wisdom has *not* arisen, so a person on this second level may sometimes slip back, make mistakes. But on the third level, on the level of Real Going for Refuge, you don't slip back or make mistakes. You go forward all the time until you reach *bodhi* or Enlightenment.

In our new Buddhist movement, particular importance is attached to passing from provisional to effective Going for Refuge. Provisional Going for Refuge is not enough. At the least, there must be effective Going for Refuge. One who reaches and maintains that level more or less consistently is known in our movement as a Dhammachari or Dhammacharini. Some of them live at home with their families and work part-time for the Dhamma. Others live in spiritual communities and work for the Dhamma full-time. Groups of them work together around Dhamma centres and retreat centres and so on. They conduct a wide variety of social, educational, medical, and cultural activities. They work together for the sake of their own spiritual development and for the sake of other people, for the sake of society. They work together in the spirit of brotherhood, unity and harmony, *maitrī* and *karuṇā*, and they try to set an example to all Buddhists.

Nagpur is very fortunate because it now has five Dhammacharis living and working here, and I hope we will soon have more. I think we need at least a hundred Dhammacharis and Dhammacharinis in Nagpur.[339] But whether there are five or a hundred, I hope that you will give them your full support and cooperation in their work for the

Dhamma. The work that they are trying to do is for your benefit, so help them to help you.

Now I must warn you, it's not easy to become a Dhammachari or Dhammacharini. It's not easy to pass from the level of provisional Going for Refuge to the level of effective Going for Refuge. It's not easy to become a member of the Order. First you become what we call a *sahayak*, a Friend. You attend classes and programmes organized by Dhammacharis. Maybe you come only occasionally, just as you please. Then you become a Dhammamitra. You keep up a regular meditation practice, at least twenty minutes a day. You develop spiritual friendships with Dhammacharis. You spend as much time as you can in their company – to help them, to discuss the Dhamma with them. And also, if you're a Dhammamitra, you stop attending other Buddhist groups. And you help the Dhammacharis in whatever practical way you can, including financially. If you fulfil these four conditions, then you are considered a Dhammamitra.[340] And finally, you become a Dhammachari, a member of the Order. But before you become a Dhammachari, you have to attend special Dhamma study classes and special Dhamma *shibirs*. All this will take time, especially if you live at home with your family and have an ordinary full-time job. I'm not sure how long it takes to become a Dhammachari nowadays here in India, but in England it usually takes four or five years from becoming a *sahayak* to becoming a Dhammachari. Sometimes it may take even eight or ten years. This is not surprising. It's not easy to be a Dhammachari. It's not easy to be a one-hundred-percent Buddhist. As I reminded you, Dr Ambedkar said 'Buddhism is a religion that is very difficult to practise.'

But we shouldn't allow this to trouble us too much. The Buddha himself said, 'Progress in my Dhamma is gradual.'[341] We have to go step by step. We have to move from a lower level of Going for Refuge to a higher level. And the fact that we *can* progress in this way, that we *can* go from a lower to a higher level, is very encouraging, very inspiring. Indeed, the very idea that progress is possible is encouraging. If there's no hope of progress, we feel down and lifeless, we feel that life is mere drudgery, not worth living. That's why Dr Ambedkar stressed the importance of enthusiasm. In his speech on 15 October 1956, the day after the great mass conversion ceremony, he quoted the words of the Maharashtrian poet-saint: 'If a man lacks enthusiasm, either his mind or his body is in a diseased condition.'[342] We need enthusiasm, and this applies to all aspects of human life. Without enthusiasm, we cannot achieve anything.

Nagpur people are famous for their energy. They're supposed to be a bit fiery. So it shouldn't be difficult for all of you to be very enthusiastic about the Dhamma. I hope in the months and years to come you will have enthusiasm for the message of Dr Ambedkar. I hope you will progress from one level of Going for Refuge to another. I hope you will attend Dhamma classes and Dhamma *shibirs*, and give all possible help to the Dhammacharis working in Nagpur, and any Dhammachari who visits Nagpur from outside. I hope many of you will become Dhammamitras, and, after the proper training, Dhammacharis and Dhammacharinis. I hope you will progress in your spiritual life, in your Buddhist life, and also in your worldly life. I hope you will be successful in all respects.

Before concluding I need to sound a note of warning. We know that Buddhism does not sanctify or ennoble poverty. Dr Ambedkar emphasized this point. Equally, however, Buddhism does not sanctify or ennoble materialism. Nowadays, materialism is very strong in the world, especially in the West. Materialism means placing the highest value on material things like job, house, car, scooter, television set, refrigerator, washing machine. It's not that these things are bad but the purpose of human life is not to live simply to own and enjoy these material things. Unfortunately, materialism, or consumerism, has started creeping into India. It has even started affecting some of the followers of Dr Ambedkar, some of whom seem concerned only to raise their standard of living, and not so concerned to raise their standard of life. This is a sad state of affairs. Please don't misunderstand me. I'm not saying that we should not raise our standard of living if we possibly can. But we should also do our best to raise our standard of life, to improve our practice of the Dhamma.

Thirty-five years ago, Dr Ambedkar started his great Dhamma Revolution. It was not just a political or social revolution. It was very much more than that. We can only call it a Dhamma Revolution. Dr Ambedkar wanted to bring about a complete transformation of human life – an individual transformation and a collective transformation. He didn't want simply to enable his followers to lead comfortable middle-class lives. That was *not* the purpose of his great Dhamma Revolution. So please make sure that you progress on all fronts. Yes, make sure that you progress materially. Make sure that you improve your standard of living, but also make sure that you progress spiritually. Make sure that you improve your standard of life. Make sure that you become better human beings. If you can do this, you'll be real Buddhists and true followers of your great leader, Dr Ambedkar.

In conclusion, let me say it has given me great pleasure to be with you all this evening and to have the opportunity of sharing my thoughts with you. Please think about what I have said, and try to remember it and practise it. And above all, give your cooperation to the noble band of Dhammacharis who, here in Nagpur, are doing their best to spread the message of Dr Ambedkar and the Buddha.

THE TEN ORNAMENTS OF THE BUDDHIST[343]

South Nagpur, 20 January 1992

Brothers and sisters in the Dhamma, my present visit to India is a short one. I am staying for only four weeks, already almost half over. So far I have visited Poona, where I have seen the magnificent new Mahavihara, Ahmednagar, Aurangabad, and Ajanta, Bordharan, where I have seen the new retreat centre, and now at last here I am in Nagpur. I am very happy to see so many people on this occasion. I am happy to see that the Dhamma Revolution is continuing to make good progress, and that you are continuing to honour the memory of your great leader, Dr Ambedkar. On my previous visits to India, I gave a great many lectures, especially in the winter of 1981–2. On that occasion I visited well over fifty towns and villages, mostly in Maharashtra, and gave well over fifty lectures. This time, I am giving only four lectures, and out of those four, I am giving three here in Nagpur. (I gave the other one in Poona.)

The reason I am concentrating on Nagpur on this visit to India is partly because it is my first visit here for twenty-five years, but also because Nagpur occupies such an important place in Dr Ambedkar's Dhamma Revolution. Tonight's lecture is my last in Nagpur, and my last in India, at least for the time being, and I've been wondering what I should speak to you about. In my first lecture on this visit I spoke about my earlier visits to this city, and especially about the visit that took place on 6 December 1956. I also spoke about the importance of the twenty-two vows. Yesterday evening, in Mahendra Nagar, Kamptee Road, I told you something about what I have been doing in the UK during the last twenty-five years, about the new Buddhist movement I have started, and why I started it. So what shall I speak about tonight here in south Nagpur? What will be my last message to my Buddhist brothers and sisters here?

I thought about this for quite a long time, and in the end I decided to talk about something quite down-to-earth, something quite simple and practical. I am going to talk about what I have called the ten ornaments of the Buddhist. People are very fond of ornaments. Ladies like to wear bangles, necklaces, and earrings, and in some parts of India nose-rings and toe-rings too, and young men like to wear gold chains around their necks or on their wrists, or even earrings. But why do people wear ornaments? Well, we all know the reason – to make themselves look more beautiful. Nothing wrong with that.

It is just the same with the ten ornaments of the Buddhist. We wear them to make ourselves look more beautiful – not in the worldly sense, of course, but in the spiritual sense. But there is another difference too. Ordinary ornaments can be taken away from us, they can be lost or stolen, but the ten ornaments of the Buddhist cannot be taken away from us because they are part of us. So what are these ten ornaments that every Buddhist should wear? We already have the Three Refuges and the Five Precepts. We have the twenty-two vows, and the Noble Eightfold Path. But in addition to these we also need the ten ornaments of the Buddhist. So let me tell you just briefly what they are, and this will be my last message.

The first of the ten ornaments of the Buddhist is meditation. People used to think that meditation was only for *bhikkhus*, that if you wanted to practise meditation, you could do so only if you lived permanently in a vihara. But this is not correct. All serious Buddhists should meditate at least from time to time, because all Buddhists should practise the Dhamma.

In the TBMSG we teach mainly two kinds of meditation: the mindfulness of breathing, and the *mettā bhāvanā*. Perhaps I should make it clear that the mindfulness of breathing is quite different from *prāṇāyāma*, of which some of you may have heard. The mindfulness of breathing is much easier and simpler than *prāṇāyāma*. It simply involves watching our breathing, counting the breaths as they come in and go out. In this way the mind becomes calm and quiet. We feel peaceful and happy, we are able to think more clearly and steadily, and we become physically more relaxed.

Mettā bhāvanā means developing feelings of friendliness towards all living beings. *Mettā* (Pāli) or *maitrī* (Sanskrit) is connected with the word *mitra* or friend, and *mettā bhāvanā* means learning to see everybody in the world as our friend, beginning with the people living in our own house and our own street. I have no time this evening to explain these two practices in detail. If you want to learn them, go to one of our meditation classes, or better still, go on one of our retreats. Only a few days ago I visited Bordharan, where I had the pleasure of opening our beautiful new retreat centre. I hope many of you will be able to go there and learn the mindfulness of breathing and the *mettā bhāvanā*. Once you have learned them on retreat it is easier to practise them by yourself at home.

The second ornament of the Buddhist is Dhamma study. In Buddhism there is no such thing as blind faith. We follow Buddhism because we

The opening of the Hsuan Tsang Retreat Centre, Bordharan

understand it; we follow it to the extent that we understand it. But how do we come to understand the Buddha's teaching? Through study. It is not necessary to study a lot of books. We need study only a few. There is, for instance, the *Dhammapada*, one of the most famous of all the Buddhist scriptures. There is also Dr Ambedkar's *The Buddha and His Dhamma*, or we can study the articles in a Buddhist magazine like *Buddhayan*, which is published by TBMSG. But it is not easy to study the Dhamma by oneself; one can easily get distracted. We therefore have Dhamma study groups. I do not know if such groups have yet been started here in Nagpur, but if not, I am sure they very soon will be. In Dhamma study groups we do not just sit and listen to the teacher. We ask questions and discuss the Dhamma, because this is the way to understand it, and if we do not understand it, we cannot practise it properly.

The third ornament of the Buddhist is spiritual friendship. In TBMSG we attach very great importance indeed to spiritual friendship. In fact, the Buddha himself attached great importance to spiritual friendship. As you know, Ānanda, the Buddha's disciple and cousin, spent a lot of time with him, and for many years accompanied him wherever he went. He used to ask the Buddha questions, and sometimes he would present the Buddha with his own ideas. One day, for some reason or other, Ānanda said to the Buddha, 'Lord, I think that spiritual friendship is half of the holy life.' But the Buddha did not agree with him. The Buddha said 'No, Ānanda. Do not say that. Spiritual friendship is not half the spiritual life; it is the whole of it.'[344] This suggests the tremendous importance that the Buddha attached to spiritual friendship. Spiritual friendship is quite different from ordinary friendship. Ordinary friendship is usually a bit selfish, and may even be very selfish. We are friends with someone because we want to get something out of him. We are not friends with him for his sake, but for ours. Maybe we want to get money from him, or we want him to use his influence on our behalf or help us get promotion. Maybe we want him to be our friend so that we can pass the time with him, going to the cinema, or drinking and gambling. But spiritual friendship is not like that. It is based on the fact that you are both committed to practising the Dhamma. Spiritual friendship means that you help one another to practise the Dhamma, encouraging each other in your spiritual life, meditating together, going on retreat together, working for the Dhamma together.

The fourth of the ornaments of the Buddhist is kindly speech. As we know, abstention from false speech is one of the five precepts, but it is not nearly enough simply to abstain from false speech and speak the truth. We have to speak the truth kindly, sweetly. This is very important. If you speak roughly and harshly to people, you will hurt their feelings. They may get upset or angry. They may even want to injure you. But if you speak kindly and sweetly to them, they will feel happy, they will love you and want to help you. Unfortunately, there is a great deal of harsh speech in the world. Masters and mistresses often speak harshly and unkindly to servants. Husbands speak harshly to wives, and wives speak harshly to husbands. Not only that; there is a lot of foul and indecent speech in the world. Buddhists should not engage in such speech; they should always speak the truth kindly and sweetly, and in this way unity and concord will be promoted.

The fifth ornament of the Buddhist is abstention from taking intoxicants and drugs. Abstention from intoxicants is of course one of the five precepts. Intoxicants destroy the peace and balance of the mind, and can make a man or woman into a devil. Under the influence of intoxicants, one might commit any sort of crime – even murder one's best friend. If one indulges in intoxicants, it is very difficult, perhaps impossible, to practise the Dhamma. Buddhists therefore abstain from taking intoxicants. But even this is not enough. Buddhists should also abstain from taking drugs. In the West, during the last twenty or thirty years, there has developed a craze for taking drugs of various kinds. This craze seems to have started in America, from where it spread to Europe. Some of these drugs are even more harmful than alcohol. People quickly become dependent on them, and if they cannot get them, they may even go mad and die. Very often they die even if they do get them. Unfortunately this craze for drug-taking has spread to India, especially to big cities like Bombay, Calcutta, and Delhi. I don't know if this evil has yet reached Nagpur, but if it has, Buddhists should have nothing to do with it. As Buddhists we seek to keep our minds clear. We want to be able to think clearly, so we should take neither intoxicants nor drugs.

The sixth of the ornaments of the Buddhist is simplicity of life. The Buddha said that human beings really need only four things – that is, four material things, four things apart from the Dhamma. Firstly, we need food to eat. Secondly, we need clothing to cover ourselves, to protect ourselves from heat and cold, and for the sake of decency.

Thirdly, we need shelter, a house. And fourthly, we need medicine when we fall sick. These are the four basic needs of human life. Everything else is extra. If we get just these four things, we can live happily, we can practise the Dhamma. That is why the Buddha authorized his monk disciples to accept only these four things from householders: food, clothing, shelter, and medicine. The Buddha himself lived a very simple life, even when he was a very old man, and he believed in the simple life not just for *bhikkhus*, but for everybody. As Buddhists we should not try to see how much we can get, how much we can consume, but should try to see how little we can live on. Of course, this is not the modern tendency. The modern tendency is that if you've got one car, you want two. A few years ago I was reading about someone whose name you've probably heard: Bhagwan Rajneesh of Poona, more recently known as Osho. He was then living in America, and I read that he had more than ninety Rolls-Royce cars – the most expensive and luxurious kind of car. And this he had the impudence, the audacity, to say that he was a Buddha. Can you imagine a Buddha having ninety cars? Nowadays, even so-called religious teachers do not want to lead a simple life. They want to live like kings and princes. Well, let them live like kings and princes, but let them not call themselves religious teachers. Let them not make pretence of teaching the Dhamma.

So let us, as Buddhists, try to lead a simple life. There are two advantages to this. In the first place, our greed will decrease. We will feel happier and more contented. Secondly, there will be more for other people. If we take more than our fair share, there will be less for others. So let us take just what we really need, and give the rest to other people. In the world there are great inequalities, especially inequalities of wealth, and the inequalities are getting greater all the time because some take more, sometimes very much more, than they need.

The seventh ornament of the Buddhist is working for the Dhamma. I myself have now worked for the Dhamma for more than forty years, and I can assure you that it brings great happiness, more than working just for oneself, or for one's family, one's caste, or one's community. There are many ways in which one can work for the Dhamma. I have worked for it mainly by giving lectures and writing books, and by starting a new Buddhist movement, but there are many, many other ways. One can work for the Dhamma by organizing meetings, distributing pamphlets, putting up posters, collecting funds, selling copies of *Buddhayan*, or publishing books. There are hundreds of ways in which one can work for the Dhamma. But there is one way in which we must all work for the Dhamma, regardless of whatever else we do. We must work for the Dhamma by practising the Dhamma, by setting an example. In fact, we cannot work for the Dhamma without at the same time practising the Dhamma. If we do not practise the Dhamma, no one will believe us or cooperate with us. So let us work for the Dhamma in whatever way we can, but first of all let us work for it by practising it.

The eighth ornament of the Buddhist is pilgrimage, going to holy places. For Buddhists pilgrimage means going to places associated with the life of the Buddha: to Lumbinī in Nepal, where he was born, to Bodh Gaya in Rajgir, where he gained Enlightenment, to Sarnath, near Benares (Varanasi), where he started teaching, and to Kusinara, where he finally passed away. For the Buddhist, pilgrimage also means visiting Shravasti, Rajgir, Nalanda. Visiting these places makes the Buddha and his teaching seem more real to us, helps us to realize that the Buddha was a real human being who lived and walked on this earth.

But there is another kind of pilgrimage of which you may not have heard. You can call it the TBMSG pilgrimage. If we live in Nagpur, we can visit the TBMSG centre in Poona and see the Dapodi Mahavihara. If we live in Poona we can visit the TBMSG centre in Nagpur. If we live in England, we can visit TBMSG centres in India, and if we live in India we can visit FWBO centres in England and other western countries. If we go on this TBMSG pilgrimage, we will get an all-round experience of our new Buddhist movement, and the bonds of friendship between us all will be strengthened. So let us practise both kinds of pilgrimage. Let us visit the traditional Buddhist holy places, and let us also visit other TBMSG centres.

The ninth ornament of the Buddhist is cooperation. Without cooperation, human life, social life, is impossible. Without cooperation there can be no Dhamma Revolution. Without cooperation there can be no new Buddhist movement. People have to learn to work together. This may sound easy, but in fact it is often very, very difficult. Why? In a word, ego. Everybody wants to do things in their own way, and if others do not want to do things our way, then we do not want to have anything to do with them. But if we want to cooperate, we have to learn to get rid of our ego, or at least keep it under control. We have to learn to discuss things, to compromise, to listen to other people. We have to realize that sometimes their ideas may be better than our own. We have to learn to practise patience, receptivity. Cooperation is the foundation-stone of the Dhamma Revolution. No one is so great, so brilliant, that he can achieve the Dhamma Revolution by himself. We can achieve the Dhamma Revolution only if we work together.

The tenth and last ornament of the Buddhist is forgiveness. We must not forget that human beings are only human and may make mistakes, and those mistakes may affect and even injure other human beings, even those who are near and dear to us. Sometimes we may get angry with someone and speak harsh words to them. Then they get angry and speak harsh words to us. We get angrier still and there are more harsh words. In this way, a bad feeling develops between two people. Maybe one of them does something against the other, and that person does something back. In the end a feud develops. Other people become involved, and parties are formed. This sort of thing happens in all walks of life. Unfortunately it even happens sometimes amongst Buddhists. And there is only one solution. If we have made a mistake, we must admit it, confess it, and apologise. We must not try to defend our mistake. And if someone has committed a mistake against us, we must forgive them, especially if they confess and apologise. Only a big-hearted person can confess and apologise. So, we must learn to confess and to forgive. Only in this way will we be able to live and work together.

These, then, are the ten ornaments of the Buddhist: meditation, Dhamma study, spiritual friendship, kindly speech, abstention from intoxicants and drugs, simplicity of life, working for the Dhamma, pilgrimage, cooperation, and forgiveness. So my request to all of you is please wear these ten ornaments. If you wear them, you will look more beautiful – not in the worldly sense, but spiritually beautiful. Wear these ornaments when you go for Refuge. Wear them when you observe the five or the ten precepts. Wear them when you observe the twenty-two vows. The more you wear these ornaments, the more beautiful you will become. The more you wear them, the more they will become part of you. So this is my last message to you, to the people of Nagpur, to the Buddhists of India – for the time being. I hope you will all live happily. I hope you will all play your part in the Dhamma Revolution.

THE OPENING OF THE BOYS' HOSTEL AT DAPOLI

Brothers and sisters in the Dhamma, I'm very happy to be here today, and to see that you've gathered in such numbers, and above all I'm very happy to have had the opportunity to declare open the memorial to Dr Ambedkar and the new hostel building. I was not expecting to say anything on this occasion, but some of my friends have insisted that I say just two words. So I shall say just two words. They won't be like Lokamitra's two words! They will be nearer to two words than his.

Some five years ago I wrote a book called *Ambedkar and Buddhism*. I wrote it in English, of course, and it's been translated into Marathi by Vimalakirti. The book consists of a number of chapters, one of which deals with the life of Dr Ambedkar. As I was sitting here this morning, I was remembering that when I wrote about his life as a small boy, I wondered what sort of place he grew up in and tried to imagine it. But I was not able to do so. I knew where he lived as a child, but what the place was like I didn't know. But now I know, and if I was to write about his early life now, I could write quite a nice description of the place he grew up in. Yesterday we came from Bombay to Raigad, from Raigad to Mahad, and from Mahad we came here. I visited Mahad about ten years ago but this is my first visit to Dapoli. I found the whole journey very interesting: the different kinds of trees and the particular kinds of huts. In this area the huts are square and the roofs are shaped like pyramids; I haven't seen this in other parts of Maharashtra.

This Konkan area is very, very beautiful, so Dr Ambedkar grew up in very beautiful surroundings, but there was one thing which was very ugly: the social system under which he grew up. Even as a small child, he encountered a great deal of injustice and oppression from the caste system, and he decided that he would not put up with it, either for himself or for his people. He saw education as the way forward, and he was a model student. He never wasted time. Most students like to play sometimes, but Dr Ambedkar just wanted to study. He realized the importance of education, seeing that only if he was qualified would he be able to help his people. So it's only appropriate that in this place, where he spent two or three years of his early life, we should have established a student hostel.

Dr Ambedkar loved reading. It wasn't just a duty for him, it was a pleasure. He was a great collector of books. If he had any pleasure or entertainment in his life, it was to go and buy books. I can appreciate this, because I'm the same. Books are like a window opening onto the wider world. It's very important that we read and study, not just for the sake of passing examinations and getting qualifications, but to enlarge our minds and expand our understanding. So it's only appropriate that the memorial here to Dr Ambedkar should take the form of a library and a reading room. At present the library is quite small, but I hope it will grow, and that as many people as possible will make use of it. There's also a beautiful little garden. At present the sun is shining on it rather brightly and maybe some trees will have to be planted to give shade. But I hope that when you have spare time, you'll come and take up a book by Dr Ambedkar or a book on the Dhamma and read, even a few pages. It isn't necessary to read a lot. What is important is that you put it into practice.

I'm very happy to have been with you all here on this occasion and to open these two institutions. I know they're only half finished, but I thought I'd fully open them all the same! I've fully opened them and I hope you will fully use them.

A VISIT TO THE GIRLS' HOSTEL AT VISHRANTWADI

Vishrantwadi, Poona 1992

Usually when I give lectures and talks in India, I start by saying, 'Brothers and sisters in the Dhamma', but tonight I'm just going to say, 'Sisters in the Dhamma', because this is a ladies' occasion, and what I'm going to say is meant just for the ladies. A few men are here, but what I say is not for them. I want to say something about my experience in Poona some thirty or thirty-five years ago. In those days I used to come here quite often and give quite a few lectures. In those days it wasn't easy for me to give lectures. Nowadays it's very easy. We have our community, and TBMSG makes beautiful arrangements for me to give my talks. But thirty or thirty-five years ago, there was no TBMSG in Poona, and the Buddhists were divided into many different political groups, and even different Dhamma groups. Each of them would try to catch hold of me and monopolize me. This created quite a difficult situation for me, because I didn't want to identify with any particular group. I wanted to be for *all* Buddhists. So I thought, what to do? But then I noticed that it was only the men who were divided into different groups, so I started the Poona District Women's Buddhist Organization and I was its president. All the members were women, and they organized all my meetings and lectures. We didn't have any place of our own, so meetings were held in the open air in the localities. So I'm very pleased to be here this evening. I'm very happy to see that the Buddhist women of Poona have got a place of their own. I'm very happy to see the hostel here, and the community, and this beautiful shrine-room with all these beautiful decorations. And I'm very happy to see so many blue saris. I'm so happy to see Dhammacharinis, and Dhammamitras and Dhammasahayaks, happy to see that there's a whole women's wing of our Buddhist sangha. I'm sure that this place will be a centre for Buddhist women's activities not only in Poona, but throughout Maharashtra.

I'm also very happy to have the opportunity of opening this shrine-room. I'm not quite sure what form the opening is supposed to take, but I shall just say, 'I open it.' So it is open! I've done my duty. So you've got to do your duty now. Your duty is to come here and do puja and meditation, have Dhamma study classes and discussions, and remember all the beautiful things that Lokamitra told you. But I have another duty to perform. A few days ago, Lokamitra told me that the community here has asked me for a name. Centres and communities are always asking me for names – not just here in India but in the West also – but I don't mind. Some years ago I only used to be asked to give names to babies. At the end of an evening lecture someone would be sure to come forward and say, name my baby! So I used to have to think very quickly. I would say, boy or girl? They would tell me and I gave them the name on the spot. To give a name to a community or centre is more difficult, but in the end I thought of one. It's a Sanskrit name: Śākyadhītā. *Śākya* is the Lord Buddha, *dhītā* is daughters, so Śākyadhītā means 'the daughters of the Buddha'. The members of the community are all daughters of the Buddha. They've been born from the Buddha's heart, because they're followers of the Buddha, and take Refuge in the Buddha. In a way, of course, you're all daughters of the Buddha, but the members of the community are like the big sisters, and the hostel members and the others are like the little sisters.

As you can see, I'm getting quite old, and my memory goes back a long way. I said at the beginning how thirty or thirty-five years ago I used to work with the women in Poona. It makes me very happy that now the women and girls of Poona have got this beautiful place in which to live and work, and from which to conduct Dhamma activities. Whether you are old or young, whether you've been living here a long time or whether you're visiting for the first time, you're all pioneers, all helping to keep rolling the wheel of the Dhamma, especially among the women of Poona and Maharashtra. As you know, women often have difficulties and disadvantages that men don't have, so Dhamma work among women is more necessary than ever. At the moment we

The opening of the new shrine-room, Vishrantwadi girls' hostel, Poona

don't have so many Dhammacharinis compared to Dhammacharis. We hope that after a few years there'll be just as many Dhammacharinis as there are Dhammacharis, but that depends on all of you. I can just give my blessing. So I'm very happy to give my blessing and to wish you all well in your lives and in the success of this institution. A very big *Jai Bhim!* to you all.

THE OPENING OF THE SHRINE HALL AT BHAJA

Bhaja, 1992

Brothers and sisters in the Dhamma, I'm very happy to be here with you in Bhaja today and to see that so many of you have come. I'm very happy to have had the privilege of opening the new shrine-room, and to be able to speak a few words. I'm particularly happy that I'm speaking after Lokamitra because he has said very well whatever is necessary, so I don't need to say much.

In the course of this tour, visiting so many TBMSG centres, old and new, I've noticed how TBMSG has grown in the three years since I was last here. I thought this especially when I saw the Mahavihara at Dapodi. Today we have this beautiful big vihara, the centre of so many social and dharmic activities. Three years ago, there was nothing there. Lokamitra took me to see the site from a distance. We looked from the bridge and on the other side of the river there was just some muddy ground. Lokamitra said, 'Look, that's where we're going to have our vihara.' I thought, 'What? In that place?' But when I saw it for the first time three weeks ago there had been an amazing transformation. At night, I saw the Mahavihara lit up with thousands of coloured lights and it looked like something out of this world, as we say in English. It's the same in Bordharan. Like this place, Bordharan retreat centre is not quite finished, but it's very beautiful. So much work has been done there and in such a short space of time. So once again I was amazed and very pleased. And then, in Dapoli, there's a new hostel, a memorial to Dr Ambedkar, who spent two or three years of his life as a very young child there. And only last night I was taken to Vishrantwadi and I saw the beautiful hostel for girls. We have many hostels for boys but this is our first for girls. And it's not just a hostel, but also a women's spiritual community whose residents include a Dhammacharini. Last night they had the opening ceremony of their Buddha hall, their shrine-room, and there were 250 women and girls all gathered there, wearing their blue saris. It was a very happy and beautiful occasion. I've noticed many other changes too. In Nagpur, for instance, I was very happy to see our bookshop. I happen to be very fond of books, so I was very interested to see this bookshop, and I was very happy with what I saw. And since my last visit, there are so many new Dhammacharis and Dhammacharinis, Dhammamitras, and Sahayaks. My predominant impression in the course of the last three and a half weeks has been of the growth and expansion of our TBMSG.

It's the same here at Bhaja. The first time I saw this place was from the train. Once again I saw just the land and once again Lokamitra said to me, 'That's where we're going to have our retreat centre.' I was very pleased to hear this, especially because of the association with the ancient caves of Bhaja. Last time I visited, there was just one small building, but now there's a cottage where visitors can stay, with a beautiful view, and this beautiful new Buddha shrine-room which I've had the privilege of opening this morning. I'm also pleased to see that there are many more trees here, and I hope that more and more can be planted. So I'm very happy to see that here in Bhaja, just as in the rest of our TBMSG movement here in Maharashtra, and in India, there's been so much growth and expansion. I'm especially pleased to see that so much thought has gone into the architecture of this place. As Lokamitra explained, the shrine-room has eight sides to symbolize the Eightfold Path, and there's going to be a tenfold pyramidal roof, symbolizing the ten *pāramitās*, so you won't have any excuse for not thinking of the Eightfold Path and the ten *pāramitās* when you come here. The beautiful Buddha image looks directly into the main shrine hall of the caves, so we can say that the present is looking to the past and the past is looking to the present, and in between there are 2,000 years of Buddhist history. This is something of which you can be very, very proud.

As Lokamitra mentioned, Western Buddhists don't have this sort of Buddhist tradition. In the West, if an archaeologist finds a little Buddha image hidden in the earth, maybe brought there by some merchant hundreds of years ago, they're very pleased, but such finds are rare. But here in Maharashtra, you've got thousands of large and beautiful Buddha images, and these great cave temples, so they should provide you with plenty of inspiration. Unfortunately, for hundreds of years India forgot about its Buddhist heritage. But thirty-five years ago, Dr Ambedkar revived the memory of that heritage. That is why we honour the memory of Baba Saheb, and with every year that goes by, we honour his memory more and more.

Nowadays Western Buddhists are learning not just about Buddhism, but also about the life and work of Dr Ambedkar. Previously, even in India Dr Ambedkar was not so much appreciated among those who were not his own followers, but now he's beginning to be appreciated more. We can say that Baba Saheb was like a great tree. A tree takes a long time to grow, but when it grows, it's very big and strong. Dr Ambedkar's reputation is like that. Weeds grow very quickly, but they don't last long. There are people who become famous very quickly – film stars, pop stars, politicians, journalists – but after a few years, no one remembers them. But Dr Ambedkar's reputation grows bigger and stronger every day. I'm very happy that in this place, as in so many other places, we're able to continue the work of Dr Ambedkar. We must never forget him. We all owe so much to him. We cannot be sufficiently grateful to him.

I'm very happy to have had the opportunity of participating in this occasion. Lokamitra has already congratulated those who contributed to this work, but I'd like to add my personal congratulations to the architect, the engineer, and all the workers. I have heard that they were working throughout the night. I'd like to congratulate those who helped raise the funds. And of course I have to congratulate Lokamitra. Thank you for coming here today and sharing this occasion. I hope you'll come very often, to take part in the *shibirs* which I know will be held here. As I mentioned at the beginning, this is the last public programme that I shall be attending in India on this visit. So I'd like to conclude with my very heartfelt *Jai Bhim!* to you all.

BHAJA SHRINE DEDICATION, ORDER CONVENTION

Bhaja, 1992

Dhammacharis and Dhammacharinis, Lokamitra mentioned that there are some cultural differences between England and India. One of those differences is that in India people like to receive words of advice. Wherever I go, people ask me to give them some words of advice, and it's been suggested that I might like to give two words of advice on this occasion. But in the last forty years, I've given millions of words of advice on so many occasions, in so many lectures, so many seminars, and I don't really have any more advice to give. I think it was also expected that I might have some suggestions or even criticisms after my tour, but I don't have any at all. Lokamitra has apologised more than once that so many buildings were not finished, but I didn't see it like that. I didn't think that the buildings had been finished late; I thought that perhaps I had come too early! Last year, quite suddenly, I said to Lokamitra, 'I'm coming in January', so he had to get on with things very quickly. He and others have done very well in getting things as advanced as this and I am very satisfied with the tour I've had during the last month, and very pleased to see the way in which people are working and how the whole of Dr Ambedkar's Dhamma Revolution is progressing, both spiritually and materially. Thirty or thirty-five years ago, when I gave lectures in Maharashtra, especially in the villages, people would come wearing rags. Some of you can remember that, I think. But in our meetings this time, people could afford to be better dressed. Thirty or thirty-five years ago, we never saw a single camera in our meetings, but nowadays everybody seems to have one, which shows that people are now more prosperous. I'm very pleased to see that too.

Nonetheless, in one of my lectures in Nagpur I struck a note of warning. I stressed the importance of simplicity of life. Material things are important, but spiritual things are more important. We must be very careful that we don't make the acquisition of material things an end in itself. It's very important that Order members should lead a simple life and thus set an example to the whole Buddhist movement. Also, it's very important that whatever we do for the movement, even if we work in an office for TBMSG or Bahujan Hitay, it must be done on the basis of *dāna*. We must always work from the basis of a positive mental state and we must work together, we must cooperate, we must start to make a spiritual community. We must cultivate spiritual friendship. If any personal difficulties arise between Order members or Dhammamitras, they must be resolved as quickly as possible. The longer we leave them, the more difficult they will be to resolve. So if a difficulty arises today, resolve it today, or at the very least, tomorrow. Don't let it carry on month after month and year after year.

Also, we mustn't forget the villages. Many of you, I know, go into the villages, doing Dhamma work, giving lectures, and so on. In India the majority of people still live in villages, so a very high percentage of the followers of Dr Ambedkar still live in the villages. So we must carry the Dhamma to them. We must make sure that they're able to go on *shibirs*, and if necessary we must help them socially too. Even though our activities may be centred in the cities, we must go out continually into the villages and spread our publications there. I would like to see more and more publications in Marathi, and in all the twenty-two official languages. I was even thinking that perhaps I should write something specially for translation into Indian languages. So far all my books have been written for Western Buddhists, but perhaps I should write something especially for Indian Order members.[345] You have some very good translators. I'm very pleased with what has been done so far and I want more and more to be done. So when I get back to England, I shall be keeping an eye on this aspect of our activities.

There are many ways of giving advice, some direct and some indirect. Maybe I've given just one or two words of *indirect* advice. I hope that that will be acceptable. I've already spoken more than two words, but I have one word more to say, and that is about Ratnaketu's banner of victory. You may be wondering, what is a banner of victory? In Tibetan Buddhism they usually erect them on the roof of a vihara and they represent the victory of the Dhamma over the whole world, and they make them very, very beautifully, so Ratnaketu has taken that as a model. His banner of victory, like some other things, is not quite finished. By this time I am quite used to opening and blessing things that are not quite finished! Here in front of me is the jewel which is going to go on top. I should also mention that although Ratnaketu has been responsible for this project, he's had a lot of help from Dhammacharini Vajramala in London, who has done a lot of the actual stitching. But the main responsibility has been Ratnaketu's, and he's brought it all the way from London. How he got it through Customs I don't know! From Bhaja, Ratnaketu's going to take it to Kalimpong, to the Indo-Tibetan Buddhist Cultural Institute school which was founded by Dhardo Rimpoche. I believe he's going to erect it on the roof of the school building in memory of Dhardo Rimpoche. So we're going to send him on his way with that. I'm going to chant some verses of blessing. I think we're all going to hold the banner, and then we're going to shout *sadhu!* three times and throw flowers.

INTERVIEW WITH NAGABODHI

Published in Golden Drum *no. 25 (May–July 1992)*

Is it your impression that the material condition of the Indian Buddhist community has improved since the late 1960s? If so, has this altered people's attitudes to the Dharma?

I noticed as a general feature that people do seem more prosperous in India, but the greater prosperity is not evenly distributed. This applies, on a smaller scale, among the Buddhists. Buddhists as a whole are more prosperous, in the sense that there's more money in the Buddhist community – this was apparent, among other things, in the kind of gifts I was given – but again, it's not very evenly distributed.

I have been a bit concerned lest Buddhists generally – not so much those involved with TBMSG – in the process of raising their standard of living, should just forget about the Dharma. In my lectures, in effect, I was warning against the 'bourgeoisification' of the Buddhist movement. I spoke about the importance of *quality* of life as well as standard of living. And I also urged the relatively better-off among the Buddhists not to forget the poorer and less privileged in the villages and in the slums in the cities.

I think that outside our own movement there are quite a few followers of Dr Ambedkar, in government service and so on, who are quite satisfied with their middle-class position, and in some cases do not want to acknowledge their connection with the ex-Untouchable community and therefore with Dr Ambedkar and Buddhism. This is what I had in mind. I wasn't referring to people within our own Movement, though there's always the possibility that they might eventually be affected by this trend. Certainly in the case of those I came into contact with their faith and devotion is greater than it ever was.

I was wondering about the atmosphere at the public programmes – compared with the atmosphere you used to experience in the old days ...
Perhaps there was a certain edge before, but it was an edge of desperation, you could say. It is not a bad thing that that edge of desperation is no longer there. But there is no doubt about the level of devotion and commitment.

Given that Indian society is so very different to what we are familiar with in the West, particular approaches in terms of the Buddhist movement are required. Could I ask you about family life? When I first went to India at the time of your visit in 1979, I remember you commenting that certain aspects of Indian family life were very positive. You were even slightly concerned that a Western influence might be detrimental. You seemed quite concerned that our Buddhist movement in India shouldn't undermine the positive elements of Indian society such as the extended family, and even arranged marriages. Is that something that you would still maintain?
As regards the extended family, as compared with the nuclear family, I think my impressions or opinions have been confirmed. It is quite noticeable that Order members – for instance – who belong to extended families in some respects have an easier time than those who belong to nuclear families, for the obvious reason that if they just have a nuclear family of wife plus two or three children, or perhaps in some cases no children at all, then if they go out very much, well, the wife is left alone. That isn't so in the case of the extended family, and it would seem that male Order members who are living in extended families are much less likely to experience tensions in their married life. That's not to say that there are never any problems in extended families. But I think that things are probably easier for an Order member living in an extended family.

It does seem, as people become better off, with a certain amount of mobility and more secure jobs, that the nuclear family is becoming more common.
I think there is a trend towards the nuclear family; also there's a definite trend towards family limitation, and of course within the Buddhist

community there's no 'ideological bar' to that. But I continue to hold the view that, in the Indian situation at least, the extended family – perhaps I should say a moderately extended family – is more viable than a really *nuclear* nuclear family.

Would you extend that to the idea of arranged marriages?
Again, the trend is somewhat in the direction of 'love marriages'. It's a trend in the society, especially in middle class society. But I don't think it has as yet affected the majority of Indian people, especially those living in the villages. I think I can still say that, so far as I can see, and bearing in mind the conditions of Indian society, that at the very least, the arranged marriage works as well as the 'love marriage'. Nowadays there's often a sort of compromise between the two. The 'boy' and the 'girl' – as they often call them, and which sometimes they are – do sometimes have at least the freedom to meet and exchange a few words before the actual marriage. Of course I'm well aware that within our Movement we've rather marginalized the marriage ceremony, but that may not have happened in the wider ex-Untouchable Buddhist community outside TBMSG.

When you say marginalized …
Well, immediately after the 1956 mass conversion the main Buddhist ceremony was the Buddhist wedding. At one time I used to get scores and scores of requests to perform the wedding ceremony. And they wanted it to be as lavish as possible, partly for positive social reasons, *vis-à-vis* caste Hindus, but it did come very much to occupy the centre of the stage. Two or three years after the conversion they were wanting to celebrate weddings on Wesak day [the anniversary of the Buddha's Enlightenment], and I had to refuse. Within the Movement that just doesn't happen. There are weddings, but they are smaller, quieter affairs. But there's still I think pressure for a reasonably lavish wedding.

In the West you've put a lot of effort into campaigning against the romantic ideal and our tendency to make an undue emotional investment in our sexual relationships. Would it be a hazard for Indian Buddhist society if they were to move away from their traditions?
I think obviously so.

What feelings do you have about the place of women in the Buddhist movement at the moment?
I think they could do a lot more. I think there are some women who are very capable and potentially capable. But in the context of TBMSG the whole thing is held back by the lack of women Order members. They do have the facility at Vishrantwadi now. This is a girls' hostel, but there is also a women's community, some members of which run the hostel. It has already become a focal point for women. I opened their shrine-room while I was there. It's a magnificent room at the top of the building, and there were 250 women present, all quite comfortably seated. They hold study groups there, and so on. Clearly they now have a centre, so I want to push quite hard for four or five Indian women to be ordained next year. Lokamitra thinks they could be ready, but they need some help from this end [i.e. from England]. The male Order members can only do so much. Lokamitra already does quite a bit, but he can't do everything.

Would you envisage, in the very long term, taking into account the way the Order has developed in the West, a women's wing with separate retreat centres and a separate ordination process?
I think it's even more necessary in India than here. We can see that, here, having their own independent retreat centre has given a good boost to the women's self-confidence. That would be even more the case in India.

The Buddhist movement is, I think it's fair to say, to a large extent urban. Ambedkar himself encouraged people to leave the villages and saw the move to the city as a way of escaping the oppressions of village life. Do you see our Movement going back into the villages, or is it always going to be city-based?
Well, the whole trend is away from the villages and into the cities. I'm not quite sure what we can actually do, so to speak, in the villages, except on a very small scale. But there are a few Order members who go, perhaps even quite systematically, from village to village, and they do give talks and discuss things with people. I heard of one Order member who had actually covered about 500 villages!

That harks back to the traditional Buddhist style.
Right. I emphasized in one of my talks that we should not forget the villages. I certainly encouraged individual Order members to engage in

that kind of work. I hadn't realized quite how much work had been done particularly in the Konkan region in that way.

I guess one of the elements that would be in the mind of an ex-Untouchable considering conversion to Buddhism would be: 'Will I be able to marry my daughter to a Buddhist?' I get the impression that that's something the Muslims have always made a very strong feature of. When someone converts to Islam, they become part of that homogenous community, whereas clearly the Christians have maintained caste.
Yes, I read a very striking instance of that as regards Muslims in a magazine. I think it was in the Punjab, during the Partition period, that a Sikh was chased and captured by Muslims and tortured until he agreed to become a Muslim. So he was made a Muslim. He was even circumcised. They gave him a terrible time. But as soon as he became a Muslim he was their brother. And when one Muslim just happened to use a word of abuse to him another Muslim said, 'No, you can't do that – he's a Muslim.' Instantly, almost, there was that switchover. This is a very strong feature of Islam. And, yes, he could marry any Muslim's daughter.

That way of fully recognizing that someone has really joined the Buddhist community – is that something we should perhaps be introducing into our Movement?
I think we should – not just on a communal basis, but as a recognition that someone else has decided to bring about certain changes in their life.

With regard to India's political life, you've lectured in the past on the importance of the secular state, and this was something Ambedkar felt very strongly about. Do you see the secular state as being a practical proposition in modern India?
I see it as more necessary than ever. I think if the Hindu political parties gain in strength, there's sure to be a reaction, at least from the Sikhs, possibly even from the Christians.

People who criticise the notion of the secular state often tend to talk of it in terms of it being a grafted Western idea that is not naturally at home in Indian society. How would you respond to that?
Well, I would say it is a Western idea, but even assuming it is, it is still indispensable to the survival of India as we know it.

What do you actually mean by the term 'secular state'? Do you mean an absence of religion?
I don't mean an absence of religion. There should be complete religious freedom. But the state, as such, would not support exclusively any one particular faith.

Should it support all faiths?
I think that it should not support at all, in the sense of financing – except to the extent to which it came under the heading of archaeology or something like that.

One of the areas in which religion and the state do overlap to a considerable extent is that of education. Do you feel that schools which have a particular religious flavour should be encouraged or discouraged? Obviously there are a lot of Christian missionary schools.
I think that in the present climate in India, their tendency cannot but be divisive.

But to take that into our own work: we have our hostels, and there are the beginnings of some schools. Would you extend those thoughts in that direction as well?
Well, our hostels are open to all; they are not open only to Buddhist boys and girls. But clearly they have a Buddhist flavour. I would hope that the Buddhist flavour was not in any way comparable, in terms of divisive potential, to the religious elements in other schools. That really follows from the very nature of Buddhism itself – though there is of course the unfortunate example of Sri Lanka, where the Buddhist majority has not been very kind to its Hindu minority, but in my view they departed from real Buddhist principles a long time ago. So even though our hostels may have a Buddhist flavour – because all our work is based upon Buddhist principles – I would hope that our hostels or schools would continue to be open to children from all communities, and that there was no compulsion to join in with the Buddhist activities.

What is your impression of the Indian Order in terms of the sort of things that we try to engage with in our chapters here in the West, such as harmony, working through conflicts, developing our Going for Refuge, our sense of purpose?

They're concerned with exactly the same issues. I would say that my general impression was that the Order in India has grown. It's grown of course in terms of numbers, but it's also grown in maturity, and more people are taking more responsibility.

How do you see that reflected?
Well, they take on more organizational responsibility. Lokamitra has been able to hand over quite a lot of his jobs and responsibilities, and I'm sure he'll be shedding more in the future.

One of the things I remember about India was the way in which anybody at all deeply involved with our Movement was expected to be involved in teaching the Dharma and organizing activities in localities. Obviously that was very appropriate at the time of getting established. But I wonder whether you think that this pressure to teach puts undue strain on people. In the West we have Order members who are not actively teaching the Dharma.
In India, of course, the teaching of the Dharma is more necessary even than it is here. There you have people who say that they are Buddhists but who don't know anything about Buddhism and who therefore need instruction on the very lowest level. So even the humblest mitra can do very useful work. Mitras have a kind of scope there which they do not have here. Order members obviously have even more scope.

Are we the poorer in the West for not having those demands and responsibilities?
I think it would be good for people in the West, especially Order members, and mitras even, if more demands were made of them and they were stretched. As I often say, we have a pretty easy time of it here.

What makes the average Indian Order member tick? Why have they become involved with our Movement? Why are they Going for Refuge?
I think they are still close enough to the oppressions of the past to experience a sense of liberation. And having given up Hinduism a great vacuum was created in their lives and they just had to fill it. Those who are taking their Going for Refuge, or their conversion, seriously and are becoming more involved with TBMSG, are absolutely delighted that that void has been filled, and that they've got a real meaning and purpose in

their lives – not that some of them don't have doubts and difficulties. But that is the overwhelming impression I get. And Dr Ambedkar is still very much alive among them. He is still very much a source of inspiration. There's no letting down on that that I could see.

Even though in effect we have a new generation?
Even though we have a new generation. Again, however, my experience is limited to TBMSG, to my direct experience. We do, as they would say, 'take the name' of Dr Ambedkar quite a lot, because in a way everything is still very much based on that, everything follows from that.

In one of your Nagpur lectures you referred to the fact that Dr Ambedkar is becoming better known in the West. Do you think this is something we still need to pursue?
I think it is very important that we see our Movement as one movement, that its Western and Eastern 'wings' interpenetrate, that there is quite a lot of contact between them, that Indian Order members come over here, Western Order members go over there. Obviously one of the things that penetrates from the East to the West is the whole Ambedkarite side of things. I think it is quite important that we make Ambedkar's life and work far better known in the West. I think knowledge of his life and work has become a contribution, through the Indian wing, to the whole FWBO.

I'd like to finish by asking you where you would like to see the Movement in India in five years' time.
Assuming that I'm still around in five years' time, which no one can guarantee, I'd obviously like to see more of everything: more Order members, more mitras, more city centres, more country meditation retreat centres. I'd like to see more publications – in fact lots and lots more publications, more bookshops, a more vigorous distribution of our literature. I'd like to see many more social projects. I would like to see the women's side of things develop much more dramatically. I'd like to see more attention devoted to Buddhist arts and I'd like to see our buildings surrounded by beautiful gardens. Yes, I'd like to see us spreading into all the different states of India, and to begin with, or at least as a beginning, drawing people into our ranks from all the scheduled caste communities. I'd like to see us having centres in all the major Buddhist holy places.

Those are the sort of developments that I would like to see becoming established over the next five years. I'd also like to see quite a few more Indian Order members visiting the West. And, oh yes, another wish: I'd like to see more anagarikas in India – as of course I'd like to see a few more, at least, here in the West.

So there's really no question of a separate Order in India from that in the West?
Well, a unified Movement means a unified Order. It does seem that the structures which were originally established in the West are perfectly adapted to the situation in India.

WISDOM BEFORE WORDS: AN EXPLORATION OF THE *UDĀNA*

With Udāna *verses translated from the Pāli by Dhivan Thomas Jones and narrative sections retold (in abridged form) by Vidyadevi.*

On the Udāna *seminar in the tent in Cornwall*

EDITORIAL NOTE

As Sangharakshita explains at the beginning of this commentary on the *Udāna*, the original Pāli text consists of prose passages and verses, possibly from different periods, which have been pieced together to tell the Buddha's story from the moment of his Enlightenment until the very end of his life. Although the text would have been passed down by word of mouth for many years before it was written down, Sangharakshita perceives a shaping editorial hand at work, crafting the material into a narrative.

Perhaps the commentary presented here has something in common with that approach. The text is drawn from two seminars given in 1974 and 1975, in the very early years of the Buddhist movement then called the Friends of the Western Buddhist Order (later the Triratna Buddhist Community). The first of these seminars in particular has a special place in the tales of those early days. Dharmacharini Dhammadinna was there:

> I remember the seminar very vividly. Bhante was on sabbatical in a beach hut in Cornwall and a number of us were invited to the seminar. Most of us camped in a field nearby, while others stayed in the village. Every day Bhante would come to join us in the main tent and lead us through the text. I was ordained in 1973, and was really more interested in Tibetan Buddhism, but through this text Bhante introduced me to the Buddha's life and teaching in a vivid way. Also, the Buddha of the *Udāna* was living a simple outdoor

> life which chimed with our camping experience. Every evening Bhante would walk up the field to the brow of the hill and then disappear. At the same time an owl would appear on the branch of a tree close to the campsite. I always imagined it was Bhante keeping an eye on us!

Not all the recordings from that tent in Cornwall survived – and it seems amazing that the occasion was recorded at all – but Sangharakshita gave another seminar on the whole text the following year, and the two have been woven together into this commentary. The seminars had a strong basis in F. L. Woodward's translation of the *Udāna*, first published in 1948, but idiosyncrasies occasionally led the discussion on rather a wild goose chase. In 2018, not long before Sangharakshita died, I discussed this commentary with him, and we considered using a more recent translation. It was at this stage that Dhivan mentioned that he had made a translation of the *udānas* (the verses) himself, and at his generous suggestion we decided to use his translations of the verses, to which I added my own retellings of the prose sections of the text, based on all the English translations I could find, including those of F. L. Woodward, John Ireland, and Peter Masefield. The initial reason for producing our own retellings was to abridge the stories for the purpose of this edition, but we found that they added to the storytelling nature of the *Udāna* to which Sangharakshita often draws attention; the same goes for the titles we devised. I'm grateful for Dhivan's advice on Pāli terms, explanatory endnotes, and many other matters.

The result is a patchwork of retold stories, retranslated verses, and conversation woven into narrative, with reference where appropriate to the original Woodward translation which was the basis of everything that followed. Padmavajra, for whom this text is very important, and whose welcome views on this commentary helped us to shape it, told me:

> I think Sangharakshita's seminars on the *Udāna* are foundational for the Order and Movement. At times during the seminars it seemed that he was seeing parallels between the very early days of the Buddha's teaching and what he was doing.

I have had the same feeling as I've grown acquainted with the text, through which blows the fresh air of the days when 'Buddhism' did not yet exist, when it was 'simply' a question of the newly Enlightened Buddha working out how on earth he was going to express his experience in a way that other people could understand, and responding to whomever he happened to meet, whether they were a haughty brahmin or a wise leper, a woman with difficulties with her pregnancy or a crowd of little boys tormenting a snake. Among the famous stories – the great ocean and the taste of freedom, the blind men and the elephant, 'In the seen only the seen'– are so many that are less well known, some quirky, some funny, some profound, and some heartrending. Then, they were all new Buddhists – and so are we.

INTRODUCTION

In the ancient Indian Buddhist world, various recensions of the scriptures, all based on oral tradition, arose, for the reason that Buddhism spread throughout India while the early canons were still in the process of formation. Of these recensions, fragments have been preserved in the Sanskrit, Prakrit, and Gāndhārī languages, and there are translations into Chinese and Tibetan. Only the Pāli canon of the Theravādins has survived intact in the original language. It was compiled originally in India, maybe in the course of two or three hundred years after the death of the Buddha, and wasn't committed to writing until the first century CE, probably in Sri Lanka rather than India, so that as a literary document it belongs to the beginning of the Christian era.

The Pāli canon is arranged in three great divisions or Piṭakas – the Sutta, the Vinaya, and the Abhidhamma. The Sutta Piṭaka contains mainly discourses and sayings of the Buddha, plus a few discourses by disciples. There's the *Dīgha Nikāya*, the *Long Discourses of the Buddha*; there are 32 of those. Then there is the *Majjhima Nikāya*, the *Middle Length Discourses*, 152 of those. Then there is the *Saṃyutta Nikāya*, which is a collection of fragments, short sayings, and verses, some of them also appearing (in either the same form or another form) in the *Dīgha* and the *Majjhima Nikāyas*, and others quite original, and all arranged according to subject, making it a collection of anthologies including sayings and teachings and verses on the gods, on Stream Entry, on the Buddha, on virtue, on householders, on monks, on nuns, on trees, on the ocean, and so on. Then there's the *Aṅguttara Nikāya*, where the topics are arranged numerically: the one of this, the two of that, the three of something else, right up to eleven. And lastly, there is the *Khuddaka Nikāya*, a vast miscellany of all sorts of things that weren't included in the earlier *nikāyas*. *Khuddaka* means miscellaneous, and the *Khuddaka Nikāya* is a very mixed collection of texts indeed, a real rag-bag. It contains fourteen works, including some of the earliest material in the whole Pāli canon, and also some of the latest. It includes the *Dhammapada*, the *Jātaka* books, and even quasi-Abhidhamma works like the *Paṭisambhidā-magga*. And it also includes the collection called the *Udāna*.

Each section of the *Udāna* has a prose passage followed by a verse or verses, which are called *udāna*s. In a few cases the prose seems to reflect the circumstances in which the *udāna* originated, but sometimes we can see quite clearly that an *udāna* has been tacked on to a prose narrative to which it is not really relevant. We shall see that for ourselves; anyone can see it. You can see it with half an eye, as it were. Sometimes it's just mildly inappropriate or irrelevant, but in a few cases there seems to be a conflict between the content of the prose narrative portion and the content of the *udāna*. The language of the verses is similar to that of the *Dhammapada*, which goes back to an early stage of Buddhist literature, though not as early as the more ancient parts of the *Sutta-Nipāta*. So with the verses of the *Udāna* we evidently get very near to the original source of the teaching. It is even possible that some of the *Udāna* verses are the Buddha's own words, or based on them. The prose sections with which the verses are associated clearly come from a later stage of the formation of Buddhist literature, but I would guess that some of them probably do go back to original teachings and traditions and situations and represent them quite faithfully. We sometimes see two different levels of Buddhism in the verses and in the prose portions and this is rather quaint and interesting. They don't always quite fit. We can see that something has happened in the interval – there's been some kind of development, not always for the better.

Udāna literally means an 'up-breathing'. According to an Indian tradition about the five breaths, the five *prāṇas*, there are five different kinds of breath governing different physiological functions. For instance, there's the downward-going breath by which we expel waste matter from the system, and the in- and out-going breath, which is the breath that keeps us alive. The *udāna* is the upward-going breath. In the context of Buddhist literature an *udāna* is a saying, or even an exclamation, forced out by great emotional and spiritual pressure as a result of feeling very stirred or moved by something, even, as we say in English, inspired, though the word inspired literally refers to a breathing in. When we say something out of the fullness of our spiritual realization, that is an *udāna*.

Sometimes people translate *udāna* as 'verse of uplift', or, better, 'inspired utterance', but the Pāli simply says that the Buddha 'up-breathed this up-breathing'. The verses represent the Buddha's utterance at crucial moments when he was very moved and spoke rhythmically in a kind of verse, with a measure and a beat. When you feel strongly you tend to speak rhythmically, and Pāli is a language that goes very easily into metre.

The prose parts of the text have become connected with the verses over the course of time and occasionally throw light on them, though we may notice that the spirit of the verses seems a little different from that of the prose. The verses are not only more archaic in diction but simpler; they seem to reflect the very early, undeveloped stage of Buddhism, perhaps the Buddhism of the Buddha himself, so far as we know. Most of the earliest material in the Pāli canon is in verse. The archaic material in the *Sutta-Nipāta* is in verse, and the first book of the *Saṃyutta Nikāya* is called the *Sagāthāvagga*, or 'book [of discourses] with verses', and is like the *Udāna* in form, with prose sections and verses. Scholars tell us that the language is archaic compared with other portions of the canon, and as we will see, the teaching is very new, very fresh. The Buddha uses the expressions of ordinary, current speech. Nothing is systematized as yet. It is certainly a long way from the Abhidharma – or rather, the Abhidharma is a long way from it.

I
THE BODHI TREE

1.1 SEEING THE NATURE OF CAUSATION

> Seven days after the Buddha had gained Enlightenment, while he was still sitting under the bodhi tree at Uruvelā, by the river Nerañjarā, he emerged from concentration and began to give thought to conditioned co-production. He saw: 'This being, that becomes. From the arising of this that arises.' He saw how from the condition of ignorance arises the whole sequence of processes which results in birth, old age and death, sorrow, grief, and despair. And realizing the significance of what he had seen, he breathed out these words:
>
> When the constituents of experience manifest
> to the ardent, meditating brahmin,
> then all one's doubts disappear
> since one clearly knows the nature of causation.

So right at the beginning, the Buddha is located at a certain place in north-eastern India, at a certain time, a certain moment, even, in his life – just after his attainment of Enlightenment. He has been seated on the bank of the river Nerañjarā at the foot of the bodhi tree for seven days, experiencing the bliss of release. I don't know whether one is to take the seven days literally. I wouldn't rule it out as literally possible, but I just wonder, because in earlier parts of the canon, in the Vinaya, for example, there are accounts of how the Buddha spent the first four weeks after the Enlightenment,[346] but in later accounts those four become seven weeks – seven times seven days, almost like the forty-nine days of the *Tibetan Book of the Dead*. So I wonder whether we're concerned with ordinary chronological time at all. Maybe what is happening is happening in some other dimension with some other time, as it were. It's difficult to say. The Buddha may have sat quite literally for seven days, maybe just easing his posture occasionally. It isn't impossible. In the history of Western mysticism you hear of saints who remained immobile in prayer day and night, and these are quite well authenticated. One can be very intensely absorbed and concentrated and be quite oblivious to what is happening outside for quite long periods. After all, you can sleep for ten hours, so why can't you remain in *samādhi* for ten hours? It doesn't seem all that extraordinary from a purely biological point of view. I wouldn't be prepared to insist that the Buddha literally sat there for seven days by the calendar, but perhaps he did. I don't feel the need to be dogmatic about it one way or the other. But what one can be sure of is that there was a tremendous inner absorption for a very long time. After all, the Buddha had gained Enlightenment. He had been looking for it for so many years, and at last he was there, so all his energy poured into that, like a waterfall falling from a tremendous height. Everything goes over, there's nothing left behind. It's quite conceivable that it was only after some days that he even started directing his attention to the nature of existence. Maybe in a sense that was at a slightly lower level, or at least a different dimension, a different facet of the whole experience.

Then, during the first watch of the night, rousing himself from his absorption, he saw things arising in dependence upon causes and conditions. It is quite important that this comes first. Right at the beginning, the first thing that he saw was universal conditionality. But it is rather interesting that in this text we get only half the story. We don't get what I call the positive *nidānas*, but only the cyclical *nidānas*. We will return to this later. I think we have to try to look at this whole passage imaginatively. The formula, as it stands, is very cut and dried, but I'm sure the Buddha didn't see things in that way. He saw the whole vast process of individual existence: how it comes into existence, develops, and passes away, and how the whole thing is involved with suffering. But he didn't sit down and say to himself, 'Ah yes, first of all comes ignorance and then there's the formations.' He saw it in one great flash, as it were, in a vivid and immediate fashion of which the formula recorded in this account gives very little hint, especially if we don't use our imagination. We have to try to feel our way back into at least some measure of what it must have been like when the Buddha started looking around and saw how individual beings came into existence as a result of what they had done in previous lives, how they perpetuated the whole process, and how they passed into other lives. He saw all this quite directly, in a way of which the stereotyped formula gives us only a very dim and distant glimpse.

We don't know when the prose section became associated with the verse, though we do know that it was the product of a later textual compilation, because the verses were circulated independently and collected in the *Udānavarga*, which was preserved in Sanskrit.[347] But together, the narrative and the verse create a picture, or even tell a story, of the inspired seer, almost the primitive shaman, becoming completely possessed with what he has seen and bursting out with an expression of it. The Buddha has just become Enlightened. For a whole week he has experienced the bliss of release. And then he looks around at existence and sees that everything arises in dependence upon causes. This is such a tremendous insight, such a revelation, that he bursts forth with his *udāna*.

Don't forget, there is no such thing as Buddhism at this stage. The Buddha hasn't started teaching. There is the Buddha, but there's no Dharma and no Sangha. And at once he comes up against a difficulty. He has something new to express, but he has to use the old language. He has to put his new wine – to use an unBuddhistic metaphor – into the old brahmanic bottles.[348] The term 'brahmin' here simply stands for a holy man, someone with some spiritual insight. As Buddhist literature shows, Buddhists were constantly trying to give different meanings – one might say more spiritual meanings – to the old Vedic terms, but the terms resisted, as it were. The Buddha tried hard to spiritualize the term brahmin, but the brahmins by birth would not allow it, and Buddhism never succeeded in doing it. But at this stage the Buddha has no option but to use the word nearest to hand, so he refers to himself as a brahmin. The word *buddha* doesn't occur at all, nor even the word *bhagavan*, and this may well reflect an actual historical process. The word Buddha originally had a much more general meaning than it later assumed in Buddhist scriptures. It didn't mean the Enlightened One who had realized Nirvāṇa; it just meant a wise man in a very general way. Bhagavan was also used in a general way to refer to a respectable person. There are instances here and there in the Pāli texts where the older usage persists. It's the same with various other words: '*arhant*' had a general, broad meaning – a worthy person, a worshipful person – but eventually it was applied to one who had realized Nirvāṇa. It's as though this verse goes right back to the very early days of the Buddha's post-Enlightenment career, when he was still using the old brahminical terminology.

What *brahmin* originally meant is not agreed. The well-known definition that 'a brahmin is a knower of Brahma' may come much later than the Buddha's time, but the word itself goes right back to Vedic times and seems originally to have suggested a shaman-like figure, a sort of inspired seer, or just a wise man, a rishi. By the time of the Buddha, though, the term had become debased. The Buddha protested against the debased brahmin, the brahmin by birth, but he fully upheld the ideal of the real brahmin. In the *Dhammapada* we get the *Brāhmaṇa-vagga*, the chapter of the brahmin, in which the brahmin is equated with the *samaṇa*, the ideal person, the Enlightened person,[349] so we can see quite clearly that the Buddha was trying to upgrade the word *brahmin*. In the end the effort failed. The weight of what became orthodox Brahmanism, orthodox Hinduism, was so strong that Buddhism wasn't able to keep the word *brahmin* for use in a purely spiritual sense and it was appropriated by hereditary castes. But here we see the Buddha as it were spontaneously using the word *brahmin* to refer to himself at the time of his Enlightenment (if in fact this work does go back to that time).

The Pāli word *tapas*, literally 'heat', is the oldest Indo-Aryan word, found in the Vedas and the Upanishads, for what we now call spiritual practice. It means spiritual heat, spiritual energy, the fiery quality you develop as a result of your intense spiritual endeavour. It brings to mind the *uṣmagata* or 'warmed up' stage of the path of preparation (*prayoga-mārga*) of the Sarvāstivāda system, a stage of spiritual practice when your impurities and your conditionality start melting away like wax, this immediately preceding the arising of Insight. However, *uṣma*, 'warm', is a different and unrelated Sanskrit term. The word being used here, *tapas*, is always used specifically in relation to asceticism, austerity.

'One who is meditating' translates the Pāli *jhāyant*, 'meditating', 'practising *jhāna*', experiencing the absorptions, the states of superconsciousness. His doubts disappear because he sees the universal truth that everything that arises does so in dependence upon causes and conditions. This makes the important point that your doubts don't vanish until you see things as they really are, until things grow plain to you in the course of your spiritual life. When you see how everything arises in dependence upon causes and conditions, you have no more doubts.

So here we have a simple, almost primitive, picture: the meditating holy man who has burned up all his impurities and is glowing with spiritual heat and no doubt giving off spiritual light as well, who is absorbed in the *dhyānas*, who is seeing things as they really are, and whose doubts, therefore, have vanished. There is only doubt when you don't know, when you haven't experienced something for yourself. You get the idea of this tremendous fiery energy aroused and this higher state of consciousness in which you are constantly dwelling, and becoming Enlightened, becoming a true brahmin. We're at a very archaic level of Indian thought and expression, though the experience behind it, the Buddha's experience, is something unique. He's just making use of whatever language lies to hand. There's no such thing as Buddhism or Buddhist terminology, or a separate Buddhist tradition. He's just taking the words that have come down from the Vedas and Upanishads and using those. It's pre-Buddhistic Buddhism, you can say.

And what does he see? He sees causation (*sahetudhamma*), the truth of how all things arise in dependence on conditions, and cease to exist when those causes are no longer there. In other words, he sees the truth of universal conditionality in all its forms. But as I said, this *udāna* gives us only half the story. In fact, the whole story is told only once in the entire Pāli canon, in the *Upanisā Sutta* of the *Saṃyutta Nikāya*, which alone, as well as listing the twelve cyclical *nidānas* of *paṭicca-samuppāda*, lists the twelve *nidānas* of the spiral,[350] giving expression to what I would term the positive *nidānas*. Why did the tradition lose sight of this vital teaching? We can only surmise, but it seems that very soon after the death of the Buddha, or possibly even in his lifetime, a preference arose for purely negative statements. That might be connected with the rise of the Abhidharma, but it can't be put down entirely to the development of the analytical side of the Buddhist tradition.

Perhaps it was due to the development of a one-sided monasticism. But there is no doubt that we get an emphasis on the cyclical *nidānas* and a neglect of the positive *nidānas*, although they are described as 'transcendental dependent arising' in a para-canonical Pāli work called the *Nettippakaraṇa*.[351] Fortunately, lists of positive *nidānas* survive in the canon in various forms, but they seem never to have been made the basis of any systematic teaching or brought into discussions of the principle of universal conditionality, although without that important link of the positive *nidānas* with the teaching of *paṭicca-samuppāda* you get so one-sided a presentation of the teaching that it amounts to a serious distortion.

This was rectified to some extent in the Mahāyāna through its emphasis on the six *pāramitās*. Soon after the Buddha died, one part of the sangha was more involved with his teachings, whereas another focused more on his example and life. It was from among the latter group that what came to be called the Mahāyāna developed, with its very positive emphasis. But even in the Mahāyāna, that positive emphasis was not specifically linked with the *nidāna* teaching, which was only presented as a whole in modern times, when Barua and Mrs Rhys Davids started digging into it a bit.[352] It seems astonishing that so important a thing should have been lost sight of. It is as though one spoke entirely in terms of getting rid of reactivity and never said a word about creativity. In an abstract way the two amount to the same thing, but psychologically speaking they represent a completely different emphasis. Without a basis of emotional positivity, very little spiritual development is possible, so it is very important indeed to stress those aspects of the teaching that encourage the development of positive states of consciousness, especially the series of positive *nidānas*: faith, joy, rapture, bliss, and so on. We must have a strong emphasis on the emotionally positive – not just a theoretical emphasis, but the actual generation of positive emotional states – otherwise we will not get very far.

1.2 THIS NOT BEING, THAT DOES NOT BECOME

> Seven days after the Buddha had gained Enlightenment, while he was still sitting under the bodhi tree at Uruvelā, by the river Nerañjarā, he emerged from concentration and began to give thought to conditioned co-production. He saw: 'This not being,

that does not become. From the non-arising of this that does not arise.' He saw how from the condition of ignorance arises the whole sequence of processes which results in birth, old age and death, sorrow, grief, and despair. And realizing the significance of what he had seen, he breathed out these words:

When the qualities of experience manifest
to the ardent, meditating brahmin,
then all one's doubts disappear
since one knows the dwindling of conditions.

This is exactly the same as the previous passage, except that it speaks not of the arising of things but their cessation. This is the sort of repetitive presentation you get throughout the Pāli canon, which is one reason why it is so bulky.

1.3 SCATTERING THE ARMIES OF MĀRA

Seven days after the Buddha had gained Enlightenment, while he was still sitting under the bodhi tree at Uruvelā, by the river Nerañjarā, he emerged from concentration and began to give thought to conditioned co-production. He saw how 'This being, that becomes. From the arising of this that arises.' And he saw how 'This not being, that does not become.' He saw how from the condition of ignorance arises the whole sequence of processes which results in birth, old age and death, sorrow, grief, and despair, and how from the ceasing of ignorance, the whole sequence of processes ceases. And realizing the significance of what he had seen, he breathed out these words:

When the qualities of experience manifest
to the ardent, meditating brahmin,
one stands firm, scattering the armies of Māra
like the sun lighting up the sky.

In the prose section both the *anuloma* and *paṭiloma* sequences of *paṭicca-samuppāda* are mentioned,[353] and the verse adds an extra element: the scattering of the armies of Māra. A strict translation of the first line of each of these three verses would be 'when the constituents of experience become manifest'. More interpretively, one could say 'when things become clear'. That would be a simple, non-technical way of referring to what later on came to be described as the development of insight, or even wisdom. Insight develops when things grow plain and clear, when you see without confusion, without projection, without conditioning, when you just see things as they are. That is all that insight, or wisdom, really is. One could even say that these three terms – 'being ardent', 'meditating', and 'qualities of experience becoming manifest' – refer to what in later tradition became known as the threefold path, *śīla*, *samādhi*, and *prajñā*, but put in language which is closer to the original experience.

In this third verse there's a bit of popular mythology: when the brahmin, having roused his energy, glowing with spiritual fervour and absorbed in higher states of consciousness, sees things clearly as they are, he disperses all the forces of evil, like the sun lighting up the whole sky. This is the primitive imagery of the victory of light over darkness found in the solar mythologies of all the high religions of the world, the light of the sun symbolizing Truth, Reality. The language is so simple. There is no such thing as Buddhism, nor even any such thing as the Dharma. The Buddha, out of the depths of his own experience, is just represented as using ordinary language to explain to himself, as it were, what is happening.

These first three sections have all been concerned with what happened at Uruvelā under the bodhi tree after the Buddha had been seated there for seven days after his Enlightenment, and the three events they describe take place during the three watches of the night. We get the same sort of subdivision in other texts which describe the Enlightenment itself. During the first watch of the night, the Buddha saw his own previous lives going back and back, and in the second watch of the night he saw beings being born and then dying and being reborn according to their deeds. In the third watch of the night he realized that he'd destroyed the *āsavas*, the defilements, and was Enlightened.[354] This passage follows the same sort of pattern except that it's seven days later. The prose parts are especially concerned with conditioned co-production in direct order, reverse order, and both together. It's as though conditioned co-production is the first thing understood, or the first way in which things are seen, as soon as one moves from the direct sense of Enlightenment and starts looking around. You see conditions, you see them arising and passing away in dependence on causes, arising when the causes are there and passing away when the causes are no longer there, and that's the key to Enlightenment. But the verse in this third section adds something, the routing of the hosts of Māra, a mythological image. It's figurative speech, and obviously it's the germ of what is later expanded into the whole episode of Māra's temptation of and attack on the Buddha-to-be.[355] This could be the oldest reference to it, though it's possible that the Buddha's encounter with Māra described in the *Sutta-Nipāta* is even older.[356] 'One stands firm, scattering the armies of Māra like the sun lighting up the sky.' In this verse we see the Buddha as it were from the outside. The first two verses describe his inner experience, but here we have what it would look like to a spectator. You've also got solar imagery, the Buddha compared with the sun, which points the way forward to Vairocana, the Sun Buddha.[357] So there's quite a lot here in germinal, archaic form. You're left with the image of the sun in the middle of the sky. There are no clouds, just the sun radiating its light in all directions, having evaporated the clouds. That's the image or picture of Enlightenment. There's no analysis, no concepts, you're just left with that picture, which is very powerful and effective even though it's so condensed, just sketched in with broad strokes as it were. You can begin to see even in the first three sections a great difference of level, or certainly a difference of approach, between the prose part and the verse.

As we have seen, the possibility is that these prose passages were compiled when (apparently quite early in the history of the Theravāda School) the positive series of *nidānas* was more or less forgotten, or at least not taken very much notice of. The process is definitely there in the Pāli scriptures but for some reason the negative emphasis began to predominate. But in the verses the question doesn't arise, because they don't go into conceptual details. You've just got a broad general picture. One has to read these texts a bit critically, bearing these sorts of things in mind.

One can well understand the compilers of this collection starting off with what they considered most important, and quite rightly they put the Buddha's Enlightenment first. They seem to have had at their disposal two sets of traditions – the verses and the prose – and they fitted them together as best they could, but in this case we can see a certain difference of level, a certain gap. Despite the story of the First Council and Ānanda reciting everything,[358] it's much more likely that different communities made their own collections of the teachings in the early days. In fact, there is an account of this happening in the *Udāna* itself, as we shall see. We shall see that the Buddha asks a monk to recite what he knows of the teaching (not the scriptures, for there were no scriptures yet) and he recites a couple of chapters of what is now the *Sutta-Nipāta*. So it's quite clear that different groups of monks made their own collections of the teachings, which they learned by heart, and much later on they all pooled what they remembered and it was compiled into one vast collection, one version of which we have in the Pāli canon.

I used to tell the story of how at a conference of monks, which took place in what is now Sri Lanka in the first century BCE, a hypothetical question was raised: between meditation and the scriptures, if one had to be dispensed with, which should it be? They decided it should be meditation, which might seem surprising.[359] But I think that what they had in mind was not meditation in the highest sense of Enlightenment, but meditation in the *dhyāna* sense, which can be lost. They made the point that if you preserved the scriptures, you had the guide to the whole path and anybody could follow it, but if you only had people meditating, well, that's more or less the situation that you had before the Buddha. There was access to the higher superconscious levels, but the transcendental experience remained untouched until the Buddha came along; that was his great contribution. It was the study of the scriptures that showed that there was a transcendental dimension, beyond meditation even. It was a question of either that or meditation experience in the ordinary sense, not the scriptures versus Enlightenment. I should add that when I originally told that story in our sangha I wanted to emphasize the importance of study at a time when hardly any Order members read anything about Buddhism!

1.4 WHO IS THE REAL BRAHMIN?

> Seven days after the Buddha had gained Enlightenment, while he was still sitting under the goatherd's banyan tree at Uruvelā, by the river Nerañjarā, emerging from concentration, he was approached by a haughty brahmin who exchanged polite greetings with him and then asked, 'How, Master Gotama, is one a brahmin, and what are the things that make one a brahmin?' In response the Buddha breathed out these words:

That brahmin who has banished evil states,
without grumbling or bitterness, self-restrained,
an expert in wisdom, who has lived the holy life –
such a one might rightly speak about the divine,
who is not bloated about anything in the world.

So here we have another tree – the goatherd's banyan tree. Early tradition depicts the Buddha as moving around in the vicinity of Uruvelā from one tree to another, and the eventual fully developed version says it was seven days, seven trees, seven weeks, in a sort of archetypal pattern. But it seems very probable that the Buddha was moving from the foot of one tree to the foot of another as he explored different dimensions of the Enlightenment experience. A lot was happening to him: various things were opening up in different dimensions, as it were, and there he was, sitting for a while under this tree, a while under that tree, a week here, a week there. Anyway, he's sitting under the goatherd's banyan tree when along comes a brahmin.

I think we can take it for granted that people had been supplying the Buddha with food. A later addition to the narrative tells us that Sujātā brought him some milk-rice on the eve of his Enlightenment,[360] and surely something like this must have happened – village folk coming up with something for him to eat and then quietly going away. The word probably got around that there was a holy man seated underneath that tree and that he'd been there for quite a while, and he looked a bit different from other people, and so a local brahmin, or maybe a wandering brahmin, came along to see what was happening, who this was.

The commentaries, and modern scholars, have different things to say about the brahmin's name, which is Huhuṅkajātika. The commentary to the *Udāna* calls him 'the brahmin who goes around saying "humph!"', suggesting that he has a contemptuous, arrogant attitude towards everything.[361] After all, he occupies the topmost rung of the orthodox hierarchy. He seems to want to know 'Who is this Buddha who claims that he is the real brahmin?' – though as yet the Buddha has not yet said anything to anyone at all, let alone claimed anything. Some say that Huhuṅka-jātika means 'reciting the mantra *hūṃ*', but it seems more likely that the other explanation is correct. Apparently there were other brahmins known as Susukka brahmins, and Huhuṅka might have been a corruption of Susukka. Anyway, he was a brahmin, that point is quite clear – a brahmin by birth, a brahmin by caste – and he came to the Buddha, and on meeting him greeted him courteously and stood at one side. As Woodward's translation has it, 'As he thus stood, that brahmin said this to the Exalted One, "Pray, Master Gotama…"' 'Master' translates *bho*, a courteous greeting. He doesn't say Bhagavan, he's not recognizing him as the Enlightened One (well, presumably no one knows yet that he is Enlightened), but he can probably see that there is something unusual about the Buddha, so he asks him, 'How is one a brahmin, what are the things that constitute a brahmin?'

It is interesting that according to the *Udāna*, a brahmin by birth is the first person the Buddha meets after Enlightenment, as if after his Enlightenment, the first problem the Buddha comes up against is that of the indigenous culture. The brahmin's question suggests that he is aware that the Buddha has a different view from the traditional one. Here we see what became a universal religion coming into contact with ethnic religion, the brahmin by virtue of his knowledge coming into contact with the brahmin by birth.

So the Buddha makes his position clear, though he is still having to use the old vocabulary. He says, 'A brahmin is one who has abandoned evil and unskilful states, and is free from arrogance.' In other words, he is not like you. The true brahmin does not have a contemptuous attitude towards others. He does not regard himself as the highest person in the socio-religious hierarchy. He is without bitterness and has the self controlled: he has not eradicated the self, but has controlled, sublimated, those energies that are referred to by the term 'self'.

Some translations say not that the true brahmin is 'expert in wisdom' (*vedagū*), but that he is 'in Vedas versed', which could mean that he knows the Vedas (that would be three Vedas out of the Hindu four, as the fourth was added after the Buddha's time). The Buddha's revalorization of the word *vedagū* is similar to how he reuses *tevijja*, the 'three knowledges', which in Brahmanism refer to knowledge of the three Vedas, but in early Buddhism refer to the three higher *abhiññā*s: the knowledge of one's own previous existences, the knowledge of the coming into being and passing away of beings according to their karmas, and the knowledge of the destruction of the *āsravas* (Pāli *āsavas*).[362] The latter would make 'brahmin' equivalent to how the term *arhant* came to be used in the Buddhist tradition.

'Holy life' translates *brahmacariya. Brahma* means high, noble, exalted, supreme, so the *brahmacariya* is the high, noble, supreme or, as we would say, spiritual life. Later it came to mean simply celibacy, but in the Pāli texts the word *brahmacariya* is constantly used, sometimes in the sense of celibacy, but more often as the general term for the whole spiritual life. For instance, when the Buddha sent out the first sixty Enlightened disciples, he said, 'Make known the perfectly pure *brahmacariya*.'[363] This is the Brahma life: to follow or practise the *brahmacariya*, the sublime, noble life – you could say, the spiritual life in the highest sense. It implies celibacy (certainly in the Buddhist context) but it certainly isn't confined to it.

The Buddha describes the brahmin as one 'who has banished evil states'. In the Pāli, the word 'banished' is *bāhita*, so the Buddha is using a popular, non-scientific etymology to link the word *brāhmaṇa* with the verbal root *bah*, 'banish'. 'The brahmin who has banished evil states' brings to mind a verse in the *Aṅguttara Nikāya* which says 'The mind is pure by nature – the defilements are adventitious'[364] – that is, they come in from outside. Much Mahāyāna and Vajrayāna teaching is based upon the insight that the mind in its depths, the true mind, is essentially pure, not psychologically but metaphysically, and one has simply to get rid of the defilements. It is interesting to find this anticipated in this Pāli text. Here the brahmin, the Enlightened man, is one who has realized that 'all these impurities don't belong to me, they are just excrescences, they are nothing to do with me, my own inner mind is pure', and who realizes that pure inner mind and discards all the excrescences, all those conditions that don't belong to him in the deepest sense. ('Excrescence' is Woodward's translation of *ussada*, here rendered as 'bloated'; it could also be rendered 'swellings'.)

Obviously this approach, though valid, is prone to misunderstanding, especially in the form of the Zen idea that your mind is pure, that you are Buddha, that there is nothing to be added to your basic perfection, which can mistakenly be construed as meaning that you don't have to engage in any spiritual practice. In one Zen story, Master So-and-so finds a monk meditating and asks, 'What are you doing?' 'I am meditating to purify my mind.' So the master picks up a stone and starts polishing it. The disciple says, 'What are you doing?' and he says, 'I'm polishing this stone to make it into a mirror.'[365] In other words, what's the use? You can't do it. There is no need to polish the stone. Realize that you are the mirror. Realize that you are pure already. The danger is that the ordinary, unillumined self may appropriate this perfect nature as an attribute of itself, rather than dissolving itself in order to realize that perfect nature, which is possibly why that approach – though in principle valid – has never been stressed within the Theravāda, or even within Buddhism as a whole.

We must not forget that originally these teachings were communicated by teachers to their disciples when they thought the disciples were ready to hear them. Nowadays anybody can pick up a book that says, 'You don't have to do anything. Just realize that you are Buddha.' Perhaps thinking that 'realizing' means understanding intellectually, people think, 'Well, yes, I *am* Buddha. There's no need for me to do any religious practice.' It may be helpful for some people, at a certain stage in their meditation, or if they feel a bit discouraged, to reflect, 'Well, after all, Buddhahood is there, in the depths of my own being. I have only got to work very hard and I will realize it.' But to tell that to someone who has not yet done any spiritual practice at all, whose ego is perhaps well developed and who may have spiritual or intellectual pretensions, is dangerous. Unfortunately, such people nowadays have easy access to writings on this subject and may even write books of their own about it. It is the opposite extreme from declaring yourself a miserable sinner who can't do anything for himself. The emphasis we find in Buddhism on development and growth, gradually weeding out unskilful states of mind and strengthening skilful states, is much more helpful.

So here we see the beginnings of the conflict between the real brahmin and the pseudo-brahmin – the true individual and the ethnic 'superior' – which runs right through the history of Buddhism in India, and which, in the end, Buddhism lost. It didn't betray its principles, but it was circumvented by the ethnic orthodoxy. It shows how careful you have to be when you use somebody else's language.

As far as Western Buddhism is concerned, the danger perhaps lies in our use of the language of psychology. We may try to inject a spiritual meaning into psychological terms, but if we are not careful the original psychological meaning will reassert itself. This is happening in some circles. For example, I read something recently which referred to *pratītya-samutpāda* as 'situational happening'. You can imagine this going down well at some seminar – it sounds very snappy and up to date – but you can see how easily it could be drawn into the psychotherapeutic orbit, losing sight of the original Buddhist meaning. Maybe in the end you would stop talking about universal conditionality and the twelve links in favour of 'situational happening', and thus get right away from the Buddha's teaching.

If you start thinking of Buddhist methods as therapy, the danger is that you insensibly replace the Buddhist goal, Enlightenment, with the psychotherapeutic goal of mental health. For instance, a Tibetan institute I heard of spoke of 'prostration therapy'. Doing the prostration practice means Going for Refuge, and Going for Refuge is the central and most sacred act of the Buddhist life. How can you regard it as a therapy? If anything is sacrilege, that is. You are using the language of Going for Refuge for therapeutic purposes. You might draw in a few people by calling it prostration therapy, but they will be after therapy, not Going for Refuge. They might progress to that, but it is a big risk to take. To translate traditional Buddhist language into psychological terms and then forget about its original significance leaves you merely with psychology with a few exotic trimmings, no doubt to be dispensed with sooner or later.

So let's try to paraphrase this verse. A brahmin, an ideal man, an Enlightened man, who is usually considered to be, or defined as, one who has excluded all evil, is not of a carping nature (according to one interpretation) or (in another interpretation) doesn't belong to the brahmin caste by birth. If you are such a person, you are completely pure and free from stains. You have a developed and disciplined self, and higher spiritual knowledge. You live devoted to the spiritual life, devoting yourself to realizing sublime states of consciousness. You have realized that all evil things don't belong to you – they are excrescences – so you have discarded them. This is the brahmin, the ideal person, the Enlightened one. This is roughly what the *udāna* is saying, and it is also suggested in the previous section, in which the Buddha applied the term brahmin to himself. When the brahmin comes along and asks, 'What is a brahmin?' obviously he's not clear or sure in his own mind. At the same time, he's got no idea of Enlightenment, because he himself isn't Enlightened, so he's a bit in the dark.

The Buddha takes up the term brahmin and gives it his own content, his own definition, making it into a term for the Enlightened man himself. As mentioned, eventually that was not successful because the debased meaning of the term brahmin reasserted itself, so perhaps it would have been better if the Buddha had coined an entirely new term, but perhaps that wasn't possible. Buddhists later on did reserve the term Buddha for the Enlightened One and they dropped the word brahmin, even though it was there in the scriptures as a synonym for the Buddha, because of that confusion with caste brahmins. Even now in India, a brahmin by birth will say, 'Brahmin doesn't mean brahmin by birth. It's a *brahmajāni* who is the real brahmin', but the fact that the word brahmin is used at all, however defined, helps the old system to perpetuate itself. You're much better off with an entirely new term, as the Buddhists eventually realized. Originally there was no word for the Buddha, because he represented a new phenomenon, something for which there wasn't any term or name, so various names were tried out, and eventually the name that stuck was Buddha, and then Tathāgata and Jina (though Jina was also used by the Jains in a rather different sense for their ideal).

In English translation we say 'Enlightened One', but that invites misunderstanding in the same sort of way, because of the eighteenth-century rationalistic enlightenment. I remember reading a report written by a Sinhalese monk about his visit to Europe and he said that in the course of his tour he had encountered many enlightened Western Buddhists. He was evidently using the word 'enlightened' quite unmindfully, almost in the eighteenth-century sense, meaning rationalistic, intellectual people. That's the same sort of confusion. If we speak of the Enlightened One and Enlightenment, we can be misunderstood, because that word has a meaning in English already and that meaning will tend to assert itself. There's still a sort of tug-of-war going on as to whether we will succeed in giving the full Buddhist meaning to the word Enlightenment, and if we don't succeed, to say that the Buddha is Enlightened would be to put him on the same level as Voltaire or Diderot or even Robespierre. But what are we to do, apart from retaining the Sanskrit or Pāli word? Well, we could use the word 'awakened', that being the literal meaning of the word 'Buddha'. Similarly, 'Lord Buddha' doesn't have the right sort of resonance. When Swami Vivekananda was in the West he wrote a letter to his disciples in Calcutta who had started referring to Ramakrishna (who was Vivekananda's teacher) as 'Lord Ramakrishna', 'What is this? If you call him Lord, why don't you call him Earl or Duke?' He was very scathing about it. Lord Jesus maybe doesn't sound very good, and Lord

Buddha sounds even worse. *Bhagavan* doesn't mean Lord or Exalted One; it's more like 'richly endowed one'.

There is definitely a great difficulty of communication. One has to struggle with language all the time, especially when a spiritual tradition goes from one culture to another, or from one part of the world to another. You can imagine someone new to Buddhism wandering around a bookstall and picking up this text, especially in one of its older translations, and saying, 'What's this got to do with Buddhism?' In Woodward's translation, this verse says, 'A brahmin, who has barred out evil things, is not a man of humph and pshaw.' What could that possibly mean? And sometimes terms are left in Pāli, so you are left in the dark, exactly where you were before.

We shall see throughout this chapter that the Buddha is quite concerned about this question 'Who is the real brahmin?', because others come up and ask the same thing. It is significant that this initial chapter is devoted to that question. Right from the beginning there is a direct conflict between the values of the universal and the values of the ethnic religion.

1.5 THOSE WHO WANDER, ALWAYS MINDFUL

> Once the Buddha was staying near Sāvatthī in the Jeta Wood at Anāthapiṇḍika's park. Seeing in the distance a group of his disciples approaching, the Buddha said to the *bhikkhus* he was with, 'These are brahmins coming!' Hearing this, one of the *bhikkhus* asked the Buddha what makes a brahmin, and in response he breathed out these words:
>
> Those who wander, always mindful,
> having banished evil states,
> awakened ones, fetters worn away –
> they are truly brahmins in the world.

Now there is a change of scene. The previous four episodes have all taken place in the vicinity of the bodhi tree immediately after the Buddha's Enlightenment, but now we are a few hundred miles away, at Sāvatthī (Sanskrit Śrāvastī), the present-day Balrampur, which was the retreat – not really a monastery – established for the Buddha some years after his

Enlightenment by the merchant Anāthapiṇḍika.[366] So we have moved on in time, perhaps six or seven years at a guess. Sāvatthī became important as a centre a bit later on, after Anāthapiṇḍika had presented his park to the Buddha and built the lodging – not a monastery, just some huts. Probably the original Buddhist *bhikkhus* stayed in little leaf shelters in the forest. They didn't have monasteries, so we shouldn't translate the word vihara in this context as a monastery and imagine some palatial building. We can tell that time has moved on also from the fact that now there is a band of followers. Different recensions of the text give different groups of disciples: most agree that Sāriputta and Moggallāna have turned up, and some include Ānanda and several others. Some, though not all, even include Devadatta, who was later to defect from the sangha.[367]

When the Buddha says to the *bhikkhus* around him, 'These are brahmins coming!' perhaps he means, 'They are the real brahmins, these disciples of mine.' He can't be referring literally to their caste, for we know that many of them, Ānanda for example, were Kshatriyas, not Brahmins, by birth. So then one of the monks asks the same question: what is a brahmin? He was a brahmin by birth, so he had been accustomed to the old ethnic definition, but the Buddha is describing as brahmins all these prominent disciples of his. What does he mean? What is his definition of a brahmin? And in the *udāna* the Buddha gives a brief definition. Being a brahmin has nothing to do with birth, rites, or reciting the Vedas. It is a matter of individual spiritual development. It is rather as if we in our order started using the word 'clergyman'. If a 'real' clergyman heard someone describing Order members as clergymen, he would say, 'In what sense are they clergymen?' We would say, 'They have no homes of their own, they work full-time for our movement, they meditate every day. That is what we mean by clergymen', and it would be clear that that was very different from the sense in which the questioner was himself a clergyman, because he would probably have a wife and family at home, and he probably wouldn't be meditating every day. But even if (for some reason) we did adopt this term, we might not be able to retain our use of it. Hundreds of years on, members of the Order might become clergymen in the old-fashioned sense, as some of the Buddhist monks eventually became, especially in Nepal, where they married and settled down with their wives and families in the viharas and became just priests.

They are 'awakened' and 'always mindful' in the sense of being awakened to Reality, seeing things as they are. 'Awakened' translates *buddha*, and at this time that was simply what the word *buddha* meant. We shall encounter this again – that words which later acquired a precise doctrinal significance are used in this early text in a general, ordinary way, bringing us nearer to their original usage and thus the life of the Buddha and his disciples.

Arhant is an example of a word that has been upgraded but also narrowed. In Mahāyāna literature it sometimes comes to mean a cold, selfish, individualistic person, which was certainly not the original meaning of the term. It means 'worthy', and came to mean spiritually worthy, a spiritually developed person, and then someone who has realized Enlightenment. Officials were addressed as '*arhant*' at the time of the Buddha, just as we say 'his worship the Mayor', but the term was gradually upgraded, so that the monks and those leading a spiritual life were the worthy ones; they were worship-worthy, deserving of worship. But then *arhant* became a highly technical term and the meaning was fixed perhaps rather narrowly. We find in early Buddhism as reflected in the *Udāna* that everything is quite fluid; there is nothing rigid or Buddhistic about it. That is one reason why it is such a valuable text.

It is interesting that the *Udāna* opens just after the Buddha's Enlightenment and remains in the vicinity of the bodhi tree for four sections, and then the scene moves to Śrāvastī, which was the most important centre of the Buddha's activity; he spent more rainy seasons there than in any other place. Later, we move to Rājagaha or Rajgir, another very important scene of his activities. We shall gradually see that the *Udāna* has been put together with a certain amount of what may be described as literary skill, although it was originally assembled in oral form. It has definitely been compiled with art and care.

You notice that though the scene has changed we are still concerned with the brahmin; that seems to be the thread connecting all the verses in this section. In appropriating and upgrading the word brahmin the Buddha was trying to encourage brahmins by birth to think in terms of being real brahmins, i.e. to strive for Enlightenment. This is very characteristic of Buddhism, trying to take whatever existed, whether in the way of terminology or custom and tradition, and improve it and give it a nobler leaning – not abolish it, not criticize it, not go against it, but try to lead people on from there. So here in the *Udāna* the question

'Who is the brahmin?' really means, 'What is the nature of the spiritual ideal?' Obviously, it is the first thing to be made clear. It is significant that almost the first thing the Buddha does after enunciating the law of universal conditionality is to clarify the nature of the spiritual ideal. There was confusion because the Buddha had to use the old language, so the question arises, 'Are you using the language in the old sense or in a new sense of your own? If the latter, what is that new sense? What do you say the spiritual ideal is?'

There's another aspect of the question too. From the point of view of brahmins by birth, they, as the true brahmins, were the only ones who could teach. At the time of the Buddha the caste system wasn't nearly as rigid as it afterwards became, but it was rigid enough, it seems. The brahmins, even at that time, objected to the Buddha teaching, on the grounds that he was not a brahmin by birth, and teaching was a monopoly of the brahmins. Lower castes were definitely looked down upon and the brahmins regarded themselves as higher caste. One of the reasons they gave was that they were of fair complexion, and the lower castes were of darker complexion. It must have meant going against quite a lot of conditioning for people who were brahmins to be considered equal with people who weren't. It is remarkable that quite a lot of brahmins did become followers of the Buddha; some of his most prominent disciples were brahmins. It's quite clear that the brahmins had a very definite spiritual and cultural tradition. They were the clerisy, the educated people. They were selfish as a class; among them were some quite gifted individuals who took to Buddhism, but the caste as a whole seemed to remain relatively unaffected. The brahmins made a determined bid for recognition of their social and religious supremacy on grounds of birth; the Buddha came right up against this, and Buddhism came up against it throughout its history in India. One of the reasons why Buddhism disappeared from India was the hostility of the brahmins by birth because Buddhism refused to recognize their credentials. Although many individual brahmins became followers of the Buddha, the brahmins as a caste have always remained strongly opposed to Buddhism, right down to the present. It was one of my first experiences after being ordained as a *śrāmaṇera* at Kusinara. As we wound our way up to Nepal, aiming for Lumbinī, we got lost shortly after leaving Kusinara, so we stopped and asked somebody to direct us.[368] He happened to be a brahmin, and at once asked us who and what we were, and where we were coming from. When we explained that we were coming from Kusinara and that we were Buddhists, his attitude became remarkably hostile. The brahmins have inherited a tradition of hostility to Buddhism, even though they usually know nothing about it. Here we find this clash between the spiritual ideal and the ethnic ideal right at the very beginning of Buddhism, as if to say that the universal religion, which upholds the realization of truth by the individual, at once has to be sharply distinguished from the old ethnic tradition.

1.6 KASSAPA REFUSES DINNER FROM THE *DEVAS*

> Once, the Buddha was staying near Rājagaha, in the Bamboo Wood at the Squirrels' Feeding Ground. At that time, the Venerable Mahākassapa, who was staying in the Pipphali Cave, became very ill. After a while he recovered and decided to go into Rājagaha for almsfood. As it happened, 500 *devatās* were busy preparing almsfood for him, but he refused their offerings and headed into Rājagaha, going to the streets of the weavers, where the poor lived. There the Buddha saw him walking along and breathed out these words:
>
> Not supporting anyone, unrecognized,
> tamed, established in the essential,
> with pollutants exhausted and impurity expelled –
> that one I call a brahmin.

Now the scene shifts to Rājagaha or Rajgir, the capital of the kingdom of Magadha, and we get another definition of the brahmin. The Bamboo Grove was situated outside the gates of Rājagaha, and one can still see the site today. Kassapa was one of the leading disciples, famous for his practice of asceticism. He lived a very austere and simple life, even more so than the other disciples.

This is the first appearance in this text of the *devas* – that is to say, the gods, beings inhabiting higher planes of existence than the human but still subject to birth, death, and rebirth, still on the wheel of life. Quite a few parts of the Pāli canon describe crowds of *devas* hovering round the Buddha and his followers, eager to listen or to be of service, and if you choose not to take this literally, you have to give some sort of meaning to it. It is as though there are all sorts of subtle or psychic influences, or even powers, around in the air or within the field of the Buddha's aura, and these can spark off events, or one can even manipulate them, get things done by them or through them. In the case of Mahākassapa, there is a whole cloud of *devas* buzzing around, and as soon as they see Kassapa, sick and frail, going off to Rājagaha to beg for alms from door to door – quite a laborious business for a sick old man – they think, 'Ah, here's an opportunity! We can fill his bowl by magic so he won't have any trouble and we can earn a great deal of merit.' But Kassapa rejects that; it's cheating. There's a similar story told about the Buddha-to-be when he was meditating and practising asceticism before his Enlightenment. The *devas* offered to inject a sort of celestial nourishment into him when he was fasting and he said, 'No, that would be cheating.'[369] It's as though the *devas* represent the magical side of existence which the Enlightened person could invoke, but he deliberately doesn't. He just relies on ordinary human methods and means. Likewise, Mahākassapa, being an *arhant*, could conjure up food for himself, but he doesn't. Even though he's ill he goes out begging as usual into the poorest quarter, where the food he gets is going to be of the roughest quality.

Whether there are actually *devas*, and whether they represent magic or not, the meaning is quite clear: as a spiritually developed person you don't make use of your spiritual development or anything associated with it in order to aggrandize yourself personally. Where your personal needs are concerned, you just rely on ordinary human factors. This seems to be what is happening. Kassapa rejects the possibility of getting food by magical means. As he is an *arhant*, he could come to no harm through using such powers, but he does not do so – maybe to set a good example. The whole archetypal magical realm is at his disposal, but he's not making use of it. Of course, that's just Kassapa. It's not that you mustn't or you shouldn't use such powers; it's good if you don't, but it's not bad if you do. For instance, Padmasambhava made full use of them, not for personal aggrandizement but to spread the Dharma.[370] But Kassapa is a specialist in asceticism, a sort of shining light in that respect. Though he is Enlightened, he does things in the ordinary human way.

Also, he seeks out that part of the city where the poor dwell – the streets of the weavers, who were a low-caste community according to the orthodox Hindu system. Perhaps his choice to reject the *devas* and go among the poorest and most despised of human beings has a general significance. The *devas*, especially the *devas* of the lower planes, stand for the aesthetic, for sensuous enjoyment, indulgence, so in a way it's a rejection of superficial aesthetics. He doesn't dally with the *devas*, who are only a little higher than the ordinary human level. He doesn't play around with these supranormal forces. He isn't interested. Kassapa lived alone in the forest much of the time, and perhaps one could say that he did not even care for the company of *devas*.

The Buddha sees him going for alms and that prompts an *udāna*. 'Not supporting anyone' translates *anaññaposī*, which literally means 'not nourishing another'. He isn't responsible for anyone else, but just wanders by himself. Perhaps this doesn't mean very much to us, but the ancient Indian, especially if he was a family man, was very conscious of his responsibility for looking after other people. There was no insurance, no Social Security, and you had no means of limiting the number of children you had. You had to think of people, look after people, feed people, all the time. Sometimes there were droughts, famines, wars. To be free from all that responsibility, from a spiritual point of view, if you took it positively, not just negatively, would be a very great thing. Think what it must be like if for years and years you've had to support and worry about your children, your parents, and any other relatives who need help, and then one day you hand all that responsibility over to somebody else and just go out on your own. It's a tremendous relief. In our culture we know that people will be looked after, no one's going to starve, but in ancient India you didn't have that assurance. If you left your family, maybe your eldest son would look after everybody, but maybe not. It was a risk. The state wouldn't help. The state meant the revenue man collecting taxes, not giving anything. The king thought he was doing his bit if he protected you from enemies and didn't plunder you too much.

The commentary gives two interpretations of *aññāta*: recognized (as an *arhant*); and unknown (because of humility, as though it's a virtue to keep yourself hidden).[371] He can't be fathomed. The *devas* certainly can't know him, because they are not Enlightened. The Buddha knows him because the Buddha is the Buddha, but to others he is unknown. In the *Majjhima Nikāya* the Buddha says that the Enlightened One is, like the great ocean, unfathomable.[372] This applies to the *arhant* too. It is not simply that the ignorant weaver folk don't appreciate Kassapa; no worldly person could know him, because he has gone beyond their range.

Instead of 'established in the essential', Woodward prefers the translation 'fixed in the core'. 'The core' is *sāra*, also sometimes translated as the essence or pith. There is an antithesis in the first chapter of the *Dhammapada* between *sāra* and *asāra*, usually translated as 'the real' and 'the unreal'. He who knows the real as the real goes to the real, but he who mistakes the unreal for the real does not attain the real.[373] But maybe translating it as 'the real' is too metaphysical. It is literally pith, essence. For instance, in Pāli the heartwood of the tree is called the *sāra*. *Sāra* represents the essence of the matter or the real substance, though not in a metaphysical sense. The brahmin is one who is established at the centre of things, in what is substantial, not in the superficial. Its meaning here is not metaphysical or technical, but quite straightforward. Maybe 'essential' is the best translation. A brahmin is one who is established in what is essential. The pith, the essence, the core, the heart of the matter: all these terms point to Nirvāṇa or Enlightenment. *Sāra* is a very strong and meaningful word. It rather fades out of the picture later on in the tradition, but it's the word that is used here, signifying one who is established at the heart of things, really centred, transcendentally centred, one who takes their stand on the essence of things. Kassapa is doing that in a practical everyday, almost Zen-like way. He's sticking to the basics, the essence of the matter, which is getting food, but he's also in a much higher sense sticking to the essence of things, sticking to Nirvāṇa, established in Enlightenment.

The pollutants or taints are the *āsavas* (Sanskrit *āsravas*). Probably the term is not being used in its later, technical sense, in which it appears among the three of this and the ten of that and so on,[374] but in a general psycho-spiritual sense.

So in the conception of a brahmin here, that is, the conception of the Enlightened person, we see that if you are such a person, you don't have to look after anybody else in the way of ordinary human attachment; you have reached such a pitch of spiritual development that you cannot be fathomed by others who are not on that level; that you have yourself fully under control and take your stand firmly upon what is essential in life; and that you have got rid of all imperfections.

In the next line a very strong term is used: 'his impurity expelled' or even 'spewed up'. The Pāli word is *vantadosa*: a *dosa* is a 'fault' or an 'impurity', and *vanta* means 'vomited', 'expelled'. The word *dosa* is medical terminology: imbalance of *dosa* is responsible for illness. You can have such an utter revulsion against aspects of yourself or even your old self, that you feel like vomiting it all up, really getting rid of it. In the Vajrayāna context, the figure of Vajrasattva, the bodhisattva who embodies primordial purity, stands, among other things, for this spewing up and in that way cleansing oneself, and here we have this strong and down-to-earth idiom that the brahmin, in the Buddha's sense, is one who has completely spewed up the impurities or faults. He has spewed up the whole of mundane existence, and even the heavens.

1.7 A DARK AND STORMY NIGHT

> Once, on a pitch-black rainy night, the Buddha was staying at Pāvā, at the Ajakalāpaka Shrine, the dwelling place of the *yakkha* Ajakalāpaka. The *yakkha*, wanting to frighten the Buddha, came up to him and three times cried out a terrible cry, shouting, 'There's a goblin for you, recluse!' In response, the Buddha breathed out these words:
>
> When a brahmin is gone beyond
> in regard to their own experience,
> then they overcome this demon
> and its horrible gabbling.

The Buddha is staying at the shrine where the *yakkha* Ajakalāpaka lives. So here again we get a bit of mythology. A *yakkha* is a particular kind of spirit. Perhaps one could translate it *daimon* in the Greek sense. It's not evil; in Indian thought there are no evil spirits in the Western sense. Even Māra, while he's a mischievous nuisance, is not evil in the sense that Satan is meant to be evil. The *yakkha* (Sanskrit *yakṣa*), appears again and again in Buddhist literature – in Mahāyāna literature as well as the Pāli canon. He is a powerful, almost sublime spirit, something very much belonging to the world of nature, an awe-inspiring natural force which sometimes functions in a helpful, sometimes in a harmful way. The Buddha himself is sometimes hailed as the great *yakkha* or *yakṣa*[375] because he impressed ordinary people as being like a spirit. They could not understand him. He appeared here and there – strange and mysterious, rather awe-inspiring, with something uncanny about him. The early Mathura-type images of the Buddha, according to some authorities, are modelled upon *yakkha* images – very sturdy, powerful figures.

There are constant references in the Pāli scriptures to shrines, usually called *caityas*, and you still get them in India today. Recently I was reading about ancient Greece, and there were constant references to shrines and little temples all over the place, where local heroes and gods and demigods were honoured, but we don't have that in the modern West because it's all been destroyed since pagan times. These shrines represent focuses of energy as it were, and this is quite important on its own level. 'Shrine' may seem to suggest a building, but any sacred spot was called a *caitya*. The term, derived from a word meaning 'to heap up', means something heaped up or gathered together and regarded as a shrine. It may be a group of trees with coloured threads tied around them or a few stones piled up. Local tradition associates that spot with some spirit, some presence or force, and offerings are made there. In some of those spots there may be quite a strange atmosphere.

In the Buddha's day, as still in India, there were folk shrines to local spirits all over the countryside. Sometimes there were huts and shelters there, and sometimes the Buddha used to stay in such places. In his day, the whole of northern India was covered with dense jungle, with villages and a few towns here and there, and paths leading from one place to another. The Buddha and his disciples spent their time in the open air among the trees, much more in contact with nature than with other human beings. You can imagine that the monk, or wanderer as he was called then, would stay most of the time in the forest, in a hut or under a tree or in a cave. He would go to the nearest village once a day for alms, then come back and spend the day surrounded by nature, deep in the forest. If he was practising meditation, he would become very sensitive. He might pick up all sorts of influences, or even feel that a tree was speaking to him. In the Pāli canon there are many stories of monks staying in the forest, and 'then a tree god spoke to him'.[376] It's not necessarily that in a crude, literal sense a god appeared before him; it could be that he was in the midst of the trees and feeling something coming from the living things around him. He was reflecting or meditating, and in the midst of it all it was as though a voice came to him. Even a teaching would come sometimes, a reminder from a *rukkha-devatā*, a tree god or spirit, or an encouragement to get on with his meditation. The Pāli canon is full of this intimate connection between the monks and nature.[377] It is not insisted upon or described in great detail, but it is there in the background all the time. Most of these teachings originated in such circumstances, not in buildings or monasteries – there weren't any monasteries then, just little shacks put up in someone's garden or park, or a camping spot at the foot of a tree. There was a strongly animistic background to early Buddhism, in a healthy and positive way. The monks were in close contact with nature all the time, but they did not romanticize or idealize it as people sometimes do today; it was just the natural background of their lives and practice.

We can well imagine the scene described here. The Buddha was sitting one night in the pitch dark. There was no moon; the sky was inky black. 'The sky god was raining' – that's an idiom, just as we say 'it rained' without there being any 'it' – and this *yakkha* wished to frighten the Buddha. So how can one interpret this? There's something in the atmosphere of that shrine, or that spot, which is uncanny, which would make an ordinary man afraid. There's a hair-raising sound, the 'hullabaloo' (as Woodward says) of this Ajakalāpaka. According to one interpretation, Ajakalāpaka means 'goat-cry', so the note says.[378] It's a very eerie, very strange sound. But on hearing this noise at this fearsome spot, the Buddha was not at all disturbed by these powerful natural forces, and simply responded with his *udāna*.

Sometimes it seems as though these episodes were manufactured to explain the lines of the verse, and I feel that a little here, though something like this could well have happened. The commentary gives two explanations for *sakesu dhammesu* (translated as 'gone beyond in regard to their own experience'): (1) the things (*dhamma*s) that are the constituents (*khandhas*) of an individual existence; (2) a person's positive qualities (*dhamma*s), starting from ethics.[379] So it's an ambiguous phrase, but if we take the first of the commentary's alternatives, the general sense is that when he has 'gone beyond' all the things that concern him as an individual, the brahmin is beyond this sort of thing. The Buddha's attitude towards the *yakkha*'s hullabaloo is dismissive. He is not bothered by it at all. In other words, when you are Enlightened, you can go into the most eerie of places and all sorts of things can happen and you are just not affected. Perhaps we could say that it links up with the previous section, which refers to the gods and not taking advantage of them and their services. Here it's not being afraid of spirits. So we can see the calm attitude of Buddhism towards ordinary archetypal-cum-magical-cum-spiritist phenomena. This section in the most general sense pertains, of course, to the conquest of fear. The brahmin or the Buddha is fearless. Whatever may be the occasion of possible feelings of fear, he doesn't experience them.

1.8 FREE FROM ALL TIES

> Once the Buddha was staying near Sāvatthī in the Jeta Wood at Anāthapiṇḍika's park. Saṅgāmaji came to see him, and hearing this, Saṅgāmaji's former wife followed him there, taking their child with her. When Saṅgāmaji was resting in the middle of the day, his ex-wife came up to him and three times asked him to support her and their son. Each time, Saṅgāmaji remained silent. So she put the child down in front of him and went away, saying, 'This is your son. Support him.' But Saṅgāmaji neither looked at the child nor spoke to him. Looking back and seeing this, his ex-wife thought, 'This recluse does not even want his son!' And she went back and took the child away. The Buddha, seeing with the divine eye this discourteous behaviour on the woman's part, breathed out these words:
>
> He does not delight in her arriving,
> he does not grieve at her going away.
> Saṅgāmaji, who is freed from ties –
> that one I call a brahmin.

We have come across the word translated in the prose section as 'support', *posa*, before, in section 1.6, where the brahmin is described as *anaññaposī*, 'not supporting anyone', with nobody other than himself to look after. That is what the woman in this story is asking for on behalf of herself and the child – support, care, nourishment. There is a little pun here. The name Saṅgāmaji (meaning 'victorious in battle') includes the word *saṅga*, which means 'bonds' or 'ties' and the pun is that Saṅgāmaji is *saṅgā mutta*, 'free from bonds'. The Buddha is saying that to be victorious in battle is really to be free from bonds. The values implied here are completely the opposite of those of modern times. The modern view would be that Saṅgāmaji was at fault for leaving his wife and child and not taking them back. But the traditional Indian view, and the Buddhist view, was that she was at fault in trying to draw him back after he had become an ascetic monk.

You notice that his former wife doesn't say, 'He doesn't need even me.' That's an interesting side-light on Indian psychology. First of all, she appeals for support for herself and the child, and when he doesn't respond, she leaves the child, which suggests that normally the child would be an even stronger tie than the wife, an even bigger temptation to come back. The son is the extension of the father, and was sometimes regarded as sharing the soul of the father, so the attachment to the son was very strong in Hindu society, as perhaps in all primitive societies. The Hindu belief was that if you didn't leave a son to make offerings to your spirit after your death, you would not go to heaven. You had to have a son, and preferably several, so that if your eldest son died, the next eldest could take on the responsibility. It was considered to be a terrible thing to die without issue. The Chinese had the same sort of idea. You needed someone to make offerings not only to your spirit but to the spirits of the ancestors for seven generations back. In the *Dhammapada* the Buddha gives as the characteristics of the spiritually immature person that he says 'this son is mine' and 'this wealth is mine'.[380] In thinking, 'This son is mine', the spiritually immature man is showing his attachment to his own individuality and its extension in his son. That is regarded, it seems, as an even stronger attachment on the part of the spiritually immature person, the *bala*, than attachment to wealth. In that same *Dhammapada* verse, the Buddha says, 'He does not even belong to himself' – never mind possessing a son or wealth.

So if a man had surmounted even his attachment to his son, he was free indeed. Even the sight of his son cannot move Saṅgāmaji. Indeed, he does not even look, and that's what makes his former wife realize that he has no attachment to anything at all. You can read a deeper meaning into it too. If he is Enlightened, why does he need to bother about heaven? He doesn't need a son to make offerings for him after he is dead. He has gone beyond heaven. He has transcended all the old ethnic values. He is an Enlightened individual. The contemporary view would be that he was very selfish, and no doubt there is a form of taking up the religious life which is selfish and not the result of any idealism. In the Buddhist view, if you really feel the spiritual urge, it is legitimate to leave, but obviously it must be a genuine urge, not just a shelving of responsibilities for unspiritual or even anti-spiritual reasons. It is that that you have to ascertain within your own mind before taking any action of this sort.

The Buddha was not within the range of ordinary human sight, but saw this happening at a distance with his *dibba-cakkhu*, his divine or clairvoyant vision. It's interesting that the Buddha refers to the former wife and not to the child. It seems to me that the story and the verse don't quite fit. You can imagine the verse referring to a quite different story, with quite different circumstances. But the prose part does epitomize the conflict which must have been very real for many people in India, during the Buddha's day and afterwards, between one's family responsibilities and the call of the spiritual life and feeling that one couldn't combine the two. It was a clear choice that you had to make. We are not told very much about Saṅgāmaji, but it must have been very difficult for him, if he wasn't already Enlightened, to sit there at the foot of the tree. His former wife comes and his son is left there and he just doesn't say anything. Maybe there's a tremendous struggle going on in him all that time. We are not told. But the Buddha sees what happens, and if the verses do refer to the episode, he approves. Of course, it's difficult for Saṅgāmaji's former wife too. She's left alone, and an Indian wife on her own doesn't have a very easy time bringing up a child. So there is a very real conflict here, but the sympathy of the tradition, or the spiritual sympathy, is very much on the side of the recluse, whereas in modern times, sympathies would probably be the other way round.

This is one of the questions I was often asked when I came back from India: why did the Buddha leave his wife and son? Wasn't that an uncompassionate act? Certainly there is the question of motivation, but I think nowadays the danger is in the other direction. People are far more likely to try to rationalize attachment than to rationalize what seems to be a selfish detachment. The test is whether you repeat the same pattern. You sometimes hear people say, 'I'm really fed up with worldly life and relationships, and I want to give it all up.' And indeed, maybe they do give it up, but after a couple of months they are just doing the same thing all over again. They just wanted a change of pattern – well, not even a change of pattern: the pattern is the same, but the colours are different, that's all. So that's the test. If there's anything suspect in your motive, sooner or later you'll get back into the same pattern. If Saṅgāmaji's former wife had seen him sitting at the foot of the tree socializing with some other men, she would have been fully justified in complaining and dragging him back home to look after her and their son, but since he's sitting there trying to gain Enlightenment, she hasn't got that right. Sometimes people think they are becoming disenchanted with relationships and want to develop spiritually when all they want is a change, maybe because they are not working hard enough at that particular relationship. If you've really come to the end of a relationship, or that kind of relationship, fair enough, but if you just want to experiment a bit, that isn't very good.

1.9 YOU DON'T BECOME PURE BY BATHING

> Once, the Buddha was staying at Gayā Head. It was the season of snowfall, and Jaṭila ascetics were plunging in and out of the water, pouring water on themselves and then performing sacrifices, thinking that that's how you become pure. Seeing this, the Buddha breathed out these words:
>
> One does not become pure through water:
> here many people bathe.
> In whom there is truth and virtue –
> that one is pure, and is a brahmin.

This takes place at a different location: at Gayā Head, which is very near the present Gaya railway station, about twelve miles from Bodh Gaya. Gayā Head is a low hill, and there is still a famous Hindu temple there. This is the place to which the Buddha led his disciples after he had converted the Kassapa brothers, who were fire worshippers, and where he preached – if that is the right term – the Fire Sermon.[381] The weather in those days in India seems to have been a bit different; I don't think there would be snow there now, even in the winter.

There was a strong belief in the Buddha's time that purity could be attained by means of ceremonial ablutions and burnt offerings, but the Buddha says here that the true brahmin is not simply one who engages in ceremonial practices or believes that purity can come about by bathing, though even in India today thousands of people still bathe in the waters of the Ganges, believing that this has some sort of spiritual benefit.

Here the Buddha is gently remarking on popular practice, not exactly criticizing it, but pointing beyond it. He says one doesn't become pure through water even though many people bathe here. 'In whom there is truth and virtue, that one is pure, and is a brahmin.' Again he is paraphrasing the ideal of what he is calling the brahmin. It's the brahmin who's really pure, and he's pure not by bathing but because he has realized the truth and virtue, or truth and the Dharma, as some translations have it, in the sense of the higher spiritual principle. Truth and Dharma are a linked pair; it is difficult to tell where one ends and the other begins. We often get this pair, for instance in the *Dhammapada*.[382] One could say 'one in whom is truth and virtue'. Perhaps Dharma suggests being in accordance with an objective moral and spiritual law or principle, and 'Truth' being true to yourself, but I offer that only as a suggestion. There is nothing very clear-cut.

1.10 IN THE SEEN, ONLY THE SEEN

> Once the Buddha was staying near Sāvatthī in the Jeta Wood at Anāthapiṇḍika's park. At that time a man called Bāhiya of the Bark-cloth was living by the seashore at Suppāraka. He was respected, honoured, and supported by local people as a holy man, but one day, when he was alone, he wondered, 'Am I an *arahant*, or on the path to becoming one?' A *devatā* who had once been a relative of Bāhiya read his mind and said to him, 'You are neither an *arahant* nor on the path to becoming one, because you're not doing the right practice.' The *devatā* went on to tell Bāhiya that in Sāvatthī he would find the Buddha, the fully Enlightened One, who would teach him the way to become an *arahant*. Bāhiya left straight away and travelled as fast as he could to Sāvatthī, where the Buddha was staying in the Jeta Wood, at Anāthapiṇḍika's park. But when he got to the Jeta Wood, the *bhikkhus* there told him that the Buddha had left on his almsround.
>
> So Bāhiya headed into Sāvatthī and saw the Buddha walking there, lovely to see, with calmed senses and tranquil mind, calm and controlled, like a perfectly trained elephant. Bāhiya immediately flung himself at the Buddha's feet and said: 'Teach me Dhamma, Lord, so that it will be for my good and happiness for a long time.' The Buddha said that it wasn't the right time; he was

on his almsround. But Bāhiya persisted. He said, 'It's difficult to know how long you will live, or I will live. Please teach me now.' The Buddha again said that it wasn't the right time, but Bāhiya asked the same question yet again, and then the Buddha said:

'For you then, Bāhiya, as regards things seen, heard, sensed or cognized, there will be in the seen only the seen, in the heard only the heard, in the sensed only the sensed, in the cognized only the cognized. When you experience things in that way, then who you are will not be defined by that; and then who you are will not be found in that. And when who you are is not found in that, then who you are will neither be here, nor in the beyond, nor in between. Just this is the end of suffering.'

On hearing this brief teaching, Bāhiya was immediately freed from the taints without grasping. Soon after that, he was killed by a cow with a young calf. The Buddha asked some of the *bhikkhus* to take away Bāhiya's body, burn it, and make a cairn for it. Having done so, the *bhikkhus* asked the Buddha what Bāhiya's destiny would be. The Buddha said that Bāhiya was a wise man who practised according to the Dhamma and didn't vex him in the matter of Dhamma teaching, and declared that he had reached final Nibbāna. And so saying, he breathed out these words:

Where neither earth nor water
nor fire nor wind find a footing,
there the stars do not glimmer,
nor does the sun spread its light;
there the moon does not shine
nor is darkness to be found.
And when a sage, a brahmin, knows this
for themselves, by sagacity,
then they are released from the realm of form,
from the formless, from pleasure and pain.

Here the Buddha is staying at Sāvatthī in north-western India, at the Jeta Grove in Anāthapiṇḍika's Park, where he spent twenty four rainy seasons after his Enlightenment; and 'Bāhiya' – the outsider, the foreigner – 'of the Bark-cloth' is staying at Suppāraka on the seashore. Suppāraka has recently been excavated. It is north of Bombay, and there is a Buddhist vihara there now. In those days it was a great port, with trade connections with Babylonia, for there was a connection between Babylonia, the Sumerian civilization, and the Indus Valley civilization. Suppāraka is just south of that Indus Valley region. Bāhiya might even have been from there, but he is probably simply an example of a non-Buddhist Indian ascetic. The commentary explains that his 'bark garment' was a cloak made of bark.[383] There are references in the Upanishads to ascetics who wore bark garments, so it is a reference to a style of extreme asceticism that the original audience would probably have known about. It seems that in the ancient world generally, including ancient Greece and ancient Egypt, people, especially those connected with religion, sometimes avoided wearing animal products, not so much for reasons of non-violence, but for magical reasons. The Egyptian priests didn't wear wool or skins, but cotton if they could get it, though that was very rare, or linen, or some kind of bark fibre garment.

Bāhiya seems to have been a sort of teacher, a spiritual leader, 'being esteemed, honoured, thought much of, worshipped and with deference paid to him, and he got plenty of robes and almsfood, bed and seat, comforts and medicines for sickness'.[384] It's quite possible, therefore, that here we've got the follower of some Middle Eastern cult, possibly coming from that area and now living on the west coast of India, which has connections with Sumeria and Babylonia. He's established himself as a sort of teacher, he's looked up to as a shaman or something of that sort, and he wonders, 'Have I really got there, or is there something beyond, something higher?' We can well imagine this sort of thing happening in those days. The way he is honoured and respected is described in Buddhistic terms, as though he was a monk, but he isn't a Buddhist monk. But anyway, he wonders whether he's gained real knowledge and real Enlightenment. Again, it's put in pre-Buddhistic terms: he wonders whether he is an *arhant* (Pāli *arahant*). The word *arhant* later on had a technical meaning, but in early Buddhism it means one who is spiritually worthy, or even just worthy. The word cannot be being used in the later Buddhist sense because Bāhiya apparently knew nothing about the Buddha's teaching. He had never heard of the Buddha, as we shall see. Anyway, a doubt arose as to whether he in fact was a spiritually developed person, even though he was regarded as such by the people of that locality.

Bāhiya is told by a *devatā* that the Buddha dwells in the far-off district of Sāvatthī. We often have these *devatās* appearing in the Pāli canon,[385] very disconcertingly for the rationalistically-minded reader. They are sometimes tree *devatās* or water *devatās*, but they appear, and very often they are blood relations of the person to whom they appear, either in that very life or in a previous life. You get the idea that a *devatā* is someone who was a human being in a past life but has now been born in a higher state of existence, from which they can look down on the earth, and is still interested in their old friends and relations, and tries to help. This *devatā* was formerly a relation of Bāhiya's, apparently, and he knew what was going on in his mind, and out of compassion and desire for his welfare he told him, 'No, you're not an *arhant*, nor even on the path to becoming one.' You can take this any way you like. You can take it literally. Maybe he consulted an oracle, as people did all over the ancient world in those days – Greece, the Middle East, North Africa. Or maybe the *devatā* spoke to him in a dream or a vision, or he heard a voice, or thought he heard a voice. Or perhaps it's just that a rumour reached him that there was an Enlightened being living in a town hundreds of miles away. But somehow the message gets to him: 'I'm not Enlightened, I'm not what I'm supposed to be, there's something more.' And he acts upon the advice. The *devatā* tells him that there is an Enlightened one living far away to the east in Sāvatthī, and Bāhiya at once sets out.

He stays only a single night at each place throughout the journey and when he gets to Sāvatthī, he presses on until he gets to the Jeta Grove, where the *bhikkhus* tell him that the Buddha has gone into the town for almsfood. Bāhiya goes that way and he sees the Buddha: 'lovely to see, with calmed senses and tranquil mind, calm and controlled, like a perfectly trained elephant'. The comparison of the Buddha to an elephant is quite common in Pāli literature, especially the tamed elephant, because there is tremendous strength but it is perfectly under control. There is also the elephant-look. The elephant, according to Indian legend, never just turns his head – he always swivels his whole body round – and likewise the Buddha gives you the whole of his energy and attention. He confronts you completely. He is all in line, as it were.

Bāhiya asks the Buddha to teach him the Dharma. The Buddha says that it is not the right time. It was the Buddha's custom, when he went collecting alms, not to speak to anybody. But Bāhiya has an answer –

why delay? There are more important things than collecting almsfood. There's the whole question of the shortness of life. You may die, if we wait, or I may die before I have time to ask you again. It's as though Bāhiya has a premonition that he is going to die soon, and indeed he is killed shortly afterwards. Perhaps he is psychic, because there he was, staying at Suppāraka, and he heard this voice, this *deva*, telling him to go to the Buddha, and now he has a premonition that life is short, or at least is going to be short for him. So he urges the Buddha: 'You ask me to wait, maybe only an hour, but who knows whether you or I will live that hour out? Let me have the teaching. It is very urgent.' The second time the Buddha refuses, but the third time the request is made the Buddha grants it. We often find in the Pāli tradition that if the Buddha is asked something a third time, he replies, however devastating the reply may be for the questioner. So what does he say?

His first piece of advice is just to be aware. In the seen, only the seen. In the heard, only the heard. In other words, the teaching that the Buddha gives is pure mindfulness. If you see something, just see it. Don't read anything into it, don't project anything on to it, just see what is there. In the same way, just hear. If you listen to the wind, you can stay with that experience or you can start thinking, 'Oh, it's windy. It might rain later on. I wonder what we shall do if it rains? Oh, I would be annoyed. In fact, I would be quite angry.' That's all produced by the mind. You are not staying with the experience itself, which is just wind. So in the heard, let there be only the heard, in the seen only the seen, and in the thought only the thought. If thought is needed, then fair enough, think! If something has to be done, think about how to do it, but go straight from A to B, as it were, don't go the long way round. Just know, without unnecessary mental activity.[386] It is not that thinking is excluded, but there need be no unnecessary or neurotic thinking. For instance, if you're working out how to get somewhere, you can think: 'First I have to go to the bus stop and get such-and-such a bus, which will take me so far. Then I can get such-and-such a train.' That is necessary, objective thinking. But if you start worrying, 'Suppose the bus doesn't come? Suppose I get on the wrong bus by mistake? Suppose I forget to take any money with me? Suppose the train is late? Suppose there is no train? Suppose there is a breakdown? Suppose I'm killed?' this is all neurotic thinking, worry. That sort of thinking is excluded. Apparently even imagination is OK so long as you are aware of what is happening. You can even fantasize, daydream, but be aware. So that's the teaching the Buddha gave Bāhiya, for which he'd come a thousand miles or so on foot, stopping only one night in every place, in his bark garment.

> When who you are, Bāhiya, is not defined by that, then who you are will not be found in that. When who you are, Bāhiya, is not found in that, then who you are is neither here, nor in the beyond, nor in between. Just this is the end of suffering.

This is quite an obscure passage, but it means there will be no speculations, no going from one thing to another, no comparisons, but just remaining with what is present here and now. In Woodward's translation there will be no 'thereby' – in other words, there won't be any mental activity explaining anything. The mind won't be saying, 'Because of this, therefore that; this comes about because of that; on account of that, thereby this' and so on. There'll be, in a sense, no meaning to it, because you won't be asking about any such thing as meaning; if you get rid of the idea of 'herein', there's no here, no there, and no in-between; these are all conceptual distinctions. And when all conceptual activity whatsoever stops, then you're Enlightened, you've reached Nirvāṇa, that's the end of suffering. In other words, what the Buddha is saying is that the way to Enlightenment is the present experience without any sort of interpretation, without any sort of conceptual judgement or evaluation. It may sound easy, but obviously it's very difficult. There's no time. There's no going from this to that, so there's no in-between, no here or there. You've just got the experience as it is at that very moment. This is mindfulness only, or pure mindfulness. It's just sitting if you happen to be sitting, or just standing or just walking, as the case may be.

There is a great possibility of misunderstanding this and developing alienated awareness,[387] just looking at everything from the outside, but not experiencing it at the same time. It's probably better to think of it in terms of the mirror-like wisdom, as an aspect of Enlightenment is described.[388] Just be like a mirror, just reflect. But that image is limited too, because the mirror may suggest something cold and hard, just reflecting, not really feeling, not experiencing, not participating, but this kind of awareness isn't like that. It doesn't mean reflecting without feeling. It's a question of not projecting, not reading into, not misunderstanding, just seeing things as they are, starting with your ordinary sense experience. It also means no *saṃskāras*, no setting up of any karma which would ripen in the future. You create karma in the past and you reap the consequences in the future. But if you remain in the present and are simply aware – if you just see and hear, just imagine, just cognize, if you don't set up any *saṃskāras*, nothing will happen on account of those *saṃskāras*. It is usually said that 'here' refers to this world, 'beyond' to the other world, heaven, and 'in between' to the intermediate state, but one can look at it more profoundly than that. There should be no comparison whatsoever, no going from one thing to another. You are just with what is actually present here and now.

Not long after this, Bāhiya was killed by a cow with a young calf, and the Buddha asked the *bhikkhus* to cremate the body and erect a cairn or primitive stupa over the ashes. 'Cairn' is *caitya*, the heap of stones, or perhaps even a heap of earth, which was the original form of the stupa. It was the custom, even before the Buddha's day, to pile up a heap of earth or stones over the ashes of the cremated body of a king, chief, or revered person, and this was continued by the Buddhists. First of all, some of the disciples of the Buddha were commemorated in that way on the Buddha's instructions, and then, after his death, the Buddha himself was commemorated in the same way. Gradually the *caitya* or stupa, as it was later called, became more and more elaborate, assuming certain symbolical values and becoming the best-known type of Buddhist monument.

The *bhikkhus* asked what Bāhiya's future destiny would be, the kind of question the Buddha was frequently asked. On this occasion he remarked that Bāhiya was a wise man who practised according to the Dharma and did not 'vex him in the matter of Dharma-teaching'. But how might one vex the Buddha in this way? By asking unnecessary questions, by disputing and carping, or by being unreceptive, as some of the people who came to see him were.

In the *udāna* the Buddha is saying that Bāhiya has reached a higher state of consciousness, a state in which the four elements are not present, the stars are not present, there is no sun, no moon, but no darkness. It's pure light, a spiritual light. Having reached the level of Reality, having gone beyond all pairs of opposites, he is completely Enlightened, completely released from the *rūpaloka* and from the *arūpaloka*, not only from pain, but even from pleasure. There's even a higher state than that, and that was the state that Bāhiya had reached by the time of his death, as a result of realizing that teaching of the Buddha. This verse comes quite close to the Perfection of Wisdom, the *prajñāpāramitā*. It goes beyond the cosmos, concerning the transcendental plane beyond the triple mundane sphere.

Note that they 'know this for themselves'. It isn't at second-hand. This is a characteristic Buddhist emphasis. One also notices that everything is firmly embedded in the concrete historical context. You don't often get this in Indian literature. If you read, for instance, the *Purāṇas*, which are popular Hindu works, you don't get so much as a glimpse of concrete human historical life. It is all very vague, almost woolly. There is a lot of teaching and many abstract ideas, a lot of supernatural happenings, but no historical detail.

The Buddha does not say that Bāhiya is a brahmin (in the new sense he's giving to the word) but that is the suggestion. All the verses in this first chapter have continued that theme. The word 'brahmin' has recurred in different ways, different contexts, from different points of view, and the Buddha uses it to express the state, or the stage, that he himself realized at the time of his Enlightenment. One can get a good feeling for what the Buddha was getting at from the verses, which simply describe the ideal human being of early Buddhism, before any specifically Buddhist terms are introduced. The term '*arhant*' is used in the prose portions, but the verses use the term 'brahmin', the pre-Buddhistic term to which the Buddha is trying to give a new meaning. The prose parts give one an idea of the background of the teaching and the context, the environment, in which the Buddha lived and taught. That couldn't have changed all that much in the one or two hundred years before the text was compiled, so we get a vivid picture of India at the time of the Buddha and the sort of teaching that he was originally trying to communicate through these verses. It wasn't even teaching, in a way; very often it was just a kind of communication. He was asked a question and he responded. The verses are inspiring, direct, and completely non-technical. The Buddha is using the ordinary language of his day and trying as best he can to express his new vision through the medium of that language.

It is significant that the compilers, whoever they were, started the *Udāna* in this way. Perhaps, since Sāvatthī figures prominently in this work, this collection was put together by monks living in that area;

it was their gospel, as it were. It reads very much like a gospel – the nearest thing to a gospel in the Christian sense that we have in the whole Pāli canon. It is about the same length as one of the gospels. It is self-contained. It begins at the beginning, with the Buddha's Enlightenment, and there is a certain chronological sequence, or at least development, throughout, as we shall see as we go on. It is pre-Buddhistic Buddhism, you could say, archaic Buddhism.

The scene is north-western India. There is mention of the place that we now call Bodh Gaya, which then was simply the village of Uruvelā. We also visit Gayā, Rājagaha, and the place now called Suppāraka, or Sopara, on the western sea coast. Cities are mentioned: Sāvatthī and Rājagaha are big cities, and then in the forest there are villages, with little patches of cultivation around them, and people going to and fro and ascetics and monks travelling around and coming to see the Buddha. The Buddha himself is travelling around and begging his food every day, and his followers are living in simple lodgings on the outskirts of the towns or in the woods, some alone, some in little groups, and all in contact with each other. It's quite a vivid picture. You feel that a real historical period is being described. A bit of Indian mythology comes in, with references to *devas* and a *yakkha*, and to religious practices and customs – the *caitya* that is set up over the ashes of the deceased monk. There is the settlement of Anāthapiṇḍika – the *ārāma*, the rest place, probably some huts put up in a park – and the Bamboo Grove, where the Buddha sometimes stays, outside the gates of Rājagaha. Though the *suttas* are short, they give vivid pictures of the life of the Buddha and the sort of people he met, how he lived and what was said. There's a general air of earnestness and sincerity – this comes across very strongly – and a sense of the very simple life they were living.

The teaching in this chapter is very simple too. The Buddha is concerned to define what he means by the ideal human being as distinguished from the old-fashioned brahmin, to distinguish the new spiritual ideal from the old ethnic ideal. We really are right at the beginning. There is no doctrine in the ordinary sense, apart from the twelve *nidānas* in a rather truncated form. It is just the ideal: the sort of life the Buddha wants to see. In the verses especially, we see the Buddha being very direct and straightforward, speaking out his new vision of the spiritual ideal, what human beings should try to become. So in archaic Buddhism the ideal is the ideal of the brahmin, the ideal described in contemporary Indian terms. Later on came the *arhant* ideal, which was the same, but described in terms of a systematic Buddhist tradition, and the bodhisattva ideal is the same thing presented even more fully and correcting some misinterpretations that had crept in since the Buddha's time.

I get a feeling from the text that there's quite a kinship between ancient India and ancient Greece, as though the world was much more one in those days. An ancient Greek going to India would be quite at home with all the little shrines and the teachers and the simple way of life. I got the same feeling from reading the ancient Greek historian Herodotus, who covered Egypt and Asia Minor and Persia. It was as though it was just one area, almost one civilization, though there were differences within it. There was a lot of communication over this vast area, people travelling to and fro. Herodotus himself went up as far as southern Russia and down into the Euphrates valley and Babylon, and Pythagoras went to India. If we accept the traditional date, the Buddha was an almost exact contemporary of Darius the Great, and the Persian invasion of Greece was in the next generation after that. The Persians invaded Greece at practically the same time that the Magadha empire invaded the Śākya territory.

In the *Udāna* there are two poles, basically. There's the Buddha's Enlightenment experience – we definitely start with that, and the first three or four episodes are centred on it – and there's the attempt to express Enlightenment in terms of the brahmin ideal redefined, to use the whole idea of brahminhood as a means of communicating what the Buddha was talking about when he spoke of Enlightenment. Let's take an example: suppose there was no such thing as Buddhism around at the moment and no one knew anything about it and there was only Christianity. Suppose you did experience Enlightenment and wanted to find some word, or term, or image to communicate that from the existing cultural heritage. Which one would you use? Which one would you think was the nearest? Which one would you try to improve on and upgrade? You might talk in terms of Super Christhood or something like that, but if you did that, some people would misunderstand and try to restore the original meaning of Christhood in the Christian sense, forgetting the new meaning that you tried to give to the word. It isn't easy to communicate a new idea, or a new experience, or a new feeling, using the old words. Sometimes the words get the better of you and reassert their original meaning. But we are left with this picture of the Buddha having this tremendous experience in the India of 500 BCE and all that that meant, and then trying to communicate it in the best way he could. That was the starting point of everything.

2
MUCALINDA

2.1 THE SERPENT KING SHELTERS THE BUDDHA

Seven days after the Buddha had gained Enlightenment, while he was still sitting under the bodhi tree at Uruvelā, by the river Nerañjarā, there was a great rainstorm out of season, and for seven days it rained and blew a gale. Then Mucalinda the great serpent, the *nāga* king, encircled the Buddha's body with his coils and spread his hood over the Buddha's head, to protect him. After seven days, the Buddha emerged from concentration and the rain stopped. Mucalinda took on the appearance of a youth and stood before the Buddha, saluting him with folded hands. And the Buddha breathed out these words:

Solitude is bliss for the contented one,
who has learned the truth and who sees.
Non-harming towards the world is bliss,
restraint towards all living beings.

Dispassion is bliss in everyday life,
the overcoming of sensual desires.
The removal of the conceit of self –
this indeed is the ultimate bliss.

At the start of this chapter we have gone back to the beginning, to the time just after the Buddha's Enlightenment. Mucalinda is a species of tree (*Pteraspermum suberifolium*), and Mucalinda the snake king has the same name, presumably because he lives in the vicinity of that tree, or perhaps he is a sort of snake-cum-tree-spirit. The verse the Buddha utters does not seem to have a very close connection with the prose episode. He simply describes his own mental state at that moment, giving a spontaneous expression of his state of complete happiness as he sits at the foot of the tree shortly after his Enlightenment. He even says why he is happy. He is happy because he has learned the truth; he has seen things as they really are. He is happy because he's full of love and goodwill towards all living beings. He is happy because he has no neurotic desires, so he has no need of any object of the senses. Above all, he is happy because he doesn't think any more that 'I am I'; he's gone beyond that. There is no 'I', no empirical ego or self, no 'conceit of self' as the final two lines of the verse say.

Perhaps we need to pause for a moment to consider the idea of 'the removal of the conceit of self'. That doesn't mean that the sense of 'I' is annihilated in a functional sense. It's not as though there's a blank where you were before. There's the physical body – that's still there – and there's the mind working, but they are not at the centre any more. It's as though your vision has overlapped a wider dimension of which your empirical self is just a very small part, so your consciousness is no longer identified with 'you'. The 'you' is still there, but you are equally identified with all the other 'yous', which are also 'I's. It's more like that. It is not that there is something actually existing in the metaphysical sense first and then it is annihilated, but more that what we experience as the empirical self or ego is expanded, one can even say to infinity. The empirical self is still 'there', but it is part, as it were, of a larger whole. That is probably the only way one can put it. When you are in the midst of a dream, you are completely identified with it. When you wake up, you may remember your dream vividly, so your dream experience is still there, but it is part of the larger whole of your waking consciousness. It is something like that. The 'self' isn't a thing that is taken from one place to another, but more like a limitation that is removed. The space that was bounded by the limitation is still there, but it is no longer limited.

We have to be very careful not to take any talk of annihilating the self too literally. We need a healthy self-confidence. The question is whether you are being really self-confident or whether you are doing a cover-up operation, not being self-confident but merely egoistic. Sometimes it is difficult to tell. Be very careful, if you disagree with anybody, not to attribute their convictions to ego as a convenient way of countering their argument. Something else that one has to watch out for is what has been called the tyranny of the weak over the strong. If you can't oppose someone openly and honestly because you lack self-confidence, you may try to undermine them, and one way you can do this is by labelling their genuine self-confidence as egotism, which at once places you in the superior position of the unegoistic person seeing through someone else's egotism. If you are vested already with a sort of spiritual authority, it is very easy to label everybody else's opinions, when they disagree with yours, as manifestations of egotism. One should think carefully before ever labelling anybody else, even momentarily, as egoistic.

Throughout the Pāli canon, the Buddha strikes one as a very self-confident person. He didn't hesitate to make his views known clearly and unmistakably, or to tell the conceited and egoistic what he thought of them. There was no false humility; he was self-confident in the best and most spiritual sense. When he spoke about 'removing the conceit of self', it was not the weak trying to tyrannize over the strong. After entirely divesting himself of the conceit of self, he remained in the world functioning vigorously as an unmistakably individual person. It is much more helpful to speak in terms of growth, development, and expansion than in terms of getting rid of the self or the ego. That negative language is hardly ever helpful. It is better to speak of a new dimension of consciousness, a new, comprehensive, or open point of view. Saying 'you must get rid of your ego' is bound to irritate people at once, obviously.

2.2 TALK ABOUT THE DHARMA OR KEEP QUIET

> Once the Buddha was staying near Sāvatthī in the Jeta Grove at Anāthapiṇḍika's park. One day the *bhikkhus* got together in the *dharmasala* after their almsround and started discussing which of two kings was wealthier and more powerful, Bimbisāra, the king of Magadha, or Pasenadi, the king of Kosala. They talked round and round this topic, not reaching a conclusion. In the evening, the Buddha emerged from his seclusion and found that they were

still talking. He asked them what they were talking about and they explained. He told them that it wasn't right that, having gone forth to the homeless life, they should talk about something like that. When they gathered together, they should either engage in Dhamma-talk or maintain noble silence. And he breathed out these words:

The bliss of sense-pleasure in everyday life
and that bliss which is divine,
these are not worth a sixteenth part
of the bliss of exhausting craving.

Once again the scene shifts back to Sāvatthī, to Anāthapiṇḍika's park. *Anātha* means 'one without a protector' (*nātha* means protector), i.e. an orphan, a destitute person with no one to look after him. *Piṇḍa* is food, especially balls of rice (*piṇḍa* is literally a ball). So 'Anāthapiṇḍika' means the one who gives food to the poor and to the orphans; his personal name was Sudatta. The site of the Jeta Grove is still there, and it's been partially excavated. One of my friends, Bhikkhu Sangharatana, lived there and tried to revive the whole area as a pilgrimage centre and Buddhist centre.[389]

By this point in the *Udāna* things are developing. There's now a *dharmasala* in which the *bhikkhus* gather in this story. A *dharmasala* is a sort of large hall. You find them on the outskirts of villages even now in India. They are large barn-like structures, mainly just a roof, sometimes with no walls at all and sometimes roughly walled in with wattle and daub. People use them for their village meetings and wandering ascetics are put up there so that people can come and visit them in the public space. Sometimes the village folk store things there during the winter.

This is the first time Bimbisāra and Pasenadi make their appearance in the *Udāna*. Bimbisāra was the ruler of the kingdom of Magadha, corresponding roughly to the present-day state of Bihar in north-eastern India, and Pasenadi was the king of Kosala, corresponding roughly to the state of Uttar Pradesh, so they were rivals. The great political question during the greater part of the Buddha's life was whether Magadha would swallow up Kosala or whether Kosala would swallow up Magadha, and both the great kingdoms were expanding and swallowing up their smaller, usually republican, neighbours. During the Buddha's lifetime his own state, the Śākya territory, was swallowed up by the kingdom of Kosala and lost its independence,[390] and after the Buddha's death, Magadha swallowed up Kosala. Two or three centuries later it was to become the great Magadhan empire of Aśoka, which was one of the biggest empires India has ever seen, extending right up into Afghanistan and right down into South India, practically to the tip. You can imagine that the *bhikkhus* were aware of the competition between these two great kingdoms, and it was no doubt natural that they were talking over the politics of the day while the Buddha was meditating in his own quarters, but they seem to have talked about it for a very long time. They had to finish eating by noon – at least, that became the rule. I myself followed this rule quite strictly for about twelve or fifteen years, and it's surprising how used to it you can get. You just don't think about food after twelve o'clock and you don't seem to feel the lack of it. You seem to be just as energetic as everyone else, it's quite strange. Anyway, the *bhikkhus* seem to have begun talking about this topic once they had eaten and 'this chance talk was unfinished when the Exalted One rose from his solitude at eventide', as Woodward puts it. That was perhaps six or seven o'clock in the evening, so they'd apparently been talking for five or six hours on this one topic.

The story has the ring of authenticity. Indeed, this sort of episode occurs more than once in the canon: *bhikkhus* gather together and instead of talking about the Dharma they engage in talk about other things.[391] I assume that the Buddha was not saying that there shouldn't ever be a reference to anything political, but the length of the discussion suggests they were rather obsessed with the matter, perhaps to the extent that they lost their mindfulness and forgot about all their spiritual life and the Dharma and why they'd become monks. Presumably it was this that the Buddha was remonstrating with them about. It's very easy to get carried away and lose mindfulness when you're talking. One can tell immediately when the mood of the conversation changes. There's a difference between being really interested or concerned and getting carried away. Maybe you identify with something emotionally. Something else has taken over; some factor within you that you are not fully conscious of has come up and is getting its satisfaction. You are not fully in control of yourself. Presumably this can happen when you are ostensibly discussing religion too. You can tell that this has happened if you feel not stimulated but worn out at the end of the conversation. You don't feel satisfied, as though you've expressed yourself and said something meaningful. You feel vaguely disturbed or unhappy, even if you were rather pleased or even jubilant during the discussion. Quite often you find something that you all agree about and you really let yourselves go on that topic, even if it's only grumbling about the weather. It's a very low level of communication, if it can be called communication at all.

On this occasion the Buddha tells the *bhikkhus* that they should either engage in Dharma-talk or keep quiet. But can he mean that they are literally never to talk about anything except the Dharma? I don't think so. The Pāli term here is *dhammakathā*, which can be translated as 'conversation about the Dharma'. We could say that it is talk which is in accordance with Dharma, in accordance with the truth or reality of things. This is not talk about Buddhism in a narrow sense. It means not talking about anything without going into the underlying principles. If you go into any subject deeply enough, that could be said to be *dhammakathā*, because Dharma is not just Buddhism in the narrow sense as a religion. Dharma (Pāli *dhamma*) means truth, or reality, or law, or principle. Superficial gossip is ruled out, but if from political events and historical happenings you go deeply into the principles of human life, this could be considered as *dhammakathā*, though obviously you have to watch yourself. Francis Bacon said, 'Histories make men wise' – meaning that the study of history makes you wise, because you become acquainted with the vicissitudes of things – 'and the study of the poets makes them witty.'[392]

The verse that follows seems a little inconsequential. One wonders whether it's just a question of tacking a verse onto the story, or perhaps it's suggested by the reference to the two kings. They are supposed to have everything – land, property, money, chariots, soldiers, women, all sorts of pleasures – but however happy they are, all that put together doesn't amount to one sixteenth of the happiness you experience when you get rid of all neurotic desire, all craving. Usually people consider that if a craving is satisfied, that is happiness. But the Buddha says that not to have any craving at all for anything mundane, or even anything heavenly, is the real happiness. Craving itself is a sort of affliction, and the satisfaction of that craving is like putting a plaster on a wound. That's soothing, but it is better not to have the wound at all. Nowadays people find it difficult to accept or even understand that to be in a state of no craving is a positive experience, that pleasures of the senses and even meditation give us only a fraction (the text says a sixteenth, this being an idiom) of the bliss that comes with the end of craving. People think in terms of the satisfaction of craving as constituting happiness. Every advertisement suggests that.

One can even say that unfortunately the state of many people is so dull that they have to stir up some craving to make life interesting, and then satisfy that craving to get a bit of happiness. This is usually considered normal. But where does that craving come from? You can have the experience of sitting quite happily on a garden bench. Everything is calm and pleasant; the sun is shining, the birds are singing, and you feel quite peaceful. Then suddenly you feel bored or restless, and you want to go and do something. Why is that? Why can't you just go on sitting there contentedly? You are enjoying yourself, but it is as though you don't want to go on enjoying yourself. There is an inner restlessness, as though you want to be dissatisfied. You start craving to crave. If you're sitting there happy and content, it is as though something is wrong. It is such an unfamiliar state, perhaps. In the same way, some people find that when their meditation is going well, they feel like sitting on for a while longer and could do so quite easily, but they don't. It is almost as though they feel they shouldn't.

In South India I came across a well-known female yogi[393] who had a very interesting theory. She said that the happiness that people experience when sense desires are satisfied is not on account of the satisfaction of the desire but on account of the desire's cessation. It is this that the Buddha is talking about, indefinitely prolonged. In our case this kind of experience may not last very long, but for the time that you are free from craving, you can experience a sort of contentment. Unfortunately, the craving reawakens, and then you have the desire to satisfy it again, but at least the momentary cessation gives you a glimpse of what is possible, and then you can start thinking how nice it would be to experience that all the time. The important thing to understand is that cessation comes about not by satisfying the craving, but by resolving it. Many people make the mistake of thinking that you can get to that state by satisfying craving again and again, but you can't. In fact, the law of diminishing returns operates.

2.3 THE BUDDHA TEACHES SOME BOYS NOT TO BE CRUEL

Once, when the Buddha was staying near Sāvatthī in the Jeta Wood at Anāthapiṇḍika's park, he was going to the village to collect almsfood when he came upon some boys hitting a snake with a stick. And he breathed out these words:

Those who injure with a stick
beings who wish for happiness,
themselves seeking happiness,
do not obtain happiness after death.

Those who do not harm with a stick
beings who wish for happiness,
themselves seeking happiness –
they obtain happiness after death.

This is a sight you often see in India – boys ill-treating a snake, or a dog, or a cat – and of course this sort of thing happens everywhere. The Buddha comments that it is natural for all beings to seek happiness. You don't wish your own search for happiness to be obstructed, so don't obstruct the search for happiness of others. In other words, do as you would be done by, in the language of that old children's story, *The Water Babies*. It's quite a simple ethical reflection, though at the same time it's quite profound. We don't like painful things being done to us, but we don't realize with equal vividness that other people don't like painful things being done to them either. It's a question of putting yourself imaginatively in the place of others, which is quite difficult to do.

The Buddha is also saying that if you obstruct the happiness of others, your own chances of obtaining happiness may be reduced. It is the law of karma. Basically, the state of mind that would lead you to perform such actions will lead you into unhappy situations. It's as though you put yourself on a wavelength that attracts trouble. If you are quarrelsome and aggressive, you may cause others to suffer, but that same quarrelsomeness and aggression may lead you into contact with people who are even more quarrelsome and aggressive than you, and who will make you suffer.

But why might someone torment others? The boys were probably tormenting the snake because they were not aware that animals could experience pain. It seems that children are often not aware of this, and they have to learn it. If you are aware of it, but you persist in tormenting others, it is perhaps because you are not happy yourself. And there are various subtle ways of tormenting people – not just physically, but restricting them and causing trouble for them, or inhibiting them. When you trouble others, it may well be either because you are unaware of what you are doing, as in the case of the young and inexperienced, or because you are not happy yourself, maybe because of your own unsatisfied cravings.

2.4 THE BUDDHA'S ADVICE ABOUT HANDLING CRITICISM

> When the Buddha was staying near Sāvatthī in the Jeta Wood at Anāthapiṇḍika's park, he and the order of *bhikkhus* were respected and honoured, and they were given clothing and food, lodging and medicines. Wanderers of other views, not being respected in the same way, were envious, and when they saw *bhikkhus* in the village or the forest, they insulted and provoked them. The *bhikkhus* told the Buddha about this, and he breathed out these words:
>
> When touched by joy or pain, in village or in wood,
> one ought not consider them as from self or other.
> Contacts touch dependent on appropriation;
> without that, by what would contacts touch?

There is a parallel between this section and the previous one – the boys tormenting the snake and the wanderers of other views tormenting the *bhikkhus* with their criticisms. We are still at Sāvatthī, and we see that the Buddha's movement is a success. We have gathered from previous sections that he now has quite a number of disciples, and his fame has reached even as far as the west coast, and now the wanderers of other opinions are becoming envious of his success. This sort of inter-religious jealousy seems familiar. The Buddha and his disciples, having become well-regarded, are being supplied with everything they need. The wanderers of other views (that is, those who are not followers of the Buddha) aren't getting very much, and they start becoming rather upset and jealous, and even abuse the Buddha and his followers. The word translated as 'wanderer' is *parivrājaka* (Sanskrit) or *paribbājaka* (Pāli), someone who has left home and is wandering around, living on the charity of the public, either following a teacher or looking for one. There were swarms of wanderers going around in the India of the Buddha's day. No one really knows why this suddenly happened, but there has been quite a bit of discussion among scholars about it. Some say the wanderers were gypsies, others that they were unsettled people who were disturbed by the changes in the world around them. They were probably a bit like the modern Indian sadhu, or the wandering teachers of the Hellenic world. T. W. Rhys Davids discusses the phenomenon in his book *Buddhist India*.[394] They weren't all spiritual seekers; some apparently just got fed up with settled home life, so they left home and wandered about, out of a sort of wanderlust.

The only people in the Pāli canon who are represented as moving from place to place apart from the wanderers are merchants and kings in the course of their administration, collecting taxes and so on. Everybody else stayed put. You could spend your whole life in the village you were born in. For people of a more adventurous disposition, this was intolerable. With no books, radio, or television, wandering was the only way of learning anything new. In ancient India, unlike ancient Greece, there were no openings in politics. The king was the supreme landowner and autocrat. There was no democratic political life, except in the republics to some extent, but they were breaking up and being absorbed by the monarchies. Restless, dissatisfied people therefore just left home and wandered.

It was perhaps a manifestation of prosperity. The whole Gangetic valley was well settled and the little villages were established. There were quite a few prosperous and flourishing cities, and people had plenty of food and fairly secure living conditions, so there was quite a bit of surplus to support the non-productive wanderers. Maybe this is the socio-economic explanation for it, but it only seems to have happened in India. We don't seem to find it in the Middle East, in the valley of the Tigris and the Euphrates, among the Sumerian and Babylonian civilizations. A very few of the Indian wanderers wandered with their families – we'll encounter one such family group later on in the *Udāna*. The majority of them seem to have had some religious or spiritual interest, though some were just people who couldn't settle down to conventional life. Various leaders among them gathered together groups of wanderers and formed brotherhoods; there were six well-known ones in the Buddha's day apart from his own sangha, including Mahāvira, the leader of the Jains – Nātaputta, as he is called in the Pāli texts. The Buddha himself was a wanderer for a while, and most of his leading followers were recruited from these wanderers.

Bhikkhu means one who lives on alms or *bhikkhā* (Pāli; Sanskrit *bhikṣā*). So now we have left behind the term *brāhmaṇa* or brahmin, and the terminology is becoming more specifically Buddhist, as it were. In the *Dhammapada*, *brāhmaṇa* and *samaṇa* form a pair, and *samaṇa* (Sanskrit *śramaṇa*) and *bhikkhu* (Sanskrit *bhikṣu*) are overlapping terms for alms-mendicants.[395] In the Buddha's day alms-giving wasn't systematized, but the general feeling, which afterwards crystallized into a definite doctrine, was that giving alms to wanderers was meritorious. This was the mutual arrangement between what afterwards became the monks and what afterwards became the lay people. The monks were able to give up the world and be supported by the lay people because the lay people believed that by giving monks alms they were acquiring merit, which would redound to their benefit in this life itself and also after death in the form of a happy heavenly rebirth. But probably at the beginning, almsgiving was more connected with the tradition of hospitality, receiving the guest as someone from outside. Maybe no one had come to your village from the outside world for a long time, and you were pleased to see someone who could bring news about what was happening elsewhere. You didn't mind him staying overnight, and you gave him food. The wanderer might also be a source of advice, even medical advice. Even today in India, people tend to ask a monk of any kind for advice on all sorts of subjects, and very often he gives it – whether he is qualified or not – and they accept it with great faith.

There is no doubt that the Buddha gathered a regular band (called a sangha or *gaṇa*) around himself, as did the other teachers, but it was quite loosely organized, though in the course of the *Udāna* we see it developing a little. According to the narrative presented to us by the text's compiler, though *bhikkhus* have been mentioned, and the nature of the ideal has been made clear, there has been no hint of any form of organization or any rule. We will encounter these things a little later on in the text, but still in a rudimentary form. We are at a very early stage in the development of the Dharma and the Sangha.

Later on we will come across instances where the Buddha ordains someone, but even that hasn't arisen yet, though it is not necessarily excluded, because this is only a selection of episodes. When the Buddha describes Sāriputta and Moggallāna, Mahākassapa, Ānanda, Devadatta, and the others as 'brahmins', they are introduced suddenly. We are not told in this particular text how they came to be the Buddha's disciples. Perhaps the compiler didn't regard it as important. But the Buddha to some extent found his disciples ready-made so far as way of life was concerned. They were already wanderers. They had already gone forth; having freed themselves from worldly ties they had taken the negative step already. The positive step was to accept his teaching, practise it, and realize it.

It was the time immediately after the Buddha's Enlightenment, and as yet there was no such thing as Buddhism. The Buddha was struggling to express himself using the terms of contemporary speech and religious terminology. There was no organization, there were no precedents; everything was new, everything was purely creative. In those days, everything was so intense, so heightened, that to meet the Buddha, to hear the teaching, to practise it, and to become Enlightened, could happen remarkably quickly. You were Enlightened before you had time to be ordained in any formal sense. So, in a way, ordination was hardly necessary. It was only in later, more benighted days that that formal step had an important place. Later on, we shall find someone formally Going for Refuge after hearing the Buddha's teaching – but not yet.

We can tell from the *Udāna* and other texts that even during the Buddha's lifetime changes did take place. Things became a little more organized, a little more formalized; rules began to be formulated. In the Vinaya the Buddha is represented as saying at the end of his life, 'When I started my mission, there were many *arhants* and few rules, but now we have many rules but few *arhants*.'[396] You can't help this development, apparently. There has to be a constant effort to keep things creative and prevent them from crystallizing. By the time of the rise of the Mahāyāna, things had become so crystallized that the Mahāyāna had to make what was practically a new beginning, and the Vajrayāna did the same thing later on when the Mahāyāna itself had become petrified in scholasticism. It is instructive to compare the way of life depicted in the *Udāna* with contemporary Buddhist practice in the East, and see what great changes have taken place; perhaps justified, perhaps not.

All that we've got so far, and this is going to continue for the greater part of the *Udāna*, is the Buddha moving about teaching, and staying at certain recognized localities. There are already a few places with which he is associated: Uruvelā (Bodh Gaya), Sāvatthī (Śrāvastī), Rajgir. There is no word as yet of anything like a monastery. The Buddha's followers spend most of their time in the open air. The Buddha is teaching but as yet there is no such thing as a sermon. There are no lengthy discourses, just sayings and responses to questions, often in verse. There is no organized instruction, no recognizable organization. All that is in the future. So you can see how things were, right at the beginning.

The contemporary Indian would have known about the social and political scene. He would have known that there were such people as wanderers, and that some were more prominent than others and had formed little brotherhoods, and then he'd hear more and more, as the years went by, about a particularly remarkable wanderer called Gautama who seemed to be getting a larger following than anybody else, not only from among the wanderers but from among people who were living at home, even merchants, kings, and princes. It would become clear that Gautama was at the head of a growing movement. Then, one day, maybe he would meet a disciple of the Buddha or the Buddha himself, and become caught up in his movement and his mission.

We have to be careful not to read back later developments into those early days. In contemporary Buddhist art in the East you see the Buddha beautifully dressed in a neatly pressed yellow robe with a bag over one shoulder, a neat little begging-bowl and his hair nicely cropped, with a column of monks, dressed in exactly the same style, with the same expressions, even, but slightly smaller in scale, following behind; and behind them sometimes you will see a great monastery. It wasn't like that at all in the Buddha's day, but Buddhist art gives us that non-historical picture.

The commentary says that *upadhi* is connected to the sense of owning, identifying with, this human existence (i.e. the five *khandhas*) – hence translated 'appropriation' in the *udāna*.[397] Śāntideva says something similar in the *Bodhicaryāvatāra*. Here, the *bhikkhus* have been abused by wanderers of other opinions, and that abuse has rather upset them, but how has it reached them? Through the sense of hearing. And how do they come to have ears? Because they have bodies. How do they come to have bodies? Through their previous karmas – previous cravings, previous ignorance, previous *saṃskāras*. It is because they have the body, equipped with ears, that they can hear abusive speech, and in that way their minds become upset. So whose fault is that? It is not simply the fault of the people who are doing the abusing. As Śāntideva says, referring to someone beating you, 'He has taken the stick, but you have taken the body.'[398] It is when the two come together that you suffer. It is not entirely your fault that you are suffering, but it is also not entirely due to other people. Here the *Udāna* is suggesting a comparable aim to that proposed by Śāntideva: to develop insight into the dependently-arisen nature of *vedanā*. This might be considered a rather negative point of view, but one should consider the practical function of this reflection, which is to help you to control anger. Don't be angry with someone else for harming you, because you are at least partly responsible for your painful experience. That is the practical message.

Of course it assumes, as Buddhism generally assumes, that you've taken, or gravitated towards, the body because your psyche was of such a nature before rebirth that it wanted to be embodied. It was seeking physical experience, sensuous impressions. Now you've got what you wanted, but that experience includes things like sticks and unpleasant words. The same body that can experience pleasure can also experience pain. You can't have the one without the other. In fact, the more exquisitely sensitive you are, and the subtler the pleasures that you can appreciate, the subtler the pains you can experience too. If you're a coarse, insensitive soul, you may not experience all those ecstatic pleasures, but you don't suffer very much either. The only refuge from this is a spiritual dimension where these conditions don't exist. If you don't want the pain and suffering, you've got to give up the sensuous pleasure too. You've got to be ready to have both or to give up both.

If your mind is absorbed in meditation, or even in something greater than that, then what is normally regarded as pleasure and pain won't influence you so much and you'll be less motivated and oriented by those things, and that will be reflected in your behaviour. You won't go after everything that everyone else is going after. Your mind is absorbed in higher things, so you won't be motivated as most people are motivated. Your feeling of competitiveness and having to get on in a worldly sense will be weakened. That competitive spirit can't function fully while your mind is absorbed in higher things. We are dominated and directed most of the time by what we think is pleasant and what we think is painful. We are completely non-objective. We instinctively go after what is pleasant and agreeable and avoid what is unpleasant and disagreeable. But if our mind is absorbed in some higher dimension, that sort of motivation is much weakened and our whole life is reorganized on a different basis. We are not seeking satisfaction all the time as people usually are.

I don't think we realize the extent to which we are dominated by the pleasure/pain principle. We can't ignore it completely because we are at least partly a physical organism, but we can't allow ourselves to be completely dominated by it. Sometimes we have to quite definitely accept situations which are not pleasant from the ordinary point of view and insist on remaining in those situations because that is the way that we are going to evolve. Not that we automatically evolve when there's pain, but we can't avoid some incidental pain if we want to evolve in the long run. You don't have to deliberately inflict suffering on yourself as a sort of discipline. If you can evolve and have a pleasant time too, why not? But you mustn't make pleasure the criterion for what you do. The Buddha does say that there are four types of people as regards spiritual evolution: those who have it easy all the way, those who have it difficult all the way, those who have it difficult at the beginning and easy towards the end, and those who have it easy at the beginning and difficult towards the end.[399] I've seen this to be true in people I've known. But even if it's painful all the way, people can feel that that doesn't matter. They recognize that what is really important is happening and they are quite prepared to put up with the trouble they meet on the way. In a sense they don't mind, in a sense they don't suffer, but the pain and difficulty and stress are there and they don't attempt to disguise the fact.

2.5 THE BUDDHA AND THE BUSINESSMAN

> Once, when the Buddha was staying near Sāvatthī in the Jeta Wood at Anāthapiṇḍika's park, a lay follower from Icchānaṅgala arrived in the area on business, and when his work was completed he went to see the Buddha. 'At last you've managed to find the opportunity to come here!' said the Buddha. 'I've been wanting to come for a long time,' said the businessman, 'but I've been so busy I couldn't get away.' And the Buddha breathed out these words:

Those who have nothing are happy indeed,
who are learned and have mastered the teaching.
See how those who have things are oppressed.
People tend to bind themselves to people.

Once again the verse does not seem to be very closely connected with the story. We are still at Sāvatthī, and an *upāsaka* comes to see the Buddha. We have had mention of *bhikkhus* before, but this is the first appearance in the *Udāna* of an *upāsaka*, here meaning simply one who is a disciple of the Buddha but who stays at home. A *bhikkhu* is a disciple of the Buddha who was either a wanderer before he met the Buddha or became a wanderer after meeting him. It is not that the *bhikkhu* has one kind of ordination and the *upāsaka* has another. There is no question of monk and layman in the later sense, much less still of priest and layman in the Christian sense. They are both followers, but the *upāsaka* followers are somewhat more restricted, as we see in this episode.

Upāsaka is usually explained as 'one who worships and is devoted to something (*upāsati*)', in the Upanishadic tradition one who practises a particular kind of worship. More etymologically, *upāsana* is also explained sometimes as meaning one who sits near – *upa āsana* – that is to say, one who sits near a teacher, one who is learning a spiritual tradition. It has the general significance of someone engaged in some kind of spiritual practice.

The *upāsaka* has come on business to Sāvatthī and takes advantage of the opportunity to visit the Buddha. He would like to visit him more often, but he is restricted in a way that the *bhikkhu* isn't. It is in this sense that we sometimes speak of the *bhikkhu* as the full-time follower and the *upāsaka* as the part-time follower. There is no difference in principle between them; the difference is in external circumstances. No doubt the *upāsaka* put himself into his family situation – originally, at least – but he is just as much a follower of the Buddha, and later on we shall find examples of *upāsakas*, and *upāsikās* (women lay followers) too, gaining high levels of spiritual development.

We must be careful that we don't have at the back of our minds any assumptions derived from Christian tradition. In orthodox Christianity, especially in the Catholic church, the priest is entirely different from the layman, inasmuch as only the priest can celebrate the mass and administer the sacrament, but both the *bhikkhu* and the *upāsaka* are followers of the Buddha, both go for Refuge, both are committed. At this stage, there is no difference in precepts. Indeed, no precepts are even mentioned. That is quite significant. Later on, the difference is indicated by the number of precepts taken and the thoroughness with which they are observed, but this is a difference of degree, not of kind. The only difference in terms of principle is that, other factors being equal, the *bhikkhu* will be a more wholehearted and thoroughgoing follower of the Buddha, one who applies the teaching more completely, or makes his Refuge more effective.

There's not a great deal to the story, but it's quite representative. It's the sort of thing that seems to have happened then and still happens now. The businessman has faith in the Buddha, but he's a householder, he's got various responsibilities, so he can't often come and see the Buddha, though he'd like to. And that's how it is. Nothing happens. He presumably just sits there quietly for a little while and then he goes home, and maybe the Buddha doesn't see him again for a few more years. Presumably the householder doesn't feel any urge to get out of that situation. The Buddha is saying, 'Look, here's this man, he'd like to see me, but he can't come often; he's busy with his various business activities, he's got to make a lot of money. Why? He's got a lot of people to support. Why has he got to support them? He's connected with them, they are relations, kinsfolk, children, and he's got entangled with them – but why? Not out of any objective reason, not because he feels an impartial *mettā* towards them, but just because of his own attachment. So, this is his life.' That's how it is: it's just a calm, objective comment on the situation. One finds in quite a few episodes in the Pāli canon that things are just stated. There's no attempt to make anything of it. It isn't, 'Oh, how terrible! You're a wicked man. You ought to come more often.' That's just the situation – it's up to him.

And then the Buddha utters the verse. If there is any connection between the story and the *udāna* that follows it, we can say that the Buddha is reflecting on how bound the poor *upāsaka* is. He wants to see the Buddha, wants to lead a spiritual life, but he's so tied up with worldly responsibilities and with other people that he is oppressed by his possessions. The Buddha is saying that one who has mastered the Dharma, who understands the truth, who has received much spiritual instruction or has heard much from spiritual teachers, never thinks that all is well with him from a worldly point of view. He knows that having possessions is only a source of trouble, and that being involved with other people in the usual worldly way is a hindrance. *Upadhi*, here translated 'appropriation' is sometimes (for example by Woodward) translated 'possessions', in the subjective sense of the 'state of mind of possessing'. 'Possessions' can thus be understood in a psychological-cum-spiritual sense. In the *Sutta-Nipāta* the Buddha says that a characteristic of the awakened being is that he is *akiñcana*, literally 'without anything, having nothing', and in another *Sutta-Nipāta* passage, the *arhant* or 'awakened person' is characterized as *akiñcana*, 'without possessions'.[400] So the man with possessions is the man who is not an *arhant*. You could even say he is an egotist, one who has substantial investments in craving, aversion, and delusion and is drawing a good income from them.

One can't necessarily infer that the *bhikkhu* will be more dedicated to spiritual practice than an *upāsaka*. Even after taking formal monastic ordination, even under the system prevailing in the Buddha's day, *bhikkhus* had to be concerned with worldly things to some extent. At least they had to mend their robes. The practical question is at what point your involvement with the spiritual life becomes so thoroughgoing that your Going for Refuge to the Three Jewels can be considered truly effective. In our Triratna community that is the point at which one is ordained. As we say, commitment is primary, lifestyle is secondary, so one should be cautious about speaking in terms of full-timer and part-timer, as though spiritual commitment was a question of external occupation rather than inner attitude. At the same time, the inner attitude will naturally find expression externally. You can meet people who lead a very worldly life but say that they are monks at heart, but that isn't good enough.

What you don't want in Buddhism is a sort of clergy or priesthood. A few hundred years after the Buddha's time, the wanderers settled down and most of them ceased to wander. The huts they had occupied during the rainy season were replaced by large buildings, eventually known as monasteries, and the monks, as they now were, lived in them all the time. They had gardens and servants – even slaves in Sri Lanka, which was not at all a happy development. You see the dangers, and how easy it is to settle down. This is why in our own order we place the emphasis entirely on the Going for Refuge, which is the common factor for everyone. Distinctions such as full-timers and part-timers, monks and laymen, *bhikkhus* and *upāsakas*, pale into insignificance in comparison with the fact that you are all Going for Refuge. That is the important thing, and you try to implement it as fully as you can, according to your circumstances.

2.6 HAPPY INDEED ARE THOSE WHO HAVE NOTHING

> Once, when the Buddha was staying near Sāvatthī in the Jeta Wood at Anāthapiṇḍika's park, the pregnant wife of a certain brahmin wanderer asked her husband to get some oil to use at her delivery. The wanderer didn't know where to get oil, but after his wife had asked him three times to go and get some, he had an idea. At that time, King Pasenadi of Kosala was offering recluses and brahmins as much oil or ghee as they wanted to drink, but not to take away. The wanderer decided to go to the king's storehouse and drink as much oil as he could, then go home and vomit it up so that his wife could use it. But he could neither vomit it up or excrete it, and ended up rolling around in excruciating pain. The Buddha, seeing this, breathed out these words:
>
> Happy indeed are those who have nothing;
> for experts in wisdom are people without anything.
> See how those who have things are oppressed.
> People have hearts tied up with people.

This is the first reference in the *Udāna* to wanderers with families. As already mentioned, there were a few, though they were the exception rather than the rule. These wanderers are brahmins, so evidently a spiritual restlessness affected them as well as the members of other castes. The story is interesting from an anthropological point of view, because we encounter married wanderers, and the woman is about to give birth to a child. One can see that being married and living in those circumstances isn't very easy. She can't get the things that she needs, so she asks her husband to go and look for them.

We also notice, for the first time in the *Udāna*, the pairing of *brāhmaṇa* and *samaṇa*, brahmin and recluse, a combination that appears again and again throughout Pāli literature. It stands for renunciates in general, but each of the terms has a particular connotation. *Śramaṇa* (to use the

Sanskrit form of the word) means a wanderer of non-Vedic tradition (literally a striver). The Buddha and his followers were *śramaṇas*, and so were Mahāvira and his followers. The brahmins were those who adhered to the Vedic tradition and performed the Vedic rites and ceremonies, who believed in brahminical law and in the supremacy of the Brahmin caste. The authorities usually treated both alike, as the king does here in his distribution of ghee or oil.

Usually the *brāhmaṇas* were settled, so if a brahmin by caste becomes a wanderer, it suggests that he has broken loose from the Vedic tradition. Sāriputta and Moggallāna were brahmins by birth, but became wanderers, as the *śramaṇas* were. The *brāhmaṇas* tended to live with their wives and families, very often in villages built on land donated by the king, earning money by performing Vedic rites and teaching the brahminical traditions to young brahmins who came to them as students. By contrast, the *śramaṇas* wandered from place to place and did not perform any rites or ceremonies. The *śramaṇas* and *brāhmaṇas* of ancient India were rather like the friars and priests of the middle ages, if you could imagine the priests being married – though often they had concubines anyway. The friars wandered from place to place and did not have to perform religious ceremonies, whereas the priests were attached to a particular church and performed mass for the faithful. Likewise, you could say that the brahmins were the secular clergy and the *śramaṇa*s were the wandering ascetics. You can see a need for both up to a point. Society seems to require people to perform domestic ceremonies. There were lots of those for the ordinary person, and the brahmin used to perform them. But in ancient India the person who performed ceremonies of that sort was always sharply distinguished from the person who was devoted to spiritual practice.

The verse does not have a close connection with the episode, but the meaning is fairly clear. If one takes it as applying to the episode, it seems a little severe, but it doesn't go particularly well with the story. It's almost the same as the previous verse, which was attached to a quite different sort of tale and which suggested that happiness consists not in the satisfaction of craving but in the cessation of craving. Here it is stated that happiness comes not from owning things but from not owning anything at all. The less you own, the happier you are. 'Happy indeed are those who have nothing; for experts in wisdom are people without anything.' There's quite a profound meaning in this. It's not just about external possessions. One doesn't consider oneself as being anything or having anything even in a psychological or spiritual sense, and that is wisdom: to have this sense of non-possession even with regard to oneself. 'For experts in wisdom are people without anything' lifts the whole conception of being without possessions on to a higher level. As we have seen, in the *Sutta-Nipāta akiñcana*, being 'without possessions', is an epithet of an awakened being, and the same word is used here. It is not simply one without physical, material possessions, as the wanderers were, but one who has no mental belongings, no opinions, and no problems. This ties up with the Perfection of Wisdom approach of the Mahāyāna. It is the conception of ownership that is referred to, rather than the possession of material things. If you don't have a conception of 'I' you won't have a conception of 'mine', and in that sense you are free from possessions.

Not having any possessions at all, or getting pretty near that, is quite an experience. In my wandering days in India, I did without money for nearly three years, which meant virtually doing without possessions, apart from the clothes I was wearing. If you have no money, you really don't have anything, because you can't fulfil your desires. However much you want something, you just can't have it. It is quite a strange state to be in. You feel quite free, but you can at times feel impotent, because money is power, though it shouldn't be, or at least you shouldn't feel it as such. You are at the mercy of circumstances and people, though often in a positive way. In India, people would come up to me and say, 'Where have you come from?' I'd say, 'From such-and-such a place.' 'Where are you staying tonight?' 'I don't know yet.' 'Well, come and stay with me. Have you eaten?' When I started using money again, it seemed a very artificial and unnatural transaction to hand over coins and notes and receive goods in exchange.

This verse transposes the concept of ownership and freedom from ownership onto the intellectual and even the spiritual plane: you don't regard anything as yours, so you cannot be threatened through anything which is not you. You don't even regard any ideas or views, or any ideology, as yours, so if an idea is attacked, you don't feel threatened or get upset. You can look at it quite calmly and objectively. The suffering of people who have possessions, not simply material possessions but intellectual possessions, to which they cling, is clear. But how is being bound to others tied up with the question of possessions? One could say that people are bound to one another because they regard one another as their possessions. The word used, *paṭibaddhacitta*, means having a heart (*citta*) bound up or infatuated. That is why in the *Dhammapada* the Buddha represents the spiritually immature person as saying to himself, 'This son is mine. This wealth is mine.'[401] Of course, what is suggested is not an attitude of cold indifference; that would be the opposite extreme. The suggestion is to be warm, friendly, compassionate, but not possessive.

All this consideration of possessions seems a bit too sweeping to refer just to the few mouthfuls of oil that the wanderer managed to swallow, which is why I rather feel that the verse doesn't really belong to the story. I'm sure the episode happened, it rings quite true. It's a rather pathetic story that the wanderer tries to get oil for his wife in this way and suffers on account of it. You could even say that he suffers on account of his good nature, not on account of being attached to possessions. It's sad, it's unfortunate, but this is the sort of thing that happens if you're trying to lead the life of a wanderer along with your wife and family. Perhaps the connection with the verse comes at the end of the story when the brahmin takes the oil and thinks he will be able to bring it up, but when it comes to doing so, he can't. Without pressing the point, this is symbolic. He can neither vomit it up nor pass it down, like the snake in the Indian fable. A snake tries to swallow a frog, but the frog is so big that the snake can neither swallow it down nor vomit it up, so it chokes. Sometimes you may find yourself in this position: you can neither assimilate something, nor give it up, so you are sort of stuck with it. Likewise, because the wanderer has a wife, he can neither get fully into the wandering life nor give it up. I'm inclined to think that there's some suggestion of that because one feels that the compilers, whoever they were, were quite subtle-minded. There are interesting little juxtapositions and contrasts, as though the whole text has been carefully and thoughtfully edited.

2.7 DON'T FALL INTO THE KING OF DEATH'S POWER

Once, when the Buddha was staying near Sāvatthī in the Jeta Wood at Anāthapiṇḍika's park, the beloved only son of a lay follower died, and after the funeral a number of lay followers with wet hair and clothes approached the Buddha in the middle of the day, prostrated themselves, and sat down to one side. When the Buddha asked them what they were doing there at that time of day in such a condition, they explained what had happened, and the Buddha, seeing its significance, breathed out these words:

The tiered gods, the human masses,
are tied to enjoying what is beloved.
But, sorrowful and suffering pain,
they fall into the King of Death's power.

But those who both by day and by night
are heedful and let go what is beloved,
they certainly dig out the root of grief,
Death's lure, so hard to pass beyond.

This was a very common story in ancient India, as it is in India today. Someone dies and the body is cremated, often on a river bank. According to the ancient Indian belief, having anything to do with a dead body is polluting, so after the cremation you all have to go and have a dip in the river. You go in fully clothed and come out with your clothes and hair streaming wet. So here an *upāsaka*'s son had died, perhaps during the night, and after the cremation, just as they were, their hair and clothes wet, they came straight to the Buddha, even though it was an untimely hour – that is, before the midday meal. Probably feeling the need for consolation, they just wanted to be with the Buddha. It's no doubt quite obvious what has happened, but anyway, the Buddha asked, and he was told the reason.

In the *udāna* the Buddha reflects on how people, due to their attachment to other human beings, especially to their children, develop a strong attachment to existence as such. Then, when they die, under the law of karma, back they have to come. It's quite a solemn verse. The Buddha is saying, in effect, you come here and you're all suffering, especially the father, because he's lost his child, and the child was very dear to him. It's a natural, universal thing that if someone (or something) is dear to you, you are attached to them, and when you lose them, you suffer. You have put yourself in that situation because you are attracted to dear and delightful things, and in that way you submit yourself to the King of Death's power. Not only men but even gods are drawn down into the circle of birth and death.

To let go of the *piyarūpa*, the one 'of a beloved nature', means casting aside one's attachment to the beloved. Those who are heedful (*appamatta*) night and day and who get over their attachment 'dig out the root of grief' – that is, they get rid of the cause of suffering. The digging up of the root of suffering is a quite common Pāli idiom. You don't merely cut it down; you dig up the root. One could say that in therapy you just trim the leaves a bit, whereas in the spiritual life you really dig down to the root. Grammatically, 'death's lure' is 'grief', but the word is in apposition to 'what is beloved'. Death is out to ensnare you, so in his trap he puts a beloved so that you will fall into his power through the operation of the law of karma. The whole process of birth and death and rebirth is 'hard to pass beyond' – that is, hard to escape from on account of one's attachment, especially to those who are dear to one.

The Buddha is saying that there is only one way to be free from this sort of suffering, and that is not to be attached. Enjoy your companionship with your children and do what you can for them – bring them up, do everything for them – but to the extent that you are attached, to that extent you are going to suffer, and you can only get beyond the suffering by getting beyond the attachment. This is what those who are spiritually devoted do. Some sadness at loss is inevitable, but to the extent that there's non-attachment (which means attachment to something higher) there won't be any suffering, or rather you'll suffer without suffering. When someone near and dear to you dies, you may be sad, but you don't suffer, because you aren't attached. It also depends on the depth of your contact. If your contact is not limited to the physical level, then you won't feel out of contact even when that person has died. Ramana Maharshi is supposed to have said to his disciples, who were upset when he was about to die, 'Why are you so upset? Do you think that I'm going away?' If it's just the 'lovely form' that you are attached to (in the words of Woodward's translation of this verse), then when that goes, everything has gone and you feel completely lost, but if you are also in contact with something more than that – the 'spirit' of the person himself or herself – and you still feel that, then the absence of the 'lovely form' doesn't matter so much. I have experienced contact after death a number of times, even with people I haven't known very well, especially if I've performed the funeral ceremony. Even if there's something unfinished about the relationship, you can't finish everything. You can't tie up all the ends neatly, that's just impossible. There's something always left undone.

2.8 A DIFFICULT PREGNANCY

Once, the Buddha was staying at Kuṇḍiya, in the Kuṇḍhiṭṭhāna Wood. At that time a Koliyā woman called Suppavāsā had been pregnant for seven years. Now at last in the midst of the pains of a difficult labour which had lasted seven days, she had the presence of mind to think three things. She thought, 'The Buddha taught the Dhamma for the abandoning of suffering such as this. His Order is on the path to abandoning such suffering. And Nibbāna is perfect bliss, where such suffering is not found.' She asked her husband to go to the Buddha and tell him about her difficult labour, and that she had been thinking about these three things, and when the Buddha heard about it, he said: 'May Suppavāsā be well and healthy and give birth to a healthy son.' And after the Buddha had said this, Suppavāsā became well again and her son was born in good health.

Her husband was astonished at the Buddha's powers and delighted at the result. Suppavāsā said to him, 'Go and see the Buddha again and invite him and his Order to come and eat with us for seven days.' Her husband duly issued the invitation. As it happened, a certain lay follower, the supporter of Mahāmoggallāna, had already invited the Buddha and the *bhikkhus* for a meal the next day, so the Buddha asked Mahāmoggallāna to go and tell his supporter that the meal with him had better be postponed on account of Suppavāsā's invitation. The man agreed to this on condition that Mahāmoggallāna would guarantee him wealth, life, and faith. Mahāmoggallāna agreed to be his surety for wealth and life, but said that faith was up to him, 'You are surety for yourself', and his supporter agreed to the postponement on that basis.

So Suppavāsā served the Buddha and his Order with sumptuous food for seven days, and she made her son pay homage to them all. Sāriputta asked the boy whether he was now well and healthy, and the child said, 'How can I be well? I have spent seven years in a cauldron of blood!' Observing Suppavāsā fondly watching her boy conversing with the famous Sāriputta, the 'general of the Dhamma', the Buddha asked her, 'Do you wish you could have another son like that?' and she said, 'I wish I could have seven more such sons!' And seeing the significance of this, the Buddha breathed out these words:

The unpleasant in the form of the pleasant,
the disliked in the form of the beloved,
suffering in the form of happiness –
these overcome the heedless.

There are several points in this story. First of all, the three thoughts on which Suppavāsā keeps her mind give us the first reference in the *Udāna* to the Three Jewels as a triad, so perhaps this episode represents a slightly more developed form of the Buddha's movement and teaching. 'Seven years' seems to represent an indeterminate period, a long time. The Indians love to exaggerate. The fact of the matter seems to have been that Suppavāsā was pregnant for an unusually long time and had an unusually difficult delivery. She sets quite a good example of a mindful attitude towards pain. She experiences the pain, it's part of the business of living, part of conditioned existence, but she keeps her mind on three thoughts. She remembers the Buddha, she practises *buddhānussati* as it were, and she remembers that he teaches the Dharma so that one can get beyond pain such as she is at that moment experiencing. She keeps her mind also on the order of disciples who are following that path which leads to the abandoning of pain. She bears in mind that true happiness is Nibbāna, wherein there is no such pain. And out of her faith in the Buddha she sends her husband to him to ask for his blessing at that critical time, and apparently the Buddha's blessing worked, so she is very grateful.

To show her gratitude to the Buddha and his disciples, she does the only thing she can: supply them with food. Indeed, she invites them for seven days running. This was a not uncommon practice, and you find it in Buddhist countries even today when people want to celebrate some special occasion. She invites them after she has recovered, but the text does not say how long after; it suggests almost immediately, but it could have been days, weeks, months, or even years, so we can either regard the boy's speaking at a few days old as a sort of miracle or conclude that the feast must have been some years later. We are not definitely told, but the Indian mind, even the Indian Buddhist mind, is always prone to the marvellous, the miraculous, the extraordinary.

However, there was a prior invitation, and it was a convention among the Buddha's followers – it was afterwards made into a rule – that you couldn't reject an earlier invitation in favour of a later one unless the people inviting you agreed among themselves to change the arrangements.[402] This was so that the monks were not tempted to reject a poor person's invitation in favour of a rich person's subsequent one. When Suppavāsā gave her invitation, apparently the Buddha and his disciples had already been invited by a lay devotee who was a supporter of the venerable Moggallāna. So the Buddha sends Moggallāna to ask if the devotee will give up his precedence and allow the monks and the Buddha to go to Suppavāsā's house first. We can see that the Buddha is very particular about these things. Moggallāna raises the matter with his supporter and he says, 'All right, if you'll guarantee me three things: wealth, life, and faith. If you can guarantee that in a week's time I will still have enough money to be able to feed you, that I will still be alive, and that I will still have faith in the Buddha, Dharma, and Sangha, then OK.' But Moggallāna says, 'You are the guarantor for yourself.' This is very Buddhistic indeed. Moggallāna, don't forget, is the disciple with the greatest psychic powers, and he also has a sense of humour. He says, in effect: 'By virtue of my magic power I can guarantee that you will still have money and that you will still be alive. But only you can guarantee that you will still have faith. That is beyond the sphere of my powers.' His follower appreciates the point. 'All right. You've guaranteed that I'll still be rich enough, and I'll still be alive. It's up to me whether I still have faith', and he agrees on that basis. This humorous exchange stresses the fact that you yourself are responsible for your own faith; nobody else has any control over that.

So the invitations are switched and Suppavāsā entertains the Buddha and his disciples to a meal. With her own hands she serves them food both hard and soft – hard, baked things and also soft rice and curries – and makes them eat their fill. Then she gets her child to salute the Exalted One, as the Buddha is called here. This is still the custom in Buddhist countries; parents bring in their small children and make them salute the monks, and they bump the heads of the babies on the floor in front of the monks, and sometimes the babies cry. If we assume that by the time of the invitation the child is old enough to speak, there is no need to assume any miracle. Sāriputta, who is known as the *Dhammasenāpati*, the commander-in-chief of the Dharma, the Buddha's leading disciple, enters into conversation with the child and makes the usual polite inquiries – 'Well, child, are you at ease? Have you food enough? Have you any pain?' – and the child is represented as saying, 'How can I be well? Think of that terrible time I had in the womb!' Maybe his mother has been telling him all sorts of horror stories about it.

The proud mother is very pleased to see her son so precociously entering into conversation with the Buddha's leading disciple. The Buddha sees this and asks her, 'Would you like to have another such son, even though his birth caused you so much pain and difficulty?' And she says, 'I would like to have seven!' Evidently she has forgotten what she's been through. She does not even say, 'Yes, for the sake of another such son, I would go through it all again.' No: she has such a lust for sons that she wants seven! This sort of thing often happens. After a painful experience, people say, 'Never again!' But within a few weeks, there they are in the same situation, the pattern repeating itself once more. You forget what it was like once it's over. Hope triumphs over experience, as Dr Johnson said with regard to someone's second marriage.[403]

As the daughter of the Koliyā raja, Suppavāsā was presumably rather an important lady, the Koliyās being a tribe or community in north-western India. They may have been republican and it may be that there was a sort of council, all the members of which were called raja. But she was clearly the daughter of a prominent man, and she was married to a member of the same community, possibly of less social consequence than she was, as we are not even told his name. She orders him to do this and do that, and he does it obediently, so maybe she was the stronger character of the two, or perhaps even the head of the household, being the daughter of a raja. Several strong-minded ladies appear in the Pāli scriptures, and we are going to come across the most strong-minded of them all, Visākhā, in the next story.

Suppavāsā has a certain amount of faith in the Buddha, the Dharma, and the Sangha. Even in the midst of her pain she remembers them. But she is concerned mainly with blessings, with magical protection. This is very much the attitude of the average lay Buddhist in the East – they are not interested so much in the teaching as in the magic powers of holy men. When you get into difficulties, you ask for their blessing and hope that it will help you, or perhaps you have faith that it works, but you are not so concerned to follow the teaching. So this story reflects the fact that in the India of that day, as in the world today, the realization of the spiritual ideal only matters to a few people. The majority are prepared to accord it a certain respect and even believe in it, but not really for what it is, more for its magical side effects, which can sometimes be harnessed to their benefit. To the ordinary Indian, who believed in holy men and in magic and blessings, the Buddha was not so much the Enlightened One as the great magician, the great wonder worker, the great source of blessings and miracles. You find this in India even today. If you go around as a sadhu or holy man, people often come up to ask for worldly advice or a blessing, or want you to tell their fortune. The Buddha is always represented as being prepared to give his blessing; that was not his principal function, but most ordinary people thought it was. Perhaps it is difficult for us in the West to understand this because we have got so far away from that sort of set-up, but it was widespread until quite recently. The Buddha seems to have accepted that situation, inasmuch as he seems to have given everybody whatever he could, though the disciples figure much more prominently in the scriptures, and he gives his main attention to them.

The verse seems quite appropriate to the story. Once you lose your mindfulness and the recollection of the pain that was followed by joy, you think only of the pleasant side of things, and so you go into it all over again. If you do it mindfully, that's all right. You could think, 'Having another child will mean a lot more suffering, but never mind, I want another child, so I'll put up with the suffering.' But usually people forget about the suffering, so preoccupied with joy and pleasure that they just go heedlessly plunging in all over again. You hear people say, 'I'm never going to do that again', whatever it is. But when they do, and when you say, 'What about last time?' they say, 'Oh, this time it will be different.' So the general moral here is clear: pleasure and pain are bound up with each another, but once the pain is over, we remember only the pleasant side of things and go after that again, forgetting that there will be a price to pay. It isn't that if you experience pleasure, you must necessarily experience pain. It's attachment that brings about the pain, not the pleasure itself. Pleasure need not be succeeded by pain at all, but if you are attached to the pleasure, and the pleasure arises from something conditioned and therefore transitory, sooner or later you are going to lose it, sooner or later it's going to change. That possibility is always there, so if you are attached, you are going to suffer sooner or later. Pleasure and enjoyment don't necessarily or logically give rise to suffering, and if you can manage to enjoy pleasure without being attached, you won't suffer, but that is very, very difficult.

2.9 BEING UNDER ANOTHER'S POWER IS ALL SUFFERING

> Once, the Buddha was staying near Sāvatthī in the Eastern Park at the house of Visākhā, who was called Migāra's mother. On this particular day, she had some business to do with King Pasenadi of Kosala, and the king didn't conclude it as she hoped. She went to see the Buddha in the middle of the day, and he asked her what she was doing there at that time. She explained, and the Buddha breathed out these words:
>
> Being under another's power is all suffering;
> being in control is all bliss.
> Sharing is oppressive,
> for subjection is hard to overcome.

Visākhā, generally known as Migāra's mother, is quite a character. She seems to have been a strong-minded, independent woman, and she came from a family of followers of the Buddha. When she was only sixteen, she was given in marriage to Migāra, who belonged to a Jain family. She was very displeased by the Jain ascetics and compared them unfavourably with the Buddhist *bhikkhus*, so she eventually converted the whole of her husband's family to the Buddha's teaching. Her husband, Migāra, was so delighted to have been converted that he said that in future he would regard her not as his wife but as his mother, because she was a sort of mother in the Dharma to him. So she was generally known as Migāra's mother, even though she was actually his wife, and her personal name was Visākhā. A lady of great enterprise, she was always going to the Buddha with ideas about this, that, and the other. One of her most famous suggestions was that the nuns should be made to wear bathing dresses instead of being allowed to bathe naked as was the former custom.[404] She seems to have been a bit of a Mrs Whitehouse;[405] she was always urging upon the Buddha regulations of this sort. She had a very strong sense of public decency and there's quite a colourful story attached to the bathing dresses, but she got her way: all the nuns had to put on these garments before taking a dip. She made some useful suggestions too (probably even the bathing dresses were quite useful); but anyway, she was a rather forceful, busy character.

In this story we see that she even deals with a king in relation to some business transaction of her own. She seems to have been a rather emancipated woman. Coming from a *seṭṭhi* merchant family – the word *seṭṭhi* (Sanskrit *śreṣṭhin*) means 'merchant', 'banker' – she was very wealthy and had lots of property of her own, and she is represented here as conducting her own affairs, and as having direct access to the king. But the king, being the king, doesn't bring the matter to a conclusion, so she has to go away without having finished her business. She goes to see the Buddha, who says, 'Well, Visākhā, how is it that you come at an unseasonable hour?' and she explains what has happened. So the Buddha says, 'Being under another's power is all suffering.' The king is the king and she is only a subject. Though she is wealthy and influential, she has to wait at his convenience. That is painful. 'Being in control is all bliss.' For the king it is all right. He is in the position of controlling, but very few can be in that position. Even sharing is not easy: 'sharing is oppressive'. So it is very difficult to escape from pain. That is the Buddha's comment on it all.

So this is quite an interesting little vignette. We've got this bustling, capable woman who had been to see the king and couldn't quite get her way and has wasted her morning in town and so comes to see the Buddha in the middle of the day, and he just says, 'Well, what can you expect? That's worldly life. It's very difficult.' You notice there isn't much of the transcendental in these episodes. They are quite down-to-earth and deal with almost everyday situations. Nowadays the equivalent would be having to wait three or four hours at the employment exchange or the Department of Health and Social Security, and not getting what you had hoped for in the end anyway. You get it in India nowadays too: waiting for officials to give you the necessary form and the necessary appointment. It takes days and weeks and sometimes a bit of bribery.

2.10 AH, WHAT BLISS!

> Once, when the Buddha was staying at Anupiya in the Mango Orchard, there was a *bhikkhu* called Bhaddiya who used to go to meditate in the forest and was heard saying over and over again, 'Ah, what bliss! Ah, what bliss!' Other *bhikkhus*, hearing him saying that, assumed that he was dissatisfied with life as a *bhikkhu*, because until he went forth he had been an aristocrat, and they thought that was the bliss he was talking about. They told the Buddha what they had heard, and he called Bhaddiya to come and see him. Bhaddiya confirmed that he had indeed been saying, 'Ah, what bliss!' and when the Buddha asked him why, he explained that in his previous royal life, although he was guarded and protected, he was constantly fearful and distrustful. But now he lived fearlessly in the forest, confident and unafraid, his needs satisfied, his mind like that of a deer. This is why he constantly said, 'Ah, what bliss!' Realizing the significance of this, the Buddha breathed out these words:
>
> One who is rid of inward irritation
> and gone beyond life's vicissitudes
> whose fear has gone, happy and griefless –
> the gods are not able to observe them.

Here, a disciple is witnessed giving expression to an *udāna* of his own. The point of this episode is how easy it is to misunderstand people. When the Buddha calls Bhaddiya and asks him his reason for saying 'Ah, what bliss!' it turns out to be just the opposite from what the *bhikkhus* guessed. Far from being discontented with living in the forest and thinking about what a good time he'd had when he was living at home as an aristocrat and enjoying himself, he is delighted when he thinks how anxious he used to be, and how he is now living in the forest, free from all that. It suggests that it is very easy to misunderstand another person – hence the Buddha's *udāna*. Even the gods, with their supernormal vision, cannot see what he is really like. Unenlightened human beings, who do not have that supernormal vision, certainly can't see another person's mind; they don't know what the real situation is. In the same way, the *bhikkhus* could not understand the real state of Bhaddiya's mind.

The episode is a warning about jumping to conclusions about people from what they do or say. It is not that the *bhikkhus* had any evil intention, apparently. Perhaps they repeated what they thought to the Buddha because they were genuinely concerned that Bhaddiya might be backsliding and thought the Buddha might want to do something about it. But even so, it was based on a misunderstanding. They didn't know what Bhaddiya's *udāna* really meant. We can also understand from this that kings led an anxious life, and we see this elsewhere in the canon too, in the story of how Ajātaśatru is taken by Jīvaka to see the Buddha at dead of night. Though Jīvaka has said that 2,500 monks are living in the forest with the Buddha, Ajātaśatru can't hear a sound, so he suspects that Jīvaka may be leading him into a trap.[406]

In the India of the Buddha's day, the republics were being ousted by the monarchies, and some scholars, looking at the Buddha's life from a purely humanistic point of view, are of the opinion that one reason he created a sangha was to preserve, at least to a limited extent, the freedom and democracy that he was accustomed to in the Kshatriya community – on, as it were, a higher level.[407] The Buddha was not at all in favour of arbitrary rule or authority. Certainly, the whole tradition of the sangha suggests that. He didn't appoint a successor. The sangha would look after its own affairs.

Bhaddiya is represented as saying that he lives in the forest fearlessly and confidently. Great importance is attached in early Buddhism to being free from fear and anxiety. Being 'rid of inward irritation', Bhaddiya, has 'gone beyond life's vicissitudes'. The Pāli here is idiomatic – literally it says, 'gone beyond various existences thus' – in other words, gone beyond any form of conditioned existence within the wheel of life. Even the gods can't see his true nature; he is beyond their vision.

We get the impression, reading through this second chapter, that we are a little further on in the history of the Buddha's movement. True, it goes back to the beginning again, but from that beginning it seems to have moved further on. It is a little more in contact with the world, and there is perhaps a bigger following by this time and a certain amount of opposition and envy. There are also several prominent and well-to-do supporters.

3
NANDA

3.1 BEARING THE CONSEQUENCES OF YOUR ACTIONS

> Once, when the Buddha was staying near Sāvatthī in the Jeta Wood at Anāthapiṇḍika's park, a certain *bhikkhu* was sitting cross-legged nearby, holding his body upright, mindful and enduring without complaint painful, sharp, and severe sensations that were the ripening of former action. Seeing this and realizing its significance, the Buddha breathed out these words:
>
> The monk who has given up all action,
> shaking off the dust of what he has done,
> unselfish, stable, and authentic,
> has no need to talk to people.

Once again, there is not a very close connection between the *udāna* and the prose section, which recounts a common enough occurrence, both then and now: someone sitting meditating and experiencing physical pain. The text here says that the pain is on account of former actions, but that should not be taken to mean that the aches and pains you get when you sit and try to meditate are the result of past karma. They may be; they may not. Unless there is a Buddha around to tell you, you can't know. But whether pain is due to past karma or not, the important thing is to do as this *bhikkhu* did and bear it mindfully, composed, and uncomplaining. It could be rather comforting to believe that it's due to your past karma: 'I've brought it upon myself, I'm paying now for something I once did', but you don't know that. It may seem to be purely accidental, and therefore thoroughly unjust. But it's not really so, because, as the Buddha sees things anyway, you have involved yourself in existence, where things like that happen.

There is no reference in the Pāli canon to how you should sit. It merely says – and even this is not an injunction, only a description – to 'hold your body upright'. This episode makes it clear that whatever discomfort arises when you are sitting, if it is unavoidable, it is just to be accepted. When you meditate you should be upright and relaxed, without being tense or strained, but you find that as you become concentrated, your posture automatically adjusts. It is almost as though an energy arises within you which quite literally pulls you up. If you are not in that deeply concentrated state, you have to put yourself deliberately into that posture until such time as it happens naturally, but there is no virtue in maintaining a posture that is so painful that you can't even begin to meditate. Some of the Zen people insist that this is necessary, and that thereby one is expiating something, and maybe there are times when you have to bear the pain and carry on as best you can, but don't make that into a general rule, or think that the more it hurts, the more good it's doing you. People in the West who take up Buddhism with lingering feelings of guilt tend to feel that if it's hurting it must be doing them good, or at least they are not suffering to no purpose, but that sounds more like a Christian attitude than a Buddhist one. You find absolutely nothing like it in the Pāli canon. If it hurts, that is unfortunate. If it doesn't hurt, so much the better.

The link, such as it is, between the *udāna* and the prose section is in the first line. The prose refers to the *bhikkhu* as enduring pain that was the fruit of former action, but the verse suggests that he has left all karma behind. He is 'mindful, composed, and uncomplaining', so he is not making any fresh karma. He is bearing the results of past karma, but he is not reacting. He is 'shaking off the dust of what he has done'. The word for 'dust' is *rajas*, which means both 'dust' and 'impurity'. He does not talk to people because there is no need so far as he personally is concerned. If he does talk to others, it is to help them, as when he teaches the Dharma.

The episode suggests that even when you have at last got yourself on the right path, you may still have to experience the consequences of things you did when you were on the wrong path. Sometimes you can find yourself in the ironical position that, on account of things you have done in the past, you have, if not to suffer, at least to be involved with consequences which are completely inconsistent with your present state of mind; you can't help it, because those consequences have sprung out of things that you did in the past. That is when one has to develop *kṣānti*, patience, in respect of the consequences of one's past actions. It is no use getting upset. You have committed those actions and you are now bearing the consequences, so there is no point in making the situation worse by rebelling or getting depressed or annoyed or resentful. Just quietly and cheerfully accept: 'Yes, this may well be the consequence of my own actions. OK, I shall bear the responsibility, and within this situation I shall now do the very best that I can,' – just as the *bhikkhu* in this story did. At least don't create any fresh karma.

3.2 NANDA AND THE NYMPHS

> Once, when the Buddha was staying near Sāvatthī in the Jeta Wood at Anāthapiṇḍika's park, his half-brother Nanda told a number of other *bhikkhus* that he was fed up with the holy life and was going to give up the training. One of the *bhikkhus* reported this to the Buddha and the Buddha asked Nanda why he was so discontented. Nanda explained that when he was leaving home, a lovely Sākyan girl with her hair half-combed looked at him and said, 'May you return soon, master', and she had been on his mind ever since.
>
> Hearing this, the Buddha took Nanda by the arm and as quickly as a strong man might flex his arm, the two of them vanished from the Jeta Wood and appeared among the *devas* of the Tāvatiṃsa heaven, where they found five hundred pink-footed nymphs ministering to Sakka, the ruler of the *devas*. The Buddha asked Nanda whether that Sākyan girl or the pink-footed nymphs were more beautiful, and Nanda said frankly that compared to the nymphs, the Sākyan girl was like a mutilated monkey. The Buddha told him to rejoice, because he would indeed obtain five hundred pink-footed nymphs. If the Buddha could guarantee that, said

Nanda, he would be content to continue living the holy life. And the Buddha took his arm again and like a flash they reappeared in the Jeta Wood.

It wasn't long before the other *bhikkhus* heard about this, and they started saying that Nanda was only living the spiritual life for the sake of nymphs, and calling him 'hireling' and 'menial', which humiliated Nanda very much. Going to practise alone, remote, energetic, ardent, exerting himself, he realized that which is the goal of spiritual life and became an *arhant*. When the night was far advanced, a beautiful *deva* who lit up the whole Jeta Wood came to tell the Buddha that Nanda had realized 'here and now through his own direct knowledge the taintless liberation of heart and liberation by wisdom'. And the Buddha knew that it was true.

At the end of the night, Nanda came to the Buddha and released him from his promise of the five hundred pink-footed nymphs. The Buddha responded that at the point Nanda's mind was released from the taints without grasping. And he breathed out these words:

That monk who has escaped the mud,
crushed the thorns of sense-pleasures,
reached the exhausting of confusion,
does not tremble at pleasures and pains.

Leaving aside the slightly mythological context, what is the real significance of this episode? The Tāvatiṃsa heaven, the 'heaven of the thirty-three' is the lowest of the heavens, within the *kāmaloka* still, not yet even into the *rūpaloka*, the world of pure form, but certainly higher than this human world. Sometimes it's referred to as a lower archetypal world, but you could also regard it as the world of the arts, the world of aesthetic delight, or even the world of imagination. The nymphs are sometimes described as 'dove-footed', which means pink-footed, because doves have pink feet, and there's an Indian custom of women painting their feet with red dye.

In the full story Nanda ungallantly declares that in comparison with the heavenly nymphs his former love is no better than a she-monkey with her nose and ears cut off. This is not to suggest that she has no beauty, for there are degrees of beauty. That the higher beauty is higher does not mean that the lower beauty is not beautiful, much less still that it is ugly. Another story in the Buddhist scriptures makes this clear. The Buddha tells the ascetic Bhaggava that, contrary to what some people say of him, he does not say that when one reaches up to the liberation called the Beautiful one sees the whole universe as ugly; what he does say is that when one reaches up to the liberation called the Beautiful one knows indeed what Beauty is.[408]

One can take the Heaven of the Thirty-Three – the number referring to the thirty-three gods of Vedic tradition, who are regarded by Buddhism as inhabiting the lowest of the heavenly worlds – as referring to meditative experience which goes somewhat beyond the ordinary sense level, but still not into the *dhyānas* proper. Soon after you take up meditation you may well have visionary experiences. Nanda's experience was probably that kind of thing, perhaps due to a powerful aura emanating from the Buddha, or simply the impact of the Buddha's personality. Maybe he got on a bit better with his meditation for a while, or at least he saw that there was something in the spiritual life after all.

He was jeered at by the other *bhikkhus* for his mercenary attitude to the spiritual life, for not continuing with the *brahmacarya* because he wanted to, but just to get a reward, like a servant who is working for wages, not like a son of the house who does things there because it is his home. This mockery seems to have prodded him to feel ashamed of himself, but obviously this is not to be applied as a general technique for helping people. You have to be quite careful, because you can make people depressed and even resentful, instead of 'remote, heedful, ardent, with resolute self'. This word *pahitatta* is interestingly ambiguous, perhaps deliberately so. We can take it to mean 'exerting himself' or 'with self given up', but there is no question here of annihilating the ego. It is more ordinary language – developing self-confidence, you could say. Maybe Nanda lacked self-confidence, and perhaps that was why he was always hankering after the Sākyan girl, 'the fairest in the land'.

The story also reminds us of the importance of the arts and everything aesthetic and imaginative to the spiritual life. Otherwise, it becomes very dry and unappetizing, and there is nothing for the emotions to latch on to. I don't mean to suggest that everybody should appreciate the arts, but there needs to be an imaginative and archetypal component to your spiritual life, such as when you set up a shrine with a beautiful image and flowers and lighted candles.

What is rather striking is that Nirvāṇa is not mentioned. The text says 'that' for the sake of which people leave home for the homeless life, 'that' which is the 'goal of the spiritual life', but not a word is said about the content of that goal. This is what has sometimes been called the metaphysical reticence of early Buddhism. It doesn't even say that the goal is Nirvāṇa or Enlightenment. It is 'that' for the sake of which people start on their spiritual quest, but it is not precisely indicated. It is left a conceptual blank, because it can't really be defined. But whatever it was, Nanda realized it.

There is a discrepancy between the verse and the prose, inasmuch as the prose represents Nanda as ascending through a series of worlds, each representing a successively higher, more refined sublimation of feeling, but the verse speaks in terms of an abrupt cutting off of the coarse feeling, the unsublimated energy. It amounts ultimately to the same thing, but this latter language can be misunderstood – as though you merely cut off the gross, which often means just repressing or suppressing it. It remains unsublimated, and then you are making a willed, forced effort which doesn't get you very far, whereas the episode of Nanda makes it clear that the energy is to be progressively sublimated through a series of successively higher levels.

There's no point in criticizing people for their attachment to the lower realms unless it is possible for them to have a glimpse of the higher realms in one form or other. The Buddha could have given Nanda a sermon, but instead he just showed him another possibility. There is no moralistic element here. Throughout the Pāli canon – in fact, throughout Buddhist tradition – there is a clear distinction between the lower and the higher levels, and it is made abundantly clear that to be entangled on the lower levels is not very satisfactory in the long run – you really will suffer – and the higher you can get the happier you will be. But there is no attempt to make you feel guilty for your attachment to the lower levels and no puritanical attitude towards life on those levels. Nanda was worried and humiliated, but he was worried and humiliated at being called a menial, at the idea that he was following the spiritual life not for the sake of Nirvāṇa but for something less than Nirvāṇa.

3.3 THE BUDDHA AND THE NOISY *BHIKKHUS*

Once, when the Buddha was staying near Sāvatthī in the Jeta Wood at Anāthapiṇḍika's park, about five hundred *bhikkhus* came to see him, headed by Yasoja. They made such a row as they greeted the resident *bhikkhus* and sorted out their lodgings that the Buddha asked Ānanda, 'What's all that noise? It sounds like fishermen landing a catch of fish!' Ānanda explained, and the Buddha asked him to bring the visitors to see him. When the Buddha asked them what all the noise was about, Yasoja told him, and the Buddha told all the *bhikkhus* to go away. 'Very well,' they said, and prostrating before the Buddha and keeping their right sides towards him, they collected their robes and bowls and walked off on tour to the land of the Vajjians. There they made leaf-huts beside the river Vaggumudā and began the rains retreat. Yasoja told them that the Buddha had dismissed them out of concern for their well being and they ought to live in such a way that the Buddha would be pleased with their way of living. They agreed, and within that very rains retreat they all realized the three knowledges.[409]

Meanwhile the Buddha, having stayed at Sāvatthī for as long as he wanted, departed on tour for Vesālī, where he stayed in the Great Wood, in the Hall of the Gabled House. Then, becoming aware of the minds of the *bhikkhus* sitting by the river Vaggumudā, he said to Ānanda that it seemed to him that light and radiance was coming from that direction. He asked Ānanda to send a message to the *bhikkhus* asking them to come and see him. They duly made the journey, vanishing from their lodgings by the river and appearing in the Hall of the Gabled House. When they got there, they found that the Buddha was sitting in imperturbable concentration, and perceiving this, they all sat down and entered the same state of concentration.

At the end of the first watch of the night, Ānanda came to the Buddha and pointed out that the visitors had been waiting a long time, and perhaps it was time for him to greet them. But the Buddha remained silent. The same thing happened at the end of the second watch of the night, and the third. At that point the Buddha emerged from his concentration and said, 'You wouldn't say that, Ānanda, if you knew the truth of the situation. These five hundred *bhikkhus* and I have all been sitting here in imperturbable concentration.' And he breathed out these words:

That monk who has conquered the thorns
of sense-pleasures, scolding, violence, and ties,
firm as a mountain, imperturbable,
does not tremble at pleasures and pains.

This is another fairly lengthy episode, and we can tell that it is later in the Buddha's life than any episode so far because Ānanda was his attendant during the last twenty-five years of the Buddha's life. The Buddha is at Sāvatthī, where he spent more time than at any other place, and 500 *bhikkhus* come to see him, headed by Yasoja. Apparently they have not met him before, and we gather that the Dharma is spreading very rapidly because 500 of them arrive all at once. We must not imagine, of course, that they were arriving at a great big monastery. The word *vihāra* simply means a lodging, from the verb *viharati*, meaning to dwell, to stay. No doubt Anāthapiṇḍika's park was a few acres in extent, and there were plenty of trees in the Jeta Grove and quite a few little huts. The Buddha used to live there with a few companions and people would visit him there. On this occasion 500 *bhikkhus* turned up, so there was quite a hubbub, because no doubt they were saying hello to the *bhikkhus* who normally lived there and finding places to stay – a corner in a leaf hut or an unoccupied tree root – and there was a lot of talking and noise.

The Buddha, who is quietly sitting somewhere, hears all this and wants to know what's going on. He says: 'It doesn't sound like *bhikkhus* arriving, it sounds like fishermen catching fish!' We can imagine that these would be fishermen not with a quiet rod and line but with nets, so when the net is drawn in and there's a big catch, they get very excited and there is a lot of shouting. The Buddha is so displeased with the noisy *bhikkhus*, apparently, that he just sends them away for their own good. So their first encounter with the Buddha is a reprimand.

They travel quite a long way; it's nearly 300 miles from Sāvatthī to Vesālī. When they get there, they go on their almsrounds and then find a place on the bank of a river to spend the rainy season. They make leaf huts for themselves, and Yasoja, at least, realizes that they were badly behaved when they arrived at Sāvatthī, so he suggests that they spend their rainy season retreat in a manner of which the Buddha would approve, and devote themselves energetically to their practice. So that is what they do. At the end of the rainy season retreat, the Buddha, having apparently spent it in Sāvatthī, goes to Vesālī. He comes to know – by his supernormal faculties, evidently – how the *bhikkhus* have been spending their time and that they have become spiritually advanced, so he sends for them.

What happens next is quite interesting. The Buddha is seated in imperturbable concentration, and the 500 *bhikkhus* perceive that, so they sit down with him and also enter into imperturbable concentration. Ānanda is in attendance. He was responsible for making the Buddha's appointments, ushering in visitors, and seeing that the Buddha saw them all in the proper order and separately when necessary. He also had a vast memory; he remembered everything the Buddha said, so that after the Buddha's decease, he was able to repeat all the teachings. But in certain respects, Ānanda was not very spiritually developed. He was not particularly good at meditation and he had no psychic powers, so he was not aware that the Buddha and the 500 newly arrived *bhikkhus* were so concentrated.

So, at the end of the first watch of the night, he coughs – 'Ahem!' – and says, 'Lord, the *bhikkhus* have come.' He thinks the Buddha doesn't know, and maybe the *bhikkhus* are a bit upset that he is not taking any notice of them, so he nudges the Buddha and says, 'Maybe you should exchange greetings with these *bhikkhus*. They have been sitting here a long time.' There are many references in the Pāli texts to the way the Buddha would exchange friendly greetings with people as they arrived. Ānanda thinks that the Buddha is unintentionally being a little rude, so he tries to rouse him, but the Buddha just goes on meditating. At the end of the second watch, Ānanda says the same thing, and at the end of the third watch, he says, 'Look, the whole night has passed. These poor *bhikkhus* have been sitting here all this time and you haven't greeted them. Don't you think you should?' But the Buddha says, 'If you knew what was really going on, Ānanda, you wouldn't ask such a question.' What does he mean?

Ānanda is suggesting that the Buddha should greet the *bhikkhus*, but the greeting has been going on all the time, though Ānanda doesn't know it due to his lack of psychic development. That is the important point: that real communication is being in the same imperturbable concentration, *āneñja samādhi*. The Buddha and the 500 *bhikkhus* are on a level where greetings are unnecessary. They are aware of each other's mental states, so there is no need for friendly exchanges; they are in perfect communication, though Ānanda doesn't know that. What a change in those *bhikkhus*!

There is a link with the previous episode – one of those little editorial touches. Just as the other monks teased Nanda for being a hireling and a menial, and that helped him and goaded him on, in the same way the Buddha's peremptory dismissal of those noisy *bhikkhus* helped them. They realized that it was for their own good – or Yasoja realized it, anyway – and they acted accordingly.

Once again, there is not a very close connection between the prose section and the *udāna*, though certainly the Buddha and the 500 *bhikkhus* were all sitting 'like mountains', in imperturbable concentration.

3.4 SĀRIPUTTA SITS LIKE A MOUNTAIN

> Once, when the Buddha was staying near Sāvatthī in the Jeta Wood at Anāthapiṇḍika's park, Sāriputta was sitting cross-legged nearby, having brought mindfulness to the fore. Seeing this and realizing what it meant, the Buddha breathed out these words:
>
> Just as a mountain, solid rock,
> is unmoving, well-established,
> so the practitioner, from exhausting confusion,
> like a mountain, does not tremble.

This is quite a simple little episode. Sometimes the meditator is described as 'setting up mindfulness before him', which is often understood as using concentration on the in-and-out breathing as a means of entering into the absorptions, the *dhyānas*, but the line can also be translated as 'bringing mindfulness to the fore', a less specific direction. This is a translation issue regarding the word *parimukhe*. It means 'in front', so it can be taken (as the commentaries took it) to mean 'around the mouth and nose', or it can be taken to mean 'to the fore' in a more abstract sense.

As in the previous verse, the meditator is compared to a mountain. There isn't much to say: it is a plain, straightforward comparison, the mental imperturbability of the meditator, in this case Sāriputta, and the stability of the great mountain. You get this sort of comparison quite often in the Pāli canon.

3.5 MINDFULNESS OF BODY AND NIRVĀṆA

> Once, when the Buddha was staying near Sāvatthī in the Jeta Wood at Anāthapiṇḍika's park, Mahāmoggallāna was sitting cross-legged nearby, having mindfulness of the body well established within him. Seeing this and realizing what it meant, the Buddha breathed out these words:
>
> Attending with mindfulness of the body,
> restrained in the six spheres of contact,
> a practitioner who is always composed
> can know Nibbāna for themselves.

This is similar to the previous episode, but there is a slight difference. Moggallāna is described as having mindfulness of the body – one of the basic forms of mindfulness, as described in the *Satipaṭṭhāna Sutta* – whereas Sāriputta was more generally said to have set up mindfulness before him.

The 'six spheres of contact', *ṣaḍāyatana*, i.e. the six senses, include the mind in the ordinary sense. Mindfulness of the body should not be interpreted as applying just to the physical body. It applies to the whole psychosomatic being as it exists on a fairly low level – not only the physical body but the *kāmāvacara*, the sense-sphere consciousness, as well, or the physical body and the consciousness bound up with that body on the body's own level. This is only suggested here; it is not directly stated. You cannot be restrained in the senses unless you are first of all mindful of the body. This is often called guarding the gates of the senses. You keep watch. You are aware of your ear and your eye and your nose and your tongue and your skin, and you are aware that 'through the eye such-and-such impressions are reaching me; there is a possibility of such-and-such sensations and such-and-such desires arising, so I'd better be careful.' If you keep up this sort of watchfulness with regard to the gates of the senses, there is less chance of unskilful thoughts arising. But that presupposes that you are aware of the body as a whole, and of how the senses are operating, what impressions are coming in and whether they are likely to give rise to skilful or unskilful mental states. The Buddha is making an apparently extraordinary statement: that if you can practise mindfulness of body, and if as a consequence you are restrained in the six spheres of sense and composed, Nirvāṇa is very close. It also suggests that mindfulness of the body is quite difficult. The Buddha doesn't say definitely that Nirvāṇa will be reached – he says a practitioner *can* know Nirvāṇa for themselves – but it becomes a possibility. It comes within reach, as it were. *Jaññā* is the verb *jñā* (know) in the optative mood, expressing possibility.

Practice can't be purely negative, just trying to get rid of something. It must consist essentially in the effort to develop something positive or allow something positive to manifest. It reminds me of something a friend of mine in Bombay, who was quite a yogi in his way and had quite a few followers and a small movement,[410] used to say: 'People' (meaning mainly Hindus) 'are always talking about detachment: "be detached from this" and "be detached from that". But I think that's all wrong. You should be thinking in terms of attachment. Attach yourself to what is positive. Attach yourself to the Buddha. Attach yourself to meditation. Don't always be thinking in terms of detachment from this, that, and the other.' There is a great deal of truth in that. It is much better to think in terms of the cultivation of the positive *nidānas* – faith, delight, joy, bliss – than in terms of getting rid of craving. Why do you crave? Because you're neurotic. And how do you stop being neurotic? By being healthy. So it is a question of being healthy. Everything else follows.

Unfortunately, the language of many Buddhist texts is negative, at least grammatically, though the implications are usually positive. For instance, in the *Dhammapada* there is a line: 'Hatred only ceases through non-hatred.'[411] Although 'non-hatred' is grammatically negative, it means love, but in English 'hatred only ceases through non-hatred' sounds quite negative, while 'hatred only ceases through love' is a quite different statement. The positive emphasis is very important. True, we need to give things up, but as a consequence of positive growth and development, not as an end in itself. Otherwise, all spiritual life looks like a process of whittling away – whittling away all your negative aspects – and then it doesn't seem as if there will be much left.

3.6 FIVE HUNDRED LIVES OF CONDITIONING

> Once, when the Buddha was staying near Rājagaha in the Bamboo Wood at the Squirrels' Feeding Ground, there was a *bhikkhu* called Pilindavaccha who was going about calling the other *bhikkhus* outcastes. The Buddha got to hear about this and asked Pilindavaccha to come and see him. Pilindavaccha confirmed that what the Buddha had heard was true. Thinking about Pilindavaccha's former lives, the Buddha told the other *bhikkhus* not to be irritated by his behaviour, explaining that Pilindavaccha had been born into the brahmin caste for five hundred births without interruption, so he had become habituated to calling others outcastes. And the Buddha breathed out these words:
>
> In whom there is no deceit or pride,
> whose greed is exhausted, selfless, wishless,
> whose anger is expelled, whose self is quenched –
> that one is a brahmin, an ascetic, a monk.

When the Buddha tells the *bhikkhus* not to be irritated by Pilindavaccha, it seems to me that he is being a bit ironical. I think he often is, but the irony is often missed. He is saying, 'He's calling you outcastes not just because of a fault he has in this life. It's much worse than that. He can't help being so stupid. It's due to a conditioning going back 500 previous lives – a conditioning of pride and superiority and arrogance.' Perhaps indirectly the Buddha is telling him off. You could look at it differently, but I think the Buddha's irony is to be taken seriously. It is an indirect way of telling Pilindavaccha that it is a fault, and a very serious one. It is also a gentle dig at the brahmin mentality. Brahminical arrogance was a byword in those days, especially among the Buddha's disciples. You can just imagine the Buddha saying, 'Don't think that he is addressing people like this out of any inward fault; it's simply that he's been a brahmin for 500 lives, and everybody knows how arrogant brahmins are!'

Perhaps the lack of *māyā* – 'deceit', 'fraud', 'hypocrisy' – of the real brahmin is also important. Perhaps Pilindavaccha didn't realize how arrogant he was being, didn't realize the extent of his brahmin conditioning, whether in this life alone or also in previous lives.

Abhinibbutatta means 'whose self is completely quenched or extinguished'; the commentary glosses this compound as *kilesaparinibbānena abhinibbutacitto sītibhūto*, 'whose heart is completely quenched through the total *nirvānizing* of the afflictions, who has become cool'.[412] The 'self that has become cool' is a typical idiom of early Pāli Buddhism. Passion and desire and craving are regarded as a sort of heat, a fever almost, and as you get rid of those, you become cool. This is appropriate to a hot country. It is as though, after the fever of the passions, becoming free from them is like going into the cool shade of a tree out of the heat of the sun.

In the last line – 'He is a brahmin, he is an ascetic, he is a monk' – the Buddha equates these three ideals, the *brāhmaṇa*, the *samaṇa*, and the *bhikkhu*. The *brāhmaṇa* is the orthodox Vedic term for the spiritual ideal, the ideal man, a term which the Buddha tried to spiritualize, the *samaṇa* is the non-Vedic term for the same ideal, and the *bhikkhu* is the somewhat later, specifically Buddhist, term for that same ideal. So if in you there is no self-deception, no pride, and so on, you are fulfilling that spiritual ideal which is indicated by these three terms.

3.7 THE KING OF THE GODS MAKES CURRY FOR KASSAPA

> Once, when the Buddha was staying near Rājagaha in the Bamboo Wood at the Squirrels' Feeding Ground, Mahākassapa was staying in the Pipphali Cave. Having sat for seven days in a state of concentration, he emerged and decided to go into Rājagaha for almsfood. Five hundred *devatās* were preparing almsfood for him, but he refused their offerings and went into town. Wanting to give almsfood to Mahākassapa, Sakka the ruler of the *devas* disguised himself as a weaver. Taking Mahākassapa's bowl, he filled it with boiled rice, but when he handed over the bowl, it was filled with all kinds of delicious curry and sauce. Mahākassapa, wondering who had the power to do this, realized that it must be Sakka, and told the ruler of the *devas* not to do such a thing again. 'We *devas* also need *merit*,' urged Sakka. And then, rising into the sky, he said that giving to Kassapa was the best kind of almsgiving. The Buddha, who heard this with his divine hearing, breathed out these words:

The gods envy that authentic one,
the monk who wanders for alms,
self-supporting, not nourishing others,
pacified and always mindful.

This episode suggests that the *bhikkhu*'s life, especially the life of the *bhikkhu* who has realized the truth, is superior even to that of the gods, and that even the gods envy that kind of life. One could say that one purpose of episodes of this sort – and there are quite a few of them in the canon – is to demote the gods, as it were, to show people that although the gods live longer and are more powerful than human beings, they are not on the same level, spiritually speaking, as those who are leading the spiritual life and trying to realize Nirvāṇa. It is intended to impress upon the minds of ordinary people that spiritual values are superior to mundane ones, however refined or exalted a form the latter take.

Representing the *devas* as inferior in merit to the spiritual person could be regarded as a subtle social-cum-political criticism. The episode is saying that you shouldn't be impressed merely by a difference of degree. The gods are no better than you are. They are a bit more powerful, a bit longer-lived, and they have a few more pleasures at their disposal, but essentially they are the same as you. But the *arhant*, the enlightened man, is a different kind of being. He is the one you should respect. Even the gods themselves worship the Enlightened man. This sort of passage represents an attempt to reorientate the ideal of the average person from worldly values to spiritual ones. One could also say that putting the Enlightened *bhikkhu* higher than the *devas* worshipped by the ordinary folk is one aspect of the 'humanism' of Buddhism. This is why in early Buddhist sculptures the Buddha is often represented as being attended by Brahma and Sakka (Sanskrit Śakra), also called Inda (Sanskrit Indra), the two gods who were most widely worshipped at that time in India. They appear as humble attendants of the Buddha, representing the fact that even the highest mundane position is inferior to that of the Enlightened man.

That suggestion wouldn't necessarily have produced a negative reaction in the followers of those gods at the time of the Buddha. There's no record of that. The worship of the gods had no degree of doctrinal precision. It was folk religion – folklore, practically. People were quite open to the suggestion that the Enlightened man was higher than the gods. At the time of the Buddha, as far as one can see, most Hindus had a vague sense of these higher powers, but they hadn't really thought about whether they were eternal or merely more long-lived than themselves, any more than the ordinary Christian thinks much about the exact nature of angels.

Brahmin pandits at the time of the Buddha wouldn't have been angry about that treatment of the gods either, because they did it too, in a different way. They maintained that through the Vedic sacrifices, correctly performed by the brahmin, you could control the gods, that the gods were only humble assistants at the sacrifice. As far as we can tell, in the earlier stages the gods were predominant, but with the growth of ritual and the importance of the brahmin as the performer of the rituals, the gods were gradually as it were brought under control. It was a common primitive idea that through your sacrifices you kept the whole order of nature stable: through them the sun rose, and the moon went through its phases, and the rain fell at the proper time. Thus you controlled the gods; this was the brahmin theology. They didn't mind the gods being demoted, provided they could keep their hereditary position.

Theism – belief in one God who is all-powerful and has created everything – is certainly referred to in the Pāli texts (as *issara-nimmāna* – 'creator god')[413] but it doesn't seem to have been widespread or popular. Most people just worshipped spirits – *yakṣas* and *devatās*, gods of different kinds – and respected the brahmins for their control over nature through their rites. They had a simple ethical code, and various tribal beliefs and practices, but theism in the fully developed sense, though known, was not very influential in the India of the Buddha's day. It certainly wasn't the norm of religion as it became in the West – and in India to some extent, after the disappearance of Buddhism.

3.8 THE ADVANTAGES OF GOING FOR ALMS

> Once, when the Buddha was staying near Sāvatthī in the Jeta Wood at Anāthapiṇḍika's park, a number of *bhikkhus*, having had their meal, fell into conversation about the merits of almsfood-collecting. When you're out collecting alms, they reflected, from time to time you get to see agreeable forms, hear agreeable sounds, smell agreeable odours, taste agreeable tastes, and touch agreeable

objects. And all the while, you are respected as a collector of alms. They agreed that they would all be alms-collectors, and this conversation went on and on. In the evening, the Buddha asked them what they had been talking about, and they told him. But he responded that it was not right for those who had gone forth into homelessness to talk about something like that. They should either engage in talk on the Dhamma or maintain noble silence, he said. And he breathed out these words:

The gods envy that authentic one,
the monk who wanders for alms,
self-supporting, not nourishing others,
but not if they depend on words of praise.

In the Buddha's day, there were two ways in which the *bhikkhu* could get his food: by accepting invitations to the houses of the lay people or begging from door to door. Most *bhikkhus* did both, but the stricter ones – Mahākassapa is a good example – made it a rule that they would never accept invitations, because that was too easy and also they might get involved in worldly life. They were generally highly regarded by the lay people as being very austere. In some Buddhist countries today, a few monks do not accept invitations to the houses of the laity. Some *bhikkhus* I knew used to say it wasted a lot of time. The meal would be at about eleven o'clock, but you were expected to turn up at about nine. The people in the house would serve you with a cup of tea and some betel, and engage you in conversation. Then at eleven o'clock would come the meal, which would take a long time to serve. After the meal, and sometimes before it as well, you would have to chant various verses, and you might have to give a discourse and answer questions, and then there would be general discussion, family matters would be brought up and your advice asked, and usually you wouldn't get away before four or five o'clock. Serious-minded monks didn't want to spend all that time in the houses of the laity, so they tried to avoid invitations, but the lay people were always trying to invite them, especially famous monks, because it conferred prestige on the family.

This episode represents *bhikkhus* deciding to engage in the more austere practice entirely for the wrong motives, in the hope of getting the chance of 'seeing forms delightful to the eye, hearing sounds delightful to the ear'. The commentary describes the monks as hoping to enter householders' houses and see innocent sights, hear nice sounds like songs, smell the flowers, and so on, but other passages tell us that what they really have in mind is the forms and sounds of women. Other Pāli canon texts relate how *bhikkhus* going for alms had the chance – strict *bhikkhus* would say the misfortune – of seeing scantily clad women taking their dip in the river.[414] If they were mischievously inclined, the women might even call out to the monks. And these worldly-minded *bhikkhus* are saying that this is one of the advantages of going for alms.

I don't think they're just having a joke. They may not be very well-instructed. All sorts of people came to the Buddha and somehow or other were ordained. They're being rather naive in thinking that they will be respected as collectors of alms despite their secret ulterior motive. And, of course, the Buddha comes to know about it. He doesn't directly tell them off, but he does say that when you gather together, that is not the way to talk. You should either engage in discussion about the Dharma or remain silent. Then he utters a verse which suggests that he is not very happy about their desire for words of praise. He makes it quite clear in the final line what the position is. Ascetic practices are good, but not if you do them for the wrong reason.[415]

Later in the history of Buddhism, once the position of the *bhikkhu* was established as respectable and honourable, no doubt many people took up the spiritual life for dubious reasons. Similar things happen in all religions. Even as early as the time of the Emperor Aśoka many people joined the sangha on seeing how well the monks were looked after, how much they were respected, and what an easy time they had. According to some sources, Aśoka had to purge the sangha of those unworthy elements.[416] When you become successful, a lot of people get on the bandwagon who would not have been with you out of belief in your cause when you were going through a difficult time in your early days. Nothing succeeds like success. So long as you are unsuccessful or not very well known, or really having to work hard, you don't have to bother about the sort of people who are joining you, but once you become successful and well established, you have to be very careful whom you allow to join you, because people may come from entirely the wrong motives.

3.9 ELEPHANT-CRAFT AND OTHER MATTERS

Once, when the Buddha was staying near Sāvatthī in the Jeta Wood at Anāthapiṇḍika's park, a number of *bhikkhus* starting talking about crafts. One of them thought that elephant-craft was the best, and another horsemanship. One praised accountancy, another writing, another poetry, another political science, and so on. This conversation went on and on. In the evening, the Buddha asked them what they had been talking about, and they told him. But he responded that it was not right for those who had gone forth into homelessness to talk about something like that. They should either engage in talk on the Dhamma or maintain noble silence, he said. And he breathed out these words:

Living lightly, without a trade, wanting the good,
with faculties restrained, completely released,
wandering without a home, selfless, wishless,
giving up pride, solitary – that is a practitioner.

This list of crafts gives some idea of occupations in those days. Craft, or trade, is *sippa* (Sanskrit *śilpa*). There is another word, *vijjā* (Sanskrit *vidyā*), for the specialist knowledge, or science, of various 'arts', like geomancy, medicine, etc. Elephant-craft is knowledge about elephants – how to breed them, train them, look after them, tend their illnesses. Chariot-craft is how to build a chariot, how to drive it, how to control it, how to decorate it, and so on.

One gets the impression that coming into the sangha at this time were quite a lot of people who hadn't been wanderers before, swept into the movement as it became more successful. Towards the end of the Buddha's lifetime, quite large numbers came in who were not completely committed and sometimes created quite a lot of trouble for the Buddha and his true disciples. There was a notorious group called the 'band of six'.[417] Certainly there were naughty and troublesome monks of many kinds. It seems to have been a very lively religious world in those days in India.

Usually people think of control of the senses as bondage, but here the Buddha is saying that it's liberty. When he says 'wandering without a home' he has in mind not only being literally homeless, but having nothing in which to even mentally settle down. 'Pride' here is *māna*, the individualistic attitude, basic egotism, almost metaphysical rather than psychological. The conceit is not the feeling or experience of self so much as the feeling or experience of self as distinct from other selves, and therefore to be affirmed, if necessary, at their expense, or used as a basis for unskilful action with regard to them.

3.10 THE DIFFICULTY OF COMMUNICATING ENLIGHTENMENT

> Seven days after the Buddha had gained Enlightenment, while he was still sitting under the bodhi tree at Uruvelā, by the river Nerañjarā, he emerged from concentration and examined the world with the Buddha-eye, and he saw beings tormented by torments and consumed by feverish longings born of passion, hatred, and delusion. Seeing the meaning of what he saw, he breathed out these words:
>
> This world is full of torment. Affected by contact,
> one speaks of what is disease as one's self;
> for, however one imagines,
> it is otherwise than that.
>
> The world is attached to existence that is becoming otherwise.
> Affected by existence, one rejoices just in existence.
> One rejoices in what is dangerous.
> One is afraid of it, this suffering.
> It is for the abandoning of existence that this spiritual life is lived.
>
> Whatever ascetics and *brāhmaṇas* have said that liberation from existence is through existence, none of them has been liberated from existence, so I say. And whatever ascetics and *brāhmaṇas* have said that the escape from existence is through non-existence, none of them has escaped from existence, so I say.
>
> For dependent on appropriation this suffering is produced. From the exhaustion of all appropriation there is no production of suffering. Look at the beings in this world – individually affected by ignorance, they have come into being, they delight in what

they have become, and they are not released. Whatever existences there are, always and everywhere, all of those existences are impermanent, unsatisfactory, and of a nature to change. From seeing what is actually the case in this way through perfect wisdom, craving for existence is given up, and one does not rejoice in non-existence. Nibbāna is fading away and cessation without remainder, because of the total exhaustion of craving.

For that monk who has attained nibbāna,
due to non-appropriation there is no renewed existence.
Māra has been overcome, the battle has been won.
The Authentic One has gone beyond all existences.

One gets the impression from these verses, which are quite obscure, their grammatical construction being rather difficult, that the Buddha is finding it difficult to communicate his experience. It is just after the Enlightenment, don't forget, so it would naturally be difficult for the Buddha to bring his Insight down to the level of ordinary thought and speech. Presumably he remembered these words that he spoke just after his Enlightenment and told them to Ānanda, or maybe Ānanda asked: 'What happened then? What did you say?' From a more sceptical scholarly point of view, one might suppose that later compilers put a frame story around these obscure older lines.

The first verse is reminiscent of the Fire Sermon, in which the Buddha says that everything is on fire, everything is blazing with craving, hatred, and delusion.[418] It is suffering through the five senses, because 'whatever one imagines, it is otherwise than that.' However ordinary people imagine or conceive of the reality of things, the truth is otherwise – things are always changing, and in any case have no fixed essence.

The second verse reflects on how everything is 'endlessly becoming', changing into something else all the time. This whole process of existence is a becoming, one thing after another. The Pāli word *bhava* means existence and also becoming. Becoming is existence, existence is becoming; it's a process, not anything that remains the same. So 'the world is attached to existence that is becoming otherwise' – that is, people delight in this process. Becoming is a source of suffering, changing from one thing into another is a source of suffering, changing from pleasure to pain is suffering, but still people are delighted at this whole process of becoming, which is the world – mundane existence – itself. The whole purpose of the spiritual life is to get away from becoming, from existence within the wheel of life.

Then the Buddha lapses into prose.

> Whatever ascetics and *brāhmaṇas* have said that liberation from existence is through existence, none of them has been liberated from existence, so I say.

In other words, you don't get released from the conditioned by means of the conditioned. There is no psychological solution to psychological problems, only a spiritual, a transcendental, solution.

> And whatever ascetics and *brāhmaṇas* have said that the escape from existence is through non-existence, none of them has escaped from existence, so I say.

That is a remarkable statement, going against what is usually said in Theravāda circles, and even in some texts. The word *nissaraṇa* means 'escape', but what does the statement mean? True, you don't escape existence – that is, you don't gain Enlightenment – by means of becoming; you don't get rid of becoming by means of becoming. You don't get rid of the conditioned by means of the conditioned. But neither do you reach the Unconditioned merely 'through non-existence', by annihilating the conditioned. Another way to talk about this is to say that there must be a positive side to your spiritual life. This is what it really means, and it is very different from the first episode of the *Udāna*, when release or Nirvāṇa is spoken of merely as the cessation of those twelve links of the wheel of life, and nothing is said about the positive links. It's very Perfection of Wisdom-like; 'perfect wisdom' (*sammappaññā*) is even mentioned in one of the verses. Sometimes the cessation of those twelve *nidānas* is regarded as equivalent to Nirvāṇa itself, but this passage makes it quite clear that that is not so.

There is no escape from becoming merely by killing yourself. Nirvāṇa does not come about by the prolongation of the saṃsaric process, in whatever form we find it, nor by the cessation of that process. It comes about only by the experience of a totally different element or dimension, which is the Unconditioned. It is almost as though the non-production of *dukkha* is distinguished from the realization of Nirvāṇa or Enlightenment, whereas in Theravāda Buddhism the cessation of *dukkha* is usually regarded as Nirvāṇa, though not, of course, in the Mahāyāna, which would not be content with a purely negative statement.

But the one who manages to destroy craving doesn't rejoice in that destruction. In other words, he doesn't have a sadistic attitude towards his own weaker side. That is quite remarkable. In a sense, it means being compassionate to your weaknesses. It doesn't mean that you should give in to them, but you should treat them kindly even as you firmly try to eliminate them. Sometimes people adopt a much more severe attitude. I remember a lecture by Christmas Humphreys at one of the Buddhist Society summer schools in which he described the spiritual pilgrim climbing the mountainside to the peak and lightening his load by 'hacking off great bleeding lumps of self', which doesn't sound at all healthy – like a sort of spiritual butcher's shop. So don't be harsh to yourself. It is really the good old super-ego taking it out on the ego and the id, especially the id.[419] Don't divide yourself from yourself and allow your so-called higher self to be cruel to your so-called lower self. That is not spiritual development. Certainly you are happy that craving should come to an end, but don't enjoy destroying it, don't enjoy crushing your weaker side. That wouldn't do you any good. To divide yourself into two, one half establishing a victory over the other, would be a very one-sided pleasure. That is not the sort of integration that one should be aiming at.

But surely, when craving is ended, that part of you doesn't exist? Well, it exists, but in a sublimated form. Being cruel to yourself prevents the process of sublimation occurring. You perpetuate a division by disowning that other side. As long as you regard it as 'not you', there is no communication with it, no possibility of its developing into something higher, or of 'something higher' absorbing its energy. This is quite an important point.

The last verse makes it clear that there's no question of any passive attitude. 'Māra has been overcome, the battle has been won' – this is active and dynamic enough, virile enough, one might say, or heroic enough. But there's no element of masochism in it. One could even say that to take a self-punishing attitude towards oneself is a partial suicide. You feel resentment towards other people, but you can't take it out on them, so you take it out on yourself, as in some cases of suicide. There is a quite different feeling to a positive process of growth and expansion. Again it comes back to this emphasis on developing what is positive in oneself rather than crushing what is negative.

4
MEGHIYA

4.1 MEGHIYA AND SPIRITUAL FRIENDSHIP

Once, the Buddha was staying on Cālikā Hill, with Meghiya as his attendant. One morning, Meghiya approached the Buddha, prostrated, and said, 'I wish to go into Jantu village for almsfood, revered sir.' 'Do what you think it is time to do, Meghiya,' said the Buddha. So Meghiya went into the village for food, and on the way back, as he walked by the river, he saw a delightful mango grove. He thought, 'That's just the place for a young man of good family like myself to meditate. I'll ask the Buddha if I can have his permission to go there.' So he told the Buddha about the mango grove and asked his permission to meditate there. The Buddha said, 'As we're alone here, Meghiya, wait until another *bhikkhu* comes.' But Meghiya said, 'It's all right for you. You've done everything you need to do. But I still need to make an effort in meditation. Please let me go and meditate in that mango grove.' For a second time the Buddha asked Meghiya to wait, but again the young man pleaded to be allowed to go. And after the third time of asking, the Buddha said, 'Since you talk of endeavour, Meghiya, what can I say? Do what you think it is time to do.'

So Meghiya hurried off to the mango grove and sat at the foot of a tree. But to his surprise, his mind was beset with unskilful thoughts: sensual thoughts, malevolent thoughts, and cruel thoughts. 'How very strange!' he thought to himself. 'Here I am, having gone forth into the homeless life, and my mind is full of all these unskilful thoughts!' And he went back to the Buddha and explained what had happened.

The Buddha said, 'Meghiya, when mind-deliverance is immature, five things lead to its maturity. The first thing is having good friends, and the second is to train carefully in the training rules you've accepted. The third thing is seeking out talk that opens up the mind and conduces to turning away, dispassion, peace, direct knowledge, Enlightenment. The fourth thing is vigorously to abandon unskilful states of mind and persevere with skilful states. And lastly, you need to develop wisdom, the understanding of the rise and disappearance of things which leads to the complete ending of suffering. If you have good friends, the other four things will follow.

'And when you're established in those five things, cultivate four more: the contemplation of the unattractive for overcoming lust; loving-kindness for overcoming malevolence; the mindfulness of breathing for cutting off discursive thinking; and impermanence for the removal of the conceit "I am". For, Meghiya, when one perceives impermanence, the perception of not-self is established, from this the conceit of "I am" is removed, and that is called Nibbāna here and now.' And seeing the significance of all this, the Buddha breathed out these words:

Low thoughts and refined thoughts,
arisen along with mental excitations –
not knowing these thoughts as belonging to mind,
one runs here and there with a mind out of control.

But knowing these thoughts as belonging to mind,
one restrains them, ardent and mindful.
Mental excitations which have not yet arisen –
these the Awakened One has completely given up.

This episode represents a quite important development in the *Udāna*. So far we have had the expression of the ideal in general terms, and some indication of qualities to be cultivated and qualities to be got rid of, but this is the first time that anything like a systematic path of progress has been mapped out, even though it is still quite rudimentary.

The moral of the episode that gave rise to the teaching is that Meghiya wasn't ready to go off on his own, and when he insisted on going, against the Buddha's advice, he was unsuccessful, to his surprise. In other words, he didn't realize the extent to which he depended for his positive mental state on his association with the Buddha, and as soon as he parted company with the Buddha, even for a single day, his mind was assailed by all these unskilful thoughts. You notice that the Buddha doesn't force him to stay. Meghiya asks three times, and twice the Buddha refuses, but the third time he says, 'What can I say? How can I stop you practising concentration?' Here again he is speaking ironically. He means, 'I have advised you to strive for concentration, and you say that that is just what you are going to go away and do. How can I object?' He knows Meghiya isn't in a position yet to strive for concentration on his own. He merely thinks that he is. But he also knows that if he told Meghiya he wasn't ready, he might be annoyed, so he lets him go off and find out for himself.

Meghiya is convinced he is in the right. He says to the Buddha: 'It's all right for you. You don't have anything left to do. You have gained Enlightenment. But I haven't. I ought to practise concentration while I have the opportunity. There's this beautiful, cool mango grove where I can get on with my practice very well.' He is ready with all the arguments. He doesn't really believe that the Buddha knows better.

The mango grove is a common feature of the Indian scene. Practically every village has its own grove, providing not only fruit in season but also shade. The leaves of the mango tree grow close together, so they provide a thick, cool shade even on the hottest day. Clearly Meghiya thought that this opportunity was too good to miss. It is as if someone in our sangha was to discover a little cottage tucked away in the country, miles from anywhere and felt compelled to go there, even though perhaps they aren't yet ready to practise on their own.

Another point you notice is that Meghiya doesn't seem to care about the Buddha being left without any attendant, though the Buddha says quite specifically, 'Wait a little, Meghiya. I am alone till some other *bhikkhu* arrives.' Apparently it was considered proper that the Buddha should always have someone with him to do things for him and receive visitors. Ānanda, of course, was the last and most famous of his attendants.

So what do we learn about Meghiya from this? First of all, he was a bit headstrong. He didn't know his own mental state very well, and he didn't consider the convenience of the Buddha very much. Also, he was good at thinking up plausible arguments so that he could do what he wanted to do. No doubt he was not a particularly bad disciple. He was just a bit misguided.

And of course he comes back that evening to tell the Buddha what has happened. Quite appropriately, in his reply the first thing the Buddha mentions is spiritual friendship, *kalyāṇa mittatā* (Sanskrit *kalyāṇa mitratā*). *Kalyāṇa* means good, positive, noble, spiritual. It is only natural, in the circumstances, that the Buddha should speak about that first, but probably it *does* come first for most people: to be in contact with like-minded people who can help you to develop skilful mental states simply by your association with them.

The Buddha then advises Meghiya to train carefully in the training rules – the Pāli word here is *pāṭimokkha* (Sanskrit *prātimokṣa*), which came to refer to the rules of conduct observed by the *bhikkhus*, although, as we shall see later, this is not quite what the term meant in these early days. This piece of advice is connected with the first. If you are living with like-minded people, you will tend to follow the same way of life. It is not about observing the rules that they are observing. You just spontaneously get into their way of doing things, simply by association with them. You find yourself following what may appear to other people to be rules quite naturally. (In any case, as we shall see, at this stage there are no 'rules' in the way they were developed later.)

I have noticed this in the East. You can read about all the rules that the monks are supposed to observe, and some of them seem quite odd. You might get the impression that becoming a *bhikkhu* and starting to observing so many rules is a highly artificial process, but leaving aside those rules that are out of date and aren't observed anyway, it isn't like that at all. When you become a monk and go to live in a monastery, you just do what everybody else does. You don't think in terms of rules exactly. You just – I won't say unconsciously, but spontaneously – go along with what other people are doing. If they are all vegetarians, you are too. You are not following a rule not to eat meat. Vegetarian food is supplied, so that is what you eat. It's the same with other things. There is no rule that you shall chant three times a day, but everybody is doing it, so you do too. It is part of the lifestyle of the monks of that monastery. If you drew up a list of the things that the monks are doing and not doing, it might look like a set of rules, but for those who are living in that way, it isn't like that at all. You could make a summary of your own life and make it look as though you were forcing yourself to obey a set of rules: you get up at seven in the morning and you put on your trousers and shirt, then you have your breakfast, and so on. The monks are just living their life. It is outsiders who think in terms of rules, not the monks themselves – or, at least, not to the same extent. If they are thinking in terms of rules, perhaps they are not very much into the way of life.

So, out of your spiritual fellowship with those who are also following the path, you adopt their lifestyle. In this way, you find yourself practising the precepts, functioning in a skilful manner. What comes next? Discussion of the right sort: positive talk, which produces a positive emotional effect. The striking thing about the Buddha's description of positive talk is that he specifically mentions talk (*kathā*) which is conducive to qualities including disenchantment (*nibbidā*) and dispassion (*virāga*), two qualities that also feature in the positive *nidānas*. That suggests that the right sort of talk can have the same effect on one's emotional state as meditation, right up to the point where the transcendental part of the series of positive *nidānas* begins. This often happens in the scriptures: someone hears a discourse by the Buddha, and he is in such a positive state that insight arises immediately. There is no need for meditation in the formal sense. He is in an equivalent state simply by virtue of that positive discussion. That is very important. It means that positive discussion can get you into virtually the same positive mental state as meditation, and can prepare the way, therefore, for the arising of insight in much the same way that meditation does. Among the kinds of talk that is helpful, the Buddha says, is talk of *sīla*, talk of *samādhi*, and talk of *paññā*, the first mention in the *Udāna* of that famous triad of three successive steps.[420] (They are virtually there in chapter 1, but not in these precise terms.)

So you see the sequence. First of all, there's spiritual fellowship. Then, in consequence of the spiritual fellowship, there is the almost insensible taking on of the way of life of your spiritual friends. Then, within the context of spiritual friendship, there is discussion of a highly encouraging and inspiring sort, which is in its emotional effect virtually equivalent to meditation and which even paves the way for the arising of insight. Next comes the vigorous abandonment of unskilful states of mind and the vigorous persevering with skilful states of mind. This suggests the fourfold right effort to which the texts often refer: preventing the arising of the unarisen unskilful thought; getting rid of the arisen unskilful thought; maintaining the arisen skilful thought; and bringing into existence the unarisen skilful thought.[421]

You notice that these five things that conduce to the heart's maturity are not quite in progressive order. The first three are, but the fourth doesn't seem quite to fall into that sequence. That's where it's becoming much more of an individual thing. You're taking more initiative yourself. First of all, you have spiritual fellowship, and you take on the lifestyle of those with whom you have spiritual fellowship. Then their positive talk and discussion encourages and inspires you; you may even have a glimpse of the truth. But it will only be a glimpse; you can't go the whole distance just by getting inspired by other people, though it can certainly start you off. You have to assume responsibility yourself, take the initiative, and, as it were, traverse that ground again by your own efforts. And the fifth thing that leads to maturity is insight. So there's a definite sequence here, amounting practically to a systematic path of development.

Then the Buddha goes further, listing another four qualities to be 'made to grow'. He doesn't say exactly at which stage this is to be done, but it seems to me that it is in connection with the development of energy. These four things that are to be made to grow correspond to different types of meditation practice. In fact, they are four of the later five basic methods of meditation. There is a slight difference from the later list of five, but it is virtually the same and covers much the same ground. First, the unattractive (*asubha*) is to be developed for the giving up of passion. Then there are two practices which are exactly the same as in the later list: *mettā* is to be developed for the giving up of ill-will and mindfulness of breathing is to be developed for the cutting off of discursive thoughts. In the context of the five basic methods, reflection on impermanence is usually said to get rid of attachment, either in the drastic form of contemplating the stages of decomposition of a corpse or simply reflecting on death or impermanence in general, but here, the perception of impermanence is to be developed for the uprooting of egoism (*asmi-māna*). In the list of the five basic meditation methods to overcome the five poisons once taught to me by my teacher Mr Chen, one reflects upon the six elements in order to get rid of conceit or egotism, and upon the chain of the *nidānas* to get rid of ignorance.[422] But there is the same type of pattern. There are certain unskilful mental states, the antidote for which is one of the basic meditation methods. So one sees this sort of list quite early on.

In the concluding verse, *bhantacitta* literally means 'wandering mind', but 'a mind out of control', as it is translated here, is a good description of the state of complete unmindfulness that overcomes one when one is possessed by an extremely pleasant experience. When things are going very well and you feel very pleased with yourself, you start becoming unmindful. It's a quite dangerous state. There's a story about a Zen master who, to test a disciple, asked him to climb to the top of a tree. There were very few branches and he could easily have made a false step, slipped and fallen, and broken an arm or a leg. The master watched the disciple climb to the top and then climb down again. When he was quite near the bottom, the master called out, 'Be careful!' Afterwards the master was asked, 'Why didn't you call out "Be careful!" when he was at the top?' The master said, 'It was more dangerous when he got close to the bottom. He would have started thinking that he was safe, because he was nearly there.' It is a little like that. When things are going well, we tend to be so pleased that we start becoming unmindful, intoxicated with pleasure and self-satisfaction, and that's when we have to watch out.

4.2 A HOME TERRITORY OF PERFECT EMOTION

> Once, the Buddha was staying near Kusinārā, in the *sāl*-tree grove of the Mallas. A number of *bhikkhus* were living in huts nearby, and they were turbulent, arrogant, frivolous, garrulous, unmindful, and unconcentrated. Seeing this, and realizing what it meant, the Buddha breathed out these words:
>
> With a body unguarded by mindfulness
> and gone under the sway of wrong views,
> through being overcome by lethargy and sleep,
> one falls into the power of Māra.

Therefore, one should have a guarded mind,
a home territory of perfect emotion,
with perfect vision brought to the fore,
knowing how phenomena rise and fall.
A practitioner overcoming lethargy and sleep
should abandon all bad post-mortem destinations.

Here we have the first mention in the *Udāna* of Kusinārā, where the Buddha eventually passed away. The Mallas were a republican tribe, many members of which were followers of the Buddha. The verse emphasizes the importance of right view and speaks of the monk as being 'overcome' or (in Woodward's translation) 'ruined' by wrong views, *micchā-diṭṭhi* – quite a strong expression.

This is the first time this topic has been introduced in the *Udāna* – the importance of getting rid of false or perverse view and cultivating right or perfect view. Sloth-and-torpor, *thīna-middha*, is twice mentioned, translated here as 'lethargy and sleep'. It's striking that succumbing to it comes immediately after being 'gone under the sway of wrong views', and overcoming it comes immediately after establishing right view and seeing the rise and fall of all things. Sometimes sloth and torpor is produced by conflict, as if your energies are cancelling each other out.

4.3 THE BUDDHA AND THE COWHERD

> Once, the Buddha was travelling among the people of Kosala with a large number of *bhikkhus*. Stepping off the road, he was sitting at the foot of a tree on a seat prepared for him when a cowherd came up to him, prostrated himself, and sat down. The Buddha gave the cowherd a talk on the Dhamma which gladdened his heart, and the cowherd invited the Buddha and the order of *bhikkhus* to a meal on the following day. The Buddha consented by silence, and the cowherd went away and prepared a large quantity of rice-gruel and some ghee. The next day, the Buddha and the *bhikkhus* arrived, and the cowherd served them a meal with his own hands. The Buddha gave another talk on the Dhamma before leaving. And not long after the Buddha's departure, the cowherd was murdered. When the *bhikkhus* told the Buddha this news, realizing its significance, he breathed out these words:

> Whatever foe might do to foe,
> or hate to someone hated,
> thoughts wrongly directed will
> do worse to you than that.

What is the moral of this little episode? Or is there a moral? You notice that the cowherd was much enthused by the Buddha's talk, but there is no question of any insight arising, as often happened after the Buddha had given someone a teaching. Positive emotional states are created in the cowherd's mind as a result of the Buddha's discourse, but nothing more than that, though even that is good, as far as it goes. But the verse is interesting.[423] It is as though the Buddha is saying, 'It doesn't really matter what this cowherd's enemy has done to him in killing him. If his own mind had been in an unskilful state, that would have done him even greater harm.' Your own unskilful mind can do you more harm than any external foe.

It is as though the Buddha says that you should not think that all is well with you just because you escape being killed. You may be doing yourself much more harm than that by your own unskilful mental states. All is not well simply because you remain alive. You are your own worst enemy when you get into an unskilful mental state. The harm that others do to you is very little by comparison. It is very rarely that other people abuse you or beat you, let alone kill you, but you are harming yourself by your own unskilful thoughts practically all the time.

4.4 SĀRIPUTTA GETS A SLIGHT HEADACHE

> Once, when the Buddha was staying near Rājagaha, in the Bamboo Wood at the Squirrels' Feeding Ground, at the same time Sāriputta and Mahāmoggallāna were staying in the Pigeons' Glen. One night, Sāriputta was sitting meditating in the open air, his newly shaved head gleaming in the moonlight. Two *yakkhas*, who were travelling from north to south on some business or other, saw Sāriputta's shining pate, and the one said to the other, 'I've a good mind to give that recluse a blow on the head!' 'Take care,' said his friend. 'He's a recluse with great supernormal powers.' A second and a third time the first *yakkha* repeated his inclination to whack Sāriputta over the head, and each time his friend warned him against it.

Not heeding his friend's warning, the *yakkha* hit Sāriputta such a blow on the head that it might have felled an elephant or split a mountain. And immediately the *yakkha*, crying out 'I am burning! I am burning!', fell into the great hell. Moggallāna, who had superhuman divine vision, saw all this happening, and went and asked Sāriputta how he was. 'I am well,' said Sāriputta, 'Although I do have a slight headache.' 'That's amazing!' said Moggallāna. 'Just now a *yakkha* gave you a blow on the head that might have felled an elephant, and your only trouble is a slight headache?' And Sāriputta replied, 'What's really amazing is your supernormal power, that you can actually see a *yakkha*. Personally, I couldn't even see a mudsprite!'

The Buddha heard with his divine hearing this conversation between his two great disciples and breathed out these words:

Whose mind is like a rock –
stood firm when being shaken,
dispassionate towards excitements,
not angry at aggravation –
one whose mind has been developed like this,
how can they come to suffer pain?

This episode connects a little with the previous one, especially with its *udāna*, inasmuch as it shows that it is much easier to hurt yourself than to hurt others. In being an enemy to others you are a much worse enemy to yourself.

It is difficult to say when the custom of the shaving of heads started. The Buddha himself is never represented in art as shaven-headed, though the disciples usually are. Anyway, Sāriputta had definitely shaved his head, as his bald head was shining in the moonlight. Sāriputta and Moggallāna were good friends from an early age, and they entered the sangha together, but they were of very different temperaments. Sāriputta was famous for his wisdom and power of exposition, but he had no psychic gifts at all; that is why he does not even see the *yakkha*. Moggallāna had great psychic gifts and could see what was happening on other planes and in other worlds, and what other beings were doing, but that is just a psychic gift; it has little to do with real spiritual attainment. What is important is that they are rejoicing in each other's merits. They appreciate each other's qualities, even though they are very different, whereas only too often people depreciate qualities which they do not themselves possess, and appreciate only their own qualities.

In the last line of the verse, the Buddha suggests that real harm can come only from yourself. If your mind is right, no real ill can come from outside. You may have to suffer, but things are all right, because your own mind is in a skilful state. This is the teaching of Seneca, that harm cannot befall the wise man.[424] Nothing really bad can happen to him because his own mind is under firm control, so there is no such thing as misfortune for the sage.

4.5 THE BUDDHA AND THE ELEPHANT SEEK SOLITUDE

> Once, the Buddha was staying near Kosambī, at the Ghosita monastery. There he was surrounded by *bhikkhus* and *bhikkhunīs*, male and female lay followers, kings and ministers, sectarian teachers and their disciples, and he was most uncomfortable. Wishing for solitude, one day he went into Kosambī for almsfood, then went back and set his lodgings in order, took up his bowl and cloak, and went off by himself, without informing his attendant or saying goodbye to the *bhikkhus*. Reaching Pārileyyaka, he stayed there in a protected forest, at the foot of an auspicious *sāl*-tree.
>
> At the same time, a certain bull elephant was living hemmed in by a whole herd of elephants who ate the branches he broke down, muddied the water he wanted to drink, and jostled him so that he was not at all at ease. 'Why should I live like this?' the elephant thought. 'Why don't I go off and live on my own?' So the bull elephant left the herd and went to Pārileyyaka. When he reached the place where the Buddha was staying, the elephant kept the place free of grass and brought in his trunk water for the Buddha to use.
>
> The Buddha compared his former uncomfortable living situation with his current life of ease, and the elephant too rejoiced in his freedom from his former discomfort, and in how he could now eat the branches he broke down, drink clear water, and live unjostled. And the Buddha, understanding the thoughts of the elephant, breathed out these words:

The mind of the awakened *nāga* is in tune
with the mind of the *nāga* elephant,[425]
who has tusks like carriage-poles:
both love solitude in the forest.

We can see that things are progressing. By this time, Buddhism has become very popular indeed. There is apparently a big new centre at Kosambi in Ghosita Park, and people are arriving there all the time wanting to see the Buddha – not only *bhikkhus* and *bhikkhunīs*, *upāsakas* and *upāsikās*, but kings and royal ministers, sectarian teachers and their followers; so the Buddha never has any time to himself and is never able to be at ease. He decides to get away from it all without telling anybody, so he goes off into the forest, and a certain bull elephant does likewise. This suggests a feeling for animal life. You find this very much in early Indian literature. Animals are not sentimentalized or treated as human, but they are definitely seen as living beings and treated well. There is a feeling of sympathy between human beings and animals. In the verse we see that the same feelings are attributed to the human being – in this case the sage – and the elephant. They both like forest solitude. No doubt the ancient Indians observed that some bull elephants did like to go off on their own, away from the herd.

There is also the interesting point that even the Buddha was not prepared to put up with just anything. Even the Buddha has his rights, as it were. You might think that he ought to have gone on enduring discomfort indefinitely, but no, even though he is an Enlightened human being, the Buddha is still a human being. He still apparently needs – or at least would like – some time to himself.

4.6 PIṆḌOLA THE RAG-ROBE WEARER

Once, the Buddha was staying near Sāvatthī in the Jeta Wood at Anāthapiṇḍika's park. At the same time, not far away, Piṇḍola Bhāradvāja was sitting cross-legged, holding his body erect. He was a forest dweller, an almsfood collector, a rag-robe wearer, a three-robe wearer, one of few wishes, contented, secluded, solitary, energetic, an ascetic, devoted to the higher mind. Seeing him thus, and seeing what it meant, the Buddha breathed out these words:

Non-abuse, non-injury,
restraint according to the monastic rules,
moderation in eating,
living in solitary retreat,
and practising meditation –
this is the teaching of the Buddhas.

This is quite a well-known verse which occurs in several other places in the canon.[426] Piṇḍola is given this name because he searches for alms. Apparently he joined the sangha originally thinking he would get food, which is probably why he is sometimes called 'Scrap-hunter'.[427] He was a forest-dweller, an almsfood collector (that is to say, he didn't accept invitations to meals at people's houses), and a rag-robe wearer. He didn't have a spare robe. He was a meditator, and elsewhere in the canon the Buddha describes him as 'foremost among lion-roarers' – that is, among preachers – in a discourse in the *Aṅguttara Nikāya* where the Buddha refers to all his leading disciples and says in what respect each is the chief.[428]

4.7 SĀRIPUTTA APPARENTLY DOING NOTHING

Once, the Buddha was staying near Sāvatthī in the Jeta Wood at Anāthapiṇḍika's park. At the same time, not far away, Sāriputta was sitting cross-legged, holding his body erect. He was one of few wishes, contented, secluded, solitary, energetic, an ascetic, devoted to the higher mind. Seeing him thus, and seeing what it meant, the Buddha breathed out these words:

There are no sorrows for the sage
trained in the ways of sagacity,
attentive and heedful, the authentic one
who is pacified and always mindful.

It seems that the Buddha was in the habit of making these little comments on various disciples, maybe to encourage the others. You notice that all these leading disciples, even though they are presumably *arhants*, whatever that might have meant at that stage, are keeping up their meditation practice, or perhaps this was just the natural way for them to behave. Maybe they just liked sitting there, apparently doing nothing, giving natural expression to their state of mind. It is what the Zen people call practice after Enlightenment.

4.8 THE *BHIKKHUS* ARE ACCUSED OF MURDER

Once, the Buddha was staying near Sāvatthī in the Jeta Wood at Anāthapiṇḍika's park. He and the order of *bhikkhus*, being much respected there, were given food, lodgings, and robes. But the wanderers of other sects were shown no such respect. Unable to tolerate the reverence with which the Buddha and his followers were treated, they approached Sundarī, the woman wanderer, and asked her if she would do something useful for them. She said she would do anything for them, even give her life for them, and asked what she could do; and they told her to go often to the Jeta Wood. This she did, and when they were sure that everyone had noticed this habit of hers, the wanderers murdered her and buried her in a ditch in the wood. Then they went to King Pasenadi of Kosala and told him that Sundarī was missing and that they suspected she might be in the Jeta Wood. The king told them to search for her there, and they dug up her body and took it to Sāvatthī, where they aroused people's indignation by saying that the murder was the work of the Buddha's followers. 'They claim that they live the holy life, but they are shameless and immoral, and do not deserve the status of recluse. Look, they have raped and murdered Sundarī.' And that rumour spread around, so that when the *bhikkhus* entered Sāvatthī for almsfood, people insulted and abused them. When they told the Buddha about this, he told them that the commotion would only last seven days, and advised them that when people abused them, they should respond with this verse:

Those who speak falsely go to hell,
and those who say they did not do what they did.
Both kinds of human beings of low deeds
share the same fate after death, in the hereafter.

So the *bhikkhus* learned this verse and repeated it whenever local people abused them. People started to say that the Buddha's followers must be innocent, and as the Buddha had predicted, the commotion lasted only seven days. The *bhikkhus* were astonished at this, but the Buddha breathed out these words:

Unrestrained people pierce one with speech,
like an elephant in battle pierced with arrows.
Hearing harsh speech stirred up and spread,
a practitioner should endure with a mind unbowed.

In previous sections we saw that the Buddha's teaching was spreading more and more widely and becoming more and more popular, but now we see a reaction from some of the other wanderers, who became envious of the success of the Buddha and his teaching. There is another reference to a woman wanderer, and you notice a touch of dramatic irony in her reply. She says she would give her life for them, little knowing that they intend to murder her. She seems rather compliant; she does exactly as they ask without bothering to enquire what it is all about.

This whole episode shows that envy and jealousy are terrible things and that even in religious circles they can arise and produce disastrous consequences. The idea of the wanderers of other views was that the public should get the idea that one of these wicked followers of the Buddha, or even more than one, had had an affair with Sundari and, in order to hide the fact and prevent her talking about it, had murdered her and hidden the body – a nasty little plot. But it doesn't come to anything. The Buddha takes no steps about the matter, except to ask the *bhikkhus* to recite that little verse, and the people come to understand – they are not such fools – that the *bhikkhus* are, as it were, putting themselves on oath. You notice the somewhat dismissive way in which the Buddha refers to all this uproar. He probably knows that the king of Kosala, Pasenadi, has full confidence in him and his disciples. After all, it is only the king who can take steps in response to a murder, and the king is apparently not intervening.

For the wanderers of other views, it was a matter of economics. It wasn't just that they were not shown respect in the way the Buddha's followers were; they also weren't given offerings. Things were becoming pretty desperate for them; their very livelihood was at stake, so they stopped at nothing, even slander and murder. The story reminds me of George Bernard Shaw's comment on Mahatma Gandhi's assassination:

'It shows it is dangerous to be too good.'[429] In order not to provoke any reaction, it is wise sometimes not to be too openly successful, but to play it down a bit.

The concluding *udāna* is a verse of general advice in a situation of that sort. There are several rather similar verses in the canon. People are almost bound to say unpleasant things from time to time and there is not much one can do about it. One just has to bear it without allowing one's mind to become disturbed.

4.9 REJOICING IN MERITS

> Once, when the Buddha was staying near Rājagaha in the Bamboo Grove at the Squirrels' Feeding Ground, his disciple Upasena Vaṅgantaputta, who was living in seclusion, thought to himself: 'Aren't I fortunate! The Buddha is my teacher, I have gone forth into homelessness, my companions in the holy life are ethical, and I too have mastered the ethical virtues and concentration of mind. I am an *arhant*, free from the taints, and I have gained great supernormal power. My life is fortunate, and my death will be too.' And the Buddha read his disciple's mind and breathed out these words:
>
> Whose life is not painful
> and who does not grieve at the end, at death,
> that wise one, who has seen the state of peace,
> does not grieve in the midst of sorrows.
>
> The cycle of birth is utterly exhausted
> for one whose craving for existence is cut off,
> that practitioner whose mind is at peace,
> for whom there is no repeated birth.

Once again one sees the hand of the editor at work. In an interesting contrast, which is no doubt no coincidence, whereas the previous episode revolved around envy, this one revolves around rejoicing in merits. Upasena rejoices in the merits of others and of himself quite impartially. He is grateful to the Buddha and to his fellow disciples, and he is happy that he has the opportunity of leading the spiritual life, becoming an *arhant* and so on. In the *Aṅguttara Nikāya*, Upasena is described as foremost among those who are 'altogether charming' (*samanta pasādika*).[430] He seems to have had a very charming nature, which is expressed in the fact that he is rejoicing in the merits of others and himself.

Some people find it difficult to practise rejoicing in merits, perhaps because they associate it with flattery, but rejoicing in merits is the natural outcome of a positive emotional state, so if we find it difficult to do it, it is our emotional state that we have got to tackle. It is so important that there should be a positive atmosphere in the sangha. Sooner or later rejoicing in merits will develop quite naturally if people are happy.

4.10 SĀRIPUTTA REVIEWS HIS OWN CALM

> Once, the Buddha was staying near Sāvatthī in the Jeta Wood at Anāthapiṇḍika's park. At the same time, not far away, Sāriputta was sitting cross-legged, holding his body erect, and reviewing his own state of peace. Seeing him thus, and seeing what it meant, the Buddha breathed out these words:
>
> The cycle of birth is utterly exhausted
> for one whose mind is peaceful and calm,
> that practitioner who has cut the leash.
> That one is freed from the bonds of Māra.

Once again Sāriputta is sitting cross-legged and upright. This time, he is *attano upasamaṃ paccavekkhamāno* – 'reviewing his own calm'. He is mindfully and happily reviewing, though not thinking about, what he has achieved. This is quite important in Buddhism generally: not only that you should experience something but that you should know that you experience it, and even know that you know. It is not simply that you have destroyed the *āsravas*, but you *know* that you have destroyed them.[431] As an *arhant*, he doesn't need to develop further. It is like a rich man who doesn't need to acquire any more wealth but spends the evening reviewing his investments and looking through his portfolio. It is also akin to rejoicing in merits; he is appreciating himself, though not with any suggestion of egotism. One should recognize what one has done, and if it is something positive and creative, recognize that too, but don't let the ego come in.

5
THE ELDER SOṆA

5.1 NO ONE DEARER THAN ONE'S OWN SELF

> Once, the Buddha was staying near Sāvatthī in the Jeta Wood at Anāthapiṇḍika's park. At the same time, King Pasenadi of Kosala and Queen Mallikā went to the upper storey of the palace to talk. The king asked the queen whether there was anyone dearer to her than she was to herself. Queen Mallikā said there wasn't, and asked the king the same question. King Pasenadi too said that no one in the world was dearer to him than he was to himself. He went to see the Buddha and told him about this conversation, and the Buddha, seeing what it meant, breathed out these words:
>
> Traversing all the directions in one's thought
> one finds no one dearer than one's own self.
> In this way, each individual is dear to themselves.
> Thus, loving one's self, one should not harm others.

We have already come across references in the *Udāna* to King Pasenadi, who was devoted to the Buddha, but this is the first time he is directly introduced, along with his queen, Mallika. It's a pleasing little scene. The king and queen have gone by themselves to the upper storey of the palace. From ancient times Indian palaces were built in several storeys, each one smaller than the one below, and you'd go to the upper apartments to enjoy the cool breeze, especially in the evening. The king and queen seem to have got on rather well together, judging by all that we know from other places in the canon and the commentaries. The only problem we know about is that the queen was rather troubled by the fact that she was excessively plain. She consulted the Buddha about this once, according to one quite well-known passage, and the Buddha said that it was because she'd been rather ill-tempered in previous existences.[432]

The moral of the story here is obvious: 'Loving oneself, one should not harm others.' It's all summed up in that. Mallikā and Pasenadi agree that we all love ourselves more than we love anybody else, but the Buddha draws a practical conclusion: remember that others are as dear to themselves as you are to yourself, and do nothing to them that you would not like to have done to yourself. There is nothing wrong with a healthy self-love. Everybody is dear to their own self, no one likes to be harmed, no one likes to suffer. So reflect that others are the same as you in that way. Just as you can suffer, so can they. If you don't want harm to be done to you, don't do it to others. If you want others to consider you, consider others. This seems to be the plain straightforward ethical meaning. We just need to recognize that there are a plurality of selves and that they are all dear to themselves. That is even extended to the animal world.

Perhaps this *sutta* underlines the fact that we don't very often really feel that others are the same as us. We don't often consider that they also suffer, that they have their own independent existence, just as we do. We obviously don't feel others' aches and pains as we feel our own, so it requires a real effort of sympathetic imagination to identify with them, and at least imaginatively realize that they feel just as we feel. It's the same with animals; they too feel pain, they too want to live.

There's been quite a bit of discussion about this episode of the *Udāna*, some scholars, especially Indian Hindu scholars, trying to inject into it a definitely metaphysical meaning and saying that when Mallikā says that 'there is no other dearer than the self', this means the supreme Self of the Upanishads, but that doesn't seem very likely given the whole trend of Buddhist teaching. It is presumably to be understood in a quite ordinary, empirical sense.[433] It all revolves around this question of the self. One can either take it in a quite ordinary empirical sense, i.e. oneself, or the Self with a capital S, the great spiritual Self of some of the Upanishads.

The general Upanishadic view is that there is an *ātman* or self that is equally the self of all empirical selves, and that all empirical selves are metaphysically identical through their common identity with this metaphysical self – that there is only one universal subject, as it were, of existence, and that you wrongly imagine that you are Such-and-such or So-and-so. In reality, it is said, there is one self ultimately behind all bodies, minds, wills, and so on, and you have to get back to that ultimate, residual, universal, metaphysical self. Buddhism does not agree with that, and that is clear in early Buddhism, but not so clear in later Buddhism, in view of the Mahāyāna teaching that the Buddha-nature is in all, and the concept of the *ālaya* or store-consciousness.[434] In fact, Mahāyāna thinkers are often accused of smuggling in the Upanishadic self. I don't agree with that, but it is easy to understand how it might be thought. The main difference is that in the Upanishadic or Vedāntic tradition, this self is conceived of as something substantial, a metaphysical entity, whereas the Buddha-nature is, as it were, an absence of entities. It is not an ontological principle. In fact, in Buddhism there are no ontological principles. Ontological means relating to being as such, not being anything in particular, but merely being. The term is synonymous with the Western concept of 'metaphysical' inasmuch as the metaphysical pertains to that which is ultimately real, what ultimately exists, the true nature of being. In Buddhism, when one says that all beings have the same Buddha-nature, it is not that they share a common ontological principle but that they are all equally devoid of ultimate determination. That must not itself be reified into an ontological principle.

The reason why this comes up in relation to this episode in the *Udāna* is partly that there is an Upanishad, the *Chandogya Upaniṣad*, where there is a conversation between a brahmin and his wife around this very topic. There, the self which is meant is very clearly the metaphysical self of the Upanishads, the supreme self. Some scholars think that this *sutta* reflects that point of view, that that particular Upanishad doctrine was current in these royal circles, and that this is what the king and the queen are discussing. Others say that they are purely talking about the empirical self, that there's no metaphysics, no Upanishadic thought here, and that seems to be borne out by the appended verse, where the application is quite clearly just ethical and where self is taken simply in the sense of oneself. Hindu scholars like Dr Radakrishna are inclined to see Upanishadic influence in early Buddhism, but there doesn't seem to be much of that to me. It's well known that the leading doctrine of the Upanishads, the identity of the *ātman* and the *brahman*, is not mentioned or even remotely referred to anywhere in the Pāli canon, so it would seem that these Upanishadic speculations weren't in fact current in circles which were in contact with Buddhism. It's rather doubtful whether there's any metaphysical overtone at all in this little discussion; it's just a plain, straightforward, honest exchange.

5.2 THE PATTERN OF THE BUDDHA'S LIFE

> Once, the Buddha was staying near Sāvatthī in the Jeta Wood at Anāthapiṇḍika's park when Ānanda came to see him and, for some reason, remarked on how amazing it was that the Buddha's mother had lived for such a short time, only seven days after the *bodhisatta*'s birth. The Buddha told him that indeed the mothers of *bodhisattas* live only seven days after the *bodhisatta* is born, and then the mother is reborn into the *tuṣita* heaven of the *devas*. And he breathed out these words:
>
> Everyone who has come into being or will exist
> will each travel onward when they leave the body.
> The expert, knowing this, the loss of everything,
> should live the holy life ardently.

This is the first time the word bodhisattva (or rather, the Pāli form *bodhisatta*) has been mentioned in the *Udāna*, and here it simply means a future Buddha, but we can say that this episode represents the beginning of the growth of the legend of the Buddha. It seems that Ānanda hasn't been meditating, he's just been thinking. He's been thinking about the Buddha, and about his life, and the fact that his mother died seven days after he was born, and wondering why this was. So as soon as he can decently go and disturb the Buddha, he goes and asks why his mother died seven days after he was born. The Buddha replies that the mothers of future Buddhas always die seven days after the birth of the *bodhisatta*. That is no answer at all, is it, strictly speaking? It's like asking, 'Why does an apple fall from a tree?' and being told, 'Well, apples always fall from trees.' The real answer is 'Well, she just died after seven days.' But in the

Buddha's words, 'Short-lived are the mothers of *bodhisattas*!' the whole bodhisattva doctrine is implied. There's a reference to bodhisattvas in the plural, and this is indirectly a reference to Buddhas in the plural. A reference to Buddhas and bodhisattvas in the plural suggests the whole background of cosmic development, periods in which Buddhas appear or don't appear, and so on. In other words, we've gone beyond the immediate historical situation.

We can't be sure of this, but I think we may be at a stage of doctrinal development which is even after the *parinirvāṇa*. We can't be absolutely sure that it represents a development within the Buddha's lifetime. It seems that this verse is very ancient, but it may well be that the prose part isn't. From the scholarly point of view, in the development of this bodhisattva doctrine you get a sort of extrapolation: what happens to this Buddha is what happens to every Buddha, it's a rule. Then, of course, you can turn it round and explain what happens to this Buddha by reference to what happens to all Buddhas. You can say that Buddhas always gain Enlightenment under a tree of some kind, at the age of thirty-five, sitting on the diamond throne or *vajrāsana*; and the mothers of bodhisattvas always pass away seven days after they are born; and they always have a charioteer, and two chief disciples. It's as though there's a standard pattern of a Buddha's career, generalized from the life of the historical Buddha, and once that pattern is firmly established, the career of the historical Buddha is explained by saying that it had to be like that because that's the way Buddhas always live. In other words, you derive the archetypal pattern from the historical situation and then you explain the historical situation as an exemplification of the archetypal pattern. The Buddha doesn't explain (looking at it from a modern point of view); he merely says, well, that's the rule, suggesting knowledge of the general rule and thereby indirectly all the other cases.

So the Buddha's life began to be regarded as a pattern, an embodiment of the ideal, and even the accidents of his life came to be regarded as part of that pattern. This occurs in the *Mahāpadāna Sutta* of the *Dīgha Nikāya*, and has parallels in other traditions, so it is an early Buddhist tradition, and also crops up in later Theravādin works, in which there is mention of previous Buddhas, each of whom has a tree under which he is Enlightened, two chief disciples, and so on, just like the historical Buddha Śākyamuni; only the names differ.[435] The life of the Buddha becomes a norm or pattern in its accidents as well as in its essential features, and in this way the Buddha legend develops. But although a Buddha always embodies the same spiritual ideal, why should every Buddha have two chief disciples? He might have ten, or two, or one, or none. The fact that the accidents of the Buddha's career are made part of the universal pattern should not be taken too seriously. It is simply meant to reinforce the universality of the ideal. You have to be careful about thinking that an ideal person like the Buddha always behaves 'like this', so that everyone who aspires to Enlightenment has to behave like that too. That is all right as regards the essentials, but not the accidentals of his life. It is the distinction between being so inspired by somebody that you try to follow the same principles and copying them in unimportant, accidental details.

You also notice how Ānanda wonders about things. Presumably he ought to be meditating, but instead he is wondering why the Buddha's mother died seven days after his birth. It could be that the Buddha is just putting him off gently by saying, 'It's always like that, Ānanda', but after that, everybody took it literally. The irony of some of the Buddha's statements is often missed, and I think there may be a touch of irony here. After all, whether it is after seven days or seven years or seventy years, everybody dies in the end. *That* is the truth that has to be reflected on.

This episode draws attention to thinking in terms of a pattern being repeated, even if the pattern is good in itself. You could even say that the repetition of the individual is the negation of other individualities. It limits the possibilities of growth. For instance, if you try to stick to the literal pattern, someone might be Enlightened, but if, wanting to find out whether he is a Buddha, you ask whether his mother died seven days after he was born and learn that she didn't, you might conclude, well, he can't be a Buddha. You get caught in a sort of net.

In this story comes the first reference in the *Udāna* to the *tuṣita devaloka*. We've already had Indra's *devaloka* (i.e. the *tāvatiṃsa devaloka*). The *tuṣita devaloka* is even higher and that is the world where (according to later developments) bodhisattvas wait before they are reborn for the last time. According to this way of thinking, this is where Maitreya, the future Buddha, is supposed to be even now, having practised all the perfections and traversed all the *bhūmis*, in the *tuṣita devaloka*, the realm of the happy *devas*, awaiting the appropriate moment to be reborn for the last time.

With this *sutta*, whether it originated rather late in the Buddha's own lifetime or even after the *parinirvāṇa*, we are getting into doctrinal developments. We haven't really encountered this before in the *Udāna*. We're in a slightly different world, there's a slightly different atmosphere. Up till now we've been concerned with practices and spiritual and psychological experiences and situations. Here, we've moved a bit into the legendary-cum-doctrinal. You presumably cannot verify this unless you become fully Enlightened and you discover that this is what happens, whereas up till now you could verify everything we've encountered within your own experience, perhaps even long before you become Enlightened.

There is an interesting progression through the whole text. With the previous *sutta* there was perhaps a very faint, distant reminiscence of some previous Upanishadic tradition, and here there's a very faint, distant anticipation of later Buddhistic doctrinal developments. But with the verse we are back with archaic Buddhism. 'The expert, knowing this, the loss of everything, should live the holy life ardently.' The old term is still being used, *brahmacarya*, not *bodhisattvacarya*, the spiritual life, the holy life. Seeing the way in which all living creatures come into existence and then pass out of it, seeing this whole saṃsāric process, any person of moderate intelligence and education and decent cultural background would almost automatically take up the spiritual life. This is more or less what the verse is saying. It's as though for anyone who's been brought up in reasonable comfort, is not crushed by toil and hardship, and is reasonably intelligent and cultured, it's the natural thing, once they have observed the whole process of life, to want to take up the spiritual life.

5.3 THE BUDDHA GIVES A PUBLIC LECTURE

> Once, when the Buddha was staying near Rājagaha in the Bamboo Grove at the Squirrels' Feeding Ground, there was living in Rājagaha a poor leper called Suppabuddha. One day when the Buddha was sitting teaching the Dhamma to a large group of people, Suppabuddha saw the crowd and thought that some food must be being distributed, so he went closer, to see what he could get. But then he realized that in fact the people were gathered to listen to the Buddha, so Suppabuddha decided to listen too.

Aware of the minds of all those gathered around him, the Buddha realized that the only person present who was capable of understanding the Dhamma was Suppabuddha, so he addressed his remarks solely to the leper. Having talked for a while about generosity, renunciation, and so forth, the Buddha saw that Suppabuddha's mind was ready, and taught him unsatisfactoriness, arising, cessation, and the path (which became known as the four noble truths). Just as a clean cloth without stains will take up dye, in Suppabuddha's mind arose the vision that whatever is subject to origination is subject to cessation. And having plunged into the Dhamma and become free from uncertainty, Suppabuddha arose from his seat, prostrated before the Buddha, expressed his delight in the Dhamma, declared his Going for Refuge to the Three Jewels, and asked the Buddha to accept him as a lay follower.

Soon after that, Suppabuddha was killed by a cow with a young calf. The *bhikkhus* asked the Buddha what Suppabuddha's destiny would be, and the Buddha said that he was now a Stream Entrant, bound for Enlightenment. Someone asked the Buddha how it was that Suppabuddha had been a poor leper, and he replied that in a former life, Suppabuddha had been a rich merchant in the very same city, Rājagaha. On his way to the pleasure-garden, he saw the *paccekabuddha* Tagarasikhī going for almsfood. Thinking, 'Who is that leper wandering about?', he spat at him and disrespectfully turned away, turning his left side towards Tagarasikhī. As a consequence of that action, he spent many years in hell, and even when he was reborn in Rājagaha, it was as a pitiful, wretched person. 'But now,' said the Buddha, 'having met the Dhamma, he has been reborn in a heavenly world, where he surpasses all the other *devas* in beauty and splendour.' And so saying, the Buddha breathed out these words:

Just as one with good eyesight, endeavouring,
would avoid all dangerous ways,
so, in the world of living beings,
the wise person avoids bad deeds.

By this time the Buddha was very popular, and here we find him teaching a great multitude in the Bamboo Grove. Suppabuddha the leper thought that some rich man must be giving away food. He hadn't come for the Dharma, but when he saw that the Buddha was delivering a discourse, he decided to stay and listen. This is quite interesting: his motivation is originally quite worldly, but he ends up listening, realizing something of the truth, and Going for Refuge. We often find this happening: people's motives change. They originally come along to a Buddhist centre for one reason, but end up staying for another. It doesn't really matter, in a sense, how people come into contact with Buddhism, or with what motivation, so long as they come into contact with it and begin to get some sense of what it's all about. They may come along to a Buddhist centre for a bit of social life or a friendly atmosphere. Never mind, that's okay, they've come along. It's up to the committed Buddhists they meet there to help them to feel something more.

We haven't come across the Buddha giving a public lecture before. The systematic teaching given to Meghiya was apparently just for him, but here the Buddha is delivering a set discourse on generosity (*dāna*), virtue (*sīla*), heaven (*sagga*), the danger, degradation, and affliction of sense-pleasures, and the benefit in renunciation, according to the full list given in the text. Apparently before he starts speaking, he looks around to see who is ready, almost reading the minds of the people in the audience. The phrase used here is *bhabbo dhammaṃ viññātuṃ* – 'able to understand the teaching', and the Buddha is said to single out Suppabuddha as capable of understanding the Dharma before he starts the progressive discourse (*anupubbikathā*). First he talks about alms-giving, because it was to an alms-giving that Suppabuddha thought he was coming. Then he goes on to the next thing, *sīla*, and then to the advantages of being reborn in a higher heavenly world. But then you find out the disadvantage: that that heaven is impermanent. So if even heaven isn't the true goal, and the desires that bring one to heaven, even the virtues that bring one to heaven, then what is? Then the Buddha comes on to his own distinctive teaching, as it's now said to be, the four noble truths. He prepares the way step by step.

We are so used to public lectures that we don't realize that at one time they were an absolute innovation. So far as India is concerned, it seems to have been the Buddha who first adopted the practice of speaking about spiritual things to large numbers of people by way of a set discourse. We are also told that he frequently stood up to speak instead of sitting, as was the custom before that. We might even say that the Buddha invented the lecture, or the sermon. Where else in the world do you get this, before his time? Confucius gave no lectures, just sayings. The Greeks made speeches, but they were political. But the *sutta*, the discourse, came to be regarded as the classic form of Buddhist scripture. At the same time, we must not overlook the fact that throughout his career the Buddha taught for the most part in short sayings responding to questions put by individuals. Some of the later *suttas* are not really reports of discourses by the Buddha, but a stringing together of his teaching on various topics, and even an expansion, in some cases, to make up a discourse which was then attributed to him as a whole. A lot of the *suttas* in the Pāli canon are literary compositions, though it is possible that they were composed with the aim of suggesting the Buddha's teaching style; one could compare this with Plato's reconstructions of Socratic dialogues.

You notice in this *sutta* that there are a few new concepts or doctrinal terms, things we haven't come across before in this text, though they are quite familiar in what we may call Buddhism. There's the *paccekabuddha* concept, the three fetters, and Stream Entry. This *sutta* seems much closer to some of the other *suttas* in the Pāli canon, especially the *Majjhima Nikāya*, than it does to some of the other material in the *Udāna*. It seems that we've come to a later, slightly more systematized, stage of the Dharma, though still perhaps within the lifetime of the Buddha. I would judge that it is not later than the previous little *sutta*, and perhaps earlier. Also there's this series which we haven't come across before in this work but which occurs again and again in the Pāli canon generally: *dāna*, *sīla*, rebirth in heaven, and the danger of sense desires and the profit of getting free of them. This is also the first mention in the *Udāna* of the four noble truths, so that's also significant. It's the opinion of some scholars, and my own personal feeling, that the four noble truths is a relatively late formulation, though it may have emerged in the lifetime of the Buddha.

So this *sutta* represents a stage of the development of the teaching as a doctrine, more systematic than anything we've encountered so far. You've got some familiar categories emerging which weren't necessarily in circulation during the first fifteen, twenty, or even thirty years of the Buddha's teaching career, which makes this quite an important *sutta* from the point of view of the development of the sequence within this work. It feels to me as though with this *sutta* we start to find ourselves in the familiar atmosphere of what afterwards became Theravāda Buddhism, whereas before we seemed to be at a stage preceding all such developments. We are now with the Buddhism out of which all the schools later on developed, though it's still very near the sources and origins.

For the first time in this text there is a specific mention of Going for Refuge, in response to the tremendous impact of the teaching, as a result of which Suppabuddha has become a Stream Entrant on the spot. 'Then Suppabuddha the leper, who had seen the Dhamma, got the Dhamma, understood the Dhamma, and had plunged into the Dhamma, who had crossed over his doubts and removed his questionings, who had obtained full confidence and was no longer dependent on others for the teacher's teaching....'[436] 'No longer dependent on others' translates *aparappaccaya*, 'not having other people as condition', not having to take it at second hand from another person. You again notice the similes which often recur: 'Just as if, revered sir, one should set upright what is overturned, or should uncover what is concealed, or should point out the path to one who is lost, or should bring an oil-lamp into the darkness so that those with eyes could see.'[437] That is how he feels – as though he had fallen and has been lifted up, as though he has discovered something that had previously been hidden from him. He feels that now he has a definite way to follow, that he has seen the light, as it were. In other words, it has all been a revelation to him, and in consequence he goes for Refuge.

This is also the first reference to a *paccekabuddha* (Sanskrit *pratyekabuddha*) – but no one really knows what a *paccekabuddha* is. The term originally meant 'solitary Buddha', one who was Enlightened by himself and for himself alone. In later times there was an attempt to classify the different kinds of Buddha, and the nub of the difficulty is that by the time this doctrine of different kinds of Buddha was systematized, the meaning of the word '*buddha*' had changed. Originally it simply meant a wise man, so the term *paccekabuddha* probably meant someone like a rishi, a wise man living alone, without a teacher and without disciples, not an Enlightened One in the later Buddhistic sense. In a way, a private or solitary Buddha is a contradiction in terms, but since the early Buddhists had no idea about historical or doctrinal development, they took the 'Buddha' in *paccekabuddha* quite literally in the later sense of 'completely Enlightened One', so they had to try to explain what a completely Enlightened One was doing leading a solitary life, and that was very difficult; in fact, they never managed to do it.

There is much the same sort of thing with regard to the Refuges. We are told that Suppabuddha goes for Refuge to the Dharma and the order of monks – the *bhikkhu* sangha. But if you take '*bhikkhu*' in the later, coenobitical sense, you narrow the Refuge. '*Bhikkhu*' is clearly used at this early stage simply to mean someone who follows the ideal of Enlightenment, as in the *Dhammapada*, where *bhikkhu* is equated with *brāhmaṇa* and also with *samaṇa*, and where it is said that, even though you live at home and even though you are well clad and richly ornamented, if there is truth and righteousness in you, then you are a *brāhmaṇa*, a *samaṇa*, and a *bhikkhu*.[438]

In this episode we find an example of the mode of address changing. To begin with, Suppabuddha referred to the Buddha as Gotama the recluse (in Woodward's translation) but later on he calls him the Blessed One. Gotama the recluse would be '*samaṇa* Gotama'. It means that Gotama was just one of the *samaṇa*s, no more than that. He becomes 'Bhagavan' when Suppabuddha recognizes him as an embodiment of Enlightenment, as his teacher, as an object of Refuge. The name Suppabuddha means 'wide awake', *pabuddha* meaning 'woken up' (from sleep), and the word *buddha* itself originally simply meaning 'aware, awake'.

From our perspective it is open to us to think in terms of historical development, for example of the way the usage of words changed over time, but it is important to realize that there was no sense of development until quite recently in human history. It became popularized only after Darwin's work in the sphere of biology. Before that, there was no sense of historical development, or any idea that language could develop and words could change their meanings. This was understood within certain limited fields; for instance, Chinese scholars were aware that characters occurring in the classics did not have the same meaning as they had 1,000 years later during the Tang dynasty. But 150 years ago in Britain, practically everybody took the *Genesis* story literally and thought that human history went back only to 4000 BCE. It was Lyell's work in geology that shook that idea,[439] and Darwin confirmed the general trend; until then, especially in the sphere of religion, people took doctrine as something static.

There's an interesting example of this in the classification of the *sūtras* by the famous Chinese master, Zhiyi.[440] He couldn't conceive that there might have been a development of Buddhist doctrine over 1,000 years, with different works produced at different times. He took it that all those texts must have been preached by the Buddha personally in the course of his lifetime, but he saw clearly, being a highly intelligent man, that there was a doctrinal development, so he came up with the idea of five periods of teaching of the historical Buddha: the Deer Park period, the *Avataṃsaka* period, and so on. He was on the right track, except that that development took place not in the course of the Buddha's lifetime but over several hundred years. If a Buddhist scholar is reading a text written hundred years after the Buddha and it contains technical terms which also occur in earlier texts, if he doesn't distinguish them as early and late, he takes the term as always meaning the same thing, so there is a tendency to read later meanings back into earlier texts. That is what has happened with the word *buddha*, which in the early days did not have the specialized meaning it acquired later. It's the same with the word *bhikkhu*. It is very important to remember that.

We learn that not long after this, Suppabuddha was trampled to death by a cow. It could be a blessing in disguise, because he's reborn in a happy heavenly world. He's assured, since he's a Stream Entrant, of a good rebirth on earth with opportunities of further progress after his period in the *devaloka* is ended. It's not exactly symbolical, but it may be significant, that when there's any marked change in one's life from a spiritual point of view, any dramatic development, repercussions in other spheres occur, about which it's very difficult to say sometimes whether they are good or bad. You might say, 'Well, how unfortunate! No sooner had he become a Stream Entrant than he died!' But not necessarily so: he went straight to a *devaloka*, and he was assured of coming back into a good healthy body and carrying on from there. So who knows? His very attainment of Stream Entry might have precipitated that happening. Being a leper was a very miserable life, after all. One was segregated from other people. It's interesting that as compared with the Christian gospel records, the Buddha is never shown, as far as I recollect, as curing disease. It may be, of course, that in the case of the gospels all these incidents are pseudo-historical renderings of symbolical things: the disease is a spiritual disease, the death is spiritual death, and it wasn't that Jesus literally went around healing sick people or bringing the dead back to life, but that he brought a spiritual healing, making the blind see in a spiritual sense. That idiom is used here: in Woodward's translation, '... show a light in the gloom, saying, "Now they that have eyes to see can see shapes."' That's like 'making the blind to see'. According to some scholars, in the case of the Christian gospels there was no question of historic fact as regards the healing ministry. There were certain idioms used by Jesus in his teaching that were later on interpreted as healing incidents.

The little verse that follows the story doesn't seem to say very much, and there's not a great deal of connection with the episode, though it does continue the metaphor of sight.

5.4 DO YOU FEAR SUFFERING AND DISLIKE PAIN?

> Once, the Buddha was staying near Sāvatthī in the Jeta Wood at Anāthapiṇḍika's park when, on his way to collect almsfood, he came upon a group of boys tormenting the fish in a pool. Seeing this, he asked the boys, 'Do you fear suffering and dislike pain?' They said they did. And seeing the meaning of it, the Buddha breathed out these words:
>
> If you are afraid of suffering
> or if suffering is disagreeable to you
> don't do actions which are wrong
> whether in the open or secretly.
>
> For if you do something very bad
> either now or in the future,
> there is no release from suffering for you,
> though you try to run away.

This episode is like the one we had earlier, and the moral is similar too. Going out for alms is a set routine: if no food is cooked where you are staying, having to go and get food determines the structure of your day. At the Buddha's time most people would have been engaged in agriculture, so if you went to a village you had to get to the houses after people had cooked but before they had all gone out to work.

The phrase at the end of the story, 'seeing the meaning of it', which is repeated throughout the *Udāna*, is rather mysterious. It means seeing the reality of the situation – not the meaning of words, but the meaning of life, as it were. The Pāli word is *attha*: meaning, or value, or significance. When the Buddha saw the truth of the situation, the *udāna* arose quite spontaneously.

5.5 THE TASTE OF FREEDOM

Once, the Buddha was staying near Sāvatthī in the Eastern Park at the house of Migāra's mother. It was the day of the *uposatha* observance, and when the night was far advanced, Ānanda approached the Buddha and asked him to recite the *pāṭimokkha* to the *bhikkhus*. But the Buddha remained silent. Again and yet again, as the night wore on, Ānanda made the same request. At the third time of asking, the Buddha said, 'Ānanda, the gathering is not pure', and pointed out that it would be inappropriate for a Buddha to observe the *uposatha* and pronounce the *pāṭimokkha* to an impure gathering. Ānanda wondered who the Buddha was talking about, but Mahāmoggallāna could read minds and saw that in the midst of the order of *bhikkhus* was someone who was no recluse, though pretending to be one, an immoral man who kept secret what he was up to. Mahāmoggallāna approached this man and told him that he'd been spotted, and that he should get up and leave, but the man did not move. Mahāmoggallāna said the same thing again, and yet again, and then – still receiving no response – took the man by the arm and pulled him through the gate, which he then locked. Returning, he told the Buddha that the assembly was now pure. The Buddha said it was remarkable that the man was so slow to gather what was happening that he stayed until he was made to leave. Then, turning to the assembly of *bhikkhus*, the Buddha told them that from that time on he would no longer participate in the *uposatha* observance or recite the *patikmokkha*, for he couldn't do so in a gathering that was not pure.

The Buddha went on to describe the eight wonderful qualities of the great ocean: (1) it gradually shelves, with no sudden precipice; (2) it is stable and does not exceed the limits of the tide-line; (3) it rejects a dead body; (4) whatever rivers flow into it, they lose their identity in the great ocean; (5) although all the rivers of the world flow into it and rain falls from the sky, the ocean is never full;

(6) it has one taste, the taste of salt; (7) it contains many precious substances; (8) it is the abode of mighty creatures.

Likewise, said the Buddha, the *Dhamma-Vinaya* has eight wonderful qualities, in which the *bhikkhus* delight:

1. Just as the ocean gradually shelves, in the Dhamma there is a gradual training, a gradual progression, with no sudden penetration to final knowledge.
2. Just as the ocean does not exceed the limits of the tide-line, the Buddha's disciples do not transgress his training rules, even for the sake of their lives.
3. Just as the ocean casts a dead body onto dry land, when a person is not practising the Dhamma though pretending to do so, when a person is suspect and secret in their behaviour, the Order does not associate with them, and when it has met together, soon throws them out. Even though that person may be sitting in the midst of the Order, he is far from it, and it is far from him.
4. Just as rivers lose their names when they flow into the ocean, those who have gone forth lose their former identity and become just recluses, followers of the Buddha.
5. Just as though rivers and rain flow and fall into the ocean, it never lessens or fills up, although many *bhikkhus* attain nibbāna without remainder, there is no lessening or filling up of the nibbāna-element.
6. Just as the ocean has one taste, the taste of salt, the Dhamma has one taste, the taste of freedom.
7. Just as the ocean contains many precious substances, the Dhamma contains many precious things, such as the four foundations of mindfulness, the four right efforts, the four bases for successful accomplishment, the five spiritual faculties, the five powers, the seven enlightenment factors, and the Noble Eightfold Path.
8. Just as the ocean is the home of mighty creatures, the Dhamma is the home of the Stream Entrant and the one who is on the way to realizing the fruits of Stream Entry, the once-returner and the one who is on the way to realizing the fruits of once-returning, the non-returner and the one who is on the way to realizing the fruits of non-returning, the *arhant* and the one who is on the way to arhantship.

And realizing the significance of these eight wonderful qualities, the Buddha breathed out these words:

The rain soaks through what is covered,
but does not soak through what is open.
Hence, you should open up what is covered,
so the rain will not soak through it.

One could consider this as the central section of the whole *Udāna*, a watershed. The teaching has reached a more developed form than in any other part of the text, and the Buddha's movement has reached its highest point of development, as recorded here. This episode must occur in the latter part of the Buddha's career inasmuch as Ānanda appears to be his attendant. It takes place at Sāvatthī, the Buddha's informal headquarters, 'in the Eastern Park, in the house of Migāra's mother'. We have come across this place before. It was apparently a wooden building, perhaps a sort of summer-house, and we can tell that it was a proper building because the full text describes it as having a porch and a bar across the door.

So here are the Buddha and the *bhikkhus*, holding a meeting in a proper building. This is the first reference to such regular meetings in the *Udāna*. The *uposatha* days are the day of the new moon, the eve of the full moon, and the two quarter days of the lunar month in between. So the Buddha and his disciples are meeting together on a fixed day, or at least they happen to be all in the same place on a certain day according to the lunar calendar, and we see the Buddha celebrating a simple observance.

Where did the observance come from? Apparently it was a common practice for the *samaṇera*s of different traditions to celebrate those four days by getting together, at least in an informal manner. It was suggested to the Buddha that he should introduce this practice into the sangha and he agreed.[441] From this and later accounts, it appears that the celebration took a twofold form: first the Buddha and the disciples sat together and meditated, and then there was a recitation of verses known as the *pāṭimokkha*. Already in the course of the *Udāna* we have seen the Buddha and his disciples sitting together quietly meditating, all enjoying the same state of higher consciousness, and this was apparently one of the things that they did on the *uposatha* night. They had what we might describe as a group meditation, clearly a very ancient practice in Buddhism. But what about the *prātimokṣa* (Sanskrit), or *pāṭimokkha* (Pāli)?

In our day, the term *pāṭimokkha* is affixed to the long list of rules that the *bhikkhu* is expected to observe, and nowadays when the *uposatha* day is observed by *bhikkhus*, a prominent feature of the proceedings is the recitation of the clauses of the complete *pāṭimokkha*. This practice has been going on for a long time, so when we read that the Buddha or the early disciples recited the *pāṭimokkha* on the occasion of the *uposatha*, it is usually assumed that that *pāṭimokkha* referred to was a recitation of the clauses of the monastic rule. But was it? This has been discussed at great length, especially by S. Dutt in *Early Buddhist Monachism*, and the position seems to be that the term *pāṭimokkha* originally applied to verses of the teachings which were recited at the *uposatha* meetings.[442] We have already seen the Buddha uttering various *udāna*s, and even giving the *bhikkhus* verses to learn and recite. It would appear that the earliest stage of the practice was that when they gathered together on the *uposatha* days, they recited verses summarizing the Dharma, and these were known as *pāṭimokkha*.

In the Pāli canon there are verses of this kind which are actually referred to as *pāṭimokkha*, including a famous set of three verses in the *Dhammapada*, beginning with the verse which is supposed to summarize the whole teaching: 'Abstention from all evil, doing of good, purifying the heart: this is the teaching of all the Buddhas.'[443] These verses are known as the *pāṭimokkha* of the Buddha Vipassī. According to Dutt, the fact that they are attributed to Vipassī, who was the previous Buddha, living thousands of years before Śākyamuni Buddha, suggests that they are of great antiquity and probably belong to the very early phase of Buddhism, in the sense of Gautama the Buddha's Buddhism.[444] So it would seem that when the early *bhikkhus* got together for the *uposatha* meetings, what they recited after the group meditation was not a set of rules, but a verse summary of the teaching. That seems quite likely, because we know that in those early days there were no rules. According to Dutt, much later on, probably after the Buddha's decease, when the sangha had become much more highly organized and the *pāṭimokkha* had been drawn up, the recitation of the Dharma stanzas was dropped, and instead the *pāṭimokkha* in the sense of a list of rules was recited and the observance of the monks was compared with that set of rules, so the *uposatha* became a sort of confessional service. If a monk had broken a rule, he had to confess it, and action was taken. Then there was a third stage of development, and this is still the practice today. Now the confession takes place before the recitation, a younger monk confessing to an older or senior monk, so that the recitation becomes a formality. That is the present position in those countries where the *pāṭimokkha* in this sense is still recited on the *uposatha* day – most parts of the Theravāda world, and the parts of the Mahāyāna world where the *bhikkhu* tradition continues.

We must not imagine, therefore, that in the *Udāna* the Buddha has been invited by Ānanda to recite a list of rules. One can hardly imagine the Buddha, as we have encountered him so far, reciting a list of 150 rules four times a month at a meeting of all the *bhikkhus*. But it seems quite consistent with what we know of him so far that he should recite verses expressing the teaching and get the *bhikkhus* to repeat them after him.

These two things – the group meditation and the recitation of verses – represent two important principles to be borne in mind in connection with such gatherings. Firstly, those present are sharing in a higher reality. They are all in the same state of consciousness. And secondly, the common recitation of the Dharma stanzas stands for a common ideal. These are the two essential features of those meetings: that there is a common mental state and that everyone is working towards a common ideal. Obviously, a common list of rules is much less important. Elsewhere the Buddha advises his followers that when they come together, they should either observe the noble silence – which suggests meditation – or engage in *dhamma-kathā*, discussing the Dharma or, presumably, reciting Dharma stanzas.[445]

In our sangha these days, discussion about organizational matters tends to be a feature of most regular meetings, but perhaps the early sangha didn't need to do that because their way of life was so settled. They went for alms in the morning, they listened to the Buddha's teaching and discussed the Dharma with one another, they meditated in the afternoon, and so on. Everything was so simple that there was nothing to discuss, and the Buddha was there taking all the important decisions. After the Buddha's decease they did call *saṅgīti* – communal recitations – at which there seems to have been some discussion about what to do, but in the Buddha's day things were very simple indeed.

The translation of *pāṭimokkha* as 'obligation' reflects much later usage. If you look at it in the light of the later interpretation, the situation is that a certain monk has broken certain rules, but in the older sense the situation is that a monk is not living up to the ideal; he is not a real follower of the Buddha. And once again we see Moggallāna exercising his psychic powers.

No doubt the practice of the Buddha and the disciples getting together for a sort of festival on the occasion of the full moon, sitting together in silent meditation and chanting Dharma verses together, was an ancient institution, but here we see the Buddha separating himself from it and saying, 'From now on you can observe it by yourselves. I'm not going to take the lead any more.' According to this passage, this was prompted by the fact that there was someone present in the assembly who was not truly a member of the community. But why might the Buddha have decided not to observe the *uposatha* or pronounce the *pāṭimokkha* any more? Perhaps it is similar to his absenting himself and going off into the forest sometimes: he hopes it will bring his disciples to their senses. Or perhaps he realizes that sooner or later they are going to have to manage on their own and that this is a suitable opportunity for him to withdraw and leave them to it.

Then we get a famous set of similes, also found elsewhere in the canon.[446] Leaving aside the qualities of the ocean, let us go straight on to their application to the *Dharma-Vinaya*. This is the first time we have encountered this term in the *Udāna*, and this again indicates a fairly late stage in the development of the Buddha's teaching during his lifetime. Dharma means the teaching in general and *vinaya*, although later on it came to mean the monastic rule, as in Vinaya Piṭaka, here means the practical side of it, the actual observance or way of life. So *Dharma-Vinaya* means the whole teaching of the Buddha in its principle and application. It's very important to notice that the *bhikkhus* take delight in it, though apparently the one who was ejected didn't. The Dharma and the *vinaya* are to be enjoyed, and if you are not taking delight in them, there is something wrong somewhere.

The first wonderful quality, the gradual nature of the training, raises the question of the gradual path and the abrupt path, as they are sometimes called, especially in the Zen context.[447] Here the Buddha's position is made very clear: the approach to insight is gradual. It is a progression along the whole sequence of the positive *nidānas*. There is no sudden penetration of knowledge. Even in the case of Suppabuddha, his progress wasn't sudden. It's more that all the *nidānas* were traversed quite rapidly. The Buddha prepared the way and roused and fired and gladdened him first, and then, when Suppabuddha was ready, the Buddha set forth his distinctive teaching. Don't forget that the Buddha looked round that whole assembly and saw that Suppabuddha was ready, and he preached, as it were, just for him. Suppabuddha had already done the preliminary work himself. He had come to that point where the Buddha could lay down a teaching into which he would immediately penetrate. The Buddha was just putting the finishing touches. There is no abrupt transition from a highly unskilful to a highly skilful state of mind. There are various intermediate steps, and in Suppabuddha's case he seems to have gone through them before he even came in contact with the Buddha, whereas no one else in the assembly had done that preliminary work. In other words, you don't go from an ordinary state of consciousness directly to insight. You have to go through the positive *nidānas* and develop the positive emotions first, and then you are in a position to develop knowledge and insight. That is what happened in the case of Suppabuddha.

Secondly, the Buddha says, just as the ocean doesn't go beyond its boundary, the *bhikkhus* don't transgress the training he has taught them, even for the sake of their own lives. Here, 'training' obviously doesn't mean a set of rules but a whole ideal – the meaning and purpose of the way of life. This passage raises the question of the place of rules as distinct from principles, and even whether rules have any place at all. In the Hīnayāna, the *bhikkhu* ideal quickly became codified in the form of a list of rules, often very elaborate and detailed. To what extent is that necessary? The rules were originally drawn up so that one could, as it were, check off one's behaviour against the ideal and see whether one was living up to it. But if one is not careful this very quickly becomes an external conformity, neglecting the spirit of the thing. I have already quoted the Buddha's remark about there being many *arhants* and few rules at the beginning of his career, and many rules but few *arhants* towards the end. It is probably good to hold off from the laying down of rules for as long as possible; it is always a sign of decline. Only when something went wrong did the Buddha lay down a rule to prevent things from going wrong again in that way. He did not sit down at the beginning of his career and draw up a list of rules. The rules were laid down – even according to the Theravādin account – only in accordance with situations that developed. Had those situations not developed – had certain *bhikkhus* not misbehaved – presumably there would not have been any rules at all.

It seems sad that at the beginning of the Buddha's career there were many *arhants* and few rules and at the end it was the other way around. It is almost axiomatic that beyond a certain point the more people join a movement, the lower the level of the movement will be. But that point is difficult to determine, and the movement can always be renewed. There were times in Buddhist history when its whole spiritual movement underwent tremendous renewal, a sort of rebirth which took place because of actions taken by certain energetic individuals, like Tsongkhapa in Tibet. The possibility of renewal is always there, but it usually starts with one individual who communicates it to a few others. Then the new movement will become big and successful, as the Gelugpa tradition did in Tibet, and again people will start being attracted for the wrong reasons and you have to start all over again. This is inevitable.

Where there are rules or precepts, it should be made clear that they are concrete applications of principles; it is the principle that is to be understood and assimilated, and no amount of rules can fully express the spirit of the principle. You can't just make sure that you are following the rules and forget about the principles, although some people sincerely try to do that. It is much less trouble, you could say; but it doesn't work. It might keep you on the right path in a sense, but in a rather unintelligent, unaware way, and you might find yourself externally conforming, but not appreciating the principles behind the rules at all. The ten precepts are simply prominent applications of ten principles.

The third quality is that, just as the ocean rejects a dead body, the sangha throws out one who is not truly conforming to the ideal, like the healthy physical body expelling germs. Someone who does not belong sooner or later finds himself outside. Any person who doesn't really belong to the sangha – isn't really following the Dharma – will automatically leave, even without anyone taking the sort of action that Moggallāna did. In our own time too, people come along and join the sangha, but because they are not on the same wavelength, not really trying to lead a spiritual life, sooner or later they drift away, or even break away. If they are coming into an assembly where everyone is in a meditative mood and is devoted to the Dharma, and if they are not feeling that way themselves, sooner or later they just won't feel happy there, and they'll leave. The *bhikkhu* in this story seems incorrigible. He can't say to the others, 'Look, I'm making a complete mess of it. Please help me.' Even when the Buddha says, 'There is someone among us who doesn't really belong', he doesn't take any action; he doesn't even say anything.

The fourth strange and wonderful thing is the way those who have gone forth abandon name and caste, like rivers reaching the ocean. This means that the sangha is a purely spiritual community in which all ethnic differences are transcended. It exists on a quite different level. On the whole, this has been kept up through the ages in the Buddhist East, with one or two unfortunate exceptions. In Sri Lanka some sections of the sangha did not accept those of so-called low caste, but I have heard that that has been changed. In the West – in Britain, anyway – it is class and nationality that correspond to difference of caste. It is very important that our sangha is classless and not only international but supranational. It would be a great mistake for the Order, or the Movement as a whole, to identify itself with Anglo-Saxon cultural assumptions. A lot of the things that we take for granted could be just assumptions, and have nothing to do with the Dharma. There should be no conflict of national interests or loyalties within the Order, nor ideally within the movement as a whole. We have to try to transcend local patriotisms in every sense.

It is important to realize that in the Buddha's time caste feeling was terribly strong, and it remained so. Buddhism did its best to mitigate the caste system, and it was not observed within the sangha, but one reason why Buddhism was eventually forced out of India was the opposition of the brahmins. It is very important that within the spiritual community these differences of class and nationality – and caste, in India – should simply not be observed and should not count. They are so strong that we have to take active steps to discourage them.

In China, where family and clan feeling was very strong, the Buddhist monks adopted 'Śākya', or its equivalent in Chinese, as their clan name. They couldn't get away from the clan system altogether, so they made a separate, non-hereditary clan of the Śākyas, which drew from all the ethnic faiths. In Kenneth Ch'en's *The Chinese Transformation of Buddhism* he shows how family feeling in the Tang dynasty was so strong that people could not get away from it altogether, so the sangha was turned into a big family, and everything was transposed into spiritual terms.[448] This is why lineage became so important in Zen, as a legacy from Chinese ethnic ideas. Just as the Chinese thought that it was important to be able to trace back your descent not only to your father but to your grandfather, your great-grandfather, and your great-great-grandfather, they did this within Buddhism too: your teacher's teacher's teacher's teacher.

So we come to the fifth of the comparisons of the Dharma with the mighty ocean. This seems to be a warning against taking metaphors too literally. Just as streams flow into and rain falls into the ocean, many monks attain Nirvāṇa, but one must not think of Nirvāṇa as a limited quantity which is increased by more monks gaining it. Nirvāṇa doesn't become over-full. There's a new technical term: 'that condition of nibbāna which has no remainder', as Woodward renders it, that is, the *nibbāna* which occurs after the physical body drops away. This is the first time that this technical term occurs in the *Udāna*: *anupādisesa-nibbāna*, it's called, as distinct from *kilesa-nibbāna*, or *sa-upādisesa-nibbāna*, 'the nibbāna with a residue of appropriation'. Sometimes it's called *khandha-nibbāna*: the *nibbāna* of the five *skandhas* as opposed to the *nibbāna* of the passions. In other words, Nirvāṇa is not an entity, but neither is it a subjective state of mind, however exalted. Nirvāṇa is often called *nibbāna-dhātu* – *dhātu* suggesting something that exists as it were independently of the mind. It is not just a psychological state.

The standpoint of the Pāli scriptures is commonsensical, not critical in the philosophical sense. Nirvāṇa is spoken of as though it were a transcendental object 'out there'. From other contexts it is clear that it is not an object as opposed to a subject, but so long as you are a subject you can only think of that which is neither subject nor object as an object. If you say that such-and-such transcends the distinction of subject and object, the mere fact that you are referring to it makes it into an object, but that is just the limitation of thought and speech. From a commonsense point of view Nirvāṇa is therefore spoken of as an object, but one must not draw any conclusions from that. It cannot but be thought of, or referred to, as something 'out there', but even though one cannot help doing that, one must not take it too literally and conceive of it as an entity, something with quantitative limitations which can be increased or decreased by additions or subtractions from outside. Nirvāṇa remains the same whether people realize it or not, like the ancient city which is there in the midst of the jungle whether discovered or not. At the same time, you notice that Buddhism does not say 'Nirvāṇa is in you all the time'. It is 'out there' all the time; it is something for you to work towards, so the pitfall of the actual and the potential is avoided.

The sixth comparison, that just as the ocean has one taste, the taste of salt, so the Dharma has the taste of freedom, is particularly important because it suggests the basic function of the whole Dharma and all its formulations: to lead to liberation of mind, *vimutti*, translated as release or emancipation or freedom. From whichever part of the ocean you take water, it still tastes of salt, and in the same way, whatever aspect of the Buddha's teaching you consider, it will bring about emancipation of mind. If it doesn't have that flavour – if it doesn't produce that result – it isn't to be considered part of the Dharma. This is also an aspect of the Buddha's advice to Mahāpajāpatī Gotami, his aunt and foster-mother: the essential characteristic of the Dharma is that it conduces to freedom.[449] It is sometimes better not to insist on this because people might think it means doing just as you like; the 'you' being the purely subjective or even neurotic 'you' indulging itself. It's about learning what freedom really is. Sometimes a distinction is made between 'freedom from' and 'freedom to'. The word translated here as taste is *rasa*, which also occurs in Indian aesthetics, the word for aesthetics being *rasa-śāstra*, the science of flavour, sometimes translated as 'aesthetic relish'. It has a much more strongly emotive – well, taste – than the English word 'taste'.

Much of the sense of the archaic term *vimutti* is conveyed when we speak in terms of growth and development. In fact, that is a more positive way of speaking of the same thing. 'Freedom' in the sense of simply becoming 'free from' is too negative. It is not just breaking *away* but developing *to* a higher level. You could say that the concept of becoming liberated is contained in the concept of growth and development and the Higher Evolution. Instead of saying that like the ocean the Dharma has one taste, the taste of release, you could say, as the Buddha said to Mahāpajāpatī Gotami, that the Dharma has one flavour, the flavour of growth and development. Whatever helps you to grow and develop and get rid of your past conditioning, that is the Dharma. The conditioning could be represented by last year's dead leaves, which you have to shed, and the growth and development by the buds that are going to blossom.

There is something suggestive in the use of the word flavour, because a flavour is subjective, something that you can only experience. A verse in the *Dhammapada* says that the wise man can detect the flavour of the Dharma just as the tongue detects the taste of soup.[450] In other words, the characteristic of the Dharma, if we take this word *rasa*, taste or flavour, as significant, is that its true nature cannot be comprehended abstractly, but only by way of an actual experience akin to an aesthetic experience. You can't convey the Dharma conceptually. You have to say, 'Come and taste it yourself.' To put it extremely, one could say that understanding the Dharma is more like eating than thinking. And to go further – though this is a little fanciful – it is perhaps not a coincidence that among all the flavours, the Dharma is compared here to salt. According to Indian cookery and medicine there are six flavours: the sweet, the sour, the salty, the pungent, the astringent, and the bitter. Out of these six, the Dharma is compared to salt because salt brings out the flavour of everything else. Without a pinch of the Dharma, everything else is flavourless.

The seventh wonderful quality of the Dharma gives us the first list of lists that we have had in the *Udāna*, which shows again that the teaching is becoming more systematized. Just as in the great ocean there are many gems, so you've got these doctrinal categories: the four *satipaṭṭhāna*s (the establishments or foundations of mindfulness), the four right efforts, the four bases of psychic power, the five faculties, the five powers, the seven awakening factors, the Noble Eightfold Path. What one notices about all these early lists is that they are lists of methods, not philosophical doctrines. Some have been mentioned before in the *Udāna*, others not. We have come across the four right efforts. The four bases of psychic power, the four *iddhipādas*, is quite an obscure aspect of the path.[451] The five faculties and the five powers are the same: faith and wisdom, energy and meditation, and mindfulness. When you are exercising the faculties all the time in their fully developed state, they can be called powers. There are the seven awakening factors and the Noble Eightfold Path – the first time that this formulation of the Path has been mentioned in the *Udāna*. The important point is that they are all methods, practices, things to be done. The Dharma is compared to a great ocean in which there are all sorts of jewels, and the jewels are the various methods. Of course, one doesn't usually think of these lists of practices as being jewels in this poetic way. Usually one thinks of them as rather dry and boring.

The eighth quality lists the eight *ariyapuggalas*.[452] In the very early texts there seem to be references only to the Stream Entrant and the *arhant*, both in a general way and without being correlated with the breaking of a certain number of fetters, but here we get the fully developed doctrine of the four pairs of Noble Persons, though the fetters are not mentioned. The once-returner and the non-returner are part of a much more detailed classification, and one which we can't be certain was introduced by the Buddha himself, but if it was, it would have been towards the end of his career. In any case, the great milestones are Stream Entry and arhantship. Only too often we think of these categories in an abstract, schematic way, but that is not how they are presented here. The *Dharma-Vinaya* is represented as a vast ocean, and swimming about in its depths are these great spiritual beings, which to ordinary people might look like monsters. That way of thinking about them gives one a quite different feeling of what they represent. They are at home in the depths of the ocean.

It would be good to select from the Pāli scriptures all the more poetic presentations of the Dharma and leave aside all the analytical, conceptual ones. One could also make an anthology of all the stories and parables in Buddhist literature. That would correct a one-sided impression we may get of the Pāli scriptures and of Buddhist teaching in general, because there are so many of these lists, and much of it is so drily analytical. Perhaps it is better to have an impression of these great beings moving about in the depths of the ocean of the *Dharma-Vinaya* than to define them and check off the number of fetters that each has broken. Of course, even when you are in sight of the ocean, you can't see the great beings in its depths. You have to penetrate into those depths yourself. Sometimes you only have an inkling that these monsters are around when they come to the surface, and then they plunge down again; you see a bit of their back or a fin and you are left to guess at their dimensions. Otherwise you might think you knew all about Stream Entrants and so on; after all, you know exactly how many fetters they break, and exactly what each fetter means. But you haven't really got any feeling of what those beings, those *ariyapuggalas*, are like. They are very powerful creatures indeed, moving about in the ocean of the *Dharma-Vinaya*. In Woodward's translation, the Buddha describes these creatures as up to 500 *yojanas* in length. A *yojana* is generally considered to be the distance that oxen can pull a cart without having to be unyoked – the words *yojana* and yoke are related. That's seven or eight miles, so if some of them are four or five hundred *yojanas* in length, they are pretty big creatures.

The *udāna* presents quite a paradox, the first time we've had paradox in this text – indeed, paradox doesn't crop up much in the Pāli canon as a whole. Thinking back to the original incident of the monk who wouldn't own up, the Buddha is saying that you will be protected if you open up. The truth is your protection, or, as the Buddha says elsewhere: 'The Dharma protects him who practises the Dharma.'[453] That monk thought he would be protected if he covered up his very unspiritual life, but he would really have been protected if he had been more open and had confessed and asked for help. If you cover up, the rain will come through; you will suffer, you will be found out, or something will happen to you. But if you don't try to hide anything, you will be perfectly safe in the long run. This ties up with the whole ideal of bringing things out into the open – not in a self-indulgent, exhibitionist way, of course. True openness is so important because it allows you to make a fresh start. You have to recognize where you are, even though it may be a very unpleasant and undesirable place; otherwise you can't move on from there. If you try to keep up a pretence that you are not there at all, you are in a false position, and progress is precluded.

In the case of that particular *bhikkhu*, since he was apparently a far-gone case, he was merely ushered out rather firmly by Moggallāna. One wonders what happened to him afterwards. But if you feel that someone is not being completely honest or is trying to cover up, you can very gently tackle them about that, for their own good and for yours too, and for the good of the whole spiritual community. If everybody is covering up, even to any slight degree, there is no real communication and therefore no community. This may tie up with the 'private life' *micchā-diṭṭhi* – that what you are covering up is your so-called private life, the bit that you don't want to be seen.

No doubt fear is involved – not fear of being hurt, because the *bhikkhu* would surely have realized that the Buddha would have been the most sympathetic and compassionate of listeners. Perhaps it's fear of facing up to one's karma, or the desire to keep on doing what one is doing. It's true that in some situations people get exploited or hurt when they reveal things about themselves – in police states and so on. It should be very different in the spiritual community, but maybe there is an instinct of self-preservation. Clearly that *bhikkhu* had no faith in the Buddha or in his fellow *bhikkhus*, and maybe no faith in the Dharma either. For him there was no spiritual community; he just couldn't see it. This is why the Buddha says (in Ireland's translation): 'Even though he may be sitting in the midst of the Order of *bhikkhus*, yet he is far from the Order and the Order is far from him.'[454] We should try to trust that the spiritual community is a safe situation. Without that trust, we go on hiding. If you're afraid that if you open up, someone is going to tread all over you with their big boots, you need to remember that you're not such a tender little blade of grass as you think. Maybe you're quite a sturdy sapling and can withstand a few hobnail boots. I think one has to beware of preciousness – 'My feelings are so tender and delicate, I mustn't expose them with all these rough, unsympathetic, insensitive people around.' And the sympathy that one gets should be of a robust, bracing quality, not just something tender and consoling and sentimental.

One should be careful not to rationalize one's unwillingness to open up, saying, 'If I open up, then this, that, and the other will happen to me.' In a way, it is better that it does; it's the lesser of two evils, because you have been open and that will help you and everybody else. If someone tries to exploit you through your honest confession, what does he make himself look like? It doesn't do any harm to you really. So at all costs, within the spiritual community, open up and never mind the consequences. And let it be a deep and genuine opening up – not just an airing of your little weaknesses in a self-indulgent way, expecting lots of love and sympathy, not just baring your soul theatrically. If you are not honest about your weaker side and your inability, at least for the time being, to work towards the ideal, you are just keeping up a big act. The best thing you can do is drop the act, admit what the real situation is, and say, 'Please help me,' or 'Please advise me,' or at least, 'Please bear with me for the time being.' There is no need to wallow in it, but at least be honest.

Of course, certain steps may need to follow your confession. If the *bhikkhu* had confessed what he had done and the Buddha had said to him, 'You need to leave us for a while. Go into the forest and meditate by yourself', the *bhikkhu* would not have been justified in feeling that the Buddha had used his openness against him. In view of the facts that had come to light, the Buddha, and perhaps others in the sangha, would objectively need to take certain action. It isn't just that you are open and then that's that. Confessing what you have done may lead to consequences that you are not very happy about. For instance, it is not enough to own up to having embezzled money; you have got to pay the money back. You must be prepared for the consequences of your openness, if what you're open about is something of a serious nature, and not think of it in terms of exploitation, or manipulation, or taking advantage.

5.6 SOṆA LEARNS THE DHARMA BY HEART

> Once, the Buddha was staying near Sāvatthī in the Jeta Wood at Anāthapiṇḍika's park, and at the same time Mahākaccāna was staying with the people of Avanti near Kuraraghara on Pavatta Hill, with the lay follower Soṇa Koṭikaṇṇa as his supporter. One day Soṇa brought to mind Mahākaccāna's teaching that it is not easy for one living at home to live the holy life, and thought that perhaps he should shave hair and beard, clothe himself in yellow robes, and go forth. Soṇa went to see Mahākaccāna and told him what he was thinking, but Mahākaccāna told him that living the life of a *bhikkhu*, with its one meal a day and living in solitude 'as long as life lasts', was also hard, and advised him to stay at home for the moment and try having just one meal a day and sleeping alone, to see how he found it. For a while Soṇa forgot about going forth, but then the idea occurred to him again. Again he asked Mahākaccāna's permission, and again he was advised to stay at home. When he asked a third time, Mahākaccāna gave his permission, and Soṇa went forth, but there weren't many *bhikkhus* living locally, and it took Mahākaccāna three years to gather together the necessary group of ten *bhikkhus* to give Soṇa the higher ordination.
>
> Then, one day after the rainy season, Soṇa emerged from his meditation and decided he'd like to visit the Buddha. Mahākaccāna gave him his blessing and asked him to give the Buddha his greetings, so Soṇa went to Anāthapiṇḍika's park and gave the Buddha his preceptor's good wishes. The Buddha asked if Soṇa had had a good journey and told Ānanda to arrange lodgings for him. Ānanda reflected that usually when the Buddha asked this, it was because he wanted to spend some time alone with the visitor,

so he arranged lodgings for Soṇa in the place where the Buddha was staying. The Buddha spent a great part of the night seated in the open air and he got up before dawn, and Soṇa did likewise. In the morning, the Buddha asked him to recite the Dhamma, and in response Soṇa chanted all sixteen sections of the *Aṭṭhaka-vagga*. The Buddha was extremely pleased, praising Soṇa for his good memory of the verses and his fine voice, which made the meaning clear. He asked how many years Soṇa had been in the Order, and Soṇa said he had been ordained just a year ago. 'What made you delay so long?' the Buddha wanted to know, and Soṇa explained that the household life, with all its things to be done, held him back. And hearing this, the Buddha breathed out these words:

Seeing the danger in ordinary experience,
knowing the state of non-appropriation,
the noble one does not delight in evil,
in evil a pure person does not delight.

There are several things to comment on here. First of all, we see the Buddha's teaching and his disciples beginning to spread south. Avanti is in central India. Another point is that although Soṇa observes that it is not easy to live the holy life at home, the suggestion is that someone living at home can follow the Dharma to some extent, even to a great extent, if not to absolute perfection. We shall see later on that even living at home you can get a very long way indeed.

Mahākaccāna makes Soṇa live the life of a monk before ordaining him as a monk. In other words, he becomes a sort of *anagārika*, in the later usage of the term. Mahākaccāna tells him that living *eka-seyyā* is no easy thing. *Eka-seyyā* literally means 'sleeping alone', so it is not so much solitude as the state of singleness: not being dependent upon others emotionally, not being afraid to do things without the company of others. The sangha is not a group, not a cosy place to be.

Soṇa's fancy for wandering may quieten down. Mahākaccāna sees that and wants him to be really ready before he is ordained. Also, there is the practical difficulty of getting a chapter of ten monks together in that region. Even after deciding to ordain Soṇa, he can't do it for three more rainy seasons, so Soṇa is on probation for quite a few years. That is why, when the Buddha learns that he has only been a monk for one year, he is surprised, because his behaviour and knowledge of the Dharma suggest that he has been ordained for many years.

By now the sangha has clearly reached a fair degree of organization. The Buddha has permitted *bhikkhus* to accept others into the community on his behalf, and he has apparently already laid down the rule that only ten monks gathered together can do this, though he relaxed that rule subsequently for districts far from Magadha, where five monks could admit someone to the Order. This is still the practice. They still follow the rule of ten within Magadha, even though until very recently there weren't any monks there, whereas in Sri Lanka and Burma five is enough even though there are thousands of monks.

But the Buddha is still alive, so naturally a newly ordained monk will want to go and see him personally, having up to that time merely heard about him. Here the Buddha is again at Sāvatthī; he seems to spend more time there than anywhere else. And when Soṇa arrives, we're told that the Buddha asks how he is. This is very characteristic of him. Many other teachers, so we are told, would never be the first to speak. To be the first to speak was apparently to make yourself a sort of inferior. If you were superior, like the king, the other person had to speak first and greet you and then you would greet him in reply. But the Buddha was always the first to welcome and greet someone. So here he says to Soṇa something along the lines of 'Are you all right? Have you had a good journey? Did you have any trouble on the way?' Notice Ānanda's thoughtfulness too. He arranges for the newly arrived monk to share a lodging with the Buddha so that they can have a little personal contact. It's all very friendly and informal. The Buddha isn't like a modern abbot. He's got his own room, where presumably Ānanda usually also stays, but when a monk arrives who's never seen the Buddha before, Ānanda thoughtfully arranges that the monk should share the same lodging as the Buddha, so that during the night when they are alone together they can have a quiet exchange. If you went into a modern monastery in, say, Thailand or Japan, the abbot wouldn't treat you in this way, but the Buddha behaves quite naturally and simply. You notice too that the Buddha doesn't sleep very much. He spends a great part of the night seated in the open air and he gets up before dawn, and Soṇa does likewise.

What is remarkable is what happens when the Buddha asks Soṇa to recite the Dharma. He has learned a whole series of Dharma stanzas by heart, presumably from Mahākaccāna. This makes it clear that even during the Buddha's lifetime the practice had developed of the Dharma being summarized in verses – maybe by the Buddha, maybe by others – and learned by heart and regularly recited. We have already seen that this is what happened at the *uposatha* gatherings. So here we see Soṇa, newly arrived from central India, reciting in front of the Buddha the Dharma stanzas he learned in Avanti. Even more remarkably, we know what these verses are. They are recorded in the *Aṭṭhaka-vagga*, the Chapter of the Eights, in the *Sutta-Nipāta*, which along with the final section of the *Sutta-Nipāta*, the *Pārāyana* is quite possibly the oldest section of the entire canon, though it also contains some later material, especially in the last part.[455]

It's a very important work, the *Sutta-Nipāta*, although the language of those two sections, the *Aṭṭhaka-vagga* and the *Pārāyana*, is very difficult, and so is the thought. These verses that Soṇa recites are very, very important. They represent a completely unsystematized teaching. The Chapter of the Eights is quite difficult – the Pāli is difficult, and the thoughts are not easy to grasp, but they are not a systematization of the teaching. Those verses are so old that they are cited even within one of the relatively older parts of the canon like the *Udāna*. If we can be sure of anything as representing the Buddha's original teaching pretty faithfully, we can be sure of the verses of the *Aṭṭhaka-vagga*, which was no doubt an independent work at that time and afterward became a chapter of the *Sutta-Nipāta*. When you read it, you are very close indeed to the original Dharma. We may even have it in the very form in which it was taught by the Buddha, or at least approved by him. He may have been responsible for those verses himself or a disciple may have composed them to summarize his teaching. According to this episode, the Buddha heard them and approved the recitation, and seems in fact to have approved the general practice of monks learning Dharma verses by heart and reciting them to themselves and to one another. Even these days it is good to memorize short texts, repeat them at the time of meditation, and reflect upon them.

The task that the early monks set themselves of handing down all this material orally, and arranging it, editing it, and collecting it, was a tremendous feat. The Dharma was preserved by word of mouth for up to 500 years. The collection of which the *Udāna* is a part is only one section of what became the Pāli canon, and every detail was remembered and handed down, generation upon generation. According to internal evidence, it does faithfully reflect the time. There are no anachronisms, except of a general nature, like adding a few clauses to a list when it was recited at a later period, to make it more complete. One had to be careful to get it exactly right. That is why the Buddha praises Soṇa: 'You are blessed with lovely speech, clearly enunciated and faultless, making the meaning clear.' If you slurred the pronunciation, one word might be substituted for another in the course of time, and that would change the meaning. It is very important that you should not say *kāma* instead of *kamma*, or *kamma* instead of *kāma*,[456] which would change the whole meaning, and there is no written text to check yourself by, though at the *saṅgīti*, the communal recitation when the monks would all chant together, if a monk got it wrong he could be corrected. This faithfulness of oral transmission is something that we need to attend to ourselves, when it comes to passing on what we have heard in our own sangha. Sometimes people give a version of what they have heard which is the opposite of what has been said, or cite an authority to support their own view. To give an example from my own experience, I once spent a few days with some Order members in the New Forest, and in a report of our two-day discussion, one sentence was quoted: 'Everything can be changed except the Three Refuges.' Several of those who were present said how extraordinary it was that out of all the things I had said, this particular thing had been fastened upon and reproduced entirely out of context. It almost suggested that the person who selected it for publication was eager to find an excuse to change everything, which was not at all what I meant. Leaving aside the context of the discussion, the general idea was to emphasize the importance of the Refuges, not to provide *carte blanche* to change everything.

In the verse, 'noble one' here translates *ariya* (Sanskrit *ārya*), the first time this has been used in this way in the *Udāna*. Originally it meant 'Sanskrit-speaking', but in the Pāli canon it is used in the sense of a spiritually superior person, even one who is definitely on the way to Enlightenment. The Āryasaṅgha consists of Stream Entrant, once-returner, non-returner, and *arhant*, for instance; and there is the Āryan Eightfold Path. Here we also see the Buddha rejoicing in merits, even the merits of this very new *bhikkhu*, appreciating his recitation and expressing approval.

5.7 PASSING BEYOND DOUBT

> Once, the Buddha was staying near Sāvatthī in the Jeta Wood at Anāthapiṇḍika's park. At the same time, not far away, Revata was sitting cross-legged, holding his body erect, and reviewing his own purification by overcoming doubt. Seeing him sitting there, and seeing what it meant, the Buddha breathed out these words:
>
> Whatever doubts there are about here or beyond
> in one's own experience or that of others,
> meditators give up all of them,
> ardent ones who live the holy life.

The word translated as 'meditators' here is *jhāyino*, 'those who have *jhāna*' (Sanskrit *dhyāna*), so the suggestion is that the effect of the *dhyāna* states is to dissolve doubts. Of course, in one sense doubt is one of the five hindrances that you have to overcome before you enter upon the first *dhyāna*. The word used here is *kaṅkhā*, which means 'uncertainty' rather than 'indecisiveness', but the commentary glosses *kaṅkhā* as *vicikicchā* so perhaps there's an overlap of meaning.[457] The hindrance of *vicikitsā* (Pāli *vicikicchā*), sometimes translated as doubt, is more like indecisiveness, or doubting so that you can put off the moment of decision. It is almost pretended, culpable doubt. You are raising difficulties because you don't want to decide, because decision means commitment. It is not honestly being unsure, really having a question. If you get into the *dhyānas*, that sort of pretended doubt disappears. You cannot resolve it on the intellectual level. You have to get into the *dhyānas* or higher levels of consciousness. So there's a clear indication here that it's only actual experience of meditation and the spiritual life that resolves doubts. You're not going to resolve your doubts theoretically beforehand and then start. Your doubts get resolved only in the course of your own spiritual experience, only as you get into higher stages of consciousness in pursuit of your *brahmacarya*, your spiritual life. You can't work it all out intellectually first and then begin. Doubts evaporate gradually as you progress. This causes problems for intellectual people, who find it very difficult to get started when they don't know or are not certain or haven't got all the answers. Trustful people who don't think so much get started much more easily. At least twice in the *Udāna* the Buddha says, referring to a certain disciple, 'He did not bother me with questions about the Dharma' i.e. he just got on with it.

Your doubts being resolved doesn't necessarily mean that you get answers to your questions, but you're dwelling in a state of mind where doubts no longer bother you because the questions on which the doubts are based no longer bother you. Sometimes you find yourself in a state where you don't worry any more, although nothing has changed. You haven't got any more knowledge and the situation isn't any different, but you just stop worrying. Suppose you're short of money and you've been worrying how to get some, but then the next morning when you wake up, you're not worried about money in the least. The objective situation is the same but you're just not worried about it in the same way. It's rather like that. Resolving doubts doesn't necessarily mean getting answers to your questions. It means – at least sometimes – that the question ceases to be a question. But a doubter usually wants to get rid of the doubt by finding an answer, and when you give him the answer he raises a further difficulty.

Sometimes when you feel tired, dull, or depleted you start having doubts just because of lack of energy, and when you get into a more zestful state of mind they dissolve. You haven't suppressed them; they are just symptoms of your rather lifeless state. As long as you can maintain yourself at a more positive level, doubts don't arise. It isn't suppression any more than the symptoms of disease are suppressed when you are healthy. When you are in a state of health, the symptoms of disease are simply not there. Persistent doubt suggests great insecurity and anxiety.

Revata is 'reviewing his own purification by overcoming doubt'. One of the *suttas* of the *Majjhima Nikāya* lists the seven stages of purification, and one of these is the stage of purification through overcoming doubts. Although these seven stages are enumerated only once in the whole Pāli canon, Buddhaghosa uses them as part of his double schematic basis for the *Visuddhimagga* or *Path of Purity*. The whole work is constructed according to the double framework of the three trainings, *śīla*, *samādhi*, and *prajñā*, and the seven stages of purification. In that *sutta*, the *Rathavinīta Sutta*, in which the teaching is attributed to Puṇṇa Mantānīputta, the illustration is given of a relay chariot race, the way one passes from one stage of purification to the next being compared to the way one moves from one chariot to the next and in that way gets to the goal. Though the succession of chariots gets you there, it is not one and the same chariot taking you the whole distance. The first chariot leads you to the second, the second chariot leads you to the third, and in this way, you traverse the ground. In the same way, the first stage of purification gets you to the second, and the second gets you to the third, until you reach Nirvāṇa.[458]

5.8 DEVADATTA DECIDES TO BREAK AWAY

> Once, when the Buddha was staying near Rājagaha in the Bamboo Grove at the Squirrels' Feeding Ground, Ānanda went into Rājagaha for almsfood. Devadatta saw him there, came up to him, and said, 'From now on, friend Ānanda, I shall keep the *uposatha* observance and enact the business of the Order apart from the Buddha and the Order of *bhikkhus*.' On his return, Ānanda told the Buddha what Devadatta had said, and added that this action on his part would divide the Order. Realizing the significance of this, the Buddha breathed out these words:
>
> The good do what is good with ease,
> the good do bad with difficulty.
> With ease the bad do what is bad,
> but it's hard for nobles to act badly.

Here we see Devadatta at work. We've encountered him once before simply as one among a number of monks, but here we see him creating a schism. The scene is Rājagaha, the Bamboo Grove, and it's the full-moon day, the time when the Buddha and all the other monks gather together. Devadatta says, 'I'm not going to join in with the common assembly. I'm going to go off with a group of my own followers and have an assembly of my own.' When the monks spread out, when the Dharma spread out over a vast area, they couldn't all meet together at the same time, so there may well have been other meetings being held at the same time in other places; but when you are all in the same place but you deliberately won't join together, that is schism, which is disastrous, and this is what we find Devadatta planning here. The text says he meets Ānanda in the street on the day of the full moon, and he knows that the meeting is that evening, but he says, 'I'm not going to be there. I'm going to have a separate meeting.' The motive – though we are not told so, it's implied – is separatism and pride and the desire to have one's own little group. They are going to observe the *uposatha* which the Buddha had laid down, but they are not going to join in with the 'common assembly'. They are going to break away from the rest.

Devadatta wasn't an *arhant*. An *arhant* couldn't have done that. He wasn't even a Stream Entrant, we're told. But he had meditated and gained psychic powers, and these misled him. He became puffed up, apparently, and deviated into magic and miracle-working and even a bit of black magic. He wanted to set up his own show. You know the type. So what does the Buddha do? He doesn't do anything. He just sees what's going on and says, 'With ease the bad do what is bad, but it's hard for nobles to act badly.'

You notice the contrast with that little scene in Avanti in the previous section. Soṇa, who has been ordained and has learned the scriptures (as they afterwards became), is practising faithfully. He has not even seen the Buddha, but he is loyal to the movement as a whole and even wants to go and visit the Buddha. But Devadatta, who is living in the same place as the Buddha, wants to break away and have his own separate group in Rājagaha instead of participating in the one held by the Buddha and the other *bhikkhus*. Ironically, he was presumably planning to recite the Buddha's own Dharma stanzas, but in a separate, breakaway meeting.

This episode doesn't tell us the whole story, but in the Vinaya Piṭaka we are told how Devadatta suggested that now the Buddha was getting on in years, he should take it easy and hand over the leadership of the Order to Devadatta. The Buddha rejected that suggestion sternly, saying that he would not hand over the leadership of the Order even to Sāriputta and Moggallāna, and he certainly wouldn't hand it over to Devadatta. Devadatta was very angry and tried to murder the Buddha.[459] Again one sees ambition and envy, and their disastrous consequences. The Buddha once said, 'I do not consider that I lead the sangha. If anyone considers that he leads the sangha, let him come forth.'[460] Obviously he was the guide of the sangha, he had initiated it and taught everybody in it, and everybody looked up to him, but he wasn't a sort of boss or party leader. That would be one extreme, and the other would be the extreme of chaos, with everybody going their own way, as Devadatta tried to do. It is a difficult middle way to find: the stability and harmony of the spiritual community which comes about without having a leader and also without breaking up into fragments. But this is what establishing a spiritual community involves; it can't be a flock of sheep under a shepherd, but nor can it be sheep all going their own way.

5.9 WHY DO PEOPLE GO ON TALKING?

> Once, when the Buddha together with a large group of *bhikkhus* was travelling among the people of Kosala, a number of young men passed by in a mocking way. Seeing this, the Buddha breathed out these words:
>
> Those who are apparently wise but deluded,
> speaking what is in the range of speech,
> wish only to stretch their mouths wide.
> What leads them, they do not know.

This is rather scathing, as scathing as anything the Buddha has said so far in the *Udāna*. People just don't know why they go on talking and talking. It's neurotic. They don't know why they are doing it. I remember being puzzled by this when I was a small child. I noticed that my family, especially the womenfolk, used to go on talking about all sorts of what seemed to me very uninteresting things hour after hour. I just couldn't understand how they could keep it up or what they got out of it. What is it that 'leads them', as the Buddha says? Perhaps we can call it neurotic verbosity. Sometimes it is an attempt at confession, an effort to come to the point and a constant failure to do so. But often it's just a desire to fill up the time, a fear of being left on your own with nothing to say and nothing to do.

5.10 SETTING UP MINDFULNESS BEFORE HIM

> Once, the Buddha was staying near Sāvatthī in the Jeta Wood at Anāthapiṇḍika's park. At the same time, not far away, Cūḷapanthaka was sitting cross-legged, holding his body erect, having set up mindfulness before him. Seeing him sitting there, and seeing what it meant, the Buddha breathed out these words:

With body and mind made steady
while standing, sitting, or lying down,
the practitioner resolving to be mindful
will obtain distinctions, one by one.
Obtaining distinctions, one after another,
they go beyond the King of Death's vision.

It seems to have been the practice that after the Buddha's followers had eaten and digested their food, they'd scatter and find a place in the neighbourhood under a tree or in a shady nook to sit quietly meditating or reflecting, and then maybe they'd gather in the evening and the Buddha would give a talk and there'd be some discussion. So maybe the Buddha saw this *bhikkhu* sitting nearby and made this comment. It seems a quite idyllic sort of life that they used to lead – or reading about it makes it sound quite idyllic, let's put it that way.

Here again the importance of mindfulness is stressed, whatever one is doing. The text represents Cūḷapanthaka as sitting cross-legged and setting up mindfulness before him, which would refer to concentrating on the in-and-out breath, but the Buddha's *udāna* refers to the practitioner practising the *satipaṭṭhāna* in general, and being aware of all the different postures. Again, the word is *parimukhe*, 'in front', which the commentaries interpret as 'around the mouth and nose', but which probably had a more abstract meaning of 'to the fore', as here, where the *bhikkhu* brings mindfulness to the fore in relation to the positions of the body.

6
BORN BLIND

6.1 WHY DIDN'T ĀNANDA ASK THE BUDDHA TO LIVE LONGER?

Once, the Buddha was staying near Vesālī in the Great Wood in the Hall of the Gabled House. One morning, having been into Vesālī for almsfood and returned, he asked Ānanda to get a mat and come with him to the Cāpāla Shrine, where he would spend the midday period. So Ānanda followed close behind, and they made their way to the Cāpāla Shrine. Having remarked on the pleasantness of the spot, the Buddha mentioned that, like anyone who had developed the four bases of successful accomplishment, he could live for the rest of the aeon if he wished to do so. But although the Buddha gave him this broad hint, Ānanda failed to understand it, his mind being possessed by Māra, so he missed the chance to ask the Buddha to live for the rest of the aeon, out of compassion for the world. A second and a third time the Buddha said the same thing, but Ānanda still didn't take the hint. The Buddha dismissed him, and Ānanda went and sat down at the foot of a tree nearby.

Not long after Ānanda had left, Māra the Evil One approached the Buddha and suggested that now was the time for the Buddha to attain *parinibbāna*. 'After all,' said Māra, 'you've said that you wouldn't attain final Nibbāna until your disciples, both men and women, both monastic and lay, were wise, confident, disciplined, and expert in the Dhamma, practising according to Dhamma, and teaching it in a convincing way. Well, now they are. Also, you've said in the past that you wouldn't attain *parinibbāna* until the holy life was successful and prosperous, widely spread and disseminated among many. But now that is the case. Surely now is the time for your *parinibbāna*.'

When Māra had said all this, the Buddha replied, 'You can rest easy, Evil One. It won't be long now. In three months' time the Tathāgata will attain final Nibbāna.' In that moment, at the Cāpāla Shrine, the Buddha relinquished the life-force. There was a great earthquake, and a hair-raising rumble of thunder. And the Buddha breathed out these words:

The sage relinquished his life-force,
comparing life with the incomparable.
Internally delighting and unified, he broke
his personal existence like a coat of mail.

This episode obviously belongs to the very end of the Buddha's life, three months before his decease. Both the prose section and the *udāna* have been the subject of a lot of discussion and even speculation, but leaving aside the question of whether Māra was a personality as it were separate from that of the Buddha or whether he represented a train of thought arising in the Buddha's mind, the fact that seems to emerge is that although he had no will to do so, the Buddha could have lived longer had he been requested to fulfil the natural span of his life. He had already lived eighty years and according to Vedic ideas the full span of life was considered to be a hundred years. There are some references to that in the Pāli canon.[461]

Normally, Ānanda was quick to penetrate the Buddha's meaning. You remember that when the monk Soṇa arrived, Ānanda understood that the Buddha wanted to lodge with that monk, though he did not directly say so. But here he seems to be quite obtuse. The text attributes this to the intervention of Māra, but whether Māra is a personification of that obtuseness or a separate entity influencing Ānanda's mind it is very difficult to say. One would have thought that the Buddha would respond to the need, but apparently not. There is the possibility, evidently, of his staying longer, but perhaps it is not strictly necessary. The Buddha has done his work, but he could stay on a few more years if he was asked. No one asks him, so he rejects, as it were, the remainder of that span. It is quite an odd and even mysterious episode. We can conjecture that after the Buddha's decease there would have been quite a bit of discussion: could he not have lived longer? Some people do live for a hundred years; why didn't he? He wouldn't have any desire to live longer and his work was done, but perhaps, if he had been asked, he might have stayed longer. The obvious person to ask him was Ānanda, but perhaps, even though the Buddha did hint that he could live longer, Ānanda was not quick enough to take it up. You can imagine a tradition of this sort developing after the Buddha's decease. They don't want to blame Ānanda too much, so they say it was Māra influencing Ānanda's mind. One could look at it in that way, if one is not disposed to take the episode as a faithful reflection of what happened.

Every species has a natural span, and in the case of a human being, in the present world-period, this is often taken to be a hundred years. So what factors could cause you not to fulfil the full term of the period of life natural to your species? The lack of the will to continue living. Disease. Karma. And there is another factor which is considered quite important in the Buddhist tradition: the 'life-faculty' (*jīvita-indriya*), the natural vitality that keeps you going. The Tibetan long-life ceremony is performed to reinforce the life-faculty and also, through accumulation of merit, to counteract any bad karma which would cut short your life span. Of course, the ceremony cannot prolong your life beyond the natural span; it can't make you live two or three hundred years. But in the case of an Enlightened person, there would not be a will to live, because the Buddha has done everything necessary, and Māra points this out. The Buddha has thoroughly trained all his disciples, so there is no need for him to stay around any longer. But his natural span of life, taking it to be a hundred years, has not been exhausted. Presumably there was no karma that would cut it off, there was no serious disease, as far as we know, and he seems to have been energetic and active right up to the very end, so there was no failure of the life-faculty. The suggestion seems to be that after the Buddha's Enlightenment under the bodhi tree, what functioned in him in place of the ordinary will to live was what is generally referred to as compassion. He remained alive simply because there was something to be done: principally the preaching of the Dharma and the founding of the Sangha.

Perhaps it is appropriate that the Buddha makes this remark to Ānanda under these particular circumstances in this particular place. Vesālī was a town in which the Buddha had quite a large number of followers, so apparently he had gone on his almsround there, he had eaten his meal, and then he had told Ānanda that they would go to the Cāpāla Shrine for their noonday rest. After they had sat down, the Buddha commented on what a lovely spot it was, with its shrines dotted here and there, presumably under groups of trees in little groves. That suggests, first of all, the Buddha's appreciation of natural beauty, but also that it is a natural situation in which the Buddha might raise that sort of matter.

According to the Buddhist tradition, the so-called psychic powers, the four *iddhipādas* (Sanskrit *ṛddhipādas*), are operated to any degree of efficacy only on the basis of a strong experience of the fourth *dhyāna*. These powers are operated through or by your active and powerful aura – using this expression rather loosely – and it is through this that you see at a distance, hear at a distance, and even cause things to happen from a distance. So the fourth *dhyāna* is the basis of *iddhi*, which means simply potency, power, in the widest sense. It is not necessarily magical power. For instance, when the monks were discussing the two kings Bimbisāra and Pasenadi, they used the same word to refer to their potency, their royal *iddhi*, which meant the power of the king in the broadest sense. We are still concerned with mundane things, nothing transcendental. Even Devadatta had some of these powers, though they didn't do him much good. When I say mundane, I mean the *lokiya* (Sanskrit *laukika*) as distinct from the *lokuttara* or transcendental. If you have a very powerful, intense, concentrated consciousness which functions around you like a sort of aura and which can project itself, as it were, into the world, things may start happening even without your conscious knowledge or intention, but you can deliberately cultivate this. There are four different ways, the *iddhipādas*, the four ways or bases of psychic power; and the Buddha has these. It is suggested here that one who has developed these four bases of psychic power can, among other things, prolong his life so as to fulfil the whole of the natural term.

First of all, there is *chanda*. *Chanda* is intense will, a sort of concentrated volition. Then there is *vīrya*, which is great energy. Thirdly, there is *citta*, mind or consciousness. I am not quite sure what it means in this context, but obviously mind or consciousness must be present. Perhaps it suggests that one cannot develop the *iddhis* or psychic powers to the full extent unless one has the conscious intention of doing so. They don't just happen. And fourthly, there is *vīmaṃsā*, which is investigation, presumably investigation into the nature of what you want to do.[462] The Buddha has these four bases of psychic power, so he has the ability to prolong his life if he can be induced to do so. But, though Ānanda is given this broad hint, Māra – so we are told – clouds his mind and he doesn't respond.

The Buddha said to Māra that he would not pass away until his monks could 'refute any wrong view arising which may well be refuted by right reasoning', in Woodward's translation, suggesting not only being able to see a *micchā-diṭṭhi* when it crops up, but being able to refute it. This comes at the end of the list the Buddha gives, as though it is a culmination of their accomplishments, which suggests how important it is to be able to refute a *micchā-diṭṭhi*, and how difficult *micchā-diṭṭhis* are to refute. The Buddha seems to suggest that some *micchā-diṭṭhis* can't be refuted in that way and you just have to let them alone.

It probably isn't a coincidence that the Pāli canon opens with the Sutta Piṭaka, the Sutta Piṭaka opens with the *Dīgha Nikāya*, and the *Dīgha Nikāya* opens with the *Brahmajāla Sutta*. The *Brahmajāla Sutta* is the great net of sixty-two wrong views which the Buddha drags up, as it were, out of the ocean of misunderstanding and brings to land, exposing them for what they really are. People holding some of these views are called 'eel wrigglers' because they evade the issue: they slither and slide, and twist and turn.[463] No doubt this wasn't the first discourse delivered by the Buddha, and maybe he didn't even give a discourse in that particular form. The compilers may have anthologized his refutations of *micchā-diṭṭhis* at different times; it is difficult for us to know. But certainly they thought the refutation of *micchā-diṭṭhis* was sufficiently important to be placed at the very forefront of the Tipiṭaka, as if to say, 'Let's clear all these wrong views out of the way first, then we can get on with the Dharma.' To expose *micchā-diṭṭhis* for what they are requires not only some understanding of the Dharma and a measure of practice, but also a fair degree of intelligence, mental alertness, and penetration. It is not everybody who can expose and refute a *micchā-diṭṭhi*, and it may well be one of the last accomplishments to be developed. It implies a degree of confidence, though not just that, otherwise you might be refuting with full confidence something that was a right view, a *sammā-diṭṭhi*.

This is the first description in the *Udāna* of an earthquake, but did it really happen, or does it have a symbolical significance? The earth gets a great shock which underlines the importance of the occasion. In later tradition the earth is described as shaking in six different ways. This is described as occurring, for instance, when the Buddha becomes Enlightened, when he passes away, and on this occasion. It is as though there is a tremendous repercussion on the whole of conditioned existence. Here we are being warned, as it were, that the Buddha's life is nearly over.

Again one has the sense that the *Udāna* is a sort of gospel. It isn't exactly a biography, but you get a sense of chronological sequence, though the episodes are not arranged in strict chronological order. We go back in time and then forward again sometimes, but there's an impression of progression, of the original Enlightenment, the proclamation of the ideal, and then more detailed teaching about qualities to be developed and faults to be abandoned. We see followers gradually coming in, people becoming disciples, the movement growing and spreading, then encountering envy, opposition, and so on. The teaching develops, becoming more complete, more systematic, and we get an impression of the organization, the sangha, developing, and a sense that Sāvatthī is at the centre of things.

6.2 THE BUDDHA AND THE KING'S SPIES

> One evening when the Buddha was staying near Sāvatthī in the Eastern Park at the house of Migāra's mother, he was sitting outside the gate when he was joined by King Pasenadi of Kosala. At that moment a crowd of ascetics of various kinds, all with hairy bodies and long nails, came along the road, passing quite close to the Buddha. King Pasenadi rose from his seat, knelt on the ground, folded his hands in the direction of the ascetics, and announced his name three times. And having done so, he sat down again and asked the Buddha, 'Sir, could any of those ascetics be *arhants*, or on the path to arhantship?'
>
> The Buddha replied, 'Great king, as you are a layman, enjoying the pleasures of the senses and living at home among your children; it's going to be difficult for you to know whether or not these men are *arhants* or on that path. You can tell someone's virtues only if

you live with them for a long time, and after careful consideration – and even then you have to be a wise man, not a fool.'

The king said that this was wonderfully well said, and revealed that in fact the wandering ascetics were not ascetics at all, but spies in disguise, whom he had employed to gather information for him. The Buddha, realizing the significance of this, breathed out these words:

One should not strive in every pursuit.
A person should not belong to another.
One should not live depending on another.
One should not live by trading on religion.

Once again we are in Sāvatthī, at the house of Migāra's mother – that is to say, the house donated by Visākhā to the Buddha and the sangha. Having spent the afternoon by himself, the Buddha is sitting just outside the porch of the house, and from what follows we can understand that there is a main road quite near. The king of Kosala, Pasenadi, comes to see the Buddha and as they sit there together, there comes along the road a company of ascetics and wanderers of all kinds.

First of all, there are seven long-haired ascetics. You see these in India even today. They wear their hair very long. They never cut it, they braid it, and sometimes they artificially lengthen their braids – they can be twenty or twenty-five feet long – and coil them round their heads. Their hair is matted and dusty and sometimes they rub ashes on themselves. Then there are seven *nigaṇṭhas*. *Nigaṇṭhas* literally means those free from bonds, and it is a term used to describe the Jains, as we call them now, the followers of Mahāvira. Then there are seven naked ascetics, seven wearing only one cloth, and seven who didn't cut their hair or trim their nails, so that they had long nails and hairy armpits (normally Indians would shave the hair from their armpits). So you have got this motley crowd of ascetics and wanderers coming along the road in the evening with their bundles on their shoulders, as the Buddha and King Pasenadi are sitting there.

King Pasenadi is quite an old man – he is supposed to be exactly the same age as the Buddha – and he is very pious. He is a follower of the Buddha, and he supports religious people generally, so as this crowd of holy men is passing by, he rises from his seat and politely salutes them in the way that lay people, even those in a prominent position, do salute ascetics and holy men even nowadays in India. He announces his own name, as is also customary.

After they have all gone, he turns to the Buddha and puts what we afterwards come to understand is a loaded question: amongst all these ascetics, are there any who are actually Enlightened? Are there any *arhants* among them? The question is loaded because he knows who and what they really are, as we see later on. Perhaps he is wondering whether the Buddha can be taken in by appearances.

The Buddha does not reply directly. After all, he is the Buddha; it is not so easy to catch him out. So first of all, he points out that it is hard for someone like the king to determine something like this. In other words, he takes the opportunity of gently rebuking the average religious-minded lay person's eager desire to know 'Is this person Enlightened, or is that person Enlightened?' You often get this, in India and elsewhere, with regard to different teachers. People always want to know, 'Is he Enlightened or not?' and they often ask the question in a way that suggests there is a definite answer which they are capable of understanding. One comes across this sort of attitude in rather strange forms. People come up to you and assure you that some guru or another is the Perfect Master and really Enlightened, and they absolutely know it, though they may not even have met him. They have only read the leaflets, but they want to insist on this and force it upon you too. This is absolute presumption; how can they possibly know? This is the sort of thing that the Buddha is getting at, saying, 'How can someone like you know? What is the use even of asking? Even supposing I said yes, you would have to take it on trust. That wouldn't help you really to know.'

With his next statement, the Buddha is saying, 'Never mind knowing who is and is not an *arhant*; it is difficult to know any human being. It is only by association that you know whether someone has integrity. It is only when you have seen someone in trouble that you know whether they have fortitude. It is only by talking with someone that you can know whether they are wise, and then only by thinking about it for a long time, not just giving it a passing thought. Even then, only if you yourself are wise can you know what another person is really like. Here you are, all eager to know whether any of these people is an *arhant*, but even to know what an ordinary man is really like is not easy, so don't expect a quick answer to this sort of question.'

King Pasenadi is very impressed, and then reveals that these wanderers are in fact his spies. Even in those days government informers used to go around disguised as sadhus, picking up information and reporting back to the king. To paraphrase the commentary, Pasenadi explains to the Buddha that he saluted them to help them keep up their disguise, saying, 'If I don't play my part and treat them as sadhus when they are disguised, they may keep back some information from me, so I pretend that I think they are sadhus and salute them accordingly.'[464]

If the Buddha had said, 'Well, yes, maharaja, very probably some of them are *arhants*', the king would not have had much faith in the Buddha. But the Buddha is not to be so easily caught out, and maybe he does see through the whole thing. He sees that they are not really sadhus from their mental states and the way they carry themselves. Maybe he could even see something fishy about the way the king saluted them and the way they responded. But for the ordinary person, even the ordinary wise person, it is not easy to penetrate another person's character. The maharaja asks him for a snap judgement, but he very gently takes the maharaja down a peg or two.

People are too ready to judge. This is the general principle that emerges. One should be very reluctant to come to a value judgement about somebody. You can assess an action, but you have to be careful about proceeding from that to a judgement about the person as a whole. You need to know them for a long time and in many different situations, and talk to them quite a lot, and you also need to be rather wise yourself before you can form any estimate of them, especially about their degree of spiritual development. People who are not even attempting to live a spiritual life are certainly not fit judges of those who are trying to do so, though that doesn't stop them from being critical: 'I thought you were a Buddhist! Why are you doing such-and-such?' If someone who is trying to lead a spiritual life happens to lose his temper, those who have never made any attempt to be mindful or to keep their anger under control are apt to say, 'I thought Buddhists were not supposed to lose their temper.' You know that only too well. It is very presumptuous of people to talk in this way. They don't know what it's like to try to make a spiritual effort, with all the repercussions that that sets up in different parts of one's being. Here the Buddha says, 'Unless you yourself are on the spiritual path, you don't know what it's like and you are not in a position to judge.'

The *udāna* seems to have some connection with the episode, but what does the Buddha mean by 'One should not strive in every pursuit'? That seems a little obscure. The commentary explains *sabbattha*, everywhere or in every pursuit, as *sabbasmiṃ pāpadhamme*: one should not spread one's effort, as it were, over every bad and unskilful mental state and activity.[465] One should only make an effort to do what is good and skilful. And one should not be dependent in the way those pseudo-ascetics were, living in dependence upon the king. This is reminiscent of an earlier verse (*Udāna* 2.9) in which it was said that 'being in control is all bliss. Sharing is oppressive'.

The Pāli word *issara* (Sanskrit *īśvara*) does not occur either in the prose section or the *udāna*, but the commentary explains 'one should not live depending on another' as 'one should not carry on one's life depending on another such as *issara*, having thoughts such as that "my pleasures and pains are bound up with him"'.[466] The Pāli term *issariya* (Sanskrit *īśvarīya*) means 'rulership' or 'supremacy' in a literal, not a psychological sense, but in this context it is worth considering that it doesn't so much suggest rulership over others as that you are yourself autonomous, not dependent on anybody or anything else. *Īśvara* is the standard Sanskrit term for God, because he is autonomous in a way that human beings are not, and in Indian thought you come across the related conception of *aiśvarya* again and again. It is not quite independence in the Western sense, but more like a positive autonomy. It is the state of being a ruler; you don't necessarily have anybody to rule over, but there is nobody ruling over you. It is pointed out that the standard Hindu conception of *ātman* involves *aiśvarya*; the *ātman* is autonomous, self-governing. Buddhism, by contrast, points out that the *ātman* as experienced by us, our empirical self, is not independent or autonomous in that way, but dependent and contingent. For instance, you get the argument in the Pāli canon that you cannot say to yourself, 'Let me be so-and-so or let me be such-and-such.'[467] This shows that you have no *aiśvarya*, no rulership, no autonomy, otherwise you could be in whatever state you wished to be. When you wished to be happy, you could be happy, and if you can't, this shows that you have no *aiśvarya*. So you are not a self of the Upanishadic metaphysical type. There is no such self, in fact, according to Buddhism. This is one of the arguments used by the early Buddhists against the Upanishadic concept of self: that that concept involves, as part of its definition, this concept of *aiśvarya* or rulership or lordship, but that is not characteristic of our empirical self, which is therefore *anātman*. In Buddhist terms – though Buddhism doesn't quite say this – an ethical and spiritual *aiśvarya* is possible, but that is something to be developed, not something that naturally belongs to you.

'One should not live by trading on religion.' The Buddha did not really approve of what Pasenadi was doing, perhaps. He suggests here that it isn't right to make use of the respect enjoyed by ascetics in society for unworthy purposes. These pseudo-ascetics are using the pretence of living the ascetic life as a means of livelihood. Of that the Buddha can hardly approve. But the expression 'trading on religion' has much broader implications than this particular instance. It's using the Dharma for worldly ends, as a sort of secular profession. This has happened, of course, in all religions to some extent, though probably less in Buddhism than in any other tradition. You certainly find it among the Christian clergy of the Middle Ages, when religion really did become a trade on a grand scale, and that's how the Reformation came about.

Several important points emerge from this episode. First, those not leading a spiritual life should not try to judge those who are trying to do so. Secondly, it is very difficult to know what someone else is really like. And thirdly, one shouldn't make a trade of the Dharma.

6.3 THE BUDDHA REVIEWS HIS STATE OF MIND

> Once, when the Buddha was staying near Sāvatthī in the Jeta Wood at Anāthapiṇḍika's park, he sat reviewing the unskilful states he had abandoned and the skilful states he had developed through meditation, and was moved to breathe out these words:
>
> First it was and then it was not.
> First it was not and then it was.
> But it was not and it will not be
> and it does not exist even now.

Although the verse doesn't quite say so, one could relate this to the fourfold right effort. (See section 4.1.) At first there was an unskilful thought, but then it was removed, at first certain skilful thoughts were not present, but then they were brought into existence, and so on. The general sense is quite clear. The Buddha is reviewing his own past development and seeing how he removed unskilful mental states and developed skilful mental states to the full. But there is something mysterious here too, hinting at the way in which the Dharma is not an existent entity.

6.4 THE BLIND MEN AND THE ELEPHANT

Once, when the Buddha was staying near Sāvatthī in the Jeta Wood at Anāthapiṇḍika's park, there were all kinds of recluses and wanderers living in the area who had all kinds of views and opinions, ranging from 'the world is eternal' or 'the world is not eternal' and 'the world is finite' or 'the world is infinite' to 'the life-principle and the body are the same', or the opposite, or 'The Tathāgata does not exist after death', or the opposite. Each declared about his own view, 'Only this is true and any other view is false', and they all began to quarrel, saying, 'Dhamma is like this, Dhamma is not like that!' A number of *bhikkhus* went to see the Buddha and told him what was going on, and in response the Buddha told the story of the blind men and the elephant:

Once upon a time there was a king in Sāvatthī who invited all the blind people of the city to come and be introduced to an elephant. The king's servant allowed some of the blind people to feel the elephant's head, others its tusk, others its trunk, and so on. And then the king asked the blind people what an elephant was like. Those who had felt the head thought an elephant was like a water jar, those who had felt the tusk thought it was like a ploughshare, and so on. And they all began to fight each other, saying 'An elephant is like this! An elephant is not like that!' – much to the king's amusement.

The Buddha said that the wanderers of various sects, with all their views, were similarly blind, and realizing the significance of this, he breathed out these words:

Some brahmins and ascetics seem
to be attached to their own views.
Like people seeing one sidedly
they dispute and they argue.

The main point of this well-known parable is that the blind men mistake the part for the whole. They are in contact with the elephant to some extent, and they describe it according to their experience of it, but their experience is limited because they are blind. It is only the man with Perfect Vision who sees the elephant – sees the truth – as it really is, in all its aspects, completely and totally. It is not so much that the blind men are wrong as that they are only partly right. In a sense you could say everybody is right – in a way. This is perhaps why William Blake says that everything possible to be believed is an image of the truth.[468] You can't ever be totally wrong. There is always some truth in what you say, because it is based on some experience, however limited, however partial, however one-sided, however much in need of qualification.

Also, it suggests that you don't arrive at the truth merely by adding together the various partial views. Suppose without knowing what an elephant was or ever having experienced one, you merely said, 'All these views are partly right. Yes, the elephant is like a ploughshare, it is like a winnowing basket, it is like a granary, it is like a pillar. It is like all these together.' That wouldn't give you an idea of what an elephant was like at all. This is the syncretistic approach, on a purely intellectual level. To see the whole, and to see how all the partial views are partly right, you need a totally different vision, on a totally different level. You need eyes. This is very, very important. The truth cannot be represented by the sum total of partial views. The truth is a sort of gestalt, we might say; it is a whole, complete in itself. When you see the whole truth, you can understand how the partial visions represent parts of the truth, but you don't get any idea of the truth merely by adding together all the partial visions without a total vision of your own. You just get something monstrous, a jumble. You can't arrive at the truth by putting together what different people have said about it at different times and in different places, and trying to get all the pieces of the jigsaw to fit. You need a total vision which is one vision, an integral vision. That is what perfect vision, *samyag-dṛṣṭi*, is – or at least *samyag-dṛṣṭi* is the beginning of it. You don't arrive at the total vision by getting as many blind men as possible, yourself included, to tell you what they perceive. You arrive at a vision or knowledge of the total truth by opening your inner eyes and becoming Enlightened. Some people do try to arrive at the truth about something by adding one bit to another, but that is not the way. You have to see the thing as a whole, even if not at first very clearly, and then gradually get to know that total picture in greater and greater detail, more and more thoroughly, more and more clearly.

This is what happens with people of limited mystical experience. They have a certain experience, but then they start thinking they know the whole truth. You can overcome this only by being connected with a tradition in which all the aspects of the truth are – if one can speak in that way – understood and taken into consideration, and where any one-sidedness on one's own part can be checked and corrected.

I can't help thinking of what William Blake says about the fourfold vision – not just single vision, as he calls it, the vision of a one-sided and degenerate intellect, but the vision of the whole man, the fourfold man, that is to say the vision that takes into consideration not only reason but emotion and imagination, and even instinct as well.[469] The fourfold vision is all of these blended together, seeing totally. I don't want to insist upon Blake's version, particularly from a Buddhist point of view. There is just the general idea of the total truth being apprehensible only by the total individual. You can't apprehend it with just one of your faculties, any more than a blind man – or, for the matter of that, any number of blind men – can apprehend the total truth which is the elephant. The total vision is undivided – indivisible, even – and so long as you are a divided and fragmented being, you will never see it.

This is one of the most important parables in the whole Pāli canon. You notice how the Buddha tells it: 'Once upon a time there was a king in Sāvatthī.' It begins almost like a *Jātaka* story. I suspect that some of the stories told by the Buddha have been taken too literally as regards their locale. It really is more like saying 'Once upon a time' (*bhūtapubbam*), as though it is a sort of fairy tale, not to be taken literally. I don't think he intends to say that at some former period of history there was a raja of Sāvatthī who actually conducted this experiment.

According to this story there seems to have been quite a variety of views held by different wanderers. Some of these views are barely intelligible to us today. We can hardly imagine people holding them, they seem so bizarre. Others we can get a sense of – for instance, the question of whether the world is limited or unlimited is something we still think and talk about today. Some people say that the universe contains so many thousands of millions of worlds or galactic systems, but it is a certain distance across, and beyond that there is nothing, void, no world, no universe. Others say, 'No, it just goes on and on, it is infinite.' This is one of Kant's antinomies, an antinomy being a sort of contradiction, but not just a contradiction. You can't say that the universe is both finite and infinite. These views are contradictory. An antinomy arises when you can find equally good and bad reasons on both sides. There are conclusive arguments against both positions, but there is no third position, apparently. Kant pointed out that antinomies arise when you consider (in this case) space as objectively existing, rather than as part of the way we apprehend things.[470] It is in this sense that Kant's philosophy is called critical philosophy and all pre-Kantian philosophy is called pre-critical – that is to say, Kant takes into consideration the way in which we apprehend existence. He criticizes the form of our knowledge. He doesn't take it for granted. This is a crude summary of a complicated subject, very much oversimplified, but to the extent that one regards space as something objectively existing, as a sort of box out there in which things are – whether those things are tables and chairs or universes and galactic systems – to that extent the question will arise as to whether it is finite or infinite. The antinomy arises when you find reasons to support both the view that the universe is finite and that it is infinite. The question cannot be settled one way or the other in those terms, so the wanderers go on disputing indefinitely. The subjectivity of space comes out quite clearly in some of the *suttas* in the *Dīgha Nikāya* where the Buddha says quite clearly, 'Within this body' – in other words in one's own mind – 'is the arising and passing away of the world, or the universe.'[471]

Among the views expressed, some say that the Tathāgata exists after death and others say that he does not. The commentary interprets *tathāgata* as *satta* or 'living being', and goes on to interpret the first view in terms of eternalism and the second in terms of annihilationism (which I would call nihilism).[472] These are the two extreme views: eternalism, that there is a self that persists unchanged after the death of the physical body, and nihilism, that the self is cut off, as it were, at the time of death. Buddhism teaches a middle way between eternalism and nihilism, maintaining that there is a continuity of the ever-changing process from life to life, but not the continuation of any unchanging psychical element, nor the abrupt cutting off of a psychical element at the time of death so that nothing is left.

The Buddha pointed out that it is not necessary to take up a philosophical position in order to lead the spiritual life. All you are concerned with is the fact that suffering exists, that your present state of being is not satisfactory, and that you can do something about it. He refused to answer any questions as to whether the world is finite or infinite, eternal or non-eternal, or whether or not the *jīva*, the soul, what makes you alive, is the same as the physical body, saying that these questions did not need to be answered in order to lead the spiritual life, and leading the spiritual life would lead you to a point at which you understood the basis for such questions.[473] It is a remarkable attitude, in a way. Many questions, or rather pseudo-questions, arise out of naive realism, whether with regard to thoughts or terminology. The Buddha is saying that to get started on the spiritual path it is not necessary to have arrived at the solution to purely theoretical questions which are antinomial in any case and therefore incapable of an answer on their own terms. If you are trying to get an answer to these questions before you even start on the spiritual path, you will never get started. This is, of course, the purport of another well-known parable, that of the man wounded by the poisoned arrow.[474]

The verse suggests that brahmins and recluses who are honoured merely by virtue of the fact that they are, or call themselves, brahmins and recluses are wasting their time in clinging to one-sided views. For those who are supposed to be leading an active spiritual life, this purely theoretical disputation about views which don't matter one way or the other from a spiritual point of view is not appropriate. It is useless to preoccupy oneself with the *avyākṛta vastūni* (Pāli *avyākata vatthūni*), the undetermined or unexplained topics, which are pairs of antinomies, or the more complex *catuṣkoṭi* formulation.[475] But there are other general reflections which are useful, and sometimes the Buddha mentions these. For example, it is profitable to reflect that there are in the world beings who have attained a higher level of consciousness, even Buddhas. It is profitable to reflect that there is a law of karma, a law of the conservation of moral effort, and that there is benefit to be derived from making an earnest spiritual effort.[476] It is antinomian propositions that have no direct bearing on the spiritual life that the Buddha is discouraging people from taking sides about. Also, it becomes clear that quite a few so-called philosophical and so-called religious views, opinions, doctrines, beliefs, are only rationalizations of limited perceptions, or even of misunderstandings.

6.5 SINKING IN THE MIDDLE OF THE FLOOD

> As in the previous story, the text describes the wanderers of various sects and their views, each believing his own view of the Dhamma to be the only correct one. To the views mentioned earlier is added a dispute as to whether pleasure and pain, the self and the world, are made by oneself or by another. When he heard about them, the Buddha said that they were blind, not knowing what is beneficial and what is harmful, not knowing what is Dhamma and what is not, and thus they were quarrelsome. And realizing the significance of this, he breathed out these words:
>
> Some brahmins and ascetics seem
> to be attached to their own views.
> They sink in the middle of the flood
> not having found a firm footing.

This is virtually the same episode as the last one, without the illustrative parable and with a different list of opposing views. The views here seem a bit more sophisticated than those in the previous episode, and there is one particular pair that is of special, almost contemporary, interest: 'whether pleasure and pain, the self and the world, are made by oneself or by another'. Some apparently hold that your state of happiness depends entirely on your own effort, and others that it depends entirely upon your environment. These are two extreme views, and we could say that the truth is somewhere in between, that they are interdependent. Maintaining a positive mental state is not entirely dependent upon yourself, irrespective of environment, nor entirely dependent on the environment. The truth lies somewhere in between, and both have to be taken into consideration.

It seems as though the recluses and brahmins have got some way towards crossing the stream. They are at least *samaṇas* and *brāhmaṇas*, so they have made a start, but they have got into deep water through these one-sided views, so they sink as it were in midstream. They are trying to find a firm footing by insisting on those views in a dogmatic way, but firm footing is to be found only in one's own spiritual experience.

> Again, the Buddha heard about the wanderers who disputed and quarrelled about the nature of the Dhamma, and he responded by breathing out these words:
>
> People are intent on self-agency,
> connected with the agency of others.
> Those who have not recognized this
> have not seen it as an arrow.
>
> But for one who has seen this as an arrow,
> it does not occur to them, 'I act',
> it does not occur to them, 'another acts'.
>
> This humankind is full of conceit,
> tied by conceit and bound by conceit.
> Captivated discussion of wrong views
> will not transcend cyclical existence.

This is the same episode as before, but with a different *udāna*. The first two verses are concerned chiefly with the idea that 'I am the agent' or 'another is the agent'. As in Śāntideva's verse discussed in section 2.4, you grasp the body, he grasps the stick, and the pain that arises is the result of those two conditions coming together. One should try to think not so much in terms of I did this or he did that, but more in terms of causes and conditions coming together and producing an effect. In other words, instead of seeing things in terms of exclusive, solely responsible agents or causes, one tries to see things in terms of conditioned co-production. The third verse depicts humanity as being quarrelsome through their views, which is a great pity. They may be supposed to be religious or philosophical views which are meant to help us to develop, but instead become occasions of attachment and clinging and dispute and ill-feeling, and in that way we become bound still more tightly to the wheel of life.

The *udāna* is not completely clear, but it clearly refers to people who have not seen adherence to any of these one-sided views as a thorn, an affliction, a hindrance to insight. For one who has seen this as an arrow, it does not occur to them, 'I act', or 'another acts'; they see what happens in terms of conditioned co-production. But do you see the difference between the two attitudes? One puts the whole responsibility for a situation on an agent, either you or me, as it were; and the other tries to understand all the factors involved and see objectively that the situation has arisen out of the interaction of those causes and conditions.

Suppose, for instance, you organize a successful meeting. You could adopt the attitude 'I am the agent; the success is all due to me.' But if you look at it carefully, the meeting was held in a hall which was built by other people. Others distributed leaflets and prepared advertisements, which were typeset and printed by still others. People distributed the newspapers in which those advertisements appeared, others read those newspapers, and others drove the buses and trains that brought people to the meeting. The success of your meeting was the result of a vast complex of causes and conditions, among which you were only one. Reflecting like that, you see that the meeting's success was the result of interaction between many factors. You could trace it back to the whole universe, or at least the whole social system within which the meeting took place. Maybe you were an important factor, but you were not the only one, and you would not be justified in having the attitude 'I was the agent.' This is the kind of thing that is meant here. We tend not to see all the other factors involved, but attribute everything to the part that we play, if it is something we are proud of. If it is something we are not happy with, we attribute it to somebody else. If the meeting went badly, we don't say, 'I didn't organize it properly,' but 'There was a strike that day. People would have come in great numbers, but there weren't any trains,' or, 'The people responsible for advertising didn't do their job properly,' or, 'The acoustics were all wrong. People don't like that hall.' Anything rather than say, 'It was my fault.'

To generalize, one could say that when craving is predominant – and craving, of course, is connected with pleasure – we tend to think of the self as the agent. When aversion is predominant, when the situation is displeasing, we tend to think of the other as the agent. People are happy to accept the credit when things go right, but not to take the blame when things go wrong. In both cases, they tend to think in terms of one agent, not a whole complex of conditions in which they are just one. Perhaps sometimes you are the decisive one, but you can't always tell. This way of reflecting obviously lessens the strength of what is popularly called egotism.

There is another aspect of this which is much more difficult to express. This we may describe as the self, or the agent, even, as an alienated subject – a subject abstracted from the concrete process of action and then regarded as pertaining to that alienated subject. To give an example, suppose you say, 'I am walking.' Is there a you that is walking, a walker, apart from the process of walking? Buddhism, of course, says no, but that what you think of as the self is only a label for the sum total of all those processes. Those processes do not belong to a fixed self, a self which is itself not a process but an unchanging thing. Sometimes you may have an eerie feeling of not being at one with what you are doing. You are aware of it not in a mindful way, but in an alienated way. There is a fictitious, rather ghostly little self which has somehow got separated from the process and is regarding it. It doesn't exist apart from it, it is not the agent separate from the process. It is a little split-off bit of the process which is as it were standing aside from it in an uneasy way, and not able to feel at one with the process, not able to feel that it is doing what it is doing. Then, of course, you feel very unreal.

It isn't necessarily the same as how it feels to meditate when you don't feel like it. Sometimes you can recognize, or even accept, that part of you doesn't like doing something, but consciously make a decision that you are going to do it all the same. This would not result in the alienated situation. But if you don't recognize that there is a part of you that doesn't want to do it, if you try to ignore that and go ahead, you may very well get this sensation of being alienated from what you are doing, or at least not being fully into it.

If you look back over your life, you may come to the conclusion that there were not many situations in which you felt completely at one with what you were doing. I am not thinking of situations of total unawareness – they can hardly be counted – but situations in which you were completely into what you were doing, and at the same time quite aware, but not in an alienated way. Very often these are situations in which you are doing something creative, something in which you really believe and into which all your energies can flow. Then the idea of a doer, paradoxically, does not arise. When you are fully into what you are doing, you are completely absorbed. There is no mental activity, including the mental activity that says I am doing this or he is doing that. You can have a working relationship with somebody else in which there is no thought of what you do and what he does, especially where there is something rhythmical about the job or you know each other very well. You just have the awareness of a situation in which you are both functioning. You get this, no doubt, in a smoothly functioning team of any kind, and I imagine it's the same in some sports. It is quite spontaneous, as it were.

In an objective, skilful discussion, you consider the subject being discussed and see it from your point of view and express that; and then somebody else sees it from his point of view, and he expresses that. You don't identify any remark or line of thought as 'mine', with the idea that you must defend that at all costs. You just see all these different contributions being made – some more valuable than others – and gradually adding up to the total discussion. It may be that in the course of discussion certain points of view are dropped, because they obviously don't belong, and others become clearer and stronger; and then a conclusion emerges. It is a cooperative process. But if it is my opinion against your opinion, it becomes a ding-dong battle, and this is not at all skilful. It is quite easy to tell whether it is discussion or just dispute. You get a completely different feeling from the whole thing. Sometimes it changes from one to the other and back again. But it is quite important to think in terms of putting forward a point of view, even one with which you are identified in a healthy way, not as 'this is my point of view', so that if someone differs from it you feel attacked or threatened, and feel the need to defend or retaliate.

It's best to try to see your own contribution as one factor in a situation, and have a sense of the other factors, especially when those other factors are other people, rather than having a one-sided consciousness of what you are doing and what others are doing in an alienated way. Aim to be fully and completely into and with whatever you are doing, and not have a part of yourself split off from that and watching as it were from the outside. Perhaps the best word to describe it is wholeheartedness: 'Whatsoever thy hand findeth to do, do it with all thy might', as the Bible says.[477] You have to find something in which you can really believe; then you can do it with all your energy, all your interest, all your enthusiasm, not just with a part of yourself, not with doubts and reservations. If you don't know what there is for you to do in that way, it is sometimes best not to do anything and just wait.

Sometimes, though, we hold back when it would be better to make more effort. Very few situations are ideal, but if we put more of ourselves into them, we will find them more satisfying. If you have got to do it, resolving to do it really well is much better than doing the minimum you can get away with out of resentment at being in the situation at all. Do the best you can, even if it isn't the situation that you would have chosen. The idea that it isn't good for you to do something you don't want to do can be misapplied. Who is it that doesn't want to do it? Is it the best you or the worst and weakest? Some people seem to have lost the capacity to act in a potent way and can express themselves only by not acting, or getting in the way of others acting. In other words, their mode of expression has become negative rather than positive. You say, 'Let's do so-and-so,' and they can't respond with 'Oh, yes!' – there's not enough oomph there. They can only say 'Oh, no, I don't think so,' or 'I don't think you should do it.' To quote Blake again, he says, to paraphrase, that the hindering of action is not virtue, that virtue is in the action itself.[478] If you think of virtue in terms of abstention from action, you tend to think of yourself as propagating virtue when you are hindering other people from action. Sometimes people are very good at finding reasons for not doing something.

There may be social or even historical reasons why you find it difficult to get into what you are doing. You may find you have a little fund of resentment, but that is no excuse. But if there are quite a lot of things that you feel you have to do half-heartedly, to the extent that you feel you are only half functioning, it is probably best to stop doing anything for a while. Wait until you really feel like doing something and then do that; and then wait again until you feel like doing something else. Then cautiously start thinking about what it would be best for you to do, what you ought to do – not 'ought' in the sense of obligation but in the ideal sense – and then make up your mind to do that, completely and wholeheartedly. Doing what you like in the sense of following your whims and fancies is not a very healthy thing. If you have been doing a lot of things that you weren't really interested in, it may be necessary for a while to do what you feel like doing until deeper and more genuine desires start coming up, but most people need to make a much more determined effort to put energy into what they are doing – assuming that it is not something unskilful.

If you see that you could be doing a particular thing, and only a weak and reluctant part of you is stopping you, you may have to grit your teeth and force yourself to do it, but you shouldn't have to do that too often. You have to ask yourself what in you doesn't want to cooperate, and why? Is it a part with legitimate needs that are not being fulfilled, or a weak part that has to be allowed to wither away as quickly as possible? For the time being, you are probably relatively unintegrated, and in formulating your long-range strategy, you have to take the needs of all these aspects of yourself into consideration. For example, if you have an open-air side that likes walks in the country and sunshine and exercise, it would be unwise to occupy yourself exclusively with studies, meetings, lectures, meditation, and so on. Sooner or later you will feel unwilling to carry on, because there will be a pull from your outdoor side. Inasmuch as that is a healthy aspect, you need to keep it happy so that it won't disturb you in pursuing your overall objective. But if it is something merely neurotic – say you want to go and see your mother every weekend and feel upset because you can't do that – you shouldn't give way to that. The more you give way to it, the more clamorous it may become. You need to make up your mind which aspects of yourself are healthy and deserving of consideration and then formulate your long-range objectives and your way of life, trying to distinguish between healthy needs and neurotic craving – which is, of course, sometimes quite difficult. It may be a good idea to consult your friends. They may have a more objective view than you have yourself.

So here there are virtually three different versions of the same episode. Out of these three, one is illustrated with the parable, and they have all got different verses. Perhaps it was repeated quite often; maybe it was regarded as a particularly helpful teaching. As several historians have pointed out, in the India of the Buddha's day there was a ferment of intellectual opinion, a multiplicity of views, among ascetics and brahmins especially. The Buddha himself described it as a forest of views, a wilderness of views, a tangle of views.

6.7 THOUGHTS BURNED UP LIKE INCENSE

Once, the Buddha was staying near Sāvatthī in the Jeta Wood at Anāthapiṇḍika's park. At the same time, not far away, Subhūti, the foremost of those who dwell remote, was sitting cross-legged, holding his body erect, having attained a non-discursive concentration. Seeing him thus, and seeing what it meant, the Buddha breathed out these words:

One whose thoughts have been burned up like incense,
wholly cut back as if well trimmed within,
overcoming that bond, perceiving the formless,
gone beyond the four yokes – that one is not reborn.

The commentary takes 'the formless' (*arūpa*) here to be Nirvāṇa. *Avitakka samādhi* means 'a meditative concentration without thought', and the commentary adds 'but here the meaning of the *avitakkasamādhi* is the *samādhi* of the *arhant* which has the four *jhāna*s as its basis'.[479] The general idea is clear. He is not scattered and unconcentrated. All discursive conceptual thinking has disappeared; there is just pure, bright, clear awareness. Thoughts won't come back again; discursive thinking, apart from what is objectively necessary, has been permanently transcended. He can 'perceive the formless'; he is conscious of that which cannot be put into thought, which has no determinate nature, which cannot be identified as this or that; in other words, *śūnyatā*. The four yokes (*yoga*) are the same as the four floods (*ogha*): *kāma*, *bhava*, *diṭṭhi*, *avijjā* (sense-pleasures, continued existence, views, and ignorance)[480] – in other words, anything that binds one to *saṃsāra*, to the wheel of life. And the result is that he becomes free from the cycle of rebirth. There is no renewal of conditioned existence.

This is freedom from neurotic thinking, not thinking which is objectively necessary, as when you think how to get from here to there. It is important to distinguish between these two forms of what may seem to be the same thing. Healthy thinking is objective and constructive, and oriented to a definite goal, purposeful; but neurotic thinking is just a mental ticking over, based on anxiety and insecurity. A lot of so-called philosophizing belongs to this second kind of thinking.

You notice, incidentally, that the different leading disciples are frequently described as sitting cross-legged with body upright and as having reached a certain level of concentration, but their approaches are practically all different. We haven't had this particular one before. Subhūti is *etad agga* of those 'who dwell remote'. This is different from the praise given him on the well-known occasion when the Buddha singled out his leading disciples and said who was best at what. In that context, he was praised as being foremost among those worthy of gifts.[481] Subhūti – presumably the same Subhūti – reappears in the *Diamond Sūtra*. His being represented here as dwelling in that concentration which is empty of thought may be a link with his appearance in the *Diamond Sūtra*, which of course deals with *śūnyatā*. Subhūti was associated with that line of thought and experience which culminated in emptiness, *śūnyatā*, so it is quite natural that he should be the Buddha's interlocutor in that particular Mahāyāna *sūtra*.

6.8 A FIGHT OVER A COURTESAN

> Once, when the Buddha was staying near Rājagaha in the Bamboo Grove at the Squirrels' Feeding Ground, there were two factions who were both enamoured of a certain courtesan. They kept attacking each other, with their fists and with weapons, and some of them died, or were left close to death. Hearing about this, the Buddha breathed out these words:
>
> What has been gained and what is to be gained – both of these are strewn with dust for the miserable, misguided follower. Those who take the training as essential, who take their conduct and vows, livelihood, celibacy, and service as essential – this is one extreme. And those who hold the belief that there is no fault in sense-pleasures – this is a second extreme. Thus these two extremes add to the cemeteries and the cemeteries increase wrong view. Not comprehending these two extremes, some remain stuck and some go too far. But those who have comprehended them are not in either, they have not imagined themselves thereby, and there is no round of existence for them to make known.

This is a rather obscure passage, but we can make some sense of it in a general way. Evidently the two extremes that add to the cemeteries include both over-concern for worldly gain and overemphasis on virtuousness and religious rituals, but what does that mean? It is evidently not an extreme asceticism that is being described. It may be that two different pairs of opposites have got mixed up. This is how I look at it. The opening sentence says that what has been gained and what is to be gained are both 'strewn with dust'. What is said subsequently has to be interpreted in the light of that. You've got two situations, one in which something has been attained, and another in which something is to be attained in the future. You could say that those who are engaged in a virtuous way of living are doing it for the sake of future recompense in heaven. This is inadequate from the Buddhist point of view, and it can go to the extreme of self-torture and asceticism, becoming self-mortification for the sake of rebirth in heaven.

To put it in a more general way, if one is thinking merely in terms of something conditioned, especially conditioned happiness, it doesn't make much difference whether you have pleasure now and pain afterwards, or pain now and pleasure afterwards. Ascetics have pain now and pleasure later, sensualists have pleasure now and pain later. Both ways only perpetuate *saṃsāra*, only feed the grave, as we would say, and what you have to do is transcend both.

According to the commentary, adding to the cemeteries means the increasing of the craving and ignorance that are called cemeteries in the sense of what is desirable by blind worldlings.[482] It is as though the extreme courses that are followed intensify craving and ignorance, and that gives rise to a fresh crop of false views. In this way a vicious circle is created. Your actions strengthen your view and your view reinforces your actions, because your wrong way of life confirms your basic ignorance and craving, and results in a fresh rationalization of what you are doing, in the form of a fresh version of a wrong view. For example, wrong livelihood would strengthen your wrong views, and on account of your wrong views you would tend more and more to follow wrong livelihood.

A few general words can be said about these two extremes of self-indulgence and self-mortification, translating them into more modern terms. They are the two extremes set forth by the Buddha according to what is called the First Discourse at Sarnath, the two extremes between which comes the middle way in the form of the Noble Eightfold Path.[483] Self-mortification is like repression, almost in the Freudian sense: when you try violently (and in Freud's view unconsciously, because repression is always unconscious) to keep down what is negative in yourself, not to recognize it, look at it, or even be aware of it. And the opposite, self-indulgence, is a constant pandering to neurotic cravings. The middle way consists in neither ignoring one's unskilful, even neurotic side, nor indulging it. It means not being repressive and not being permissive, one could say.

A Buddhist movement has to be careful to steer a middle way between these two extremes. You don't want to say to people either, 'Buddhism says you must do this or that,' or, 'Buddhism says anything goes.' Perhaps it's best just to say, 'Develop what is skilful; don't develop what is unskilful.' But it is difficult for those who are trying to be individuals to follow this middle way, especially for many people in the West. They tend to veer to one extreme or the other. Some people even feel guilty if they are quite skilfully happy. Repression is often associated with guilt, self-indulgence is often associated with neurotic needs, and both are associated with a lot of rationalization. Probably we have to be more careful not to go to the extreme of self-indulgence. This seems to be the current ethos. But don't counteract that by the repressive extreme. You need to find a healthy, truly skilful middle way.

One of the things to be appreciated about ancient India is that when they went in for self-mortification, they did it heroically, and when they were sensual and hedonistic, they were gloriously so, without any apologies or excuses. The Buddha thus had these two clear-cut extremes between which his middle way ran. Nowadays ascetics are a bit apologetic about being ascetic and hedonists are even more apologetic about being hedonists. There are not even any decent extremes any longer! But the whole principle of the middle way is very important.

There are different aspects of the middle way. There is the ethical middle way between the two extremes of self-indulgence and self-mortification. Then there is what may be called the psychological middle way. Here the two extremes are the belief in the continued existence of the unchanging self beyond death and the sudden annihilation of that unchanging self at death, the middle way being the continuity of the ever-changing process of cyclical existence. Then there is the metaphysical middle way between the extremes of existence and non-existence, thinking in terms of absolute being and absolute non-being, the middle way being conditioned co-production, a network of conditions or factors arising in dependence upon other factors. The world is neither absolutely existent nor absolutely non-existent. It represents an ever-changing play of conditions. The Madhyamaka school is most concerned with this third level, the middle way in metaphysics.

6.9 LIKE MOTHS THAT FALL INTO THE LAMP'S FLAME

> One dark night when the Buddha was staying near Sāvatthī in the Jeta Wood at Anāthapiṇḍika's park, he was sitting in the open air and oil-lamps were burning, and many insects were destroying themselves by flying into the flames of the lamps. Seeing this, and realizing what it meant, the Buddha breathed out these words:
>
> Going too far they do not reach the essence,
> but increase their ever-renewing bonds.
> Like moths that fall into the lamp's flame
> some have thus settled in the seen and heard.

This episode describes what is still a familiar scene in India. It is night-time, the oil lamps have been lit, and swarms of insects come fluttering in from all directions and fly towards the flame, sometimes just missing it, sometimes landing right in it, sometimes singeing their wings and sometimes getting badly burned. The Buddha, witnessing this scene, thinks that those insects behave just like human beings. Deeply stirred by this reflection, he utters the *udāna*.

In this one *udāna*, the light of the lamp is compared to two quite different things, first to the Real, the essence, and then to *saṃsāra*. In the first few lines, the human beings to whom the Buddha is implicitly comparing the winged insects are buzzing up to the light and missing it. Human beings are attracted by Reality; there is something that draws them to it – maybe they don't know quite what it is, or why they are drawn to it. But instead of diving into it, they swerve at the last minute and go right past it. Carrying the comparison a little further, what attracts you from a distance is the light, but as you get nearer, you start feeling the heat, it starts becoming uncomfortable, and you swerve when the heat gets too much to bear. When you see the light in the distance, when you see all those people treading the spiritual path and hear all about Enlightenment, it seems beautiful. As you get a bit nearer, though, it starts becoming uncomfortably warm. You start feeling a bit singed and in danger of being burned up, so at the last minute you make a sudden swerve. In this way the same old pattern goes on repeating itself, over and over again.

Then comes a quite different comparison. Like moths falling towards the flame, people are entranced by the sights and sounds of the world.

It is not simply that people see and hear, but they are intent upon what they see and hear. It is not just objective, aware seeing and hearing. There is attachment to the things you see and hear, to the way in which you interpret your experience. There is nothing wrong with the senses. It is being intent upon what comes to you through them, becoming attached to it, hankering after it, that causes all the trouble. That way, captivated by what comes to them through their senses, people fall into the fire – not in a positive, purifying way but in a very negative way. In other words, they bring about their own suffering.

6.10 THE SUN AND THE GLOW-WORMS

> Once, when the Buddha was staying near Sāvatthī in the Jeta Wood at Anāthapiṇḍika's park, Ānanda approached him and remarked that when there are no Tathāgatas in the world, wanderers of other sects are revered and respected, and given food and clothing, but when Tathāgatas appear, wanderers of other sects are not respected in the same way. Only the Buddha and his order of *bhikkhus* are now venerated and supported. Agreeing with this and realizing what it meant, the Buddha breathed out these words:
>
> Just as the glow-worm glows and shines
> as long as the sun has not come up,
> but when that brilliance has arisen
> their glow goes out and shines no more,
> in this way mere speculators only shine
> as long as Buddhas do not arise in the world.
> Thinkers are not purified, nor their followers.
> Those with wrong views are not freed from suffering.

Here the Buddha and his teaching are compared to the sun, and the one-sided views held by others – like the limited perceptions of the blind men in the parable – are compared to the light of the glow-worm. In other words, all partial visions are swallowed up in the total vision, or the lesser lights in the greater light. So long as the sun has not risen, glow-worms may look bright and beautiful, but when the sun rises, they are no longer to be seen.

'Speculators' translates *takkikā*, which literally means 'mere reasoners', those who speculate or reason from, or draw conclusions from, limited experience. Sometimes it is translated as 'logicians', and *takka* or *tarka* does mean logic in later Indian thought, but here it means those who arrive at general or even universal conclusions from limited experience. What the Buddha is saying is that there are many views based upon limited experience, and that these are popular only so long as a complete and total truth has not yet been discovered. This is what one finds today in the West: all sorts of fashions in thought are current for a while and then disappear. This is possibly an abnormal situation. In ancient Egypt, for example, they had one philosophy, one way of life, practically one religion. In the religious sphere there were some differences of detail between one part of Egypt and another, but there was no confusion of thought – maybe a rivalry between great temples, but nothing more than that, just one wisdom existing at different levels. We can't imagine a completely unified civilization, but that is virtually what the civilization of ancient Egypt was. Modern Western society echoes Indian society at the time of the Buddha, with all these trends and fashions, though probably our society is in even more of a mess than theirs was, so from time to time we come into contact – not to say conflict – with various wrong views, *micchā-diṭṭhis*. It is interesting that these are exposed as *micchā-diṭṭhis* only when we are trying to follow the path, or trying to get clear about what following the path involves. A *micchā-diṭṭhi* is seen as a *micchā-diṭṭhi* only in the light of a higher truth. In other words, you only see the glow-worms as glow-worms when the sun rises, when there is some standard of comparison. Until then, you may be tossed from one fashionable *micchā-diṭṭhi* to another.

7
THE LITTLE CHAPTER

7.1 BHADDIYA THE DWARF GAINS INSIGHT

> Once, when the Buddha was staying near Sāvatthī in the Jeta Wood at Anāthapiṇḍika's park, Sāriputta, by a variety of means, was instructing, rousing, inspiring, and gladdening Bhaddiya the dwarf with a talk on the Dhamma, in the course of which Bhaddiya's mind was freed from the taints without grasping. Seeing this, and realizing what it meant, the Buddha breathed out these words:
>
> Liberated above, below, all around,
> one who does not observe that 'I am this',
> liberated like this, has crossed the flood,
> uncrossed before, to unrenewed existence.

Here we encounter the interesting fact that Bhaddiya the dwarf becomes an *arhant* simply as a consequence of hearing Sāriputta's discourse. First he is, as it were, softened up; he is roused and made happy. The discourse puts him in a positive state of mind, and then, as Sāriputta expounds the Dharma, he sees the truth on the spot: breaks the fetters, destroys the *āsravas*, becomes an *arhant*. That suggests that the development of the positive *nidānas* is not exclusively associated with sitting and meditating. What is important is the sequence of mental states you go through, and these you can experience in any posture, as it were.

This is also the first time the text has mentioned anyone other than the Buddha having a hand in bringing about insight in someone else directly through communication, which means that the Dharma has now been fully transmitted. Sāriputta is able to work the same spiritual miracles, as one might describe them, as the Buddha himself, though, as we shall see, Sāriputta still has his limitations. The text seems to suggest that Sāriputta's discourse was very lengthy, with many illustrations, parables, digressions, explanations, analyses, and so on. He was going on and on, getting more and more enthusiastic, more and more carried away, and so was Bhaddiya the dwarf, and in this way they went on until Bhaddiya became Enlightened. And there was the Buddha apparently, just observing it all and ready with his contribution, his *udāna*, which is quite a plain, straightforward statement. 'Above' means the realms of form and the formless realm; 'below' means the realm of sense-desire.

But does it happen like that? Is there actually a point at which you become an *arhant*? As we have seen, *arhant* simply means worthy, and originally it seems to have been applied to those of advanced spiritual experience – those who had more than entered the Stream. Later on, it came to be considered a designation for one who had realized Nirvāṇa. But whether Nirvāṇa represents the last link in the series of positive *nidānas* is quite another question. According to Dr Beni Madhab Barua in his essay 'Buddhism as Personal Religion', Nirvāṇa only indicates the last perceivable link in an ongoing process, a process which – though this is only in a manner of speaking – goes on to infinity.[484] We mustn't superimpose on spiritual experience our limited linear modes of thinking and think in terms of there being a precise 'point at which'. It is more like a horizon beyond which we can't see. But certainly by all accounts the *arhant* was one who had gone well beyond the point of no return, and was hurtling in the direction of Nirvāṇa.

Nirvāṇa is an action noun from the verb *nir-vā*, 'go out' (of a flame), hence translations like 'extinguishing' or 'quenching'. The term *nibbuto* in Pāli is a past participle, and the way it is used in early Buddhist texts combines two meanings: 'quenched' or 'extinguished', and 'happy' or 'satisfied'. There is a verb, *parinibbāyati*, which one might translate as 'Nirvānize' or 'attains Nirvāṇa'; in the *Dhammapada* we find the related verb *parinibbanti*, 'they are Nirvānized', 'they attain Nirvāṇa', or in my translation 'they become utterly Cool'.[485] It is not a state you attain, but a way of functioning, an uninterrupted creative process which need not have any end. You are seen disappearing into some other dimension, and the so-called full stop is the point at which you enter that further dimension, which is not perceivable to the person who is observing you. We must be careful not to regard the Buddha as having come to a full stop called Buddhahood; that is just our way of thinking. It is all right for practical purposes to think in that way, but don't take it too literally.

Barua explains this quite clearly, basing himself upon the exposition of the Buddha's disciple Dhammadinnā, who says that Nirvāṇa is reckoned as the last link so as to be able to complete the enumeration, as it were, for the sake of avoiding an infinite progression. You've got to stop somewhere. The term *nirvāṇa* is just where you stop counting, and *parinirvāṇa* is going over the horizon as regards the physical body. When the texts speak of the Buddha at the time of his death gaining *parinirvāṇa* they don't mean he had a new experience – it was just the same experience going on – but simply that that experience was now dissociated from the physical body.

7.2 SĀRIPUTTA DOESN'T REALIZE BHADDIYA IS AWAKENED

> Once, when the Buddha was staying near Sāvatthī in the Jeta Wood at Anāthapiṇḍika's park, Sāriputta, by a variety of means, was instructing, rousing, inspiring, and gladdening Bhaddiya the dwarf with a talk on the Dhamma, in the course of which Bhaddiya's mind was freed from the taints without grasping. Sāriputta made a special effort because he considered Bhaddiya to be still a learner. Seeing this and realizing what it meant, the Buddha breathed out these words:
>
> They broke the wheel, reached desirelessness:
> the dried-up river no longer flows,
> the broken wheel no longer turns –
> just this is the end of suffering.

A footnote in Woodward's translation says that Bhaddiya the dwarf was '*etad agga* (foremost) of those who have a sweet voice'.[486] And the taints are the *āsravas* (Sanskrit), or *āsavas* (Pāli). You notice that Sāriputta, though he has succeeded in sparking Bhaddiya off to such a transcendental extent, doesn't fully realize what has happened. He goes on teaching him, considering him still to be a learner, and Bhaddiya apparently goes on enjoying the discourse. 'Learner', *sekha*, has a technical meaning here – that is, one who is not yet an *arhant*. An *arhant* is termed *asekha*, literally the non-learner, sometimes translated as 'one beyond training'. He has nothing more to learn. All others – even the Stream Entrant, the once-returner, and the non-returner – are still learners. Such was Sāriputta's enthusiasm and so intent was he on preaching the Dharma that he didn't notice that Bhaddiya had actually gained Enlightenment, so he went on teaching him, but the Buddha sees what has happened, as expressed in his *udāna*. Evidently Sāriputta doesn't have complete insight, certainly as regards other human beings, in the way the Buddha has.

7.3 STUCK ON PLEASURE'S TIES

> At a time when the Buddha was staying near Sāvatthī in the Jeta Wood at Anāthapiṇḍika's park, the people of Sāvatthī lived excessively attached to sensual pleasures, passionate, greedy, enslaved, infatuated, addicted, completely intoxicated with sensual pleasures. When the *bhikkhus* told the Buddha about this, realizing its significance, the Buddha breathed out these words:
>
> Intent on sensuality, stuck on pleasure's ties,
> not seeing any problem with the fetters,
> surely those attached to fetters and ties
> have not crossed the flood, so large and wide.

Quite a straightforward statement, but you notice the accumulation of epithets, a progression, or rather retrogression, from living 'passionate', then 'greedy,' then 'enslaved', then 'infatuated', then 'addicted', and finally 'completely intoxicated with sensual pleasures'. Looking at that sequence more closely, and using the imagination a little, one could say that you start off by feeling lustful for some particular sense object. As a result of your lustful feeling, you experience that sense object and you enjoy it. You enjoy it again and again, and you want to go on enjoying it. In this way, you become greedy. And having become greedy, although you can't always be enjoying it – you have to do other things sometimes – when you are not able to enjoy it you are longing for it and thinking about it. Then you reach a state of mind in which, whether you are enjoying it or not, you can think about nothing else. You then become infatuated. Because you are not able to think of anything else, things start to go wrong. Reactions start occurring, or other aspects of your life get into a mess and start creating difficulties, but you don't care; you are completely possessed and carried away, intoxicated. This is how it usually develops. It is a powerful sequence of terms: passionate, greedy, enslaved, infatuated, addicted, and finally intoxicated. Needless to say, it can be applied to a variety of situations, depending upon the nature of the original passions.

As the Buddha says, those in this state don't see any problem with the fetters. That is the strange thing: those who are in bondage in this way don't see anything wrong with it, think it's quite natural, quite justified, and so there is absolutely no possibility of their crossing the flood of the *saṃsāra*, which is wide and mighty anyway, and reaching the other shore.

7.4 LIKE FISH IN THE MOUTH OF A NET

> Once, when the Buddha was staying near Sāvatthī in the Jeta Wood at Anāthapiṇḍika's park, the people of Sāvatthī clung excessively to sensual pleasures, addicted to and intoxicated by them. Observing this for himself when he went into Sāvatthī for almsfood, and realizing its significance, the Buddha breathed out these words:
>
> They are blind to sense-desires, trapped in a net,
> covered with a covering of craving.
> They are bound by Māra, the friend of negligence,
> like fish in the mouth of a net.
> They move closer towards ageing and death,
> like a calf drinking its mother's milk.

A funnel-net has a very wide mouth, so fish hardly notice they're getting into it, but it narrows, and there's a small opening at the end which admits them to a larger, closed net. And, of course, they can't then easily turn round and find their way out. It's a good metaphor. You don't know at first that you are swimming into the net of desires. Not only that, people go to old age, decay, and death 'like a calf drinking its mother's milk'. They go to what is fundamentally unpleasant as though it was something pleasant; they rush upon their own destruction.

No need to labour the point; it is sufficiently obvious, and things haven't changed very much since the Buddha's day. Never mind the people of Sāvatthī; you can see the men and women of London, and everywhere else, doing these very things. It is just the human condition.

7.5 A BEAUTIFUL ROYAL CHARIOT

> Once, when the Buddha was staying near Sāvatthī in the Jeta Wood at Anāthapiṇḍika's park, he was approached by Bhaddiya the dwarf, following behind a number of *bhikkhus*. The Buddha said to the *bhikkhus* around him, 'Do you see that *bhikkhu* coming along behind the others – the one who is ugly, deformed, and generally despised?' 'Yes,' they said. And the Buddha told them, 'Bhaddiya has great supernormal power. It is not easy to find any attainment which he has not already attained. He has realized here and now through his own direct knowledge the goal of the spiritual life for which people rightly go forth from home to the homeless life.' And realizing the significance of this, the Buddha breathed out these words:
>
> With faultless parts and white parasol,
> the one-spoked chariot rolls on.
> See the unagitated one coming along,
> whose stream is cut off, without bonds.

Once again we are warned not to go by appearances. Bhaddiya the dwarf follows in the footsteps of a great number of monks, he doesn't push himself forward, but the Buddha recognizes his attainments, singles him out, knows what the state of his mind is and points it out to the other *bhikkhus*. They weren't very kind to Bhaddiya, apparently; according to the commentary, the meaner ones used to pull his hair and tease him. Bhaddiya the dwarf may have been ugly and deformed, but the Buddha isn't misled by appearances.

The verse is quite poetic. The commentary goes into its various riddles, concluding:

> Thus, the teacher [the Buddha], comparing [him] to a well-enclosed, well-fitted chariot with a thoroughbred [horse], shows that the venerable Bhaddiya the dwarf had a good wheel with the fruit of arhantship at its hub; a very excellent parasol is the liberation which is the fruit of arhantship; it had a good spoke in well-established mindfulness; was unagitated through not being agitated by the afflictions; undefiled through not being defiled by craving; without bonds through the non-existence of the fetters and so on.[487]

So this is the Buddha's poetic description of Bhaddiya the dwarf as he comes along, ugly as he is; the Buddha sees him as he really is, just like a beautiful royal chariot rolling along the road. Bhaddiya the dwarf seems to have been a bit like Socrates, whom Alcibiades in the *Symposium* compares to a satyr, in Greek mythology an ugly creature which can be opened to reveal the figure of a god.[488] Socrates was notoriously ugly, with a snub nose and protruding eyes, a flat forehead and a thickset body. He was also very sweet of speech, like Bhaddiya the dwarf. But people do very much go by outward appearances.

7.6 WORKING ON ALL YOUR IMPERFECTIONS AT ONCE

> Once, the Buddha was staying near Sāvatthī in the Jeta Wood at Anāthapiṇḍika's park. At the same time, not far away, Aññāta Koṇḍañña was sitting cross-legged, holding his body erect, and contemplating his release by the destruction of craving. Seeing him thus, and seeing what it meant, the Buddha breathed out these words:
>
> Without a root and without earth,
> without leaves, how could a tree grow?
> That steadfast one who is free from bonds –
> who is fit to censure that person?
> Even the gods praise that person,
> who is praised even by Brahmā.

Aññāta Koṇḍañña was one of the first five disciples who were with the Buddha in the days before he became Enlightened, who left him in disgust when he gave up self-mortification, whom he sought out after his Enlightenment, and to whom he first taught the Dharma. Aññāta Koṇḍañña was the first of those five to realize the truth of the Dharma. Koṇḍañña is a clan or family name, and Aññāta, according to tradition, is a nickname, meaning 'one who has understood'.[489]

So he was 'contemplating his release by the destruction of craving'. That was the particular route of his spiritual path, and he is reflecting upon it. Seeing him so engaged, the Buddha gives utterance to this *udāna*, which is poetic and slightly riddling. A possible interpretation might be that inasmuch as views are the product of craving and ignorance, if you consider craving and ignorance as the branches, since there are no branches there are no leaves in the form of false views. There has been a complete reversal; his root is in the sky, in Nirvāṇa. You sometimes get the image in Indian literature of the sacred fig tree with its roots in the sky. It suggests this whole idea of turning upside down, or turning around (*āśraya-parāvṛtti*), in the language of the *Laṅkāvatāra Sūtra*,[490] or what Nietzsche called a transvaluation of all values.[491] It's as though you don't tackle the whole mass of delusions and conditionings simultaneously. You work away at one aspect, and through that aspect you get at the whole bundle. In Aññāta Koṇḍañña's case he had been working to overcome craving, possibly with the help of the *aśubha-bhāvanā*.

It is very difficult to start working on all your imperfections at once. If you are very methodical, you could work on abandoning craving on Monday, aversion on Tuesday, and so on through the week. Or, to take up something more positive, you could devote a day of the week to each of the six perfections of the Mahāyāna tradition. On Monday you could make a special effort to be generous in body, speech, and mind; if you can do nothing else, at least give something to somebody, not only material things but time, energy, interest, and so on. On Tuesday you could try to be especially scrupulous about the precepts, and on Wednesday you could try to be patient, tolerant, and friendly. Then Thursday would be *vīrya* day! Of course you aim to be energetic all the time, but on Thursday you could try to be particularly zestful, not wasting a minute. Then on Friday you relax and devote more time to meditation. Saturday would be *prajñā*, wisdom, so that might mean spending more time than usual going through scriptures or revising your notes, or even preparing lectures. And on Sunday, the big day, you could make a special effort to develop all six perfections as occasion required, which is obviously quite difficult. People sometimes attempt this practice in Mahāyāna countries. It is just a question of working systematically.

The *udāna* raises the question of who is worthy to censure him – a rhetorical question, as the gods and Brahmā praise him. You often get the idea in the Pāli canon that the Enlightened human being is praised by the gods, which suggests that an Enlightened One occupies a much higher level than the gods, who are still only mundane beings, and also that the gods have no envy; they are quite happy to praise the Enlightened One.

7.7 THE ABANDONMENT OF PROLIFERATION

> Once, when the Buddha was staying near Sāvatthī in the Jeta Wood at Anāthapiṇḍika's park, he sat reviewing the abandoning of perceptual and conceptual proliferation. And realizing this, he breathed out these words:
>
> The world with its deities does not despise
> that sage who lives without craving,
> in whom there is no proliferation and persistence,
> and who has overcome the tether and the bar.

So here again we see the Buddha contemplating an aspect of his own Enlightenment, the one consisting in 'abandoning perceptual and conceptual proliferation', which can be understood in terms of abandoning the tendency of the mind to actively generate perceptions and thoughts based on underlying afflictive tendencies, a process called *prapañca*. The commentary says that 'proliferations are the afflictions (*kilesa*) – greed, hate, delusion, craving, views, conceit, all together'.[492] The manifoldness, it's sometimes called, or the many-ness.

7.8 MINDFULNESS OF THE BODY IS ENOUGH

> Once, the Buddha was staying near Sāvatthī in the Jeta Wood at Anāthapiṇḍika's park. At the same time, not far away, Mahākaccāna was sitting cross-legged, holding his body erect, having mindfulness with regard to the body set up and well

established within him. Seeing him thus, and seeing what it meant, the Buddha breathed out these words:

> One whose mindfulness would always be
> attending to the body continuously –
> 'there might not be and there might not be for me,
> there will not be and there will not be for me' –
> in that state, dwelling in gradual stages,
> one might in time cross over entanglement.

In this episode Mahākaccāna is practising mindfulness of the body, as we saw in a previous *udāna*. This *udāna* suggests that mindfulness, even mindfulness of the body, is enough; you are practically there if you can practise that. Mindfulness of the body is one of the four basic forms of mindfulness, the others being mindfulness of feelings, thoughts, and the teachings, as explained in detail in the *Mahāsatipaṭṭhāna Sutta* of the Pāli canon.[493] There is no suggestion of progressive stages; apparently all four are equally foundations, equally to be established. If you list them you have to enumerate them one after another, but that doesn't necessarily suggest a linear progression. It could be just going round the petals of the lotus.

To interpret the riddling line 'there might not be and there might not be for me', this could mean that my actions may not be based on the afflictions in the past, and there might not be the arising of self in the present. Likewise, 'there will not be and there will not be for me' could mean that due to the empty nature of the self and what belongs to self, revealed through mindfulness, in the future there will not be anything that is taken as 'I' and 'mine'. The emphasis here is that through Mahākaccāna's mindfulness of the body unskilful mental states are prevented from arising, and he goes on considering their non-arising and the fact that they are being kept at bay. If you can go on doing this indefinitely, you will come to the end of all unskilful thoughts, and even the possibility of their arising.

7.9 THE BUDDHA AND THE WELL

> Once, when the Buddha was travelling among the Mallas with a large party of *bhikkhus*, they came to the brahmin village of

Thūna. The villagers heard they were coming and filled the village well with grass, so that the 'shaven-headed ascetics' would not be able to get water to drink. When the Buddha arrived, taking his seat beneath a tree, he asked Ānanda to fetch him some water. Ānanda explained what the villagers had done, but a second and a third time the Buddha asked for some water. So Ānanda went to the well, which, as he approached it, threw up all the grass from its mouth so that it stood filled to the brim with pure, clean water. As he filled a bowl and took it to the Buddha, Ānanda thought how amazing the Buddha's powers were. And realizing the significance of the event, the Buddha breathed out these words:

What would one do with a well
if there was water everywhere?
Having cut off craving at the root
for what would one go in search?

From this episode we can understand something of the hostility towards the Buddha of some members of the brahmin caste. So far in the *Udāna* we have only seen this in the hostility of the wanderers, some of whom were of brahmin origin, but here it is specifically the brahmin householders, *gahapatika*, of Thūna. Later on, the hostility of the so-called orthodox brahmins to the Buddha and his teaching became quite pronounced, and there are many instances of it elsewhere in the Pāli canon.

The Buddha is going his rounds among the Mallas, a republic of tribal people. It seems that a particular village, or perhaps a particular area of land, had been donated to the brahmins, so that they can live there and follow their Vedic practices, possibly supported by the people. But they are clearly not at all friendly to the Buddha and his disciples. 'Shaven-headed ascetics' is *muṇḍaka* in Pāli; it means 'the shaven ones', the contemptuous expression the orthodox brahmins used to refer to the Buddha and his disciples.

When one is wandering, one obviously needs water. It is very hot, you get very thirsty, and there may not be a river. The brahmin householders no doubt guessed that the Buddha would need water to drink, so they blocked up the well with grass and husks so that he couldn't get any. But there is a miracle, and the Buddha does get water. It has been pointed out that one can look at this episode as having not exactly a symbolical but perhaps an allegorical meaning. The brahmins tried to monopolize religious truth, whereas the Buddha made it available to anyone who could benefit from it. The brahmins charged for their teaching and for the performance of sacrifices, whereas the Buddha and his disciples gave everything freely, without any thought of remuneration. In fact, the Buddha is represented in the Pāli canon as saying, 'I am not one who has the closed fist of the teacher and who keeps something back.'[494] The brahmins always wanted to keep something back, something that only they knew, but you can't do this with spiritual truths. You can do it with information, even quasi-religious information; you can do it with doctrines and traditions; but you can't do it with real spiritual truth, just as you can't communicate spiritual truth to someone who is not in a position to receive it. But in those days the brahmins considered that they had a monopoly on culture, learning, education, and what passed as spiritual wisdom, and that they were entitled to keep that monopoly. One of the criticisms of the Buddha made by orthodox brahmins, a criticism that continued right down into the Indian middle ages, was that despite being a Kshatriya by birth he dared to teach, which was the function of the Brahmin caste. There is a work called the *Mīmāṃsā Śloka Vārttika*, by an orthodox Vedic brahmin called Kumārila Bhaṭṭa, who lived in the seventh century, which says that the Buddha's teaching, even though it may be true, should not be accepted. To paraphrase, he says, 'Milk is drinkable, it's pure, but if milk came to you in the skin of a dog, you wouldn't touch it. In the same way, what the Buddha says may be true, but since it comes from the lips of a Kshatriya who, not being a Brahmin, has no right to teach, it should be rejected.'[495] This is the typical orthodox brahmin view, which continues, in a diluted form, right down to the present day. The brahmin is quite literally the born teacher. It was this sort of thing that the Buddha was up against. This is the main reason for the hostility of the brahmins to the Buddha and his teaching: he undermined their monopoly and criticized their pretensions.

So this stopping up of the well suggests that the brahmins tried to close up the well of religious knowledge, even spiritual knowledge, to prevent others having free access to it, but the Buddha, by his magic power as it were, defeated the brahmins' attempts to keep spiritual wisdom to themselves. He made it available to everybody who could drink it. Some historians take this line of thought too literally, suggesting that the brahmins actually possessed certain spiritual truths, and that the only difference between them and the Buddha was that the Buddha, having possession of those same spiritual truths, made them available to all and sundry. This can't be accepted inasmuch as real truth is of such a nature that it naturally communicates itself. If you really have the truth, if you really have that degree of insight, you can't think in terms of keeping it to yourself, so if you can even think of keeping it as a private possession for yourself or your caste or your community, it can't be Enlightenment. We mustn't think, as some seem to have thought, that the brahmins had mastered certain secret teachings which were true, and it was simply these secret teachings that the Buddha broadcast more widely. That is much too literalistic. One could perhaps see some significance in the fact that the brahmins choked the well with grass and husks, because husks are empty shells. All that the brahmins really had was the husks. And in preventing others from having access to the water, you also interfere with your own access to it.

I had some personal experience in India of what the Buddha's attitude might have meant to the people of India – the ordinary people, the non-brahmins – of his time. When I was going around among the Dalits and giving talks about Buddhism, the people attending those lectures were not only extremely interested in the content but enraptured at the idea that they were being permitted to listen to a religious teaching at all. Formerly, when they were Hindus, they were not allowed access to any religious teaching – at best, a bit of devotional singing, and certainly nothing of a Vedic nature. They weren't even supposed to hear the verses of the Veda. According to the *Manusmṛti*, which is the best known of all the orthodox Hindu law books, if a Shudra, that is, someone of the lowest of the four castes, happens to hear the words of the Vedas, red-hot lead is to be poured into his ears.[496] This is quoted, apparently with approval, by Śaṅkara in one of his commentaries, he being the greatest of the orthodox Hindu philosophers and commentators on Vedic texts, especially the Upanishads and the *Bhagavad Gītā*. This is still very much in force – not that actual punishment, but the attitude of keeping religious knowledge away from the members of the lowest castes. This is why the Dalits were thrilled by the mere idea that religious knowledge was not being withheld from them by the Buddhists as it was by the Hindus. This was perhaps very much the way in which many people in the Buddha's day received his teaching: here was a great teacher who felt that they were worthy to listen, who didn't just go off into the forest with a few disciples who could pay him for his teaching, but went about teaching all who could benefit from it.

It must have upset the brahmins that here was someone going about giving real spiritual instruction, real help – and free, so that their services, for which there was not so much of a demand as before anyway, were rendered even more superfluous, and their whole position in society was undermined. Even some Hindus with whom I was in contact were not quite happy that Dalits should be taught Buddhism. There was no doubt that they were just as intelligent as anybody else and could follow everything just as well, but one could still see that brahminical attitude at work. Some orthodox Hindus reconciled themselves to it by saying, 'Ah well, Buddhism will keep them happy, but it isn't, of course, such an advanced teaching as that of the Vedas.' We can see from instances of this sort what the Buddha himself was up against, the sort of opposition he had to face from the brahmins. In a hot country like India, choking up the well is a particularly mean thing to do, and against all traditions of hospitality.

The verse goes off at a bit of a tangent: 'What would one do with a well if there was water everywhere?' Perhaps the well is a source of spiritual truth, but the Buddha, being Enlightened, had an inexhaustible source of spiritual truth within himself, so did not need to seek it from any other source. For him, water is everywhere. He doesn't have to have recourse to any particular practice. It's a bit like the Zen idiom of selling water by the river. Someone who has the river, i.e. the source of spiritual truth, within himself, does not need a well. He is himself the ocean now. But we must be a bit careful about thinking that spiritual truth is everywhere as far as we are concerned. When water is not everywhere, when you don't have any water at your disposal at all, you certainly do need a well. The water being everywhere shouldn't be just an idea or a concept; it should be something that you actually experience, otherwise you become like the pseudo-Zen person who says, 'Truth is everywhere, so what need is there to study books? I'm the Buddha, so what need have I to follow any particular practices or methods?' That's just words. One should make sure that the water actually is everywhere, because if it isn't everywhere for you, you need a well, and the sooner you find one the better.

In the same way, and with much the same sort of meaning, 'Having cut off craving at the root, for what would one go in search?' If you have no craving, you have gained Enlightenment. What else is there for you to seek? Or, changing the metaphor for the traditional Buddhist one, once you have reached the further shore, what use do you have for a raft?[497]

7.10 THE WOMEN OF THE HAREM GAIN INSIGHT

> Once, when the Buddha was staying near Kosambī in the Ghosita monastery, the women's quarters in the royal park of King Udena burned down and five hundred women, headed by Sāmāvatī, were killed. A number of *bhikkhus* asked the Buddha what the future birth of these women lay followers would be, and he told them that some of the women were Stream Entrants, some once-returners, and some non-returners. 'Not fruitless was the death of any of those women,' he said. And realizing the significance of this, he breathed out these words:
>
> Tied up in confusion, the world
> is seen as agreeable in nature.
> The fool, tied to acquisitions,
> is wrapped around in darkness.
> It appears as if it is eternal, but
> one who sees holds on to nothing.

The *udāna* doesn't seem to have much of a connection with the episode, but perhaps it doesn't matter. Kosambī is the present-day Allahabad, a town in north central India. It is interesting that among the women of the harem of Raja Udena, there were some who were Stream Entrants, some once-returners, and some non-returners. Perhaps it was because they had plenty of time for spiritual practice. Some rajas had harems of hundreds of women, and they didn't see the raja from one year's end to the next. They were maintained, if not in luxury, certainly in comfort, and some of the more serious-minded no doubt took up religious practices and practised meditation. Some, we know, were disciples of the Buddha. In those propitious circumstances, they could attain a considerable degree of spiritual development. We have to look at these things not in accordance with modern prejudices but according to the ideas of the time, when to be a concubine in the harem of a king or nobleman was quite an honourable career. For a religious-minded woman, it was almost an ideal environment. There was no temptation in the form of men, there was only the king, and you only saw him once or twice a year. It was almost like a nunnery. No wonder some of them made such good spiritual progress. And the Buddha was apparently quite aware of this.

The story underlines the spiritual capacity of women, and the benefit for them of a sheltered, supportive, and pleasing environment. That need for an appropriate environment might be something to do with why the Buddha appears to have been reluctant to ordain women, because he made it quite clear that there was no doubt about their capacity to gain Enlightenment. Ānanda asked the straightforward question, and he gave a categorical reply in the affirmative which, so far as Buddhist tradition is concerned, settled the matter once and for all.[498] The Buddha was extremely reluctant to allow women to go forth as wanderers as the men did, but there is no question of his being reluctant to allow them to go for Refuge or practise the Dharma. It was the wandering lifestyle that he was unwilling to open to them, because of its special dangers for women. But he emphasized the capacity of women to gain Enlightenment, and here again we find it being emphasized.

There is also the important point that among those women, there are Stream Entrants, once-returners, non-returners, but no *arhants*. The feeling seems to have been that you could go quite a long way along the spiritual path and still remain a layman or laywoman, but when you became an *arhant*, no compromise was possible. You just had to give up the lay way of life. That didn't necessarily mean getting ordained in the technical, ecclesiastical sense, but once you became an *arhant*, you just had to lead a spiritual life not only internally but also externally. The mere fact that the harem women were living a lay life, in however refined a way, means that they cannot have been *arhants*. There may have been women among them who became *arhants*, but they would then have left the harem, not because it was a bad place, but because they would have wanted to be completely free from lay life. It's encouraging that there are so many *arhants* in the early Pāli canon. There was this tremendous outburst of spiritual energy, which was the beginning of Buddhism. But we mustn't take the word *arhant* too literally. It means someone worthy, someone spiritually advanced, not necessarily someone who has gained Nirvāṇa in the fullest sense.

Not that spiritual development is synonymous with monastic life. In the Indian middle ages, when Buddhist monastic life had become highly organized, when you became Enlightened you would tend to leave the monastery and become a yogi, as did some of the Tantric *siddhas*. Monastic life had become a sort of celibate lay life, and once someone became Enlightened they couldn't live like that any longer and went roaming around, as the *bhikkhus* did in the old days. The important point is that once you reach a certain degree of spiritual development, there are things that you just can't do any more. Later Buddhist texts, even later Pāli scriptures, express this in a quaint way which has been the basis of much misunderstanding: that when you become an *arhant*, if you are not already a *bhikkhu*, you at once become one – miraculously if necessary. There are instances of a layman becoming an *arhant* and at once a yellow robe appears on him, his hair disappears, and a begging-bowl appears in his hand. But though it is put in this simple-minded, literal way, there is a truth behind it: not that he becomes a monk in the formal, external sense, but that when he becomes Enlightened this must show itself in a change of lifestyle. But it's not necessarily true the other way around. You could carefully refrain from doing all the things that laymen do, but still not be an *arhant*. By giving up certain habits which are roughly speaking the habits of the layman, you might well have a more skilful mental state, but you wouldn't become an *arhant* automatically.

This sort of thing happens at lower levels too: as a result of a change of mental attitude, you feel compelled to change your way of life. Before you started meditating, you might have liked going to parties every weekend, but once you're getting satisfaction from meditation, you may not feel like going to parties, and if you find yourself in the midst of one, you may have to leave. It's rather like that, except that it's not just a party, it's the whole of worldly life – though one mustn't make too formal a distinction between the secular and the so-called religious. It is not that, from then onwards, you can only occupy yourself with 'religious' activities, though it is often looked at in that way. It raises the question of 'What is worldly? What is religious?' You can technically be a monk but be busy with all sorts of worldly things – running some thriving pilgrimage centre, say, which is perhaps no more than just a business, though a comparatively innocent one.

It is quite important that one's lifestyle and ways of behaving do change. Otherwise, it is doubtful whether anything is happening inside. This is one of the things I noticed when I came back to England. English Buddhists seemed no different from other English people. They went along to the Buddhist Society or the vihara once or twice a week, just like other people went to church on Sundays, but there was no other difference. A very few were vegetarians, but most were not. They lived in exactly the same way as other people. I concluded that they had very little belief in the Buddha's teaching, never mind practice or insight. Even the suggestion that people could change was not always happily received. In fact, some people said quite strongly that English Buddhists should try to be as like other English people as possible – if anything, more English. They should be just as conventional, have the same sort of cars, watch the same sort of television programmes, and have the same sorts of jobs and houses. The only difference should be that they were Buddhists. When I started suggesting otherwise, people were surprised and quite resistant. This is one reason why we eventually started up our own Buddhist movement. There must be some external change. William James used to say, 'A difference which makes no difference is no difference at all.'[499] A theoretical difference has to have a practical corollary, otherwise the difference is unreal – it doesn't even exist theoretically.

As to what changes might take place, simplicity of lifestyle might be one. It is said of the *arhant* that he finds it difficult to possess anything apart from his bowl and robes. You might become a vegetarian, in accordance with the first precept. If you had political views, they would no longer be dependent on the way you were brought up. You would see things more clearly. You might find that you could only have deep friendships with people on the same path, though obviously that could give rise to difficulties, and quite a lot of heart-searching and even heartache, because you might be reluctant to recognize that your old friends could no longer be your friends. There's also work – moving towards right livelihood. There's your attitude to alcohol, and drugs, and even sweets. When it came to food, you would become more aware, more discriminating – though not in a gourmet way. You would be happy whatever you had to eat, apart from the question of vegetarianism. You could enjoy a dry crust of bread just as much as a beautifully prepared curry. And there's the sense of security, in the sense that perhaps you used to do a lot of things and collect a lot of things and build up a lot of things to provide yourself with a certain security for the morrow. For many people, their job is security – the fact that they can look forward to forty years of uninterrupted employment, with a pension at the end, though that sort of job security is becoming a thing of the past anyway – but once you have evolved beyond a certain point, you don't feel the need for that sort of security any more. Another change: you might look happier. And probably you wouldn't need so much entertainment – in other words, distraction. Also, you could no longer act violently; perhaps you wouldn't even feel like swearing.

The *udāna* is quite a general verse. Confusion (*moha*) is a synonym of ignorance (*avijjā*), which underlies all the thoughts, words, and actions of the spiritually immature person. Spiritually immature people seem to themselves, and maybe to others like them, as though they are going to go on and on for ever. But the one who sees clearly is the one who has developed insight and wisdom, and thus holds on to nothing.

8
PĀṬALI VILLAGE

8.1 NEITHER EARTH NOR WATER NOR FIRE NOR WIND

> Once, when the Buddha was staying near Sāvatthī in the Jeta Wood at Anāthapiṇḍika's park, he gave the *bhikkhus* present an inspiring, gladdening, rousing Dhamma talk about Nibbāna, and the *bhikkhus* listened attentively with their whole minds. Realizing the significance of this, the Buddha breathed out these words:
>
> *Bhikkhus*, there is that sphere where there is neither earth nor water nor fire nor wind; neither a sphere of infinite space, nor a sphere of infinite consciousness, nor a sphere of no-thing-ness, nor a sphere of neither perception nor non-perception. There is not this world, nor another world, neither is there sun or moon. There is no coming, no going, no staying, no dying, no rebirth. Not established, not moving, it has no basis. Just this is the end of unsatisfactoriness.

This *udāna* is often quoted because it makes it clear that for the Buddha, Nirvāṇa was not merely a state of the cessation of ignorance and craving, but had what, for want of a better way of putting, it we can call a positive content. Normally, the Buddha doesn't say very much about Nirvāṇa at all, focusing more on what has to be done to get to Nirvāṇa, but here he makes it as clear as it can be made through the medium of words what Nirvāṇa is. Even though in this passage there are a number of negative statements, the general impression it gives is that Nirvāṇa isn't simply the cessation of the mundane. It does as it were exist in its own right. It is noticeable that the Buddha speaks about Nirvāṇa in this way at a time when he finds that the *bhikkhus* are listening attentively.

When the text says, 'There exists that condition wherein is neither earth nor water nor fire nor air', it is not referring to a cosmic principle like those of some of the pre-Socratic Greek philosophers, or even a psychological or mental principle. It is not the sphere of infinite consciousness or no-thing-ness, or neither consciousness nor unconsciousness.[500] In fact, it is beyond this world altogether; there is no world, no sun, no moon. Also, it is a state outside time; there is no coming to be, no going. There is no duration. It is not a process. Inasmuch as it isn't something that goes on as a process within time, there can't be any falling away from it, nor any arising. At the same time, it isn't fixed – yet it doesn't move on. It isn't based on anything else. It is completely autonomous and sovereign, ultimate. Here the Buddha is trying to give us some idea of it, and we get the impression that there is an 'it' about which he is trying to give us some idea.

Probably this is the most quoted passage in the whole of the *Udāna*, and the same teaching is to be found in the *Ariyapariyesanā Sutta* of the *Majjhima Nikāya*, in which the Buddha speaks about his own early reflections. As a young man he reflected that at present he himself was conditioned and he was going in search of conditioned things.[501]

8.2 ONE WHO SEES HOLDS ON TO NOTHING

> Once, when the Buddha was staying near Sāvatthī in the Jeta Wood at Anāthapiṇḍika's park, he gave the *bhikkhus* present an inspiring, gladdening, rousing Dhamma talk about Nibbāna, and the *bhikkhus* listened attentively with their whole minds. Realizing the significance of this, the Buddha breathed out these words:
>
> What is called 'the uninclined' is hard to see,
> for the truth is indeed not easy to see.
> One who knows has pierced through craving.
> One who sees holds on to nothing.

For one who truly sees, one who has developed insight, nothing of a conditioned nature remains. He is no longer bound to conditioned existence; indeed, so far as conditioned existence is concerned, he has become a 'man of naught', as discussed earlier. This *udāna* seems complementary to the previous one. In the first one the Buddha did his utmost to give the monks some idea of what Nirvāṇa is like, but now he reminds them that truth is very hard indeed to see. It isn't easy to see the real, the true, the infinite; but if one can see it, then one pierces through all craving, all conditionality.

8.3 THE UNBORN, UNBECOME, UNMADE, UNCONDITIONED

> Once, when the Buddha was staying near Sāvatthī in the Jeta Wood at Anāthapiṇḍika's park, he gave the *bhikkhus* present an inspiring, gladdening, rousing Dhamma talk about Nibbāna, and the *bhikkhus* listened attentively with their whole minds. Realizing the significance of this, the Buddha breathed out these words:
>
> *Bhikkhus*, there is that which is unborn, unbecome, unmade, unconditioned. If there were not that which is unborn, unbecome, unmade, unconditioned, no escape could be discerned for that which is born, become, made, conditioned. But, *bhikkhus*, because there is that which is unborn, unbecome, unmade, unconditioned, an escape is discerned for that which is born, become, made, conditioned.

This third section is connected with the previous two, but here the Buddha goes a step further. In the first of the three *udāna*s he makes it clear that Nirvāṇa doesn't consist merely in the cessation of craving, aversion, and delusion, but has a positive nature of its own. Then in the second *udāna* he goes on to say that Nirvāṇa is not easy to see. And in the third *udāna* he draws the conclusion that if there was no such thing as Nirvāṇa as a positive entity, as it were, there could be no escape from *saṃsāra*. This suggests that the Unconditioned is not a mere absence or cessation of the conditioned but has a positive nature of its own, and also that it is only by, as it were, grasping hold of this Unconditioned that one can escape from the conditioned. Standing on the conditioned, you can't negate the conditioned.

In view of what the Buddha says here, it is unfortunate that in later formulations of the teaching so much is made of the negative side. No doubt one shouldn't think too literally of Nirvāṇa as existent, but from a practical point of view it is better to think of it in crudely positive terms than in purely negative terms. If you think of it in positive terms, however crude, at least you've got something to which you can go forward, and you can refine your conception of it in the light of your experience and your deeper understanding. But if you have a negative conception of Nirvāṇa, if you think of it merely as the cessation of the conditioned, there is nothing of a positive nature to attract you. All you can do is chip away at the conditioned until there is nothing of it left, and then there is nothing left at all. You just as it were fall through the void – the void in the sense of vacancy – except there isn't even any 'you' left to fall through. Probably it is best to think in terms of growing into Nirvāṇa. The Buddha makes it clear that it is only because there is an actually existent higher spiritual, even transcendental state, as it were waiting to be reached, waiting to be realized, that such a thing as the spiritual life is possible. The spiritual life consists in the realization of this higher transcendental principle, not merely in the annihilation of the conditioned. There is quite a difference between getting rid of the conditioned in order to reach the Unconditioned, and getting rid of the conditioned and finding that the state of having got rid of the conditioned *is* the Unconditioned. The practical conclusion is that there cannot be a purely negative conception of the spiritual life. It is the progressive achievement of something positive in the highest sense.

Indian language is often grammatically negative even when the meaning is positive. For instance, the word *amata* means the immortal, the deathless; that's a good example, because in English we have similarly got 'immortality', which is a negative term, grammatically speaking – 'not mortal' – but conveys a positive impression. If you speak in terms of 'immortality' you mean not mere absence of death, but endless life. The passage certainly doesn't leave us in any doubt that there is an Unconditioned, quite separate, as it were, from the conditioned and with, as it were again, a positive nature of its own. And the Buddha points to that as the end of suffering. In fact, there cannot be an end of suffering just as an end of suffering. There can only be a realization of the Unconditioned, upon which there is an end of suffering. When *dukkha* ends, it is not like a process which is going on and on, and then the process comes to an end and after that there's nothing, though this is sometimes how Buddhism is interpreted, and Nirvāṇa is interpreted as that nothing. You can't lift yourself up by your own bootlaces. You have to take hold of a branch above you and pull yourself up by that, so that branch has to be there. In order for it to be possible for you to grow, you need an ideal which is as it were outside of you, ahead. It is not enough to think, 'I must get rid of this and get rid of that. I must overcome my anger and eliminate my craving.' You need a positive goal in front of you, the attraction of which you can feel, towards which you can feel yourself moving. This is not how the Buddha's teaching is usually explained, but this important passage makes it quite clear, though its full import isn't always brought out.

> But then, monks, I thought, why do I, being myself of a nature to have been born, of an ageing, ailing, mortal, sorrowful and afflicted nature, go in search of what is similarly of a nature to have been born, of an ageing, ailing, mortal, sorrowful and afflicted nature? What if I, being myself of a nature to have been born, of an ageing, ailing, mortal, sorrowful and afflicted nature, aware of the danger in what is of a nature to have been born, of an ageing, ailing, mortal, sorrowful and afflicted nature, were to go in search of the unborn, unageing, unailing, deathless, griefless and unafflicted, unexcelled security from bondage, Nibbāna?[502]

This is the *ariyapariyesanā*, the noble quest, and the other, a conditioned being going in quest of the conditioned, is the *anariyapariyesanā*, the ignoble quest. *Esanā* is an Upanishadic word which means seeking in a very strong sense, going ardently in pursuit of; questing is not nearly strong enough. The *ariyapariyesanā* is the going ardently in search of the Unconditioned or the Absolute on the part of a conditioned being, while for a conditioned being to go ardently in pursuit of things which also are conditioned is the ignoble quest or the ignoble seeking. The Buddha describes how he transferred from the ignoble quest to the noble quest and went forth, became a wanderer. This also suggests that the Unconditioned, Nirvāṇa, is a positive state, not merely the cessation of the conditioned.

8.4 THERE IS AGITATION FOR ONE WHO IS DEPENDENT

> Once, when the Buddha was staying near Sāvatthī in the Jeta Wood at Anāthapiṇḍika's park, he gave the *bhikkhus* present an inspiring, gladdening, rousing Dhamma talk about Nibbāna, and the *bhikkhus* listened attentively with their whole minds. Realizing the significance of this, the Buddha breathed out these words:
>
> There is agitation for one who is dependent; there is no agitation for one who is independent. When there is no agitation, there is calming down. When there is calming down, inclination does not exist. When inclination does not exist, there exists no coming nor going. When there is no coming nor going, there exist no death nor rebirth. When there is no death nor rebirth, neither here nor there nor in between exist. Just this is the end of unsatisfactoriness.

'There is agitation for one who is dependent.' For example, suppose you're on retreat but you've left someone behind, back in London or wherever. You think, 'What are they doing now?' Then, because of the dependence, there is agitation. 'Should I phone, just to find out? Or perhaps I should write? Or should I ask someone to go and check up on what they're doing?' One could give hundreds of other examples. You might have a strong dependence on sweets or cigarettes and think, 'Should I go into the village and get some? If I do, what will other people think? But I'd like to have some.' Much of the time we are in this state of doubt and indecision, not being sure what to do, not because of any objective situation but just on account of our dependence: 'If I do this, I shall lose that; if I get involved in this, I can't get involved in that; if I win on the swings I shall lose on the roundabouts.' But with no agitation comes peace of mind, calm.

Woodward translates *nati* not as 'inclination' but as 'bending', which seems to suggest a habitual stance of dependence that results in a constant pendulum-like swinging between pairs of opposites, and especially between birth and rebirth or life and death. This is the way the reactive mind works. It swings to and fro, from one extreme to the other, and all on account of dependence. 'Bending' seems to suggest bending towards the conditioned, as though you are permanently bent in that direction.

It suggests that if you constantly cling, you become frozen in a posture of clinging, permanently oriented in the direction of the conditioned, the cyclic process. If you are completely calm, completely balanced, there is no reason why you should move in one direction rather than another, so far as your subjective feelings are concerned. This is how you can feel when you are meditating – balanced, poised, calm, ready to roll in any direction as it were, but not under any inner compulsion to do so.

This ties up with the idea of the *antarābhava*, the six intermediate states as described in the *Tibetan Book of the Dead*, and the general principle of the intermediate state, the *bardo*, the point at which, between two opposites or two extremes, there is rest, where the action of one extreme has come to an end and the action of the other has not begun.[503] There is an intermediate point where the pendulum, just for an infinitesimal instant, stops. This, one could say, is the end of suffering, except that you've got to try to stay all the time at that point. If you can do that, there is complete calm, therefore there is stability, and an end of suffering.

One could look at the 'in between' as the intermediate state between death and rebirth in the literal sense. If there is no death and no rebirth, there is no in-between state. Birth and death not being, there is no 'here' or 'there' – 'here' meaning this life, especially the end of this life, and 'there' meaning the next life, especially the beginning of the next life; nor any intermediate state. The Theravādins, incidentally, don't believe in an intermediate state, although there are references to it here and there in the Pāli canon. The Sarvāstivādins did believe in the intermediate state, and it is from them that the Tibetans took it up.[504]

It is important to see the significance of this *udāna*, lifting it out of its immediate doctrinal context.[505] It tells us that there is a state of agitation which is due to dependence, a state of oscillating between extremes. The important thing is to come to rest at a central point. If you can do that, you will make contact, as it were, with something beyond the opposites, beyond the conditioned. One can take it even within the limits of the present lifetime, with reference to this oscillatory movement between contradictory emotions, all based upon dependence. Once dependence goes, agitation goes; when agitation goes, you are calm, you are at rest. When you reach this state of calm, even in a quite ordinary sense, you feel centred. And from that experience of centredness within yourself, you can begin to contact the Unconditioned.

8.5 THE BUDDHA'S LAST MEAL

Once, when the Buddha was travelling among the Mallas with a large party of *bhikkhus*, they came to the village of Pāvā, where the Buddha stayed in the mango grove of Cunda the smith. After the Buddha had gladdened Cunda with a Dhamma talk, the smith invited him and the *bhikkhus* for a meal the following day. The next day, Cunda prepared the food himself, including a quantity of *sūkaramaddava*. The Buddha asked Cunda to serve him with the *sūkaramaddava* and give the other food to the *bhikkhus*, and this was done. Once he had eaten some of the *sūkaramaddava*, the Buddha told Cunda to bury the rest of it in a pit, 'For I do not see in this world any being, whether *deva*, *brahma*, Māra, or human, who could eat and digest this food, except myself.' Cunda did this, and then returned to the Buddha's side to hear another talk about the Dhamma.

After the Buddha had eaten the *sūkaramaddava* he was very sick with dysentery and terrible pain. He bore it mindfully and without complaint, and said to Ānanda that they would now travel to the city of Kusinārā. On the way, the Buddha felt tired and went to sit under a tree by the side of the road, asking Ānanda to bring him some water. Ānanda pointed out that hundreds of wagons had just gone past and the nearby water had been churned up, but after the Buddha had asked him three times for water, Ānanda went to get some and found that the water was now flowing pure, clean, and unmuddied, and he marvelled at the power of the Buddha.

Having drunk the water, the Buddha, together with a large crowd of *bhikkhus*, went to the river Kukuṭṭhā, where he bathed and drank. Then he went to a nearby mango grove, where he told a *bhikkhu* called Cunda that he was tired and wanted to lie down. Cundaka folded the Buddha's robe in four to act as a sort of couch, and the Buddha lay down. At this point the Buddha said to Ānanda that someone might make Cunda the smith feel bad that the Buddha had gained *parinibbāna* after Cunda had given him his last meal, but that Ānanda should reassure Cunda that he had heard from the Buddha's own lips that it was a great thing that he had given the Buddha his last meal. The Buddha explained that two kinds of almsfood produced much more merit than any other kind: the almsfood given to the Buddha for his first meal after his Enlightenment, and that which he ate just before gaining *parinibbāna*. Cunda's action would thus be conducive to his long life, beauty, happiness, heaven, fame, and supremacy, and there was no need for remorse on his part. And realizing the significance of what had occurred, the Buddha breathed out these words:

Those who are generous increase their merit.
The restrained do not heap up more hatred.
Experts give up what is bad, and are quenched
through the end of greed, hate, and confusion.

In this section we come very near to the end of the Buddha's life. It is a fairly lengthy section, almost like a short *sutta*, and it seems to be a compilation with a few minor inconsistencies, due no doubt to the putting together of material from different sources.[506] There has been quite a discussion about what the Buddha's last meal consisted of, whether it was mushrooms, truffles, boar's flesh, or what not. *Sūkaramaddava*, 'pig-tender', could be truffles (a foodstuff delicious to pigs) or pork (the tender meat of a pig). People also wonder why the Buddha said it could not be digested by anybody except a Buddha, but it seems to me quite simple. Cunda, in his enthusiasm and devotion, prepared a dish of truffles, or whatever it was, for the Buddha, and served the Buddha first. It was so rich and indigestible that after eating some himself, out of politeness, the Buddha asked Cunda to bury the rest. He said nobody else would be able to digest it. Perhaps, in view of his well-known irony, we can imagine that he said, 'Cunda, only a Buddha could digest this meal!' That is much more likely than the far-fetched magical explanations that some of the commentaries give to the effect that, for instance, all the *devas* in the universe had infused tremendous fiery energy into that food, so that only a Buddha was able to digest it. There is a much more ordinary explanation. It is just another example of the Buddha's thoughtfulness. He didn't want Cunda to feel remorseful or responsible for the Buddha's death, but he also wanted to make sure that none of the *bhikkhus* were given this over-rich, indigestible food, so he asked Cunda to go and bury it somewhere. There may be some symbolical meaning too, but that isn't clear to us. The immediate occasion of the Buddha's death seems to have been this heavy and indigestible meal, whatever it was, and the Buddha didn't want Cunda to feel remorse. But we are not given the whole story in this section of the *Udāna*.

You will notice that the section concludes with the *udāna*, not saying anything more about the last hours of the Buddha. Why that is so we shall be seeing a little later on, but there does seem to be a definite artistic reason. We have now practically traversed the Buddha's entire life. Even though the *Udāna* isn't a biography, or even mainly biographical, and though it doesn't keep to strict chronological sequence, there is a progressive movement from the time just after the Buddha's Enlightenment right up to a few hours before his death. We get a definite feeling of the gradual growth and development of the teaching and the whole movement, the sangha, and even to some extent its growing complexity. The *Udāna* is a very good, complete little work, practically like a gospel, as I said before. Though it is only a very small part of the Pāli canon, it gives us a small-scale picture of the whole thing, more or less complete in all its parts. We don't get all the teachings or all the episodes, but what we get gives a faithful impression of the whole. The material seems comparatively unworked up compared with some of the other elaborations, which gives the sense that we are pretty close to what the Buddha actually did and said and thought, and the way he lived, the experiences he had, the people he met, the milieu in which he lived and worked. If I had to choose any one work from the Pāli canon to give people an idea of what it was like to be alive in the Buddha's day and to encounter him and listen to his message, I would probably recommend the *Udāna*.

8.6 THE BUDDHA GIVES THE VILLAGERS TIPS ON ETHICS

> Once, when the Buddha was on tour among the people of Magadha with a large party of *bhikkhus*, they came to the village of Pāṭali. The villagers invited the Buddha to stay in the village rest house and prepared it by covering the floor, providing a water jar, and setting up an oil-lamp. On arriving there, the Buddha washed his feet and then sat down by the middle pillar facing east. The order of *bhikkhus* sat down near the western wall facing east, with the Buddha in front of them, and the lay followers of Pāṭali also came in and sat down, sitting near the eastern wall with the Buddha in front of them.

The Buddha proceeded to give them a Dhamma talk about ethics. He explained that there are five disadvantages for the immoral person: he loses money; he gets a bad reputation; if he has to appear in public, he lacks confidence; he dies confused; and after death he will be reborn in an unhappy state. By contrast, through his diligence, a moral person gains five advantages: he becomes rich; he gets a good reputation; he approaches any assembly with confidence; he dies unconfused; and after death he is reborn in a heavenly realm. The Buddha spoke to the people of Pāṭali on these themes for much of the night and then, commenting on the lateness of the hour, sent them away to do whatever they thought best. Pleased with what they had heard, they made their salutations and left, and the Buddha retired to an empty room.

At that time Sunīdha and Vassakāra, two government ministers of Magadha, were building a city at Pāṭali. Thousands of *devatās* lived in the area, and wherever powerful *devatās* are around, that encourages powerful kings and ministers to build settlements there; likewise, when middling and minor *devatās* are around, that encourages middling and minor kings and ministers to build there. With his divine eye, the Buddha saw all the *devatās* around Pāṭali, and he asked Ānanda who was building a city there. Ānanda told him that it was Sunīdha and Vassakāra, and the Buddha said it was as though the two ministers had consulted the *devas* of the Tāvatiṃsa heaven before deciding to build a city at Pāṭali to ward off the Vajjians. The Buddha went on to predict that Pāṭali would become the chief city of the area, whose trade routes would spread as far as his own influence, but that the city would suffer three disasters: from fire, from water, and from the breaking of an alliance.

Sunīdha and Vassakāra invited the Buddha and the *bhikkhus* to a meal the next day, and by his silence the Buddha consented to come. The two ministers served the food with their own hands, and the Buddha thanked them with verses in which he said that wherever a wise man set up his home, he should feed those leading a holy life and make offerings to the local *devatās*, who would respond with compassion which would bring good fortune. With this, the Buddha departed, and the two ministers followed him, deciding that whichever gate the Buddha left by would henceforth be called the Gotama Gate, and the ford by which he crossed the river Ganges would be called the Gotama Ford.

But when the Buddha reached the river Ganges, it was so full that a crow standing on the bank could drink from it. On the banks there were some people searching for a boat or floating log by which they might cross, and others were making a raft. But in the time it would take a strong man to extend his flexed arm or flex his extended arm, the Buddha and the order of *bhikkhus* vanished from the bank of the river and reappeared on the far bank. And the Buddha breathed out these words:

Those who cross the river in flood
build a bridge and leave the lakes behind.
While people bind a raft together,
the wise have already made the crossing.

There are quite a few points of interest here. It is set in a familiar scene. The Buddha is on tour, on this occasion among the people of the Magadha area. Together with a great company of monks, he reaches Pāṭali, and the lay followers, having heard a rumour that the Buddha is in the area, invite him to stay at an *āvasathāgāra*, a rest house. The commentary describes it as a *mahāsālā*, a large hall in the middle of town, big enough to accommodate tradespeople, travellers, the homeless, and the ill without their touching each other. It seems that every village, especially where there was a republican form of government in the area, had such a hall (in modern India it would be called a *dharmasala*) in which to hold their meetings, conduct their judicial business, listen to lectures by wanderers on tour, and accommodate those wanderers. This is very much the situation in India even today; in practically every village there are one or two *dharmasalas* put up by devout and wealthy people. Nowadays they are not used for courts or assemblies – they are entirely for religious purposes – but any wandering monk can stay there, and very often the local people will arrange for him to give a talk and they will all come in the evening and listen, just as in the Buddha's day.

In the course of his stay at the community hall in Pāṭali, the Buddha gives a little talk. It would appear from the nature of the discourse that the villagers are rather new disciples, not spiritually very advanced but mainly occupied with their worldly lives, so the talk is mainly about virtue, *śīla*, pointing out the five disadvantages, so far as they are concerned, of not practising *śīla*, starting with simple, practical, ordinary things which they can understand. He doesn't even start by talking about generosity, *dāna*, as he often does. He simply advises them to lead an ethical life and points out to these practical people the practical consequences of unskilful behaviour like not attending to your work, not going to the fields regularly, gambling, and squandering your money.

One of the first consequences of an unethical life, the Buddha says, is loss of wealth. Probably this is an argument that will appeal to the thrifty householders of that village. You can imagine them shaking their heads and saying, 'Oh yes, that's true indeed! Living it up in the big city really costs money; leading an immoral life just wastes wealth.' The argument from thrift is not exalted or noble, but at least it will convince them and get them started.

And, the Buddha says, the next consequence is that you get a bad reputation. Obviously, in a small village, to be well thought of by your fellow villagers is quite important, and to have a good reputation you need to be sober and thrifty and industrious and kind and helpful. People who live in cities can't imagine what it's like living in a small village and how much importance is attached to having a good name. If you manage to offend the community, very often you have to take steps to rectify that. You may have to give a feast for the whole village to make things right. In the city, if you offend the group of people that you are usually associated with and you don't want to do anything about it, you just cut off contact with them and make new friends, join a new group; but in a small village you have to live with one another so you can't afford to displease others too much. No doubt this is one reason why some people became wanderers: they found this situation very narrow, especially if it was a very small village. This is why in the Pāli scriptures you find people saying, 'Dusty is the household life. Free as the air is the life of the wanderer.'[507] And then they go forth, shaking the dust of the village from their feet. But to those living and working and bringing up their families in the village, it was a cogent argument that if you led an ethical life you would enjoy the good opinion of your fellow villagers.

Thirdly, the fact that you are leading a virtuous life and enjoy the good opinion of your fellows will give you confidence at the village assemblies. You will feel that you are a solid, worthy citizen and everybody esteems you, and this will give you the confidence to speak your mind. This, for some reason, was very much insisted upon in the Buddha's time. Again and again the Pāli scriptures say that if you are leading an ethical life you will not feel abashed in the company of other people, as if people attached a lot of importance to being at ease socially, being able to walk into any gathering with confidence. Part of the reason may be that in those days you had to speak up for yourself. If there was a dispute, there would be a meeting of the elders in the community hall, and the head man of the village would preside. You would have to state your case yourself – there weren't any lawyers – and the other party to the dispute would speak up for himself, and all your fellow villagers would sit there nodding approval at some things you said and shaking their heads in disapproval at others. They would perhaps ask questions and then give their opinion, and eventually the presiding elder would pass a judgement which was binding upon both parties. It was important in such situations to be able to speak up for yourself. So here the Buddha uses a positive version of the argument *ad hominem*, as it's called: you would like to be wealthy, respected, and influential, and by leading a moral life, you will be able to be all these things. If someone says, 'I don't want wealth. I don't care what people think of me. I want nothing to do with public assemblies', this argument falls to the ground. But the Buddha knew his audience. He knew what sorts of argument would appeal to them.

Fourthly, if you lead a virtuous life, you die a peaceful death. There won't be anything to reproach yourself with, so you won't be afraid of what might happen afterwards. You will die with a clear conscience, having led a virtuous life, accumulated your wealth, brought up your children, enjoyed the esteem of your neighbours, wielded a certain amount of influence within your community, not done anyone any harm. The Buddha points that out as a fourth advantage, and the opposite, of course, as a disadvantage. If you have led a virtuous life – here he introduces a directly religious argument – after death you will have a happy, heavenly rebirth. So he is leading them step by step from the lower to the higher consideration. But he breaks off there. He speaks far into the night simply along these lines. It may be that these householders, though devoted to the Buddha, are a worldly lot, and maybe they need quite a lot of persuasion. He has advocated skilful action for very down-to-earth, worldly, practical reasons, but he can't get any further than that, apparently. He can't go on even to *dāna*, and certainly not on to meditation or the four noble truths. He does what he can, and then he brings the discourse to a conclusion, saying, 'The night is far spent. Do whatever seems good to you' – the customary formula. And the villagers, delighted with the Buddha's words, salute him and return to their homes. At least the Buddha has laid the foundations; at least he has impressed upon their minds the importance of *śīla*, and they have accepted that happily.

Now, the lay people having withdrawn, something quite interesting occurs. Pāṭali was at that time a small village, but it was strategically situated. The kingdom of Magadha was expanding, and the king, Ajātaśatru, was thinking about breaking up the Vajjians, a strong confederacy of eighteen different tribes, and in this way gradually swallowing them all up. At that time the capital of Magadha was Rājagaha or Rajgir, but because Ajātaśatru wanted to conquer the Vajjian confederacy and seize their territory, two ministers of the king were strengthening and enlarging the village of Pāṭali, which was on the border. According to some authorities they wanted to build a fortress there, a base from which to launch an attack on the Vajjians. Here it says that these two ministers were building a town on the site of Pāṭali to ward off the Vajjians, which suggests that they were expecting an attack, but we never read about the Vajjians thinking of attacking the kingdom of Magadha; it is always the other way around. So maybe it is the well-known argument of the conqueror – 'this is all for defensive purposes' – while the real purpose is offensive.

Anyway, they were building this town on the site of the village, and we are told that great numbers of *devatās*, of gods or spirits, had gathered there. And we are further told, as a piece of folklore, that wherever *devatās* gather, they bend the minds of ministers and others to building there. We are told that the Buddha sees this, and from the fact that there are so many *devatās* gathered together he first foresees and then foretells that there will be a great city on that site. According to Western scholars this is not a real prophecy, but shows that this episode was inserted into the scriptures later on, when Pāṭali had become a great city. But it is difficult to say; we mustn't jump to that kind of rationalistic conclusion too easily. The Buddha sees that there are other forces at work – this is probably the best way of putting it – causing people to build at one spot rather than another. It is as though there are certain energies in certain places which influence people to build and settle there. The Buddha sees that there is a powerful complex of energies at that spot, drawing the minds of ministers and others to build there, so he sees that there is going to be a great city on that site. But he predicts various kinds of disaster for that city in the future. The involvement of the *devas* is as if to say that what happens on this earth is affected, or even sparked off, by happenings on higher planes. One sees that there are certain sites where people build again and again, even though the settlements may be destroyed again and again, and there are other apparently quite suitable spots where people seem never to think of building. Why is that? This passage suggests that people are moved to build in particular places by psychic forces or subtle energies of which they are not altogether conscious.

The Buddha says in the verses he recites by way of thanksgiving that one should be on good terms with those forces, but there is a widespread belief in Buddhist circles that they only affect worldly affairs, although traditionally in Buddhist countries people do tend to take account of them even where spiritual things are concerned. They like to choose a site for a monastery or temple according to the influences that prevail there. Obviously one can lose oneself in the maze of this sort of thing, but certainly some spots feel as if they are more positive than others. The spirits that move people to build great cities may not be very healthy. They are certainly not very 'spiritual' spirits, if one can use that expression; they are perhaps rather *asura*-like, wanting a big city to be built, where there will be a lot of trade, a lot of wealth, a lot of power. One need not go along with this sort of thing, but the Buddha does suggest that one should be on good terms with the local *devatās*. Perhaps that simply means that one should have a positive attitude towards one's environment, not just use it in a selfish way. If you worshipped the spirits of the trees around you, you could hardly go on cutting down the trees ruthlessly until there were none left. Perhaps it suggests a sensitive, almost reverential attitude towards one's environment, not just pillaging it in a selfish exploitative way, and that one should be sensitive to the influences by which one is surrounded and harmonize with them when they are positive and healthy. Very clearly the Buddha suggests that if your attitude towards the forces of nature is positive, they will cooperate with you. One shouldn't carry this too far, but there is a certain amount of traditional wisdom in it. The important consideration is that the householder, the one who is living and working and earning and producing, shouldn't do so only for himself, or even only for his family. He should also help to support those who wander from place to place, those who live on alms, those who are leading a spiritual life. This comes first, before making offerings to *devas*.

This seems a mundane episode so far. The Buddha visits these village folk and gives them a practical discourse, confining himself to matters of ethics. Then he is entertained by the officials who are building a town on the site of that village, and he sees that there are psychic factors involved in the building of that town. He thanks the officials and draws attention to the importance of supporting holy men and remaining on positive terms with one's environment. The Buddha refers to 'those leading a holy life', whether they are wanderers or not, presumably, but normally it would only be wanderers who would come to the door for alms.

Then there is that little incident of the gates being named after the Buddha, and the Buddha crossing the river Ganges apparently by the exercise of his supernormal power; and that leads us on to the *udāna*, in which while some people are still preoccupied with making a raft, others have already crossed the river. This suggests that while everybody else is getting ready to follow the spiritual life, the sages are actually doing that; in fact, they've done it, while you're just making the preparations. There's nothing supernormal or magical about it. They have simply got down to the business of leading the spiritual life in a more practical, businesslike manner than you have. They've been getting on with the job while you've just been talking about it or thinking about it or making preparations.

The mention of Pāṭali, which is going to become Pāṭaliputra, brings to mind the emperor Aśoka, who made that city the capital of his subcontinent-wide empire and the centre of his dissemination of the Buddha's teaching far beyond the boundaries of India. So here perhaps we get a glimpse of the future and start becoming aware, just before the Buddha's death, of those possibilities. It is to Pāṭaliputra that Greek envoys went in the time of Candragupta Maurya, so we get a hint here not only of the expansion of Pāṭali into Pāṭaliputra – the little village into the capital of a great empire – but also perhaps of the expansion of Buddhism itself from the teaching of a comparatively obscure Indian teacher into a world religion. This is another example of the sense that there is a definite editorial skill at work in this text.

8.7 THE BUDDHA AND THE FOOLISH DISCIPLE

> Once, the Buddha was journeying along a road among the people of Kosala, accompanied by a *bhikkhu* called Nāgasamāla. At a fork in the road Nāgasamāla suggested going one way, but the Buddha said that the other road was the way they should take. Nāgasamāla repeated his suggestion a second and a third time, and then put the Buddha's bowl and cloak down on the ground and went off on his own. But as he went along the road he had chosen, robbers attacked him and broke his bowl and tore his robe. He went back to the Buddha and told him what had happened. Realizing its significance, the Buddha breathed out these words:
>
> Travelling together, living as one,
> the expert in wisdom mixes with the ignorant.
> Knowing this, one leaves the bad person
> like the milk-drinking heron leaves the water.

Clearly one can take this little episode literally, allegorically, or both. It seems to belong to the period before the last twenty-five years of the Buddha's life, because the Buddha is attended not by Ānanda but by another monk, Nāgasamāla, and the two disagree about which way to go when they reach a fork in the road. One would have thought that, whatever Nāgasamāla might have thought himself, he would have gone along with the Buddha, but he is so obstinate that he is prepared to leave the Buddha there and go on by himself. Being the attendant, he has been carrying the Buddha's spare robe and his bowl, so he just puts them down by the side of the road. He observes the formalities, but what is the use, one might ask, of being polite when you are being thoroughly disobedient and stupid at the same time?

Retribution is in store for Nāgasamāla, as one might expect. Robbers fall upon him, he is beaten, kicked and – a stroke of poetic justice – his bowl is broken and his robes are torn to tatters. So he has to come back to the Buddha. He salutes him and sits down at one side – very subdued, probably – and tells the Buddha what happened. The Buddha doesn't make any direct comment, but in the *udāna* he speaks about how the wise leave behind bad people just as the milk-drinking heron leaves behind the water.

There are quite a few references in the Pāli scriptures – in the *Dhammapada*, for example – to the painful experiences that come upon one through keeping company with a fool, with a spiritually immature person.[508] The word translated as 'the ignorant' is *aññajana*, 'a person who doesn't know', 'an ignorant person'. Here the Buddha is making that general comment, as if to say, 'Well, what was I to expect? This Nāgasamāla is ignorant. Here am I walking with him from place to place. It would be better to leave him and go on by myself.'

Of course, you can also look at it allegorically: the Buddha says, 'That's the middle way, that's the Eightfold Path', but then you go some other way and sooner or later you come to grief. But we have to be careful not to interpret this in an authoritarian or goody-goody way: 'The Buddha knows best. You mustn't do anything that the Buddha says you mustn't. You must always be good and obedient.' *Koñca* means a heron or a crane. The commentary says that just as a heron, when presented with milk mixed with water, will drink only the milk, likewise the wise person (*paṇḍita*) will leave behind the person of little wisdom.[509] The same thing is said about the *haṃsa*, the swan or goose, in Sanskrit literature. It is usually considered to represent the separation of the essential from the inessential, the point being that if you have been accustomed to the essential, you will reject the inessential. If a heron is accustomed to drink milk rather than water, it will reject the water; and similarly the wise man, having been brought up, as it were, on the company of the wise – certainly on the company of his own skilful mental states – won't care for the company of the fool.

This again draws attention, though in a rather negative way, to the importance of *kalyāṇa mitratā*. The Buddha says sometimes, as in the *Dhammapada*, that if you can't find good spiritual company it is better to be on your own.[510] Of course, if you can find spiritual friends to travel with, that's best. The second best is to fare on alone. The third best, or third worst, is to try to fare on in the company of fools – those who don't know what is good for them or good for you, and who have no interest in the spiritual life. And the worst situation of all is to be a fool in the company of another fool.

8.8 THE DEATH OF VISĀKHĀ'S GRANDCHILD

Once, the Buddha was staying near Sāvatthī in the Eastern Park at the house of Visākhā, who was called Migāra's mother. Visākhā's beloved grandchild had just died, and she approached the Buddha in the middle of the day with wet clothes and wet hair. The Buddha asked her what she was doing there at that time and in that condition, and she explained what had happened.

The Buddha asked her a question: 'Would you like to have as many children and grandchildren as there are people in Sāvatthī?' And Visākhā said she would. But, given how many people die in Sāvatthī every day, she would never be without wet clothes and wet hair, the Buddha pointed out. Visākhā, seeing what he meant, discarded the idea of having so many children and grandchildren. The Buddha told her, 'Those who are attached to a hundred things have a hundred sorrows, those who are attached to ninety have ninety sorrows, and so on – but those who are attached to nothing whatever are sorrowless, stainless, without despair.' And realizing the significance of this, the Buddha breathed out these words:

Whatever griefs and sorrows there are,
the many kinds of suffering in the world,
dependent on love these originate:
love not being, they do not become.

So they are happy and without grief
who have nothing dear at all in the world.
So those desiring the griefless and dust-free
don't make anything in the world dear.

Here we are obviously concerned with the subject of death. Just as in the earlier episode when people came to the Buddha with wet hair and clothes after cremating a dead body, Visākhā has had to attend to the cremation of a 'dear and lovely granddaughter'. In modern India, women never have anything to do with funerals, and probably they didn't usually in the Buddha's day, but Visākhā, as we know, was an independent and strong-minded woman, so it may be that she acted more or less like a man on this occasion, accompanying the corpse and attending the cremation and afterwards having a purificatory bath. The Buddha at once goes to the root of it all, asking, 'Would you like to have as many children and grandchildren as there are people in Sāvatthī?' And Visākhā, despite her piety, is so biologically greedy – she has such a lust for reproduction – that she says, 'Yes, I would indeed.' This is as it were nature speaking through her mouth, and saying, 'Let's multiply. The more men and women there are in the world the better.' But then the Buddha says, 'Just think how many people die in Sāvatthī every day.' The other side of the coin of birth is death. All right, you'd have hundreds of children and grandchildren, but you would also have so many funerals to attend. As the Buddha says, in, we may imagine, a slightly ironic or humorous manner, 'You'd never be without wet hair and wet clothes!' She hadn't thought of that. She'd only thought of life, she hadn't thought of death. She'd not seen the other side of the coin. But now she sees it, so she says, 'Enough for me, sir, of so many sons and grandsons!' She is quick to see the point once the Buddha puts it to her. Then the Buddha tells her that those who are attached to a hundred things have a hundred sorrows, but if you are attached to nothing, you have no sorrows at all. We have to be quite careful how we interpret this passage. It does not exclude positive skilful emotions. In Pāli, there are a clear distinction between friendly love, *mettā* and 'sticky affection', *pema*, or sometimes *sneha*. You can't have too much *mettā*, but *pema* is not friendliness but a sort of infatuation which can be very painful. The Buddha is not saying you shouldn't be friendly, you shouldn't be kind, you shouldn't have positive emotions. He is saying you shouldn't have attachment, you shouldn't have infatuations, because then you will have sorrows.

If we translate *mettā* as 'friendliness', which is quite literal, it may sound a bit weak, because in English the conception of friendliness tends to be overshadowed by 'love'. It is misleading, however, to translate *mettā* as 'love', because the word 'love' has an ambiguity about it while the meaning of *mettā* is crystal clear. It is connected with *mitra*, which is 'friend', and friendship in ancient India was evidently a much more positive emotion than it seems to be in the modern West. We tend to think of friendship as something quite tepid, just a sort of liking that develops upon acquaintance, but *mettā* is a very strong, powerful, positive thing, and we're advised to cultivate it as much as we can. Loving-kindness is perhaps the best translation.

The verse seems to be quite straightforward. It certainly doesn't mean that you shouldn't have positive feelings towards other people, but they should be skilful positive feelings. Once again we come up against the rather negative mode of expression of some of the Pāli canon, but elsewhere in the canon the importance of *mettā* and the desirability of its cultivation is quite strongly insisted upon.[511]

8.9 DABBA ATTAINS FINAL NIRVĀṆA

> Once, when the Buddha was staying near Rājagaha, in the Bamboo Grove at the Squirrels' Feeding Ground, Dabba Mallaputta approached him and said, 'Now, Sugata, is the time for my final *nibbāna*.' And the Buddha said, 'Do now what you think it is time to do.' So Dabba Mallaputta got up, prostrated himself before the Buddha, and keeping his right side towards the Buddha, rose up into the air. As he sat cross-legged in space, he entered into the fire element, emerged, and attained final *nibbāna*. His body was completely burned up so that no part of it remained behind, just as when oil is burned, no ash or soot remains. And realizing the significance of this, the Buddha breathed out these words:
>
> The body gave out, perceptions ceased,
> all felt-experience became cool.
> Determining factors calmed right down.
> Consciousness arrived at its end.

Once again we are concerned with death. Not many episodes ago we came within a few hours of the Buddha's own decease, but the *Udāna* stops there so far as the Buddha is concerned. It is as though the compiler doesn't want to say anything directly about the Buddha's death. One practical reason would be that the Buddha couldn't have spoken a verse about it! And in the next section, the Buddha does have the last word, not about his own death, but somebody else's. If you exclude the Buddha's own *parinirvāṇa*, he is left with the last word. But there could have been an episode dealing with the *parinirvāṇa* before the end, because the text is not strictly chronological in its arrangement. Perhaps the collection was compiled quite soon after the Buddha's decease, and the thought of the Buddha having passed away was still quite painful, so the compilers don't like to bring it in very directly. They carry you to within a few hours of the Buddha's death, but they don't say anything about it. Instead, there's a little episode about death in general, and then somebody else's death, and then, as we will see, in the final episode the Buddha comments upon that. Death is brought in, the Buddha is brought in, and he gets the final word. You are left with the suggestion of death, and the awareness that the Buddha has passed away, but nothing is directly stated.

Here we get a legendary element that is very rare in the *Udāna*, though elsewhere in the canon we find the Buddha rising into the air when he performed the twin miracle, the supernormal feat of emitting from his body alternately flames of fire and streams of water.[512] In that case, the Buddha rising into the air represents the fact that whatever happens after that happens on another plane, in another dimension, it's not to be taken literally, it's not historical. Perhaps we can say this also of Dabba the Malla's rising into the air. It is an archetypal death, a sort of spiritual death. Don't forget, we are still concerned with the Buddha's *parinirvāṇa*, and that would be a special kind of passing away, because he was the Buddha. It would be the dropping away of the physical body, but with no change in the spiritual state. He remained the Buddha. Before he was a Buddha with a body, now he is a Buddha without a body. That's the only difference. The death of the Buddha's body symbolizes the final disappearance of everything conditioned, and this is also what Dabba's miraculous death and disappearance seems to represent. The burning of his body symbolizes the burning up of everything conditioned consequent upon one's attainment of the Unconditioned. Dabba the Malla's physical body is consumed by fire, but the Buddha has consumed everything conditioned in his own nature, and he is now purely the Unconditioned. Perhaps this episode is meant to throw light on the Buddha's *parinirvāṇa* and bring out its significance, or perhaps to draw our attention from physical death, the death of the body, to spiritual death, the complete disappearance of the conditioned. When the Buddha 'dies', only the Unconditioned side as it were of his nature is left. In a sense, it wasn't a death, for spiritually speaking he died when he gained Enlightenment under the bodhi tree. He doesn't really die, it's only the worn-out physical body dropping off after eighty years. The Buddha as Buddha is, as it were – we don't want to be too existentialist here – still there. The Buddha doesn't die. Perhaps, very skilfully and indirectly, the compiler is suggesting something like this. The literal burning up of Dabba's physical body without remainder becomes a symbol of the Buddha's, or any Enlightened person's, burning up of the conditioned so as to leave only the Unconditioned which can't be expressed. It seems quite a skilful piece of editing.

8.10 UNWAVERING HAPPINESS

> Once, when the Buddha was staying near Sāvatthī in the Jeta Wood at Anāthapiṇḍika's park, he addressed the *bhikkhus* present and told them about how Dabba Mallaputta gained final *nibbāna*. And realizing the significance of what had happened, the Buddha breathed out these words:
>
> Just as the future state is not known
> of an iron bar that has been wrought
> in the furnace, with its heat and flame,
> and which now gradually cools down;
> likewise, for the perfectly liberated ones
> who have crossed the flood of bondage to pleasure,
> no future is to be discerned for those
> who have reached unwavering happiness.

In this final section of the *Udāna* our attention is shifted from the Buddha's death to Dabba's death, enabling the Buddha to have the last word, so that the whole text concludes with an *udāna* of the Buddha. The state of the Enlightened One after death, he says here as he also says elsewhere,[513] cannot be fathomed, not on account of his death, but because his state cannot be fathomed even during life. It's as though there is nothing more to be said. The Buddha has not only gained Enlightenment; the physical body that was associated with that Enlightened state for forty-five years has now dropped off. There is only the Enlightened mind left, but you can't say what that Enlightened mind is like. It is unfathomable, indescribable.

It is not that when the spark dies there is nothing left. The spark passes into a state which cannot be perceived. One scholar has pointed out that we must bear in mind the ancient Indian belief that when a fire was extinguished, it didn't go out in the sense that it ceased to exist, but passed from a gross to a subtle state. This is the significance of what the Buddha says here. The spark, having gone out, exists in a subtle state which cannot be apprehended. The Buddha's physical body having disappeared, the Buddha Mind exists in a subtle, purely transcendental state which cannot be perceived by the unenlightened person.

By this ingenious device the compiler has the Buddha virtually commenting upon his own *parinirvāṇa*. As we have seen, the *Udāna* as a whole is a sensitively put together anthology. It has carried us practically through the Buddha's whole life, from shortly after his Enlightenment to shortly before his physical death, with many episodes in between, allowing us to see the spread of the teaching, the consolidation of the Order, and much of the social and religious and even political and economic life of India, and it closes on this solemn and inspiring note.

It is interesting that there is a reference to *acalaṃ sukhaṃ*, 'unwavering happiness', 'unshakeable bliss'. It is not just a cessation of suffering that has been attained, or a state of no-lusts, but a state of unshakeable bliss. Even though there have been many negative ways of putting things in the course of the *Udāna*, it closes, as it began, on a very positive note. It is as though the compiler wants to leave us with a positive impression, and no doubt he is very wise in wanting to do that. The *Udāna* begins with the Buddha under the bodhi tree, with a statement of the spiritual ideal in positive terms, using the old word brahmin or *brāhmaṇa*, and it closes with a reference to the inexpressible but highly positive nature of the Enlightened state. Or, to put it another way, it begins with Enlightenment with a body and ends with Enlightenment without a body, and the rest of the text tells us what the Buddha did in between....

Appendix 1
DR AMBEDKAR'S TWENTY-TWO CONVERSION VOWS

1. I shall not consider Brahma, Vishnu, and Mahesh as gods, nor shall I worship them.
2. I shall not consider Rama and Krishna as gods, nor shall I worship them.
3. I shall not believe in 'Gauri', Ganapati, and any other gods and goddesses of Hinduism, nor shall I worship them.
4. I do not believe that god has incarnated.
5. I do not and shall not believe that Lord Buddha was the incarnation of Vishnu. I believe this to be sheer madness and false propaganda.
6. I shall not perform 'shraddha' nor shall I give 'pind-dan'.
7. I shall not act in a manner violating the principles and teachings of the Buddha.
8. I shall not get Brahmins to perform any ceremonies.
9. I believe that all human beings are equal.
10. I shall endeavour to establish equality.
11. I shall live according to the Noble Eightfold Path taught by the Buddha.
12. I shall practise the Ten Paramitas taught by the Buddha.
13. I shall be compassionate towards all living beings and nourish and protect them.
14. I shall not steal.
15. I shall not tell lies.

16. I shall not commit sexual misconduct.
17. I shall not drink alcohol.
18. I shall lead my life bringing together the three Buddhist principles of wisdom, morality, and compassion.
19. I renounce Hinduism, which is detrimental to the fulfilment of human beings, and which considers human beings as unequal and degraded, and I embrace the Buddha Dhamma.
20. I firmly believe the Dhamma of the Buddha is the *saddhamma*.
21. I believe that I am taking a new birth.
22. Thus I vow to lead my life according to the Buddha's teachings.

Translated from Marathi by
Mangesh Dahiwale and Dhammachari Lokamitra

Appendix 2

AMBEDKAR AND BUDDHISM, REINSTATED PASSAGE

Due to uncertainty about the author's intentions, a passage was omitted from later editions of chapter 8 of Ambedkar and Buddhism, *and thus also from* Complete Works *volume 9. It now appears that it was Sangharakshita's intention to restore that passage to the book, so we reproduce it here. It should be placed between the two paragraphs on volume 9, on p. 139, i.e. between 'sufficient to reveal' and 'As we have already seen'.*

Before embarking on such an account, however, we shall have to try and clear up some of the doubts by which the work became surrounded at the time of its original appearance, nearly a year after Ambedkar's death, and which for some of his followers surround it still.

These doubts find expression in two closely related questions: Was *The Buddha and His Dhamma* published in exactly the same form that Ambedkar himself left it at the time of his death? And, had Ambedkar really been able to complete the work in accordance with his original intentions? With regard to the first question, it would appear that the published version of *The Buddha and His Dhamma* differs from Ambedkar's own version in at least one respect, that is, in not including the Preface that he wrote for it on 15 March 1956. This Preface, as we have already seen, did not appear in print until 1980, when Bhagwan Das, a well known Punjabi Buddhist littérateur, included it in his *Rare Prefaces Written by Dr Ambedkar*. But though the Preface itself did not appear in the published version of *The Buddha and His Dhamma*, all the points that Ambedkar makes in it concerning his early religious impressions, the origin of the book, and the circumstances under which it had been compiled, were faithfully incorporated in the publisher's Foreword. All the points, that is, except one. This point related to Ambedkar's illness and to the help he had received from his wife and Dr Malvankar. It would therefore appear that the reason the Preface which Ambedkar had written for *The Buddha and His Dhamma* on 15 March 1956 did not appear in the published version of that work was that it contained a reference to Mrs Ambedkar, for after the great leader's death his widow had become *persona non grata* to many of his followers and the publishers must have decided to omit the Preface out of consideration for their feelings.

With regard to the question of whether Ambedkar had really been able to complete *The Buddha and His Dhamma* in accordance with his original intentions, it is necessary to go back to the speech that he delivered at Dehu Road on 25 December 1955. In that speech he told his audience that he was writing a book explaining the tenets of Buddhism in simple language for the benefit of the common man, that it might take him a year to complete the work, but that when it was finished he would embrace Buddhism. Yet by February 1956 the last chapters of *The Buddha and His Dhamma* had been written and on 15 March he was able to compose his Preface. How was this possible? How had Ambedkar, then a very sick man, been able to complete in less than two months a task that he had thought might take him twelve? One can only assume that, realizing he did not have much longer to live, he had decided that instead of trying to complete *The Buddha and His Dhamma* in accordance with his original intentions he would bring it out just as it was and embrace Buddhism immediately afterwards. He was, in fact, extremely anxious that his book should be published without delay. On 5 May 1956 he wrote to S. S. Rege, the librarian of Siddharth College, Bombay: 'There is one urgent matter which I want you to attend to and that is the publication of my book *The Buddha and His Dhamma*.... I am in a great hurry and I want the book to be published by September the latest.'[514] The wingèd chariot was hurrying near, and Ambedkar could hear it. Less than three weeks later, on 24 May, he announced that he would embrace Buddhism in October 1956 – in other words, a month after the expected publication of his book.

What *The Buddha and His Dhamma* would have been like if Ambedkar had been able to complete it in accordance with his original intentions we can only speculate. There is little doubt, however, that its contents would have corresponded more closely to those of his proposed 'gospel of Buddhism', as described in 'The Buddha and the Future of His Religion', and that in addition to 'a short life of Buddha' and 'some of the important dialogues' it would have contained the 'Chinese' *Dharmapada* and 'Buddhist Ceremonies for birth, initiation, marriage, and death'. There is also little doubt that, in accordance with his own dictum that 'in preparing such a gospel the linguistic side of it must not be neglected',[515] Ambedkar would have given more attention to the literary style of the work. In the form in which we have it, *The Buddha and His Dhamma* is, stylistically speaking, quite rough in texture. This is particularly true of Book 3 and of Book 4, Parts 1 and 2. Indeed, it is at times difficult to resist the impression that one is reading notes that Ambedkar did not have time to work up properly or which he did not intend for publication – an impression that is reinforced by the fact that he was revising the proofs of the book right up to the time of his death. It is also likely that besides incorporating more material in *The Buddha and His Dhamma* and improving its style Ambedkar would have included a Table of Reference showing the sources he had utilized in compiling the work (as Carus had done in the case of *The Gospel of Buddha*), thus making his book more useful to the serious student.

But speculations of this sort need not be carried too far. Even though Ambedkar was unable to complete *The Buddha and His Dhamma* in accordance with his original intentions it is, nevertheless, a monument to his untiring industry, his exemplary devotion to the Buddha and his teaching, and his heartfelt desire to understand that teaching and relate it to the needs of his people – and it is these things that really matter. *The Buddha and His Dhamma* can, in fact, be compared to a well planned, solidly built, and beautifully decorated palace, some apartments of which the architect was obliged to leave unfinished. Though they are unfinished, so splendid is the palace as a whole, and so perfectly inhabitable, that as one enters the lofty portals and starts looking around one is struck less by any incompleteness in the execution of the work as by the genius of the architect and the grandeur of his overall design.

SOURCES

REMEMBERING AMBEDKAR

'Remembering Ambedkar' is edited from a talk given at the London Buddhist Centre in October 2006. The interview with Dhammachari Maitriveer Nagarjuna took place in Birmingham in 2011. 'B. R. Ambedkar, a great Buddhist' is an excerpt from a talk, 'Great Buddhists of the Twentieth Century', given in 1995 at the London headquarters of the Maha Bodhi Society and previously published by Windhorse Publications as a booklet.

BUDDHA AND THE FUTURE OF HIS RELIGION

This is edited from the transcript of a 1986 question-and-answer session on Dr Ambedkar's article 'Buddha and the Future of His Religion'.

THE MASS CONVERSION AND THE YEARS AFTER

The articles in this section from the *Maha Bodhi* were also included in the collection *Beating the Drum*; see *Complete Works*, vol. 8. The original handwritten manuscript of 'A whirling programme at Nagpur' by A. R. Kulakarni is held in the archive at Urgyen House, Adhisthana. The extract from Triyana Vardhana Vihara, Kalimpong Report 1957–1962 comes from a booklet published in Kalimpong in 1963; a copy is held in the archive at Urgyen House. Sangharakshita's handwritten talk notes are held in the archive at Urgyen House.

A NEW BUDDHIST MOVEMENT

This section is made up of edited transcripts of talks given in India in 1979, 1983, 1988, and 1992, and in England in 1983. Some of them have been published previously in India as *Dhammamegha* booklets: 'Dr Ambedkar's true greatness' in *Dhammamegha* no. 23 in January 1986, 'Buddhism in one word' in *Dhammamegha* no. 33, July 1988, 'The ten ornaments of the Buddhist' in *Dhammamegha* no. 53 in July 1992, and 'The path of the Dhamma' as *Dhammamegha* no. 52 in April 1993.

WISDOM BEFORE WORDS

This commentary was produced by editing and combining two seminars on the *Udāna* given in 1974 and 1975.

NOTES AND REFERENCES

FOREWORD

1 A speech delivered by Dr Ambedkar in Kathmandu, Nepal on 20 November 1956 at the Fourth Conference of the World Fellowship of Buddhists; see B. R. Ambedkar, *Buddha or Karl Marx*, Critical Quest, New Delhi 2005, p. 28.

2 'Dr Ambedkar and his Egalitarian Revolution', in Dr Babasaheb Ambedkar, *Writings and Speeches*, vol. 17 (part 3), Government of Maharashtra, Bombay 2003, p. 503.

3 The *varṇa* system is an oppressive hierarchical social stratification based on castes with descending order of respect. Four basic categories are defined: Brahmins (priests), Kshatriyas (warriors), Vaishyas (traders), and Shudras (workers/labourers, artisans). A social hierarchical structure defines caste-based occupation and divides humans on the basis of birth.

4 'Constitution Assembly Debates', in Dr Babasaheb Ambedkar, *Writings and Speeches*, vol. 13, Education Department, Government of Maharashtra, Bombay, 1994, p. 1217.

5 'Castes in India', in B. R. Ambedkar, *Writing and Speeches*, vol. 1, Government of Maharashtra, Bombay 2016, p. 9.

6 'Dr Ambedkar and his Egalitarian Revolution', in B. R. Ambedkar, *Writings and Speeches*, vol. 17 (part 3), Government of Maharashtra, Bombay 2003, p. 407.

7 B. R. Ambedkar, *The Buddha and His Dhamma*, book 3, part 1, Samyak Prakashan, New Delhi 2007, p. 227.

8 *Udāna* 1.4. For Sangharakshita's commentary, see pp. 436ff below.

9 *Sutta-Nipāta* 1.7, verse 21; for this translation see H. Saddhatissa, *The Sutta-Nipāta*, Curzon Press, Richmond 1994, p. 14.

10 2011 Census of India.

11 B. R. Ambedkar, *Annihilation of Caste*, in *Writings and Speeches*, vol. 1, Government of Maharashtra, Bombay 2016, p. 57.

12 B. R. Ambedkar, *Riddles in Hinduism: An Exposition to Enlighten the Masses*, *Writing and Speeches*, vol. 4, Government of Maharashtra, Bombay 1987, pp. 283.

13 Ibid.

14 This was the phrase the Buddha used when he exhorted his first disciples to go out and teach the Dharma 'for the welfare of the many'. See Vinaya Piṭaka i.21 (*Mahāvagga* 1.11), in I. B. Horner (trans.), *The Book of the Discipline*, part 4, Pali Text Society, Oxford 1996, p. 28.

15 A speech delivered by Dr Ambedkar in Kathmandu, Nepal on 20 November 1956 at the Fourth Conference of the World Fellowship of Buddhists; see B. R. Ambedkar, *Buddha or Karl Marx*, Critical Quest, New Delhi 2005, p. 28.

16 B. R. Ambedkar, *The Buddha and His Dhamma*, *Writings and Speeches*, vol. 11, Government of Maharashtra, Bombay 2016, p. 301.

17 B. R. Ambedkar, *Annihilation of Caste*, in *Writings and Speeches*, vol. 1, Government of Maharashtra, Bombay 2016, p. 75.

18 Ibid., p. 68.

19 See Appendix 1.

20 Dr Ambedkar's speech while embracing Buddhism, 15 October 1956, at the Diksha Bhumi.

21 Sangharakshita, *The History of My Going for Refuge*, in *Complete Works*, vol. 2, p. 439.

22 Personal conversation with Urgyen Sangharakshita at Adhisthana, UK, May 2018.

23 *Maha Bodhi*, Vaishak Number, vol. 58, Calcutta, May 1950; see also p. 71 below.

24 Speech delivered by Dr Ambedkar in Kathmandu, Nepal on 20 November 1956 at the Fourth Conference of the World Fellowship of Buddhists; see B. R. Ambedkar, *Buddha or Karl Marx*, Critical Quest, New Delhi 2005, p. 28.

VOICES FROM THE DHAMMA REVOLUTION

25 Jnanasuri's memories are edited from an interview with Vassika during the International Order Convention at Bodh Gaya, India, in February 2013.

26 Dharmarakshita's memories are edited from a conversation with Nagabodhi at Bhaja Retreat Centre in 1985. For a longer version, see Terry Pilchick (Nagabodhi), *Jai*

Bhim! Dispatches from a Peaceful Revolution, Windhorse Publications, Glasgow 1988, pp. 121–3.

27 For the published version of these lectures, see *Complete Works*, vol. 16, pp. 227ff.

28 This conversation was published as an appendix to the 1990 edition of Dr Ambedkar's *Annihilation of Caste*, Arnold Publishers, New Delhi.

29 *Dhammapada* 6.

30 FWBO *Newsletter* no. 41, winter 1979.

31 Terry Pilchick (Nagabodhi), *Jai Bhim! Dispatches from a peaceful Revolution*, Windhorse Publications, Glasgow 1988.

32 The lectures appear in edited form in *Complete Works*, vol. 9, pp. 163ff.

33 Padmasuri, *But Little Dust*, Windhorse Publications, Birmingham 1997.

34 From 'A Life for the Dharma', a talk about Atīśa given in Birmingham UK in 1999; see *Complete Works*, vol. 12.

35 We meet the two merchants at Vinaya Piṭaka i.4 (*Mahāvagga* 1.4); see I. B. Horner (trans.), *The Book of the Discipline*, part 4, Pali Text Society, Oxford 1996, pp. 5–6.

36 The Manuski Trust is a charity based in Pune, whose mission is 'to develop an All India Network of Social Activists inspired by the vision of a caste-free society and working towards community mobilisation to realise human and civil rights of marginalized people'.

37 For a powerful account of the conditions of women in India, see Valerie Mason-John (Vimalasara), *Broken Voices: untouchable women speak out*, India Research Press, New Delhi 2008.

38 Tarahridaya is the coordinator of the women's ordination process team in India, and Abhayanavita, after a very difficult early life, got involved with the Triratna community at the age of 13, learned to fight against social injustice and gender discrimination through the Ashvaghosha Project, which educates people through plays and songs, and now (2021) runs a hostel for vulnerable and abused women.

REMEMBERING AMBEDKAR: AN INTRODUCTION

39 Sangharakshita set up the Kalimpong branch of the Young Men's Buddhist Association (YMBA) in May 1950, soon after his arrival in Kalimpong. As well as lectures, debates, and recreational activities, there were free tutorials to help with examinations on which depended the futures of the many young men from diverse backgrounds who came along. See *Facing Mount Kanchenjunga*, in *Complete Works*, vol. 21, pp. 36–8.

40 Sangharakshita describes how he came to edit the *Maha Bodhi* in his memoir *In the Sign of the Golden Wheel*; see *Complete Works*, vol. 22, pp. 62ff.

41 For a facsimile and transcript, see pp. 30 and 32.

42 Rajgir, a town in Bihar, is the modern name for Rājagṛha ('house of the king'), which at the time of the Buddha was the capital of the ancient kingdom of Magadha in north-east India. Bimbisāra, long a disciple of the Buddha, was the king there until he was usurped by his son Ajātaśatru, and Rājagṛha was a centre of Buddhist activities from the early days. The First Council after the Buddha's death took place there, and the Vulture's Peak, where the Buddha gave many of his teachings, is close by. Dr Ambedkar's house in Bombay, which was named after the historical Rajgir, is now a museum dedicated to Dr Ambedkar's life.

43 Sangharakshita describes this situation and how it was resolved in his memoir *In the Sign of the Golden Wheel* in *Complete Works*, vol. 22, pp. 64–7.

44 Dr Ambedkar founded the People's Education Society on 8 July 1945, and the society established its first educational institution, Siddharth College of Arts and Science, in Bombay (re-named Mumbai) on 20 June 1946. It is still going strong as Siddharth College of Arts, Science and Commerce.

45 Sangharakshita describes his meeting with and ordination by U Chandramani in his memoir *The Rainbow Road from Tooting Broadway to Kalimpong*, *Complete Works*, vol. 20, pp. 403–13.

46 This was a Mr Bhandari. The Scheduled Castes Federation (SCF) was an organization in India founded by Dr Ambedkar in 1942 to campaign for the rights of the Dalit community.

47 For Sangharakshita's article in the *Maha Bodhi*, see pp. 93ff. below.

48 For a list of the twenty-two vows, see Appendix 1, p. 657.

49 'Buddha or Karl Marx', in Dr Babasaheb Ambedkar, *Writings and Speeches*, vol. iii, Education Department, Government of Maharashtra 1987, pp. 441–62.

50 For Sangharakshita's report of his tours in 1958–1961, first published in a report from his vihara in Kalimpong, see pp. 116ff. below.

51 Dhammachari Maitriveer Nagarjuna (Dr Santosh I. Raut) teaches in the Department of Aesthetics and Philosophy at the EFL University, Hyderabad.

52 Sangharakshita describes this in his memoir *In the Sign of the Golden Wheel* in *Complete Works*, vol. 22, pp. 64–7.

53 A. R. Kulkarni was the secretary and founder of the Buddha Society in Nagpur when Sangharakshita first

visited the city in 1953. For Sangharakshita's description of that visit and his impressions of Dr Kulkarni, a lawyer and brahmin who 'saw himself as a Hindu follower of the Buddha rather than as a Buddhist', see *In the Sign of the Golden Wheel*, in *Complete Works*, vol. 22, pp. 154–65. For Kulkarni's own memories of Sangharakshita's visit in 1956, see pp. 95ff. below.

54 For a description of these tours, and notes of the some of the talks given, see pp. 116ff. below.

55 The lecture was given at the London Buddhist Vihara in Chiswick, which was founded as the London branch of the Maha Bodhi Society in 1926 by Anagarika Dharmapala, whose biography Sangharakshita wrote and first published in 1952. For Sangharakshita's account of the writing of the biography, see chapter 18, 'Discovering Dharmapala', in *Facing Mount Kanchenjunga*, in *Complete Works*, vol. 21, pp. 367–89; and for the biography itself, see *Complete Works*, vol. 8.

56 Dr Ambedkar described some of his early experiences in a short volume called 'Waiting for a Visa', in Vasant Moon (ed.), Dr Babasaheb Ambedkar: *Writings and Speeches*, vol. xii, Education Department, Government of Maharashtra, Bombay 1993, part 1, pp. 661–91.

57 At a meeting in Poona (now Pune) on 21 May 1932, Dr Ambedkar is reported to have said,

> At present I am the most hated man in Hindu India. I am represented as a traitor, I am denounced as an enemy of the Hindus, I am cursed as a destroyer of Hinduism, and branded as the greatest enemy of the country. But believe me when I say that, when after some days the dust settles down and a review of the proceedings of the Round Table Conference is dispassionately taken by future historians, the future generations of the Hindus will acclaim my services to the nation. If they do not recognise, well, I would not care for their disapprobation.

Quoted in Dhananjay Keer, *Dr Ambedkar: Life and Mission*, third edition, Popular Prakashan, Bombay 1971, p. 201.

58 For an account of this speech see Dhanajay Keer, *Dr Ambedkar: Life and Mission*, Popular Prakashan, Bombay 1981, p. 253.

59 These twenty-two vows are listed in the Appendix 1, p. 657.

BUDDHA AND THE FUTURE OF HIS RELIGION: A COMMENTARY ON DR AMBEDKAR'S ARTICLE.

60 *Maha Bodhi*, Vaishak Number, vol. 58, Calcutta, May 1950.

61 This seems to have been the case. In the preface of *Dhamma as told by Dr Ambedkar* (ed. D. C. Ahir, Dalit Sahitya Prakashan, New Delhi 1990), Ambedkar is quoted as saying

> In 1950, the editor of the Maha Bodhi Society's journal of Calcutta asked me to write an article for the Vaisakha Number. In that article I argued that the Buddha's religion was the only religion which a society awakened by science could accept, and without which it would perish. I also pointed out that in the modern world, Buddhism was the only religion which it must have, to save itself.

62 *Vedanta Kesari* is a periodical which has been published by the Ramakrishna Mission since 1895. The May 1950 edition included an article called 'Buddhism and Dr Ambedkar'.

63 It's clear that this Kṛṣṇa / Kaṇha is a human being, not a god. He just happens to be called Kṛṣṇa, which means 'Dark One'. The sage Kaṇha appears in the *Ambaṭṭha Sutta*, *Dīgha Nikāya* 3; M. Walshe (trans.), *The Long Discourses of the Buddha*, Wisdom Publications, Boston 1995, pp. 111–124; or T. W. Rhys Davids (trans.), *Dialogues of the Buddha*, part 1, Pali Text Society, London 1973, pp. 108–22. Incidentally, the theme of this *sutta* is the pride of the Brahmin Ambaṭṭha.

64 *Dhammapada* 276: 'By you must the zealous effort be made. The Tathāgatās are only proclaimers of the Way.' (trans. Sangharakshita).

65 Aśvaghoṣa, *Buddhacarita*, i.9–10. See E. H. Johnston, *The Buddhacarita*, Motilal Banarsidass, Delhi 1984, p. 3.

66 Devadatta, who was a cousin of the Buddha, became a monk when the Buddha first returned to Kapilavatsu after his Enlightenment. His practice was exemplary and the Buddha praised it (*Udāna* 3.4). But then, having begun to develop psychic powers as a consequence of his diligent meditation, Devadatta became proud, and began to feel that the Buddha was not strict enough in teaching ascetic practices. He demanded that the Buddha should insist on five specific forms of asceticism, and when the Buddha refused, on the basis that the middle way should be followed rather than going to an extreme of asceticism, Devadatta and his followers separated from the Buddha and his followers, thus bringing about a grievous split in the Sangha. This

story is told at Vinaya Piṭaka ii.188 (*Cullavagga* 7.3); I. B. Horner (trans.), *The Book of the Discipline*, part 5, Pali Text Society, Oxford 1996, p. 264. For the full story and all its sources, see Reginald A. Ray, *Buddhist Saints in India*, Oxford University Press, New York and Oxford 1994, pp. 162–8.

67 See the *Kevaddha Sutta*, *Dīgha Nikāya* 11 (i.215); M. Walshe (trans.), *The Long Discourses of the Buddha*, Wisdom Publications, Boston 1995, pp. 175–6; or T. W. Rhys Davids (trans.), *Dialogues of the Buddha*, part 1, Pali Text Society, London 1973, p. 279.

68 For an account of what is called the 'Great Miracle', see Eugene Watson Burlingame (ed.), *Buddhist Legends*, part 3, Luzac, London 1969, pp. 45–7.

69 *Bhagavad Gītā* 4.7.

70 For example, in a speech given at the Constituent Assembly of India on 25 November 1949, Ambedkar said:

> *Bhakti* in religion may be a road to the salvation of the soul. But in politics, *Bhakti* or hero-worship is a sure road to degradation and to eventual dictatorship.

Bhagwan Das (ed.), *Thus Spoke Ambedkar*, vol. ii, Bheem Patrika Publications, Jullundur n. d., p. 185.

71 This is the *Mahāsīhanāda Sutta*, *Majjhima Nikāya* 12 (i.69–71), which describes the Buddha's ten powers; see Bhikkhu Ñāṇamoli and Bhikkhu Bodhi (trans.), *The Middle Length Discourses of the Buddha*, Wisdom Publications, Boston 1995, pp. 166–7; or I. B. Horner (trans.), *The Collection of the Middle Length Sayings*, vol. i, Pali Text Society, London, Henley & Boston 1976, pp. 93–5.

72 In the Pāli canon Mahāvira is called Nigaṇṭha Nātaputta, and his claim to omniscience is often discussed and disputed. For one of many examples, see the *Cūḷadukkhakkhandha Sutta*, *Majjhima Nikāya* 14 (i.93); Bhikkhu Ñāṇamoli and Bhikkhu Bodhi (trans.), *The Middle Length Discourses of the Buddha*, Wisdom Publications, Boston 1995, pp. 187–8; or I. B. Horner (trans.), *The Collection of the Middle Length Sayings*, vol. i, Pali Text Society, London, Henley & Boston 1976, pp. 122–3.

73 For example, the Buddha, asked by Vacchagotta whether it is true that, as he has heard, the Buddha claims to be omniscient and all-seeing, clarifies that this is a misrepresentation, but that he has the 'threefold true knowledge': knowledge of his past lives, knowledge with regard to the unfolding of the lives of others in accordance with their karma, and knowledge that his mind

has now been freed, the *āsavas* having been destroyed. *Tevijjavacchagotta Sutta*, *Majjhima Nikāya* 71 (i.482); I. B. Horner (trans.), *The Collection of the Middle Length Sayings*, vol. ii, Pali Text Society, Oxford 1994, pp. 159–61; or Bhikkhu Ñāṇamoli and Bhikkhu Bodhi (trans.), *The Middle Length Discourses of the Buddha*, Wisdom Publications, Boston 1995, pp. 587–8.

74 See Sangharakshita, *The Rainbow Road from Tooting Broadway to Kalimpong*, *Complete Works*, vol. 20, pp. 196–202, p. 336.

75 See ibid., pp. 279–80.

76 See *Kūṭadanta Sutta*, *Dīgha Nikāya* 5; M. Walshe (trans.), *The Long Discourses of the Buddha*, Wisdom Publications, Boston 1995, pp. 133–141; or T. W. Rhys Davids (trans.), *Dialogues of the Buddha*, part 1, Pali Text Society, London 1973, pp. 173–85.

77 See Sangharakshita, *The Rainbow Road from Tooting Broadway to Kalimpong*, *Complete Works*, vol. 20, p. 134.

78 For example, see the *Kūṭadanta Sutta*, in which the Buddha explains to Kūṭadanta, who has planned a great sacrifice of cows, goats, and sheep, that a much more profitable sacrifice is Going for Refuge to the Three Jewels and practising the precepts. Convinced, Kūṭadanta sets free the animals he had intended to slaughter: 'I grant them life, let them be fed with green grass and given cool water to drink, and let cool breezes play upon them.' See *Kūṭadanta Sutta*, *Dīgha Nikāya* 5; M. Walshe (trans.), *The Long Discourses of the Buddha*, Wisdom Publications, Boston 1995, pp. 133–41; or T. W. Rhys Davids (trans.), *Dialogues of the Buddha*, part 1, Pali Text Society, London 1973, pp. 173–85.

79 See Dr B. R. Ambedkar, *The Untouchables*, Bharatiya Buddha Shiksa Parishad, Shravasti 1977, pp. 117–9. Also Dr Babasaheb Ambedkar, *Writings and Speeches*, vol. vii, Education Department, Government of Maharashtra, Bombay 1990, pp. 346–7.

80 See the *Jīvaka Sutta*, *Majjhima Nikāya* 55 (i.370); Bhikkhu Ñāṇamoli and Bhikkhu Bodhi (trans.), *The Middle Length Discourses of the Buddha*, Wisdom Publications, Boston 1995, p. 474; or I. B. Horner (trans.), *The Collection of the Middle Length Sayings*, vol. ii, Pali Text Society, Oxford 1994, pp. 34–5.

81 D. T. Suzuki (trans.), *The Laṅkāvatāra Sūtra*, chapter 8, 'On Meat Eating', Motilal Banarsidass, Delhi 1999, pp. 211–21.

82 *Bṛhadāraṅyaka Upaniṣad* 4.4.1–7 is an early account of karma and rebirth; and there is also the *Chāndogya Upaniṣad*

5.10.7, although this looks like an interpolation.

83 The teaching of the Dharma by the various Buddhas is based on the two truths; namely, the relative (worldy) truth and the absolute (supreme) truth.

Nāgārjuna, *Mūlamadhyamakakārikā*, xxiv.8. See K. Inada (trans.), *A Translation of the Mulamadhyamakakarika*, Hokuseido Press, Tokyo 1970, p. 146. See also Sangharakshita, *A Survey of Buddhism*, *Complete Works*, vol. 1, p. 206.

84 *Bhagavad Gītā* 4.13.

85 See Dr B. R. Ambedkar, *The Untouchables*, Bharatiya Buddha Shiksa Parishad, Shravasti 1977, pp. 190–5, 204. Also Dr Babasaheb Ambedkar, *Writings and Speeches*, vol. vii, Education Department, Government of Maharashtra, Bombay 1990, pp. 372–5, 379.

86 Dr Ambedkar tells the stories of a number of low caste and outcaste disciples of the Buddha in *The Buddha and His Dhamma*, People's Education Society, Bombay 1991, pp. 129–33, 137–40. The stories of most of them come from the *Theragāthā*, for which see, for example, C. A. F. Rhys Davids (trans.), *Psalms of the Brethren*, Pali Text Society, London 1980: for Sunīta's story, pp. 271–5; for Sumaṅgala, pp. 47–8; for Suppiya, pp. 36–7; for Sopāka, pp. 37–8; and for Upāli, pp. 168–9. Another element of the story of Upāli the barber is told at Vinaya Piṭaka ii.182–3; see I. B. Horner (trans.), *The Book of the Discipline*, part 5, Pali Text Society, Oxford 1996, pp. 256–7. The story of Suppabuddha the leper is told in the *Udāna*; see below, pp. 549–56 and p. 563. And the story of Prakṛti, who gave Ānanda some water from the well, is told in *Divyāvadāna* 33, along with the ensuing complications; Sangharakshita discusses this story in *The Eternal Legacy*, in *Complete Works*, vol. 14, pp. 68–9), stating:

> The *Divyāvadāna* ... contains the highly popular story of Ānanda and Prakṛti. The latter, an outcaste girl from whom Ānanda had once begged water, falls deeply in love with the noble monk, and with the help of her mother, an enchantress, draws him to her house by means of spells. At the critical moment he is saved by the miraculous intervention of the Buddha. Prakṛti eventually becomes a nun. This gives rise to fresh complications, as the Hindu public strongly objects to a despised outcaste being given ordination, and complaints are made

to the king. Through the medium of a 'story of the past', with whose characters he identifies, the Buddha vindicates his own universalist outlook and severely criticizes the whole theoretical basis of the Brahminical caste structure.

The Buddha himself had difficulty getting water from a well which had been choked up by local Brahmins; see below pp. 622–6.

87 B. R. Nanda, *Gandhi and his Critics*, Oxford University Press, Delhi 1986.

88 B. R. Ambedkar, *What Congress and Gandhi have done to the Untouchables*, Thacker and Co., Bombay 1945.

89 See, for example, Dr Babasaheb Ambedkar, *Writings and Speeches*, vol. v, Education Department, Government of Maharashtra, Bombay 1979, pp. 131–3.

90 *Bhagavad Gītā* 3.35.

91 Christmas Humphreys (1901–1983) was an English barrister, and later a judge, whose theosophical interests led him to Buddhism. He wrote many books, widely read at a time when there was little available in English on Buddhism. The Buddhist Lodge of the Theosophical Society was one of the first Buddhist organizations in Europe. In 1926, breaking with the Theosophical Society, it was renamed the Buddhist Society. Humphreys was its president until the end of his life. Its activities continue to the present day.

92 The five orders of conditionality, or *niyamas*, are enumerated by Buddhaghosa in his commentary on the *Dhammasaṅgaṇī*, the first book of the Abhidhamma Piṭaka, vol. ii. See Pe Maung Tin (trans.), *The Expositor*, ch. 10, ed. C. A. F. Rhys Davids, Pali Text Society, London 1921, p. 360; also Buddhaghosa's commentary on the *Dīgha Nikāya*, ed. W. Stede, Pali Text Society 1920, p. 360 (not available in English translation). Sangharakshita's source is C. A. F. Rhys Davids, *Buddhism: a Study of the Buddhist Norm*, Williams and Norgate, London 1912, pp. 118–9. For Sangharakshita's account of them see, for example *The Three Jewels*, in *Complete Works*, vol. 2, pp. 69–70.

93 The Dalit population of India is now (2021) about 166,000,000 (16.6% of the population).

94 This refers to the affirmative action scheme established in 1950 whereby a quota of places in education and employment are reserved for people from 'Scheduled Castes, Scheduled Tribes, and Other Backward Classes'.

95 These riots in Ahmedabad and elsewhere in Gujarat began in

February 1985 and went on for about six months, during which many people were killed, through caste-related violence and also other community violence, particularly against Muslims.

96 For example, the Buddha describes the duties and rewards of employers and workers in the *Sigālaka Sutta*, *Dīgha Nikāya* 31 (iii.191); see M. Walshe (trans.), *The Long Discourses of the Buddha*, Wisdom Publications, Boston 1995, pp. 468; or T. W. and C. A. F. Rhys Davids (trans.), *Dialogues of the Buddha*, part 3, Pali Text Society, London 1971, p. 182. Sangharakshita discusses this text in *What is the Sangha?*, in *Complete Works*, vol. 3, pp. 585–8.

97 Published as Samuel Beal (trans. from Chinese), *Dhammapada: with accompanying narrative*, Susil Gupta, Calcutta 1952.

98 Eugene Watson Burlingame (ed.), *Buddhist Legends*, Luzac, London 1969.

99 Karl Marx wrote this passage in 1843 as part of the introduction to a book that criticized philosopher Georg Wilhelm Friedrich Hegel's 1820 book, *Elements of the Philosophy of Right*. The introduction was published in 1844 in a small journal. The book itself was published posthumously.

100 Molly Lefebure, *Samuel Taylor Coleridge: A Bondage of Opium*, Gollancz, London 1974.

101 The 'positive group' is one of a number of terms Sangharakshita used to describe the journey from being a group member to being a true individual. One is naturally a member of all kinds of groups based on family, nationality, occupation, and so on, in the context of which one may be an individual only in a statistical sense. In Sangharakshita's words, the goal is to become an individual in the sense of being one who is 'sufficiently integrated as an individual as to be able to make a valid commitment to the path to Enlightenment'. The relationships between individuals form the network of the spiritual community, which is at the heart of a wider network which Sangharakshita called the 'positive group': still a group, but one whose activities have one purpose: to help people grow and develop as individuals. See, for example, chapter 7, 'The positive group and the new society', in *What is the Sangha?*, in *Complete Works*, vol. 3, pp. 457–8.

102 See S. Radhakrishnan, *Indian Philosophy*, Oxford University Press, India 2009 (but first published in 1927), in which, as one critic puts it, 'S. Radhakrishnan explains away the radical project of Buddha and Buddhism

and portrays it as a part of Hinduism.'

103 Sangharakshita describes this situation and how it was resolved in his memoir *In the Sign of the Golden Wheel* in *Complete Works*, vol. 22, pp. 64–7.

104 The World Fellowship of Buddhists, founded in Sri Lanka in 1950, continues to meet, and has regional centres in many countries.

105 The situation changed over the years, Taiwanese Buddhists, for example, being supportive of many Triratna projects, as Lokamitra explains on p. li in the Foreword to this volume.

106 Dalit literature first emerged in the 1960s in Marathi, and it soon began to appear in other languages: Bangla, Hindi, Kannada, Punjabi, Telugu, and Tamil. Through poems, short stories, and autobiographies, the writers express their experience of caste discrimination and Dalit life. Once Dalit literature was recognized, it was considered to include writings of the past as well as more recent works.

107 The bodhisattva Mañjuśrī or Mañjughoṣa is indeed depicted wielding a sword, but the sword symbolizes not violence but discriminating wisdom which cuts through all delusion.

108 The Buddha's exhortation to his disciples to go forth and preach 'out of compassion for the world, for the welfare and happiness of gods and men' is to be found at Vinaya Piṭaka i.21 (*Mahāvagga* 1.11). I. B. Horner (trans.) *The Book of the Discipline*, part 4, Pali Text Society, Oxford 1996, p. 28.

109 These are said to have been the Buddha's last words to his disciples: *appamādena sampādetha* – 'With awareness (or mindfulness) strive.' *Mahāparinibbāna Sutta*, *Dīgha Nikāya* 16 (ii.156); M. Walshe (trans.), *The Long Discourses of the Buddha*, Wisdom Publications, Boston 1995, p. 270; or T. W. and C. A. F. Rhys Davids (trans.), *Dialogues of the Buddha*, part 2, Pali Text Society, London 1971, p. 173.

110 See note 31.

111 This talk was published as a booklet by Windhorse Publications in 1984 and appears in *Complete Works*, vol. 12.

112 This refers to the fundraising effort which began as the Poona Project and became the charity Aid for India founded by members of the Western Buddhist Order in 1980, and in 1987 renamed the Karuna Trust. The charity states,

> Since 1980, Karuna and its supporters have enabled people to overcome caste discrimination, finally gaining their own dignity and realising their potential as human beings. Based in the UK, we work with

in-country partners towards achieving the UN's Sustainable Development Goals of eliminating inequality, ensuring access to humane and decent work and basic education for all.

Projects supported are diverse, including the provision of medical, social, and educational support through clinics, hostels, and in many other ways. The charity raises funds through door-to-door fundraising appeals carried out by volunteers who live together in community for the period of the appeal; Karuna's fundraising approach is motivated by Buddhist ethics. For more information, visit www.karuna.org.

113 In February 2021 there were 710 Order members in India, 531 men and 179 women.

114 This happened, and continues to happen. In 1986 Order members in the West started a fund to help Indian Order members to come to the UK for Order conventions, and many have done so, as well as coming to the West to participate in all kinds of other activities.

115 See *Complete Works*, vol. 9, pp. 1–159.

THE MASS CONVERSION AND THE YEARS AFTER: 1956–1969

116 Sangharakshita was involved in the ceremonies that surrounded the return of the Sacred Relics to India; see *Facing Mount Kanchenjunga*, in *Complete Works*, vol. 21, chapter 10, pp. 170ff.

117 Vijayadashami (the ten-day victory) is a Hindu festival celebrated to commemorate the victory of the god Rama over the demon Ravana. (The story is told in the great Sanskrit epic the *Rāmāyaṇa* and is said to represent the triumph of the forces of good over the forces of evil.) 14 October is the day on which, in c.261 BCE, Emperor Aśoka converted to Buddhism. To the Buddhists of India, therefore, 14 October is known as Ashok Vijayadashami.

118 See note 58.

119 Reference to this editorial can be found in *In the Sign of the Golden Wheel* in *Complete Works*, vol. 22, pp. 350–2.

120 See note 53.

121 i.e. the Three Refuges and Five Precepts.

122 Dr Ambedkar included this famous mantra (that of Avalokiteśvara, the bodhisattva of compassion) in a puja book he published to coincide with his conversion to Buddhism (*Bauddha Puja Paath*, Bharatiya Bauddha Mahasabha, Bombay 1956). Sangharakshita chose to speak to the new Buddhists on this subject on many occasions, to explain its significance.

123 If this account reflects what Sangharakshita said on this

occasion, he subsequently came to see the sangha very differently. In 1961 he published an article called 'Wanted: A New Kind of Bhikkhu', followed the next year by 'Wanted: A New Type of Upāsaka', and in *The Three Jewels*, also written in 1961, he wrote:

> The Sangha is primarily the community of those who, by virtue of their immediate or remote approximation to Enlightenment, stand in spiritual relation to the Buddha and dwell spiritually in his presence. It is the community of those who, through their relationship with him, are also spiritually related to one another. (*The Three Jewels*, in *Complete Works*, vol. 2, p. 138.)

In other words, as he said many times, 'Going for Refuge is primary, lifestyle is secondary'. For much more on this subject, see part 3 of *The Three Jewels* and also *What is the Sangha?*, in *Complete Works*, vol. 3. See also pp. 265ff and pp. 385–6 below.

124 The twenty-four-spoked wheel (chakra) of the Dharma appeared on many of the stone pillars on which the edicts of the Emperor Aśoka were engraved, and the wheel was chosen as the emblem of the Indian flag adopted in 1947. One account of the wheel's symbolism has it that it reflects an aspect of the Buddha's teaching, the twenty-four spokes representing the twelve *nidānas* and their cessation.

125 Reference to this editorial can be found in *In the Sign of the Golden Wheel*, in *Complete Works*, vol. 22, pp. 366–7.

126 Venerable U Chandramani (1876–1972) was a Burmese *bhikkhu* based from 1904 in Kusinārā. He campaigned for the restoration of Buddhist viharas and stupas not only there but also at Sarnath, Lumbinī, and other Buddhist holy sites. It was at Kusinārā, in May 1949, that he conferred on Sangharakshita the *sāmaṇera* or novice ordination (*The Rainbow Road from Tooting Broadway to Kalimpong*, *Complete Works*, vol. 20, pp. 408–10).

127 From John Milton, *Samson Agonistes*, lines 986–7: 'my tomb / With odours visited and annual flowers.'

128 In 1978 building began on a stupa on the Diksha Bhumi that can accommodate more than 5,000 people. The monument was completed in 2001, and the site includes a Buddhist vihara and a bodhi tree as well as Buddha statues. The agricultural college was subsequently built at Akola.

PREACHING TOURS

1958–1961

129 Triyana Vardhana Vihara, Kalimpong Report 1957–1962, Kalimpong 1963, pp. 17–28.

130 'In Magadha' probably refers to the words of Brahma Sahampati imploring the Buddha to teach the Dharma after his Enlightenment. The story occurs in various places in the Pāli canon, but the speech beginning 'In Magadha' occurs in Vinaya Piṭaka i.4–7 (*Mahāvagga* 1.4–6):

> In Magadha there has appeared till now
> Impure law, thought out by men still stained.
> Open the Deathless Gateway. Let them hear
> The Law the Immaculate has found.

This translation is taken from Bhikkhu Ñāṇamoli, *The Life of the Buddha*, Buddhist Publication Society, Kandy 1978, p. 38. See also I. B. Horner (trans.), *The Book of the Discipline*, part 4, Pali Text Society, Oxford 1996, pp. 6–10.

In the *Brahmajāla Sutta*, which is the first *sutta* of the *Dīgha Nikāya*, the Buddha draws clear distinctions between the beliefs and practices of 'some ascetics and Brahmins' and his own views and practices; presumably that is what is meant here.

And perhaps the 'words to Subhadra' relate to the Buddha's teaching to Subhadra (Pāli Subhadda), who was the last person the Buddha taught, having approached him as he lay on his death-bed. Subhadra asks whether all the 'ascetics and Brahmins' of the day have realized the truth, as they make out they have, but the Buddha tells him not to worry about that, but that wherever the Noble Eightfold Path is found, it is there that true ascetics are to be found. See the *Mahāparinibbāna Sutta*, *Dīgha Nikāya* 16 (ii.148–52); M. Walshe (trans.), *The Long Discourses of the Buddha*, Wisdom Publications, Boston 1995, pp. 268; or T. W. and C. A. F. Rhys Davids (trans.), *Dialogues of the Buddha*, part 2, Pali Text Society, London 1971, pp. 166–8.

131 This is an allusion to the *White Lotus Sūtra*; see, for example, Bunnō Katō et al. (trans.), *The Threefold Lotus Sutra*, Kosei Publishing, Tokyo, 1975, pp. 246–8; and for Sangharakshita's commentary, see *The Drama of Cosmic Enlightenment*, in *Complete Works*, vol. 16, pp. 48–9.

132 Perhaps this is a reference to the story of Vakkali told in the Pāli canon. Vakkali is ill, and when the Buddha visits him, he says that his one regret is that he hasn't been able to see the Buddha before now, as he wasn't strong enough. But the Buddha says, 'Enough, Vakkali! What is there to see

in this vile body? He who sees Dhamma, Vakkali, sees me; he who sees me sees Dhamma. Truly seeing Dhamma, one sees me; seeing me one sees Dhamma.' See the *Vakkali Sutta*, *Khandasaṃyutta*, *Saṃyutta Nikāya* iii.120; F. L. Woodward (trans.), *The Book of the Kindred Sayings*, part 3, Pali Text Society, London & Boston 1975, p. 103; or Bhikkhu Bodhi (trans.), *The Connected Discourses of the Buddha*, Wisdom Publications, Boston 2000, p. 939.

133 *Sambhogakāya* is a term from the *trikāya* doctrine of the Mahāyāna, referring to archetypal, as distinct from historical, Buddhas. For a brief introduction to the five Buddhas of the mandala, see *What is the Dharma?*, in *Complete Works*, vol. 3, pp. 373–5.

134 *Śīla*, *samādhi*, *prajñā* (ethics, meditation, wisdom) are the steps of the threefold path, one of the Buddha's most frequent descriptions of the Buddhist path. I would guess that 'Bodhidharma' refers to a story Sangharakshita often told. It's said that an emperor once asked Bodhidharma to explain to him the Buddhist teaching, and was surprised to be told simply, 'Cease to do evil, learn to do good, purify your mind.' 'That's so simple a child of three could understand it,' he protested. But Bodhidharma said, 'Yes, but an old man of eighty couldn't put it into practice.' This legendary conversation is variously ascribed, frequently being held to have taken place between Bodhidharma, regarded as the first patriarch of the Chinese Chan tradition who lived in the fifth–sixth centuries CE and Xiao Yan, Emperor Wu of Liang (reigned 502–549). The verse he quotes to the emperor is *Dhammapada* 183. According to Dōgen, the exchange took place between Haku Kyo-i, the governor of Hangzhou, and Zen master Choka Dorin. See Master Dōgen, *Shōbōgenzō*, book 1, trans. Gudo Nishijima and Chodo Cross, Windbell, Woking 1994, pp. 106–8. Also quoted in Thomas Cleary (trans.), *Rational Zen: The Mind of Dōgen Zenji*, Shambhala Publications, Boston 1995, pp. 91–4.

135 A sequence *of suttas* on this theme is to be found at *Aṅguttara Nikāya* ii.95–100. See Bhikkhu Bodhi (trans.), *The Numerical Discourses of the Buddha*, Wisdom Publications, Boston 2012, pp. 476–80; or F. L. Woodward (trans.), *The Book of the Gradual Sayings*, vol. ii, Pali Text Society, Oxford 1995, pp. 104–7.

136 This is perhaps a reference to this observation of the psychoanalyst C. G. Jung. which Sangharakshita sometimes quotes:

Among all my patients in the second half of life – that is to say, over thirty-five – there has not been one whose problem in the last resort was not that of finding a religious outlook on life. It is safe to say that every one of them fell ill because he had lost that which the living religions of every age have given to their followers, and none of them has really been healed who did not regain his religious outlook. This of course has nothing to do with a particular creed or membership of a church.

'Psychotherapists or the Clergy' (1932), in Carl Gustav Jung, *Collected Works*, vol. 11, Routledge and Kegan Paul, London 1958, p. 334.

137 The Tathāgata, bhikkhus, the Arahant, the Perfectly Enlightened One, is the originator of the path unarisen before, the producer of the path unproduced before, the declarer of the path undeclared before. He is the knower of the path, the discoverer of the path, the one skilled in the path. And his disciples now dwell following that path and become possessed of it afterwards. This, bhikkhus, is the distinction, the disparity, the difference, between the Tathāgata, the Arahant, the Perfectly Enlightened One, and a bhikkhu liberated by wisdom.

Khandhasaṃyutta, *Saṃyutta Nikāya* iii.66. See Bhikkhu Bodhi (trans.), *The Connected Discourses of the Buddha*, Wisdom Publications, Boston 2000, p. 901; see also also F. L. Woodward (trans.), *The Book of the Kindred Sayings*, part 3, Pali Text Society, London & Boston 1975, p. 58. For discussion of this point see *A Survey of Buddhism*, *Complete Works*, vol. 1, pp. 50–6.

138 According to tradition, Sumedha was a Brahmin who lived countless ages ago at the time of the Buddha Dīpaṅkara. When Sumedha lay down in the mud so that Dīpaṅkara could walk across him, Dīpaṅkara realized that Sumedha would be a Buddha in the future – and indeed he is said to have become the Buddha of our own era, Śākyamuni. For Sumedha's story, see *The Three Jewels*, *Complete Works*, vol. 2, pp. 17–18; also (for Sumedha's *Jātaka* story) see T. W. Rhys Davids (trans.), *Buddhist Birth-Stories*, George Routledge, London 1950, pp. 83–112. A *kalpa* is an almost unimaginably long period of time, the time it takes for a whole world system to evolve and disappear. Traditionally, the duration of a *kalpa* is illustrated by the

following simile: suppose that every hundred years a piece of silk is rubbed once on a solid rock one cubic *yojana* in size; when the rock is worn away by this, one *kalpa* will still not have passed. See *Saṃyutta Nikāya* ii.181; Bhikkhu Bodhi (trans.), *The Connected Discourses of the Buddha*, Wisdom Publications, Boston 2000, p. 654; or F. L. Woodward (trans.), *The Book of the Kindred Sayings*, part 2, Pali Text Society, Oxford 1997, pp. 121–2.

139 In one of the *Jātaka* stories of the *Khuddaka Nikāya*, Prince Vessantara is shown giving away all that he has, from his elephant to his beloved children; see E. B. Cowell (ed.), *The Jātaka*, vol. 6, Pali Text Society, London 1895, pp. 246–305, and M. Cone and R. Gombrich (trans.), *The Perfect Generosity of Prince Vessantara*, Clarendon Press, Oxford 1977.

140 The Kanheri Caves are a group of caves and rock-cut monuments cut into a massive basalt outcrop in the forests of the Sanjay Gandhi National Park, on the former island of Salsette in the western outskirts of Mumbai, India. They contain Buddhist sculptures and relief carvings, paintings and inscriptions, dating from the first to the tenth centuries CE.

141 The *paritrāṇa* (Pāli *paritta*) is an ancient Buddhist practice. The word means 'protection' and the ceremony involves the chanting of Buddhist texts such as the *Mettā Sutta*.

142 The story of the tiger and the sheep is told below, p. 237.

143 This is a reference to the Buddha's advice to Kevaddha, a lay follower, and was that rather than miracles performed as demonstrations of magical powers, the true miracle was conversion to the Dharma. See the *Kevaddha Sutta*, *Dīgha Nikāya* 11 (i.214); M. Walshe (trans.), *The Long Discourses of the Buddha*, Wisdom Publications, Boston 1995, p. 176; or T. W. Rhys Davids (trans.), *Dialogues of the Buddha*, part 1, Pali Text Society, London 1973, p. 279.

144 Ambedkar and his entourage went on an expedition to a place in the neighbourhood of Mahad in order to see the excavations of some ruins that were believed to date from the time of the Buddha. Deeply moved by the sight of the sculptures that had been unearthed, Ambedkar described to the members of his entourage how the Buddha's disciples had lived lives of poverty and chastity and selflessly devoted themselves to the service of the community. In a reverential mood, he asked them not to sit on the ancient stone benches that formed part of the ruins since these may have been the seats of Buddhist monks.

Sangharakshita, *Ambedkar and Buddhism*, *Complete Works*, vol. 9, pp. 52–3.

145 See note 42 and above on p. 4.

146 Dhananjay Keer, *Dr Ambedkar: Life and Mission*, third edition, Popular Prakashan, Bombay 1971, p. 201.

147 Speech delivered by Dr Ambedkar to the Bombay Presidency Mahar Conference, 31 May 1936.

148 See above pp. 31ff.

149 Archimedes said, 'Give me a place to stand and with a lever I will move the whole world.' *The Library of History of Diodorus Siculus*, Fragments of Book 26, as translated by F. R. Walton, in *Loeb Classical Library* (1957), vol. xi.

150 Sangharakshita discusses the book in more detail in chapter 8 of *Ambedkar and Buddhism*; see *Complete Works*, vol. 9, pp. 136–49; also Appendix 2 in this volume.

151 This is 'The Deserted Village', published in 1770 by the English poet Oliver Goldsmith.

152 This was the organization founded by Sangharakshita's friend Dr Dinshah Mehta, whom Sangharakshita first met in Bombay in 1955. For Kalyanaprabha's account of the friendship, see 'The Monk and the Prophet', *Complete Works*, vol. 21, pp. 599–619.

153 For this translation, see *Complete Works*, vol. 17.

154 P.E.N. is an international association of writers. The PEN Club was founded in London in 1921, the initials standing for 'Poets, Essayists, Novelists'; this was later expanded to include playwrights and editors. It is now known as PEN International and has branches in many countries; among its aims is 'to create a world community of writers that would emphasize the central role of literature in the development of world culture'.

155 The Second Buddhist Council took place in Vaiśālī about a hundred years after the Buddha's *parinirvāṇa*. It was here that there was a doctrinal split between two groups of monks, the Theravādins and the Mahāsāṃghikas, in which can be seen the beginnings of Mahāyāna Buddhism. For more details, see *A Survey of Buddhism*, *Complete Works*, vol. 1, pp. 186–7.

156 'The teaching of the Dharma by the various Buddhas is based on the two truths; namely, the relative (worldy) truth and the absolute (supreme) truth.' Nāgārjuna, *Mūlamadhyamakakārikā*, xxiv.8. See K. Inada (trans.), *A Translation of the Mulamadhyamakakarika*, Hokuseido Press, Tokyo 1970, p. 146. See also Sangharakshita, *A Survey of Buddhism*, *Complete Works*, vol. 1, p. 206.

157 The three *yānas* (vehicles) are the three historical phases of the development

of Buddhism: the Hīnayāna (more neutrally referred to as early Buddhism), the Mahāyāna, and the Vajrayāna. In Tibetan Buddhism the three *yānas* came to be seen as constituting successive stages of the path. For more about this, see Sangharakshita, *Tibetan Buddhism*, *Complete Works*, vol. 13, p. 12 (and there are other references in this work).

158 *Abhiṣeka* literally means 'a sprinkling', but the inner meaning is 'transmission of power', the transmission that occurs when a teacher initiates a disciple into a Tantric practice; 'Tantric meditation cannot be practised without a guru'. See *Tibetan Buddhism*, *Complete Works*, vol. 13, pp. 88–91.

159 The *satkāryavāda* line of reasoning was 'held at the time of Nāgārjuna by the [Hindu] Sāṃkhya School,... it may be regarded as the representative Brahminical view of causation'; the *asatkāryavāda* 'was upheld by the Sarvāstivādins and Sautrāntikas, and is the representative Hīnayāna view.' Sangharakshita, *A Survey of Buddhism*, *Complete Works*, vol. 1, p. 314, quoting Surendranath Dasgupta, *A History of Indian Philosophy*, vol. 1, Motilal Banarsidass, Delhi 1975, p. 115.

160 *Puṇya anumodanā* is 'rejoicing in merits', a key Buddhist practice, and *śraddhā* is 'faith', but the point is obscure.

161 *Dhammapada* 165.

162 A *dhāraṇī* is a 'sort of protective mantra' which 'has some sort of magical potency'; see *The Inconceivable Emancipation*, *Complete Works*, vol. 16, pp. 496–7. The *Saddharma Puṇḍarīka* (*White Lotus Sūtra*) has a chapter of *dhāraṇīs* (chapter 26) and another example is the 'Great Crown' *dhāraṇī* at the end of the *Śūraṅgama Sūtra* in Dwight Goddard (ed.), *A Buddhist Bible*, Beacon Press, Boston 1970, p. 272. And see also the *Sūtra of Golden Light*: 'I will bestow ... a Dhāraṇī for the sake of preventing the loss of its memory.' R. Emmerick (trans.), *The Sūtra of Golden Light*, Pali Text Society, London 1979, p. 44.

163 See note 158.

164 *Issara-nimmāna-vāda* (belief in a Creator God) is described in *Brahmajāla Sutta*, *Dīgha Nikāya* 1 (i.19); M. Walshe (trans.), *The Long Discourses of the Buddha*, Wisdom Publications, Boston 1995, p. 76; or T. W. Rhys Davids (trans.), *Dialogues of the Buddha*, part 1, Pali Text Society, London 1973, p. 31. The *avyākatas* (Sanskrit *avyākṛtas*) are the 'indeterminate questions' identified by the Buddha, such as 'Is the world eternal?', 'Is the self the same as the body?', 'Does the Buddha exist

after death?'. The Pāli texts give only ten, the Sanskrit texts fourteen questions. But the Buddha said that such questions are unprofitable. See, for example, Bhikkhu Ñāṇamoli and Bhikkhu Bodhi (trans.), *The Middle Length Discourses of the Buddha*, Wisdom Publications, Boston 1995, p. 591; or I. B. Horner (trans.), *The Collection of the Middle Length Sayings*, vol. ii, Pali Text Society, Oxford 1994, pp. 164–5.

165 Anagarika Dharmapala, who was born in Sri Lanka, did much to restore the Buddhist sacred sites and founded the Maha Bodhi Society. For Sangharakshita's account of his mission work to London, see *Anagarika Dharmapala: A Biographical Sketch*, Ibis Publications, Ledbury 2013, pp. 62–3; see also *Complete Works*, vol. 8.

166 Mahāpajāpatī Gotami (Sanskrit Mahāprajāpatī Gautami) was the Buddha's aunt, and her question to the Buddha was 'How can I tell what is your teaching, when different people give such different accounts of it?' The Buddha told her that whatever conduced to dispassion, contentment, solitude, frugality, and so on could be considered to be his Dharma. The story is to be found at Vinaya Piṭaka ii.258–9 (*Cullavagga* 10.5); see I. B. Horner (trans.), *The Book of the Discipline*, part 5, Pali Text Society, Oxford 1996, p. 359. Also *Aṅguttara Nikāya* iv.280; E. M. Hare (trans.), *The Book of the Gradual Sayings*, vol. iv, Pali Text Society, Oxford 1995, pp. 186–7; or Bhikkhu Bodhi (trans.), *The Numerical Discourses of the Buddha*, Wisdom Publications, Boston 2012, p. 1193. For the parable of the raft, see note 197. For Sangharakshita's commentary, see, for example, the introduction to *What is the Dharma?* in *Complete Works*, vol. 3, pp. 165–6.

167 This refers to the Buddha's saying that just as the ocean has one taste, the taste of salt, the Dharma has but one taste: the taste of freedom. This is the sixth of the eight qualities of the great ocean described by the Buddha in the *Uposatha Sutta*, *Udāna* 5.5. See below p. 557.

168 *Dṛṣṭis* (Pāli *diṭṭhis*) are 'views', so 'formulate *dṛṣṭis*' may refer to the need to cultivate right view, *samyag-dṛṣṭi*, the first stage of the Noble Eightfold Path. *Mithyā-dṛṣṭis* (Pāli *micchā-diṭṭhis*) are wrong views. The importance to Buddhist practice of the removal of wrong views is indicated by the fact that the net of views (sixty-two in total) is the major subject of the first *sutta* of the *Dīgha Nikāya*, the *Brahmajāla Sutta*. Wrong views are not generally consciously adopted; they

tend to be the way we see things, whether we are aware of it or not, and one way to see Buddhist practice is in terms of the identification and overturning of wrong views so that Perfect Vision may arise. For a sense of the kinds of views meant, see, for example, Sangharakshita, *The Meaning of Orthodoxy in Buddhism*, in *Complete Works*, vol. 7, pp. 514ff.

169 *Udāna* 6.4 (*Paṭhamanānātitthiya Sutta*); see below, p. 594–6.

170 See note 159.

171 *Ātmavāda* refers to the Hindu conception of the spiritual path (the 'way of the soul'). In his 1948 article 'Progress and Religion' Sangharakshita discusses it (as Ātmanism), saying: 'The materialist and Ātmanist views ... are, in spite of the fact that in one sense they represent opposite poles of thought, identical inasmuch as they equally invalidate the ideal of progress and in fact preclude it altogether.' See *Early Writings*, Ibis Publications, Ledbury 2014, p. 186; also *Complete Works*, vol. 7, pp. 129ff.

172 Pāli *suttas* list 'the one freed by faith', *śraddhā-carita*, as one of the seven types of person, the others being

> the one who is freed both ways, the one freed by means of intuitive wisdom, the mental realizer, the one won to view, the striver after dhamma, and the striver after faith.

See, for example, the *Kīṭāgiri Sutta*, *Majjhima Nikāya* 70 (i.478–9); Bhikkhu Ñāṇamoli and Bhikkhu Bodhi (trans.), *The Middle Length Discourses of the Buddha*, Wisdom Publications, Boston 1995, pp. 580–1; or I. B. Horner (trans.), *The Collection of the Middle Length Sayings*, vol. ii, Pali Text Society, Oxford 1994, pp. 151–3. The *Buddhānusmṛti*, *Dharmānusmṛti*, and *Saṅghānusmṛti* are the practices of recollecting the Three Jewels, and *iti'pi so* is the opening of the *Tiratana Vandanā*, the salutation to the Three Jewels.

173 See note 122.

174 For a brief introduction to the *Kāraṇḍa-vyūha Sūtra*, see *The Eternal Legacy*, *Complete Works*, vol. 14, pp. 177–8. An English translation of the *sūtra* by Peter Alan Roberts is titled *The Basket's Display*.

175 This story is of a fish who had lived all its life in a lake and one day happened to meet a turtle who had been for a wander on dry land. The turtle tried to describe the land to the fish, but the fish could make no sense of the idea of something which wasn't wet or cool, or transparent, or any of the other qualities of water, and concluded in the

end that dry land could be 'nothing'. But the turtle said, 'Anyone who knows what is water and what is land would say that you are a silly fish, for you think that anything you have never known is nothing just because you have never known it.' The story is told in Maha Thera Narada, *The Buddha and His Teachings*, Apothecaries Co., Colombo 1973, pp. 288–9.

176 The *cintāmaṇi* is the 'wish-fulfilling' jewel, which in Buddhism has come to symbolize the *bodhicitta*, the aspiration for Enlightenment for the benefit of all. See 'The Jewel in the Lotus', chapter 7 of *The Drama of Cosmic Enlightenment*, *Complete Works*, vol. 16, pp. 174–5.

177 These are the first two words of the first verse of the *Dhammapada*: 'Experiences are preceded by mind'. The full verse is: 'Experiences are preceded by mind, led by mind, and produced by mind.' (trans. Sangharakshita)

178 This is how Śāntideva described the *bodhicitta*. See Śāntideva, *Bodhicaryāvatāra* iii.27.

179 The Buddha's vision of humanity like a bed of lotuses is described at *Saṃyutta Nikāya* i.138; see Bhikkhu Bodhi (trans.), *The Connected Discourses of the Buddha*, Wisdom Publications, Boston 2000, p. 233; or C. A. F. Rhys Davids (trans.), *The Book of the Kindred Sayings*, part 1, Pali Text Society, London, Henley & Boston 1979, p. 174. See also Vinaya Piṭaka i.6; I. B. Horner (trans.), *The Book of the Discipline*, part 4, Pali Text Society, Oxford 1996, p. 9.

180 As pink lotuses, sweet-scented and lovely, spring from a heap of rubbish thrown in the highway, so among those who have become (as) rubbish, (among) ignorant, ordinary people, the Disciple of the Perfectly Enlightened One shines forth exceedingly in wisdom.

Dhammapada 58–9, trans. Sangharakshita.

181 Just as the great ocean gradually shelves, slopes, and inclines, and there is no sudden precipice, so also in this Dhamma and Discipline there is a gradual training, a gradual course, a gradual progression, and there is no sudden penetration to final knowledge.

Udāna 5.5 in John D. Ireland (trans.), *The Udāna and the Itivuttaka*, Buddhist Publication Society, Kandy 1997, p. 71. See also below pp. 557–8.

182 The spiritually immature person vexes himself (thinking), 'Sons are mine, riches are mine'. He himself

is not his own, even; how
then sons? how then riches?

Dhammapada 62, trans. Sangharakshita.

183 This may be a reference to the famous discussion by the fourth-century St Augustine of Hippo (in *Faith and Grace*) as to whether salvation comes through faith alone or through faith and works. In his memoirs Sangharakshita describes how as a teenager he himself argued the case for faith and works. See *The Rainbow Road from Tooting Broadway to Kalimpong*, *Complete Works*, vol. 20, p. 44.

184 A sequence of *suttas* on this theme is to be found at *Aṅguttara Nikāya* ii.95–100; Bhikkhu Bodhi (trans.), *The Numerical Discourses of the Buddha*, Wisdom Publications, Boston 2012, pp. 476–80; or F. L. Woodward (trans.), *The Book of the Gradual Sayings*, vol. ii, Pali Text Society, Oxford 1995, pp. 104–7.

185 Tathāgata is a title of the Buddha. It can mean 'one thus gone' or 'one thus come'. A Buddha goes from the world through wisdom – seeing its illusory nature. He comes into it through compassion – in order to teach living beings how to put an end to suffering.

186 For the four additional *pāramitās*, see *A Survey of Buddhism*, *Complete Works*, vol. 1, pp. 448–50; and for more about the elements of *upāya-kauśalya*, see *The Inconceivable Emancipation*, in *Complete Works*, vol. 16, pp. 485–91.

187 *Pramāṇa* means 'valid cognition'. In Buddhism, it refers to the tradition, principally associated with Dignāga and Dharmakīrti, of logic and epistemology. According to this tradition, Buddhism accepts only two *pramāṇas* as valid means to knowledge: *pratyakṣa* (perception) and *anumāna* (inference).

188 See note 109.

189 It's possible that the Japanese story referred to is one that Sangharakshita liked to tell about a young man who wanted to learn from a meditation teacher, but couldn't remember on which side of the door he had left his umbrella, and was asked to come back when he had learned to be more mindful. See *What is the Dharma?*, *Complete Works*, vol. 3, p. 286; and *The Purpose and Practice of Buddhist Meditation*, *Complete Works*, vol. 5, p. 72.

190 This was the Buddha's teaching to Bāhiya of the Bark-cloth, who asked the Buddha three times – even though the Buddha was on his almsround – to give him a teaching 'for my good and happiness for a long time'. The Buddha finally told him

to train himself thus: 'In the seen, only the seen....' *Udāna* 1.10; John D. Ireland (trans.), *The Udāna and the Itivuttaka*, Buddhist Publication Society, Kandy 1997, p. 21; for Sangharakshita's commentary, see below pp. 458–65.

191 *Saṃyutta Nikāya* v.115 (*Mahāvagga* 46.53); Bhikkhu Bodhi (trans.), *Connected Discourses of the Buddha*, Wisdom Publications, Boston 2000, p. 1607; or F. L. Woodward (trans.), *The Book of the Kindred Sayings*, part 5, Pali Text Society, London, Henley & Boston 1979, p. 98.

192 See note 190. The key point here is that according to the text, 'the mind of Bāhiya of the Bark-cloth was immediately freed from the taints without grasping'. In other words, Insight immediately arose.

193 'Thou canst not travel on the Path before thou hast become that Path itself.' H. P. Blavatsky in *The Voice of the Silence* (published 1898), a Theosophist work.

194 This refers to the famous trial in 1960 of Penguin Books for the publication of D. H. Lawrence's novel *Lady Chatterley's Lover*. Penguin won the case.

195 Sangharakshita discusses this classification further in his lecture 'The Glory of the Literary World'; see *Complete Works*, vol. 14, pp. 302–4.

196 The text of the *Tiratana Vandanā*, which is often chanted in the context of Buddhist ritual, is found in several places in the Pāli canon, notably in the *Mahāparinibbāna Sutta*, *Dīgha Nikāya* 16 (ii.93); M. Walshe (trans.), *The Long Discourses of the Buddha*, Wisdom Publications, Boston 1995, p. 241; or T. W. and C. A. F. Rhys Davids (trans.), *Dialogues of the Buddha*, part 2, Pali Text Society, London 1971, pp. 99–100. Buddhaghosa discusses the elements of the text in great detail at *Visuddhimagga* 198–221; Bhikkhu Ñāṇamoli (trans.), *The Path of Purification*, Buddhist Publication Society, Kandy 1991, pp. 188–215; or Pe Maung Tin (trans.), *The Path of Purity*, Pali Text Society, London 1975, pp. 227–56. For Sangharakshita's commentary on this phrase, that the Dharma is well communicated, see *What is the Dharma?*, *Complete Works*, vol. 3, pp. 160–2.

197 In the parable of the raft, the Buddha conjures up the image of a raft that is used to cross the water, but can then be discarded, as it is no longer required, and compares it to the Dharma, which is no longer needed once the flood of *saṃsāra* has been crossed. The parable is told in the *Alagaddūpama Sutta*, *Majjhima Nikāya* 22 (i.134–5); Bhikkhu Ñāṇamoli

and Bhikkhu Bodhi (trans.), *The Middle Length Discourses of the Buddha*, Wisdom Publications, Boston 1995, pp. 228–9; or I. B. Horner (trans.), *The Collection of the Middle Length Sayings*, vol. i, Pali Text Society, London, Henley & Boston 1976, pp. 173–4.

198 See Nāgārjuna, *Mūlamadhyamakakārikā* xxiv.15:

> When you foist on us
> All of your errors
> You are like a man who has mounted his horse
> And has forgotten that very horse.

Jay L. Garfield (trans.), *The Fundamental Wisdom of the Middle Way*, Oxford University Press, New York 1995, p. 69.

199 *Saṃyutta Nikāya* v.115 (*Mahāvagga* 46.53); Bhikkhu Bodhi (trans.), *Connected Discourses of the Buddha*, Wisdom Publications, Boston 2000, p. 1607; or F. L. Woodward (trans.), *The Book of the Kindred Sayings*, part 5, Pali Text Society, London, Henley & Boston 1979, p. 98.

200 These similes are found in various places including the *Mahā-assapura Sutta*, *Majjhima Nikāya* 39 (i.276–9); see Bhikkhu Ñāṇamoli and Bhikkhu Bodhi (trans.), *The Middle Length Discourses of the Buddha*, Wisdom Publications, Boston 1995, pp. 367–9; or I. B. Horner (trans.), *The Collection of the Middle Length Sayings*, vol. i, Pali Text Society, London, Henley & Boston 1976, pp. 330–2. See also the *Mahāsakuludāyi Sutta*, *Majjhima Nikāya* 77 (ii.15–17); Bhikkhu Ñāṇamoli and Bhikkhu Bodhi, ibid., pp. 641–2; or I. B. Horner (trans.), *The Collection of the Middle Length Sayings*, vol. ii, Pali Text Society, Oxford 1994, pp. 216–7.

201 See note 159.

202 The *catuṣkoṭi* is the 'fourfold negation': the logical argument that goes 'not this, not that, not both, not neither'. It crops up often in the Pāli canon, for example in the *Aggivacchagotta Sutta*, *Majjhima Nikāya* 72 (i.484–9); Bhikkhu Ñāṇamoli and Bhikkhu Bodhi (trans.), *The Middle Length Discourses of the Buddha*, Wisdom Publications, Boston 1995, pp. 590–4; or I. B. Horner (trans.), *The Collection of the Middle Length Sayings*, vol. ii, Pali Text Society, Oxford 1994, pp. 162–7. See also the parable of the poisoned arrow, in the *Cūḷamāluṅkya Sutta*, *Majjhima Nikāya* 63 (i.427–32); Bhikkhu Ñāṇamoli and Bhikkhu Bodhi (trans.), *The Middle Length Discourses of the Buddha*, Wisdom Publications, Boston 1995, p. 533–6; or I. B. Horner (trans.), *The Collection of the

Middle Length Sayings, vol. ii, Pali Text Society, Oxford 1994, p. 99. Nāgārjuna, the founder of the Madhyamaka school of Mahāyāna Buddhism, makes great use of the *catuṣkoṭi*, for example in chapter 25 of the *Mūlamadhyamakakārikā*, considering whether Nirvāṇa exists, or does not exist, or both, or neither.

203 Lama Anagarika Govinda was a German Buddhist scholar and writer whom Sangharakshita met and became friends with in the Himalayan town of Kalimpong, the two in particular sharing a belief in the important place of art in the spiritual life. In 1947 Lama Govinda and his wife Li Gotami moved to Kasar Devi, near Almora in northern India.

204 This was D. T. Suzuki, the great proponent of Zen Buddhism, who at the age of ninety visited India for a month in 1960 at the invitation of the Indian government.

205 Huineng tells the story of how he gained Enlightenment when he chanced to hear the *Diamond Sūtra* in the first chapter of the *Sūtra of Huineng* (*Sūtra Spoken by the Sixth Patriarch*). See, for example, Dwight Goddard (ed.), *A Buddhist Bible*, Beacon Press, Boston 1970, pp. 497–8.

206 See Edward Conze (trans.), *Buddhist Wisdom Books*, Unwin Hyman, London 1988.

207 This refers to a copy of the *Diamond Sūtra* that was discovered in Dunhuang, China, in 1900 and is now held by the British Library. It is the earliest dated example of woodblock printing, and is acknowledged to be the world's earliest surviving dated complete book. It is a scroll sixteen feet long by 10.5 inches wide, made up of seven strips of yellow-stained paper printed from carved wooden blocks and pasted together.

208 Sangharakshita's commentary on the *Diamond Sūtra* (based on a seminar) was later published as part of a book called *Wisdom Beyond Words*; see *Complete Works*, vol. 14, pp. 323ff.

209 This refers to Karl Marx's argument known as historical materialism and Thomas Carlyle's statement of what has since been called the 'great man theory of history'. Thomas Carlyle (1795–1881) was a Scottish essayist and satirist, historian, and mathematician. In *On Heroes, Hero Worship, and the Heroic in History*, published in 1841, he wrote

> As I take it, Universal History, the history of what man has accomplished in this world, is at bottom the History of the Great Men who have worked here.

210 This is probably a reference to the *Sigālaka Sutta*, in

which the Buddha comes across a young man called Sigālaka standing in the river worshipping the six directions and explains that true worship of the six directions consists of carrying out one's duties in regard to six kinds of relationship. See the *Sigālaka Sutta* (also known as the *Sigālovāda Sutta*), *Dīgha Nikāya* 31 (iii.180–93); M. Walshe (trans.), *The Long Discourses of the Buddha*, Wisdom Publications, Boston 1995, pp. 461–9; or T. W. and C. A. F. Rhys Davids (trans.), *Dialogues of the Buddha*, part 3, Pali Text Society, London 1971, pp. 173–84. For Sangharakshita's commentary on the text, see *What is the Sangha?* part 3, 'The Network of Human Relationships', in *Complete Works*, vol. 3, pp. 521ff.

211 See note 57.

212 *Namkaran* is the baby naming ceremony.

213 See note 44.

214 *Udāna* 6.4 (*Paṭhamanānātitthiya Sutta*); see below, pp. 594ff.

215 To the Kālāmas of Kesaputta, the Buddha said,

> Come, Kālāmas, do not go by oral tradition, by lineage of teaching, by hearsay, by a collection of scriptures, by logical reasoning, by inferential reasoning, by reasoned cogitation, by the acceptance of a view after pondering it, by the seeming competence of a speaker, or because you think: 'The ascetic is our guru.' But when, Kālāmas, you know for yourselves: 'These things are unwholesome; these things are blameworthy; these things are censured by the wise; these things, if accepted and undertaken, lead to harm and suffering,' then you should abandon them.

Kālāma Sutta, *Aṅguttara Nikāya* i.188–93 (3.65) in Bhikkhu Bodhi (trans.), *The Numerical Discourses of the Buddha*, Wisdom Publications, Boston 2012, pp. 279–83. See also F. L. Woodward (trans.), *The Book of the Gradual Sayings*, vol. i, Pali Text Society, Oxford 2000, pp. 170–5.

216 Herbert Spencer (1820–1903) was an English philosopher who wrote about many subjects, including evolutionary theory. (It was he, not Charles Darwin, who coined the phrase 'survival of the fittest'.) This could be a reference to his thinking expressed in the book *First Principles*, which was first published in 1862, and whose main theme is what he called the 'knowable' and the 'unknowable'. He believed there is a basic and final reality beyond our knowledge, which he called the Unknowable,

and also often refers to as the Unconditioned, a term which Sangharakshita also often uses.

217 The Karle or Karla caves are a complex of rock-cut caves near Lonavala in Maharashtra. They were developed by Buddhists over a long period, from the second century BCE to the fifth century CE. Perhaps in his talk Sangharakshita made reference to the many carvings of animals in the caves: elephants, lions, and others. The nearby Bhaja caves, which have a similar history, are very close to the Saddhamma Pradeep Retreat Centre, Triratna's first retreat centre in India.

218 These are the four *pārisuddhi sīlas*, the four 'kinds of morality consisting of purification'. Nyanatiloka gives canonical references for these in his *Buddhist Dictionary*, Buddhist Publication Society, Kandy 1980, pp. 200–1, and they are listed among the tetrads identified by Buddhaghosa at *Visuddhimagga* 15–17; Bhikkhu Ñāṇamoli, *The Path of Purification*, Buddhist Publication Society, Kandy 1991, pp. 19–20.

219 At *Visuddhimagga* 102–10, Buddhaghosa identifies six 'kinds of temperament'. As well as 'greedy' and 'hating'; the other four are 'deluded', 'faithful', 'intelligent', and 'speculative'. See Bhikkhu Ñāṇamoli (trans.), *The Path of Purification*, Buddhist Publication Society, Kandy 1991, pp. 101–10; or Pe Maung Tin (trans.), *The Path of Purity*, Pali Text Society, London 1975, pp. 118–28.

220 The 'hate-type' is identified by Buddhaghosa at *Visuddhimagga* 102–10 as one of six kinds of temperament: greedy, hating, deluded, faithful, intelligent, and speculative.

In *The Purpose and Practice of Buddhist Meditation*, *Complete Works*, vol. 5, pp. 390–1, Sangharakshita notes:

> You can practise anything if you make sufficient effort, regardless of temperament; it is just a question of the degree of effort that is needed. If you were of a hate type, you might say that the *mettā bhāvanā* wasn't suited to you, but that's what you need, even though it's very difficult for you to practise it, and maybe someone of a greedy temperament will find it much easier.

221 Whether or not Sangharakashita meant to speak of 'contempt' here, he later came to refer to the near enemy of compassion as 'horrified anxiety'. In the *Visuddhimagga*, Buddhaghosa, who first referred to these 'near enemies' and 'far enemies', says that the near enemy of compassion is 'grief

based on the home life', 'since both share in seeing failure'. *Visuddhimagga* 319; Bhikkhu Ñāṇamoli (trans.), *The Path of Purification*, Buddhist Publication Society, Kandy 1991, p. 311.

222 See note 122.

223 *Yathābhūta-jñānadarśana* means 'knowledge and vision of things as they really are'. It is the eighth of the twelve positive *nidānas* or links, and represents the point of Stream Entry, or the arising of Insight. Chapter 7 of Sangharakshita, *What is the Dharma?*, 'The Spiral Path', gives a detailed account of the positive *nidānas*; see *Complete Works*, vol. 3, pp. 258–79, and for 'knowledge and vision of things as they really are' see pp. 274–5.

224 The *kasiṇa* meditation practices involve taking as an object of concentration a disc of very pure, bright colour – red or blue or green, etc., according to temperament. There are ten *kasiṇas* described in Buddhaghosa's *Visuddhimagga* 118–175; see Bhikkhu Ñāṇamoli, *The Path of Purification*, Buddhist Publication Society, Kandy 1991, pp. 118–70. See also *The Purpose and Practice of Buddhist Meditation*, in *Complete Works*, vol. 5, pp. 566ff.

225 The *Kāraṇḍa-vyūha Sūtra* is a Mahāyāna *sūtra* all about the bodhisattva Avalokiteśvara, including the origin of the mantra *oṃ maṇi padme hūṃ*. For a brief introduction to the *sūtra*, see *The Eternal Legacy*, *Complete Works*, vol. 14, pp. 177–8. An English translation of the *sūtra* by Peter Alan Roberts has the title *The Basket's Display*.

226 The 'Puruṣa Sūkta' is hymn 10.90 of the *Rig Veda*, dedicated to the *Puruṣa*, the Cosmic Being. The verse about the creation of the Varnas (verse 12) is believed by some scholars to be an insertion. For more about the verse, see *Ambedkar and Buddhism*, *Complete Works*, vol. 9, p. 77.

227 See Sangharakshita's memoir *The Rainbow Road from Tooting Broadway to Kalimpong*, *Complete Works*, vol. 20, p. 284.

228 The Republican Party of India was established by Dr Ambedkar in 1956, evolving from the Scheduled Caste Federation which he founded in 1942. It still exists, but in more recent years has tended to split into factions.

A NEW BUDDHIST MOVEMENT: TALKS IN INDIA AND ENGLAND 1978–1992

229 These were Order members who were accompanying Sangharakshita on his tour. Lokamitra, indeed, was organizing the tour, having

been living and working in Poona (now Pune) for about six months at this time, with the support of Padmavajra, and Virabhadra, a doctor, who had just arrived in India to work there. Priyananda, from New Zealand, who was living in the UK, had accompanied Sangharakshita to India, and would go with him on the next part of the tour, to New Zealand. Sangharakshita says a bit about them all in his account of this tour in the first chapter of his *Travel Letters*; see *Complete Works*, vol. 24.

230 The artist was Dharmachari Chintamani.

231 The three levels of wisdom are enumerated in, for example, the *Saṅgīti Sutta*, *Dīgha Nikāya* 33 (iii.219); see *The Long Discourses of the Buddha*, Wisdom Publications, Boston 1995, p. 486; or T. W. and C. A. F. Rhys Davids (trans.), *Dialogues of the Buddha*, part 3, Pali Text Society, London 1971, p. 212.

232 This is probably a reference to chapter 15 of the *Dhammapada*, 'Happiness', which begins:

> Happy indeed we live,
> friendly amid the haters.
> Among men who hate we
> dwell free from hate.

Dhammapada 197, trans. Sangharakshita.

233 The Windhorse was painted by Dharmachari Padmapani. In 1995, having become faded and worn, it was replaced by a mural of lotuses. Dharmachari Maitreyabandhu, who designed and painted the new mural, said that Sangharakshita requested 'an earth image this time, not a sky image'.

234 These are three of the four animals of Aśoka. For more information, see *Lecture Tour in India 1981–2*, *Complete Works*, vol. 9, pp. 366–7.

235 Among many canonical references to the five *indriyas*, *Saṃyutta Nikāya* v.193ff. describes them in various ways in a section on the faculties; see Bhikkhu Bodhi (trans.), *The Connected Discourses of the Buddha*, Wisdom Publications, Somerville 2000, pp. 1668ff., or F. L. Woodward (trans.), *The Book of the Kindred Sayings*, part 5, Pali Text Society, London, Henley & Boston 1979, pp. 169ff. See also 'The Five Spiritual Faculties', in Sangharakshita, *A Survey of Buddhism*, *Complete Works*, vol. 1, pp. 279–94.

236 For a canonical reference to the four right efforts, see the *Mahāsatipaṭṭhāna Sutta*, *Dīgha Nikāya* 22 (ii.311); M. Walshe (trans.), *The Long Discourses of the Buddha*, Wisdom Publications, Boston 1995, p. 348; or T. W. and C. A. F. Rhys Davids, *Dialogues of the Buddha*, part 2, Pali Text Society, London 1971, p. 344.

For more on the four right efforts, see Sangharakshita, *The Buddha's Noble Eightfold Path*, ch. 6 in *Complete Works*, vol. 1, pp. 552ff.

237 See note 232.

238 It was Buddhaghosa (at *Visuddhimagga* 573) who said, 'The ordinary man is like a madman' (*ummattako viya hi puthujjano*); see Bhikkhu Ñāṇamoli, *The Path of Purification*, Buddhist Publication Society, Kandy 1991, p. 591.

239 The Buddha's vision of humanity like a bed of lotuses is described at *Saṃyutta Nikāya* i.138; Bhikkhu Bodhi (trans.), *The Connected Discourses of the Buddha*, Wisdom Publications, Boston 2000, p. 233; or C. A. F. Rhys Davids (trans.), *The Book of the Kindred Sayings*, part 1, Pali Text Society, London, Henley & Boston 1979, p. 174; also Vinaya Piṭaka i.6; see I. B. Horner (trans.), *The Book of the Discipline*, part 4, Pali Text Society, Oxford 1996, p. 9.

240 This was the Buddha's advice to Mahāprajāpatī Gautami. See note 166.

241 *Maggasaṃyutta*, *Saṃyutta Nikāya* v.2; Bhikkhu Bodhi (trans.), *The Connected Discourses of the Buddha*, Wisdom Publications, Boston 2000, pp. 1524–5; or F. L. Woodward (trans.), *The Book of the Kindred Sayings*, part 5, Pali Text Society, London, Henley & Boston 1979, p. 2.

242 This perhaps refers to the Buddha's address to the Vajjians: see the *Mahāparinibbāna Sutta*, *Dīgha Nikāya* 16 (ii.73–6); Maurice Walshe (trans.), *The Long Discourses of the Buddha*, Wisdom Publications, Boston 1995, p. 231–2; or T. W. and C. A. F. Rhys Davids (trans.), *Dialogues of the Buddha*, part 2, Pali Text Society, London 1971, p. 79–80.

243 See, for example, Bunnō Katō et al. (trans.), *The Threefold Lotus Sūtra*, Kōsei Publishing Company, Tokyo 1995, pp. 126–34; and for Sangharakshita's commentary on the story, see chapter 5, 'Symbols of Life and Growth', in *The Drama of Cosmic Enlightenment*, *Complete Works*, vol. 16, pp. 116–30.

244 See Vinaya Piṭaka i.21 (*Mahāvagga* 1.11); I. B. Horner (trans.), *The Book of the Discipline*, part 4, Pali Text Society, Oxford 1996, p. 28.

245 See note 166.

246 At this time, Sangharakshita had recently edited the transcript of a study seminar on Śāntideva's *Bodhicaryāvatāra*, which was published in a cyclostyled edition with the title *The Endlessly Fascinating Cry* (now included in *Complete Works*, vol. 4, pp. 219ff). With the advent of affordable desktop publishing in the 1980s, many of the transcripts of Sangharakshita's seminars

and lectures were subsequently edited by a team of editors in close consultation with Sangharakshita, and published in book form from 1990 onwards, the most recent being the *Udāna* seminar in this volume. Most of the seminars are available online as verbatim transcripts.

247 This was published as *The Eternal Legacy*; see *Complete Works*, vol. 14, pp. 5ff.

248 The Buddha describes this as the *ariyapariyesanā*, the 'noble search': realizing that one is subject to old age, sickness, and death, one goes in search of Nirvāṇa, the 'supreme security from bondage'. See the *Ariyapariyesanā Sutta*, *Majjhima Nikāya* 26 (i.163); Bhikkhu Ñāṇamoli and Bhikkhu Bodhi (trans.), *The Middle Length Discourses of the Buddha*, Wisdom Publications, Boston 1995, p. 255–6; or I. B. Horner (trans.), *The Collection of the Middle Length Sayings*, vol. i, Pali Text Society, London, Henley & Boston 1976, p. 207.

249 This would seem to be the *Pabbajjā Sutta*, *Sutta-Nipāta* 3.1, which describes the going forth of the Buddha-to-be. The text doesn't quite refer to 'trouble and disturbances'; the second verse, in Saddhatissa's translation, is:

> 'In a home', thought that man, 'a life is stifled – impurity is everywhere like dust.' 'For the wanderer', thought that man, 'there is space – he lives out in the open, in the air.' He saw this was so and set off.'

250 Julius Ceasar was murdered in the nearby Theatre of Pompey. Sangharakshita probably had in mind the lines from *Hamlet*, in which Polonius says, 'I did enact Julius Caesar. I was killed i' th' Capitol. Brutus killed me.'

251 In the *Aggivacchagotta Sutta*, *Majjhima Nikāya* 72 (i.484–5), the Buddha is asked a whole range of speculative questions of this kind by the wanderer Vacchagotta, including whether the mind and the body are the same or different; see Bhikkhu Ñāṇamoli and Bhikkhu Bodhi (trans.), *The Middle Length Discourses of the Buddha*, Wisdom Publications, Boston 1995, pp. 590–1; or I. B. Horner (trans.), *The Collection of the Middle Length Sayings*, vol. ii, Pali Text Society, Oxford 1994, pp. 164–5.

252 *Dhammapada* 33.

253 We have been unable to trace this. It could perhaps be an interpretation of a passage in the *Aṅguttara Nikāya* which lists four kinds of people: those who gain Nibbāna with effort in this life, those who gain Nibbāna without effort in this life, those who gain Nibbāna with effort upon death, and those who gain Nibbāna

without effort upon death. See *Aṅguttara Nikāya* ii.155; Bhikkhu Bodhi (trans.), *The Numerical Discourses of the Buddha*, Wisdom Publications, Boston 2012, pp. 533–5; or F. L. Woodward (trans.), *The Book of the Gradual Sayings*, vol. ii, Pali Text Society, Oxford 1995, pp. 160–2.

254 This is an account of 'The Boy's Questions', chapter 4 of *The Illustrator of Ultimate Meaning* (*Paramatthajotikā*); see Bhikkhu Ñāṇamoli (trans.), *The Minor Readings and the Illustrator*, Pali Text Society, Luzac & Co., London 1960, pp. 78–94.

255 *Dhammapada* 197.

256 See the *Saṅgīti Sutta*, *Dīgha Nikāya* 33 (iii.209); M. Walshe (trans.), *The Long Discourses of the Buddha*, Wisdom Publications, Boston 1995, p. 480; or T. W. and C. A. F. Rhys Davids (trans.), *Dialogues of the Buddha*, part 3, Pali Text Society, London 1971, p. 202.

257 First published as *Dhammamegha* no. 52, April 1993.

258 See *The Rainbow Road from Tooting Broadway to Kalimpong*, *Complete Works*, vol. 20, pp. 432–3.

259 This is the *Tiratana Vandanā*, or 'Salutation to the Three Jewels'. See also note 196 above.

260 Vinaya Piṭaka ii.139 (*Cullavaga* 5.33). See I. B. Horner (trans.), *The Book of the Discipline*, part 5, Pali Text Society, Oxford 1996, pp. 193–4.

261

> O Bhikṣus, my words should be accepted by the wise, not out of regard for me, but after due investigation – just as gold is accepted as true only after heating, cutting, and rubbing.

Ganganatha Jha (trans.), *The Tattvasaṅgraha of Shāntarakṣita*, Motilal Banarsidass, Delhi 1986, vol. ii, p. 1558, text 3588.

262 B. R. Ambedkar, *The Buddha and His Dhamma*, People's Education Society, Bombay 1991, pp. 153–6.

263 *Rathavinīta Sutta*, *Majjhima Nikāya* 24; Bhikkhu Ñāṇamoli and Bhikkhu Bodhi (trans.), *The Middle Length Discourses of the Buddha*, Wisdom Publications, Boston 1995, pp. 240–5; or I. B. Horner (trans.), *The Collection of the Middle Length Sayings*, vol. i, Pali Text Society, London, Henley & Boston 1976, pp. 187–94.

264 For a list of the sixty-two wrong views, see the *Brahmajāla Sutta*, *Dīgha Nikāya* 1 (i.12–38); M. Walshe (trans.), *The Long Discourses of the Buddha*, Wisdom Publications, Boston 1995, pp. 73–86; or T. W. Rhys Davids (trans.), *Dialogues of the Buddha*, part 1, Pali

Text Society, London 1973, pp. 30–52.

265 This is possibly a reference to *Dhammapada* 207.

266 See Vinaya Piṭaka i.83 (*Mahāvagga* 1.54); I. B. Horner (trans.), *The Book of the Discipline*, part 4, Pali Text Society, Oxford 1996, p. 104.

267 See, for example, *Aṅguttara Nikāya* i.145 (3.39); Bhikkhu Bodhi (trans.), *The Numerical Discourses of the Buddha*, Wisdom Publications, Boston 2012, p. 240; or F. L. Woodward (trans.), *The Book of the Gradual Sayings*, vol. i, Pali Text Society, Oxford 2000, p. 128.

268 In early Pāli sources the legendary account of the four sights is only described in connection with the Buddha Vipassī; see the *Mahāpadāna Sutta*, *Dīgha Nikāya* 14 (ii.22–8); M. Walshe (trans.), *The Long Discourses of the Buddha*, Wisdom Publications, Boston 1995, pp. 207–210; or T. W. and C. A. F. Rhys Davids (trans.), *Dialogues of the Buddha*, part 2, Pali Text Society, London 1971, pp. 18–22. In later texts, for example the *Nidāna-kathā*, *Buddhavaṃsa*, and *Lalitavistara*, the story is applied to the Buddha Śākyamuni. The *Mahāvastu* gives a particularly graphic account of the four sights; see J. J. Jones (trans.), *Mahāvastu*, vol. ii, Pali Text Society, London 1987, pp. 145–53. See also Aśvaghoṣa, *Buddhacarita*, book 3, verses 26–62.

269 In most legendary accounts Siddhārtha gives his clothes to his charioteer, Chanda, though in Aśvaghoṣa's version, the clothes are swapped with those of a hunter who serendipitously appears. See *Buddhacarita* iii.34 in E. H. Johnston (trans.), *Buddhacarita*, Motilal Banarsidass, Delhi 1984, pp. 89–90.

270 Siddhārtha's teachers were called Āḷāra Kālāma and Uddaka Rāmaputta. For an account of his time with them, see the *Ariyapariyesanā Sutta*, *Majjhima Nikāya* 26 (i.167–70); Bhikkhu Ñāṇamoli and Bhikkhu Bodhi (trans.), *The Middle Length Discourses of the Buddha*, Wisdom Publications, Boston 1995, pp. 256–9; or I. B. Horner (trans.), *The Collection of the Middle Length Sayings*, vol. i, Pali Text Society, London, Henley & Boston 1976, pp. 207–10.

271 The Buddha describes his fear in the forest in the *Bhayabherava Sutta*, *Majjhima Nikāya* 4 (i.20–1). See Bhikkhu Ñāṇamoli and Bhikkhu Bodhi (trans.), *The Middle Length Discourses of the Buddha*, Wisdom Publications, Boston 1995, p. 104; or I. B. Horner (trans.), *The Collection of the Middle Length Sayings*, vol. i, Pali Text Society, London, Henley & Boston 1976, pp. 26–7.

272 These dramatic words are from the *Lalitavistara Sūtra*; see Gwendolyn Bays (trans.), *The Voice of the Buddha*, vol. ii, Dharma Publishing, Berkeley 1983, p. 439. See also Aśvaghoṣa, *Buddhacarita*, E. H. Johnston (trans.), Motilal Banarsidass, Delhi 1984, p. 186. Also the *Appaṭivāṇa Sutta*, *Aṅguttara Nikāya* i.50; Bhikkhu Bodhi (trans.), *Numerical Discourses of the Buddha*, Wisdom Publications, Boston 2012, p. 142; or F. L. Woodward (trans.), *The Book of the Gradual Sayings*, vol. i, Pali Text Society, Oxford 2000, p. 45.

273 The story of how the Buddha and Ānanda looked after the monk with dysentery is told at Vinaya Piṭaka i.301–2 (*Mahāvagga* 8.26); I. B. Horner (trans.), *The Book of the Discipline*, part 4, Pali Text Society, Oxford 1996, pp. 431–4. See also Sangharakshita's talk, 'A Case of Dysentery', in *The Buddha's Victory*, *Complete Works*, vol. 11. It was Ānanda who asked the woman for water; see note 86.

274 The Mulagandhakuti Vihara was opened in Sarnath in 1931, having been built through the inspiration of Anagarika Dharmapala, who first visited Sarnath in 1891 and lamented that the Buddhist ruins there were not being protected. The frescoes on the walls of the vihara depicting scenes from Buddha's life were created by Japanese artist Kosetsu Nosu.

275 See, for example, the *Udāna*, below pp. 427–8.

276 See *Mahā-assapura Sutta*, *Majjhima Nikāya* 39 (i.276–9); Bhikkhu Ñāṇamoli and Bhikkhu Bodhi (trans.), *The Middle Length Discourses of the Buddha*, Wisdom Publications, Boston 1995, pp. 366–7; or I. B. Horner (trans.), *The Collection of the Middle Length Sayings*, vol. i, Pali Text Society, London, Henley & Boston 1976, pp. 329–30.

277 The ascetic's name was Upaka. See the *Ariyapariyesanā Sutta*, *Majjhima Nikāya* 26 (i.172): Bhikkhu Ñāṇamoli and Bhikkhu Bodhi (trans.), *The Middle Length Discourses of the Buddha*, Wisdom Publications, Boston 1995, pp. 263–4; or I. B. Horner (trans.), *The Collection of the Middle Length Sayings*, vol. i, Pali Text Society, London, Henley & Boston 1976, pp. 214–5.

278 This story is quoted from the *Anāgatavaṃsa* (which is a poem from the Theravādin tradition on the story of Metteyya, the future Buddha, by an elder named Kassapa) in Henry Clarke Warren, *Buddhism in Translations*, Cambridge, Mass. 1906, p. 484:

When a pious king shall cause a purse containing a thousand pieces of money to be placed in a golden casket on the back of an elephant, and shall cause proclamation up to the second and third time to be made throughout the city to the sound of a drum as follows: 'Any one who knows a single stanza spoken by the Buddhas, let him take these thousand coins together with this elephant,' and yet shall fail to find any one who knows a four-line stanza, and shall receive again the purse containing the thousand pieces into the royal palace, then the disappearance of learning will have occurred.

279 The story of the Buddha's first teaching at Sarnath is told at Vinaya Piṭaka i.8–14 (*Mahāvagga* 1.6); I. B. Horner (trans.), *The Book of the Discipline*, part 4, Pali Text Society, Oxford 1996, pp. 13–21.

280 The story of Yasa can be found *at* Vinaya Piṭaka i.15–18 (*Mahāvagga* 1.7). Ibid. pp. 21–6.

281 See Vinaya Piṭaka i.21 (*Mahāvagga* 1.11); Ibid. p. 28.

282 *Mitra* is a Sanskrit word meaning 'friend'. At the time of writing (2021) the guidelines for becoming a Mitra in the context of the Triratna Buddhist Community are as follows: People ask to become a Mitra when they themselves (1) consider that they are Buddhists; (2) want to live in accordance with the five ethical precepts; and (3) believe that the Triratna Buddhist Community is the appropriate spiritual community for them.

283 See note 57.

284 See above pp. 31ff.

285 These two articles were published in the *Maha Bodhi* in October 1961 and March–April 1962. They were reproduced in an appendix to *Beating the Drum*; see *Complete Works*, vol. 8.

286 See the *Mahāparinibbāna Sutta*, *Dīgha Nikāya* 16 (ii.73–81); Maurice Walshe (trans.), *The Long Discourses of the Buddha*, Wisdom Publications, Boston 1995, p. 231–4; or T. W. and C. A. F. Rhys Davids (trans.), *Dialogues of the Buddha*, part 2, Pali Text Society, London 1971, p. 79–3.

287 King Ajātaśatru's story (Pāli Ajātasattu) is told in the *Sāmaññaphala Sutta*, *Dīgha Nikāya* 2 (i.47–50); M. Walshe (trans.), *The Long Discourses of the Buddha*, Wisdom Publications, Boston 1995, pp. 91–3; or T. W. Rhys Davids (trans.), *Dialogues of the Buddha*, part 1, Pali Text Society, London 1973, pp. 65–8.

288 These were Rie and Sten von Krusenstierna. Sangharakshita describes his first meeting with them in Singapore in his

memoir *The Rainbow Road from Tooting Broadway to Kalimpong*, *Complete Works*, vol. 20, pp. 147–8. His reunion with them in Australia is described in *Travel Letters*; see *Complete Works*, vol. 24.

289 Swami Vivekananda (1863–1902) was a chief disciple of Sri Ramakrishna and largely responsible for bringing the Ramakrishna Mission to the attention of Westerners. Among 'notes taken down in Madras, 1892–3' are his words: 'My religion is one of which Christianity is an offshoot and Buddhism a rebel child.' To be found in the *Complete Works of Swami Vivekananda*, vol. 6.

290 See, for example, Thomas Watters, *On Yuan Chwang's Travels in India AD 629–645*, Munishiram Manoharlal Publishers, New Delhi 1996, pp. 301, 340, 355.

291 This is to be found in Jonathan Swift's *Thoughts on Various Subjects, Moral and Diverting*, published in 1703.

292 The situation has changed, and at the time of writing (2021) the population of Maharashtra is 114.2 million and the population of the UK is 66.6 million.

293 Still based in Pune (was Poona), Dhammachari Lokamitra has continued to devote himself to work on behalf of the Buddhist community in India and at the time of writing (2021) has lived there for forty-two years.

294 Dharmarakshita and Dharmalochana are the ordination names of Mr and Mrs Maheshkar, who had supported Sangharakshita in many ways during his lecture tours of Maharashtra in the late 1950s and early 1960s (for an account, see *Moving Against the Stream*, *Complete Works*, vol. 23, p. 339) and were also a great support to Lokamitra when he initiated Dharma activities in Pune in 1978. Dharmarakshita was (along with Bakula) one of the first two Indian Order members, and Dharmalochana was ordained a few months later, both ordinations taking place in 1979 at Sinhagad ('Lion Fort'), about 15 miles outside Pune.

295 The Ellora Caves, near Aurangabad, are a complex of rock-cut monastery caves with Buddhist, Hindu, and Jain monuments; the Buddhist caves date from about 200 BCE to 600 CE.

296 For edited transcripts, see *Complete Works*, vol. 9, pp. 163–539.

297 See note 44.

298 *Buddhayan* is still published every three months and circulated among the Marathi speaking and reading population in Maharashtra and beyond. The circulation (in 2021) is 8,500 copies.

299 This was Rajiv Gandhi (1944–1991), the son of Indira Gandhi, who was India's Prime Minister for many years. Rajiv Gandhi was not a politician but a professional airline pilot, but after his brother's death he was pressed to enter politics, and on the day of his mother's assassination he was appointed Prime Minister, a position he held until his party's defeat in 1989. Rajiv was himself assassinated in 1991.

300 See *Complete Works*, vol. 9, pp. 347–55.

301 Founded by Sir George Trevelyan in 1971, for twenty years the Wrekin Trust provided conferences, courses, and programmes that enabled people from diverse disciplines and viewpoints to explore the spiritual nature of humanity in non-sectarian ways.

302 See *Complete Works*, vol. 9, pp. 387–95.

303 The Dalit population of India is now (2021) about 166,000,000 (16.6% of the population).

304 The film *Gandhi* was a joint British-Indian production directed by Richard Attenborough; it was released in 1982 and was very well received, winning eight Oscars.

305 *The Thousand-Petalled Lotus* is the title given by its original publishers to Sangharakshita's first volume of memoirs, later published as *The Rainbow Road from Tooting Broadway to Kalimpong*, *Complete Works*, vol. 20.

306 See p. li and note 112.

307 For an account of these tours and notes from some of the lectures, see pp. 116ff above.

308 *Mahāmaṅgala Sutta* at *Sutta-Nipāta* 2.4, verse 2.

309 See note 57.

310 Isaiah 9:2.

311 This was the Roman Stoic philosopher Seneca (c. 4 BCE–65 CE): *Tota vita discendum est mori.*

312 *Dhammapada* 6 (trans. Sangharakshita).

313 See, for example, Daw Mya Tin (trans.), *The Dhammapada Verses and Stories*, Central Institute of Higher Tibetan Studies, Sarnath 1990, pp. 150–1.

314 This refers to the parable of the good physician in the *White Lotus Sūtra*. For a translation see, for example, Bunnō Katō et al (trans.), *The Threefold Lotus Sūtra*, Kosei Publishing, Tokyo 1957, pp. 252–6. See also Sangharakshita's commentary in *The Drama of Cosmic Enlightenment*, in *Complete Works*, vol. 16, pp. 198–200.

315 For example, the *Mahāsudassana Sutta*, *Dīgha Nikāya* 17 (ii.170) evokes the sounds of the (admittedly once-upon-a-time) city of Kusāvatī:

> The city was … never free of ten sounds by day or night: the sound of elephants,

horses, carriages, kettle-drums, side-drums, lutes, singing, cymbals and gongs, with cries of 'eat, drink and be merry' as tenth.

M. Walshe (trans.), *The Long Discourses of the Buddha*, Wisdom Publications, Boston 1995, p. 279. See also T. W. and C. A. F. Rhys Davids (trans.), *Dialogues of the Buddha*, part 2, Pali Text Society, London 1971, p. 200.

316 This is the story of the farmer Kasi-Bhāradvāja, told at *Sutta-Nipāta* 1.4.

317 First published as 'Dr Ambedkar's True Greatness', *Dhammamegha* no. 23, January 1986. Also given the title Buddhism versus the secular philosophies of the modern age.

318 For the text of this talk, 'Losing and Finding the Jewel of the Dharma', see *Complete Works*, vol. 9, pp. 260–9. The story of the jewel in the garment is told in the *White Lotus Sūtra*. For a translation, see, for example, Bunnō Katō et al (trans.), *The Threefold Lotus Sūtra*, Kosei Publishing, Tokyo 1957, p. 177. See also Sangharakshita's commentary in *The Drama of Cosmic Enlightenment*, ch. 7, in *Complete Works*, vol. 16, pp. 165ff.

319 See p. 311 and pp. 337–8 above, and also note 304.

320 See note 31.

321 This is a theme of the *Brahmajāla Sutta*, in which the worldling's praise of the Tathāgata (the Buddha) for 'elementary, inferior matters' is contrasted with 'the other matters, profound and hard to see', about which 'those who would truthfully praise the Tathāgata would rightly speak'. See *Brahmajāla Sutta*, *Dīgha Nikāya* 1; M. Walshe (trans.), *The Long Discourses of the Buddha*, Wisdom Publications, Boston 1995, pp. 67–90; or T. W. Rhys Davids (trans.), *Dialogues of the Buddha*, part 1, Pali Text Society, London 1973, pp. 1–55.

322 *Dhammapada* 165.

323 B. R. Ambedkar, *The Buddha and His Dhamma*, People's Education Society, Bombay 1991, pp. 199–203.

324 This could be the *Kalandaka Jātaka* which is preserved in Sri Lanka; Indra is probably given the name Sakka. There is a similar story in the Hindu *Rāmāyaṇa*, in which Rāma encounters a squirrel carrying pebbles in its mouth in an effort to build a bridge across the sea.

325 *Saṃyutta Nikāya* v.115 (*Mahāvagga* 46.53); Bhikkhu Bodhi (trans.), *Connected Discourses of the Buddha*, Wisdom Publications, Boston 2000, p. 1607; or F. L. Woodward (trans.), *The Book of the Kindred Sayings*, part 5, Pali Text Society, London, Henley & Boston 1979, p. 98.

326 Residential hostels were set up to provide children with an environment which supports their education.

327 The book is included in *Complete Works*, vol. 9, pp. 1–159.

328 See note 58.

329 See also pp. 31ff. above.

330 For a list of the twenty-two vows, see Appendix 1, pp 657–8.

331 Bahujan Hitay is a partner of the Karuna Trust (see p. li and note 112) that runs social projects in India including several hostels.

332 See note 325.

333 'Energy in pursuit of the good', is Sangharakshita's favoured translation of a phrase from Śāntideva's *Bodhicaryāvatāra* 7.2: 'What is vigour? The endeavour to do what is skilful.'

334 Bhagwan Das (ed.), *Thus Spoke Ambedkar*, vol. ii, Bheem Patrika Publications, Jullundur n.d., p. 148.

335 The Ajanta caves, near Aurangabad, date from the second century BCE to about 480 CE. They are particularly noted for their wall-paintings, especially images of Padmapāṇi ('Lotus in Hand'), a form of the bodhisattva Avalokiteśvara, which date from the fifth century CE.

336 This is presumably a reference to the emergence of Vajrayāna or Tantric Buddhism.

337 Bhadant Anand Kausalyayan first appears in Sangharakshita's memoirs in *Facing Mount Kanchenjunga*, in *Complete Works*, vol. 21, p. 266, and more can be learned about him later in that volume (especially pp. 448–50).

338 In his 1978 lecture, 'Levels of Going for Refuge', Sangharakshita describes six levels: cultural, provisional, effective, real, ultimate, and cosmic. Sometimes he simplified them into four levels, combining the first two and the last two. (For the 1978 lecture see *Complete Works*, vol. 12).

339 In February 2021 there were 125 Order members in Nagpur.

340 See note 282.

341 *Udāna* 5.5: John D. Ireland (trans.), *The Udāna and the Itivuttaka*, Buddhist Publication Society, Kandy 1997, p. 71. See also pp. 557–8 below, and note 181.

342 See note 334.

343 First published as *Dhammamegha* no. 53, July 1992.

344 *Maggasaṃyutta*, *Saṃyutta Nikāya* v.2; see Bhikkhu Bodhi (trans.), *The Connected Discourses of the Buddha*, Wisdom Publications, Boston 2000, pp. 1524–5; or F. L. Woodward (trans.), *The Book of the Kindred Sayings*, part 5, Pali Text Society, London, Henley & Boston 1979, p. 2.

345 In 2021, approximately fourteen of Sangharakshita's

books were available in Hindi and Marathi translations.

WISDOM BEFORE WORDS: AN EXPLORATION OF THE *UDANA*

346 Vinaya Piṭaka i.1–7 (*Mahāvagga* 1.1–5). See I. B. Horner (trans.), *The Book of the Discipline*, part 4, Pali Text Society, Oxford 1996, pp. 1–10.

347 The work was published in 1892 in English translation; see W. Woodville Rockhill (trans.), *The Udānavarga*, Kegan Paul, Trench, Truber & Co., London.

348 The metaphor of putting new wine in old bottles is used by Jesus in Matthew 9:14–17, Mark 2:21–22, and Luke 5:33–39.

349 *Dhammapada* chapter 26.

350 A canonical reference to the twelve positive *nidānas* occurs in the *Upanisā Sutta* at *Saṃyutta Nikāya* ii.29–31. See Bhikkhu Bodhi (trans.), *The Connected Discourses of the Buddha*, Wisdom Publications, Boston 2000, p. 554; or C. A. F. Rhys Davids (trans.), *The Book of the Kindred Sayings*, part 2, Pali Text Society, Oxford 1997, pp. 25–7.

351 See Bhikkhu Ñāṇamoli, *The Guide*, Pali Text Society, London 1977, p. 97.

352 For more about this, see Sangharakshita, *A Survey of Buddhism*, in *Complete Works*, vol. 1, pp. 116–20.

353 *Anuloma* and *paṭiloma* mean 'forwards' and 'backwards' (literally 'with the grain' and 'against the grain'). Here, reflecting on the process of conditioned co-production, the Buddha observes both how each link in the chain arises on the basis of the previous one, and also how as each link ceases, the next one also ceases, and so on. See *A Survey of Buddhism*, in *Complete Works*, vol 1, p. 107.

354 *Mahāsaccaka Sutta*, *Majjhima Nikāya* 36 (i.248); see Bhikkhu Ñāṇamoli and Bhikkhu Bodhi (trans.), *The Middle Length Discourses of the Buddha*, Wisdom Publications, Boston 1995, pp. 341–2; or I. B. Horner (trans.), *The Collection of the Middle Length Sayings*, vol. i, Pali Text Society, London, Henley & Boston 1976, pp. 302–3.

355 For the Mahāyāna version of this story see, for example, 'The Defeat of Māra' in the *Lalitavistara Sūtra*: Gwendolyn Bays (trans.), *The Voice of the Buddha*, vol. ii, Dharma Publishing, Berkeley 1983, pp. 463–8.

356 *The Padhāna Sutta* is at *Sutta-Nipāta* 3.2.

357 Vairocana, whose name means 'illuminator', occupies the centre of the mandala of the five Buddhas. He is represented as brilliant white in colour, and holds his emblem, the eight-spoked golden wheel of the Dharma. His fingers make the

'wheel-turning gesture', which is associated with the Buddha's first teaching at Sarnath and represents the dissemination of truth in all directions, like the sun shining in all directions of space.

358 For the story of the First Council or *saṅgīti*, see Vinaya Piṭaka ii.284–93; I. B. Horner (trans.), *The Book of the Discipline*, part 5, Pali Text Society, Oxford 1996, pp. 393–406.

359 At a conference of several hundred monks held at Mandalārāma monastery in Kallagāma Janapada, a question was raised that hadn't come up before: what is the basis of the Buddha's message (*sāsana*)? Study or practice? According to the original teaching of the Buddha the practice of the Dhamma (*paṭipatti*) is of greater importance than mere learning (*pariyatti*), yet a difference of opinion regarding this fundamental idea seems to have arisen in the minds of the *theras*. The Paṃsukūlikas maintained that practice was the basis of the *sāsana*; but the Dhammakathikas held that it was learning. Eventually it was decided that learning, not practice, was the basis of the *sāsana*. See Walpola Rahula, *History of Buddhism in Ceylon*, M. D. Gunasena & Co., Colombo 1956, p. 158.

360 This part of the story is told in the *Lalitavistara Sūtra*; see Gwendolyn Bays (trans.), *The Voice of the Buddha*, vol. ii, Dharma Publishing, Berkeley 1983, pp. 406–8.

361 See Dhammapāla, *The Udāna Commentary*, trans. Peter Masefield, Pali Text Society, Oxford 1994, vol. i, pp. 99–100.

362 The six *abhijñās* (Pāli *abhiññās*) consist of five mundane (*lokiya*) powers which are attainable through concentration (*samādhi*): the ability (1) to travel any distance or take on any form at will, (2) to see everything, (3) to hear everything, (4) to know another's thoughts, and (5) to recollect former existences; and (6) the extinction of the *āsavas*, which is attainable through insight (*vipassanā*). The *abhiññās* are enumerated in many places in the Pāli canon; for example, in the *Ākaṅkheyya Sutta*, *Majjhima Nikāya* 6 (i.34–5); Bhikkhu Ñāṇamoli and Bhikkhu Bodhi (trans.), *The Middle Length Discourses of the Buddha*, Wisdom Publications, Boston 1995, pp. 116–7; or I. B. Horner (trans.), *The Collection of the Middle Length Sayings*, vol. i, Pali Text Society, London, Henley & Boston 1976, pp. 43–4.

363 Vinaya Piṭaka i.21 (*Mahāvagga* 1.11); I. B. Horner (trans.), *The Book of the Discipline*, part 4, Pali Text Society, Oxford 1996, p. 28.

364 *Aṅguttara Nikāya* i.10: Bhikkhu Bodhi (trans.), *The Numerical Discourses of the Buddha*, Wisdom Publications 2012, p. 97; or F. L. Woodward (trans.), *The Book of the Gradual Sayings*, vol. i, Pali Text Society, Oxford 2000, p. 8.

365 The monk was Mazu (sometimes spelled Baso). D. T. Suzuki tells the story in *Essays in Zen Buddhism (First Series)*, Rider, London 1958, p. 236.

366 The story of the conversion of Anāthapiṇḍika and his donation of the Jetavana, or Jeta Grove in Sāvatthī, is told at Vinaya Piṭaka ii.154–9 (*Cullavagga* 6.4). See I. B. Horner (trans.), *The Book of the Discipline*, part 5, Pali Text Society, Oxford 1996, pp. 216–23. Also see the *Dhammapada* commentary, for example, Daw Mya Tin (trans.), *The Dhammapada Verses and Stories*, Central Institute of Higher Tibetan Studies, Sarnath 1990, pp. 275–6.

367 The story of Devadatta is told at Vinaya Piṭaka ii.188 (*Cullavagga* 7.3); I. B. Horner (trans.), *The Book of the Discipline*, part 5, Pali Text Society, Oxford 1996, p. 264; see also note 66 above.

368 See *The Rainbow Road from Tooting Broadway to Kalimpong*, *Complete Works*, vol. 20, p. 414.

369 This is more or less what happens in the biography of the Buddha called the *Mahāvastu*; see J. J. Jones (trans.), *Mahāvastu*, vol. ii, Luzac, London 1956, p. 195.

370 Padmasambhava was the historical-mythical bringer of Buddhism to Tibet. For Padmasambhava as a *mahāsiddha*, an adept in magical powers, see, for example, Yeshe Tsogyal, *The Lotus-Born*, Shambhala Publications, Boston 1993, pp. 45–51.

371 See Dhammapāla, *The Udāna Commentary*, trans. Peter Masefield, Pali Text Society, Oxford 1994, vol. i, pp. 99–100.

372 *Aggivacchagotta Sutta*, *Majjhima Nikāya* 72 (i.488); I. B. Horner (trans.), *The Collection of the Middle Length Sayings*, vol. ii, Pali Text Society, Oxford 1994, p. 166; or Bhikkhu Ñāṇamoli and Bhikkhu Bodhi (trans.), *The Middle Length Discourses of the Buddha*, Wisdom Publications, Boston 1995, p. 593.

373 *Dhammapada* 11–12.

374 The three *āsavas* (Sanskrit *āsravas*) or mental poisons are listed in many places in the Pāli canon. For example, the *Mahāsaccaka Sutta*, *Majjhima Nikāya* 36 (i.249); see Bhikkhu Ñāṇamoli and Bhikkhu Bodhi (trans.), *The Middle Length Discourses of the Buddha*, Wisdom Publications, Boston 1995, p. 342; or *The Collection of the Middle*

Length Sayings vol. i, Pali Text Society, London 1976, p. 303.

375 For example, see *Upāli Sutta*, *Majjhima Nikāya* 56 (i.386). In the last verse of Upāli's praises of the Buddha, the layman says that the Buddha is 'most worthy of gifts, most mighty of spirits', the 'mighty spirit' translating *yakkha*. Bhikkhu Ñāṇamoli and Bhikkhu Bodhi (trans.), *The Middle Length Discourses of the Buddha*, Wisdom Publications, Boston 1995, p. 491; or I. B. Horner (trans.), *The Collection of the Middle Length Sayings*, vol. ii, Pali Text Society, Oxford 1994, p. 53.

376 See, for example, Vinaya Piṭaka iv.34; I. B. Horner (trans.), *The Book of the Discipline*, part 2, Pali Text Society, Oxford 1996, p. 226.

377 See, for example, *Majjhima Nikāya* i.306; Bhikkhu Ñāṇamoli and Bhikkhu Bodhi (trans.), *The Middle Length Discourses of the Buddha*, Wisdom Publications, Boston 1995, p. 406; or I. B. Horner (trans.), *The Collection of the Middle Length Sayings*, vol. i, Pali Text Society, London, Henley & Boston 1976, pp. 369–70.

378 The note is in Woodward's translation; see F. L. Woodward (trans.), *Minor Anthologies of the Pali Canon*, part 2, Pali Text Society, London 1987, p. 6. For the reference in the commentary, see Dhammapāla, *The Udāna Commentary*, trans. Peter Masefield, Pali Text Society, Oxford 1994, vol. i, p. 100.

379 See Dhammapāla, ibid. p. 106.

380 *Dhammapada* 62.

381 Vinaya Piṭaka i.34; I. B. Horner (trans.), *The Book of the Discipline*, part 4, Pali Text Society, Oxford 1996, p. 45; also *Saṃyutta Nikāya* iv.19–20; see F. L. Woodward (trans.), *The Book of the Kindred Sayings*, part 4, Pali Text Society, London, Henley & Boston 1980, p. 10, or Bhikkhu Bodhi (trans.), *The Connected Discourses of the Buddha*, Wisdom Publications, Boston 2000, p. 1143.

382 For example *Dhammapada* 393:

> One is not a brāhmaṇa on account of matted hair or (one's) clan or birth. He in whom there exists both truth and principle (*dhamma*), *he* is pure, *he* is a brāhmaṇa.

trans. Sangharakshita.

383 See Dhammapāla, *The Udāna Commentary*, trans. Peter Masefield, Pali Text Society, Oxford 1994, vol. i, p. 119.

384 G. P. Malalasekera, *The Buddhist Dictionary of Pāli Proper Names*, John Murray, London 1938, vol. i, reports:

> Bāhiya Dārucīriya: An arahant. He was born in the family of a householder of Bāhiya – hence his name – and engaged himself in

trade, voyaging in a ship. Seven times he sailed down the Indus and across the sea and returned safely home. On the eighth occasion, while on his way to Suvannabhūmi, his ship was wrecked, and he floated ashore on a plank, reaching land near Suppāraka. Having lost all his clothes, he made himself a bark garment, and went about, bowl in hand, for alms in Suppāraka. Men, seeing his garment and struck with his demeanour, paid him great honour. Though they offered him costly robes and many other luxuries, he refused them all and his fame increased. Because of his bark garment he was known as Dārucīriya. In due course he came himself to believe that he had attained arahantship, but a devatā (a Suddhāvāsā-brahmā, who had been his fellow celibate in the time of Kassapa Buddha, says the Commentary), reading his thoughts and wishing him well, pointed out to him his error and advised him to seek the Buddha at Sāvatthi....

385 See, for example, *Majjhima Nikāya* i.306; Bhikkhu Ñāṇamoli and Bhikkhu Bodhi (trans.), *The Middle Length Discourses of the Buddha*, Wisdom Publications, Boston 1995, p. 406; or *The Collection of the Middle Length Sayings* vol. i, Pali Text Society, London 1976, pp. 369–70.

386 There is a very similar passage at *Saṃyutta Nikāya* iv.72–4, in which the Buddha gives a similar teaching with an interesting preamble to Māluṅkyāputta. See Bhikkhu Bodhi (trans.), *The Connected Discourses of the Buddha*, Wisdom Publications, Somerville 2000, pp. 1175–6; or C. A. F. Rhys Davids (trans.), *The Book of the Kindred Sayings*, part 4, Pali Text Society, London, Henley & Boston 1980, pp. 42–5.

387 For more about what Sangharakshita means by alienated awareness, see chapter 10, 'The Integrated Individual', in *What is the Sangha?*, in *Complete Works*, vol. 3, especially pp. 487–8.

388 The mirror-like wisdom is the aspect of Enlightenment represented by the dark-blue Buddha, Akṣobhya, the 'Imperturbable', of the eastern quarter of the mandala of the five Buddhas. This wisdom is 'mirror-like' in the sense that it reflects experience just as it is, without distortion.

389 It was with Sangharatana that Sangharakshita first visited Bodh Gaya in 1949. See *The Rainbow Road from Tooting Broadway to Kalimpong*, *Complete Works*, vol. 20, pp. 453–6. Sangharatana invited Sangharakshita

to the celebration of the anniversary of the opening of the Mulagandhakuti Vihara: *Facing Mount Kanchenjunga*, in *Complete Works*, vol. 21, p. 97; and was present at his ordination (ibid., p. 108). Later, Sangharatana invited Sangharakshita to join him and Jagdish Kashyap as the official delegation accompanying the Sacred Relics of Śāriputra and Maudgalyāyana to Sikkim. See ibid., p. 173 and chapter 11. See also *Moving Against the Stream*, in *Complete Works*, vol. 23, p. 359, which describes Sangharatana's apology to Sangharakshita for the refusal to ordain him at Sarnath. In 1969, Ven. Sangharatana went to Sravasti and initiated the construction of the Nava Jetavana Vihara just outside the old Jetavana (Jeta Grove).

390 In the *Pabbajjā Sutta*, *Sutta-Nipāta* 3.1, verses 18–19 the Buddha-to-be tells King Bimbisāra that he comes from Kosala.

391 See, for example, the *Katthāvatthu Sutta*, *Aṅguttara Nikāya* v.128–9 (10.69); Bhikkhu Bodhi (trans.), *The Numerical Discourses of the Buddha*, Wisdom Publications, Boston 2012, pp. 1424–5; or F. L. Woodward (trans.), *The Book of the Gradual Sayings*, vol. v, Pali Text Society, Oxford 1996, pp. 86–8.

392

> Histories make men wise; poets, witty; the mathematics, subtle; natural philosophy, deep; moral, grave; logic and rhetoric, able to contend.

From Sir Francis Bacon's essay 'Of Studies', in his *Essays*, published in 1597.

393 This would have been Ānandamayi, in whose ashram Sangharakshita stayed when he was a young wanderer, as he recounts in his memoirs; see Sangharakshita, *The Rainbow Road from Tooting Broadway to Kalimpong*, *Complete Works*, vol. 20, pp. 182–213 – though this theory of hers is not mentioned.

394 See T. W. Rhys Davids, *Buddhist India*, Motilal Banarsdass, Delhi 1993, pp. 141–6, 247.

395 *Dhammapada* 142:

> If one who is richly adorned lives in tranquillity, is calm, controlled, assured (of eventual enlightenment), and devotes himself to the spiritual life, laying down the stick with regard to all living beings, then (despite his being richly adorned), he is a brāhmaṇa, he is an ascetic, he is an almsman.

trans. Sangharakshita.

396 *Saṃyutta Nikāya* ii.224. See Bhikkhu Bodhi (trans.), *The Connected Discourses of the Buddha*, Wisdom Publications, Somerville 2000, pp. 680–1; or C. A. F. Rhys Davids (trans.), *The Book of the Kindred*

Sayings, part 2, Pali Text Society, Oxford 1997, p. 152.

397 See Dhammapāla, *The Udāna Commentary*, trans. Peter Masefield, Pali Text Society, Oxford 1994, vol. i, pp. 280–1.

398 Śāntideva, *Bodhicaryāvatāra* vi. 43.

399 See note 253.

400 See, for example, *Sutta-Nipāta* 5.4, verse 11.

401 *Dhammapada* 62.

402 See 'taking food in turn', in T. W. Rhys Davids and Hermann Oldenberg (trans.), *Vinaya Texts*, part 1, Motilal Banarsidass, Delhi 1974, p. 38; or 'out-of-turn meal'; see I. B. Horner (trans.), *The Book of the Discipline*, part 4, Pali Text Society, Oxford 1996, p. 305n (which notes that this is Pācittiya 33).

403 Dr Samuel Johnson is reported to have said, 'the triumph of hope over experience' in 1770, in relation to a man who remarried soon after the death of his wife, with whom he had been unhappy, as recorded by James Boswell in his *Life of Samuel Johnson*, published in 1791.

404 Vinaya Piṭaka i.293 (*Mahāvagga* 8.15); I. B. Horner (trans.), *The Book of the Discipline*, part 4, Pali Text Society, Oxford 1996, p. 418.

405 Mary Whitehouse (1910–2001) was an English conservative activist who campaigned for many causes. In the 1960s and 1970s she was a vocal critic of the British media and the arts, especially the BBC, and won a notorious case against the publication *Gay News*. Her campaigns against swearing, obscenity, and other causes of concern to her, especially on television, were fiercely criticized by some, who accused her of demanding censorship, and approved by others who saw her as a force for the prevention of moral decline.

406 For the story of King Ajātaśatru's visit to see the Buddha, see the *Sāmaññaphala Sutta*, *Dīgha Nikāya* 2 (i.47–86); M. Walshe (trans.), *The Long Discourses of the Buddha*, Wisdom Publications, Boston 1995, pp. 91–109; or T. W. Rhys Davids (trans.), *Dialogues of the Buddha*, part 1, Pali Text Society, London 1973, pp. 65–94. See also pp. 274–5 above.

407 See, for example, Trevor Ling, *The Buddha*, Penguin Books, Harmondsworth 1976, p. 117.

408 *Pāṭika Sutta*, *Dīgha Nikāya* 24 (iii 34–5); M. Walshe (trans.), *The Long Discourses of the Buddha*, Wisdom Publications, Boston 1995, pp. 382–3; or T. W. Rhys Davids (trans.) *Dialogues of the Buddha*, part 3, Pali Text Society, London 1971, pp. 31–2. See also Sangharakshita, *The Three Jewels*, *Complete Works*, vol. 2, p. 84.

409 The three knowledges (Pāli *tevijja*) are remembrance

of former births, the divine eye, and knowledge of the destruction of the *āsavas*. The Buddha is described as having gained them in the process of his Enlightenment; see, for example, the *Mahāsaccaka Sutta*, *Majjhima Nikāya* 36 (i.249); Bhikkhu Ñāṇamoli and Bhikkhu Bodhi (trans.), *The Middle Length Discourses of the Buddha*, Wisdom Publications, Boston 1995, pp. 341–2; or I. B. Horner (trans.), *The Collection of the Middle Length Sayings*, vol. i, Pali Text Society, London, Henely & Boston 1976, pp. 303–4.

410 This was Dr Dinshah Mehta. Sangharakshita describes his acquaintance with Dr Mehta in his memoir *In the Sign of the Golden Wheel*, in *Complete Works*, vol. 22, pp. 282–303.

411 *Dhammapada* 5.

412 See Dhammapāla, *The Udāna Commentary*, trans. Peter Masefield, Pali Text Society, Oxford 1994, vol. i, p. 485.

413 For example, the Buddha refers to the belief that experience is caused by 'God's creative activity' in *Aṅguttara Nikāya* i.173 (3.61). See Bhikkhu Bodhi (trans.), *The Numerical Discourses of the Buddha*, Wisdom Publications, Boston 2012, p. 266; or F. L. Woodward (trans.), *The Book of the Gradual Sayings*, vol. i, Pali Text Society, Oxford 2000, p. 158.

414 See Dhammapāla, *The Udāna Commentary*, trans. Peter Masefield, Pali Text Society, Oxford 1994, vol. i, pp. 495–6.

415 There's an example of this in the *Susīma Sutta* at *Saṃyutta Nikāya* ii.119–28 (*Nidānavagga* 12.70); Bhikkhu Bodhi (trans.), *The Connected Discourses of the Buddha*, Wisdom Publications, Somerville 2000, pp. 612–8; or C. A. F. Rhys Davids (trans.), *The Book of the Kindred Sayings*, part 2, Pali Text Society, Oxford 1997, pp. 84–92.

416 See John S. Strong, *The Legend of King Aśoka*, Princeton University Press, Princeton 1983, p. 23.

417 The antics of the band or group of six monks are catalogued throughout the Vinaya Piṭaka, which details the many rules which had to be formulated to thwart all their various efforts to wriggle out of their ethical obligations. See I. B. Horner (trans.), *The Book of the Discipline*, part 4, Pali Text Society, Oxford 1996, to find them trying to get away with wearing multi-coloured sandals (pp. 246–7), devising ever more luxurious beds (pp. 256–7), mistreating cattle (pp. 254–5), causing senior monks to faint by overheating the sauna and blocking the door (*The Book of the Discipline*, part 5, Pali Text Society, Oxford 1996, pp. 308–9), and so on. The

following passage from Vinaya Piṭaka i.188 (ibid., Part 4, p. 250) gives an idea of the kind of people the accounts say they were.

> Now at that time the group of six monks, getting up in the night towards dawn, having put on wooden shoes, paced up and down in the open air talking in high, loud, rasping tones a variety of worldly talk....

The passage goes on to describe all the kinds of things they talked about, and points out that they disturbed the other monks from their practice and also killed a lot of insects with their tramping up and down.

418 Vinaya Piṭaka i.34; I. B. Horner (trans.), *The Book of the Discipline*, part 4, Pali Text Society, Oxford 1996, p. 45. Also *Saṃyutta Nikāya* iv.19–20; F. L. Woodward (trans.), *The Book of the Kindred Sayings*, part 4, Pali Text Society, London, Henley & Boston 1980, p. 10; or Bhikkhu Bodhi (trans.), *The Connected Discourses of the Buddha*, Wisdom Publications, Boston 2000, p. 1143.

419 These are references to Sigmund Freud's theory of the elements of human personality, first outlined in *The Ego and the Id* (published in 1923). Very basically, the id is the instinctual aspect, all about desire and drives; the super-ego is the perfectionist aspect that internalizes rules and wants to appear socially acceptable, so tends to produce guilt; and the ego is the realistic element that tries to negotiate between reality and the id's desires.

420 The Buddha often described the path to Enlightenment in terms of this threefold path and according to the Pāli canon he did so many times in the last days of his life. For example, see the *Mahāparinibbāna Sutta*, *Dīgha Nikāya* 16 (ii.81); Maurice Walshe (trans.), *The Long Discourses of the Buddha*, Wisdom Publications, Boston 1995, p. 234; or T. W. and C. A. F. Rhys Davids (trans.), *Dialogues of the Buddha*, part 2, Pali Text Society, London 1971, p. 86. For Sangharakshita's exposition of the threefold path, see *What is the Dharma?*, chapters 10–12, in *Complete Works*, vol. 3, pp. 315ff.

421 For a canonical reference to the four right efforts, see the *Mahāsatipaṭṭhāna Sutta*, *Dīgha Nikāya* 22 (ii.311); M. Walshe (trans.), *The Long Discourses of the Buddha*, Wisdom Publications, Boston 1995, p. 348; or T. W. and C. A. F. Rhys Davids, *Dialogues of the Buddha*, part 2, Pali Text Society, London 1971, p. 344. For more on the four right efforts, see Sangharakshita, *The Buddha's Noble Eightfold*

Path, ch. 6, in *Complete Works*, vol. 1, pp. 552–66.

422 Sangharakshita learned of the antidotes from his teacher C. M. Chen, whom he knew in Kalimpong. For Mr Chen's account, see C. M. Chen, *Buddhist Meditation, Systematic and Practical*, published by Dr Yutang Lin, El Cerrito 1989, chapter 8, 'The Five Fundamental Meditations to Cure the Five Poisons', pp. 326–30. See also Sangharakshita, *The Purpose and Practice of Buddhist Meditation*, Ibis Publications, Ledbury 2012, pp. 29–35 (*Complete Works*, vol. 5, pp. 29–35).

423 The same verse is found at *Dhammapada* 42.

424 Lucius Annasus Seneca, 'On Firmness', *Moral Essays*, trans. John W. Basore. The Loeb Classical Library, Heinemann, London 1928–1935, vol. 1, p. 51.

425 In Pāli, *nāga* has several meanings, including both elephant and snake.

426 For example, *Dhammapada* 185, and *Mahāpadāna Sutta*, *Dīgha Nikāya* 14 (ii.50) in M. Walshe (trans.), *The Long Discourses of the Buddha*, Wisdom Publications, Boston 1995, p. 219; or T. W. and C. A. F. Rhys Davids (trans.), *Dialogues of the Buddha*, part 2, Pali Text Society, London 1971, p. 39.

427 This part of Piṇḍola Bhāradvāja's story is apparently to be found in the *Aṅguttara Nikāya* Commentary (i.96), not yet available in English translation. Bhikkhu Bodhi also tells the story and gives some sources for other information in *The Numerical Discourses of the Buddha*, Wisdom Publications, Boston 2012, p. 1604, n. 81.

428 *Etadaggavagga*, *Aṅguttara Nikāya* i.23–6 (1.14); Bhikkhu Bodhi (trans.), *The Numerical Discourses of the Buddha*, Wisdom Publications 2012, p. 109; or F. L. Woodward (trans.), *The Book of the Gradual Sayings*, vol. i, Pali Text Society, Oxford 2000, p. 16.

429 Following their meeting in 1931, Gandhi said of George Bernard Shaw, 'I think he is a very good man.' Shaw's response to Gandhi's assassination in 1948 was 'It shows how dangerous it is to be too good.'

430 *Etadaggavagga*, *Aṅguttara Nikāya* i.24; Bhikkhu Bodhi (trans.), *The Numerical Discourses of the Buddha*, Wisdom Publications 2012, p. 110; or F. L. Woodward (trans.), *The Book of the Gradual Sayings*, vol. i, Pali Text Society, Oxford 2000, p. 17.

431 The penultimate stage of the spiral path or twelve positive *nidānas*, the last stage before the arising of Enlightenment, is 'the knowledge of the

destruction of the *āsavas*'. The three *āsavas* (Sanskrit *āsravas*) are listed in many places in the Pāli canon. For example, in the *Mahāsaccaka Sutta*, *Majjhima Nikāya* 36 (i.249); Bhikkhu Ñāṇamoli and Bhikkhu Bodhi (trans.), *The Middle Length Discourses of the Buddha*, Wisdom Publications, Boston 1995, p. 342; or *The Collection of the Middle Length Sayings* vol. i, Pali Text Society, London 1976, p. 303. A few sources list a fourth *āsava*, *diṭṭhāsava*, the mental poison of wrong views; for example, the *Mahāparinibbāna Sutta*, *Dīgha Nikāya* 16 (ii.81); M. Walshe (trans.), *The Long Discourses of the Buddha*, Wisdom Publications, Boston 1995, p. 234; or T. W. and C. A. F. Rhys Davids (trans.), *Dialogues of the Buddha*, part 2, Pali Text Society, London 1971, pp. 327–37.

432 See *Aṅguttara Nikāya* ii.202–3; E. M. Hare (trans.), *The Book of the Gradual Sayings*, vol. ii, Pali Text Society, Oxford 1995, pp. 214–8; or Bhikkhu Bodhi (trans.), *The Numerical Discourses of the Buddha*, Wisdom Publications, Boston 2012, p. 577–9.

433 Richard Gombrich (in *What the Buddha Thought*, Equinox, London 2009, p. 88) argues that this *Udāna* discourse and stanza is a response to *Bṛhadāraṇyaka Upaniṣad* 4.5.6, in which Yajñavalkya converses with his wife Maitreyī on the same topic.

434 For an explanation of the *ālaya-vijñāna* or store-consciousness, see Sangharakshita, *The Meaning of Conversion in Buddhism*, ch. 5, in *Complete Works*, vol. 2, pp. 279–81.

435 See *Mahāpādana Sutta*, *Dīgha Nikāya* 14 (ii.22–8), in which the legendary account of the four sights is described in connection with the Buddha Vipassī; see M. Walshe (trans.), *The Long Discourses of the Buddha*, Wisdom Publications, Boston 1995, pp. 207–10; or T. W. Rhys Davids (trans.), *Dialogues of the Buddha*, part 2, Pali Text Society, Oxford 1971, pp. 18–22. This is also the pattern of the stories of Buddhas told in the *Buddhavaṃsa*; see I. B. Horner (trans.), *Chronicle of Buddhas*, in *The Minor Anthologies of the Pāli Canon*, vol. iii, Pali Text Society, Oxford 1994.

436 John D. Ireland (trans.), *The Udāna and the Itivuttaka*, Buddhist Publication Society, Kandy 1997, p. 67.

437 Ibid.

438 *Dhammapada* 142.

439 Sir Charles Lyell (1797–1875) was a Scottish geologist who demonstrated the power of existing natural causes in explaining the history of the Earth. He is best known as the author of *Principles of Geology* (1830–1833), which presented for a wide

public audience the idea that the Earth was shaped by the same natural processes still in operation today, operating at similar intensities.

440 Zhiyi lived in the sixth century CE and founded the Tiantai school of Buddhism, which under his guidance undertook the classification of Buddhist teachings into 'five periods and eight teachings'. The five periods were: the period of the Buddhāvataṃsaka, which, according to the Tiantai, the Buddha taught immediately following his Enlightenment; that of the Āgamas, writings of the Sanskrit canon that coincide broadly with the Pāli canon; that of the Vaipulya (extensive) *sūtras* – that is, *sūtras* of the early Mahāyāna, including the *Avataṃsaka* and the *Ratnakūṭa*; that of the Prajñāpāramitā (Perfection of Wisdom) *sūtras*; and that of the *White Lotus Sūtra* and the *Mahāparinirvāṇa Sūtra*. This was a chronological division of the teachings; but the Tiantai held the view that the Buddha also taught the teachings of the five periods simultaneously, and therefore also systematized them into eight doctrines, four concerned with method and four with content: the sudden, gradual, secret, and indeterminate methods; and the teachings of the Hīnayāna; the general teachings common to Hīnayāna and Mahāyāna; special teachings for Bodhisattvas; and the complete, 'round' teaching – only the *White Lotus Sūtra* being considered to be fully complete or 'round'.

441 It was King Bimbisāra who made the suggestion, as recorded at Vinaya Piṭaka i.101 (*Mahāvagga* 2.1) ; see I. B. Horner (trans.), *The Book of the Discipline*, part 4, Pali Text Society, Oxford 1996, pp. 130–1.

442 S. Dutt, *Early Buddhist Monachism*, Kegan Paul, Trench, Truber & Co., London 1924, pp. 87–90.

443 *Dhammapada* 183–5.

444 S. Dutt, *Early Buddhist Monachism*, Kegan Paul, Trench, Truber & Co., London 1924, p. 87 and pp. 104–7.

445 See, for example, sections 2.2, 3.8, and 3.9 above.

446 See, for example, the *Pahārāda Sutta*, *Aṅguttara Nikāya* iv.198–203 (8.19), which opens with Pahārāda, leader of the *asuras*, approaching the Buddha and remarking that the *asuras* delight in the great ocean for eight reasons. He then asks the Buddha if the monks delight in the *Dhamma-Vinaya*. The Buddha replies that they do, for eight reasons also, and makes eight comparisons with the great ocean. The *Uposatha Sutta* which follows this in the *Aṅguttara Nikāya* also gives the eight similes. See E. M. Hare (trans.), *The Book of the Gradual Sayings*, vol. iv,

Pali Text Society, Oxford 1995, pp. 136–40; or Bhikkhu Bodhi (trans.), *The Numerical Discourses of the Buddha*, Wisdom Publications, Boston 2012, pp. 1142–7. The similes also appear at Vinaya Piṭaka ii.236–40 (Cullavagga 9.1–3); see I. B. Horner (trans.), *The Book of the Discipline*, part 5, Pali Text Society, Oxford 1996, pp. 330–6.

447 This is raised in the *Sūtra of Huineng* (or *Wei Lang*). Wong Mou-Lam's translation, in Dwight Goddard (ed.), *A Buddhist Bible*, Beacon Press, Boston 1970, pp. 517–8, says,

> While there is only one system of Dharma, some disciples realise it quicker than others but the reason why the names, 'Sudden' and 'Gradual', are given is because some disciples are superior to others in their mental dispositions. So far as the Dharma is concerned, the distinction of Sudden and Gradual does not exist.

448 Kenneth K. S. Ch'en, *The Chinese Transformation of Buddhism*, Princeton University Press, Princeton 1973, chapter 2, 'Ethical Life'.

449 See note 166.

450 *Dhammapada* 65.

451 For canonical references to the four *iddhipādas*, see *Iddhipādasaṃyutta*, *Saṃyutta Nikāya* v.283–4; F. L. Woodward (trans.), *The Book of the Kindred Sayings*, part 5, Pali Text Society, London, Henley & Boston 1979, pp. 251–7; or Bhikkhu Bodhi (trans.), *The Connected Discourses of the Buddha*, Wisdom Publications, Boston 2000, pp. 1740–6.

452 The eight *ariyapuggalas* or 'noble persons' are often listed as 'four pairs of persons': the Stream Entrant and the one who has won the fruits of Stream Entry; the once-returner (that is, the one who will live only one more human existence before Enlightenment) and the one who has realized the fruition of that stage; the non-returner (who will gain Enlightenment from a heavenly realm), and the one who has realized its fruition; and the *arhant*, who has attained Enlightenment, and the one who has realized the fruits of arhantship. The Buddha is recorded as making this fourfold classification on many occasions, for example, in the 'Mirror of Dhamma' he gave to Ānanda in the last days of his life; see *Mahāparinibbāna Sutta*, *Dīgha Nikāya* 16 (ii.93); Maurice Walshe (trans.), *The Long Discourses of the Buddha*, Wisdom Publications, Boston 1995, p. 241; or T. W. and C. A. F. Rhys Davids (trans.), *Dialogues of the Buddha*, part 2, Pali Text Society, London 1971, pp. 99–100.

453 *Dhammo have rakkhati dhammacāriṃ*. This verse

appears in *Jātakas* 447 and 510 and also in the story of Dhammika in the *Theragāthā* in C. A. F. Rhys Davids (trans.), *Psalms of the Brethren*, Pali Text Society, London 1980, p. 285.

454 John D. Ireland (trans.), *The Udāna and the Itivuttaka*, Buddhist Publication Society, Kandy 2007, p. 73.

455 The Chapter of the Eights is the fourth chapter of the *Sutta-Nipāta*, which is available in various English translations.

456 The Pāli term *kāma* means 'desire' and *karma* (Pāli *kamma*), while literally meaning 'action', of course refers to the volitional actions which bear fruit in the form of *karma vipāka* – so it's important not to get these two terms confused.

457 See Dhammapāla, *The Udāna Commentary*, trans. Peter Masefield, Pali Text Society, Oxford 1995, vol. ii, p. 787.

458 *Rathavinīta Sutta*, *Majjhima Nikāya* 24; Bhikkhu Ñāṇamoli and Bhikkhu Bodhi (trans.), *The Middle Length Discourses of the Buddha*, Wisdom Publications, Boston 1995, pp. 240–5; or I. B. Horner (trans.), *The Collection of the Middle Length Sayings*, vol. i, Pali Text Society, London, Henley & Boston 1976, pp. 187–94; and see also pp. 248–9 above.

459 Vinaya Piṭaka ii.188 (*Cullavagga* 7.3) in I. B. Horner (trans.), *The Book of the Discipline*, part 5, Pali Text Society, Oxford 1996, p. 264.

460 *Mahāparinibbāna Sutta*, *Dīgha Nikāya* 16 (ii.101); see M. Walshe (trans.), *The Long Discourses of the Buddha*, Wisdom Publications, Boston 1995, p. 245; or T. W. and C. A. F. Rhys Davids (trans.), *Dialogues of the Buddha*, part 2, Pali Text Society, London 1971, p. 107.

461 For example, see the *Rohitassa Sutta*, *Aṅguttara Nikāya* ii.48; Bhikkhu Bodhi (trans.), *Numerical Discourses of the Buddha*, Wisdom Publications, Boston 2012, p. 435; or E. M. Hare (trans.), *The Book of the Gradual Sayings*, vol. ii, Pali Text Society, Oxford 1995, p. 58.

462 For canonical references to the four *iddhipādas*, see *Iddhipādasaṃyutta*, *Saṃyutta Nikāya* v.283–4; F. L. Woodward (trans.), *The Book of the Kindred Sayings*, part 5, Pali Text Society, London, Henley & Boston 1979, pp. 251–7; or Bhikkhu Bodhi (trans.), *The Connected Discourses of the Buddha*, Wisdom Publications, Boston 2000, pp. 1740–6.

463 *Brahmajāla Sutta*, *Dīgha Nikāya* 1 (i.26–8); see Maurice Walshe (trans.), *The Long Discourses of the Buddha*, Wisdom Publications, Boston 1995, pp. 80–1; or T. W. Rhys Davids (trans.), *Dialogues of the Buddha*, part 1, Pali

Text Society, London 1973, pp. 37–8.

464 See Dhammapāla, *The Udāna Commentary*, trans. Peter Masefield, Pali Text Society, Oxford 1995, vol. ii, p. 863.

465 See ibid., p. 866.

466 See ibid., p. 867.

467 The Sanskrit word *aiśvarya* means 'the state of being a mighty lord, sovereignty, supremacy, power, sway'. It is an abstract formation from *īśvara*, meaning 'lord' or 'master'. The Pāli equivalent is *issariya*. The argument referred to here is probably this:

> Form (*rūpa*), monks, is not the self (*anattā*). For if form were the self, then it would not be disposed to affliction, and with regard to form it would be possible to say, 'may my form be like this, may my form not be like that.' But, monks, because form is not the self, then form is disposed to affliction, and it is not possible to say with regard to form, 'may my form be like this, may my form not be like that.'

Saṃyutta Nikāya iii.67 (22.59); see Bhikkhu Bodhi (trans.), *The Connected Discourses of the Buddha*, Wisdom Publications, Boston 2000, pp. 901–2; or F. L. Woodward (trans.), *The Book of the Kindred Sayings*, vol. iii, Pali Text Society, London and Boston 1975, p. 59.

468 This is one of the Proverbs of Hell in William Blake's *The Marriage of Heaven and Hell* (1790).

469 William Blake wrote of the 'fourfold vision' in various contexts, the best-known being a verse included in a letter to Thomas Butts in 1802:

> Now I a fourfold vision see,
> And a fourfold vision is
> given to me;
> 'Tis fourfold in my supreme
> delight
> And threefold in soft
> Beulah's night
> And twofold Always. May
> God us keep
> From Single vision &
> Newton's sleep!

470 The German philosopher Immanuel Kant outlined his antinomies in his work *Critique of Pure Reason*, first published in 1781.

471 *Rohitassa Sutta* at *Aṅguttara Nikāya* ii.48; Bhikkhu Bodhi (trans.), *Numerical Discourses of the Buddha*, Wisdom Publications, Boston 2012, pp. 434–5; or E. M. Hare, *The Book of the Gradual Sayings*, vol. ii, Pali Text Society, Oxford 1995, p. 58. See also *Saṃyutta Nikāya* i.62 (*Sagāthāvagga* 2.26); Bhikkhu Bodhi (trans.), *The Connected Discourses of the Buddha*, Wisdom Publications, Boston 2000, p. 158; or C. A. F. Rhys Davids (trans.), *The Book of the Kindred Sayings*, part 1, Pali Text Society, London,

Henley & Boston 1979, pp. 86–7.

472 See Dhammapāla, *The Udāna Commentary*, trans. Peter Masefield, Pali Text Society, Oxford 1995, vol. ii, pp. 875–6.

473 In the *Aggivacchagotta Sutta*, *Majjhima Nikāya* 72 (i.484–5), the Buddha is asked a whole range of speculative questions of this kind by the wanderer Vacchagotta; see Bhikkhu Ñāṇamoli and Bhikkhu Bodhi (trans.), *The Middle Length Discourses of the Buddha*, Wisdom Publications, Boston 1995, pp. 590–1; or I. B. Horner (trans.), *The Collection of the Middle Length Sayings*, vol. ii, Pali Text Society, Oxford 1994, pp. 162–5.

474 The parable of the poisoned arrow is told in the *Cūḷamāluṅkya Sutta*, *Majjhima Nikāya* 63 (i.427–32); see Bhikkhu Ñāṇamoli and Bhikkhu Bodhi (trans.), *The Middle Length Discourses of the Buddha*, Wisdom Publications, Boston 1995, pp. 533–6; or I. B. Horner (trans.), *The Collection of the Middle Length Sayings*, vol. ii, Pali Text Society, Oxford 1994, p. 99.

475 See note 202 about *catuṣkoṭi*.

476 See, for example, *Aṅguttara Nikāya* iii.71–4; Bhikkhu Bodhi (trans.), *Numerical Discourses of the Buddha*, Wisdom Publications, Boston 2012, pp. 686–9; or E. M. Hare, *The Book of the Gradual Sayings*, vol. iii, Pali Text Society, Oxford 1995, pp. 59–61.

477 Ecclesiastes 9:10.

478

> Accident is the omission of act in self and the hindering of act in another. This is Vice, but all Act is Virtue. To hinder another is not an act. It is the contrary. It is a restraint on action both in ourselves and in the person hindered, for he who hinders another omits his own duty at the time.

This is one of William Blake's annotations of his copy of Johann Kaspar Lavater's *Aphorisms on Man*, published in 1788 with annotations and a frontispiece by Blake.

479 The *animitta-vimokkha* (Sanskrit *animitta-vimokśa*) is one of the three 'entrances to liberation'. In *What is the Dharma?* Sangharakshita says,

> The second liberation, the second door to the Unconditioned, is *animitta*, the 'signless'. *Nimitta* literally means a sign, but it can also mean a word or a concept; so the *animitta* is the approach to the Unconditioned by bypassing all words and all thoughts. This is a very distinctive experience. When you have it, you realize that all words, all concepts, are totally inadequate. Not that they're not very adequate, but that actually they don't mean anything at all.

Sangharakshita, *What is the Dharma?*, in *Complete Works*, vol. 3, p. 219. For a traditional reference, see *Visuddhimagga* 657–9 in Buddhaghosa, *The Path of Purification*, trans. Bhikkhu Ñāṇamoli, Buddhist Publication Society, Kandy 1991, pp. 680–2.

480 See *Saṃyutta Nikāya* v.59; Bhikkhu Bodhi (trans.), *The Connected Discourses of the Buddha*, Wisdom Publications, Boston 2000, p. 1563; or F. L. Woodward (trans.), *The Book of the Kindred Sayings*, part 5, Pali Text Society, London, Henley & Boston 1979, p. 336.

481 *Etadaggavagga*, *Aṅguttara Nikāya* i.24 (1.14). See Bhikkhu Bodhi (trans.), *The Numerical Discourses of the Buddha*, Wisdom Publications 2012, pp. 109–113; or F. L. Woodward (trans.), *The Book of the Gradual Sayings*, vol. i, Pali Text Society, Oxford 2000, pp. 16–25.

482 See Dhammapāla, *The Udāna Commentary*, trans. Peter Masefield, Pali Text Society, Oxford 1995, vol. ii, p. 893.

483 See *Dhammacakkappavattana Sutta*, *Saṃyutta Nikāya* v.421; Bhikkhu Bodhi (trans.), *The Connected Discourses of the Buddha*, *Wisdom Publications*, Boston 2000, p. 1844; or F. L. Woodward (trans.), *The Book of the Kindred Sayings*, part 5, Pali Text Society, London, Henley & Boston 1979, p. 357.

484 B. M. Barua, 'Buddhism as Personal Religion', in *Maha Bodhi*, vol. 52, nos. 3–4, March–April 1944, Calcutta, p. 62. See also B. M. Barua, *Ceylon Lectures*, second edition, Sri Sat Guru Publications, Delhi 1986, pp. 157–62.

485 Sangharakshita used the term 'nirvanized' in an early draft of his translation of *Dhammapada* 126, but in the version published in 2001, he chose to translate the verse differently: 'Those who are free from defilements become utterly "Cool".' See also p. 515 above.

486 *Etadaggavagga*, *Aṅguttara Nikāya* i.24 (1.14). See Bhikkhu Bodhi (trans.), *The Numerical Discourses of the Buddha*, Wisdom Publications 2012, p. 109; or F. L. Woodward (trans.), *The Book of the Gradual Sayings*, vol. i, Pali Text Society, Oxford 2000, p. 16.

487 See Dhammapāla, *The Udāna Commentary*, trans. Peter Masefield, Pali Text Society, Oxford 1995, vol. ii, pp. 960–1 (which gives a slightly different translation).

488 Alcibiades claims that Socrates is like a satyr, both in appearance and in other ways as well. Marsyas, the flute-playing satyr, could produce bewitching flute-music with the power of his mouth. Socrates, Alcibiades suggests, can also bewitch people with

his mouth, though he needs no flute, using words alone. Plato's *Symposium* 215a–f.

489 See *Saccasaṃyutta*, *Saṃyutta Nikāya* v.423; Bhikkhu Bodhi (trans.), *Connected Discourses of the Buddha*, Wisdom Publications, Boston 2000, p. 1846; or F. L. Woodward (trans.), *The Book of the Kindred Sayings*, part 5, Pali Text Society, London, Henley & Boston 1979, p. 359. Also the *Dhammacakkappavattana Sutta*, *Saṃyutta Nikāya* v.424; Bhikkhu Bodhi (trans.), ibid. p. 1847; or F. L. Woodward, ibid. p. 360.

490 See, for example, chapter 5 of the *Laṅkāvatāra Sūtra* in Dwight Goddard (ed.), *A Buddhist Bible*, Beacon Press, Boston 1970, pp. 302–9. Also Aśvaghoṣa (attrib.), *The Awakening of Faith*, trans. Yoshito S. Hakeda, Columbia University Press, New York 1967, p. 47; or Dwight Goddard (ed.), *A Buddhist Bible*, p. 366. For more about the 'turning about', the *parāvṛtti*, see Sangharakshita, *The Meaning of Conversion in Buddhism*, chapter 5, in *Complete Works*, vol. 2, pp. 275–85.

491 This is the theme of Nietzsche's book *The Antichrist*, first published in German in 1985. See F. Nietzsche, *Twilight of the Idols and The Antichrist*, trans. J. Hollingdale, Penguin, London 1990.

492 See Dhammapāla, *The Udāna Commentary*, trans. Peter Masefield, Pali Text Society, Oxford 1995, vol. ii, p. 963.

493 The *Mahāsattipaṭṭhāna Sutta* is at *Dīgha Nikāya* 22. Sangharakshita's commentary on the *sutta* is found in *Living with Awareness* in *Complete Works*, vol. 15.

494 *Mahāparinibbāna Sutta*, *Dīgha Nikāya* 16 (ii.100); M. Walshe (trans.), *The Long Discourses of the Buddha*, Wisdom Publications, Boston 1995, p. 245; or T. W. and C. A. F. Rhys Davids (trans.), *Dialogues of the Buddha*, part 2, Pali Text Society, London 1971, pp. 107–8.

495 Kumārila Bhaṭṭa lived in the seventh century CE, and was a contemporary of the Buddhist philosopher Dharmakīrti; Bhaṭṭa is widely believed to have exercised an influence on his younger contemporary Śaṅkara (fl. c. 710). The legendary account of his life says that he studied at the Buddhist monastic university at Nālandā, then in its prime, and used the knowledge gained to try to counter Buddhist philosophical positions. His *Śloka Vārttika* is the first of a three-part treatise on the *Mīmāṃsā Sūtra* composed by the third-century BCE Vedic philosopher Jaimini. Kumārila Bhaṭṭa is regarded as the founder of one of the six orthodox (*āstika*)

philosophical schools of Hinduism.

496 If the shudra intentionally listens for committing to memory the veda, then his ears should be filled with (molten) lead and lac; if he utters the veda, then his tongue should be cut off; if he has mastered the veda his body should be cut to pieces.

Manusmṛti xii.4.

497 This is a reference to the well-known parable of the raft. See note 197.

498 *Aṅguttara Nikāya* iv.274–6; Bhikkhu Bodhi (trans.), *The Numerical Discourses of the Buddha*, Wisdom Publications, Boston 2012, pp. 1189–90; or E. M. Hare (trans.), *The Book of the Gradual Sayings*, vol. iv, Pali Text Society, Oxford 1995, pp. 181–5.

499 'There can be no difference that doesn't make a difference.' William James, *Pragmatism* (1907).

500 This is a reference to the four 'formless *dhyānas*' (*arūpa dhyānas*). For information about these, see, for example, chapter 7, 'On the Threshold of Enlightenment', in Sangharakshita, *The Bodhisattva Ideal*, *Complete Works*, vol. 4, pp. 156–9.

501 See the *Ariyapariyesanā Sutta*, *Majjhima Nikāya* 26 (i.163); Bhikkhu Ñaṇamoli and Bhikkhu Bodhi (trans.), *The Middle Length Discourses of the Buddha*, Wisdom Publications, Boston 1995, p. 256; or I. B. Horner (trans.), *The Collection of the Middle Length Sayings*, vol. i, Pali Text Society, London, Henley & Boston 1976, p. 206.

502 Ibid.

503 For more about the *bardo*, see Sangharakshita's lecture on the *Tibetan Book of the Dead* in the series 'Aspects of Buddhist Psychology'; *Complete Works*, vol. 12.

504 This was the subject of discussion at the Third Buddhist Council, which was held in the time of the Emperor Aśoka. The Theravādin position that there is no intermediate state (*antarābhava*) is set out in *Kathāvatthu* viii.2, 'Of an Intermediate State'; see See S. Z. Aung and C. A. F. Rhys Davids (trans.), *Points of Controversy* (*Kathāvatthu*), Pali Text Society, London 1915, pp. 212–3. For Pāli canon references to an intermediate state, one could cite, for example, *Saṃyutta Nikāya* iv.400; see Bhikkhu Bodhi (trans.), *The Connected Discourses of the Buddha*, Wisdom Publications, Boston 2000, p. 1393; or F. L. Woodward (trans.), *The Book of the Kindred Sayings*, vol. iv, Pali Text Society, London, Henley & Boston 1980, p. 170; or the *Mettā Sutta*, the eighth *sutta* of 'The Chapter of the Snake' in the *Sutta-Nipāta*, which mentions extending

loving-kindness to 'beings born and to-be-born'.

505 This *udāna* is an important and often-quoted saying of the Buddha. It appears in the *Channovāda Sutta*, *Majjhima Nikāya* 144 (iii.266); Bhikkhu Ñāṇamoli and Bhikkhu Bodhi (trans.), *The Middle Length Discourses of the Buddha*, Wisdom Publications, Boston 1995, p. 1116; or I. B. Horner (trans.), *The Collection of the Middle Length Sayings*, vol. iii, Pali Text Society, Oxford 1993, pp. 317–8. It is also found at *Saṃyutta Nikāya* iv.59; Bhikkhu Bodhi (trans.), *The Connected Discourses of the Buddha*, Wisdom Publications, Boston 2000, p. 1166; or F. L. Woodward (trans.), *The Book of the Kindred Sayings*, part 4, Pali Text Society, London, Henley & Boston 1980, p. 32. It is also cited in a para-canonical Pāli work called the *Nettippakaraṇa*, paragraph 364; Bhikkhu Ñāṇamoli, *The Guide*, Pali Text Society, London 1977, pp. 94–5. There is a parallel preserved in Sanskrit at *Udānavarga* 26.20:

> There is no agitation for one who has no dependence, and here one finds calming down. There is neither going nor passing away, called the end of suffering.

The conclusion of this *udāna*, 'neither here nor there nor in between exist. Just this is the end of suffering', also occurs at *Udāna* 1.10 (the discourse to Bāhiya) and in the *Māluṅkyāputta Sutta* at *Saṃyutta Nikāya* iv.72; Bhikkhu Bodhi (trans.), *The Connected Discourses of the Buddha*, Wisdom Publications, Boston 2000, pp. 1175–6; or F. L. Woodward (trans.), *The Book of the Kindred Sayings*, part 4, Pali Text Society, London, Henley & Boston 1980, pp. 43–4.

506 The story is also told in the *Mahāparinibbāna Sutta*, *Dīgha Nikāya* 16 (ii.126–8 and ii.135–6). See T. W. and C. A. F. Rhys Davids (trans.), *Dialogues of the Buddha*, part 2, Pali Text Society, London 1971, pp. 136–9 and 147–8; or M. Walshe (trans.), *The Long Discourses of the Buddha*, Wisdom Publications, Boston 1995, pp. 256–7 and 261–2.

507 See, for example, *Sāmaññaphala Sutta*, *Dīgha Nikāya* i.62; T. W. Rhys Davids (trans.) *Dialogues of the Buddha*, part 1, Pali Text Society, London 1973, p. 78; or M. Walshe (trans.), *The Long Discourses of the Buddha*, Wisdom Publications, Boston 1995, p. 99. See also the *Pabbajjā Sutta*, *Sutta-Nipāta* 3.1, verse 2, for the Buddha's account of his own Going Forth.

508 See *Dhammapada* 60–1.

509 See Dhammapāla, *The Udāna Commentary*, trans. Peter Masefield, Pali Text

Society, Oxford 1995, vol. ii, pp. 1058–9.

510 *Dhammapada* 61.

511 The *locus classicus* for the Buddha's teachings on *mettā* or *maitrī* is the *Mettā Sutta* (sometimes called the *Karaṇīya Mettā Sutta*) at *Sutta-Nipāta* 1.8. See H. Saddhatissa (trans.), *The Sutta-Nipāta*, Curzon Press, London 1985, pp. 15–16 for one of the many translations in English. Sangharakshita's commentary on the *sutta* is published as *Living With Kindness* in *Complete Works*, vol. 15. *Mettā* is, of course, mentioned in many other places in the Pāli canon. For example, in the *Mettānisaṃsa Sutta*, *Aṅguttara Nikāya* v.342, the Buddha explains the eleven advantages of cultivating *mettā*, which include sleeping easily and having a serene countenance. See Bhikkhu Bodhi (trans.), *The Numerical Discourses of the Buddha*, Wisdom Publications, Boston 2012, pp. 1573–4; or F. L. Woodward (trans.), *The Book of the Gradual Sayings*, vol. v, Pali Text Society, Oxford 1996.

512 For an account of the twin miracle, see Eugene Watson Burlingame (ed.), *Buddhist Legends*, part 3, Luzac, London 1969, pp. 45–7.

513 See, for example, the *Aggivacchagotta Sutta*, *Majjhima Nikāya* 72 (i.485); Bhikkhu Ñāṇamoli and Bhikkhu Bodhi (trans.), *The Middle Length Discourses of the Buddha*, Wisdom Publications, Boston 1995, p. 591; or I. B. Horner (trans.), *The Collection of the Middle Length Sayings*, vol. ii, Pali Text Society, Oxford 1994, p. 163.

APPENDIX 2

514 Dhananjay Keer, *Dr Ambedkar: Life and Mission*, second edition, Bombay 1962, p. 488.

515 B. R. Ambedkar, *Buddha and the Future of His Religion*, third edition, Jullundur 1980, p. 14.

INDEXES

INDEX 1: INDIA

To assist the reader, the index for this volume has been split into two, the first relating to the Dhamma Revolution in India, which began in 1956 (pages 1 to 418) and the second covering the commentary on the *Udāna*, *Wisdom before Words* (pages 419 to 656). Page numbers in italic refer to images.

Abhayanavita, Dhammacharini lxv, 666n
Abhidhamma Piṭaka 219–20, 673n
Abhidharma 133, 143, 163, 165, 211, 232, 238, 312
abhiṣeka 135–6, 683n; *see also* initiation
absolute, and relative, truth, *see* truths, two
ahiṃsā 64, 166; *see also* non-violence
Ahmadnagar 131, 143, 147, 161
Ahmedabad xl–xli, xlvi, xlviii, 60, 62, 108, *155*, 160, 166, 169, 170, 182, 293, 296, 363, 376, 673n
Aid for India (later Karuna Trust) li, 88, 314, 675n, 704n
Ajanta, caves 333, 372, 704n
Ajātaśatru, King 274–5, 667n, 700n
Ajmer xlviii, 12, 157, 296
Akbar 44
Alagaddūpama Sutta 141, 156, 684n, 688n
alienation 73–4
All-India P.E.N. 131, 134, 682n
altruism, and individualism 73; *see also* transformation of, 'self and world'
Ambedkar, B. R. (Dr Babasaheb) *xxxiv*, 69, 126–7, 168, 186–8, 237–8, 288–9, 310–11, 319, 343, 379, 668n
'Babasaheb' 14
background 21–2, 106–7, 668n
birth anniversary 166–7, 169, 177, 181, 185
'a bodhisattva' xxxi, 319, 321, 339
and Buddhism, *see under* Buddhism
career 3–4, 22, 24, 76–7, 107
and caste system, *see* caste system
character 5, 14, 15–16, 39, 76, 167–8, 271, 318–19, 339, 355
conversion of, *see under* conversion
death 11, 17–18, 25, 320, 325, 375
anniversary xlix, 116, 160, 181, 316
condolence meeting liv, 11–12, 18, 96–7, 313, 375
exemplification of six perfections 318–19

followers xl, lv, 12, 20, 23, 39, 40–1, 77, 108, 298, 313, 338–9, 410–11; *see also* Ambedkarite movement; Buddhists, new
  confusion about conversion xlii, 343–4, 350
  Sangharakshita and xl, 12, 20, 121
and hero worship 38–9, 670n
and Hinduism, *see under* Hinduism
and Marxism 10, 71–2, 665n, 667n
memorials 2, 112, 399–400, 405
opposition to 24, 76–7, 94, 107, 167, 271, 289, 319, 668n
and religion, *see* religion, Ambedkar and
reputation 3–4, 10, 406, 668n
Sangharakshita and, *see* Sangharakshita, and Ambedkar
true homage to 97, 100–1, 103–4, 108, 116, 167, 360
twenty-two vows of, *see* vows, twenty-two
vision xxiii, xxv, xxix–xxx, xxxi, lxi, 78, 82–3, 118, 203, 354, 362
Ambedkar, Y. 123, 126
Ambedkar and Buddhism 15, 89, 353, 359–63, 399, 659–61, 704n
Ambedkarite movement xxxviii, xlii, xlviii, lvi; *see also* Ambedkar, followers of
Amitamati, Dhammacharini lix–lxiii
amṛta 231
anagarikas 418
Anand, M. R. xliv
Ānanda 40, 208, 394, 672n, 699n
Anandamayi 41, 44
Ananda Metteyya (Allan Bennett) 139
ānāpānasati, *see* mindfulness, of breathing
anātman (Pāli *anattā*) 142–3, 157–60, 171, 176, 319; *see also* self, no
anger 173, 226–7, 249, 398; *see also* hatred
Aṅguttara Nikāya 171, 220, 228, 679n, 684n, 687n, 691n, 696n, 698n, 699n
animals 171, 201, 345–6, 692n, 694n
  sacrifice of lvii, 9, 20, 26, 45–6, 48–9, 279, 671n
anitya 159, 327–8
Annihilation of Caste xxv, xxvi, 128, 665n, 666n
appamādena sampādetha 84, 675n
Archimedes 129, 682n
arhant, ideal 68–9, 133
arhants 93, 146, 157, 225, 676n
Arjuna 33, 55–6
Arnold, E. 24, 139
art, Buddhist 99, 207–8, 384, 417
arts 68, 99, 139, 153–4, 208, 368, 370, 690n
Āryadeva 327
āryans 140, 235
āryapudgalas, four kinds of 146
Āryasaṅgha 146
Asaṅga 327
asceticism 135, 669n
ascetics
  five 263–4
  true 678n
Ashok-chakra 105, 677n
Ashok Dhammaduta programme li
Ashvaghosha Project 666n
Aśoka 120, 220, 677n, 694n
Aśok Vijayadashami 93, 676n
Aṣṭasāhasrikā Prajñāpāramitā 164
Aśvaghoṣa 36, 123, 126, 669n, 698n, 699n
atheism 138
Atīśa 135, 666n
ātman 145, 159–60; *see also* self
ātmavāda xxix, 142, 280, 685n
atomic or nuclear wars and weapons 87–8, 120, 157
Augustine, Saint 146, 687n
Aurangabad xli, 128, 293, 302, 333, 337, 358, 391, 701n, 704n
Aurobindo 160
Australia 246, 276, 283–4, 701n
Avalokiteśvara (*Mahākāruṇika*) xliii, 38, 147, 176, 227, 693n, 704n
  mantra, *see* mantras, Avalokiteśvara
avyākatas (Sanskrit *avyākṛtas*) 138, 225–6, 234, 683n
awareness 119, 231, 370, 675n; *see also* mindfulness

Bāhiya 151–2, 687n
bahujana sukhāya, bahujana hitāya xxix, 212, 665n
Bahujan Hitay 366, 367–8, 408, 704n
Bahujan Samaj Party xlviii
Bakula, Dhammachari *xlv*, 701n
banner of victory 408–9
beauty 368, 370
Benares 44, 124, 312, 397; *see also* Varanasi
beneficial activity (*artha-caryā*) 147, 176
Bhagavad Gītā 33, 37, 47, 51–6, 162, 164, 670n, 672n, 673n
Bhagwan Rajneesh (Osho) 396
Bhaja
  caves xlix, 285, 334, 405, 692n
  first women's retreat *l*
  retreat centre (Saddhamma Pradip Retreat Centre) xlvii, xlix, liv, 326, 334, 404, 405, 407, 409

bhakti 117, 138, 670n
Bhandare, R. D. (Mr Bhandari) 8, 122–3, 336, 667n
Bhāradvāja 330–1
Bharate family 355, 357, 367
Bharatiya Bauddha Mahasabha 18, 116, 117, 123, 130, 148–9, 177, 375
bhāvanā 197, 332
bhikkhunīs (Sanskrit *bhikṣuṇīs*) liv, 48, 212, 268; *see also* nuns
bhikkhus (Sanskrit *bhikṣus*) 49, 67–8, 139, 267, 680n; *see also* monks
  Ambedkar's view of 32, 67–9, 75, 80, 271, 362
  response to new Buddhists 79–80
  sangha 48, 66, 67, 68, 220, 270–1, 362, 385
  Thai 49, 79, 131
  and *upāsakas* 225, 267
bhūmis, ten 146
Bimbisāra, King 274, 667n
blind man finding a jewel 145, 686n
blind men and elephant, parable of 142, 170, 685n
Bodh Gaya xxvi, *lxiii*, lxiv, 131, 149, 206, 259, 261–2, 264, 307, 397, 665n
bodhi 125, 143, 368–9, 387; *see also* Enlightenment
Bodhicaryāvatāra 369, 686n, 704n
  seminar 215, 695n
bodhicitta 125, 145, 151, 175, 686n
bodhicitta-utpāda 175
Bodhidharma
  Chan patriarch 119, 679n
  Dhammachari 367
Bodhisattva, Buddha's previous lives as 122, 133
bodhisattva ideal xliii, 68–9, 81–2, 101, 121–2, 135–6, 153, 171
bodhisattvas 81, 121, 125, 145–7, 165, 369
  Ambedkar described as xxxi, 319, 321, 339
  vow xliii; *see also praṇidhāna*
bodhi tree 145, 207, 357, 370, 677n
bodhyaṅgas, seven 230, 368–70
body 231, 307, 683n
  and mind l, 225–6, 307, 317, 354, 696n
  speech, and mind, transmutation of 136
Bombay (now Mumbai) xl, 10, 17, 60, 71–2, 131–2, 186, 287, 291, 295, 305, 352, 682n
  Ambedkar and 4–5, 16, 71, 186, 289, 310, 336, 360
  Mahar communities in 288, 309
  mass conversion movement 363
  Sangharakshita lecture tours and visits xlviii–xlix, 20, 116, 123, 148–9, 277, 313, 336, 374, 376
    schedule December 1959 *132*
  Siddharth College, *see* Siddharth College
  State removal of Scheduled Caste facilities 110–11
  Suzuki in 164, 690n
  TBMSG and xlvii
  Worli district, *see* Worli
brahmacarya 183; *see also* celibacy
Brahmajāla Sutta 117, 138, 249, 343, 678n, 683n, 684n, 697n, 703n
Brahmanism 46, 48–9, 300, 308; *see also* Hinduism
brahma vihāras 121, 169, 171, 172–4, 196–7
brahmin, true xxvi
brahmins 21, 23, 44, 45, 50, 54, 82, 168, 186, 233, 287, 308, 361; *see also* caste Hindus
  Ambedkar and 75, 381–2
  new Buddhists and 315
  political alliances with Dalits 62
  presidents of Maha Bodhi Society 5, 16, 76
Buddha lviii, 14, 33–42, 103, 118, 121–2, 198, 234–7, 252–3, 259, 266, 326, 670n, 678n; *see also* Gautama, Siddhārtha, Tathāgata
  archetypes and symbols and 37, 679n
  birth 35–6, 261
  and caste system xxvi, 13, 47–8, 125, 186, 282, 672n, 673n
  death of, *see parinirvāṇa*
  decision to teach 145, 206, 678n
  disciples of, *see* disciples
  Enlightenment anniversary, *see* Buddha Jayanti, Vaiśākha Pūrṇimā, Wesak
  Eternal 118, 678n
  exhortation to spread the Dharma xxix, 83, 212, 665n, 675n
  not God xxvi, 36, 38, 235, 255, 362
  going forth, leaving home (*parivrajā*) 219, 221–2, 229, 257, 696n
  a guide or teacher not salvation-giver xxvi, 35, 128, 138, 150, 247, 680n
  Hindu view of 8, 38, 235, 657
  images liv, 60, 80, 126, 145, 195, 208, 215, 234, 236, 241–2, 405–6
  life of 24, 236, 255–60, 330, 397
  and monk with dysentry 260, 699n
  and omniscience 40, 670n
  previous lives 122, 133
  recollecting or meditating on 207, 214, 397; *see also Buddhānusmṛti*

supernormal powers of 36–7
three bodies of, *see trikāya*
and 'Untouchables' 54, 260, 672n, 699n
walking xxix, li, *lv*, lvi
words
to be tested like gold 246, 697n
last 150, 675n
The Buddha and His Dhamma xxii, xxvi, xxix–xxx, xlii, 170, 199, 203, 205, 219, 247, 258, 327, 343, 351, 363, 394, 664n, 665n, 672n, 697n, 703n
Sangharakshita's critique of 129, 363, 659–61
'Buddha and the Future of His Religion' xix, xxxi, 3, 15, 31–90, 128, 270, 362
Buddhacarita 36, 669n, 698n, 699n
Buddha-field (*buddha-kṣetra*) 254–5
Buddhaghosa 673n, 688n, 692n, 693n, 695n
Buddhahood 122, 136, 145–6, 369; *see also* Enlightenment
Buddha Jayanti 9, 17, 109, 111, 124, 144, 169, 177, 181–2
Buddhānusmṛti 144, 685n; *see also* Buddha, recollecting or meditating on
Buddhas, Five 118, 176, 679n; *see also* wisdom, five aspects of
Buddhayan xli, liv, 299, 316, 322, 337, 394, 396, 701n
Buddhism 119, 120, 138, 140–1, 142, 156–9, 211, 281, 327, 341–2
Ambedkar and
contact with other Buddhists 75–6
integrity of 9, 26, 100, 363, 378; *see also* vows, twenty-two
interpretation of xxvi, xliii, 40–1, 64–7, 219, 221, 351, 362–3
reasons for choosing xxix, 24, 82–3, 128–9, 169, 187, 209, 362, 379
anniversary of, *see* Buddha Jayanti
attraction for Western people 205–9
compared to other religions 63–9, 350–1
confusion and misunderstanding, in Buddhist organizations 5, 16, 76, 265, 269
confusion and misunderstanding about 8, 20, 26, 75, 132, 159, 170, 212, 240, 350
decline of 25–6, 129, 186, 265, 308
emphasis on reason and experience 37, 40, 129, 169
and Hinduism
absorption by 8, 26, 38, 117, 235, 657, 674n
compared 43–50, 117–18, 125
influence on each other 49, 50, 277–8
Hindu view of 8–9, 26, 38, 235, 279–80, 657, 701n
history of 134–5, 163, 307–8, 372, 377
'philosophy' of 126, 142–3, 152, 171, 211, 267
and religion 120, 138, 170–2, 252, 350–1, 669n
revival of xix, lxiv, 57–62, 93–4, 101–2, 112, 120–1, 127, 157, 254–5, 285
schools of, *see* schools of Buddhism
and science xxx, lviii, 117, 129, 138, 169, 226, 234, 669n
social aspect of 41–2, 172, 207
spreading, *see* Dharma, spreading xxxi, 65–7, 70–1, 80, 83–5, 87–8, 103, 675n
Tibetan, *see* Tibetan Buddhism
timeless (*akāliko*) 156–7, 245
Triyāna 134
unity of 117–18, 169, 272, 377
whole of, in *oṃ maṇi padme hūṃ* 147, 174
'Buddhism, World Peace, and Nuclear War' 87, 675n
Buddhist
definition of 385
movement, new, *see* FWBO
organizations 194, 265, 269, 298, 384–5, 673n
ten ornaments of a 392–8
The Buddhist Review 139
Buddhists
new xxi, xlii, xlvi, 12–13, 80–2, 300–4, 306
attempts to undermine unity of 169, 281–2, 362, 377
effect of conversion on xxvii, lviii–lix, 12, 19, 25, 60, 61, 110, 188, 237–8, 303–4, 314–15, 416
and fear 167–8, 303
forfeit of Scheduled Caste facilities 61–2, 109–11
not ' Hīnayānists or Mahāyānists' 169, 362, 377
and Hindu beliefs and practices 9, 20, 26, 45, 81–2, 257, 277–8, 333
prosperity of xxvii, 19, 297, 407–8, 410
response of Buddhist world to 79–80, 300
Sangharakshita and xx, xliv, 10–12, 313, 335, 676n

Buddhists, new (*cont.*)
termed 'Neo-' by Hindu newspapers 187, 281–2
treatment by caste Hindus 12, 23, 187, 301–3
Western xxi, lxiv, 88, 300, 337, 338–9, 342, 406, 408
Buddhist Society
of England 139
of Great Britain and Ireland 139
of Gujarat 169, 182
of India, Nagpur Branch 95, 98, 99
London 139, 312, 673n
But Little Dust li, 666n

Calcutta (now Kolkata) 4, 12, 46, 166, 177, 210, 267, 362, 376
canonical literature 179, 219, 221, 696n; *see also* Pāli canon
Carlyle, T. 167, 690n
caste, *see also* Classes, *varnas*
and consciousness 232–3
discrimination lvi–lvii, lx, 6, 675n; *see also* caste Hindus, treatment of 'Untouchables'
duties (*jāti-dharma*) xxv, lvii, 8, 125
hell of xxx, 11, 361, 379
Hindus, *see also* brahmins; Hindus, orthodox
opposition to Ambedkar 24, 76–7, 94, 107, 289
ratio to Dalits 59, 288
response to conversions, *see under* mass conversion, responses to
riots in Ahmedabad 62, 673n
treatment of new Buddhists 12, 23, 187, 301–3
treatment of 'Untouchables' xli, lvi–lvii, lxii, 7, 12, 21–2, 24, 59–60, 62, 78, 110, 288, 309; *see also* Ambedkar, background; Chowdar Tank case
meaning of word (*jāti*) 44
system xxiv–xxviii, xxx, 6, 21–2, 41, 44–5, 82, 186, 235, 287, 308–9, 361
basis of Hinduism xxiv–xxv, 44, 51, 125, 186, 287; *see also Chaturvarna* doctrine
four main castes 54, 186, 287, 308, 664n
laws, *see Manusmṛti* 309
in villages xli, 12, 59–60, 186, 287, 309, 329
castes
privileged xxiii–xxiv
Scheduled lv, 58, 61–2, 79, 109–10, 182, 188, 417; *see also* 'Untouchables'; Classes, Depressed; Dalits
Ambedkar's influence with 78–9, 107, 128
government and positive discrimination 61–2, 673n
causation, *satkāryavāda*, and *asatkāryavāda* views of 135, 142, 160, 683n
celibacy 43; *see also brahmacarya*
Chandramani, U. 7, 8, 26, 98, 112, 116, 378, 667n, 677n
Chan school 164, 679n; *see also* Zen
chanting lxv, 122, 216, 227, 257, 335, 681n; *see also* devotional practices, *Tiratana Vandanā*, worship
chariots, seven 248
Chaturvarna doctrine 47–8, 51–6; *see also* caste, system
China li, 134, 164, 229, 244, 254, 264, 282, 308, 690n
Chinese Buddhists, support for TBMSG projects li
Chintamani, Dharmachari 195, 694n
Chowdar Tank case 22–3, 127, 187
Christianity 122, 170, 201, 205–6, 236, 240, 277, 282, 311, 341–2, 345
influenced by secular philosophies 346–7, 350
Christian missionaries 68, 84–5
Classes
Backwards lxi, 58, 109, 185, 673n; *see also* Shudras
Depressed 110, 116; *see also* castes, Scheduled
Coleridge, S. T. 72, 674n
commitment is primary, lifestyle is secondary 27, 225, 362, 385, 677n
communication 120, 217, 224
communism 10, 71–2, 344, 347–8, 350; *see also* Marxism
community living 208, 222, 365, 366, 368, 387, 405, 413
compassion liii, 141, 176, 197, 235, 264, 687n; *see also karuṇā*
of Ambedkar xxix, 135, 168, 339
and Avalokiteśvara mantra 227
development of (*Karuṇā bhāvanā*) 173
fullness of Buddha's (*mahākaruṇā*) 125, 206, 227, 235, 261
near and far enemies of 173, 692n
and wisdom xxx, 122, 133, 145, 147, 152, 156, 243, 251, 266, 331
concentration 151, 158; *see also dhyānas, samādhi*
forty supports for (*kammaṭṭhānas*) 125, 144, 172, 176

conceptual
formulations and expressions 133, 142–3
symbols 159
conditionality 135–6, 142–3, 152, 160, 171; *see also nidānas, pratītya-samutpāda*
five orders of (*niyamas*) 56, 673n
progressive order of (spiral path) 175, 693n
conditioning, religious 301
conditions, material 347–8, 410
confession 398
consciousness xxxii, 143; *see also* mind, *vijñāna*
levels or higher states of 137, 175, 346; *see also* worlds
store (*ālaya-vijñāna*) 232, 348–9
consumerism xxii, lxii, 389
conversion (*diksha* (Sanskrit *dīkṣā*)) 125–6, 129, 170; *see also Dhammadiksha*
of Ambedkar 7, 8, 25, 26, 78–9, 93–4, 107, 128, 169, 218, 257, 339
anniversary liii, 3, 21, 149, 181
and *bodhicitta-utpāda* 175
effect on individuals, *see* Buddhists, new, effect of conversion
four means of (*saṃgraha-vastus*) 147, 176
mass, *see* mass conversion
movement liii, 10, 12, 25, 124–5
vows 657–8; *see also* vows, twenty-two
cooperation 334, 352, 382, 387–8, 390, 397–8; *see also* harmony
Councils, after *parinirvāṇa* 133, 667n, 682n
craving (*tṛṣṇā*) 136, 151, 152; *see also* greed
cultural life xlviii, 80–1, 99, 379
culture, gift of 355

Dalai Lama 38, 50, 77, 131, 135, 211
Dalits xxxviii, 3, 5–7, 58–9, 62, 65, 82, 89, 233, 673n; *see also* castes, Scheduled, 'Untouchables'
after conversion, *see* Buddhists, new
attitude to Ambedkar 39, 313
literature 81, 126, 153–5, 675n
population 58, 309, 673n, 702n
dāna 35, 122, 125, 146, 175–6, 318, 355, 357, 408
of Ambedkar 318
Dapodi
development of TMBSG activities xlix–l, 317–18, 325, 354–7, 405
Mahavihara, *see* Mahavihara
Sangharakshita's visits l, liv, 147, 254, 316, 399–400
Darwin, C. xlix, 344–7, 349–50, 691n
death 320–5, 696n
deities, Hindu 81, 100, 128; *see also īśvaras*
Delhi xlviii, 12, 159, 167, 210, 294, 296, 312, 376
Ambedkar in 9, 17, 106, 360, 375
democracy xxvi–xxviii, 38, 65, 78, 126
De Quincey, T. 153
Devadatta 36, 669n
devotional practices, *see also* chanting, *Tiratana Vandanā*, worship
Ambedkar's book of xlii, xliv, 174, 676n
Dhammacharinis lxv, 362, 387, 389, 402–3, 405, 413; *see also* ordination, in India, of women
Dhammacharis and Dhammacharinis 387, 403; *see also* Order members
Dhammadiksha 26, 350–1, 378, 385; *see also* conversion
denial of 62, 168
unwillingness to take 343, 350, 351
Dhammamitras 255, 388–9, 402, 405, 408; *see also* Mitras
Dhammapada xlvii, 35, 66, 136, 145, 146, 150, 163–4, 198, 202, 226, 231, 251, 323–4, 327, 346, 666n, 669n, 674n, 679n, 683n, 686n, 687n, 694n, 696n, 697n, 698n, 702n, 703n
Ambedkar's view of 66–7
Chinese, *see Dharmapada*
commentary (*Dhammapāda aṭṭhakathā*) 66, 674n
and *Diamond Sūtra* 163, 164
Sangharakshita teaching 118, 119, 138, 179, 394
Dhamma Revolution xlviii, lvi, 19, 25, 351, 360, 364, 378–80, 389, 397–8
Revolution
significance of 339–40, 377, 379
start of xxix–xxx, 355, 362
Sangharakshita and xxxi, xl
dhāraṇīs 136, 683n
Dhardo Rimpoche 409
Dharma (Pāli Dhamma) 46–7, 103, 133, 141, 146, 210–13, 218, 240–1, 243, 263, 266, 270, 684n, 688n; *see also* Buddhism
birth of 262, 264, 700n
Buddha's definition of 206, 212, 213, 684n, 695n

Dharma (Pāli Dhamma) (*cont.*)
Buddha's exhortation to spread xxix, 83, 212, 665n, 675n
'come and see' (*ehipassiko*) 141, 156, 243–7, 331–2, 688n
enemies of 117, 240–1
gift of 175, 231, 318
Hindu (Vedic) meaning 8, 45, 55–6, 350
liberty to 'chip and chop' 40, 41
practice in different countries 239–40, 243–5
psychological and social attitudes to 12, 41–2, 303
qualities described in *Tiratana Vandanā* 141, 156–7, 242–7, 251, 332, 688n
Revolution, *see* Dhamma Revolution
and *saddhamma* 344, 351
spreading 210, 213, 238, 264–5, 269, 275, 362; *see also* Buddhism, spreading
and Going for Refuge 269–70, 359
work of liii, lxv, 125, 202, 215–17, 230, 259, 275, 359, 396–7, 408
study lviii, 204, 214–15, 217, 370, 393–4, 398
groups 214–15, 394
and Vinaya 247
wheel of (*dharmacakra*) 105, 145, 305, 374, 677n
Dharmacharis and Dharmacharinis, *see* Dhammacharis and Dhammacharinis
dharmadūtas 108
dharmakāya 118
Dharmalochana, Dhammacharini 290, 701n
Dharmānusmṛti 144, 685n
Dharmapada (Chinese) 66, 661; *see also Dhammapada*
Dharmapala, Anagarika 21, 139, 668n, 684n, 699n
Dharmarakshita, Dhammachari xxxvii–xxxviii, *xlv*, 277, 290, 665n, 701n
dharmas (Pāli *dhammas*), Abhidharma and Mahāyāna views compared 163, 165
dharma-vicaya 369–70
dhyānas (Pāli *jhānas*) 84, 151, 158–9, 176, 228, 350
factors 159, 370
Diamond Sūtra (*Vajracchedikā-Prajñāpāramitā Sūtra*) xx, 162–6, 311, 690n
Dīgha Nikāya 37, 45, 48, 84, 125, 138, 167, 209, 220, 236, 256, 272, 275, 330, 343, 669n, 670n, 671n, 673n, 674n, 675n, 678n, 681n, 683n, 684n, 688n, 691n, 694n, 695n, 697n, 698n, 700n, 702n, 703n
diksha (Sanskrit *dīkṣā*) *see* conversion, *Dhammadiksha*, initiation
Diksha Bhumi xxxix–xl, 8, 92, 97–8, 116, 177, 364
garlanding Ambedkar's statue 2
memorial 98, 112–13, 677n
disciples
of Ambedkar xlii; *see also* Ambedkar, followers; Ambedkarite movement
of the Buddha lvi, 37, 198, 213, 236, 263–4, 274–5, 307, 325, 357, 387, 700n
exhorted to teach 83, 264, 665n, 675n
formerly Brahmins 244, 308
known as *śrāvakas* 197, 230
low caste and outcaste 672n
meeting regularly 209, 275, 695n
and oral tradition 197, 219, 230, 326–7
and Tipiṭaka 219–20, 243
relationship to teacher 135, 324–5, 683n
of Sangharakshita xlii, xliv, xlvi, 367
true, 'like a lotus' 145, 686n
Dōgen 679n
doubt and indecision (*vicikitsā*) 158–9, 175, 250
Dr Ambedkar Institute of Pāli, Buddhism and Social Sciences 131, 138–9
The Drama of Cosmic Enlightenment 678n, 686n, 695n, 702n, 703n
dṛṣṭis (Pāli *diṭṭhis*) 138, 142, 684n; *see also* views
duḥkha (Pāli *dukkha*) *see* suffering
duties 118, 125, 183, 402, 674n, 691n
caste 23, 55–6
spreading the Dharma xxxi, 71, 108, 375
of *upāsakas/upāsikas* 100, 121, 140, 143, 161, 225, 677n
Dutt, N. 177
dysentry, case of 260, 699n

education xlix, li, 101, 168, 182, 183, 288, 400, 415
gift of 318, 355
effort 346–7, 692n, 696n; *see also virya*
fourfold right 202, 694n
Eightfold Path 181, 225, 264, 657, 678n
mentioned in Sangharakshita's lectures 20, 119–21, 125, 143, 150, 175, 179, 202, 230, 290, 368, 684n
symbolized in Bhaja Shrine Hall 405
Ellora caves 293, 701n

emotions 73, 173–4, 231
enemies 196, 207, 278
of the Dharma 117, 240–1
near and far 83, 173–4, 692n
energy 199–203, 356, 704n; *see also* *virya*
Enlightenment 35, 118, 129, 243, 251, 262, 346, 674n; *see also bodhi*, Buddhahood, Nirvāṇa
Ambedkar's understanding of 38
aspiration for, *see bodhicitta*
of Huineng 690n
seven factors of (*bodhyaṅgas*) 230, 368–70
enthusiasm 83–4, 370, 388–9
equality xxvi–xxviii, xxix, li, 47, 64, 117, 120, 129, 182, 351, 657
fraternity and liberty xxiii–xxiv, xxvi, xxvii, xxviii, xxx, 63, 362, 379
wisdom of 176
equanimity, *see upekkhā*
The Eternal Legacy 219, 672n, 685n, 693n
ethics xx, 142–3, 147, 153–5, 158; *see also* morality, precepts, *sīla*
Ethiraj, D. xvii, lvi–lix
evolution, theory of 344, 345–6, 350, 691n
exemplification (*samānārthatā*) xxiii, 147, 176

faculties, five spiritual 140, 155, 158, 201, 368, 369, 694n; *see also* *indriyas*, spiritual, five
faith 135–6, 201–2, 224, 231, 331–2, 687n; *see also śraddhā*
blind 40–1, 125, 201, 246–7, 331–2, 393
follower (*śraddhā-carita*) 144, 685n
seed of 235, 331–2
family life 411–12
fear 206, 249, 258–9, 698n
fearlessness (*abhaya*) lix, 167, 175, 195, 259, 339
fearlessness, gift of 318, 355
feeling (*vedanā*) 151–2, 231
fetters (*saṃyojanas*) 146
Finland 205, 240, 245
fish and turtle story 144, 685n
food 54–5, 231, 333
forgiveness 323–4, 398
four analytical knowledges (*pratisaṃvids*) 147, 176
four necessities 172, 396
four noble truths 20, 121, 179, 230, 290
four sights 219, 221, 257, 698n
fraternity xxviii, 82; *see also mettā*
equality and liberty xxiii–xxiv, xxvi, xxvii, xxviii, xxx, 63, 362, 379
freedom xxvi, 64–5, 140–1, 153, 159, 188, 280–1; *see also* liberation, *vimukti*
'one taste of' 141, 160, 684n
seven types of person and 685n
Freud, S. xlix, 344, 348–50
Friends (*sahayaks*) of TBMSG/FWBO/ Triratna 268, 388
friendship 208, 342
spiritual, *see kalyāṇa mitratā*
Friends of the Western Buddhist Order, *see* FWBO
Furlong, M. 306, 307
FWBO xx, xxxix, 83, 185, 198, 376, 383; *see also* Triratna Buddhist Community
centres 13, 195, 205, 268, 359; *see also viharas*
and local communities 87
cooperatives 215–16; *see also* team-based right livelihood
emphasis on teamwork 301
Indian wing, *see* TBMSG
Mitras, *see* Dhammamitras, Mitras
reasons for starting 265, 383–9
start of 194–8, 204–5, 313

Gandhi, M. liii–liv, 23–4, 55, 128, 311, 313, 338, 359, 361
Gandhi, R. 301, 702n
Gandhi and his Critics 55, 673n
Gandhi film 311, 337, 702n
garlanding liv, 5, 193–4, 239–40, 306, 359, 366
of Ambedkar 2, 318
Gautam, M. 381–2
Gautama 224, 229, 242, 261, 326; *see also* Buddha
Gelug school 135
generosity, *see dāna*
globalisation 120
God xxvi, 34–5, 117, 120, 126, 150, 205, 233–5, 237, 252, 346
Buddha is not xxvi, 36, 38, 235, 255, 362
Buddha's silence about 138
creator 138, 150, 233–4, 249, 683n
word of 39–40
Godbole, W. M. 95–6, 116–17
gods and goddesses, Hindu xxxvi, 26, 45–6, 81, 287, 333, 657
Going for Refuge lxi, lxiii, 14, 208, 266–8, 316, 385–6, 671n
central or defining act of a Buddhist xxxi, xliii, 27, 225, 362, 385, 677n

Going for Refuge (*cont.*)
levels of 386–8, 704n
and ordination 269, 385
significance of mass conversion for 267
unifies all Buddhists 282–3
Goldsmith, O. 129–30, 682n
Govinda, Lama Anagarika 160, 690n
grace 117, 141, 145, 687n
gratitude xl, xliii, 13, 39, 96, 313, 406
greed 396; *see also* craving
hatred, and ignorance xxv, 103, 144, 213, 317, 370; *see also* poisons, three
group 73
and individual 43, 73–4, 674n
positive 73, 674n
guilt 173, 301
gurus 44, 136, 246–7, 274, 346, 683n, 691n; *see also* spiritual, teachers

happiness 198, 202, 228, 251, 262, 694n
'of the many' (*bahujana sukhāya*) xxix, 212, 665n
Hardy, S. 139
harmony xxix, 195–6, 249, 273, 364, 387, 408, 415; *see also* cooperation
hate-type (*dveṣa-carita*) 173, 692n
hatred (*vyāpāda*) 159, 173, 175, 231; *see also* anger
heart 72, 168, 196–7, 217, 283, 334
learning by 230, 242
Heart Sūtra 164
hero worship 37–9, 670n
hierarchy xxvii, 82, 135, 664n
spiritual 82, 235
hiṃsā, *see* violence
Hīnayāna 133–5, 163, 384, 683n; *see also* Theravāda
and Mahāyāna 133–4, 136, 163, 282, 377
monks sharing *viharas* 282
terms not applicable to new Buddhists 169, 362, 377
hindrances, five (*nivarāṇas*) 125, 158–9, 175, 226–7
Hindu
beliefs and practices, new Buddhists and 9, 20, 26, 45, 81–2, 257, 277–8, 333
view of Buddhism, *see under* Buddhism
Hindu Code Bill 3, 15, 76, 77, 107
Hinduism 170; *see also* Brahmanism
Ambedkar and xxvii, 24, 78, 94, 107, 127–8, 186–7
renunciation of in twenty-two vows xxx, 9, 26, 59, 100, 363, 378, 657–8
based in caste system xxiv–xxv, 44, 51, 125, 186, 287; *see also Chaturvarna* doctrine
and Brahmanism distinguished 48
and Buddhism, *see under* Buddhism
rituals and observances (*karmas*) 46–7, 50, 54
separate of social and spiritual life 41, 44–5
Hindus, orthodox 34, 308; *see also* brahmins, caste Hindus
and new Buddhists 187, 303
horses 44, 199–201, 248, 257; *see also* Windhorse, the
'riding but denying' 158, 689n
hostels (TBMSG) li, 89–90, 358, 366, 373, 405, 415, 666n, 676n, 704n
Dapodi 365, 399
Vishrantwadi Girls' lviii, 401–3, *403*, 405, 413
Wardha 358
Hsüan Tsang (Xuanzang) Retreat Centre, Bordharan li, liv–lv, 365–6, 391, *393*, 404
Huineng 164, 311–12, 690n
hūṃ 147, 151, 176
humanity xxiii, 37–8, 78, 101, 145, 182, 251–2, 342, 686n, 702n
human life, preciousness of 322
Humphreys, C. 56, 139, 312, 673n

ignorance (*avidyā*) 146, 151, 152, 249
images
of bodhisattvas 81
of the Buddha, *see under* Buddha
imagination 66, 153–4
impermanence (*anitya*) lviii, 327–8
India
constitution of 80, 110, 278, 309
Ambedkar and xxiii, 4, 89, 107, 186, 310, 338
independence of xxiii–xxiv
Indian Institute of World Culture 131, 140, 162
individual
and democracy xxviii–xxix
freedom of the 243, 281
and group 43, 73–4, 674n
salvation, renunciation of 122
and society xxvii, 207, 348
true lviii, 90, 674n
individualism, and altruism 73; *see also* self, and world
Indo-Tibetan Buddhist Cultural Institute (ITBCI) school 409
Indra 356, 703n
indriyas, five 150, 694n; *see also* spiritual faculties
infallibility 39–40, 48, 51

initiation xlii, 66, 98; *see also abhiṣeka, diksha*, ordination, transmission
insight 175, 688n, 693n; *see also vipassanā*
inspiration xxix, 202
interconnectedness 346
In the Footsteps of Ambedkar lii
intoxicants 175, 249, 395, 398
Isaiah 319, 702n
Islam 127, 170, 280, 293, 308, 311, 414
īśvara
  -bhakti 138
  parama- 35
īśvaras 140; *see also* deities

Jackson, R. J. 139
Jai Bhim!
  greeting 14
  book xlviii, 338, 665n, 666n
Jātakas 121–2, 680n, 681n, 703n
jealousy 174, 249
Jesus 33–6, 38–40, 255
jewel
  blind man finding 145, 686n
  hidden in garment 336, 703n
  in the lotus 147; *see also oṃ maṇi padme hūṃ*
  wish-fulfilling (*cintāmaṇi*) 145, 686n
jewels, three, *see* Three Jewels
jhānas, see dhyānas
Jnanasuri, Dhammacharini xxxv, xxxvii, xli, xliv, *lii*, 665n
joy 202, 231
  sympathetic, *see muditā*
Jung, C. G. 120, 679n

Kagyu school 135
Kālāma Sutta lix, 171, 691n
Kalimpong 3, 15, 19, 84, 210, 279, 312, 381, 409, 666n, 690n
kalpas 122, 383, 680n
kalyāṇa mitratā 208–9, 316, 359, 695n; *see also* spiritual friendship
kāmachanda 158–9, 175
kammaṭṭhānas 125, 144, 172, 176
Kaṇha 33, 669n; *see also* Krishna
Kanheri Caves 122, 333, 335, 681n
Kāraṇḍa-vyūha Sūtra 144, 176, 685n, 693n
Karle or Karla caves 171, 333, 692n
karma 56, 137, 141, 362
karma, Hindu (Vedic) meaning 47, 50, 51, 59, 670n, 671n
karmas, see rituals and observances, Hindu
karuṇā 122, 158, 212, 213, 231, 264, 351; *see also* compassion
karuṇā bhāvanā 173
Karuna Trust (formerly Aid for India) li, 88, 314, 675n, 704n
Kashyap, J. (Kashyapji) 3, 235–6
kasiṇa meditation 176, 693n
Kasturchand Park xxxvii, liv, 11, 17–18, 96, 98, 313, 365, 374–5
Kausalyayan, Bhadant Anand 381, 704n
Khuddaka Nikāya 220–1, 681n; *see also Dhammapada, Udāna, Sutta-Nipāta, Theragāthā*
kliṣṭa-mano-vijñāna 232–5, 238
knowledge
  and insight (*ñāṇadassana*) 250–1
  and insight, and seven *visuddhis* 250
  and love 224
  threefold true, of the Buddha 670n
  three kinds of 171
  'unknowable' 691n
  valid means to (*pramāṇas*) 150, 687n
  and vision of things..., *see Yathābhūta-jñānadarśana*
Korea Buddhists, support for TBMSG projects li
Kosambi 323–4
Krishna 33–5, 36, 37, 38–9, 47, 51–2, 56, 100, 255, 657; *see also* Kaṇha
Krusenstierna, R. and S. von 276, 700n
kṣānti 122, 125, 146, 175–6, 355–6, 357, 398; *see also* patience, tolerance
  of Ambedkar 318–19
Kshatriyas 54–6, 82, 186, 287, 308, 361, 664n
Kularatna, Dharmachari xl
Kulkarni
  A. R. xxxix, 17, 95, 97–9, 116–18, 123, 130, 662, 667n
  D. R. 105
  G. G. 99
Kusinara 8, 116, 312, 397, 677n

Lady Chatterley's Lover 153, 688n
lakṣaṇas, three 20, 159, 179
Lalitavistara Sūtra 259, 699n
language
  Buddha's emphasis on using one's own 133, 244
  inadequacy of 144, 159
Laṅkāvatāra Sūtra 49, 671n
Lawrence, D. H. 688n
lay people xliii, 172, 225; *see also upāsakas/upāsikas*
  and monks 25, 49, 68, 129, 172, 225, 267
  ordination of 26–7; *see also Dhammadiksha*
laziness 83–4

liberation xxix, lxi; *see also* freedom, *vimukti*
liberty, equality, and fraternity xxiii–xxiv, xxvi, xxvii, xxviii, xxx, 63–4, 362, 379
life, three levels of xlviii
lifestyle
  is secondary, commitment to Going for Refuge is primary 27, 225, 267–8, 271–2, 362, 385, 677n
  simplicity of 395–6, 398, 408
The Light of Asia 24, 139
lion liii, 167, 201, 238, 345, 692n
Lion's Roar Sutta (*Mahāsīhanāda Sutta*) 40, 670n
literalism, danger of 37, 133, 136, 175
livelihood li; *see also* right livelihood, work
logic 165, 687n
Lokamitra, Dhammachari *xlv*, *194*, 290, 299, 337, 356, 413, 416, 693n, 701n
  and Bhaja retreat centre *xlix*, 405–6
  early years in India xxxix–xli, xliii, 255
  fundraising li
  and Mahavihara 367, 404
  and Poona (Pune) xxxix–xli, 367, 694n, 701n
  and Sangharakshita's tours xxi, xliv, xlvii–xlix, lii–liii, 277, 285, 295, 302–3, 365, 376, 404, 407
London Buddhist Centre 3, 195, 199, 215, 255
  murals 199, *200*, 694n
London Buddhist Vihara 139, 668n
lotus (*padma*) 145, 146, 147, 159, 175, 686n
  'in hand' (Padmapāṇi) 704n
lotuses, humanity as bed of 145, 206, 686n, 694n, 695n
love xxviii, 82, 126, 141, 224, 231; *see also mettā*
Lumbinī 261, 397, 677n

Madhyamaka school 143, 211, 609, 690n
madness, of worldly people 204, 209, 695n; *see also pṛthagjanas*
Magadha 330, 678n
Mahābhārata 33, 35
Maha Bodhi Ambedkar Mission 155, 160
Maha Bodhi journal xix, 3, 21, 31, 61, 75, 76, 128, 667n, 669n
Maha Bodhi Society 21, 31, 93, 131, 157, 267, 298, 662, 668n, 684n
  Brahmin presidents 5, 16, 76
Mahad xlviii, 22–3, 127, 294–5, 399, 681n
Mahākāruṇika 227; *see also* Avalokiteśvara
Mahākaśyapa 308
Mahāmoggallāna (Sanskrit Mahāmaudgalyāyana) 93, 308
Mahāpajāpatī Gotami (Sanskrit Mahāprajāpatī Gautami) 206, 212, 213, 684n, 695n
Mahāparinibbāna Sutta 40, 84, 117, 209, 272, 675n, 678n, 688n, 695n, 700n
Maharashtra xlviii, li, 298–9, 309–10, 313, 317, 333, 339, 352, 358, 363, 366, 391, 407, 701n
  as *dharma-kṣetra* 254–5
Mahars 79, 285, 287–8, 309–11
Mahāsīhanāda Sutta 40, 670n
Mahavihara xlix, lii, liv, 40, *192*, 285, 354, 365–71, 404, 670n
Mahāyāna xliii, 118, 133–4, 163, 325, 679n, 682–3n, 690n, 693n
  division into *pāramitāyāna* and *mantrayāna* 136
  and Hīnayāna, *see* Hīnayāna, and Mahāyāna
Mahāyāna *sūtras* 50, 146, 164, 227, 324–5, 693n; *see also* individual *sūtras*
Maitreyabandhu, Dharmachari 694n
Maitreyanatha, Dhammachari 367
Maitreyaratna, Dhammachari lvi, lviii–lix
maitrī xxviii–xxix, 117, 138, 145, 158, 200, 227, 235, 337, 351, 368, 387; *see also mettā*
Maitriveer Nagarjuna, Dhammachari xvii, xix, xxi, xxxii, 15, 662, 667n
Majjhima Nikāya 40, 49, 156, 159, 160, 220, 248, 259, 262, 670n, 671n, 685n, 688n, 689n, 696n, 697n, 698n, 699n
Malaysia li, 272, 276, 280, 283, 386
Malaysian Buddhists, support for TBMSG projects li
Maṅgala Sutta 141, 318
maṇi 145, 147, 151, 175, 227
Maṇi Kabum 227
Mañjuśrī 81, 675n
mano-vijñāna 232
mantras xliii–xliv, 136, 144, 151, 174, 176, 683n
  Avalokiteśvara 144–7, 174, 176, 227, 693n; *see also oṃ maṇi padme hūṃ*
  Ambedkar and xliii, 144, 147, 676n
  sabbe sattā sukhī hontu 283, 318
  Tārā lxv
  tisaraṇa as 96

Vedic 23, 45–6
mantrayāna 136
Manu 309
Ambedkar as modern 310
Laws of, *see Manusmṛti*
Manuski Trust lix, 666n
Manusmṛti xxx, 23, 129, 294–5, 309, 310
burning of by Ambedkar xlviii, 23, 127, 187, 294–5
Māra 260, 281, 370
Margadata, and *Mokshadata* xxvi, 35, 128
marriage 44, 67, 182–3, 277, 308, 363, 412, 414
and dowry system 20, 183, 187
Marx, K. xlix, 72, 128, 167, 344, 347–8, 350, 664n, 674n, 690n
Ambedkar lecture on Buddha and 10, 665n, 667n
Marxism lxii, 10, 58, 70–2, 289, 311, 344, 348; *see also* communism
Ambedkar and 10, 71–2
mass conversion xxvii, xxxvi, 25, 95, 107, 128, 185, 187, 218, 254–5, 311, 339, 362; *see also* conversion
condolence meeting liv, 11–12, 18, 96–7, 313, 375
continuation of 10, 108, 124, 178, 187, 311
description of original xxxv–xxxvi, 8–9, 26–7
ground, *see* Diksha Bhumi
responses to xxxvii, 3, 9, 60, 61, 109–10, 127, 134, 165, 187, 201, 280–2, 301–2, 340, 342–3, 377
Sangharakshita
in Nagpur after xlii–xliii, 10–12, 17–18, 95–105, 289–90, 312–13, 363–4, 374–6
unable to attend original 9, 19, 374, 377
significance of xxxi–xxxii, 18–19, 93–4, 128, 314, 339–40, 342
material conditions 347–8
materialism xxii, lxii, 122, 138, 142, 389, 685n, 690n
material things, acquisition of 408
māyā doctrine 50
meditation lviii, lx, 19–20, 67, 119, 136, 179, 201, 206–7, 213–14, 231, 249, 392–3; *see also samādhi*
Ambedkar's attitude to 67–8
and spiritual truths 158
kasiṇa 176, 693n
pain during 227–8
retreats lviii, 214, 393
and state of 'no self' 223
together as a sangha 274
Mehta, D. 682n
mental states 347–8, 369–70, 408; *see also* mind
distinguishing skilful and unskilful (*dharma-vicaya*) 369
merit (*puṇya*) 267
Methodism 85–6
mettā xxix, lxi, 82, 172–4, 193, 195–8, 212, 213, 217, 231, 266, 324, 393; *see also* fraternity, *maitrī*
mettā bhāvanā xli, lviii–lix, lx, 120, 156, 173, 196, 207, 213, 245, 332, 392, 393, 692n
micchā-diṭṭhis, *see* views, wrong
middle path or way (*madhyama mārga*) 135–6, 138, 142, 160, 264, 347–9, 351, 669n
The Middle Way 139
Milarepa 135
Milinda College 128
Milton, J. 112, 340, 677n
mind xxix, 134, 145, 231, 341, 348–51, 370; *see also* consciousness, mental states
and body l, 225–6, 307, 317, 354, 696n
'experiences preceded by' 145, 686n
levels of 197, 348–50
to mind transmission 136
superconscious 349–50
unconscious (*bhavaṅga-sota*) 348–9; *see also* consciousness, store
unskilful (*akusala citta*) 226–7, 249
mindfulness *sati* (Sanskrit *smṛti*) 142, 150–1, 153, 201, 349, 356, 368–9, 687n; *see also* awareness
of breathing (*ānāpānasati*) xli, lviii, 151, 206, 213, 226–7, 332, 392–3
'is always useful' 151, 158, 356, 368, 688n
and *prajñā* 159
'strive on with' (*appamādena sampādetha*) 84, 675n
miracles 35, 36, 125, 681n
mitra, meaning of 173, 393
Mitras 13, 269, 300, 416, 417, 700n; *see also* Dhammamitras
Mohammed 33–6, 38–40
Mokshadata, and *Margadata* xxvi, 35, 128
monks, *see also bhikkhus*
four necessities of 172, 396
and laity 25, 49, 68, 129, 172, 225, 267
morality 63, 82, 137; *see also* ethics, precepts, *sīla*

morality (*cont.*)
Ambedkar view of xliii, 76, 78, 355
in Buddhism and Hinduism xxix, xliii, 43, 45–7, 63, 343, 658, 692n
contrasted to Enlightenment 141, 343, 703n
as essence of religion 43, 46–7, 63, 355, 362
muditā 172, 174, 196–7, 231
muditā bhāvanā 174
mudrās 136, 180
Mulagandhakuti Vihara 260, 699n
Mūlamadhyamakakārikā 158, 672n, 682n, 689n, 690n
Muslim, architecture 293
Muslims 19, 24, 60–1, 128, 234, 280, 293, 311, 343, 414, 674n

Nagabodhi, Dharmachari xlviii, 87, 286, 292, 665n
book on Ambedkar, *see Jai Bhim!*
interview with Sangharakshita 410–18
Nagaloka lv–lix, lxii
alumni stories lvi–lix
campus, walking Buddha *lv*
statue of Ambedkar *xxxiv*
Nāgārjuna 126, 134, 158, 327, 672n, 682n, 683n, 689n, 690n
Nagarjuna Training Institute li, lvi
Nagpur lv–lvi, 287–8, 376–7
Diksha Bhumi, *see* Diksha Bhumi
early years of TBMSG lii–liii
Kasturchand Park, *see* Kasturchand Park
Lokamitra's first visit to xxxix–xl
and mass conversions xxvii, xxxv, lvi, 95, 254–5, 372
Nagaloka campus, *see* Nagaloka
Sangharakshita in after Ambedkar's death xlii–xliii, 10–12, 17–18, 95–105, 289–90, 312–13, 363–4, 374–6
Sangharakshita lecture tours 20, 116, 124, 126, 149, 166, 177, 210, 376
Sangharakshita's first visit 374, 667n
Sangharakshita's last visit liv–lv, 372–3, 391–8
Sangharakshita's strong link with xlii, liv, 12, 193, 383
Nālandā 68, 128, 308, 397
nāma-rūpa 151–2, 231, 317, 325; *see also* mind and body
nature 120, 368
Nature (*prakṛti*) 53
negation, fourfold (*catuṣkoṭi*) 160, 689n
Neo-Buddhists, *see* Buddhists, new
New Zealand 191, 205, 245, 272, 276, 283, 284, 313, 329, 694n
nidānas 151, 152, 230, 677n, 693n; *see also* conditionality
nirmāṇakāya 118
Nirvāṇa 40, 101, 122, 136, 137, 144–5, 174–5, 176, 228, 690n; *see also* Enlightenment
and *saṃsāra* 147, 176
and seven purifications (*visuddhis*) 248–9
niyamas 56, 673n
non-returners (*anāgāmins*) 146
non-violence xxiii, 48, 71, 302; *see also ahiṃsā*
civil disobedience movement (*satyagraha*) 188

offerings 180, 239–40
oṃ 144–5, 147, 151, 174
oṃ maṇi padme hūṃ xliii–xliv, 99, 144, 151–2, 174–6, 227, 676n, 693n; *see also* mantras, Avalokiteśvara
once-returners (*sakṛdāgāmins*) 146
opposites 147, 152, 232
oral tradition 133, 136, 219, 307, 691n
Order, *see also* TBM, Triratna Buddhist Order
members 13, 83–4, 87, 269, 299, 388, 408, 416–17; *see also* Dhammacharis and Dhammacharinis
contact between, across world l, lxiv, 88–9, 290, 417, 418, 676n, 693n
and Going for Refuge 269, 387–8
in India xxxvii, liii–liv, 288, 313–14, 359, 366, 405, 411, 413, 676n, 704n
need for in India 88, 90
ordination, *see also* initiation
into WBO/TBM/Triratna Buddhist Order 269, 276, 385
and effective Going for Refuge 387–8
in India xlvi, 290, 297, 352, 366
not monastic or lay 362
training liv, lxv, 366, 388–9, 413, 666n
of women *lii*, lxv, 413, 676n, 701n; *see also* Dharmacharinis
of lay people 26–7; *see also Dhammadiksha*
of Sangharkshita 8, 26, 312, 667n, 677n
Orissa (Odisha) lvi, 254

padma 145, 175; *see also* lotus
Padmaloka Retreat Centre 320
Padmapāṇi 704n
Padmapani, Dharmachari 200, 694n
Padmasambhava 135
Padmasuri, Dharmacharini *l*, li, lii, 666n

Padmavajra, Dharmachari xl–xli, lx, 194, 290, 694n
padme 145, 147, 151
pain 227–8; *see also* suffering
Pain, J. R. 139
Pāli canon 40, 54, 133, 219–21, 225, 672n, 688n; *see also* canonical literature, Tipiṭaka
pañcasīla 119–20, 125, 161, 258, 385; *see also* precepts, five
 taking, *see* Refuges and Precepts
 teaching children 183
parables, *see also* stories
 of blind men and elephant 142, 170, 685n
 of the good physician 325, 702n
 of raft 141, 156, 688n
 of the raincloud 211, 218, 695n
paradox 160, 165
pāramitās 119, 121–2, 125, 146–7, 151, 175–6, 369, 405, 687n; *see also* perfections
 as foundation stones 355–7
pāramitāyāna 136
parinirvāṇa 9, 111, 307, 325–6, 330
paritrāṇa (Pāli *paritta*) ceremonies 124, 140, 147, 681n
path (*magga* (Sanskrit *mārga*)) 152–3, 247–50, 688n
 Eightfold, *see* Eightfold Path
 four stages of in Hīnayāna texts 146
 and fruit (*phala*) 146
 Hindu view of spiritual 685n
 motivation to follow 119, 121, 156
 of purity (*visuddhi magga*) 248–51
 spiral, *see* conditionality, progressive
 threefold, *see* threefold path or way
 yānas as successive stages of 135
patience 398; *see also kṣānti*, tolerance
pattern, in lives of great men 127
peacefulness 53, 83–4, 275
peace of mind 41, 150, 156, 197, 207, 274, 637; *see also praśrabdhi*
People's Education Society 126, 128, 168, 298–9, 667n
perception 118, 165, 231, 687n; *see also samjñā*
perfection of wisdom, *see prajñāpāramitā*
perfections xliii, 118, 318, 657; *see also paramitās*
perfect vision 685n
philosophy 142
 secular xlix, 344–50, 703n
pilgrimage 17, 125, 152, 161, 180, 381, 397–8
 Ambedkar and 106
 TBMSG 112, 367, 397
play (*līlā*) 202, 233
poetry 81, 153, 231, 318, 340–1
poisons, three xxv, 103, 144, 213, 317, 370; *see also* greed, hatred and ignorance
politics xlviii, 77–8, 120, 147, 169, 188, 243, 313, 414
 in the Buddha's day 65, 219, 221
 and religion 169, 415
Poona (now Pune) xl, 60, 180–3, 203, 218, 255, 260, 284; *see also* Dapodi
 Ambedkar in 668n
 conversion ceremonies 12, 108, 160–1, 363
 first social training course in Buddhism 179–80
 hostels, *see* hostels
 Karuna Trust and li, 675n
 Mahar communities in 288
 ordinations in xlvi, 290
 sangha 60
 as *saṅgha-kṣetra* 255
 Sangharakshita and Mrs Ambedkar in 6
 Sangharakshita lectures in xxxviii, xlix, 12, 20, 116, 123, 131, 140, 144, 161, 166–7, 181, 193, 199, 204, 210, 229, 232, 238, 251, 254, 260–1, 265, 272, 276–7, 284–5, 294, 296, 313, 316, 354, 366, 391, 401
 Sangharakshita's return visits xl, 193, 198–9, 204, 229, 232, 251, 254–5, 260, 265, 272, 276–7, 316, 366, 376
 TBMSG work in xlvii, li; *see also* Dapodi, hostels, Mahavihara, Saddhamma Pradip Retreat Centre
 women in 401–3
Poona District Buddhist Women's Association 161, *162*, 166, 181–3, 401
Poona Pact 55
Poona Project li, 675n; *see also* Aid for India, Karuna Trust
poverty xlii, li, 347
 not justified by religious belief xxx, 64, 125, 207, 362, 379, 389
powers
 supernatural 35, 36
 supernormal or psychic 36–7, 135, 669n
prajñā 137, 142, 152, 159, 163, 176, 212, 351, 356; *see also* wisdom
 and *samādhi* 143, 144, 174
prajñāpāramitā 118, 163 4
Prajñāpāramitā *sūtras* 163–4, 311
Prakṛti 53, 672n
praṇidhāna 147, 151, 176; *see also* bodhisattvas, vow

praśrabdhi 370
pratisaṃvids 147, 176
pratītya-samutpāda 136, 141, 151–2, 179; *see also* conditionality
precepts xliii; *see also* ethics, morality, *sīla*
five 222–3, 355, 385, 392, 395; *see also* *pañcasīla*
and three Refuges, *see* Refuges, Three, and Precepts
ten 14, 385, 387, 398
principles
Buddhism reduced to a single 327
spiritual xxiii, xxviii, 41, 154, 168, 223, 279
prīti 159, 176, 202, 369–70
Priyananda, Dharmachari 194, 694n
progress 346–7
in Dharma 'is gradual' 145, 388, 686n
spiritual 158, 209, 347, 388, 390, 685n
pṛthagjanas 36, 140, 235, 703n
psychic powers, *see* powers
psychoanalysis 344, 348–50
psychological
ethics 143
problems 13, 42, 86–7, 303
psychology, supernormal 158
puja 50, 179, 208–9, 214, 216–17, 245, 370, 402; *see also* worship
book of Ambedkar xlii, xliv, 174, 676n
Sevenfold (*Anuttara*) lxii–lxiii, 121
punarbhava 136, 160
Pune, *see* Poona
puṇya 267
Purāṇas 33, 35, 46, 50
purity 248, 346; *see also visuddhi*
fullness of Buddha's (*mahāviśuddhi*) 125, 235, 243, 261
path of (*visuddhi magga*) 248–51
Purna, Dharmachari 295
puruṣa 53, 186, 693n

quarrels xlviin, 273, 320, 323–4, 364
Kosambi 323–4
questions
indeterminate (*avyākatas*) 138, 225–6, 683n, 696n

Radhakrishnan 75, 674n
raft, parable of 141, 156, 684n, 688n
The Rainbow Road 44, 46, 667n, 677n, 687n, 701n, 702n
raincloud, parable of 211, 218, 695n
Rajagriha (Ambedkar's house) 4, 127, 336, 360, 667n
Rajgir (Rājagṛha) 4, 397, 667n
Ramakrishna Mission 44, 67–8, 101, 280, 669n, 701n
Ramana Maharshi 41, 44
Rāmāyaṇa 676n, 703n
rapture, *see prīti*
Rathavinīta Sutta 248, 697n
Ratnaketu, Dharmachari 408
Ratnasuri, Dharmacharini *lii*
reading 400
Reality 118, 133, 142–3, 151
reason 37, 40, 120, 129, 142, 143, 169
rebirth 135, 136, 137, 142, 160, 175
refuge (*saraṇa*) 266–7
Refuges, Three (*tisaraṇa*) 121, 125, 290; *see also* Three Jewels
difference to Three Jewels 266
and Precepts (*pañcasīla*) 108, 125, 144, 195, 217, 241–2, 266–8, 392
admin 122, 177
Ambedkar's safeguarding of 363; *see also* vows, twenty-two
and conversion or ordination lix, 7–8, 26, 106, 108
mentioned in Sangharakshita's lectures 20, 121–3, 144, 160, 290
taken and administered by Ambedkar 9, 26–7, 377–8
recitation at condolence meeting 96, 107–8
rejoicing in merits (*puṇya anumodanā*) 136, 683n
relative, and absolute, truth, *see* truths, two
religion 120, 138, 185, 301, 350
Ambedkar and xxiii, xxvii, xxx, 5, 7, 33, 43, 57–8, 78, 82, 107, 127–8, 205, 311, 342, 351
criteria for choosing 24, 63–4, 71, 128–9, 362, 379
and Buddhism 120, 138, 170–2, 252, 350–1, 669n
cultural or ethnic and universal 34, 43–4, 170, 245–6
freedom to choose 280–1
Freudian view 349
Jung on illness and 120, 680n
morality as essence of 43, 46–7, 63, 355, 362
as 'opium of the people' 72, 674n
and politics 169, 415
Sangharakshita 'prepared to die for' 340, 342
and science xxx, lviii, 63, 68, 379
repetition 108, 144, 151
Republican Party of India (R.P.I) 188, 693n
restlessness (*auddhatya-kaukṛtya*) 158, 159, 175, 201, 322, 329
retreat centres xlix, liv, 214, 333, 365, 387, 405, 413, 692n

Bhaja (Saddhamma Pradip Retreat Centre) xlvii, *xlix*, lii, liv, 326, 334
at Bordharan (Hsüan Tsang (Xuanzang) Retreat Centre) li, liv–lv, 365, 366, 391, *393*, 404
women's 413
retreats (*shibirs*) 204, 273, 330, 332–4, 358, 377, 388–9, 406, 408
Dhamma study 215
first women's at Bhaja *l*
meditation lviii, 214, 393
and transformation of self and world 331–2
revolution
Dharma, *see* Dhamma Revolution
social xxvii, 72, 389
Rhys Davids, C. A. F. 673n
right livelihood 119, 125, 139, 172, 216–17, 301, 630; *see also* work
team-based 13; *see also* FWBO, co-operatives
Rig Veda 186, 693n
rituals
Buddhist, *see* devotional practices, puja
paritrāṇa ceremonies 124, 140, 147, 681n
and observances, Hindu 46–7, 50, 54
robes 4, 293, 332
Roman Catholic church 280–1
routine 240–2
rūpa 225, 231, 317, 325
rūpa-dhyānas 350
rūpakāya 118

sabbe sattā sukhī hontu 283, 318
Sacred Books of the East 139
Sacred Relics of Sāriputta and Mahāmoggallāna 93, 676n
sacrifice 45, 48, 50, 671n
of animals lvii, 9, 20, 26, 45–6, 48–9, 279, 671n
saddhamma 344, 351, 658
Saddhamma Pradip Retreat Centre, Bhaja xlvii, *xlix*, lii, liv, 326, 333–4
Saddharma Puṇḍarīka Sūtra, *see White Lotus Sūtra*
sādhana practice lxv
Sakya school 135
samādhi 118, 137, 142, 152, 176, 201, 319, 332, 356, 370; *see also* concentration, meditation
and *prajñā* 143, 144, 174
sambhogakāya 118, 679n
saṃgraha-vastus 147, 176
samjñā 231; *see also* perception
Sāṃkhya philosophy 52–3, 683n
saṃskāras 151, 152, 231
Saṃyutta Nikāya 122, 145, 151, 158, 201, 206, 208, 220, 356, 394, 679n, 680n, 681n, 686n, 688n, 689n, 694n, 695n, 703n, 704n
sangha 209, 251, 264–6, 377, 385–6, 669n, 677n; *see also* spiritual community
Ambedkar's vision and understanding of xlviii, 270–2
and Āryasaṅgha 146
bhikṣu/bhikkhu 48, 66, 67, 68, 220, 270–1, 362, 385
and caste xxvii
future of the 261–75
as an ideal society xliii, 348
and *Mahāsaṅgha* 208, 255, 271, 385
monastic, *see bhikkhus* sangha
and politics 77–8
Sangharakshita's view of 100, 676n
splits in 133, 669n, 682n
threefold nature of 146
unity of 98, 117–18, 152, 161, 169, 272–4, 337, 364, 387, 395
Saṅghānusmṛti 144, 685n
Sangharakshita *lxiv*, *194*, 311–12, 294
and Ambedkar
continuation of work of, *see under* mass conversion
correspondence xix, 4, 15, 24, *30*, 31–2
critique of interpretations of Buddhism 37, 40–1, 64–5, 75, 129, 219, 221
first hearing of 3–4
followers of xl, 12, 20, 121; *see also under* Buddhists, new
influence of xxxi
meetings 4–10, 16–17, 336, 360
similarity of approach to Dharma xliii
view of xxxi, lxiv, 25, 129, 319, 321, 339, 342–3, 378–9
with Bakula, Dharmarakshita and Lokamitra *xlv*
Buddha Jayanti pilgrimage 9, 17
giving a talk in Ahmedabad *155*
impelled to go to Nagpur 10, 17; *see also under* Nagpur
on importance of healthcare l, 317–18
and mass conversion, *see* mass conversion
and Mrs Ambedkar *6*
ordination of 8, 26, 312, 667n, 677n
and poetry 318, 340–1
and politics 77–8
with Poona District Buddhist Women's Association *162*
preaching tours xx–xxi, xxxviii–xxxix, xliii, 12, 19–20, 124, 131, 149, 290;

see also under Bombay, Nagpur, Poona
return to Britain xxxix, 290, 298, 313
return visits to India xliv–xlvi, xlviii–l, lii–lv, 191, 291–4, 305, 363, 365; *see also under* Bombay, Nagpur, Poona
seminars xx–xxi, 663, 690n, 695n, 696n
significance in Dhamma Revolution xl
an 'unfathomable, scruffy friend' *xlv*
why he is a Buddhist 340–2
Sanghasena, Dhammachari liii, 358
Śaṅkara 160, 186
Sannyasa 48
sannyasins 37, 44, 67–8, 293
Śāntideva 369, 686n, 695n, 704n
Sāriputta (Sanskrit Śāriputra) 93, 122, 308, 387
Sarnath 116, 124, 131, 260, 262–4, 397, 677n, 699n, 700n
Sarvāstivādins 49, 683n
sati (Sanskrit *smṛti*) 150, 369; *see also* mindfulness
satipaṭṭhānas 150
Scheduled Castes, *see* castes, Scheduled
Scheduled Castes Federation 8, 336, 667n, 693n
Scheduled Tribes lv, 109, 673n
schools of Buddhism 134–5, 143, 158, 163–4, 176, 282, 682n, 683n
science 120, 153, 231
Buddhism and xxx, lviii, 117, 129, 138, 169, 226, 234, 669n
and philosophy 171
and religion xxx, lviii, 63, 68, 379
secular state 110, 278, 280, 414–15
seed
of Buddhahood 235
Dhamma xl
of faith 235, 331–2
self
Abhidharma view 163
-hatred 173
-help 117
'indeterminate questions' and 683n
-*mettā* 207
no 122, 223; *see also anātman*
and others, motivation for following path 119, 121, 156
-reliance 103, 187, 324–5
-respect xxiii, 289, 301, 303, 311, 314, 318
and world, transformation of, *see under* transformation
selfishness 146
Seneca 320, 702n
sexual relationships 412
Shakyananda, Dhammachari liii
sheep and tiger, story of 125, 167, 237–8
Shravasti (Sanskrit Śrāvastī) 330, 397
Shudras 21, 54–5, 82, 186, 212, 287, 295, 308–9, 361, 664n; *see also* Classes, Backwards
in *bhikkhu sangha* 48
effect of Buddhism on xxvi, lxi
hostility to Dalits 62
punishment for teaching 23
Siddhārtha 170, 242, 256–9, 261, 698n; *see also* Buddha
teachers 257–8, 698n
Siddharth College of Arts and Science lix, 5, 7, 16, 126, 128, 131, 137, 140, 336, 360, 660, 667n
Sigālovāda or *Sigālaka Sutta* 169, 674n, 690n, 691n
Sikkim, Maharaja Kumar of 16, 76
sīla (Sanskrit *śīla*) 137, 142, 152, 175, 180, 351, 355; *see also* morality, ethics, precepts
of Ambedkar 318
four kinds of (*pārisuddhi*) 172, 692n
purification of (*sīla visuddhi*)
śīla, samādhi, prajñā 119, 141, 142, 156, 225, 332; *see also* threefold path or way
sīlas (Sanskrit *śīlas*), five, *see* precepts, five
silence 18, 214, 243, 313
simplicity of lifestyle 395–6, 398, 408
six element practice 207
skandhas, five 135, 231
skilful means 147, 687n; *see also upāya-kauśalya pāramitā*
sloth and torpor (*styāna-middha*) 158–9, 175
social
activities lv, 314, 368
conscience or ethics 142, 347
'endosmosis' xxxii, lx
transformation, *see under* transformation
work 359
socialism xliv, 38, 125
society
changing 83, 207, 270, 315; *see also* transformation, social
concern for 68, 87
ideal xxvii, xxxii, xliii, 348
and individual xxvii, 207, 348
new xxiii, xliii, 257, 270, 296, 674n
Society of Servants of God 118–19, 131, 682n
Soren, L. lvi–lvii, lix
speech
kindly (*priyavāditā*) 147, 176, 395, 398

precepts lxi
Spencer, H. 171, 691n
spiral path 175, 693n; *see also* conditionality
Spirit 53; *see also puruṣa*
spiritual
attainment 145–6
birth 145, 261
community xlvi, 73, 82, 385, 408, 674n, 700n; *see also* sangha
and positive group 74
development 206
faculties, five 140, 155, 158, 201, 368, 369, 694n; *see also indriyas*
friendship (*kalyāṇa mitratā*) 208–9, 316, 359, 370, 377, 388, 394, 398, 408
'the whole of the spiritual life' 394
hierarchy 82, 235
life
four kinds of people and 119, 125, 146, 175, 228, 679n, 696n
and planning 222–3
practice
intense (*tapas*) 331–2
work as 408; *see also* team-based right livelihood
principles xxiii, xxviii, 41, 154, 168, 223, 279
progress, *see* progress, spiritual
teachers 223–4, 324; *see also* gurus
śraddhā 136, 201–2, 224, 231, 331; *see also* faith
śrāvakas 197; *see also* disciples, of the Buddha
Sri Lanka 75, 134, 225, 267, 271, 312, 415
Srimala, Dharmacharini *lii*
state
secular 110, 278, 280, 414–15
welfare 120
states
of consciousness/mental 347–8, 369–70, 408
higher 137, 346
stories 66–7, 81, 238, 243; *see also* parables
of the Buddha 145
emperor and Bodhidharma 119, 679n
of fish and turtle 144, 685n
frog in the well 256
of Indra and the squirrel 356, 703n
Japanese 151, 176, 687n
of low caste or outcast disciples of the Buddha 672n
of sheep and tiger 125, 167, 237–8
stream entry (*srotāpanna*) 146, 175, 225, 693n
stupas 145, 213, 677n
Subhadra 117, 272, 678n
suffering (*duḥkha* (Pāli *dukkha*)) xxix, xxxi, 158–9, 228, 326, 379; *see also* pain
Sufism 293
Sujiva, Śrāmaṇera 149, 155, 179
Sumedha 122, 680n
śūnyatā xx, 118, 143, 157–60, 163–5, 176, 319
śūnyavāda 143
supernatural powers 35, 36
supernormal
distinguished from supernatural 36
or psychic, powers 36–7, 135, 669n
psychology 158
suppression 151, 159
Surata, Dharmachari xxxix
Sūtra of Golden Light xxxix, 683n
Sūtra of Huineng 311–12, 690n
sūtras (Pāli *suttas*)
dhāraṇī chapters of 136, 683n
Mahāyāna 50, 146, 164, 227, 324–5, 693n; *see also* individual *sūtras*
Pāli canon, *see Aṅguttara Nikāya, Dīgha Nikāya, Khuddaka Nikāya, Majjhima Nikāya, Saṃyutta Nikāya*
Sutta-Nipāta xxvi, 221, 318, 331, 665n, 696n, 702n, 703n
Sutta Piṭaka 219, 220, 327
Suzuki, D. T. 164, 671n, 690n
Swift, J. 283, 701n
Sydney 272
symbolism 37, 145–6, 175, 677n
of descent in *hūṃ* 147, 151, 176
symbols, conceptual 159

Taiwanese Buddhists, support for TBMSG projects li, liv, 675n
Tantrayāna 136; *see also* Vajrayāna
Tantric
Buddhism 136, 372, 683n, 704n; *see also* Vajrayāna
traditions, six different in India 46
tapas 331–2
Tārā lxv
Tarahridaya, Dhammacharini *lxiv*, lxv, 666n
Tathāgata 141, 147, 680n, 687n, 703n; *see also* Buddha
TBM (Trailokya Bauddha Mahasangha) xlvii, 352, 415–17; *see also* Triratna Buddhist Order, Western Buddhist Order
Order members, *see* Order members
ordination, *see* ordination

TBMSG (Trailokya Bauddha Mahasangha Sahayaka Gana) xlvii, 290, 300, 337, 363, 376, 385, 394, 416–17; *see also* FWBO, Triratna Buddhist Community
centres, *see viharas*
Dharma activities liv, 199, 269, 272–3, 359, 364, 366–7, 373
in Nagpur, *see under* Nagpur
in Pune, *see under* Poona
explanation of name xlvii–xlviii, 314
formation of 363
'foundation stones' of 355–7
'Friends' *see* Friends
growth of 298–9, 354, 356–9, 366, 401, 404–5, 413
headquarters 354, 367–8
health care work xlix–l, 314, 317–18, 367
hostels, *see* hostels
Lokamitra and, *see* Lokamitra, Dhammachari
Mitras, *see* Dhammamitras, Mitras
a new kind of sangha xlviii, 362–3
Order, *see* TBM
pilgrimage 112, 367, 397
publications xlvii, liv, 299, 394, 408, 417; *see also Buddhayan*
support from China, Korea, Malaysia and Taiwan li
women and, *see* women
work in villages xlviii, li, liii, lvi, 305, 376, 391, 407–8, 413–14
team-based right livelihood 13; *see also* FWBO, cooperatives
teamwork 301; *see also* working together
temperament 144, 212, 224, 228, 685n, 692n, 693n
six kinds of (*caritas*) 172, 692n
Theosophical Society 139, 673n
Theosophists 56, 688n
Theragāthā 672n
Theravāda xliii, 164, 384; *see also* Hīnayāna
The Thousand-Petalled Lotus 312, 702n
three characteristics, *see lakṣaṇas*
'Three Chief Paths' of Tsongkhapa 131, 682n
threefold path or way 144, 151–2, 158, 171, 172, 264, 679n; *see also śīla, samādhi, prajñā*
Three Jewels 8, 20, 144, 199–200, 261, 266, 685n; *see also* Refuges, Three
salutation to, *see Tiratana Vandanā*
Tibet 4, 50, 77, 144, 164–5, 174, 176, 202, 244, 264, 308
Tibetan Buddhism 46, 134–5, 409, 683n; *see also* Tantric Buddhism, Vajrayāna
tiger and the sheep, story of 125, 167, 237–8
Tipiṭaka 138, 164, 219–21, 224, 243, 327; *see also* Pāli canon, Tripiṭaka
Tiratana Vandanā 146, 156, 242, 685n, 688n, 697n
tisaraṇa, *see* Refuges, Three
and *pañcasīla*, *see* Refuges, Three, and Precepts
tolerance 83, 283; *see also kṣānti*, patience
tradition 133, 154–5
Trailokya Bauddha Mahasangha, *see* TBM
Trailokya Bauddha Mahasangha Sahayaka Gana, *see* TBMSG
transformation, of individual mind and society li, lxii, 25, 42, 207, 278, 315
of 'self and world' xxvii, xxix, xl, xliii, lxii, 315
'Transforming Self and World in the *Sūtra of Golden Light*' xxxix
translation 244, 299, 316, 408
transmission 136, 683n; *see also* initiation, oral tradition
Trevelyan, G. 305, 702n
tribes, scheduled lv, 109, 673n
trikāya 118, 136, 679n
Tripiṭaka 117, 163; *see also* Tipiṭaka
Triratna Buddhist Community xxxix, xlviii, lx, lxiv, 13, 74, 80, 90, 417, 666n, 692n, 700n; *see also* FWBO, TBMSG
Friends, *see* Friends
international council lxiv
Mitras, *see* Dhammamitras, Mitras
and politics 77–8
Triratna Buddhist Order xxi, lxiv, 418; *see also* TBM, Western Buddhist Order
conventions *lxiii*, lxiv, 178, 407, 665n, 676n
members, *see* Order members
ordination, *see* ordination
Triyana Vardhana Vihara, Kalimpong Report 115, 662, 678n
truth 271
truths, two 50, 134, 165, 672n, 682n
Tsongkhapa 131, 135, 682n
tulkus 135

Udāna xxvi, 66, 141, 142, 145, 170, 215, 221, 388, 665n, 669n, 672n, 684n, 685n, 686n, 688n, 691n, 696n, 704n
the unconditioned xxix, 159, 692n

'Untouchability' liv, 21–4, 55, 289, 309, 361
  laws defining, *see Manusmṛti*
  in Pāli canon 54, 672n
The Untouchables 48, 54, 128, 361, 671n
'Untouchables' 6, 21–2, 54, 186, 287, 307, 308–9, 666n; *see also* Castes, Scheduled; Classes, Depressed; Dalits
  and the Buddha 54, 260, 672n, 699n
Upaka 262–3, 699n
Upanishads 50, 133, 162, 170, 211, 233, 671n
upāsakas/upāsikas 267–8, 362; *see also* lay people
  and *bhikkhus*, terms unimportant 225, 273
  duties of 100, 121, 140, 143, 161, 677n
  training course for 179
upāya-kauśalya pāramitā 147, 176, 687n
upekkhā (Sanskrit *upekṣā*) 159, 172, 174, 197, 370
upekkhā bhāvanā 174

Vacchagotta 670n, 696n
Vaiśākha Pūrṇimā 124, 170; *see also* Wesak
Vaiśālī 133, 682n
Vaishyas 54, 82, 186, 287, 308, 664n
Vajracchedikā-Prajñāpāramitā, *see Diamond Sūtra*
Vajraketu, Dharmachari 352
Vajraloka Retreat Centre 214
Vajramala, Dharmacharini 409
Vajrapushpa, Dharmacharini li
Vajrayāna 134, 136, 683n, 704n; *see also* Tibetan Buddhism, Tantric Buddhism
Vakkali 678n
vandanā 161, 179–80, 204, 217; *see also* worship
Varanasi 264, 397; *see also* Benares
varnas 52–3, 693n, *see also* caste
Vasala Sutta xxvi
Vasubandhu 327
Vedānta 50, 283
Vedanta Kesari 32, 669n
Vedas 34, 48, 51–2, 162, 186, 211, 236, 295
vegetarianism 48–50, 81, 125, 346
Vessantara, Prince 122, 681n
views (*dṛṣṭis* (Pāli *diṭṭhis*) 138, 142, 684n
  purification of (*diṭṭhi visuddhi*) 248–9
  wrong (*mithyā-dṛṣṭis* (Pāli *micchā-diṭṭhis*)) 135–6, 138, 142, 249, 684n, 697n
viharas 282, 333, 677n
  TBMSG xlvii, 118, 187, 193, 199, 215, 269–70, 317; *see also* Mahavihara
  in holy places 417, 699n
Vijayadashami 93, 95, 676n
vijñāna 151, 152, 231–2, 238, 348; *see also* consciousness
villages
  caste system in xli, 12, 59–60, 186, 287, 309, 329
  TBMSG work in xlviii, li, liii, lvi, 305, 376, 391, 407–8, 413–14
Vimalakirti, Dhammachari 367, 399
Vimalasara, Dharmacharini 666n
Vimalasuri, Dhammacharini *lii*
vimokṣas 159
vimukti (Pāli *vimutti*) 143, 160, 171; *see also* freedom, liberation
Vinaya 67, 134–5, 247
Vinaya Piṭaka xxix, lvi, 36, 83, 117, 141, 212, 219, 244, 256, 260, 264, 665n, 666n, 670n, 672n, 675n, 678n, 684n, 686n, 695n, 697n, 698n, 699n, 700n
violence (*hiṃsā*) xli, lvii, 48, 50, 55, 71–2, 86, 323, 348, 355, 674n; *see also* non-violence
vipassanā 143; *see also* insight
Virabhadra, Dharmachari l, *194*, 367, 694n
vīrya 122, 125, 146, 168, 176, 200–2, 319, 356–7, 369–70; *see also* effort, energy
  of Ambedkar 168, 319
  of the Windhorse 199–201, 202
Vishnu 34, 283, 657
  Buddha seen as *avatāra* of 8, 38, 235, 657
Vishvahindu Parisa 302
visuddhi 248; *see also* purity
Visuddhimagga of Buddhaghosa 172–3, 204, 688n, 692n, 693n, 695n
visuddhis, seven, or *visuddhi magga* 175, 248–51
Vivekananda, Bhikkhu 149, 160, 169
Vivekananda, Swami 68, 279–80, 701n
vows
  bodhisattva xliii; *see also praṇidhāna*
  twenty-two conversion xxxn, xxxvi, xlii, 9, 26–7, 100, 102, 104, 363, 378, 391–2, 398
    list of 657–8

Wadia, S. 140, 162
Wardha lii–liii, 124, 130, 353, 358, 363–4, 376
'welfare of the many' (*bahujana hitāya*) xxix, 212, 665n
Wesak 31, 412; *see also* Vaiśākha Pūrṇimā
Wesley, J. 85–6
Western Buddhist Order xxi, 222, 385; *see also* TBM, Triratna Buddhist Order
  and Aid for India (Karuna Trust) 675n
  members, *see* Order members
What Congress and Gandhi have done to the Untouchables 55, 311, 673n
wheel
  of the Dharma (*dharmacakra*) 105, 145, 305, 374, 677n
  of life 152
White Lotus Sūtra (*Saddharma Puṇḍarīka Sūtra*) 121, 211, 678n, 683n, 695n, 702n, 703n
  commentary, *see The Drama of Cosmic Enlightenment*
Who were the Shudras? 361
Windhorse, the 199–203, *200*, 694n
wisdom 151, 158, 163, 201, 235, 237, 319, 679n, 680n, 685n, 687n; *see also prajñā*
  and compassion xxx, 122, 133, 145, 147, 152, 156, 243, 251, 266, 331
  discriminating 176, 675n
  five aspects of 176; *see also* Buddhas, five
  fullness of Buddha's (*mahāprajñā*) 125, 235, 243, 261
  three levels of 125, 176, 197, 694n
  transcendental, and Real Going for Refuge 387
woman, 'untouchable,' and the Buddha 260, 699n
women 48, 161, 181, 401–3, 417, 666n
  and community living 365, 366, 413
  ordination of, *see bhikkhunīs*; ordination, into TBM/WBO/Triratna
  position in Buddhism 182–3, 222, 413
  retreats for *l*, 214, 413
word, of God 39–40
words
  of the Buddha
    to be tested like gold 246, 697n
    last 150, 675n
  danger of misunderstanding 144
work lxv, 408; *see also* livelihood
  for the Dharma, *see* Dharma spreading work
  women and 183
working together 198, 272, 275, 301, 324, 337, 387, 397–8, 408; *see also* teamwork
world 120, 315, 351
  and self, transformation of, *see under* transformation
World Fellowship of Buddhists 80, 106, 128, 664n, 665n, 675n
worldlings (*pṛthagjanas*) 36, 140, 235, 703n
worlds 137; *see also* consciousness, levels of
  three (*triloka*) xlvii–xlviii
Worli xlix, 8, 121–2, 151, 153, 285, 295, 335–7, 352, 360
worship 48, 50; *see also* chanting, devotional practices, puja, *vandanā*
  true 167, 691n; *see also* homage, true
Wrekin Trust 286, 305, 702n

Xuanzang (Hsüan Tsang) liv–v, 282

yānas, three 134–5, 682n
Yasa 264, 700n
Yathābhūta-jñānadarśana 175, 693n
Yeola Conference 127, 187
Yerawada 204, 277
yoga xxxix–xl, 228, 290
Yogācāra school 143, 211
Young Men's Buddhist Association (YMBA), Kalimpong 3, 4, 15, 666n
Yuvaraj, Dharmachari *194*

Zen 164–5, 212, 312, 679n

INDEX 2: *WISDOM BEFORE WORDS*

To assist the reader, the index for this volume has been split into two, the first relating to the Dhamma Revolution in India, which began in 1956 (pages 1 to 418) and the second covering the commentary on the *Udāna*, *Wisdom before Words* (pages 419 to 656). Page numbers in italic refer to images.

Abhidhamma (Sanskrit Abhidharma) 424, 426, 431
abhiññās (Sanskrit *abhijñās*) 438, 706n; *see also* powers, supernormal
aesthetic experience 505, 506–7, 567, 568
afflictions (Pāli *kilesas*) 515, 619, 621–2; *see also* poisons
Ajakalāpaka 451, 453
Ajātaśatru, King 501, 646, 711n
Akṣobhya 709n
alienated awareness 463, 602, 603, 709n
alms 448–9, 461, 479, 517–19, 537–8, 551, 639, 648
 -giving, *devatās* and 447, 515–16
 invitations 493, 495, 518, 533, 538, 540, 639, 642, 711n
anagārika 573
Ānanda 435, 444, 480, 508–11, 522, 528, 546, 548, 557, 572, 574, 579, 583–7, 611, 623, 628, 639, 642, 706n, 717n
Ānandamayi 475, 710n
Anāthapiṇḍika's park 443–4, 466, 472, 509, 707n
anātman (Pāli *anattā*) 592–3, 719n; *see also* self
anger 482, 591; *see also* hatred
Aṅguttara Nikāya 439, 473, 538, 542, 544, 562, 584, 597, 598, 607, 615, 628, 707n, 710n, 712n, 714n, 715n, 716n, 718n, 719n, 720n, 721n, 723n, 725n
animism 453
antinomies 597–8, 719n; *see also* opposites
anxiety 500–1, 578, 606
archetypal dimension 437, 454, 506–7, 547, 654; *see also* legend, mythology
arhant (Pāli *arahant*)
 ideal 467, 569
 use of word 430, 445, 460, 465, 628–9
arhants (Pāli *arahants*) 450, 458, 460–1, 542, 558, 569, 576, 590, 613–14, 616, 628, 708n, 717n
 and 'learners' (*sekhas*) 615–16
 and lifestyle 628–9, 630
 'many, rules few...' 480, 563–4
 recognizing 449–50, 588–90
ariya (Sanskrit *ārya*), meaning of 576
ariyapariyesanā 636
Ariyapariyesanā Sutta 633, 696, 698–9, 723n
ariyapuggalas 569–70, 717n; *see also* Āryasaṅgha
arrows 598, 600–1, 720n
arts 452, 481, 505, 506–7
Āryasaṅgha 576; *see also ariyapuggalas*
āsavas (Sanskrit *āsravas*) 450, 615, 707n; *see also* defilements, poisons, taints
 destruction of 434, 438, 542, 613, 706n, 712n, 715n
asceticism 430, 447, 448, 460, 519, 607–8
ascetics 460, 515, 588–90, 593, 609, 710n; *see also śramaṇas*
Aśoka 473, 519, 648, 723n
aśubha-bhāvanā 620
ātman 545–6, 592; *see also* self
attachment 455–6, 485, 491–2, 497–8, 507, 521–2, 611, 651, 652; *see also* clinging, dependency, possessions
 positive 492, 513
aversion 486, 601, 620, 634; *see also* hatred
awareness 462–3; *see also* mindfulness
 alienated 463, 602, 603, 709n

Bacon, F. 474, 710n
Bāhiya 458–65, 687–8, 708n
bardo, *see* states, intermediate
Barua, B. M. 432, 614, 615, 721n
beauty 505–6, 550, 586
Bhaddiya 500–1, 613–16, 618–19
Bhagavan 429, 430, 438, 443, 554; *see also* Buddha
bhikkhunīs (Sanskrit *bhikṣuṇīs*) 536, 537; *see also* nuns, women
bhikkhus (Sanskrit *bhikṣus*) 479, 484, 515–16, 554, 555, 563; *see also* monks

bhikkhus (Sanskrit *bhikṣus*) (*cont.*)
sangha 554
training rules 527, 529, 558; *see also* *pāṭimokkha*
and *upāsakas*, *see* lay followers, and monks
Blake, W. 595–6, 604, 719n, 720n
blessings 494, 496–7
blind men and elephant, parable of 594–6, 611, 685n
bliss 432, 469, 472, 475, 498, 500, 513, 592
Bodh Gaya 457, 466, 709n; *see also* Uruvelā
Bodhicaryāvatāra 481, 711n
bodhisatta, term for future Buddha 546
bodhisattva doctrine 547
bodhisattva ideal 467
bodhisattvas 548, 716n
bodhi tree 427, 434, 445
body
mindfulness of, *see* mindfulness
and *parinirvāṇa* 'without remainder' 522, 558, 566, 654–6
and stick 482, 600
brahmacarya (Pāli *brahmacariya*) 439, 506, 549; *see also* holy life, spiritual life
Brahmajāla Sutta 587, 718n
brahmin (*brāhmaṇa*), use of word 429–30, 440, 441–2, 488, 708n, 710n
brahmins (*brāhmaṇas*)
'by birth' *see* caste, brahmins
real or true 430–1, 436–40, 442–6, 454–8, 465–7, 514, 710n; *see also* individual, true
and *samaṇas* 479, 487–8, 554
Buddha 435, 442, 451–2, 461, 470–1, 546, 580, 708n; *see also* Bhagavan, Gotama, Tathāgata
death of, *see parinirvāṇa*
and discourses 551–2, 587, 608
followers, *see* disciples
and irony 514, 528, 548, 640
life of 421–3, 427–8, 434–5, 437, 547, 639–40, 656, 707n
meaning of word 429–30, 442, 445, 553–5
names and modes of address 442–3, 554
original teachings 425, 538, 575, 706n, 716n
recollecting (*buddhānussati*) 494
supernormal powers or faculties 497, 510, 623, 624, 648; *see also* miracles
use of words, *see* language
Buddhaghosa 578, 721n
Buddhahood 440, 615; *see also* Nirvāṇa
Buddha-nature 439–40, 545, 626
buddhānussati 494
Buddhas 547, 553
future, *see* Maitreya
mandala of five 705n, 709n
solitary, *see paccekabuddhas*
Vipassī 560, 715n
Buddhavaṃsa 715n
Buddhism 425, 429, 431, 440, 445, 466, 480, 507, 516, 547, 549, 560
and Hinduism 546, 626
historical, context 465–7, 472–3, 478–9, 481, 496, 501, 517, 533, 605, 646
history of 440, 446, 519, 537, 547, 564
as religion 474, 648
use of existing traditions and terminology 445–6; *see also* language
Buddhist India 478, 710n
busyness 483, 485

calm 392, 458, 461, 542, 637–8, 710n
caste
brahmins 442, 488, 514, 517, 598
opposition to Buddha and Buddhism 446–7, 488, 565, 624–6
and Buddha's disciples 444, 446, 514, 565, 623
system 446, 565, 625–6
catuṣkoṭi formulation 598, 689n
celibacy 439, 607, 629
cessation 433, 475, 522–4, 550, 632–6, 656
chariots 578–9, 618–19
Chen, Yogi 532, 714n
Ch'en, K. 565, 717n
Chih-I, *see* Zhiyi
children 454–6, 485, 491–2, 495–6
Chinese Buddhism 565–6
Christianity 484, 503
clinging 600, 637–8; *see also* attachment
commitment 486, 577
communication 474, 500–1, 511, 524, 570, 613–14
compassion 461, 490, 524, 583, 585, 642
conceit (*māna*) 470–1, 521, 527, 531–2, 600, 621; *see also* pride
conditionality 428, 431–3, 446; *see also* conditioned co-production
the conditioned, and the Unconditioned 524, 634–5, 637–8, 654–5
conditioned co-production (*pratītya-samutpāda*) 427, 428–9, 432, 433,

440–1, 705n; *see also* conditionality, *nidānas*
conditioning 434, 446, 514, 567, 620, 633
confession 561, 571–2, 581
confusion (*moha*) 434, 505, 511, 627, 631, 640; *see also* ignorance
consciousness 432, 470, 471, 512, 563, 586, 653; *see also* mental states
higher levels of 431, 434, 464, 510–11, 561, 577–8, 598; *see also dhyānas*, realms
sense-sphere (*kāmāvacara*) 512
store- (*ālaya-vijñāna*) 545, 715n
'turning about' in (*parāvṛtti*) 620, 722n
contact, six spheres of (*ṣaḍāyatana*) 512
Council
First 435, 706n
Third 723n
craving 474–5, 513, 515, 521–2, 524, 541, 601, 617, 621, 633; *see also* greed, lust
aversion, and delusion, *see* poisons
cessation or overcoming of 472, 488, 522, 619–20, 623, 627, 633–4
and ignorance 608, 620, 632
Cūḷapanthaka 581–2
Cunda 639–41

Dabba 653–5
Dalits 625–6
dāna, *see* generosity
death 490, 491–2, 582, 609, 617, 651–2, 653–4
archetypal or spiritual 654
and rebirth 637, 638, 642, 645
deathless (*amata*) 635–6
defilements 439, 721n; *see also āsavas*, poisons
delight 505, 513, 522, 550, 558, 562, 716n; *see also* enjoyment
delusion 521, 522, 620–1, 634; *see also* ignorance
demons, *see yakkhas*
dependency 324, 553, 573, 592, 637–8, 724n; *see also* attachment
Devadatta 444, 480, 579–81, 586, 707n
devalokas, *see* heavens
devas and *devatās* 447–9, 452, 461, 504–5, 515–17, 642, 646–7, 709n
Dhammacakkappavattana Sutta 608, 620, 721n, 722n
Dhammadinnā 615
Dhammadinna, Dharmacharini 421
dhammakathā, *see* Dharma, talk
Dhammapada 425, 430, 450, 455, 458, 479, 490, 513, 538, 554, 568, 614, 650, 705n, 707n, 708n, 710n, 711n, 712n, 714n, 715n, 717n, 721n, 724n, 725n
verses summarizing *pāṭimokkha* 560, 716n
Dharma (Pāli *dhamma*) 474, 558, 567–8, 593–4
compared to ocean 558–69, 716n
development of 479–81, 494, 522, 546–7, 549, 551–4, 559, 562, 568–9, 575–6, 588, 641
Zhiyi's classification 554–5, 716n
negative language of, *see* language, use of negative
as path, *see* path
quarrels about nature of 594, 599, 600
recitation of, *see* recitation
study 436, 440, 706n
talk (*dhammakathā*) 472, 474, 518, 519, 520, 527, 530–1, 561
turning wheel of 705n
Dharmakīrti 722n
Dharma-Vinaya (Pāli *Dhamma-Vinaya*) 558, 562, 569, 716n
Dhivan, Dharmachari 422
dhyānas (Pāli *jhānas*) 431, 436, 506, 511, 577, 606; *see also* consciousness, higher; *samādhi*
formless 632, 633, 723n; *see also* realms, formless
and psychic powers (*iddhipādas*) 586–7
Diamond Sūtra 607
Dīgha Nikāya 424, 501, 506, 538, 547, 580, 587, 597, 622, 624, 640, 644, 711n, 713n, 714n, 715n, 717n, 718n, 722n, 724n
dimensions, *see also* levels, planes, realms
other, higher, wider 428, 437, 470, 482–3, 523, 615, 654
disciples 440, 532, 537, 551, 563, 585, 707n, 717n
of the Buddha 444, 447, 479–80, 529, 533, 535–7, 538, 539–42, 562, 576, 583–4, 619–20
the 'band of six' 520, 712n
caste brahmins 446, 488, 514
meetings, *see uposatha* observance
upāsakas and *bhikkhus* 484–5
women 627–8
dispassion (*virāga*) 469, 527, 530
doubt (*vicikitsā* (Pāli *vicikicchā*)) 427, 431, 433, 553, 577–8, 637
dreams 461, 470
dukkha 524, 635; *see also* pain, suffering, unsatisfactoriness
Dutt, S. 560, 716n

Ecclesiastes 603, 720n
effort 507, 592, 598, 599, 604–5
  fourfold right 531, 558, 568, 593, 694n, 713n
ego 397, 440, 470–1, 524, 542, 713n; *see also* self
Egypt 460, 612
Eightfold Path 558, 568, 576, 608
elephants 520, 536–7, 540, 594–6, 714n
emotion 506–7, 532–3, 596, 638
  positive 432, 530, 534, 542, 563, 652–3
empathy 476–7, 543, 544
energy 428, 503, 507, 524, 531, 533, 568, 578, 586, 603, 620; *see also* effort, forces
  subtle or psychic 452, 647; *see also* *devas* and *devatās*
enjoyment 492, 498, 559, 562, 616–17; *see also* delight
Enlightenment 434–5, 442, 450, 463, 467, 470, 539, 554, 610, 654–6, 709n, 712n; *see also* Nirvāṇa
  factors, seven 558, 568
  by and for oneself alone, *see* *paccekabuddhas*
  women and 628
environment 647, 648
envy 501, 516, 518, 540–1, 580, 588; *see also* jealousy
ethics 453, 476, 609, 641–2, 644–5; *see also* precepts, *sīla*
evolution, Higher 483, 567, 631
existence
  and becoming (*bhava*) 522–3, 606, 609; *see also* rebirth
  craving for 521–2, 541
  human, identifying with 481–2
  liberation from 521, 523
eyes 595–6
  divine (*dibba-cakkhu*) of the Buddha 454, 456, 521, 642, 712n

faculties 510, 520, 596
  five spiritual (*indriyas*) 558, 568, 694n
  life- (*jīvita-indriya*) 585
faith 432, 493, 494, 495, 513, 568, 571
families 454–6, 484, 487–8, 490, 565–6, 644, 648
fearlessness (*abhaya*) 453–4, 500, 501
feeling (*vedanā*) 482, 622, 638
fetters (*saṃyojanas*) 443, 552, 569, 613, 616–17, 619
Fire Sermon 457, 522, 708n
fish 556, 617
forces, natural or psychic 451–3, 646–7; *see also* *devas* and *devatās*, powers
four noble truths 550, 551, 552, 646
four yokes (*yoga*), or floods (*ogha*) 606
freedom (*vimutti*) 449, 454–5, 459, 489, 505, 557–8, 567, 613, 615; *see also* liberation, release
Freud, S. 608, 713n
friendliness, *see* *mettā*
friends 527, 535, 605, 630, 652; *see also* spiritual friendship
Friends of the Western Buddhist Order (FWBO), movement 421–2, 436, 444, 551, 565, 630

Gandhi, M. 540, 714n
generosity (*dāna*) 550, 551, 552, 620, 624, 640, 644, 646
gestalt 595; *see also* pattern
God 517, 592, 712n
gods 491, 515–17, 621; *see also* *devas*
  of Vedic tradition 506
Going for Refuge 485, 486–7, 553, 554, 628
  effectiveness of 485, 486, 550, 551
  and prostration practice 441
Going Forth 456–7, 480, 572
'gone beyond' 451, 453, 455, 464, 470, 500–1, 522, 606
Gotama (Sanskrit Gautama) 436, 481, 554; *see also* Buddha
greed 514, 616–17, 621, 640, 652; *see also* craving, lust
guilt 503, 507, 609, 713n

happiness 470, 474, 476, 487, 488–9, 494, 599, 608, 631, 655, 656
hatred 513, 522, 640; *see also* anger, aversion, ill-will
heavens 451, 455, 464, 506, 550, 551, 555
  rebirth in 479, 546, 552, 608, 645, 717n
  of the thirty-three (*tāvatiṃsa*) 504–6, 548, 642
  tuṣita 546, 548
hell realms 535, 539, 550
Herodotus 467
Hīnayāna 563, 716n
holy life 439, 504–5, 546, 549, 572–3, 648; *see also* *brahmacarya*, spiritual life
householders 485, 519, 554, 572–3, 643–5, 648, 708n; *see also* lay followers
Huhuṅkajātika 436–8
Humphreys, C. 524

iddhipādas (Sanskrit *ṛddhipādas*) 568, 586, 717n
ideal
  man or person 430, 441, 515, 548; *see also* individual, true
  spiritual 446, 497, 515, 547–8, 561, 656
ideals
  brāhmaṇa, *samaṇa* and *bhikkhu* equated 515
  of brahmin, *arhant* and bodhisattva 466–7
ignorance (*avijjā*) 433, 521, 532, 606, 608, 620, 631; *see also* confusion, delusion
ill-will 531; *see also* hatred
imagination 462–3, 505, 506–7, 544, 596, 616
impermanence 527, 531
individual, true or total 440, 564, 596; *see also* brahmin, real or true; ideal man or person
individualism 445, 521
Indra (Pāli Inda) 516, 548; *see also* Sakka
insight 430–1, 434, 530–1, 534, 553, 562–3, 600, 613–14, 625, 627–31, 634, 706n
inspiration 426
integration 524, 596, 602–3, 604–5
intoxication 532, 616–17

Jains 442, 479, 589
James, W. 630, 723n
Jātakas 425, 718n
jealousy 477–8, 540; *see also* envy
jewels 568; *see also* Three Jewels
jhānas, *see dhyānas*
Jina 442; *see also* Buddha
Johnson, S. 496, 711n
joy 432, 513
  and pain 459, 464, 477, 482–3, 497–8, 505, 509, 599; *see also* pleasure, and pain

kalyāṇa mitratā, *see* spiritual friendship 650
kāma, *see* sense desire
Kant, I. 597, 719n
karma (Pāli *kamma*) 464, 476, 481, 492, 502–4, 556, 570, 585, 598, 718n
  and *kāma* 576, 718n
  and rebirth 434, 438, 491–2, 539, 550
Kassapa (Mahākassapa) 447–50, 480, 515, 518
Kassapa brothers 457
khandhas (Sanskrit *skandhas*) 453, 481, 566
Khuddaka Nikāya 425
knowledge 505, 520–1, 527, 542, 556–7, 563, 618
  of destruction of *āsavas* 438, 542, 715n
  specialist (*vijja*)) 520
knowledges, three (*tevijja*) 438, 508, 711n
Koṇḍañña 619–20
Kosambi (Allahabad) 536–7, 627
Kumārila Bhaṭṭa 624, 722n
Kusinārā 446–7, 532–3, 639

Lalitavistara Sūtra 435, 437, 705n, 706n
language
  Buddha's use of 429–30, 431, 434, 438, 441–2, 445–6, 465, 467–8, 480, 506
  development of Buddhist 554–5
  of growth and development 440, 471, 525, 567, 635–6
  limitations of 566, 720n; *see also* literalism
  misunderstanding 440–3, 507
  use of negative 431–2, 471, 513, 604, 633, 635, 653, 656; *see also* cessation
Laṅkāvatāra Sūtra 620, 722n
lay followers (*upāsakās*) 483–4, 490, 493, 536, 550, 572, 628, 641, 643; *see also* householders
  and monks (*bhikkhus*) 479, 484–5, 486, 496–7, 518–19
  and ordination, *see* ordination
  women (*upāsikās*) 484, 536, 627–8
legend and legendary elements 546, 548–9, 653, 654, 715n; *see also* archetypal dimension, mythology
levels, *see also* realms
  of consciousness, *see* consciousness
  of intellect and rationalism 461, 577, 595, 646
  of Reality 464
  sangha exists on different 565
liberation 505–6, 521, 523, 619; *see also* freedom, release
  entrances to (*vimokśas* (Pāli *vimokkhas*)) 720n
lifestyle, and commitment, *see* commitment
light 431, 433–5, 459, 464, 508, 553, 556, 610–12
literalism 447–8, 470, 548, 554, 566, 596, 625, 654; *see also* language, limitations of

love 513, 543–4, 651, 652; *see also mettā*
lust 496, 527, 616, 652, 656; *see also* craving, greed
Lyell, C 554, 715n

Mahākaccāna 572–3, 575, 621–2
Mahākassapa, *see* Kassapa
Mahāmoggallāna (Mahāmaudgalyāyana) 444, 480, 488, 493, 495, 512, 534–5, 557, 562, 564, 570, 580, 710n
Mahāpadāna Sutta 547, 714n
Mahāpajāpatī Gotami 567, 684n
Mahāparinibbāna Sutta 580, 624, 640, 713n, 715n, 717n, 718n, 722n, 724n
Mahāsatipaṭṭhāna Sutta 622, 713n, 722n
Mahāvastu 448, 707n
Mahāvira (Nātaputta) 479, 488, 589
Mahāyāna 432, 439, 445, 480, 489, 524, 545, 561, 705n, 716n
Maitreya 548
Majjhima Nikāya 424, 434, 449, 453, 461, 552, 579, 598, 633, 655, 705n, 706n, 707n, 708n, 709n, 712n, 715n, 718n, 720n, 723n, 724n, 725n
Mallikā, Queen 543–4
Manusmṛti 625, 723n
Māra 433, 435, 451, 522, 524, 532, 542, 583–5, 587, 617, 639, 705n
Masefield, P. 422, 706n
meditation 436, 482–3, 502–3, 506, 509, 511–12, 530, 559, 568, 613, 620, 629, 638; *see also dhyāna, samādhi*
  four or five basic methods 527, 531–2, 714n
  in a group 559–60, 561
Meghiya 526–41, 551
Mehta, D. 513, 712n
mental states, *see also* consciousness, higher; thoughts
  skilful or positive 528–31, 599, 629, 650
    and unskilful 513, 563, 593–4
  unskilful 512–13, 526–8, 532, 534, 592, 622, 714n
merit 448, 479, 515–16, 639–40
merits, rejoicing in 535–6, 541–2, 576
metaphor 429, 566, 617, 627, 705n
metaphysical
  perspective 439, 450, 545, 609
    on self 470, 545–6, 592
  questions, *see* questions, unexplained
mettā (Sanskrit *maitrī*) 527, 531, 652–3, 724n, 725n
Mettā Sutta 723n, 725n
micchā-diṭṭhis, *see* views, wrong
middle way 581, 597, 599, 608–9
Migāra 498
Migāra's mother, *see* Visākhā
mind (*citta*), five things leading to maturity of 527, 531
mind
  Buddha 656
  control of 536; *see also* effort, fourfold right
  essential purity of 439
  reactivity of, *see* reactivity
mindfulness 462–3, 471–4, 497, 511, 519, 532, 581–2, 619; *see also* awareness
  of body 512–13, 621–2
  of breathing (*ānāpānasati*) 511, 527, 531
  four foundations of (*satipaṭṭhānas*) 558, 568, 622
  and pain 494, 497, 502–3
  of sense experience 464, 512, 520
miracles 497, 623, 654, 725n; *see also* Buddha, powers, supernormal
Moggallāna, *see* Mahāmoggallāna
monasticism 50, 453, 486, 529–30, 574, 629
monastic rule 562; *see also pāṭimokkha*
monks, *see also bhikkhus*
  and laity, *see* lay followers, and monks
  naughty and troublesome 520, 532
Mucalinda 469–70
mysticism 428, 596
mythology 434, 435, 451, 466, 505, 619; *see also* archetypal dimension, legend

nāgas 469, 537, 714n
Nāgasamāla 649–50
Nanda 502–25
nature 452–3, 517, 586
  forces or spirits of 451–3; *see also yakkhas*
Nettippakaraṇa 432, 724n
nibbāna-dhātu 566
nidānas
  cyclic 428, 431–2, 433, 523, 532, 714n
  positive or spiral 428, 431–2, 513, 530, 562–3, 613–14, 714n
    in Pāli scriptures 435, 523, 705n
nidānas, *see also* conditioned co-production
Nietzsche, F. 620, 722n
Nirvāṇa (Pāli Nibbāna) 493, 494, 507, 522, 523–4, 527, 558, 566–7, 606, 614–15, 620, 632–7; *see also* Buddhahood, Enlightenment, Reality, the Unconditioned
Nirvānized 614, 721n

non-returners 558, 569, 576, 616, 627–8, 717n
nuns 498–9; *see also bhikkhunīs*
nymphs 504–5

ocean, compared to *Dhamma-Vinaya* 557–69
offerings 455, 457, 540, 642; *see also* alms
once-returners 558, 569, 576, 616, 627–8, 717n
openness 570–2
opposites 464, 637–8; *see also* antinomies
Order 656; *see also under* Friends of the Western Buddhist Order; sangha
ordination 480, 484, 485, 486, 519, 572, 573–4, 628, 710n

paccekabuddhas (Sanskrit *pratyekabuddhas*) 550, 552–3
Padmasambhava 448, 707n
Padmavajra, Dharmachari 422
paganism 58, 85, 452
pain 499, 502–3, 535, 600; *see also dukkha*, suffering
  mindfulness and 494, 497, 502–3
  and pleasure or joy 459, 464, 477, 482–3, 497–8, 505, 509, 599
Pāli
  canon 424–5, 435–6, 569, 575
  language 426
parables
  of blind men and elephant 594–6, 611, 685n
  of poisoned arrow 598, 720n
  of raft 627, 723n
  and storytelling 422, 429, 569, 596
paradox 570
pāramitās, *see* perfections
parinirvāṇa (Pāli *parinibbāna*) 583–8, 615, 639–40, 653–6
Pasenadi, King 471, 472, 487, 498, 539–40, 543–4, 586, 588–9, 591, 593
Pāṭali (Pāṭaliputra) 641–3, 646, 648
path 527–8, 531, 612
  gradual and abrupt 562–3, 717n
  of preparation (*prayoga-mārga*) 430
  of purity 578–9
  spiral, *see nidānas*, positive
  threefold 434, 530, 578, 713n
patience (*kṣānti*) 504, 620
pāṭimokkha (Sanskrit *prātimokṣa*) 529, 538, 557, 559–62
pattern 437, 532, 547–8, 715n; *see also* gestalt
Perfection of Wisdom (*Prajñāpāramitā*) 465, 489, 523; *see also* wisdom, perfect
  sūtras 716n
perfections (*pāramitās*) 432, 548, 620
Pilindavaccha 514
Piṇḍola Bhāradvāja 537–8, 714n
planes, higher, of existence 447, 465, 489, 647; *see also* states, realms
Plato 552, 722n
pleasure
  and pain 459, 464, 482–3, 497–8, 505, 509, 599; *see also* joy, and pain
  sense- 472, 474–5, 482, 505, 509, 551, 606–7
poisons 486, 521–2, 532, 634, 707n, 714n; *see also* afflictions, *āsavas*, defilements
possessions 485–6, 488–90, 625; *see also* attachment
powers, *see also* forces
  five spiritual (*balas*) 558, 568
  magical or psychic 448, 495, 497, 586, 707n; *see also iddhipādas*
  supernormal 534–5, 541, 618, 648; *see also abhiññās*
    of the Buddha 497, 510, 623, 624, 648
praise 518, 519, 621, 639
prajñā, *see* wisdom
prajñāpāramitā, *see* Perfection of Wisdom
prapañca 621; *see also* thoughts
pratītya-samutpāda (Pāli *paṭicca-samuppāda*) *see* conditioned co-production
precepts 530, 564, 620, 630; *see also* ethics, *sīla*, *pāṭimokkha*
  of *bhikkhus*, *see pāṭimokkha*
pride (*māna*) 438, 514–15, 520–1, 580; *see also* conceit
psychology 440–1, 492, 523, 609
purification, seven stages of 578–9
purity 450–1, 457–8
  path of 578–9
  of *uposatha* observance 557

questions, unexplained (*avyākṛta vastūni* (Pāli *avyākata vatthūni*)) 507, 598, 720n

raft 643, 648; *see also* parables
rainy seasons 445, 459, 486, 508, 509–10
Rājagaha (Rajgir) 445, 447, 466, 481, 514–15, 534, 541, 549, 579, 607, 646, 653, 667n
Ramana Maharshi 492

Rathavinīta Sutta 578–9, 718n
reactivity 432, 503, 617, 637–8
and creativity 432
real, and unreal (*sāra* and *asāra*) 450
Reality 434, 464, 561, 610; *see also* Nirvāṇa
realms, *see also* dimensions, levels, planes, states, worlds
heavenly, *see* heavens
hell 535, 539, 550
three 507, 614
of form (*rūpaloka*) 448, 459, 464, 505, 614
formless (*arūpaloka*) 459, 464, 614; *see also dhyānas*, formless
of sense desire (*kāmaloka*) 505, 614
rebirth 482, 541, 542, 546, 606, 637, 638, 642, 645, 717n
in heaven 479, 546, 552, 608, 645, 717n
intermediate states (*antarābhava* or *bardo*) 464, 638, 723n
previous lives 429, 434, 438, 461, 514, 544, 550, 712n
recitation 436, 560–1, 573, 574–6
of *pāṭimokkha* 560–1
reflections, helpful and unhelpful 598; *see also* questions
Refuges 482, 554, 576; *see also* Going for Refuge, Three Jewels
rejoicing in merits 535–6, 541–2, 576
relationships 456–7
release 567, 619–20; *see also* freedom, liberation
religion 434, 473, 516–17, 519, 554, 589, 593, 612
Buddhism as 474, 648
ethnic, and universal 438, 443, 447, 565
repression 507, 608–9
responsibility
for oneself 495, 504, 531, 601
for others 449, 454–6, 485
retreats, solitary 528, 538
Revata 577–8
Rhys Davids
C. A. F. 432
T. W. 478
right livelihood 630
rites and ceremonies, Vedic 488, 517
rulership (*issariya* (Sanskrit *īśvarīya*)) 592–3, 719n
rules 479–80, 495, 501, 529–30, 560–1, 562, 563–4, 712n

sacrifice 457, 517, 624
Sakka (Sanskrit Śakra) 504, 515–16; *see also* Indra
Śākyamuni 547; *see also* Buddha
samādhi, *see also dhyānas*, meditation
avitakka or *animitta* 606, 720n
of Buddha after Enlightenment 428, 429
imperturbable (*āneñja*) 511
saṃsāra 606, 608, 610, 617, 634
saṃskāras 464
Saṃyutta Nikāya 424, 426, 431, 462, 480, 519, 522, 568, 606, 608, 620, 650, 705n, 708n, 709n, 710n, 712n, 713n, 717n, 719n, 721n, 722n, 723n, 724n
Saṅgāmaji 454–7
sangha 432, 519, 538, 542, 554, 565, 573, 579–81; *see also* spiritual community
Ārya, *see ariyapuggalas*, Āryasaṅgha
development of 479–81, 501, 520, 573, 574, 588, 641
meeting together (*uposatha* observance) 557, 559–62, 579
someone not truly a member of 557, 558, 562, 564–5, 570–1
Sangharakshita, during *Udāna* seminar 420
Sangharatana, Bhikkhu 472, 709n
saṅgīti 561, 576, 706n; *see also* Council; recitation
Śaṅkara 625, 722n
Śāntideva 481–2, 600, 711n
Sāriputta (Sanskrit Śāriputra) 444, 480, 488, 493–4, 496, 511–12, 534–5, 538, 542, 580, 613–16, 710n
Sarnath 608, 706n, 710n
Sarvāstivāda 430, 638
Satipaṭṭhāna Sutta 512
Sāvatthī (Sanskrit Śrāvastī) 443–4, 445, 461, 466, 472, 477, 481, 509–10, 539, 559, 588, 707n, 710n
schools of Buddhism 553, 564, 609, 716n
self 438, 515, 521, 527, 544–5, 600–2, 622; *see also ātman*, ego
-confidence 470–1, 506
empirical 470, 545, 592–3
harm or mortification 524–5, 534, 536, 608–9, 620
-indulgence 608–9
-love or appreciation 524, 541, 542, 543–4
Upanishadic or Vedāntic view 544–5
selfishness 455–6
Seneca 536, 714n
sense
desire or pleasure (*kāma*) 449, 469, 472, 475, 482, 505, 509, 551–2, 576, 606–7, 614, 616–17, 718n

experience, mindfulness of 464, 512, 520
-sphere consciousness (*kāmāvacara*) 512
senses 512–13, 611; *see also* contact, six spheres of
contact 512, 521, 522
six spheres of (*ṣaḍāyatana*) 512–13
Shaw, G. B. 540–1, 714n
shrines (*caityas*) 451, 452–3, 464, 467
Shudras 625, 723n
sīla (Sanskrit *śīla*) 434, 551, 552, 644, 646; *see also* ethics, precepts
śīla, *samādhi*, and *prajñā*, *see* threefold path
silence 472, 508, 518, 519, 520, 557, 561
six element practice 532
skandhas, *see khandhas*
sloth-and-torpor (*thīna-middha*) 532, 533
snake 470, 476–7, 714n
and frog 490
Socrates 619, 721n
solitude 469, 536–7, 572, 573
Soṇa 572–6, 580
sons 455–7, 490, 491, 493–4, 496
speech 474, 503, 518, 520, 530, 539–41, 576, 619
spheres
of *dhyānas* 632–3, 723n
triple mundane 465; *see also* realms
spirits 452, 517, 647; *see also yakkhas*
spiritual
attainment 535, 555, 588–91, 618
community 570–1; *see also* sangha
death 555, 654
evolution, four types of people and 483
faculties, *see* faculties, five
friendship (*kalyāṇa mitratā*) 526–7, 529–31, 535–6, 650
life 483, 555, 591, 598, 620, 628–9, 635, 648, 722n; *see also ariyapariyesanā*, *brahmacarya*, holy life
motivation for 456–7, 478, 505–7, 519, 549, 551, 564, 598
negative and positive approaches to 471, 513, 523, 525, 567, 632, 634–5
śramaṇas (Pāli *samaṇas*) 479, 487–8, 515; *see also* ascetics, wanderers
Śrāvastī, *see* Sāvatthī
states
higher, of consciousness 431, 434, 461, 464, 635, 654, 656; *see also* realms
intermediate (*antarābhava* or *bardo*) 464, 638, 723n
Stream Entry 424, 550, 552–3, 555, 558, 569, 576, 616, 627–8, 693, 717n
stupas (*caityas*) 464, 466
Subhūti 605–7
suffering 459, 463, 489, 491–4, 497–8, 521–2, 598, 615, 635, 638, 724n; *see also dukkha*, pain
Sujātā 437
sun 434, 611, 612, 706n
Sunīdha 642
śūnyatā 606–7
supernormal powers, *see* powers
Suppabuddha 549–51, 553–5, 563, 672n
Suppāraka 458–60, 462, 466, 709n
Suppavāsā 493–6
Sūtra of Huineng 562, 717n
Sutta-Nipāta 425–6, 435, 436, 473, 486, 489, 573, 575, 705n, 710n, 711n, 718n, 723n, 724n, 725n
suttas (Sanskrit *sūtras*) 424–5, 466, 552, 554–5, 578, 597, 716n
Mahāyāna 716n; *see also* individual *sūtras*

taints 450, 459, 505, 541, 613, 615, 688n, 707n; *see also āsavas*
taste of freedom (*rasa*) 567–8
Tathāgata 442, 594, 597, 611; *see also* Buddha
Theravāda Buddhism 424, 435, 440, 523, 547, 561, 638
thoughts 462–3, 527, 531, 532, 566, 606, 622, 720n; *see also* mental states, *prapañca*
threefold path 434, 530, 578, 713n
Three Jewels 486, 494, 550; *see also* Refuges
Tibetan Book of the Dead 428, 638, 723n
Tibetan Buddhism 421, 424, 564, 585, 638, 707n
time 428, 633
tradition, or transmission, oral 424, 436, 575–6
transcendence 432, 450, 455, 565–6, 600, 606, 608
transcendental
dimension, plane or state 436, 465, 523, 530, 635, 656
object 566
principle 635
trees, gods or spirits of 452, 461, 470, 647
Triratna Buddhist Community 421, 486, 565; *see also* Friends of the Western Buddhist Order
truth 570–1, 595–6, 613, 624–6, 633–4
Tsongkhapa 564

Udāna 425–6, 588, 641
compilation of 421, 435, 465, 480, 490, 511, 522, 541, 587, 648, 653–4, 655, 656
history of Pāli text 421, 424–6, 429, 434–5, 444, 445, 465–6, 640
prose passages 421, 422, 465
and verses compared 425–6, 429, 433–4, 435, 453, 456, 465, 470, 497, 502–3, 507, 511, 522, 547
Sangharakshita's seminars on 421–2, 663
in a tent in Cornwall 420
translations 422, 706n, 708n, 715n
Udānavarga 429, 705n, 724n
the Unconditioned 524, 634–8, 654–5; *see also* Nirvāṇa
unsatisfactoriness 550, 632, 637; *see also dukkha*
Upanisā Sutta 431, 705n
Upanishads 211, 233, 430, 431, 460, 544, 545–6, 625, 715n
upāsaka, use of word 484
upāsakas, *see* householders, lay followers
Upasena 541–2
uposatha observance 517, 559–62, 575, 579, 580
Uruvelā 427, 432–4, 436–7, 466, 469, 481, 521; *see also* Bodh Gaya

Vairocana 435, 705n
Vajrasattva 451
Vajrayāna 439, 480
Vassakāra 642
Vedas 430, 431, 438, 625–6, 723n
Vedic, language 429–30, 431, 434, 438, 441–2, 445–6, 465, 467–8, 480, 506
Vedic rites 488, 517
vegetarianism 529, 630
Vesālī (Sanskrit Vaiśālī) 508–10, 583, 586
views (*diṭṭhis* (Sanskrit *dṛṣṭis*)) 489, 599, 600–1, 603, 606, 621, 715n
right (*sammā-diṭṭhis* (Sanskrit *samyag-dṛṣṭis*)) 533, 587
wrong (*micchā-diṭṭhis* (Sanskrit *mithyā-dṛṣṭis*)) 532–3, 570, 587, 594–600, 607, 608, 611–12, 620
Vinaya Piṭaka 428, 435, 439, 444, 452, 457, 480, 498–9, 522, 559, 562, 580, 705n, 706n, 707n, 708n, 711n, 712n, 713n, 716n, 717n, 718n
Vipassī, Buddha 560, 715n
Visākhā (Migāra's mother) 496, 498–9, 557, 559, 588–9, 651–2
vision
fourfold 596, 719n
perfect (*samyag-dṛṣṭi*) or total 470, 533, 595–6, 611
supernormal 456, 500, 506, 535, 550
Visuddhimagga 578, 721n
Vivekananda, Swami 442

wanderers (*parivrājakas* (Pāli *paribbājakas*)) 452, 472, 477–9, 480, 481, 486, 488, 520, 589, 591, 629, 636, 643–4; *see also śramaṇas*
with families 487
of other sects or views 477, 539–40, 594, 596, 597, 611
women 539, 540, 628
wandering, 'without a home' 520–1
wheel, of Dharma 705n
wheel of life 447, 501, 523, 600, 606
Whitehouse, Mary 499, 711n
wisdom 434, 437–8, 487, 488–9, 505, 527, 568, 620, 649
mirror-like 463, 709n
perfect (*sammappaññā*) 522, 523; *see also* Perfection of Wisdom
wives 454, 455, 456, 457, 487, 488, 490, 498
women 484, 496, 498–9, 519, 536, 539, 540, 627–8
work 630, 631
worlds 507, 535, 549; *see also* levels, realms, states
worship 484, 516, 647

yakkhas (Sanskrit *yakṣas*) 451–3, 466, 517, 534–5, 708n
Yasoja 508–9, 511
yogis 629

Zen 439–40, 503, 532, 539, 562, 566, 626
Zhiyi (Chih-I) 554–5, 716n

A GUIDE TO THE COMPLETE WORKS OF SANGHARAKSHITA

Gathered together in these twenty-seven volumes are talks and stories, commentaries on the Buddhist scriptures, poems, memoirs, reviews, and other writings. The genres are many, and the subject matter covered is wide, but it all has – its whole purpose is to convey – that taste of freedom which the Buddha declared to be the hallmark of his Dharma. Another traditional description of the Buddha's Dharma is that it is *ehipassiko*, 'come and see'. Sangharakshita calls to us, his readers, to come and see how the Dharma can fundamentally change the way we see things, change the way we live for the better, and change the society we belong to, wherever in the world we live.

Sangharakshita's very first published piece, *The Unity of Buddhism* (found in volume 7 of this collection), appeared in 1944 when he was eighteen years old, and it introduced themes that continued to resound throughout his work: the basis of Buddhist ethics, the compassion of the bodhisattva, and the transcendental unity of Buddhism. Over the course of the following seven decades not only did numerous other works flow from his pen; he gave hundreds of talks (some now lost). In gathering all we could find of this vast output, we have sought to arrange it in a way that brings a sense of coherence, communicating something essential about Sangharakshita, his life and teaching. Recalling the three 'baskets' among which an early tradition divided the Buddha's teachings, we have divided Sangharakshita's creative output into six 'baskets' or groups: foundation texts; works originating in India; teachings originally given in the West; commentaries on the Buddhist scriptures; personal writings; and poetry, aphorisms, and works on the arts. The 27th volume, a concordance, brings together all the terms and themes of the whole collection. If you want to find a particular story or teaching, look at a traditional term from different points of view or in different contexts, or track down one of the thousands of canonical references to be found in these volumes, the concordance will be your guide.

1. FOUNDATION

What is the foundation of a Buddhist life? How do we understand and then follow the Buddha's path of Ethics, Meditation, and Wisdom? What is really meant by 'Going for Refuge to the Three Jewels', described by Sangharakshita as the essential act of a Buddhist life? And what is the Bodhisattva ideal, which he has called 'one of the sublimest ideals mankind has ever seen'? In the 'Foundation' group you will find teachings on all these themes. It includes the author's *magnum opus, A Survey of Buddhism*, a collection of teachings on *The Purpose and Practice of Buddhist Meditation*, and the anthology, *The Essential Sangharakshita*, an eminently helpful distillation of the entire corpus.

2. INDIA

From 1950 to 1964 Sangharakshita, based in Kalimpong in the eastern Himalayas, poured his energy into trying to revive Buddhism in the land of its birth and to revitalize and bring reform to the existing Asian Buddhist world. The articles and book reviews from this period are gathered in volumes 7 and 8, as well as his biographical sketch of the great Sinhalese Dharmaduta, Anagārika Dharmapala. In 1954 Sangharakshita took on the editing of the *Maha Bodhi*, a journal for which he wrote a monthly editorial, and which, under his editorship, published the work of many of the leading Buddhist writers of the time. It was also during these years in India that a vital connection was forged with Dr B. R. Ambedkar, renowned Indian statesman and leader of the Buddhist mass conversion of 1956. Sangharakshita became closely involved with the new Buddhists and, after Dr Ambedkar's untimely death, visited them regularly on extensive teaching tours.

From 1979, when an Indian wing of the Triratna Buddhist Community was founded (then known as TBMSG), Sangharakshita returned several times to undertake further teaching tours. The talks from these tours are collected in volumes 9 and 10 along with a unique work on Ambedkar and his life which draws out the significance of his conversion to Buddhism.

3. THE WEST

Sangharakshita founded the Triratna Buddhist Community (then called the Friends of the Western Buddhist Order) on 6 April 1967. On 7 April the following year he performed the first ordinations of men and women within the Triratna Buddhist Order (then the Western Buddhist Order). At that time Buddhism was not widely known in the West and for the following two decades or so he taught intensively, finding new ways to communicate the ancient truths of Buddhism, drawing on the whole Buddhist tradition to do so, as well as making connections with what was best in existing Western culture. Sometimes his sword flashed as he critiqued ideas and views inimical to the Dharma. It is these teachings and writings that are gathered together in this third group.

4. COMMENTARY

Throughout Sangharakshita's works are threaded references to the Buddhist canon of literature – Pāli, Mahāyāna, and Vajrayāna – from which he drew his inspiration. In the early days of the new movement he often taught by means of seminars in which, prompted by the questions of his students, he sought to pass on the inspiration and wisdom of the Buddhist tradition. Each seminar was based around a different text, the seminars were recorded and transcribed, and in due course many of the transcriptions were edited and turned into books, all carefully checked by Sangharakshita. The commentaries compiled in this way constitute the fourth group. In some ways this is the heart of the collection. Sangharakshita often told the story of how it was that, reading two *sūtras* at the age of sixteen or seventeen, he realized that he was a Buddhist, and he has never tired of showing others how they too could see and realize the value of the '*sūtra*-treasure'.

5. MEMOIRS

Who is Sangharakshita? What sort of life did he live? Whom did he meet? What did he feel? Why did he found a new Buddhist movement? In these volumes of memoirs and letters Sangharakshita shares with his readers much about himself and his life as he himself has experienced it, giving us a sense of its breadth and depth, humour and pathos.

6. POETRY, APHORISMS, AND THE ARTS

Sangharakshita describes reading *Paradise Lost* at the age of twelve as one of the greatest poetic experiences of his life. His realization of the value of the higher arts to spiritual development is one of his distinctive contributions to our understanding of what Buddhist life is, and he has expressed it in a number of essays and articles. Throughout his life he has written poetry which he says can be regarded as a kind of spiritual autobiography. It is here, perhaps, that we come closest to the heart of Sangharakshita. He has also written a few short stories and composed some startling aphorisms. Through book reviews he has engaged with the experiences, ideas, and opinions of modern writers. All these are collected in this sixth group.

In the preface to *A Survey of Buddhism* (volume 1 in this collection), Sangharakshita wrote of his approach to the Buddha's teachings:

> Why did the Buddha (or Nāgārjuna, or Buddhaghosa) teach this particular doctrine? What bearing does it have on the spiritual life? How does it help the individual Buddhist actually to follow the spiritual path?... I found myself asking such questions again and again, for only in this way, I found, could I make sense – spiritual sense – of Buddhism.

Although this collection contains so many words, they are all intent, directly or indirectly, on these same questions. And all these words are not in the end about their writer, but about his great subject, the Buddha and his teaching, and about you, the reader, for whose benefit they are solely intended. These pages are full of the reverence that Sangharakshita has always felt, which is expressed in an early poem, 'Taking Refuge in the Buddha', whose refrain is 'My place is at thy feet'. He has devoted his life to communicating the Buddha's Dharma in its depth and in its breadth, to men and women from all backgrounds and walks of life, from all countries, of all races, of all ages. These collected works are the fruit of that devotion.

We are very pleased to be able to include some previously unpublished work in this collection, but most of what appears in these volumes has been published before. We have made very few changes, though we have added extra notes where we thought they would be useful. We have had the pleasure of researching the notes in the Sangharakshita Library at 'Adhisthana', Triratna's centre in Herefordshire, UK, which houses his own collection of books. It has been of great value to be able to search among the very copies of the *suttas*, *sūtras* and commentaries that have provided the basis of his teachings over the last seventy years.

The publication of these volumes owes much to the work of transcribers, editors, indexers, designers, and publishers over many years – those who brought out the original editions of many of the works included here, and those who have contributed in all sorts of ways to this *Complete Works* project, including all those who contributed to funds given in celebration of Sangharakshita's ninetieth birthday in August 2015, and to a further outpouring of generosity after Sangharakshita's death in October 2018. All these donors have made the publication of this series possible, and we are very grateful. Many thanks to everyone who has helped; may the merit gained in our acting thus go to the alleviation of the suffering of all beings.

Vidyadevi and Kalyanaprabha
Editors

THE COMPLETE WORKS OF SANGHARAKSHITA

I FOUNDATION

VOLUME 1 A SURVEY OF BUDDHISM / THE BUDDHA'S NOBLE EIGHTFOLD PATH
A Survey of Buddhism
The Buddha's Noble Eightfold Path

2 THE THREE JEWELS I
The Three Jewels
The Meaning of Conversion in Buddhism
Going for Refuge
The Ten Pillars of Buddhism
The History of My Going for Refuge
My Relation to the Order
Extending the Hand of Fellowship
Forty-Three Years Ago
Was the Buddha a Bhikkhu?

3 THE THREE JEWELS II
Who is the Buddha?
What is the Dharma?
What is the Sangha?

4 THE BODHISATTVA IDEAL
The Bodhisattva Ideal
The Endlessly Fascinating Cry (seminar)
The Bodhisattva Principle

5 THE PURPOSE AND PRACTICE OF BUDDHIST MEDITATION
The Purpose and Practice of Buddhist Meditation

6 THE ESSENTIAL SANGHARAKSHITA
The Essential Sangharakshita

II INDIA

7 CROSSING THE STREAM: INDIA WRITINGS I
Early Writings 1944–1954
Crossing the Stream
Buddhism in the Modern World: Cultural and Political Implications
The Meaning of Orthodoxy in Buddhism
Buddhism in India Today
Ordination and Initiation in the Three Yānas
A Bird's Eye View of Indian Buddhism

VOLUME 8 BEATING THE DHARMA DRUM: INDIA WRITINGS II
Anagarika Dharmapala and Other 'Maha Bodhi' Writings
Dharmapala: The Spiritual Dimension
Beating the Drum: 'Maha Bodhi' Editorials

9 DR AMBEDKAR AND THE REVIVAL OF BUDDHISM I
Ambedkar and Buddhism
Lecture Tour in India, December 1981–March 1982

10 DR AMBEDKAR AND THE REVIVAL OF BUDDHISM II
Remembering Ambedkar
Buddha and the Future of His Religion
The Mass Conversion and the Years After, 1956–61
Lectures in India and England 1979, 1982–92
Wisdom before Words: The Udāna

III THE WEST

11 A NEW BUDDHIST MOVEMENT I
Ritual and Devotion in Buddhism
The Buddha's Victory
The Taste of Freedom
Buddha Mind
Human Enlightenment
New Currents in Western Buddhism
Buddhism for Today – and Tomorrow
Buddhism and the West
Aspects of Buddhist Morality
Dialogue between Buddhism and Christianity
Buddhism and Blasphemy
Articles and Interviews
Alternative Traditions

12 A NEW BUDDHIST MOVEMENT II
Previously unpublished talks

13 EASTERN AND WESTERN TRADITIONS
Tibetan Buddhism
Creative Symbols of Tantric Buddhism
The Essence of Zen
The FWBO and 'Protestant Buddhism'
From Genesis to the Diamond Sūtra

IV COMMENTARY

VOLUME 14 THE ETERNAL LEGACY / WISDOM BEYOND WORDS
The Eternal Legacy
The Glory of the Literary World
Wisdom Beyond Words

15 PĀLI CANON TEACHINGS AND TRANSLATIONS
Dhammapada (translation)
Karaṇīyamettā Sutta (translation)
Living with Kindness
Living with Awareness
Maṅgala Sutta (translation)
Auspicious Signs (seminar)
Salutation to the Three Jewels (translation)
The Threefold Refuge (seminar)
Further Pāli Sutta Commentaries

16 MAHĀYĀNA MYTHS AND STORIES
The Drama of Cosmic Enlightenment
The Priceless Jewel (talk)
Transforming Self and World
The Inconceivable Emancipation

17 WISDOM TEACHINGS OF THE MAHĀYĀNA
Know Your Mind
Living Ethically
Living Wisely
The Way to Wisdom (seminar)

18 MILAREPA AND THE ART OF DISCIPLESHIP I
The Yogi's Joy
The Shepherd's Search for Mind
Rechungpa's Journey to Enlightenment

19 MILAREPA AND THE ART OF DISCIPLESHIP II
Rechungpa's Journey to Enlightenment, continued

V MEMOIRS

20 THE RAINBOW ROAD FROM TOOTING BROADWAY TO KALIMPONG
The Rainbow Road from Tooting Broadway to Kalimpong

VOLUME 21 FACING MOUNT KANCHENJUNGA
Facing Mount Kanchenjunga
Dear Dinoo: Letters to a Friend

22 IN THE SIGN OF THE GOLDEN WHEEL
In the Sign of the Golden Wheel
Precious Teachers
With Allen Ginsberg in Kalimpong (essay)

23 MOVING AGAINST THE STREAM
Moving Against the Stream
1970 – A Retrospect

24 THROUGH BUDDHIST EYES
Travel Letters
Through Buddhist Eyes

VI POETRY AND THE ARTS

25 POEMS AND SHORT STORIES
Complete Poems 1941–1994
Other Poems
Short Stories

26 APHORISMS AND THE ARTS
Peace is a Fire
A Stream of Stars
The Religion of Art
In the Realm of the Lotus
The Journey to Il Convento
St Jerome Revisited
A Note on the Burial of Count Orgaz
Criticism East and West
A Moseley Miscellany
Adhisthana Writings
Urthona Articles and Interviews

27 CONCORDANCE AND APPENDICES

WINDHORSE PUBLICATIONS

Windhorse Publications is a Buddhist charitable company based in the UK. We produce books of high quality that are accessible and relevant to all those interested in Buddhism, at whatever level of interest and commitment. We are the main publisher of Sangharakshita, the founder of the Triratna Buddhist Order and Community. Our books draw on the whole range of the Buddhist tradition, including translations of traditional texts, commentaries, books that make links with contemporary culture and ways of life, biographies of Buddhists, and works on meditation.

To subscribe to the *Complete Works of Sangharakshita,* please go to: windhorsepublications.com/sangharakshita-complete-works/

THE TRIRATNA BUDDHIST COMMUNITY

Windhorse Publications is a part of the Triratna Buddhist Community, an international movement with centres in Europe, India, North and South America and Australasia. At these centres, members of the Triratna Buddhist Order offer classes in meditation and Buddhism. Activities of the Triratna Community also include retreat centres, residential spiritual communities, ethical Right Livelihood businesses, and the Karuna Trust, a UK fundraising charity that supports social welfare projects in the slums and villages of India.

Through these and other activities, Triratna is developing a unique approach to Buddhism, not simply as a philosophy and a set of techniques, but as a creatively directed way of life for all people living in the conditions of the modern world.

For more information please visit thebuddhistcentre.com